THE COMPLETE GUIDE TO TRADITIONAL
JEWISH COOKING

THE COMPLETE GUIDE TO TRADITIONAL
JEWISH COOKING

An extraordinary culinary encyclopedia with 400 recipes and 1400 photographs
celebrating Jewish cooking through the ages, including influential cuisines and dishes
inspired by Jewish foods

Featuring dishes from Russia, Poland, Ukraine, Germany, Hungary, Romania,
Bulgaria, France, Italy, Spain, Portugal, Greece, Morocco, Egypt, Iran, Israel,
the Middle East, India, the United States and Latin America

MARLENA SPIELER

HERMES
HOUSE

Dedication: To Sophia Dubowsky, "Bachi" to all, for her love of feeding people, her appetite for life, and her chicken soup that could cure anything.

This edition is published by Hermes House, an imprint of Anness Publishing Ltd, 108 Great Russell Street, London WC1B 3NA; info@anness.com

www.hermeshouse.com; www.annesspublishing.com; twitter: @Anness_Books

If you like the images in this book and would like to investigate using them for publishing, promotions or advertising, please visit our website www.practicalpictures.com for more information.

A CIP catalogue record for this book is available from the British Library.

Publisher: Joanna Lorenz
Editorial Director: Helen Sudell
Project Editors: Susannah Blake, Margaret Malone and Catherine Stuart
Production Controller: Stephanie Moe
Contributors: Marlena Spieler, Lesley Chamberlain, Catherine Atkinson and Trish Davies
Designers: Julie Francis, Nigel Partridge and Diane Pullen
Jacket Design: SteersMcGillan
Home Economists: Joss Herd, Justine Kiggin, Kate Lewis, Christine Rodrigue and Sunil Vijayakar
Stylists: Shannon Beare, Marion McLornan and Helen Trent
Photography: Ian Garlick, Dave Jordan and William Lingwood
Picture Acknowledgements: AKG – pp12 bottom, 20 bottom, 27 bottom-right, 30, 34 bottom, 35 top and 39 top; The Art Archive – pp26 bottom and 35 bottom; The Bridgeman Art Library – pp13 and 27 bottom left; David Harris, Jerusalem/photo courtesy of the Beth Hatefutsoth Photo Archive – p25; Melvine H. Levine/photo courtesy of the Beth Hatefutsoth Photo Archive – p31 top; Hulton Getty Images – pp14 top, 15, 18 bottom, 29 left, 32 bottom, 33 top, 36 bottom, 40, 41 top and bottom; The Jewish Museum, London – pp16 and 17.

PUBLISHER'S NOTE
Although the advice and information in this book are believed to be accurate and true at the time of going to press, neither the authors nor the publisher can accept any legal responsibility or liability for any errors or omissions that may have been made nor for any inaccuracies nor for any loss, harm or injury that comes about from following instructions or advice in this book.

COOK'S NOTES
Bracketed terms are intended for American readers. For all recipes, quantities are given in both metric and imperial measures and, where appropriate, in standard cups and spoons. Follow one set of measures, but not a mixture, because they are not interchangeable.
Standard spoon and cup measures are level.
1 tsp = 5ml, 1 tbsp = 15ml,
1 cup = 250ml/8fl oz.
Australian standard tablespoons are 20ml. Australian readers should use 3 tsp in place of 1 tbsp for measuring small quantities.
American pints are 16fl oz/2 cups. American readers should use 20fl oz/2.5 cups in place of 1 pint when measuring liquids.
Electric oven temperatures in this book are for conventional ovens. When using a fan oven, the temperature will probably need to be reduced by about 10–20°C/20–40°F. Since ovens vary, you should check with your manufacturer's instruction book for guidance. The nutritional analysis given for each recipe is calculated per portion (i.e. serving or item), unless otherwise stated. If the recipe gives a range, such as Serves 4–6, then the nutritional analysis will be for the smaller portion size, i.e. 6 servings. The analysis does not include optional ingredients, such as salt added to taste.
Medium (US large) eggs are used unless otherwise stated.

CONTENTS

INTRODUCTION

The food of the Jewish people is also the history of the Jewish people. The dishes, flavourings, and traditions chronicle the resources of the lands they were exiled to and from, where they grew rich and contented, and where, conversely, they lived in poverty and constant peril. Whether communities of Ashkenazim, Sephardim, Italkim or Jews of India, Yemen or the Far and Near East, the different customs attributed to "being Jewish" have been myriad over the course of centuries.

Historical events have precipitated developments in Jewish cuisine which, in turn, have influenced how people across the world eat. During the Spanish Inquisition, for example, Jews migrating to North Africa, Eastern Europe, Portugal, England and India took their special dishes with them.

A CULINARY JOURNEY

Jews fleeing Spain for Hungary are said to have helped spread the pepper, which, when ripened in the sun and ground into paprika, now colours Hungary's entire cuisine. Jewish settlers in Greece, who had been arriving in large numbers since the second century BCE (BC), brought spices they had accrued from years of living in the east. Jewish traders often plied spices from

Below: The Jewish cuisine boasts an astonishing array of sweet treats. These almond-filled cigars hail from Tunisia.

country to country, setting up informal communications. It is said that this is how the Alsatians cultivated the use of spices in their biscuits and cakes.

Venice's Jewish community brought the pumpkin to Italy and Italian Jews who got word of the tomato and its goodness spread it to the rest of Italy. The aubergine (eggplant) made its way around Europe thanks to the Jewish affinity for this incredibly versatile vegetable. It is often able to mimic meat, at least in its savoury heartiness. As meat cannot be mixed with dairy in Jewish cuisine, this mimicry is a frequent a consideration in the food of Jewish people.

Jewish confectioners stopped along the way in Bayonne and Biarritz and set up shops plying their trade in the newly-discovered bitter-sweet cocoa bean, which was much in demand for making chocolate. In 17th-century Britain, Portuguese Jews were bringing their art of battering and deep-frying – said to have been learned by Portuguese seafarers' discovery of Japanese tempura – to the fresh fish of that isle, so beloved of the Jewish community. Almost two centuries later, when the East End of London became home to a new wave of Jewish immigrants, this time from Eastern Europe and Russia, the fish friers began adding potatoes to the fish as a means of bulking out the dish to keep the workers warm and fed. This was very probably the origin of

Above: Beetroot – shredded for soups and salads, or roasted and served with garlic or horseradish – is loved by Jews throughout the world.

Britain's traditional fish and chips. Since the food was pareve, observant Jews did not need to worry about the quality of kashrut, as they might when obtaining meat or dairy.

AN EVER-CHANGING COMMUNITY

The Jews of different cultural and ethnic groups were not really, however, part of each other's lives. It would take the 20th century to bring the Jewish people from the far-flung corners of the world back together again, in a process that is still happening in the 21st century. In 2005, for example, the Chief Rabbi of Israel recognized the Jewish heritage of the Bene Menashe. Likely to be the lost tribe of Israel, they now live in Eastern India.

The foods of the Jewish people were as varied as their looks and languages. Some communities spoke the languages of those around them, others spoke Yiddish, or Ladino, or other Jewish languages such as Judaeo-Persian, Judaeo-Arabic, Targum (Kurdish Jews) and Tajiki (the Judeo-Persian dialect of Afghan Jews).

During the last century, many Jewish communities have disappeared: many in Europe fall tragically into this category. However, a number have also reformed, either elsewhere, or in the same places with the remnants of those who survived and stayed behind, bolstered by Jewish immigrants from other nations where, suddenly, after generations or even centuries of living peacefully together, Jews were forced to seek new comfort and security in other lands. The Jewish community in France is characterized by groups of this kind; a far from homogenous combination of Ashkenazic and Sephardic Jews, with their own distinctive customs, foods and emotional scars.

Sometimes, the food is almost the only thing left of a community. After it has been destroyed, a speciality sometimes appears among a newly formed community of survivors, or endures among the non-Jews living close by. In this way, a culture and its memory are perpetuated.

KASHRUT AND THE CALENDAR

Jewish cooking is shaped by the places Jews have lived and the lives they have experienced. Jewish food tells a story, and influences those whom Jews have lived among. The thread that holds it all together is the dual balance of kashrut: the guide that tells Jews which foods are fit for them to eat (kosher literally

Below: The peel of preserved lemons is often added to the savoury dishes of North African and Mediterranean Jews.

means "fit"), and the unifying force of the year of observances: the celebrations and festivities of the year, beginning with Rosh Hashanah, the Jewish new year, through the family occasions of Shabbat, Brit Milah (circumcision), Bar and Bat Mitzvah, and weddings and funerals.

It is, above all, the rules of kashrut, setting out what may be eaten with what and what is forbidden, that have kept the Jewish people distinct from those with whom they live, more even than separate languages. This has, in turn, resulted in different situations and challenges for different Jewish groups. The Sephardim, for example, cooked with olive oil – a practice that enabled them to combine dishes of meat and vegetables and enjoy dishes of cooked dairy, yogurt and cheese. The Ashkenazim used the fat chicken shmaltz, so most meals were de facto meat meals. As the non-Jews of the area cooked in pork fat – lard – this meant that foods which could be shared with the non-Jewish community were fewer than those of the Sephardim, who shared their love of olive oil with their Muslim neighbours. The distinction and division between Jew and non-Jew in Ashkenazi lands therefore grew deeper, especially where food was concerned.

The calendar year of feasting and fasting is something in which the world Jewish community partakes. As the sun sets into Pesach, for example, Jewish families in countries around the globe sit down to the ritual meal, the Seder. At Chanukkah time there are eight days of feasting and frolicking; at Purim the Megillah is said and at Rosh Hashanah and Yom Kippur, as the previous year is being evaluated, forgiveness is begged and a new year dawns. In Jewish communities throughout the world, then, the calendar is enacted around the dinner table.

The Talmud says, "There is no festive celebration without eating and drinking" and there is no eating and drinking without thanking God. Each meal is accompanied by prayers of thanks. A basic tenet of the Jewish table is that good food is a gift from God.

Above: Challah – golden, tender bread enriched with egg – is a traditional part of the Ashkenazi Shabbat meal.

FOOD UNITES PEOPLE

The noted philosopher and physician Moses Maimonides (Moses ben Maimon, 1135–1204) of Cordoba and Cairo left a legacy of much insight and wisdom about food and eating. He emphasized the importance of having a good calm attitude of spirit, both when cooking and when eating. He stressed the value of eating healthily and of preparing food appealingly, and recommended chicken soup as a treatment for colds and flu. He also noted that sharing sociable meals not only made for happier individuals but also bridged cultural and ethnic gaps. This observation, which is so modern in its sensibility, was made hundreds of years ago.

Food, more than any other ritual, transmits the culture of a people. Sharing an appreciation of food means we are showing appreciation for one another's cultures. Since Judaism unites many cultures and peoples under a shared religion, especially regarding the kashrut, the food at the Jewish table is of utmost importance. Whether a feast for a bar mitzvah, a wedding or a ceremonial meal to celebrate the holidays, it says, "Come and share our culture. The people of Israel may be varied, but We Are One."

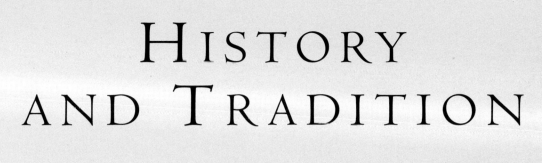

HISTORY
AND TRADITION

From the time of their first exile in 70CE (AD), Jews have adopted the flavours of the lands they dwelt in. Each time they were forced to flee they re-established their community in a new country, taking on the new foods found there, always in keeping with the basic laws of the kashrut. Even the religious table is tightly bound up with history. Holidays commemorate the events of the past and demand traditional and ritual foods, from the matzos of Pesach to the fried dishes of Chanukkah and the sweet foods of Rosh Hashanah.

The Jewish Diaspora

Exile has been a common thread throughout the history of the Jewish people. It is this, linked with intrinsic religious and cultural considerations, that has been a major factor in developing a cuisine that is as diverse as it is delicious. As communities fled from one country to another, they took with them their culinary traditions but also adopted new ones along the way.

With the destruction by the Romans of the Second Temple in Jerusalem in 70CE (AD), the Jews were banished from their holy city. Since that date, they have travelled the world establishing communities, many of which lasted for centuries, before being forced to flee once more.

Jews spread to nearly every corner of the globe and this dispersal or diaspora has helped to create the cultural and liturgical differences that exist within a single people. Following the dispersal, two important Jewish communities, the Sephardim and the Ashkenazim, were established which still define the two main Jewish groups that exist today. Each has its own individual culture, cuisine and liturgy.

The first of these communites was established in Iberia and was called Sepharad after a city in Asia Minor which was mentioned in Obadiah 20. The second was in the Rhine river valley and was called Ashkenaz, after a kingdom on the upper Euphrates, which is referred to in Jeremiah 51:27.

Iberia, which was ruled by Muslims, was a relatively tolerant society. The Jews had a revered place in it and lived undisturbed and in harmony with their Islamic neighbours for long periods. They often held influential positions as doctors, scholars or royal advisers.

In contrast, the Christian lands of Europe were restrictive, feudal, and often hostile. The Ashkenazim tended to live apart in ghettos or shtetlach (villages), away from the non-Jewish population. They spoke a different language to that of their neighbours and became very strict regarding their dietary laws, as they were surrounded by people who ate pork, rabbit, shellfish and other non-kosher foods that were forbidden to Jews.

Over the centuries, both communities blossomed in their new environments, but each developed very differently, creating its own culture. Ashkenazic Jews developed different customs, laws, liturgy, Hebrew pronunciations and cooking styles from their Sephardic cousins, despite having the same roots.

Yemenite Jews, known as Tienamim, are the third largest Jewish ethnic group today. Although, historically, they do not belong to the Sephardim, they are often grouped with them, possibly because of their Eastern culture and traditional

Below: A painting by Francesco Hayez depicting the destruction of the Jewish Temple in Jerusalem by the Romans under Titus in 70CE (AD) (1867).

spicy cuisine. Other ethnic groups that are neither Ashkenazic nor Sephardic include Jewish communities from Iran, Azarbaijan, Bukhara (Uzbekistan), Georgia, Kurdistan, India, Ethiopia and K'ai-feng (Canton).

THE SEPHARDIM

Jews who settled in Iberia spoke Ladino, a dialect of Castilian Spanish written in Hebrew script. In many respects, their lifestyle was not so very different from that of their Arab neighbours, who had a similar outlook of generous hospitality. The Arabs also prepared their food ritually: meat was ridded of blood and pork was forbidden.

Jews lived in Jewish quarters known as mellahs, generally by choice. Living together as a community helped to strengthen their culture and allowed them to be near the centres of Jewish life such as the synagogue, kosher butcher and ritual baths.

As the Iberian Jews settled and moved, four main groups emerged. Judaeo-Spanish Jews settled in the Ottoman lands of Turkey and Greece. Maghrebi or North African Jews settled in Morocco, Tunisia, Algeria and Libya. Arab Jews lived in Babylon and Persia and, for over ten centuries, Iraqi and Babylonian Jews were the leaders of world Jewry. Syria, Iraq, Lebanon and Iran all produced Jewish communities of greatness which became centres of excellence for culture, learning and commerce.

The communities could have grown in different directions, but the caravan trade allowed communication and mobility between the different groups. Matters of Rabbinical law, politics and business were communicated easily. Migration in search of new opportunities also became common.

This interaction between the different communities allowed a mingling and unification of flavours in the Sephardic cuisine. The food the Sephardic Jews ate and the way they cooked it was a blend of their own heritage and dietary laws with distinct influences from the Iberian and Arabic culinary tradition. What emerged was a cuisine which was

rich with the flavours of the region. At its heart, Sephardic cooking still has the warm undertones of Spain. It is olive oil-based, rich with fish from the sea and the vegetables of a warm climate and fragrant with garlic, herbs and spices. When meat is used in Sephardic cooking, it is usually lamb.

The Sephardim also introduced their own influences on the Iberian and Arab cuisines. Even today, if you enquire in Andalusia in Spain as to the major influences on the local cuisine, the Jewish contribution will be readily acknowledged, alongside that of the Moors who ruled there for so long.

Sephardic cooking reflected Sephardic life. Sensual and imbued with life's pleasures, this attitude is reflected

Above: An illumination from a Hebrew manuscript showing a synagogue in northern Spain (c.1350).

in the celebrations for life's happy occasions too. For example, in Sephardic tradition a wedding celebration lasted for two weeks and a Bar Mitzvah celebration lasted for a week. These traditions still live on today.

The peace and prosperity enjoyed by the Sephardim in Spain was not to last forever. Shortly before the end of the 14th century, antagonism towards Jewish inhabitants erupted into violent riots and thousands were massacred. Many of those who survived were forced, on pain of death, to convert to Christianity. These Jews were known as

Left: North African Sephardic Jews wear traditional prayer shawls in a synagogue on the island of Djerba off the coast of Tunisia (1952).

"conversos" or, less politely, "marranos" (a word associated with pigs and dirt). Cooking and eating pork was a way for persecuted Jews to show that they were Christian. It was a painful but necessary measure in a climate where inquisitors roamed the streets in search of families cooking Jewish dishes or keeping their chimneys cool and smoke-free on Saturday to observe Shabbat. If accused of following the Jewish faith, the punishment might be death.

Jews and their families often continued their religious practices in secret. At times such as these, food was a great comfort, not only because eating familiar, traditional dishes reminded the conversos of their history, but also because in their own kitchens they could observe the rituals bound up with preparation and serving. Interestingly, when Jews prepared pork, they observed their own methods of doing so, slow-cooking suckling pig as they would cook kosher meats such as lamb. A Shabbat bean and meat dish, dfina, made with layers of pork and pork sausages; is even said to have evolved into the Spanish national dish, cocido.

For a few decades these clandestine Jews flourished but they were a thorn in the flesh of the Spanish rulers. The Spanish Inquisition came about at the end of the 15th century and in 1492 all the remaining Jews in Spain were expelled. They scattered to North Africa, Europe, the Middle East and the New World. The communities of the Caribbean, Mexico and much of South America date from these times.

With each migration, Sephardic Jews encountered new flavours which they introduced into their own cooking. From countries such as Iraq, Turkey, Greece, Morocco, Egypt and Romania, they acquired a love of new and often exotic flavourings. When Iraqi Sephardic Jews migrated to India in the 19th century, they introduced Middle Eastern flavours to the Bene Israel and Cochinese Jews already there. They used spices in ways unknown before, and these methods were embraced enthusiastically by the Indian Jews.

THE ASHKENAZIM

The Jews who fled to the Rhine valley spread across Europe over the centuries. Ashkenazic Jewish communities of France, Italy and Germany, which were so numerous in the early Middle Ages, were pushed farther and farther eastwards due to persecutions from the time of the Crusades, which began late in the eleventh century. Many Jews fled to Eastern Europe, especially Poland. They spoke Yiddish, which is a combination of Middle High German and Hebrew, written in Hebrew script.

Their non-Jewish neighbours ate abundant shellfish and pork, cooked with lard and mixed milk with meat freely. None of this was permitted for Jews, so the only answer for them was to keep themselves apart. In Tsarist Russia, they were only allowed to live in the Pale of Settlement, a portion of land that stretched from the Baltic Sea to the Black Sea. The Ashkenazic Jews lived – often uneasily – in shtetlach (villages) and never knew when they would be forced to flee again.

For the Jews who settled in Germany and Austria, the age of enlightenment was the Haskalah in the 18th to 19th centuries, when the Reform movement freed them from the more restrictive bonds of religious adherence and allowed them to enter the secular world of arts, philosophy, science and music. German Jews amassed great knowledge and created a culture of depth and finesse. They became so intertwined with the culture of Germany that when the Holocaust was upon them they could not fathom how it could have happened, because they considered themselves German first and foremost.

Ashkenazic food was the food of a cold climate. Vegetables were pickled in salt and fermented; for example, cabbage became sauerkraut, which was stored to last the winter. Cucumbers were transformed into pickles, piquant treats to enliven the bland fare of winter. Fermented beetroot (beets) became russel, the basis for a traditional borscht. Fish – freshwater, rather than the sea fish enjoyed by the Sephardic Jews – was smoked and salted, as were meats. Because there was often insufficient kosher meat to go around, very small amounts would be bulked out with other ingredients and served as dumplings and pastries, or in casseroles and stews.

Grains and beans were eaten in abundance. Healthy, hearty and filling, they were also pareve, so they could be mixed with either meat or milk. Often, but most usually for Shabbat or a festival, beans were cooked slowly with meats in a dish known as cholent, which could be eaten when the family returned home from the synagogue.

Horseradish was shredded into an eye-watering condiment and fresh herbs and other aromatics such as spring onions (scallions), dill and parsley were delighted in. Ashkenazic food was often cooked in chicken or goose fat, whether it contained meat or not, rendering anything cooked with chicken or goose fat a meat meal and unable to be eaten with dairy products. Ashkenazic food was often enriched with golden onions and sometimes flavoured with honey, a tradition of which the Polish were especially fond. A variation on this was a mixture of honey and vinegar which makes a tangy sweet and sour sauce.

When potatoes were introduced from the New World, the Ashkenazic Jews adored them and incorporated them into their cuisine with great enthusiasm. Latkes and kugels, soups and dumplings were all prepared from this new and filling vegetable.

YEMENITE JEWS

The Yemenite Jewish community dates back to before the destruction of the Second Temple. In the 4th and 5th centuries, the rulers of Yemen were in fact Jewish, but after the arrival of Islam in the 8th century their lives in Yemen became prison-like and they lived in great isolation. This in fact helped to preserve the ancient rituals and customs of Judaism that were left behind by other Jewish communities. From the 1800s through to the foundation of the state of Israel, thousands of Jews made their way to what was then Palestine and in 1949

Right: A group of Ashkenazic Jews sit outside their home in Jerusalem (1885).

the newly founded state rescued what was left of the Yemenite community. Called "Operation Magic Carpet", the airlift fulfilled a Yemenite prophesy that a great bird or magic carpet would one day swoop down and carry them all off to the promised land.

Yemenite crafts, jewellery and handiwork have greatly enhanced the culture of Israel, and its food has been given an exotic, fragrant character. Yemenite spice mixtures such as hawaij, redolent of cumin, turmeric, garlic and pepper; soups of meat and vegetables, and sauces such as zchug or hilbeh have become such a part of the everyday Israeli diet that it is impossible to think of Israeli food without it.

EUROPE, CENTRAL ASIA AND THE MIDDLE EAST

The changes wrought by the twentieth century blurred the geographical distinctions once held by eastern and western Jewish cultures, with the result that Ashkenazim, Sephardim and other communities are now scattered widely throughout Europe and the Near East. The result is a wonderful array of dishes that often fuse exotic spices and zesty flavours with the wholefoods and culinary technique of colder climates.

Britain

The first Jewish migrants arrived in Britain in 1066 and were expelled by Edward I in 1290, a hundred years after

the massacre of York's entire Jewish community at the site of Clifford's Tower. In 1655, after negotiations had been held between Manashe ben Israel and Oliver Cromwell, Jews were allowed to return and live in England.

Sephardic Jews then came to settle in England. They came via Holland, bringing with them the flavours and specialities of their native Portugal, which included their favourite dish, battered or crumbed fried fish.

Today, most of Britain's Jewish communities live in north London, with smaller communities scattered in towns around the rest of the country including Brighton, Manchester, Liverpool, Glasgow and Edinburgh. Stamford Hill in north London is home to one of the largest communities of Chassidic Jews in the world. Most of the Jewish communities in Britain are Ashkenazic, though there are a few Sephardic groups and an excellent Sephardic centre in London. The well-known British families of Sassoon and Saatchi were both Sephardic, Baghdadi families who were instrumental in building the British Empire in the Far East.

Glasgow has the largest Jewish community in Scotland, though even in the remote islands pockets of Jewishness may be found. Typical Eastern European fare of strudel and pickled herring can be found alongside Anglo-Jewish fried gefilte fish and a plum pudding made with matzo meal instead of flour, for Pesach. Even a typically Scottish dish of white pudding, made with sausage and oats, bears an uncanny resemblance to the vegetarian Jewish dumpling known as kishke.

France

France is now home to the largest Jewish community in Europe, and this influence shows in the national cuisine. Foie gras, often considered typically French, originated in ancient Egypt and was undoubtedly introduced to France by Jewish immigrants – by Ashkenazim in Alsace, and possibly Sephardim in the south-west. Some say that the French cassoulet was originally cholent, the Jewish bean and meat stew baked slowly in a low oven and served warm on Shabbat, and that the spices that are so well loved in eastern France –

Chassidic Jews

This group of strictly observant Jews, recognizable by their traditional Eastern European dress – black coats and hats of cloth or fur for the men; long skirts and sleeves, stockings and (when married) headscarves for the women – originated in Poland, Galicia and the Ukraine. The movement was founded by Israel Ben Eliezer, also known as the Ba'al Shem Tov (Master of the Good Name) in the 17th century.

cumin, ginger and cinnamon – are testament to the Jewish community that flourished there. Chocolate, like aubergines, came to France with the Sephardic Jews expelled from Spain.

Scandinavia

The Jews of Scandinavia were primarily Ashkenazim and met their fate in World War II, as did so many of Europe's Jews. Communities do exist there, growing due to the arrival of Russian and Israeli Jews. As shechita (kosher slaughtering) is illegal, kosher meat must be imported, but fish is plentiful and the beloved herring of Ashkenazic Jews is also the herring of Scandinavia.

Italy

The Italian Jewish community (Italkim), which is now very small as a result of the Holocaust and post-World War II emigration, was once grand, influential and active. It is said that the true Roman is the Jewish Roman, for there has been a Jewish community in Rome longer than anywhere else.

Italian cuisine has been influenced very strongly by these long-established settlers. To this day, carciofi alla Giudia (artichokes in the Jewish manner) is a

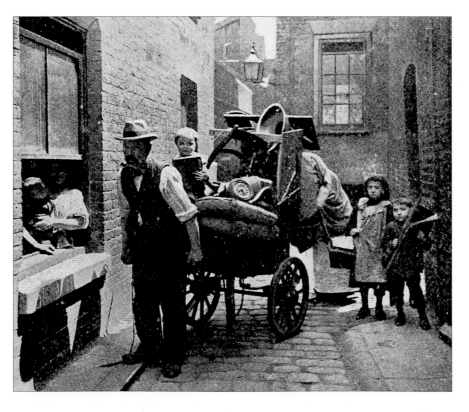

Left: Jews struggling to make a living in London's East End (1900s).

Opposite: A bakery selling matzos in the Jewish area in the 4th arondissement of Paris (1923).

speciality of Giudia, the ghetto of Rome. (The word "ghetto" originated in Italy to describe an area set aside for Jews.)

The little town of Pitigliano in Tuscany was once such an important centre of Jewish life, religious study and culture that it was known as Little Jerusalem. The Jewish community built the aqueduct there and the matzo ovens they used can stil be seen. During World War II, the Jews of Pitigliano were saved by local people, who smuggled them out of the city. Although there are no Jews there now, all of them having emigrated to either America or Israel, the citizens of Pitigliano rejoice in the fact that Jews from Israel often come to their town to be married in the synagogue there.

Greece

Both Thessalonika and the islands traditionally had large Jewish communities. In Corfu, for example, they were a very important part of the community when it was part of the Venetian empire. After the Inquisition, Jewish refugees from Spain and Portugal made their way to Zakynthos and Lefkada. At one point, it was said that the Jewish population of Rhodes was particularly dominant and many large towns on Greek islands had a Jewish area, such as that in Chania, Crete. Ties between Jewish and non-Jewish inhabitants often endured, even when pressure was brought to bear during World War II. On the Ionian island of Zakynthos, the archbishop and mayor allegedly listed themselves first on a register of local Jews extracted by the Gestapo. Despite the devastation of Greece's Jewish community by the Holocaust, the culinary legacy remains strong. One of Corfu's most delicious salads is a Jewish-inspired dish of raw fennel, delicately flavoured with oranges, olive oil and lemon juice.

Georgia

The Jews of Georgia may be the descendants of the ten tribes sent into exile by Shalmaneser, the king of Assyria (858–824BCE). On the other hand, some say that the Jews were exiled from Judah under the ruler of Babylonia, Nebuchadnezzar (605–562BCE). They were mentioned by Benjamin of Tudela from Spain in 1160, then by Marco Polo in 1272. They suffered greatly under the rule of Stalin.

Georgian Jewish food is rich with beans, vegetables, and sauces made from puréed walnuts or sour fruit such as plums and pomegranates. Tangy vinegar, garlic, chilli and cumin are favourites, with lots of herbs scattered throughout the cuisine including dill, coriander (cilantro), basil, mint and

Below: Jewish refugees crowd on the top deck of the Haviva Reik *as they arrive in Palestine (1946).*

parsley. They eat rich pilaff dishes, hearty barbecued meat and wild vegetables gathered from the forest. Cheese-filled Khatchapuri is one of Georgia's famous pastries. They enjoy a cornmeal porridge much like mamaliga, a tomato-pepper sauce much like the Hungarian lecsó and a walnut and honey crisp sweet (candy) similar to the ones eaten by Jews throughout the Middle East and the Balkans.

Uzbekistan

The cities of Uzbekistan are Samarkand and Bukhara. Samarkand was a city of great architecture on the route of the ancient silk road. When the city was destroyed by the Muslims in the 16th century, the Jews moved to Bukhara where they found an already flourishing Jewish community. Persian Jews were invited by the Emir of Bukhara who brought their traditions of poetry written in Judaeo-Persian. Today the Jews of Bukhara speak Tajiki-Jewish.

Many have emigrated to Israel, but there is still a Bukharan Jewish community. Their food, like that of the Persians, is subtle, with pasta a favourite dish (it is believed that pasta originated in this area rather than in China or Italy). Plov – a pilaff seasoned with cumin, coriander, turmeric and pepper, with ingredients that change with the season – often has lamb in it. Naan is a favourite bread and carp, fresh from the many rivers, is a favourite fish. Like so many Jewish communities, they have a favourite recipe for aubergine (eggplant) salad. In this case, it is made specifically with deliciously juicy aubergines roasted over hot coals, and garlic pounded with salt

Kurdistan

According to tradition, the Jews of Kurdistan are the descendants of the tribes Dan, Naphtali and Benjamin. Life for Jews was hard. Until the 20th century they could be sold into slavery and there were so many murders that they can be said to have lived lives of fear. From 1950–51, the Jews who lived in the area of Kurdistan that is modern Iraq fled, mostly to Israel.

Kurdish Jews are fond of a wide variety of dumplings. Known as koobe, they are made from bulgur wheat, rice and semolina and can be found in soups rich with milk, meat, or vegetables. Sometimes they are fried or stuffed and the flavourings are often cumin, turmeric, red chilli and lemon. Cabbage is a favourite vegetable, fresh or pickled, as are okra and turnip.

The Gulf

The Jewish community of Iran goes back to the destruction of the First Temple (586BCE) at the time of Cyrus the Great. One of the oldest communities in the diaspora, today it is very small and has a precarious position in Muslim Iran.

The years of the Palevi dynasty were years of prosperity and freedom for Iran's Jews; yet during the 1979 revolution of the Ayatollahs, about half of them fled. The largest communities are now in Israel and Los Angeles, where they live in a tightly knit community with separate synagogues and groups, adhering to their Persian customs and eating their traditional foods, such as

Above: Buying vegetables at a Greek market. Many Jewish dishes of fish and vegetables, as well as the famous egg-lemon sauce (avgolemono), have left their mark on Greek cuisine.

chellou, kebab, khoresht (zesty sauces of meat, vegetables and fruit) and jewelled pilaffs of rice.

The Bene Maneshe

In 1979, word arrived in Israel about another group of Jews in India, previously not in touch with world Jewry, who appeared to be the "lost tribe of Israel", Manacho. In the following decades, rabbis were dispatched to examine the customs and rituals of the Bene Menashe. They have finally been recognized as the lost tribe they claimed to be and granted the right of return to Israel. It is thought that, following their expulsion from Israel, the tribe wandered through Afghanistan and Mongolia, finally turning south to India where they settled. Their foods are heavily influenced by Indian cuisine, featuring spicy stews, kebabs, rice and flatbreads. The population is now expected to gradually emigrate to Israel, a migration that will require them to embrace new laws and customs, and to shed some of their highly observant heritage which has long been extinct within modern Jewish culture.

AFRICA

Many thriving Jewish communities and remnants of others exist throughout Africa. Some of the communities, such as those of South Africa and Zimbabwe, are Eastern European in origin, dating to the 1880s when Jews, from Lithuania in particular, sought refuge from the pogroms (violent attacks) of Europe.

Morocco and Tunisia

There has been a Jewish community in North Africa since Roman times, long before the establishment of Islam, although during difficult times a large number of Jews travelled to Spain where they lived peacefully until the Inquisition and Expulsion.

The food heritage of Morocco is that of the Moors, the Berbers, the Almohads and Almoravids and the Andalusian flavours that had dominated southern Spain for centuries. Morocco boasted a large Jewish community, in places such as Fez, Tetouan and Marrakesh, which was known for its wealth of delicately spiced dishes.

Although a vibrant civilization flourished, there were periods of persecution, martyrdom, massacres and forced conversion. After the Expulsion however, things became quieter, then the community prospered. Jews lived in cities and villages throughout the country and were famous for all manner of occupations. Their foods developed with Arabic flavours, and, with the arrival of the French in the 19th century, the latter's culinary traditions permeated their already exotic-scented Jewish-Moroccan cuisine.

The Tunisian community of Jews today numbers only about 2,000. However, there were once two large Jewish communities there, the first of Arabian language and culture, the second, European, that had coexisted for centuries with their non-Jewish neighbours. In 1948 they were for the most part forced to emigrate, mostly to Israel and France.

The luscious specialities of raw egg-filled pastries called brik (where eggs poach while the pastry is frying crisply), harissa (a hot chilli sauce), Tunisian sandwiches, and their many distinctive versions of couscous, have all added their savour to the French and Israeli table. Tunisian food is spicier than Moroccan and, while perhaps more limited in scope, is irresistible.

Ironically, the foods of North Africa, while often seen as chic and stylish in Europe and America, are viewed as the food of the poor in Israel. Israelis take the cuisine for granted much in the way that Americans take Mexican food for granted and the British take Indian food for granted. It is inevitable that the delicacies of North Africa will eventually find the same enthusiastic reception in Israel as they do elsewhere, and this is in fact starting to happen. Couscous is a great culinary ambassador, in the same way that chicken soup with matzo balls is proclamatory of being Ashkenazic.

Libya

During the Roman Empire, Libya had been both a refuge from and a place of terror and persecution. Throughout the rules of Spain, Turkey, Arabs, Italy and Britain, the Jewish community survived until the year of independence in 1951. At first, the Jews were received by the king and thanked for their support. Within a year, however, newspapers

Below: A Jewish grocer in a Moroccan souk (market) sells the specialities of his community.

were attacking them as agents of Israel. From then on, Jewish agencies were closed, Jews were forbidden to travel unless leaving a member of the family at home and Jewish property was confiscated. Finally, with the onset of the Six-Day War in 1967, pogroms swept through Libya, killing 18 Jews. The remaining 3,500 hid and many fled. Today, the largest Libyan Jewish communities are in Italy and Israel.

Libyan Jews spoke a local version of Judaeo-Arabic which included Italian, Spanish, Turkish and other influences. In public, they often spoke Italian. Libyan-Jewish food exuded the exotic aromas of other North African flavours, with a layer of Italian influence which contributed pastas and soups like minestrone. Libyan gefilte fish, called cheraimie, is a spicy poached fishcake served on a bed of tomato and chilli sauce, said to be representative of the Red Sea. Their version of cholent was called t'fina and one of their most beloved everyday dishes was maakood, a frittata filled with potatoes or bread, enriched with vegetables and/or meat, and tinted gold with turmeric.

Egypt

By the early 20th century, the Eygptian Jewish community, which has existed since antiquity, had flourished into a great cosmopolitan, sophisticated, multilingual community made up of Jews from Yemen and North Africa, Turkey, Thessalonika in Greece, and Syria. Even Ashkenazim from Russia and other Yiddish-speaking countries had responded to the lure of fortunes to be made on the building of the Suez Canal and flocked to Egypt.

The bourgeois Jewish community in Egypt coincided with an era of secularism in the formerly observant Jewish European community, and inhabitants spoke Judaeo-Spanish and French in addition to the local Arabic. Egyptian-Jewish fare came into its own at religious celebrations, where spicy stews (wat) and dishes of rice, lentils and broad (fava) beans were served alongside delicate offerings such as savoury meatballs and sweet pastries.

Ethiopia

The Jews of Ethiopia are said to be descendants of the son of King Solomon and the Queen of Sheba. Long isolated from the Jewish world, they nonetheless kept up their Jewish traditions and rituals until their arrival in Ethiopia.

In Ethiopia, they lived in their own villages away from non-Jewish Ethiopians. At one point, the Ethiopian Jews, Beta Israel, thought they were the last Jews in the world and took their guardianship of the Torah very seriously. They kept kashrut devotedly, but had only the rules laid out in the Torah. They did not, however, adhere to the meat/dairy distinction of the rest of the kosher-keeping world.

Like non-Jewish Ethiopians, the Beta Israel ate their spicy stews, and boiled vegetables, meat and salads laid out on thin pancakes of the fermented grain, teff. Ethiopian-Jewish cuisine also had a big influence on the cuisine of the rest of the country. Around 500 years ago, the Jewish merchants of Addis Ababa introduced curry powder and other aspects of Indian cooking. Combined with the local spices of Berbere, a pounded paste of chilli, garlic, ginger, fenugreek, cardomom, cloves, allspice, nutmeg, salt, white pepper and turmeric, it forms the main flavouring of the land. Dishes like spicy dried green peas or mixed vegetables are typical. Interestingly, Ethiopian Jews eat beans for Pesach but avoid fermented milk products and traditional Ethiopian matzo is made with chickpea flour.

There is a Jewish community in Ethiopia today, although it is much reduced in size since the mass exodus to Israel in the 1980s, known as "Operation Solomon". In Israel, life has not always been easy for Ethiopian Jews, yet they contribute much to Israeli culture.

Sub-saharan Africa

The Abayudaya Jews are indigenous to Sub-Saharan Africa and, while wholeheartedly embracing Judaism, have been practising only since the early 20th century. Foods are locally influenced, with rice, plantain and

Above: Doro wat, the traditional Ethiopian chicken and spices dish, is enjoyed by Jews and non-Jews alike. The egg represents life and wholeness. When preparing the dish, care is taken so that every guest receives one egg with their serving of the stew.

cassava forming a mainstay of the diet. Ghanian Jews serve a delicious peanut soup with chicken, tomatoes and curry spices. They make a special fritter called mandaz which is soaked in syrup. Variations of this are also found among Ugandan Jews.

The Lemba of Malawi, Zimbabwe, and South African Vende are endeavouring to be recognized as Jews, although to date this has not happened. They do follow their own traditions and adhere to them devotedly.

Maputo, Mozambique, once had a thriving Jewish community but at independence the community left. Similarly, the Jews of Timbuktu and Mali were almost all forced to convert to local customs and religious practice, or flee. Sao Tome and Principe had a Jewish community with the sad history of having originated as a dumping ground for Jewish children by the Portuguese during the Inquisition. Descendants of this group continued to live there for a while but no community – or culinary heritage – remains in these places today.

CHINA AND HONG KONG

Hong Kong's predominantly Sephardic Jewish community began in 1857 when the wealthy Indian-Jewish businessman, Sir Victor Sassoon, opened an office in the newly established colony and, aided by the similarly influential Kadoorie family, also of Sephardic origin, and Jewish administrators of mainly Baghdadi descent, developed trade to and from the island. The rise of the Jewish community in Hong Kong was hindered by the internment of many Jews at the hands of the Japanese during World War II. Today the community numbers about 3,000 mostly American, British and Israeli Jews and is balanced between Sephardim and Ashkenazim, Reform (Progressive) and ultra-observant Chabad Lubavitch, a branch of Chassidic Jewry. The synagogue, Kehillat Beijing, serves a mostly professional, and transient, community of international business people, university lecturers and international development workers.

The Jewish community of Kaifeng has one of the most interesting stories imaginable, a story still in the making because there are so many missing pieces. Are they a lost tribe? Are they Jewish? No one is quite sure. Over the years, seven Sino-Jewish clans have been identified, though by patrilineal rather than matrilineal descent, which does not conform to the Halacha (complete body of Jewish religious law).

The 600 or so Kaifeng Jews wear the headcovering of kippot, indicating observance. They refrain from eating pork and adhere to ritual slaughter as well as circumcision, which is often thought barbaric by their non-Jewish neighbours. They have a traditional Jewish meal, youtai, which is comprised of four courses, each symbolising the different aspects of being Jewish: bitter, spicy, sour and sweet.

Sephardic Jews began to settle in Shanghai in the mid-1800s. They were mostly observant Jews from India but originally from Baghdad. The Sassoon family endowed the first cemetery and not long after, the first synagogue was established. Ashkenazim began to arrive in the 1920s, fleeing pogroms. In the run up to World War II, over 20,000 European Jews sought refuge in Shanghai. Japan was urged by the Gestapo to put a "final solution" into place but refused, in gratitude to Jewish bankers who had helped Japan to modernize 30 years earlier. The Jews were, however, ultimately crowded into the Hongkou ghetto.

After the war, the community emigrated to Australia, America and Israel. The few who had remained were forced to flee the communists in the early 1950s. By the 1990s, Westerners were returning to China, including Jews. By 1998, Chabad Lubavitch had arrived, and today there are over 250 Jews living in Shanghai, for the most part in Western business communities.

The Harbin Jewish community was established in the late 1800s when China granted Russia the concession to build the railway across Manchuria. Russian authorities were keen to attract workers, so they encouraged minorities, including Jews, to settle there. By the early 1900s, a strong Jewish community was thriving in most spheres of local life and culture.

Jews fled the Bolsheviks in the revolution, but they were joined by fleeing Cossacks and members of the White Guard, many of whom harboured anti-Semitism. This came to an ugly conclusion after the Japanese invasion, prompting many Jews to move to Shanghai, Tianjin and Palestine.

After the Chinese Communist revolution, Jewish families lost their jobs and businesses and many ended up in Siberia. Jews fled to Israel, Australia and North and South America. By 1962, the community had disappeared. In the late 1990s, the restoration of the Jewish cemetery was begun, followed by the restoration of the former synagogue and the establishment of a Harbin Jewish research centre.

The Russian Jews of Harbin led a vital and exciting existence. Living in a Russian world surrounded by Chinese culture and eating Russian food, they often gave their traditional dishes a Chinese touch. For example, they adapted beef stroganoff into a dish based on chicken, using local black funghi instead of European mushrooms, and soy sauce instead of sour cream.

Tianjin, not far from Beijing, hosted a large Jewish community in the late 1800s, when Jews fleeing Russia looked

Left: Russian Jews living in China adapted local ingredients to their cuisine, such as Chinese cabbage for stuffing. Certain factors, such as the shortage of dairy in the Chinese diet, made this fusion quite simple.

for opportunity elsewhere. It grew in 1917 after the revolution and by the late 1930s had its own synagogue. Around 1957, Jewish businesses were nationalized and by 1958 most Jews had left.

AUSTRALIA AND NEW ZEALAND

The first fleet to Australia, which arrived in 1788, carried on it a handful of Jews; by 1841 the first synagogue was built in York Street, Sydney. The Jewish community grew in tandem with that of the pogroms in Russia at the turn of the 20th century, and once again as a result of immigration from Nazi-occupied Europe several decades later. Today, Australian Jews live in primarily urban areas, though a community is growing on the Gold Coast in Queensland. New Zealand Jews share a similar history of settlement with the Jews of Australia.

In recent years, Jews from Russia, South Africa and even a few Israelis have made their way down under, and Jewish food in the Antipodes reflects their mainly Ashkenazic heritage. Foods like borscht, kasha and knishes are found in restaurants catering to the Jewish population.

LATIN AMERICA AND THE CARIBBEAN

From its beginnings with Spanish and Portuguese Jews fleeing the Spanish Inquisition, the community of Hispanic Jews grew peacefully, though often uneasily alongside that of non-Jews in Catholic Latin America.

In the late 19th and early 20th century, the communities expanded to absorb Jews fleeing European oppression. Russia and Lithuania saw an especially large migration to countries like Peru, Mexico, Argentina, Uruguay, Cuba, Brazil and Venezuela. Before and after World War II, Jews sought refuge in Latin America, some more successfully than others.

The oldest continuous community was in Curacao. From there, fledgling Jewish communities in the New World were aided into establishment. Today, Argentina has the largest Jewish population in Latin America, pairing Sephardic and Ashkenazic communities who live side by side rather than in shared culture. Peru and Mexico have large lively Jewish communities as well.

In Lima's Jewish community, as in so many others in the diaspora, local foods are mingled with traditions from the Old Country. Yiddish meatballs of beef and fried onions are simmered in a Peruvian sauce with tomatoes, oregano, peas and mushrooms. Chicken and turkey are cooked in sauces that the Peruvians usually use for cuy (guinea pig), the nation's favourite meat. Matzo balls are stuffed with mashed chicken livers and baked into bocaditos (savoury pastries) and the traditional Polish apple cake – brought to Peru by Ashkenazic migrants – is known as pastel de manzanas.

Cuba's Jews fled Castro for the shores of Miami, the gateway for Latin American Jews heading for the USA. The Jewish community there is influential, active socially and politically, and dotes on the same food as the other exiled Cubans: black beans, rice and coffee, but, of course, no pork, shellfish or meat with milk.

Mexico's Jewish community is surprisingly large with a similar history to that of the rest of Latin America's Jews. Dishes like guacamole found their way into the daily diet. Mole, which uses mostly kosher ingredients, became as much a weekly grandmotherly dish as kishke. Chicken soup might be served Mexican style, with a wedge of lime and a dash of salsa instead of a matzo ball.

THE UNITED STATES

In the early part of the 20th century, a great wave of immigration to the United States influenced the American table enormously. The most obvious influence was the emergence of the delicatessen – or deli as it is more commonly known. In places that were home to Jewish communities from Eastern Europe such as Chicago and Old New York, delis were places where hungry men with no homes of their own could go for a good meal. These men had usually travelled ahead – often by many years – of their wives and children to establish a new life. Lodging in rented rooms and

Above: Deliciously chewy bagels were transported to the streets of New York City from Eastern European shtetlach.

working hard to save enough money to pay for their families to join them, they needed somewhere to eat that was kosher and that gave them a taste of home.

Other ethnic groups discovered delis and began to enjoy the hearty foods they served, which became the flavour of America: bagels, soups, pastrami and other robust meats, huge sandwiches, dill pickles, salads and juicy sausages.

MODERN TIMES

The 20th century saw the end of many of the great Jewish communities of the world – some 2,500 years old – and the start of others. Ashkenazim emigrating from Germany, Central Europe and Russia during the late 19th and early 20th centuries often packed little by way of possessions, but they did take the traditions of the cuisine that we typically think of as Jewish: chicken soup and matzo balls, Viennese pastries, rye bread and bagels, delicate noodles and robust chopped liver. The same dishes – familiarly called the food of the Old Country – travelled to Great Britain, Israel, Latin America and the United States with the refugees before, during and after World War II.

The Holocaust destroyed much of European Jewish culture, and communist control of Eastern Europe and Russia swept away most of the remainder, although here and there communities continued to keep the faith, albeit in secret, keeping their traditions alive.

In many places communities have regrouped. The Jewish community of Iran, which relocated to Los Angeles after the Islamic revolution, had been in Persia since 600BCE and held tight to its customs and cuisine. In Brooklyn, a suburb of New York City, there is a thriving Cochinese synagogue, where Indian Jews cook their spicy delicacies for feast celebrations. Ironically, in Cochin itself, there are barely any Jews left. In the Israeli port of Jaffa, you can eat wonderfully spicy, zesty Libyan food thanks to Libyan Jews who have relocated there. In Beijing in China, a fledgling synagogue and Jewish community has recently emerged, consisting primarily of international development workers and their families.

Traditionally, when Sephardic and Ashkenazic Jews settled in the same country, they tended to keep apart, maintaining their distinctive cultures, but that too has changed in recent times. When Askenazim from Eastern Europe and Germany emigrated to South America, they frequently found themselves living alongside Sephardic Jews from Spain. Conversely, Sephardim from North Africa moved to France after World War II and helped to breathe new life into the Ashkenazic communities destroyed by Hitler.

A NEW HOME IN ISRAEL

With the establishment of the State of Israel in 1948, hundreds of thousands of Jews who had been both isolated and stateless for generations made their way back. Each group brought with it the culinary traditions and flavours of the countries they had left.

At first, this diversity was not always appreciated. The halutzim (settlers) were eager to be integrated and to divorce themselves from a past that included what they saw as the foods of

bondage. There was great pressure to abandon individual traditions gleaned from the lands and non-Jewish cultures they had left behind, and to throw all heritage into one melting pot with the new identity of "Israeli food".

Fortunately, and at last, all this is changing. Moroccan Jews in Israel are beginning to celebrate their traditional flavours, recognizing that they are delicious in their difference and not something to be ashamed of. Yemeni restaurants are terribly chic, as are other ethnic eating houses. The waves of recent Russian and Ethiopian immigrations (the last of Ethiopia's ancient tribe of Jews were flown to Israel in 1992) have added their own ingredients to a cuisine that includes flavours from almost every corner of the globe, set against a Middle Eastern backdrop and a belief that what grows easily tastes best.

In an almost complete circle, Ashkenazic food has found a certain cachet in Israel in recent years, with classic dishes such as cholent, chicken soup with matzo balls and pickled vegetables reaching almost cult status. However, as part of the marvellous fusion of foods that has arisen with the union of the various different Jewish communities, Israeli Ashkenazim have been influenced by other cuisines. For example, classic chicken soup might be served with a spoonful of fiery zchug, the Yemenite sauce.

JEWS TODAY

As we have seen, it is at times of both celebration and commemoration that Jewish cooking really comes into its

Below: The Jewish deli is a wonderful legacy from the Ashkenazic Jews who settled in the United States.

own, whether the occasion be the weekly Shabbat meal, an annual festival such as Chanukkah or Pesach or one of the events that mark the cycle of Jewish life such as Brit Milah (ritual circumcision), Bar or Bat Mitzvah (coming of age), a wedding or a funeral. Many Jewish families celebrate the traditional religious holidays, but do not necessarily keep kosher or strictly observe Shabbat. Thus, all over the world, but especially in the USA, where Reform (Progressive or Liberal) Judaism has become mainstream, there are many different ways of being Jewish other than being strictly observant.

In the modern world, many Jews are beginning both to adapt their traditions to the exigencies of contemporary life and to make changes to their cuisine. For example, Ashkenazic Jews, with a close eye on health, often use olive oil for cooking, as in the ancient Sephardic tradition. The dishes of the Middle East are also enjoying a resurgence of popularity, and kosher convenience foods – obtained from specialist Jewish grocers and supermarkets – are increasingly used when time is short.

The laws of kashrut continue to be a focus of daily life for observant Jews. In recent years, the tendency towards liberalization, and the shedding of age-old customs in certain communities, is being increasingly balanced by a strong emergence of modern Orthodox Jewry, many of whom are returning to a strict adherence to kashrut.

Above: Yemenite Jews in Jerusalem enjoy a traditional Pesach Seder meal.

Whether the traditional Jewish table is Sephardic, Ashkenazic, Conservative, Reform (Progressive), Orthodox or Chassidic is not what matters most. The most important factor is that the food it carries reflects both a people's life and its culture. Having suffered so much during the twentieth century, world Jewry is, increasingly, learning to find room for the many surviving traditions, of diverse origins, that make up its whole. The Jewish culinary repertoire offers food for sharing with family and friends, for bringing communities closer together, and for giving reassurance in an ever-changing world.

HOLIDAYS, FESTIVALS AND OBSERVANCES

The Jewish calendar is punctuated by holidays, festivals and observances, which are shared by the entire community. Personal milestones in the lives of individuals such as Bar or Bat Mitzvahs, weddings and celebrations attending the birth of a baby are also celebrated. Each festival has a special significance, and is accompanied by its own songs, stories, admonitions, activities, prayers and, of course, foods.

The Jewish year follows the 354–5 day lunar calendar, as opposed to the 365–6 day solar year, so while each Jewish festival falls on precisely the same date in each year of the Jewish calendar, the dates will differ on a Gregorian calendar. For synchronicity, and also to keep the months in their appropriate season, a thirteenth month is added to the Jewish calendar every two or three years. In the northern hemisphere, therefore, Rosh Hashanah will always be celebrated between summer and autumn, while Chanukkah always heralds winter and Pesach

ushers in the spring, regardless of how different the actual dates will be on Christian calendars.

Jewish holidays always begin at sundown on the day before. The year of celebrations starts around September, with Rosh Hashanah, the Jewish New Year, and progresses through Yom Kippur, the Day of Atonement, which is marked nine days later. Sukkot, the harvest festival of thanksgiving, follows, ending with Simchat Torah, the festival of the Torah. Around December comes Chanukkah, the festival of lights, when gifts are traditionally exchanged. Tu b'Shevat, the Holiday of the Trees, comes next, around February, and this in turn is followed by Purim, a flamboyant festival that involves dressing up in colourful costumes, and that could be considered a kind of Jewish Mardi Gras or carnival.

Pesach commemorates Israel's deliverance from Egypt. During this eight-day festival, Jews consume particular foods and drinks, eschewing

those that contain leaven. Shavuot celebrates the Giving of the Torah, while Tish b'Av is a day of fasting, when the Destruction of the Temple is mourned.

Many communities also observe Yom Hatsmaut, Israeli Independence Day, which is celebrated on 14 May with festivities, including outdoor gatherings where falafel is traditionally eaten. Yom Ha Shoah, the Holocaust Remembrance Day, is observed shortly after Pesach, honouring the millions who died.

The most important festival and observance of them all is the Sabbath or Shabbat. This is celebrated every week, and forms a model for all the other holidays. It is a day for refraining from work, escaping the chaos of the ordinary working week, focusing on the spiritual, appreciating nature and enjoying family life.

Below: This Mizrah scroll, hung on the west wall of the house to indicate the direction of Jerusalem, illustrates the major Jewish festivals.

SHABBAT

This is the sabbath, the day of rest. It is said to be the most important Jewish holiday, and it comes not once a year, but once a week. It is the weekly island of peace amid the sea of hectic life. Even those who are not observant in other ways will often enjoy keeping Shabbat. The word "shabbat" means cessation of labour and it is a treasured time to relax with the family, perhaps taking walks through the countryside or visiting friends for lunch.

The origins of Shabbat are related in Genesis, the first book of the Bible, which describes how God created the world in six days and rested on the seventh. In the fourth commandment of the Ten Commandments, it is decreed that Shabbat is a day of rest that must be kept holy (Exodus 31:17).

A set of rules has been laid down, encompassing what it means to keep Shabbat. Observant Jews do not do any work, handle money, carry loads, light fires, tear paper, watch television or listen to the radio. They also may not cook, which has led to ingenious ways of providing warm, freshly cooked food without infringing the rule.

Below: An illumination depicting God's creation of the world (c.1530).

Above: Shabbat begins with the blessings being said over a loaf of challah and a cup of wine.

The Festive Meal

On the eve of Shabbat a festive meal is served. It begins with the lighting and blessing of the candles before sundown. Further blessings are then said over the challah, and the Kiddush (sanctifying blessing) is said over the wine.

The lighting of the candles marks the dividing line between the rest of the week and the start of Shabbat. When the candles are lit, traditionally by the woman of the household, she passes her hands lightly over the flame in a movement that seems to gather up the light, then she covers her eyes.

The greeting on Shabbat is "Shabbat Shalom", often accompanied with a kiss – or two – on the cheek, as participants wish each other a Shabbat filled with peace.

Different families have different customs regarding the blessing of the challah. It is traditional in a number of households for everyone to gather around the table, with their hands on the challah during the blessings, after which they pull it apart, making sure that each person has at least a tiny bite of the blessed bread.

A welcoming song might be sung, for example Sholem Aleichem, and/or Shabbat Shalom, a light and evocative melody that welcomes the holiday and puts everyone in a mellow mood.

The meal on Friday night usually includes chicken soup, and a chicken or braised meat. Guests will often be invited, and the table set with white linen, flowers and the finest china and cutlery. Meanwhile, the next day's meal will be simmered slowly in a low oven, as no cooking is allowed on the Shabbat itself. This is usually a dish of beans and meat taken from the Sephardi or Ashkenazi tradition.

Morning Services

Services are held on Saturday mornings in the synagogue; this is a popular time for Bar and Bat Mitzvahs. If one of these is taking place, a light celebration meal will be served at the synagogue for the whole congregation. This includes herring, salads, cookies and perhaps cakes, in addition to the Kiddush wine, challah, coffee and tea.

The main meal is served at midday or in the early afternoon as the family observes Shabbat. The steamy warm

Below: Polish Jews celebrate Shabbat in a traditional synagogue (1956).

SHABBAT BLESSINGS
Candle Lighting

As soon as the candles are lit, signifying the start of Shabbat, this blessing is recited:

Baruch Ata Adonai Elohaynu Melech Haolam, asher kedashanu b'mitzvotav, v'tzivanu l'hadleek neer shel Shabbat.

Blessed are You, Lord our God, Eternal One, who enables us to welcome Shabbat by kindling these lights.

If there are children present, then a blessing is said over them. The head of the household places his or her hands on the children and asks that they strive to carry on the traditions of the Jewish people, the boys like Ephraim and Menasshe, the girls like Sarah and Rebeccah, Rachel and Leah.

A plea is always offered for God's blessing, safety, warmth and protection, and peace.

Friday Night Kiddush

The blessing that follows is said over the goblet of Kiddush wine.

Baruch Ata Adonai Elohaynu Melech Haolam, boray p'ree hagafen.

Blessed are You, Lord God, Eternal One, who creates the fruit of the vine.

Baruch Ata Adonai Elohaynu Melech Haolam, asher kedashanu b'meetzvatov, v'rahzah banu, v'Shabbat Kodsho b'ahavah oov'rahzon heen'heelanu, zeekahron l'maasay b'raysheet. Kee hoo yom t'heela l'meekrah-ay kodesh, zaycher l'tzeeat meetzraheem. Kee vanu vacharta ohtanu keedashta meekol ha'ahmeem v'Shabbat kodshecha b'ahavah oov'ratzon heenaltanu. Baruch Ata Adonai M'kadest HaShabbat. Amen.

Blessed are You, Lord God, Eternal One, Who sanctifies us with holy acts and gives us special times and seasons to rejoice. Shabbat reminds us of the times for celebration, recalls the days of Creation of the world and how God rested from that work. Shabbat reminds us of the Exodus from Egyptian slavery. God has distinguished us from all people and given us the Shabbat full of joy. Blessed are You, Lord God, Eternal One, who sanctifies the Shabbat.

Saturday Midday Kiddush

This blessing is said over the wine to begin the Shabbat meal.

Al ken bayrah Adonai et Yom Hashabbat v'kodsho. Baruch Ata Adonai Elohaynu Melech Haolam, boray p'ree hagafen.

Behold the Eternal blessed the seventh day and called it a holy time. Blessed are You, Lord God, Eternal One, who created fruit from the vine.

Blessing over the Challah

This blessing is said over bread: challah, rye bread, matzo etc.

Baruch Ata Adonai Elohaynu Melech Haolam, hamotzi lechem meen ha'aretz.

Blessed are You, Lord God, Eternal One, who creates bread from the earth.

The Birkat Hamazon is the grace said after the meal. It is only said after meals in which bread or matzo cholent or other fragrant dish that has been keeping warm in the oven will be taken to the table, where the whole family will share it.

Both Friday night's and Saturday's meal, and indeed any meal that includes the traditional challah, should end with the saying of grace over the meal, the Birkat Hamazon, or the blessing of thanksgiving.

Shabbat is over when the first three stars are visible in the night sky. At this time Havdalah will be observed. The Havdalah ceremony comes from the word hevdal, which means different, to signify the difference or separation between Shabbat and the other days of the week.

The ceremony consists of the blessing over the wine (the Kiddush), inhaling the fragrance of sweet spices and lighting a braided candle, which is then extinguished by a few drops of wine – and so the new week begins.

Below: A braided candle and spice box used for the Havdalah ceremony.

ROSH HASHANAH

The Jewish year begins in September or October with Rosh Hashanah, which means the head of the year. This is the start of the Ten Days of Penitence, also called the Days of Awe, which end with Yom Kippur. Jews are encouraged to spend these days in retrospection,

Left: The New Year is ushered in with the saying of prayers.

considering their behaviour and how to make amends, improving their own lives and the lives of those around them.

The holidays of Rosh Hashanah and Yom Kippur are often referred to as the High Holy Days, and many Jews consider them so important that even if they observe no other festivals in the year, at this time they will go to synagogue, partake of a festive meal, and recite the prayers and blessings.

The Ram's Horn

A ceremonial shofar (ram's horn) is blown on Rosh Hashanah, as it is on Yom Kippur. The haunting sound of the shofar reminds Jews of their long history and of the ancient convenant between the people of Israel and God.

One tradition (tashlicht) calls for penitents to throw all their sins of the previous year into a body of running water. The gesture symbolizes a fresh start for the new year.

Above: The ceremonial shofar (ram's horn) is blown at Rosh Hashanah to welcome in the New Year.

Rosh Hashanah begins, as usual, at sundown on the evening before. Candles are lit, the bread is blessed, and the Kiddush is recited over the wine. A festive meal is prepared. This includes sweet foods such as apples dipped in honey, bringing the promise of sweetness in the year ahead. The challah, which is shaped into a round, rather than the more familiar oval plait, is studded with raisins or small sweets (candies). Honey replaces salt for the blessing of the challah.

Different Customs

Various ethnic groups have different customs for the holiday. Sephardim eat a whole fish with the head left intact, representing their hopes for a year rich with wisdom, with Israel as the head of the nations rather than the tail – the leader rather than the oppressed.

No sour or bitter foods are eaten at Rosh Hashanah – some communities will not even eat pickles or olives – as no sharp flavours may interfere with the sweetness of the festival. All the new season's fruits are enjoyed. In some communities, on the second night of the holiday a pomegranate is blessed and eaten. The numerous seeds of the fruit represent hoped-for fertility.

BLESSINGS FOR ROSH HASHANAH

Several blessings and benedictions attend this festival, which marks the beginning of the Jewish year. In addition to the blessings printed below, parents give thanks for their children, the challah is blessed as for Shabbat, and a slightly longer Kiddush (sanctifying blessing) is recited over the wine before it is drunk.

Candle Lighting

If Rosh Hashanah falls on the same day as Shabbat, then the blessing is modified and added to accordingly.

Baruch Ata Adonai Elohaynu Melech Haolam, asher Kiddshanu b'mitzvotav, v'tzivanu l'hadleek neer shel Yom Tov.

Blessed are You, Lord God, Eternal One, who enables us to welcome Rosh Hashanah, by kindling these lights.

Benediction

Versions of the prayer that follows – Shehehayanu – are recited on other important occasions or festivals, as well as Rosh Hashanah.

Baruch Ata Adonai Elohaynu Melech Haolam, shehehayanu, v'keeyomany v'higeeyanu laz man hazeh.

Blessed are You, Lord God, Eternal One, who has kept us alive and sustained us, enabling us to celebrate this New Year.

Honeyed Apples

When sliced apples are dipped in honey to symbolize sweetness for the year ahead, this blessing is recited.

Baruch Ata Adonai Elohaynu Melech Haolam, boray p'ree ha aytz.

Blessed are You, Lord God, Eternal One, who creates the fruit from the earth.

YOM KIPPUR

The 10th day of Tishri, the first month in the Jewish calendar, is Yom Kippur – the Day of Atonement. It is the most solemn day of the year and marks God's forgiveness of the early Israelites after they worshipped the golden calf while Moses received the tablets of the law from God on Mount Sinai.

It is a day devoted to spiritual life, when the physical is set aside. Sex is forbidden, as is wearing leather shoes, brushing the teeth, spending money, using perfumes or soap and wearing make-up. Everyone, other than children, pregnant women, and the ill or infirm, is expected to fast.

Making Amends

Jews are urged to take stock of their sins, to make amends for any wrong-doing, and to repent. The ancient Kapparot (expiations) ceremony is still observed in some circles. This involves passing a live chicken over the head of an individual, so that his or her sins may be symbolically transferred to the bird. Many prefer to use a coin instead. The coin symbolizes giving to charity.

On the day of Yom Kippur, Jews go to synagogue, greeting each other with "Have an easy fast". Much time is then spent in quiet retrospection as individuals examine their consciences with honesty, aiming to make amends for past misdeeds, and promising to do much better in the year ahead. The Yom Kippur devotions include chanting the Kol Nidre, and the Yizkor, the memorial service at which the dead are remembered and respected. Kaddish, the prayer for the dead, is recited for the deceased family members and friends of participants, and for the Jewish martyrs. Candles are also lit for the deceased.

Below: A coloured wood engraving by Julius Schnorr von Carolsfeld depicting Moses bringing the people of Israel the new Tablets of the Law after the first set was broken (1860).

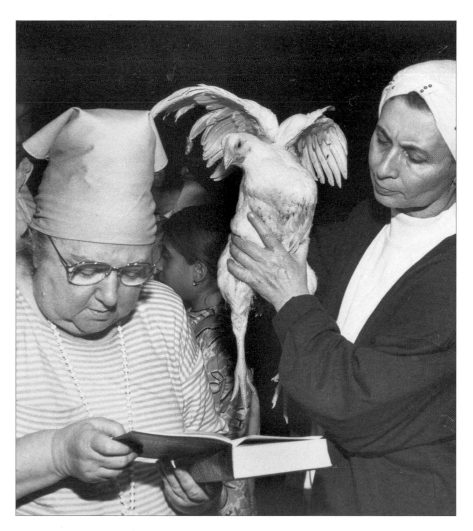

Above: During the traditional Kapparot ceremony, a live chicken is passed over the head while a prayer is recited to symbolically absorb and absolve the person's sins.

The meal on the eve of Yom Kippur is eaten in the afternoon, before sunset. Chicken soup is the preferred food, as it is for almost every festive occasion. It is probably favoured at Yom Kippur because of the traditional Kapparot ceremony involving a chicken.

For Ashkenazic Jews it is traditional to eat the soup with knaidlach (matzo balls) or kreplach filled with chicken, while for Sephardic Jews there are many different variations. In Egypt, Jews traditionally eat a simple egg and lemon soup before the fast. Sephardic Jews often follow the soup with a simple dish

such as boiled chicken with rice or couscous. The festive challah, which is enjoyed by Ashkenazic Jews on the eve of Yom Kippur, is often shaped into raised arms or wings or a ladder, rather than the traditional braided shape. The shape represents prayers being made towards heaven on this day of praying and retrospection.

All foods eaten at this time must be light and simple and not too salty or spicy as it is terribly difficult to fast with a raging thirst. It is intended that penitents should feel a few hunger pangs while they are fasting, but they should not get into any difficulty during this period.

Right: Sephardic Jews traditionally break the fast of Yom Kippur by serving eggs, which are a symbol of life.

A Day of Purity

At Yom Kippur the synagogue is decorated in white, the Torah is draped in white and the rabbi wears a kitl (a white robe), as a symbol of purity. Observant Jews also wear white in the synagogue, and shoes made from cloth rather than leather.

Unlike other festivals and holidays when candles are lit before the meal, the candles are lit after the meal – before the start of Yom Kippur and the festival observances. A pure white tablecloth is draped on the dinner table, and instead of the challah and feasting foods that are usually enjoyed for other holidays and festivals, a Bible, prayer book and other sacred religious texts are placed on the table until the observance has been completed.

Families and friends gather together for celebrations to break the fast after Yom Kippur. It is a happy occasion after the solemnity of the day's observance. Sephardim serve eggs, the symbol of life, and almost all Jews, Sephardim and Ashkenazim alike, enjoy sweet foods with mild flavours, such as honey cake and fresh fruit.

Dishes are prepared the day before Yom Kippur so that they are ready for the end of the fast and the celebrations. For Ashkenazic Jews, it is a good time to eat bagels, cream cheese, lox (smoked salmon), kugels and marinated fish such as herring.

A break-the-fast party is much like a brunch, but with a feeling of lightness of soul and a spirit of looking forward to the new year.

SUKKOT

This festival is observed by building a sukkah, which is a little three-sided hut or booth. The Mishnah (the first code of Jewish Law) lays down how this must be done. There must only be three sides, and the roof must be covered with schach, or branches of trimmed greens or palm leaves, with enough open space to permit those inside to see the stars. A sukkah must be a temporary building, so you cannot use any other permanent structure that stays up for the rest of the year. Sometimes a few families get together to share the task of building, starting at one house and then moving to the next until all the structures are complete.

If the weather permits, meals during the seven-day festival are eaten in the sukkah. The mood of Sukkot is festive; it is a wonderful outdoor celebration. Friends and family drop by, and if the weather is mild enough, families sleep in the sukkah, too. It is wonderful to catch sight of these sukkahs in big cities where you can see their greenery perched on terraces and in courtyards and gardens.

Celebrating the Holiday

The proper greeting for Sukkot is "Chag Sameach", which translates as happy holiday. Celebrants give thanks for the previous year, and express hopes for the year to come. At the end of the festival, prayers are offered for the first rains and the Hebrew dance Mayim may be performed.

Four plants – Arba Minim – decorate the sukkah, and are held in the hands during the blessings each evening. They are: the etrog (a lemon-like citron); the lulav (palm branch); the arava (willow branch); and the myrtle. Each of these has a deep significance. The etrog is shaped like a heart and symbolizes the hope of divine forgiveness for the desires of our heart; this should be held in the left hand. The right hand holds the lulav, which symbolizes Israel's loyalty to God, while the myrtle is shaped like an eye, and represents the hope that greed and envy will be forgiven. Finally, the arava, considered to be shaped like a mouth, symbolizes forgiveness for idle talk and lies. Bright cut-outs are pinned up and fresh and dried fruits are hung from the roof.

Above: Myrtle and willow branches are placed in the sukkah along with the etrog (citron) and lulav (palm branch) as directed in Leviticus 23:40.

Observing the Festival

Since it is a harvest festival, fruits and vegetables are eaten. Cabbage is stuffed in the Eastern European tradition to make holishkes, and strudel is made from apple. Pomegranates and persimmons are considered a Sukkot treat.

The eighth day of Sukkot is Shemeni Atzeret, when memorial prayers are said. The next day, Simchat Torah, is the festival of rejoicing in the Torah, when the weekly readings of the Torah in the synagogue finish and the cycle begins again. The Torah comprises B'raisheet (Genesis), Sh'mot (Exodus), Va'yikra (Leviticus), Bmidbar (Numbers) and Dvarim (Deuteronomy). It is central to Jewish life, as it contains the laws and traditions, customs and festivals, and their history.

Children are often brought to the synagogue to celebrate Simchat Torah. They are given apples and chocolate, and little Torahs and flags, to symbolize the learning of the Torah as a happy, sweet experience.

Left: A devout member of the ultra-orthodox Mea Shearim community in Jerusalem prepares for Sukkot.

CHANUKKAH

Throughout the world, beginning on the eve of the 25th of Kislev, which falls in November or December, Jews celebrate Chanukkah, the festival of lights, by lighting an oil lamp or menorah filled with candles, lighting one every night for eight nights until all are lit. A shamash (helper candle), is used to light each candle.

The festival commemorates the Maccabean victory over Antiochus IV, who was known as Epiphanes of Greece, in the year 165BCE (BC). When the Jewish Maccabees returned to the Temple, after defeating the Syrians who had attempted to annihilate Judaism, they found it pillaged, and the eternal light extinguished. They immediately lit the lamp, but there was only enough sacred oil to keep it burning for one day. A messenger was sent to get oil, but the supply was four days away, each way. However, a miracle occurred, and the holy lamp did not go out but continued to burn, until eight days had passed and the messenger returned with a new supply of oil. The miracle of Chanukkah is also that a small band of fighters could triumph over a powerful, well-equipped army.

At Chanukkah, Jews eat foods cooked in oil, to remind them of the lamp that burned and burned. On the first night, the Shehehayanu (the benediction of thanks) is recited, and each evening a blessing is said over the candles.

Right: Children spin the dreidel as part of the Chanukkah celebrations.

Customs and Traditions

Jewish children often make ceramic or papier-mâché menorahs (candelabras) or dreidels (spinning tops) with which to celebrate the holiday. All Jews gather together socially throughout the festival of Chanukkah, greeting each other with "Chag Sameach" meaning happy holiday, drinking spirits, exchanging gifts or giving money (Chanukkah gelt) and singing songs such as Ma-oh Tzur (Rock of Ages) or the Dreidel Song. This last will often accompany a game of dreidel, when small coins or nuts are gambled away on the outcome of the spinning of the four-sided top that plays such an important part in the festivities. Hebrew letters marked on the top signify "A Great Miracle Happened There", or, if one lives in Israel, "A Great Miracle Happened Here".

Potato latkes, crisp pancakes, are an Eastern European treat enjoyed by the Ashkenazim. They are relatively recent, as potatoes were not brought back

Above: Lighting candles, one for each night of Chanukkah, symbolizes the lamp that burned for eight days.

from the New World until the 16th century. Few snacks are as evocative as these crisp brown potato pancakes, especially if you grew up eating them.

The Sephardim have different Chanukkah traditions: Persians eat snail-shaped syrupy treats called zelebis; Israelis enjoy soufganiot, which are a kind of jam-filled doughnut; and Greek Jews eat loukomades, delectable airy dough balls that are fried until golden and drizzled with honey. It is said that these sweet fritters are very similar to what the Maccabees themselves would have eaten.

Chanukkah is a happy and joyous celebration. Indeed, the Shulkhan Arukh – the code of law – forbids mourning and fasting during this time, and instead encourages great merry-making and enjoying the feast.

PURIM

This festival is one of celebration and joy, feasting and drinking. It falls on the 14th Adar, around February or March, and reminds Jews of the triumph of freedom and goodness over evil.

The story that Purim celebrates took place in Shushan, which later became Persia and then Iran. The principal characters are Queen Esther, her cousin Mordecai and the evil First Minister of King Ahasuerus, Haman. The tale is told in the Megillah, the Scroll of Esther, which is read in the synagogue on the night of Purim.

The tale relates how Haman, irate that the Jew Mordecai did not show him proper respect, plotted to kill the Jews. Mordecai's cousin, the beautiful Queen Esther, went to her husband pleading for the lives of her people. And so, at a banquet that was designed to honour Haman, the tables were turned. The king hanged Haman on the very gallows intended for Mordecai, and the Jews were saved.

Below: A painting by Filippo Lippi (1457–1504) telling the story of Esther: Mordecai's lament about Israel's lot; Esther before King Ahasuerus; and the fate of Haman.

Celebrating the Story of Esther

During Purim, children come to the synagogue dressed in costume, often as Haman, Mordecai or Esther. The Megillah is read aloud and, when Haman's name is uttered, all make as much noise as they can, either by twirling the grogger (noisemaker), or just banging things together.

Wine is a sign of happiness and inaugurates all Jewish religious ceremonies, but at Purim it is essential. Indeed, the Talmud exhorts Jews to "drink so much that you can't tell the difference between Mordecai and Haman". This is because Esther served huge quantities of wine at the banquet she gave at the palace, when Haman was exposed as a villain.

Special foods are eaten for Purim. In Ashkenazi cultures, triangular pastries filled with nuts, seeds or dried fruit are served. The filling is meant to commemorate Esther, who ate only fruits and nuts in the palace, as the kitchen was not kosher. For North African Sephardim, fried pastries drenched in honey and sprinkled with nuts, called oznei Haman (the ears of Haman), are a favourite Purim treat.

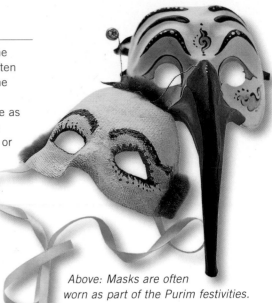

Above: Masks are often worn as part of the Purim festivities.

Gifts to Share

The giving of sweet pastries and fruit, known as shaloch manot, is a Purim observance. Charitable donation is also decreed, usually money, which is given to at least two individuals or two causes.

Some Jews observe the fast of Esther, in honour of the queen's fast before she pleaded with the king for her people's lives. Fasting, prayers and charity are all required for repentance, and the Jewish community of Shushan was saved by Esther's repentance.

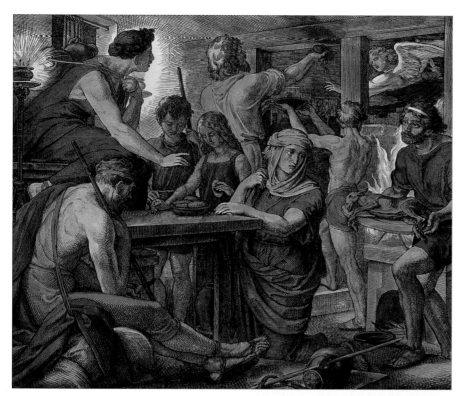

to wander for an entire generation until Moses led them to the Promised Land. The festival of Pesach takes Jews on that journey via the Haggadah; the story is relived as the ritual meal is eaten.

For eight days special foods are eaten, and many very ordinary foods permitted at other times of the year are taboo. No leavened foods are permitted, which rules out any cakes or cookies prepared with flour (because when flour comes into contact with water for a certain period of time, it naturally produces leaven).

Left: A coloured wood engraving by Julius Schnorr von Carolsfeld showing the angel of death passing over the homes of the Israelites whose doorways were splashed with blood (1860).

Below: An illustration of a father placing the passover basket on his son's head during the ritual Seder meal (from Barcelona Haggadah c.1340).

PESACH

The Passover festival, Pesach, is one of the biggest in the Jewish year. It commemorates the story of the exodus of the Hebrew slaves from bondage in Egypt, a flight that turned a tribe of slaves into a cohesive people. During this festival, Jews celebrate the flight for freedom of all humanity – the freedom of spirit as well as personal, religious and physical freedom.

"Why is tonight different from all other nights?" asks a small child, quoting from the Haggadah, the narrative read at the Pesach feast. And so the story unfolds.

Pesach falls sometime around March or April, following the Jewish calendar. The word "pesach" means passing over, and represents the passing over of the houses whose doorways the Israelites had splashed with lamb's blood, so that those inside remained unharmed when the angel of death ravaged Egypt, slaying the first-born sons. This was Egypt's final agony, the last straw that convinced Pharaoh to, in the much-quoted words of Moses, "Let my people go!" And go they did, into the desert

Special Foods for Pesach

Crisp flat breads called matzos are served at Pesach. They are a reminder of the Israelites who, in their escape to the desert, only had time to make flat breads, baked on hot stones. Instead of the two loaves of bread traditionally placed on the table during a festival, on Pesach, three matzos are served.

Because of the separation over the years of Ashkenazim and Sephardim, each group has evolved its own rules for what may or may not be eaten at Pesach. Ashkenazim forbid the consumption of corn, rice and beans (which are known collectively as kitniyot) for these can ferment and become yeasty. Sephardim, however, still eat these foods.

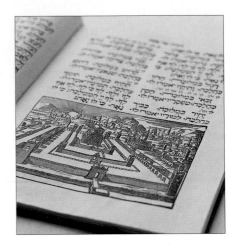

Above: Passover Haggadahs are often noted for their embellishments.

Matzos

The flour from which matzos are made may be exposed to water for no more than 18 minutes if they are to be kosher for Passover. Biblical teachings dictate that the dough must be allowed to rise for no longer than the time it took to walk a Roman mile, which has been timed as taking between 18 and 24 minutes. The number 18 is portentous, as it represents chai, the Hebrew for life.

Schmurah matzo is a hand-made matzo that some very observant Jews insist upon eating at Pesach. Bakers gather around the table while the oven is readied. A stopwatch is pressed and any matzo that is not ready in time is rejected and thrown away. Automated, assembly line baking produces matzos much more quickly, usually in about 7 minutes.

There is more to Passover matzos than the simple baking. Before the process can even begin, the flour must be inspected by the rabbi to ensure it has not come into contact with damp, and that no grains have sprouted. The inspecting rabbi turns off the water at the mill before the Passover flour arrives, and the delivery truck itself is inspected before and after loading up, then it is sealed with the rabbi's sign of inspection.

Below: Matzos are made in a Jewish factory in the Holy Land (c.1950).

In the weeks prior to the Pesach feast the house is cleaned from top to bottom, especially the kitchen. The day before the Seder or Pesach feast, the head of the household searches for anything that might contain leaven – usually there are napkins filled with crumbs left here and there for symbolic removal. Then he or she recites a blessing on the hametz (leavening) that has been gathered which is then burned. The search for hametz continues. Sometimes the searcher uses a feather, a symbolic gesture to signify that no crumbs whatsoever remain.

In addition to bread, all flour or leavened products are forbidden, as are beer and other alcoholic drinks made with yeast. Observant Jews are very careful about the dairy products they eat during Pesach. Milk should come from animals that have only eaten grass, not grain, and there must be no risk of contamination with leaven.

Sephardim eat all vegetables and some eat rice, though Ashkenazim eschew many vegetables on the grounds that they could be considered grains or ingredients to make breads or cakes. The list includes corn, green beans, peas, lentils, chickpeas, and other dried beans.

Instead of cakes based on a leavening agent such as baking powder, Pesach boasts a wealth of cakes risen with the aid of beaten eggs.

The Seder

On the first night of the festival (and the second night too, unless the participants are Reform or living in Israel) a ritual meal called the Seder is served. The word seder simply means order, referring to the fact that the meal has a specific order of events. The meal revolves around the reading of the Haggadah, the story of the exodus from Egypt and from slavery. The foods eaten often have symbolic significance and represent various elements of the story.

Many families use the Pesach Seder as an opportunity to highlight some facet of modern life or struggle that needs to be addressed. Some place an empty chair at the table to symbolize those who are still in slavery.

Wine, candles for the holiday, a plate of matzos, and the Seder plate are placed on the Pesach table. The Seder plate holds a selection of foods that have special meaning for the festival; the role of each is highlighted as the reading of the Haggadah progresses.

Below: Hard-boiled eggs dipped in salt water, representing the tears of the Israelites, are eaten at Pesach.

Above: A ritual Seder plate.

The Seder Plate

Maror (bitter herbs) are placed on the Seder plate to remind Jews of the bitterness of slavery. Horseradish is usually used as maror, but any sharp, bitter herb can be eaten. Charosset takes the next place. Also known as charosses, harosses and halek, this is a distinctive blend of sweet fruit and nuts. When mixed with wine, it becomes a tasty sludge, symbolizing the mortar used in the Hebrews' forced labour. Sometimes, in Morocco and other Sephardic communities, charosset is rolled into sticky balls and eaten as a sweetmeat throughout the holiday.

The cycle of life is represented by a roasted egg. It is also a symbol of the sacrifice brought to the Temple in ancient days, a symbol of mourning for the destroyed Temple. A bowl of boiled eggs is usually served with salt water as the first course of the Seder meal. The salt water represents the sad tears of the Hebrews.

Also to be dipped in the salt water are springtime greens such as parsley, lettuce and celery, which recall the oppression of the Israelites, as well as renewal represented by spring.

A roasted shank bone of lamb is placed on the plate as a reminder of the paschal sacrifice at the Temple. Some Sephardic communities put a big shoulder of roast lamb on to the Seder plate and eat it as the main course, but some individuals refuse to eat lamb at the Seder until the Temple is rebuilt. Vegetarian Jews often substitute a roasted beetroot (beet) for the lamb bone.

There are no specific rules about what must be on the Seder menu, apart from the restrictions of Pesach itself. Each community has developed its own traditions. A Persian custom, for instance, commemorating the beating of the slaves by their cruel masters, involves beating each other with spring onions (scallions). This helps to break the ice, relaxes all who are at the Seder table, and makes the whole room smell exceedingly delicious and oniony. It is great fun, too, for the children, who start getting fidgety after a while if there are too many prayers and not enough playing and eating and singing.

Four cups of wine (or grape juice) must be poured during the Seder. A fifth is left for Eliahu, the harbinger of the Messiah, who is said to visit every Jewish house on the night of the Seder, drinking from every cup.

Below: Four cups of wine are poured for the Seder, plus an extra cup for Eliahu.

SEFIRAH

Between Pesach and the next major festival, Shavuot, is a period called Sefirah. It is a solemn time of observance rather than a festival. Beginning at the end of Pesach, it commemorates the day when a sheaf of young barley – the Omer – was traditionally brought into the Temple in Jerusalem. Observing this period is called Counting the Omer. The solemnity of this period is thought to have stemmed from an ancient superstition. Partial mourning was observed in the hope that it would ensure a good harvest of grain.

During this time, the observant do not celebrate weddings, have other celebrations or even cut their hair.

Lag b'Omer

This happy day falls on the 33rd day of counting and is the one break in the solemn time of Sefirah. Lag b'Omer is a day made for celebrating out of doors and picnicking. For observant Jews, Lag b'Omer is the day in spring when you could schedule a wedding or have a haircut.

TU B'SHEVAT

This festival is known as the Holiday of the Trees. It is one of the four holidays that celebrate nature, as mentioned in the Mishnah (part of the Talmud). Tu b'Shevat occurs in early February, when the sap begins to rise in the fruit trees of Israel. To celebrate, it is customary to eat different kinds of fruits and nuts.

The image of trees is very important in Jewish life, for instance Etz Chaim, the Tree of Life. The Torah, too, is sometimes likened to a tree, for it protects and nourishes. Even the wooden poles around which the Torah is wrapped are called atzeem, or trees.

Tu b'Shevat is often celebrated by planting trees and collecting funds for reforestation. An old custom of holding Tu b'Shevat Seders has recently been revived. The meal progresses from fruits and nuts, through various juices, all symbolizing the awakening of nature after its slumber during winter.

Below: Lag b'Omer is a popular day for receiving a first haircut. Chassidic Jews wait until a boy is three years old. (Photograph by Ed. Toben.)

Above: Traditionally, when the Omer (a sheaf of young barley) was brought into the Temple in Jerusalem, the period of Sefirah began.

The Tu b'Shevat Seder contains three different categories of fruits and nuts: hard, medium and soft, which are said to represent the different characteristics of the Jews. The first category includes those fruits and nuts that have a hard or inedible skin or shell such as kiwi fruits, bananas, oranges, pineapples, pistachio nuts and almonds. The second category includes those fruits with a hard stone (pit) that cannot be eaten such as prunes, plums, peaches, apricots, cherries and olives. The third category includes those fruits that can be eaten in their entirety such as strawberries, raspberries, grapes, figs, pears and apples.

Certain fruits also have specific meanings. For example, pomegranates represent fertility, apples represent the splendour of God, almonds represent divine retribution (because the almond tree blossoms before other trees) and carob represents humility and penitence.

Enjoying a meal made up entirely of fruits and nuts, or simply adding fruits and nuts to a loaf of challah are all traditional ways of celebrating the festival of Tu b'Shevat.

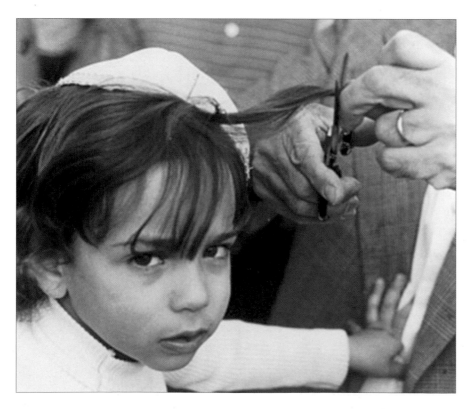

SHAVUOT

The word "shavuot" means weeks in Hebrew, as this festival comes seven weeks after Pesach. In English it is known as Pentecost, which comes from the Greek, meaning 50 days.

It is also sometimes referred to as the Festival of the Torah, because it tells the story of the Israelites wandering through the desert and commemorates the giving of the Jewish scriptures, the Torah, and the Ten Commandments to Moses on Mount Sinai. It is also the Feast of the First Fruits, one of the ancient pilgrimages to Jerusalem, when the first fruits and grains of the season were brought as offerings.

Shavuot is celebrated for one day among Israeli and Reform (Progressive) Jews and for two days in other Jewish cultures throughout the world. As with Shabbat, the holiday begins at sundown the night before. The table is set with a fine, festive cloth, wine and challah, as well as fresh flowers of the springtime.

Shavuot is also a time to enjoy meals based on dairy products, although there are no rules that say this must be done. Ashkenazim enjoy blintzes, sour cream kugels, cheese pancakes and cheese dumplings, while Sephardim enjoy cheese pastries such as borekas.

Some may say the tradition of eating dairy foods is based on the abundance of milk during spring, but Jewish

Below: Prayers for Shavuot.

scholars have added other reasonings, too. To eat milk and dairy products reminds Jews of the milk and honey in the Song of Songs, say some scholars. Another explanation is that the Israelites were away so long receiving the Ten Commandments that their milk had soured and begun to turn to cheese. Still others suggest that when the Israelites finally returned to their camp they were too hungry to wait to prepare and cook a meat meal and so just drank lots of milk for sustenance.

Above: An illuminated 13th-century manuscript from the Book of Ruth, which is read at the holiday of Shavuot.

The Book of Ruth is read on Shavuot and provides a dramatic story of a woman devoted to her adopted faith, choosing it over her own family upon the death of her husband.

Shavuot is one of the four times of the year that Yizkor, the memorial prayers in which the dead are respected, are recited.

LIFE EVENTS

From birth to death, Judaism offers ceremonies and observances to mark the rites of passage and key events in the lives of individuals. Each event, observance or celebration is always accompanied by an abundance of festive food and drink.

Brit Milah

Male children are ritually circumcised on the eighth day after birth unless they have been small at birth, ill or premature; if any of these occur, the circumcision will be delayed until the child is healthy and has achieved a specific weight so as not to endanger his health.

The ritual circumcision is called Brit Milah in Hebrew, Bris in Yiddish. It is done in the home by a community specialist called a mohel, though some Reform (Progressive) Jews have the baby circumcised in hospital by a doctor. In a traditional ceremony, the baby is given no more than a few drops of wine as a painkiller and the operation is swift. The baby scarcely gives more than a little cry, but the adults often need a bit more wine or something stronger, to fortify themselves after the baby's ordeal.

After the ceremony, which includes blessings and prayers, there is a party, because this is a very happy occasion, when the newborn baby becomes part of the world's Jewish community. And, like any happy occasion, a Brit Milah is celebrated with plenty of food and drink. There is every reason to rejoice. Not only is there a new, healthy child, but the mother has come through the rigours of pregnancy and childbirth. As the baby is passed from one adoring relative to the next, and all remark on how he has his father's nose and his grandmother's eyes, the table groans with lavish offerings such as traditional salads, delicatessen specialities, breads and cakes and sweetmeats.

At the Brit Milah, the male child is given a Hebrew name. He is often named after a favourite relative; in Sephardic tradition it is a favourite living relative, in Ashkenazic tradition it is a revered deceased relative. A girl child will usually be given her Hebrew name at the synagogue, at the age of about a month. This too is an occasion for celebration and eating, with the parents hosting a reception at the synogogue after the service. In observant families, there is a ceremony for the first-born child – Pidyon ha Ben for a boy and Pidyon ha Bat for a girl. This means redemption of the first born and marks the start of the new family.

Bar or Bat Mitzvah

The next milestone in the circle of life is a child's Bar or Bat Mitzvah. This coming-of-age ceremony marks the time when the child takes on the religious obligations of an adult.

Bar Mitzvah – the ceremony for a boy – means the son of the commandment; Bat Mitzvah, the equivalent ceremony for girls, means daughter of the commandment. After Bar or Bat Mitzvah the child may be counted as part of a minyan (quorum of ten people required to hold a religious service). In some sectors such as Orthodoxy, ten men are still required to make up a minyan, while in others such as Reform (Progressive), it is simply ten people – either male or female.

A Bar Mitzvah ceremony takes place any time after the boy's 13th birthday, while a Bat Mitzvah takes place after the girl's 12th birthday. However, many adults who have not had a Bar or Bat Mitzvah as a child decide later that they would like to study for it as adults. It is a good excuse to return to the community, and to embrace studying once again.

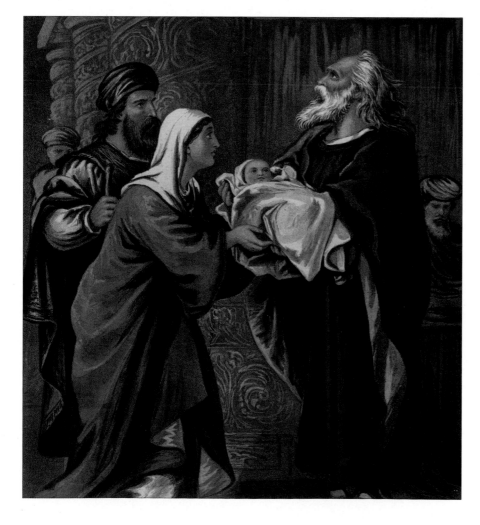

Left: An infant boy is presented in the synagogue for the ritual Brit Milah.

Each night during the period of mourning there is a gathering for the purpose of prayer, a minyan. Members of the community bring prepared foods with them when they come to offer support and comfort. Usually this will be traditional, homely foods that warm the soul and are easily digested, for grief is very hard on the body. The food, and the act of giving food, sustains the mourners through their ordeal, for even when there is no strength for the task it is still necessary to eat to survive. The preparing, bringing and eating of food is all about survival.

Sharing Food

The heart of Jewish celebration is the home. The taste of Judaism is in its kitchen, and the traditions of Jewish cooking are in the home table – the everyday eating with the family, and celebrations with extended family and friends. In Jewish celebrations, food is central to the festivities and, for Jews sharing that food, it is as wonderful an experience as eating it themselves.

There is joy in the Jewish tradition of generosity at the table. As the Haggadah says: "Let all who are hungry come and eat."

Left: A young couple stand under a traditional chuppah at a wedding ceremony in London's East End (1969).

Below: A man from a Jewish community in Morocco reads psalms at the grave of a deceased family member.

A Bar or Bat Mitzvah is an occasion for rejoicing. A large party is often given, with a festive meal. There will be dancing and general merrymaking. A boy or girl can expect to be the centre of attention and everything possible will be done to make the day a special one.

Marriage

Weddings have a special role in Jewish life. They are grand, festive and full of hope. They represent the joining of two families to create a new family and new members of the community.

They are also a great excuse for a huge party and seeing family and friends. Even older people who have been married before might have a big wedding party, for it is such a happy time.

From the moment that the glass is stamped on by the groom (the moment when the couple are officially married), the merriment begins. There will be a lavish table with foods such as smoked salmon, chopped liver, herring and rye breads, and lots of dancing of the hora.

Bereavement

Even at the end of life food plays an important role for Jews. The period of mourning is known as Shiva, and there could be nothing more comforting than food brought by friends and relations to sustain the family through this time, when the practicalities of cooking and eating can be too much to bear alongside the great demands of bereavement.

JEWISH FOODS

The foods of the Jewish table are global by nature, reflecting the flavours of the countries where Jews have settled. They also have their roots in ritual and tradition. Ashkenazic and Sephardic foods are very different but cross-cultural marriages and the intermingling of people from different backgrounds have blurred the boundaries. With the myriad Jewish communities coming together again, this is a time in which Jews can feel as well as say "Am Yisrael Chil" – We are One People.

THE LAWS OF KASHRUT

Kashrut is the set of ritual dietary laws that are set out in the Talmud. Food that conforms to those standards is described as kosher. Whether a Jew comes from a land where onions, garlic and chicken fat are freely eaten, or one whose cuisine includes hot peppers, spices and olive oil, the meals eaten in the observant Jewish household will not taste the same as food prepared from similar ingredients by non-Jewish neighbours, because the former will conform to the rules of Kashrut.

Though the basic principles of Kashrut are outlined in the Bible, they have been ruled upon and commented upon by rabbis in the Shulkhan Arukh, the code of Jewish law. There is no reason given for the laws of Kashrut, though many have suggested that hygiene, food safety and health might be contributory factors. The rabbis state, however, that no reason or rationale is needed; obeying the laws of Kashrut is a commandment from God.

Below (clockwise from top): Beef, goat and lamb, when prepared appropriately, are all permitted by the laws of Kashrut.

PERMITTED MEATS

Only certain types of meat are allowed, based on the text in Leviticus 11:3, which states: "Whatsoever parteth the hoof, and is clovenfooted, and cheweth the cud…that shall ye eat". These two conditions mean that ox, sheep, goat, hart, gazelle, roebuck, antelope and mountain sheep may be eaten, while pork, horse, camel, rabbit, hare and whale are forbidden. No birds of prey or predatory animals are allowed, nor are scavengers, creeping insects or reptiles.

PERMITTED BIRDS

The Torah is not quite so clear when it comes to identifying which birds may be eaten. Instead, it lists 24 species of forbidden fowl, which are mainly birds of prey or scavengers. Permitted fowl have in common with each other a protruding claw, a crop and a stomach that can be peeled readily of its inner lining. In general, chickens, ducks, turkeys and geese are allowed, but this can vary. Goose is popular among Ashkenazim, while Yemenite Jews consider it to be of both the land and sea and therefore forbidden by Kashrut.

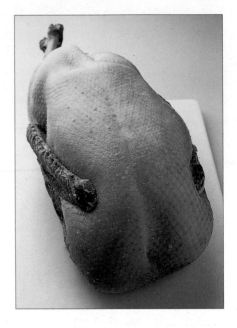

Above: Goose is very popular among Eastern European Jews who, in the past, often raised them for their fat livers and to serve at holiday meals.

RITUAL SLAUGHTER

For kosher animals to become kosher meat, they must be slaughtered ritually (shechita). An animal that dies of natural causes, or is killed by another animal, is forbidden. The knife for slaughter must be twice as long as the animal's throat and extremely sharp and smooth; even the tiniest nick in the blade renders the knife invalid for kosher butchering. The shochet (ritual slaughterer) must sever the animal's trachea and oesophagus without grazing its spine, and the knife must be wielded with care and speed; the smallest delay would bring terror and pain to the animal and render the meat unkosher.

The shochet inspects the incision to make sure the cut is smooth, and the lungs must be examined for symptoms of disease. If there is any doubt, the shochet blows air into the lungs; if they fail to hold the air, the animal is not kosher. Certain types of injury also render the animal unkosher. Some cuts of meat are considered unkosher, unless specially treated, for example the hind legs of the cow and sheep must have the sciatic nerve removed.

Kashering Meat

This is the term used to describe the removal of blood from an animal immediately after slaughter, which is essential if the meat is to be labelled kosher. To Jews, blood is a symbol of life, and the prohibition against consuming it comes from the scriptures: "Therefore I said unto the children of Israel, No soul of you shall eat blood…" (Leviticus 17:12).

Because blood is categorically forbidden by the laws of Kashrut, all meat must be kashered by soaking, salting or grilling (broiling) so that no blood remains. Hearts must be cut open, all veins removed and drained of blood. This is usually done by the butcher. It is then salted and prepared as desired. A spot of blood in an egg renders it unkosher.

How to Kasher Meat

Most kosher butchers kasher meat before offering it for sale. If your butcher does not do this, consult a rabbinical authority or follow the simple instructions below.

1 Place the meat or poultry in a large bowl or bucket as soon as possible after purchase, pour over cold water to cover and leave to stand for 30 minutes.

2 Remove the meat or poultry from the water and place on a plastic drainer, tilted to allow the juices to drain away. Leave to stand for about 5 minutes, then sprinkle with coarse kosher salt. Leave to stand for 1 hour.

3 Rinse the meat three times to rid it of all blood and salt. Pat dry with kitchen paper, then chill until ready to cook.

To kasher liver, rinse it well under cold water, then sprinkle with salt and grill (broil) on a rack or over an open fire, on each side until the flesh is cooked through.

PERMITTED FISH

To be considered kosher, all fish must have detachable scales and fins. Fish with scales that do not come away from the skin are not kosher: "These shall ye eat of all that are in the waters: whatsoever hath fins and scales in the waters, in the seas, and in the rivers, them shall ye eat" (Leviticus 11:9).

The London Bet Din (People's Court) lists the following as being non-kosher fish: abbot, allmouth, angelfish, angler, beluga, blonde, catfish, caviar, cockles, conger eel, crabs, dogfish, eelpout, eels, fiddlefish, fishing frog, frog-fish, glake, goosefish, guffer eel, huss, lumpfish, monkfish, mussels, ray, rigg, rock salmon, rockfish, roker, sea devil, sea pout, skate, sturgeon, swordfish, thornback ray and turbot. Other sea creatures that are forbidden by the laws of Kashrut include all shellfish and crustaceans, sea urchin, octopus and squid.

Below (from left): Red mullet, trout and salmon all have detachable scales so are considered kosher.

Kashrut Certification

To be sure that any packaged food is kosher, look for a symbol of recognized certification every time you buy, as additives and methods can change. There are numerous certifying boards, and many Jews will eat only packaged foods certified by specific boards. If a food is certified as Glatt Kosher it conforms to a particularly stringent Kashrut, which requires, among other things, that the lungs be more thoroughly examined.

Some observant Jews will eat foods such as canned tomatoes, for the only ingredients are tomatoes and salt. Others avoid such foods, as they could have been contaminated on the production line. Very strict Jews extend their watchfulness even to the basics, and will eat only sugar with the rabbinical supervision marking, to be sure it has not been tainted by other unkosher food products or insects.

DAIRY PRODUCTS

Deuteronomy states "Thou shalt not seethe a kid in his mother's milk." This is the basis for the rule that dairy foods and meat must not be cooked together. After eating a meat meal, a certain amount of time must elapse before dairy food can be consumed. Some communities wait six hours, while others wait only two. There is no requirement to wait after eating a dairy meal before having a meat one.

There are many non-dairy products, including non-dairy margarine, that approximate the taste and texture of dairy products. These make it possible to eat meat with creamy sauces and creamy desserts after a meat meal.

To ensure the complete separation of meat and milk, kosher kitchens have separate dishes, pans and washing-up utensils for each. These must be stored separately in the kitchen.

Cheese and Rennet

Natural rennet, the ingredient used to curdle milk for cheese-making, comes from the lining of an animal's stomach. Therefore, the cheese made from it is not kosher. Much modern cheese is made with vegetable rennet and not necessarily labelled as such, but to be sure, one should eat only cheeses that are marked "Suitable for Vegetarians", or that have the appropriate kosher certification marking.

Gelatine in Dairy Products

Because gelatine is made from animal bones, it is not kosher. Kosher gelatine made from seaweed (carrageen) is vegetarian, and must be used instead. Care should be taken with products such as yogurt, as they can often contain gelatine. For this reason, many Jews will eat only milk products that are marked as kosher.

Above: The quality of kosher wines has improved tremendously over the last few years and an excellent selection is now available.

ALCOHOL

Spirits and grain alcohol are permitted by Kashrut, as is wine, although wine (and wine products such as brandy) carry a few provisos.

Since wine has been drunk by Jews since biblical times and it is an intrinsic part of observances carried out for festivals and Shabbat, wine must be labelled kosher. This means that the grapes have been harvested, and wine prepared, processed and bottled, under rabbinical supervision.

In the not-too-distant past kosher wines were barely drinkable; now, however, there are some wonderful dry and deliciously drinkable wines coming out of Israel, California and France. Traditional sweet Kiddush wines are also available.

Left (clockwise from top): milk, Cheddar cheese, goat's cheese, fatmet cheese and yogurt are just a few of the dairy products that can be enjoyed in the kosher kitchen.

KOSHER FOR SHABBAT

"Ye shall kindle no fire throughout your habitations upon the sabbath day" (Exodus 35:3). No fire for domestic use can be lit in religious homes on Shabbat. No stove should be turned on, even if it is electric. A stove may be left on to keep food warm or to cook food very slowly, but it may not be used for actual cooking on Shabbat.

Many rules surround the definition of what precisely constitutes cooking if a warmer or low-heat gadget is used – some say that food must be partially cooked before Shabbat begins. Water must be previously boiled, then kept warm for Shabbat in an urn which must not be turned on or off.

This injunction applies to all holidays and celebrations, in addition to the weekly Shabbat, and has given rise to the many long-cooked dishes featured in Jewish cooking throughout the world such as dafina, cholent, and other bean and meat dishes that require long, slow cooking to make them succulent.

KASHRUT FOR PESACH

In addition to the requirements for the rest of the year, there is a special set of rules that applies to foods during the Passover festival.

During Pesach no leavened foods may be eaten. This means that no bread, breadcrumbs, flour, yeast, baking powder or bicarbonate of soda (baking soda) may be eaten. Cakes must also be eschewed unless they are prepared using special meal made from ground matzo. (Eggs can be used as a rising agent in cakes, as it is not the fermentation of grains that causes the cake to rise, but rather the air trapped in the beaten egg.)

Ashkenazim eschew many vegetables that could be considered grains or ingredients that could be made into breads or cakes. These include green beans, corn, peas, chickpeas, lentils and other dried beans. Sephardic Jews, however, eat all vegetables and some eat rice.

Before Pesach begins, the house must be cleared entirely of all leavened foods and ingredients. Many religious Jews simply seal cupboards that contain hametz (leaven) with tape, unsealing them again when the festivities are over.

Beer and other alcoholic drinks made with yeast are forbidden during Pesach, although kosher wine is permitted to carry out the observances and traditions of the festival.

Many Sephardim are careful about the milk and dairy products that they consume during Pesach, and will drink only milk that is marked kosher for Pesach to be sure that it is permissable under the laws of Kashrut.

Both Ashkenazic and Sephardic observant families have separate sets of dishes, cutlery and pans for exclusive use during Pesach. These are stored away for the rest of the year. To make ordinary kitchenware kosher for Pesach, it must be scalded in boiling water. Even the stove must be koshered – the fire and grill (broiler) heated until red hot – before the stove is considered fit to be cooked on for the holiday.

PAREVE FOODS

In Yiddish, these foods are known as "pareve" and in Hebrew they are "parva". These are the neutral foods that are neither meat nor dairy. They do not, therefore, have the same restrictions imposed upon them and can be eaten with either meat or dairy foods.

All plant foods such as vegetables, grains and fruit are pareve, as are eggs and permitted fish. However, if a pareve food is cooked with a fat that is derived from meat (such as chicken fat) or dairy (such as butter or cream), the food is no longer pareve.

Jews who keep kosher will not usually eat pareve foods that have been prepared outside the home as they could have been prepared using non-kosher fats.

Below (clockwise from top left): Pareve foods such as barley, onions, aubergines (eggplants), tomatoes and eggs can be eaten with either meat or dairy foods.

DAIRY FOODS

In both the Ashkenazic and Sephardic kitchen, all dairy foods are held in very high esteem, a tribute to the biblical description of the land of Israel as a "land of milk and honey". There are strict rules concerning the consumption of dairy foods, but they do not have great religious significance except during the festival of Shavuot. This is sometimes known as the dairy festival and is a time when dairy products are enjoyed for main meals, in preference to meat, which is normally enjoyed at festivals and celebrations.

MILK AND DAIRY PRODUCTS

The milk taken from any kosher animal is considered kosher. Cows, goats and sheep are all milked and the milk is then drunk or made into various dairy products such as butter, yogurt and sour cream. The influences of the past can be seen in the dairy products that are enjoyed by Jews today.

Left (clockwise from top left): Cottage cheese, cream cheese, feta and kashkaval are among the many kosher Jewish cheeses.

In the past, in Northern Europe, milk from cows was readily available and, because the weather was cool, spoilage was not a great problem. Many towns and villages had small dairies that produced sour cream, butter, buttermilk, cottage cheese and cream cheese, and families often owned a cow or two of their own. In Lithuania, however, goats tended to be kept more often than cows and were referred to as Jewish cattle. In warmer countries, especially those situated around the Mediterranean, goats and sheep were much easier to raise, and their milk was more suitable for making fermented dairy products such as yogurt, feta cheese and halloumi. Today, Israel is a great producer of yogurts and sour creams.

Left: Sour cream and smetana, a thicker, sweeter variety from Eastern Europe, are popular dairy products.

Cheeses

A wide variety of kosher cheeses are produced in modern-day Israel, including kashkaval, which resembles a mild Cheddar; halloumi; Bin-Gedi, which is similar to Camembert; and Galil, which is modelled on Roquefort. Fresh goat's cheeses are particularly popular in Israel and are of a very good quality.

Cream cheese has been very popular with Ashkenazim since the days of shtetlach, where it was made in small, Jewish-owned dairies, and sold in earthenware pots or wrapped in leaves. Soft cheeses such as cream cheese and cottage cheese were also made in the home. Cream cheese is the classic spread for bagels, when it is known as a schmear. It can be flavoured with other ingredients such as smoked salmon.

Dairy Delis
These were a great legacy of New York's Lower East Side Jewish community. Among the most famous restaurants was Ratners, known for its elderly waiters who were invariably grumpy, nosy, bossy and ultimately endearing. Dairy shops and restaurants sold specialities such as cheese-filled blintzes, cheesecake, cream cheese shmears and knishes. Among other treats were boiled potatoes with sour cream, hot or cold borscht, cheese kugels and noodles with cottage cheese.

EGGS

These represent the mysteries of life and death and are very important in Jewish cuisine. They are brought to a family on the birth of a child, and served after a funeral to remind the mourners that, in the midst of death, we are still embraced by life. They also represent fertility. In some Sephardic communities, an egg will be included as part of a bride's costume, or the young couple will be advised to step over fish roe or eat double-yolked eggs to help increase their fertility.

Eggs are pareve so may be eaten with either meat or dairy foods. They are nutritious and filling and provide a good source of protein when other sources may be lacking or forbidden due to the laws of Kashrut.

EGGS FOR PESACH

These feature prominently in the Pesach Seder – both symbolically and as a food. It is said that a whole egg represents the strength of being a whole people (unbroken, the shell is strong; broken, it is weak).

Eggs are also an important ingredient during Pesach, as raising agents may not be used for baking and eggs, when beaten into a cake mixture, can help the cake to rise.

Making Roasted Eggs

A roasted egg is placed on the Seder plate to represent the cycle of life. It is symbolic of the ritual sacrifice made at the Temple during biblical times.

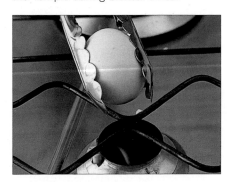

Place a hard-boiled egg over a gas flame, turning occasionally, until it is lightly browned all over. Alternatively, the egg can be roasted in the oven.

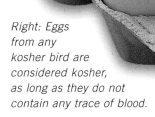

Right: Eggs from any kosher bird are considered kosher, as long as they do not contain any trace of blood.

Making Eggs in Salt Water

This simple dish is the first thing eaten when the Pesach service is over. It is only eaten at this time. Allow about 1½ eggs per person.

1 Hard-boil the eggs. Meanwhile, in a small bowl, dissolve 2.5ml/½ tsp salt in 120ml/4fl oz/½ cup warm water. Cool, then chill.

2 Shell the eggs and serve with the salt water for dipping, or place them in the bowl of salt water.

HAMINADOS EGGS

These are a Sephardic speciality. Whole eggs are cooked very slowly with onion skins or coffee grounds, to colour the shells. Alternatively, they may be added to the slow-cooked stew, dafina. They are delicious mashed with leftover cholent, in savoury pastries or chopped and added to simmered brown broad (fava) beans with a little garlic, onion, olive oil and hot chilli sauce.

Making Haminados Eggs

Cooking the eggs with onion skins colours the egg shells but does not impart any flavour to the egg inside.

1 Place 12 whole eggs in a pan and add 5ml/1 tsp each of salt and pepper. Drop in the brown outer skins from 8–10 onions, pour over water to cover and 90ml/6 tbsp olive oil.

2 Bring to the boil, then lower the heat to very low and cook for 6 hours, adding more water as needed. Shell and serve.

> ### Classic Deli Dishes
> Hard-boiled egg, chopped with onion and mixed with a little chicken fat or mayonnaise is one of the oldest Jewish dishes. In modern-day Israel, an avocado is often mashed with the eggs. Scrambled eggs with browned onion and shredded smoked chicken on rye toast or bagels make a perfect brunch.

MEAT

For observant Jews, meat must be kosher. Originally, any Jew versed in the ritual could slaughter meat, but this changed in the 13th century, with the appointment of shochets (ritual slaughterers). To qualify for this post, a man needed to be very learned, pious and upstanding.

Meat has always been an expensive but highly prized item on the Jewish table. For Ashkenazim, it was made even more costly with the levying of a hefty government tax (korobka). This, together with a community tax for Jewish charities, brought the price to twice that for non-kosher meat. None of this deterred Jews from eating meat, however; they simply saved it for Shabbat and other special occasions.

LAMB AND MUTTON

These were favoured by the Sephardim from North Africa and other Arabic lands until the early 20th century, when the strong French influence introduced beef and veal to their table. Due to the time-consuming removal of the sciatic nerve required by the laws of Kashrut, the Ashkenazim avoided eating the hindquarters of lamb and mutton until the 15th century when a meat shortage made the lengthy procedure worthwhile.

BEEF

This is very popular, especially among European Jews. Brisket is grainy and rough textured, but yields a wonderful flavour when cooked for a long time. The same applies to the short ribs and the chuck or bola. Many of these cuts are not only excellent for pot-roasting and soups; they also make good salt or corned beef and pastrami. Beef shin makes a marvellous soup.

Sausages and Salami

Both Ashkenazim and Sephardim use beef to make a wide array of sausages and salamis. The Ashkenazim tend to favour tasty cured sausages such as frankfurters, knockwurst, knobblewurst and spicy dried sausages while the Sephardim favour fresh sausages, such as the spicy merguez from North Africa and France.

VEAL

This is a favourite meat for all Jewish communities, because it is so delicate and light: shoulder roast, breast of veal, shank and rib chops are all popular cuts along with minced (ground) veal. The breast was often stuffed, then braised with vegetables; minced veal was made into cutlets and meatballs; and, in Vienna, slices of shoulder were pounded until very thin, then lightly coated in breadcrumbs and fried to make crisp, golden schnitzel.

OTHER MEATS

These include goat and deer (venison). Goat is popular in Sephardic cooking and is often used in dishes where lamb could be used such as spicy stews, curries and meatballs. Venison is cooked in similar ways to beef.

OFFAL

Historically, poorer families tended to eat cheaper cuts of meat such as feet, spleen, lungs, intestines, liver, tongue and brains. These were popular with both Ashkenazim and Sephardim, especially Yemenite Jews who are still famed for their spicy offal soups.

COOKING KOSHER MEAT

Kosher meat is usually tough because the cuts eaten tend to contain a high proportion of muscle, the meat is not tenderized by being hung but must be butchered within 72 hours of slaughter, and because the salting of meat to remove blood produces a dry result.

Because of this, meat is generally cooked slowly by stewing, braising, pot-roasting and simmering until the meat is tender. These long, slow methods are also ideal for the Shabbat meal, which can be prepared and cooked ahead of time, then left in the oven to grow beautifully tender.

Above:
Veal is the
meat used to make
classic Vienna schnitzel.

When meat is cooked quickly, for instance kebabs, the meat is marinated first to tenderize it. Chopping or mincing (grinding) meat has a similar effect, which is why so many Jewish meat recipes are for meatballs, patties and meat loaves. These dishes also allow a modest amount of meat to be stretched.

Meatballs in Many Guises

Spiced or seasoned meatballs are popular throughout the Jewish world and come in many forms.

• Russian bitkis are made from minced (ground) beef, often with chopped onion, and may be fried, grilled (broiled) or simmered, often alongside a chicken for a Shabbat or other festive meal.

• Kotleta are flattened meatballs that are fried.

• Cylindrical Romanian mitetetlai are flavoured with garlic, often with parsley, and are fried or grilled (broiled) until brown.

• The Sephardic world has myriad meatballs: albondigas, boulettes, kefta or kofta, and yullikas. They are highly spiced and can be grilled (broiled), cooked over an open fire or simmered in sauces.

Traditional Flavourings

Each region favours certain flavourings. The Polish choose sweet-and-sour flavours; the Germans sweet and fruity; the Russians savoury, with onions; the Lithuanians peppery. Sephardim favour spices and vegetables. Moroccans add sweet, fruity flavours; Tunisians prefer sharp spices; Turkish Jews add tomatoes and fresh herbs such as dill; Persians prefer delicate flavours, with herbs, fruits and vegetables and beans.

Making Meatloaf

A traditional Ashkenazic dish, meatloaf is called klops. Serve hot or cold.

1 Preheat the oven to 180°C/350°F/Gas 4. In a bowl, combine 800g/1¾lb minced (ground) meat, 2 grated onions, 5 chopped garlic cloves, 1 shredded carrot, chopped parsley, 60ml/4 tbsp dried breadcrumbs, 45–60ml/3–4 tbsp tomato ketchup and 1 beaten egg.

2 Form the mixture into a loaf and place in a roasting pan. Spread 60ml/4 tbsp tomato ketchup over the surface, arrange 2 sliced tomatoes on top, then sprinkle over 2–3 sliced onions.

3 Cover the pan with foil and bake for 1 hour. Remove the foil, increase the temperature to 200°C/400°F/Gas 6 and remove some of the onions. Bake for a further 15 minutes, or until the meat is cooked and the onions are browned.

Making Calf's Foot Jelly

This light, richly flavoured aspic, known as petcha, is a traditional Ashkenazic dish. Serve as an appetizer with slices of hard-boiled egg.

1 Cut 4 cleaned calf's feet into pieces, and place in a large pan. Pour over cold water to cover. Bring to the boil, then simmer for 5 minutes. Drain and rinse the feet well in cold water.

2 Place the feet in a clean pan and add 500g/1¼lb veal shin, 1–2 halved onions, 1 halved carrot, 1 chopped celery stick, several sprigs of parsley, thyme and rosemary, 2 bay leaves, 8–10 garlic cloves, 7.5ml/1½ tsp salt and 30ml/2 tbsp whole black peppercorns. Pour over enough cold water to cover.

3 Bring the mixture to the boil, then simmer for about 5 minutes, skimming off any scum that rises to the surface. Simmer for a further 4 hours, skimming the surface occasionally.

4 Remove the calf's feet from the pan with a slotted spoon and set aside. Strain the stock into a large bowl and stir in 30ml/2 tbsp lemon juice.

5 Remove the meat from the bones, cut into bitesize pieces and add to the stock. Chill until set, then serve.

Meats from the Deli Counter

Traditionally, Jewish delis sold either meat or dairy foods, never both. Meat delis always have a wonderful choice of cured meats and sausages – salt beef on rye, thin slices of salami, smoky pastrami or frankfurters and knockwurst with a generous helping of sauerkraut. There are cooked meats too, such as boiled brisket with a rich, brown gravy and boiled flanken, ready to eat with a little dab of hot mustard.

Right: Beef salami, salt beef and spicy pastrami are classic deli fare.

POULTRY

This is considered meat in the laws of Kashrut, and is therefore subject to all the same rules as regards slaughter and preparation. Any part of a permitted bird can be eaten.

CHICKEN

This is probably the most popular fowl for both Sephardim and Ashkenazim. Like beef and lamb, chicken was once reserved for the Shabbat or other festive meal. However, chicken was usually served more frequently as people often raised a few chickens of their own and could take them to the shochet when the time came.

Chicken is often first simmered in water or stock to make soup, then roasted for a main course. There is no more potent an image of Jewish cooking than a bowl of steaming hot chicken soup with noodles or dumplings. It has always been considered very nourishing. Moses Maimonides, the Jewish philosopher and doctor, touted its benefits in the 12th century, and in recent years, scientific studies have confirmed its value, proving the aptness of its nickname – Jewish penicillin.

Chicken backs are rich with morsels of meat and are excellent for soup; as are the feet and wings.

Meatballs made from minced (ground) chicken were a favourite food of Persian and Turkish Jews, especially when simmered along with aubergine (eggplant). Iraqis were famous for their spiced chicken croquettes, which they introduced to India and Burma. Indian Jews cook marvellous chicken curries, substituting coconut milk for yogurt, which is not permitted with chicken. A favourite Sephardic dish, eaten on the streets of Jerusalem, consists of chicken giblets and livers, grilled (broiled) until brown and crisp, and eaten with pitta bread and a hot, spicy pepper sauce.

OTHER BIRDS

Turkey, duck, goose and farmed pigeon (US squab), quail and poussin are also eaten. In Morocco, it is traditional for bridal couples to be served pigeons cooked with sweet fruits on their wedding night, to grant them a sweet life together.

In the Sephardic tradition, birds were often stuffed with couscous, spicy meat, rice and dried fruit, or with herbs and milder spices such as cinnamon. The Sephardim also liked stewed poultry with quinces or pomegranates, or flavoured with tomatoes, (bell) peppers, chickpeas or olives.

The art of raising geese for foie gras was acquired by Jews in Ancient Egypt, and it is believed that it was they who introduced the delicacy to France. In the Ashkenazic tradition, poultry necks are often stuffed with a mixture of chopped liver or kishke (stuffed derma) stuffing to make a sausage known as a helzel.

Left: Chicken is used in an array of classic Jewish dishes from chicken soup to schnitzel.

SCHMALTZ AND GREBENES

Chicken fat (schmaltz), and the crisp morsels of skin left over after the rendering (grebenes), are widely used in Jewish cooking. Schmaltz was long considered a symbol of abundance and there is a traditional Yiddish saying: "He's so lucky that even when he falls, he falls right into a schmaltz bucket!" Spread schmaltz on bread with onions or use it to flavour cholent or to make chopped liver.

Making Grebenes

One chicken won't make very much schmaltz, so save the fat and skin from several chickens and chill or freeze until you have 450g/1lb.

1 Using a sharp knife, cut the fat and skin into small pieces. Place in a large, heavy pan and pour over water to cover. Bring to the boil and cook over a high heat until the water has evaporated.

2 Reduce the heat and add about 2½ chopped onions and 1–2 whole garlic cloves. Cook over a medium heat, removing the garlic when golden.

3 When all the fat has been rendered and the grebenes are crunchy, remove the grebenes with a slotted spoon.

FISH

Permitted fish are classified as pareve, so have no restrictions with regard to combining with other foods. Its versatility makes fish very important on the Jewish table. It may take centre stage, as when a whole fish is served at Rosh Hashanah, but more often it is served as an appetizer or one of several dishes on a buffet table.

From the fresh fish counter, there is a wide choice. Sea bass, cod, sole and flounder, haddock, hake and mackerel are all popular sea fish, with perch, pike and trout among the best-loved of the freshwater varieties.

Some fish are thought of as being more Jewish than others. However, this apparent preference for certain fish has simply come about because of geography and traditional availability. Carp is a particular favourite among Ashkenazic Jews, as is pike. Carp was brought to Europe by Jews who encountered it in China when involved in the silk trade in the 15th century, while pike was introduced into the USA from Germany in the 19th century and grew in popularity as waves of Jewish immigrants arrived in the country.

Making Jellied Carp

This traditional, and delicious, dish of poached carp in jelly is a legacy of the Jews of Eastern Europe.

1 Cut 1kg/2¼lb prepared fresh carp into 8–10 slices. Heat 15ml/1 tbsp vegetable oil in a large pan. Add about 2½ chopped onions and sauté until golden brown.

2 Add 2–3 bay leaves, 1–2 parsley and thyme sprigs, 1–2 lemon slices and the carp to the pan and season well with salt and black pepper.

Above:
Carp is one of the fish traditionally enjoyed by Ashkenazic Jews. It is used to make such classic dishes as gefilte fish and jellied carp.

3 Pour 450ml/¾ pint/scant 2 cups hot fish stock and 250ml/8fl oz/1 cup dry white wine into the pan. Bring to the boil, then simmer for about 1 hour until the fish is tender. Cool slightly, then remove the carp and pack into a mould.

4 Strain the stock into a large bowl. Dissolve 2 sachets kosher gelatine in 150ml/¼ pint/⅔ cup of the stock, then stir into the remaining stock. Pour over the fish and chill until firm. Serve with lemon wedges and horseradish.

Fish from the Deli Counter

No Ashkenazic celebration is complete without some kind of fish from the deli counter. A good deli will smell deliciously of smoked and cured fish. The art of preserving fish is very much a speciality of the Ashkenazic Jews. They perfected the technique so that stocks of fish could be laid down to last all year. Methods used included salting, brining, smoking and marinating.

In a good deli you will find silky smoked salmon (lox), its natural orange colour providing a contrast to the smoked whitefish in its shimmering gold skin. In addition there will be salt herring, smoked herring, pickled herring, herring in sour cream, herring in brine and herring salad. Carp, smoked and seasoned with paprika, is known as sable and is a rare treat. It is sold only in the most traditional delis. You will find also gefilte fish in the deli, either freshly made or in jars, the liquid jellied and flavoured sweetly in the Polish manner, or peppery in the Russian or Lithuanian tradition.

Below: Spicy, piquant pickled herring rollmops and thinly sliced smoked salmon are perfect for a Shabbat brunch.

GRAINS, BEANS AND LENTILS

For Jews, grains, beans, peas and lentils have long been the staff of life and have fuelled generations. In many places, a certain type of grain or pulse (legume) actually helped to define the cuisine of the community. In Romania it was mamaliga, a cornmeal porridge that resembles polenta; in North Africa it was couscous; and for many places in the East, the staple food was rice. In Russia, Poland and the Ukraine, kasha (buckwheat) was widely eaten. Pulses are added to cholent, hamim and dafina, the slow-cooked stews that are traditionally served for Shabbat.

KASHA

This nutty, earthy grain is the partially milled grain or groat of buckwheat. It is traditionally used in Ashkenazic cooking and is very evocative for Ashkenazim who grew up eating it.

Kasha is traditionally served with roasts and pot-roasts, bathed in gravy and meat juices, or may be used as a filling for knishes and dumplings. It can also be combined with onions, wild mushrooms and noodles. Kasha varnishkes, a classic Ashkenazic dish of kasha, butterfly-shaped noodles and onions, is traditionally eaten at the festival of Purim.

Making Kasha

The grains may be fine, medium or coarse. Kasha should be toasted before being cooked, to keep it from going mushy and give it a nutty flavour. It is often toasted with egg before being simmered, to keep the grains separate.

To toast kasha, heat in a heavy pan over a medium heat for a few minutes until the grains start to give off their aroma. Add stock, bring to the boil, reduce the heat and cover. Simmer gently for 10–20 minutes until tender.

To toast kasha with egg, combine about 250g/9oz/1¼ cups kasha in a bowl with 1 beaten egg. Add the mixture to a cold heavy pan. Stir well, then turn on the heat to medium-high. Stir constantly while the grains toast and the egg sets. When the grains look dry, add stock or water and cook the kasha as above.

MAMALIGA

This golden cornmeal is widely used in Eastern Europe and is Romania's national dish. It resembles polenta and can be eaten either soft and porridge-like, or spread out on a tray and left to chill until firm, then sliced and fried or grilled (broiled). It is good hot or cold.

Mamaliga is eaten by everyone in Romania, whether Jewish or not. For breakfast, it is drizzled with honey or jam and served with sour cream; for lunch it is topped with cottage cheese or Brinza, a cheese similar to feta, and butter. It tastes great with roasted (bell) peppers and tomatoes, or for a meat meal, with a pot-roast and gravy, or grilled beef patties or sausages.

Making Mamaliga

The cornmeal used for mamaliga, like that for polenta, may have small or large grains, so the cooking time will need to be adjusted accordingly. To make mamaliga for a dairy meal, stir in a few tablespoons of butter and about 450g/1lb/2 cups cottage cheese or Brinza and serve hot.

1 Put 300g/11oz/2¾ cups golden cornmeal or polenta in a bowl with 15ml/1 tsp salt. Pour in about 250ml/8fl oz/1 cup cold water, stir well and leave to stand for a few minutes. Meanwhile, bring 900ml/1½ pints/3¾ cups water to the boil.

Left (clockwise from top left): Pareve grains such as barley, kasha (buckwheat) and bulgur wheat are important staples in both the Ashkenazic and Sephardic kitchens.

2 Gradually add the cornmeal to the boiling water, stirring constantly. Cook over a low heat for 20–35 minutes, stirring, until all the water has been absorbed. If it sticks to the pan, add more water and stir vigorously.

Grilling Mamaliga

Pour the hot, freshly cooked cornmeal on to a buttered or oiled sheet or platter and spread it out to a thickness of about 2.5–4cm/1–1½in. Leave to cool, then cut the mamaliga into fingers, brush with oil and grill (broil). Top with grated cheese, tomatoes or mushrooms.

BARLEY

This high-protein food is a good source of B vitamins. It is an indispensable ingredient in Eastern European dishes such as mushroom and barley soup, or barley with vegetables and butter (lima) beans. A small amount of meat is sometimes added.

BULGUR WHEAT

This is the partially milled grain of the whole wheat and is widely used in the Middle East. It comes in different sizes, from small and fine through to large. Bulgur wheat is sometimes eaten in place of couscous or rice, with savoury stews or soups.

COUSCOUS

This grain-like staple actually consists of tiny pellets of pasta, though it is usually categorized as a grain. It has always been very popular with the Jews of North Africa and, when they came to Israel, they brought it with them, in various different sizes. It is easy to

Right: Israeli couscous has much larger grains than regular couscous.

Right (clockwise from top right): Beans, split peas and lentils are rich in protein and can be added to stews to eke out a small amount of meat.

prepare and is usually steamed over a light and savoury spicy stew of vegetables, meats, fish or fruit. Many different types of couscous are available and they are cooked in different ways. Ordinary couscous is first moistened with cold water and left to plump up. It is then steamed over a stew. Fast-cooking couscous usually only needs to be combined with boiling water, then heated through or left to soak.

Israeli couscous, a pea-sized toasted pasta that has become a fashionable ingredient in Europe and America, is cooked in the same way as pasta. It gives a succulent result and is very good in soups and fish dishes.

RICE

This is widely eaten by Jews throughout the world. Chelou is a classic dish of the Persian Jews. As it cooks, the rice at the base of the pan is allowed to form a crisp crust (tahdeeg), which is then stirred into the tender rice, providing a tasty contrast of textures. Sometimes, thinly sliced potatoes are also added.

Many Iranian Jewish specialities use chelou as their base, topping it with herby vegetable or meat stews. At Rosh Hashanah, Iranian Jews particularly favour rice. The many tiny grains of rice represent the many grains of happiness that are hoped for during the coming year.

CHICKPEAS

These are eaten in great quantities by Sephardic Jews, and Eastern European Jews serve them to celebrate a Brit Milah. They are milled into flour and used as a thickener by Indian and Middle Eastern Jews, and are soaked and ground to make falafel, which is considered by many to be Israel's national dish.

DRIED BEANS AND PEAS

Broad (fava) beans and black-eyed beans (peas) are very popular with the Sephardim. Broad beans are very ancient and have been found at pre-pottery Neolithic B levels in Jericho. Black-eyed beans originated in Ethiopia about four thousand years ago and were recorded in Judea about 1500. Both are eaten in soups and stews. Dried broad beans are cooked and eaten with garlic, olive oil, hard-boiled eggs and a little tahini.

LENTILS

All types of lentil are made into soup, from split red lentils, which cook quickly, to the superior tasting brown variety. Yellow and green split peas are also popular. In Genesis, the story is told of how Esau sold his birthright for a potage of lentils.

VEGETABLES

Many vegetables have particular significance in celebrations to mark religious festivals. At Rosh Hashanah, pumpkin may be served; its golden colour signifying prosperity. Green vegetables will be on the table too, symbolizing renewal and happiness, while dried beans and peas signify abundance. Carrots for Rosh Hashanah are cooked in honey to signify a sweet new year. In contrast, at the Pesach Seder, bitter herbs are eaten as a reminder of the bitterness of slavery. At the same time, Ashkenazim eat broad (fava) beans, since this was what the Israelite slaves were fed during their captivity in Egypt. When Ashkenazim celebrate Chanukkah, they do so with potato latkes.

Seven different types of vegetable are used by North African Jews to make one of their specialities, a soup, which represents the seven days of Creation, with Shabbat being the seventh day.

Every year, the new season's produce is eagerly anticipated, and as each vegetable is tasted for the first time, it is customary to recite the Shehehayanu, a prayer of thanksgiving.

Below: Root vegetables such as carrots, turnips and beetroot (beets) are staple Ashkenazic wholefoods.

THE ASHKENAZIC TRADITION

Years of struggle and poverty, when Eastern European Jews were hounded from place to place, and taxed to the limit, made them increasingly inventive as to how they prepared vegetables. Carrots, cabbages, beetroot (beets), onions and turnips may have been dull and heavy but the Jews favoured their strong flavours. They frequently pickled vegetables to improve their taste, and to preserve them through the long winters. Sauerkraut, pickled cucumbers and borscht all date from this era.

When Ashkenazic Jews from Poland and Russia migrated south, they discovered a wealth of new vegetables. Peppers soon became popular, partly because they pickled well, and could be dried to make paprika. Potatoes were eaten with great gusto because they were so tasty and filling, and aubergines (eggplants), which had made their way to Romania from Spain and Italy, became widely used. Tomatoes were not widely accepted for some time, as their red colour was the same hue as blood and there was some question as to whether or not they were kosher – which may account for the Ashkenazic speciality, pickled green tomatoes.

Making Vegetable Eingemachts

Ashkenazim often made sweetmeats from vegetables. Eingemachts is a sweet preserve made from beetroot (beets), which is traditionally eaten at Pesach. It is usually eaten with a spoon along with a hot cup of tea.

1 Put 300g/11oz/scant 1½ cups granulated sugar and 250ml/8fl oz/ 1 cup honey in a large non-reactive pan and stir to combine. Stir in 20ml/4 tsp ground ginger and 120ml/4fl oz/½ cup water. Bring the mixture to the boil, then simmer, stirring occasionally, until the sugar has dissolved.

2 Peel 1.3kg/3lb boiled fresh beetroot, then grate or cut into very thin strips. Thinly slice 3 whole lemons and remove the seeds. Add the beetroot and lemons to the pan and bring to the boil, then lower the heat slightly and cook for 30–40 minutes, or until the mixture is very thick, shaking the pan occasionally.

3 Stir 90g/3½oz/scant 1 cup chopped blanched almonds into the beetroot mixture, then spoon into hot sterilized jars. Cool, then seal. Store in the refrigerator for 2–3 weeks.

Salad Vegetables

In the early days, raw vegetables and salads were not greatly appreciated by Ashkenazim raised in cold climates, where warming, filling stews were a necessity. However, radishes of several kinds were still enjoyed, along with raw turnips, cucumbers, raw onions and garlic. The young spring shoots of garlic were much prized, and were often eaten with dense black bread. Sometimes raw carrots were grated and eaten in salads, as were the young leaves of wild greens and herbs, although these were often cooked and eaten hot as well.

THE SEPHARDIC TRADITION

The Jews of the Iberian Peninsula had a much greater variety of fresh vegetables available to them than their northern neighbours. They were among the first Europeans to encounter corn, (bell) peppers, tomatoes and green beans, which were introduced from the New World, and they embraced them with enthusiasm. Jewish merchants helped to popularize these new vegetables by introducing them to the more remote parts of Spain and then, after their expulsion in 1492, to the wider world.

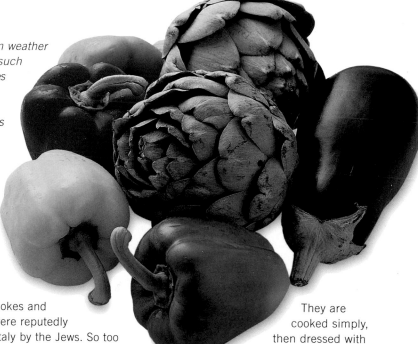

Right: Warm weather vegetables such as aubergines (eggplant), artichokes and peppers add colour to many Sephardic dishes.

Globe artichokes and pumpkins were reputedly brought to Italy by the Jews. So too were aubergines (eggplants), which were much valued for their meaty texture, particularly when meat itself was not available, or had to be omitted because of the presence of dairy foods.

Sephardic Jews have always been known for their love of vegetables. They add vegetables to stews, pilaffs and soups. Because they cook with olive oil, vegetable dishes are pareve so they may be served with meat or dairy.

They are cooked simply, then dressed with olive oil and lemon juice. Vegetables are also perfect partners for eggs. Sephardic specialities range from the North African turmeric-tinted potato omelette, a variation on tortilla, to the Sicilian spinach tortino and a Spanish-Syrian dish of aubergine with eggs and cheese. The repertoire also includes shakshouka, a delicious Arabian dish consisting of (bell) peppers, tomatoes and eggs.

From the Deli Counter

Potato salad, coleslaw, cucumber and onions, Russian salad, roasted peppers, Romanian aubergine (eggplant) salad and marinated mixed vegetables are just some of the tasty vegetable offerings that can be found in the deli. Sauerkraut is another deli staple, while dill pickles are the star attraction. American deli kosher dill pickles are not made with added sweetening or vinegar, just brine with spices and so much garlic that you can smell them down the street. More recently, specialities from Israel such as baba ghanoush have become popular.

Left: Tubs of coleslaw, dill pickles and potato salad are just a few of the delectable offerings found in the deli.

FRUITS, NUTS AND SEEDS

Since the Garden of Eden when Eve ate the proverbial apple, fruit has always been very important to the Jewish table. The first fruits of every season are the subject of specific blessings, with special affection being reserved for melons, figs, dates and grapes, because of their prominent place in the Bible. Nuts and seeds are also widely eaten, providing valuable protein and variety to many dishes.

FRUITS

All fresh fruits are considered kosher and, for some very strict Jews, it is the only food they will eat if they are not sure of the Kashrut of a kitchen. Fresh fruit can be eaten whole, uncut by treyf (not kosher) knives. There is no need for a plate or cooking pan, which might be treyf.

Israel is one of the world's leading fruit growers. Jaffa oranges, juicy grapefruit, kumquats and tiny lime- and lemonquats are grown for local consumption and export, alongside persimmons (Sharon fruit) from the Sharon valley and delicious avocados.

Below: Quinces, dates and figs are among the warm weather fruits of the Sephardic table.

Below: Apples, plums and cherries are all popular fruits of the Ashkenazic table.

Traditions

At Sukkot, a lulav (citron) is used for making the blessings over the Sukkah. At Rosh Hashanah, apples are dipped in honey, pomegranates are eaten to celebrate fertility and abundance, quinces are baked and preserved and challah often contains dried fruit.

Ashkenazim make charosset, the fruit and nut paste enjoyed at Pesach, from apples and walnuts, while Sephardim favour tropical fruits and dried fruits. At Tu b'Shevat, Jews taste their way through a variety of orchard fruit, and at Chanukkah, apple sauce is served with potato latkes.

Regional Specialities

Sephardim, living in lush, warm climates, have always enjoyed a wide variety of fruits including figs, dates, melons and citrus fruits. Quinces are traditionally made into sweet preserves for Rosh Hashanah, stuffed for Sukkot, candied for Pesach, and added to meat stews at other times. Another speciality of the Sephardic Jews, particularly those from North Africa, are preserved lemons that have been pickled in brine. They are often added to savoury dishes such as spicy meat stews.

Fruit was not as easily available to the Ashkenazim and soft and deciduous fruits were a seasonal delight for them. Raspberries, gooseberries, currants, cherries, plums, pears and apples were enjoyed in many dishes from pancakes and pastries to fruit soups, cakes and compotes. Baked apples filled with brown sugar and cinnamon are one of the classics of the Ashkenazic kitchen.

Surplus harvest was often dried or preserved and enjoyed during the rest of the year when the fruits were out of season. Compotes made of dried fruit are still very popular in the Ashkenazic kitchen. Dried fruit is used in cakes and strudels and is often added to meat dishes. Raisins are often added to meatballs and pie fillings, and the classic tzimmes (a savoury meat or vegetable stew) is enriched with dried apricots and prunes.

Making Fruit Soup

Classic Ashkenazic fruit soup makes a refreshing start or end to a meal. Plums, cherries or red berries give a good result, but any fruit can be used.

1 Chop 1.3kg/3lb fruit and place in a large non-reactive pan. Add 1 litre/ 1¾ pints/4 cups water, 475ml/16fl oz/ 2 cups dry white or red wine and the juice of 1 lemon. Stir in a little sugar, honey and cinnamon. Bring to the boil, then simmer until the fruit is tender.

2 Mix 10ml/2 tsp arrowroot with 15ml/1 tbsp cold water. Stir into the soup; bring to the boil and cook, stirring constantly, until thickened.

3 Remove the pan from the heat, stir in a little more water or wine if the soup seems too thick, then stir in a dash of vanilla extract. If using peaches, cherries or apricots, add almond extract instead. Cool, then chill. Serve with sour cream or yogurt.

VARIATION

To make kissel, purée the soup mixture, then press through a strainer into a bowl. Serve chilled, with a drizzle of cream.

NUTS AND SEEDS

These are pareve and enjoyed by both Ashkenazim and Sephardim. They may be added to sweet or savoury dishes as an ingredient or eaten on their own as a snack. Street stalls in Israeli cities sell toasted nuts and seeds, known as garinim, for nibbling.

Almonds are used in sweet and savoury dishes. Mandelbrot (hard almond cookies) are among the classic sweets of the Ashkenazic kitchen, whereas almond paste is a favourite filling used in the delicate filo pastries of North Africa and Mediterranean countries.

Coconut is used for making macaroons to serve at Pesach. In India, coconut milk is used to give meat curries a creamy quality without the need for yogurt or other dairy foods.

Pistachio nuts are enjoyed throughout the Middle East. Toasted and salted, they are a favourite snack. Unsalted pistachio nuts are crushed and layered into sweet desserts such as baklava, cake fillings and cookies.

Poppy seeds are particularly popular in the Ashkenazic kitchen. They are eaten in cakes such as the classic Russian mohn torte and sprinkled on top of breads such as bagels. Their flavour is intensified when they are roasted and ground to a paste, to be used as a filling for cakes and pastries.

Below: Almonds, sesame seeds and poppy seeds are widely used in Jewish cooking.

Treats from the Deli

The sweet aroma of baked apples welcomes visitors to the deli. Fruit compotes and jellies, and rice puddings studded with dried fruit are all available. Apricot leather – a paste of cooked apricots, dried in sheets or strips, and eaten as a confection or warmed with boiling water until it reverts to a thick paste – is also a deli speciality. Dates are coated with coconut or stuffed with nuts and sold in blocks. Delis with a large Middle Eastern clientele have jars of sweet preserves, ready to be spooned out and eaten with plain cake. Green walnuts, cherries, plums and kumquats are stewed in honey and sold in this way.

Sesame seeds can be purchased whole or hulled, raw or toasted. For optimum flavour, buy raw hulled seeds. Just before use, toast them in a heavy, ungreased pan until fragrant and golden. Toasted sesame seeds can be crushed to make halva or tahini, or simmered with honey or sugar to make sumsum, crisp confections that are sold as street food in Israel.

Walnuts are widely used in Ashkenazic cooking and are an essential ingredient in charosset.

HERBS, SPICES AND FLAVOURINGS

The Ashkenazim used the flavourings of Eastern Europe to create their robust and often piquant dishes, while the Sephardim used their own local flavourings to create a cuisine that is richly spiced and aromatic.

HERBS AND SPICES

A special place is reserved for herbs and spices in the rituals of the Jewish table. Both mild and bitter herbs are eaten at Pesach, while the sweet aroma of cinnamon, ginger, nutmeg and cloves is inhaled as part of the Havdalah ceremony that signifies the end of Shabbat, the smell of the spices welcoming the week ahead.

Ashkenazim adopted the flavours of Eastern European cooking: young dill fronds, parsley, spring onions (scallions) and tender young garlic. Spices were

Karpas and Moror

These are the herbs that feature at Pesach. Karpas is the mild herb eaten at the Seder meal. It might be leaves of young lettuce, as favoured in the Sephardic tradition, or parsley, as favoured by the Ashkenazim. Moror are the bitter herbs, eaten as a reminder of the tears shed by Hebrew slaves in Egypt. Grated horseradish is often used, or the bitter greens might be represented by chicory (Belgian endive) or watercress.

added to cakes and breads and occasionally meat dishes. A mixture of herbs and spices was used in pickled vegetables, meats and fish, contributing to their piquant flavours.

Countries with a strong German and Russian heritage introduced Jewish settlers to mustards of various kinds. In delis today you will find a large selection of mustards, such as wholegrain, smooth, sweet and herbed, ready to add their flavour to all manner of Ashkenazic dishes. In Hungary, Jewish inhabitants encountered paprika, and soon embraced it, making their own versions of dishes dominated by this warm, yet subtle, spice, such as chicken paprikash and meat goulash.

In the same eclectic fashion, Jews embraced other flavours typical of the lands in which they lived: thyme and oregano from the Mediterranean region; cumin and coriander from India; cinnamon and harissa from North Africa and chillies from Mexico.

On the wondrous palette of Middle Eastern cooking, spice mixtures are the culinary colours. They add fragrance and flavour to whatever they touch. Middle Eastern spice blends are many and varied and may be dry ground mixtures or wet pastes made with fresh chillies, garlic and herbs. Spice blends taste much more intense if they are made from freshly roasted and ground spices.

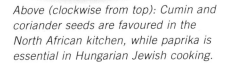

Above (clockwise from top): Cumin and coriander seeds are favoured in the North African kitchen, while paprika is essential in Hungarian Jewish cooking.

Making Harissa

This hot, spicy paste is used extensively in Tunisian and other North African cooking. It is based on medium-sized chillies with a medium hot flavour. The blend is widely sold in jars, but it is easy to make your own.

1 Put 10–15 whole dried chillies in a pan with water to cover. Bring to the boil, then remove from the heat.

2 When the chillies are cool enough to handle, remove the stems, seeds and membrane, then pound to a purée with 10 garlic cloves and 5ml/1 tsp each ground coriander, caraway and cumin in a mortar with a pestle. Add 2.5ml/½ tsp salt and about 15ml/1 tbsp extra virgin olive oil. Stir in enough cold water to make a thick paste.

Right: Fresh dill is used extensively in Ashkenazic cooking and its aroma is redolent of many classic dishes from the Old Country.

Making Hawaij

This wonderfully fragrant mixture of spices comes from Yemen. It is delicious in stews, soups and sauces.

Place 30ml/2 tbsp black peppercorns and 15ml/1 tbsp caraway seeds in a spice grinder, or use a pestle and mortar. Add 10ml/2 tsp each ground cumin and turmeric, 5ml/1 tsp cardamom seeds and several pinches of saffron threads. Process to a powder and keep in a tightly sealed jar in a cool, dark place.

Making Berbere

This Ethiopian spice mixture is based on hot chillies.

1 Mix 90g/3½oz paprika with 10ml/ 2 tsp cayenne pepper, the seeds from 20 cardamom pods, 2.5ml/½ tsp ground fenugreek seeds; 1.5ml/¼ tsp each of ground ginger and freshly grated nutmeg, and generous pinches of black pepper, cloves, ground cinnamon and allspice.

2 Lightly toast the mixture in a hot, ungreased pan for less than a minute. When cool, store in a tightly sealed jar.

Making Chermoula

This moist mixture of herbs, spices and aromatics comes from North Africa. It is mainly used as a marinade for fish but is also good with chicken, potatoes and other vegetables.

1 In a bowl, combine 75ml/5 tbsp extra virgin olive oil with 30ml/2 tbsp lemon juice, 4–5 crushed garlic cloves and 10ml/2 tsp ground cumin.

2 Stir 15ml/1 tbsp paprika, 1.5ml/¼ tsp ground ginger and 1 chopped fresh chilli or a pinch of chilli powder into the spice mixture.

3 Add 90ml/6 tbsp chopped fresh coriander (cilantro) leaves and a little flat leaf parsley or mint, if you like, to the bowl, season with salt and mix well or purée to a smooth paste.

Below (clockwise from top left): Rose water, honey and halek are widely used in both sweet and savoury dishes in the Sephardic kitchen.

FLAVOURINGS

There are a number of other flavouring ingredients that play an essential role in Jewish cooking.

Salt is not just used as a seasoning but also plays a role in ritual, especially in kashering. It is seen as a purifying agent and, in biblical times, it was sacrificed at the Temple in Jerusalem. In Morocco, Jews sprinkle salt on newborn babies, to ward off the evil eye. At the Pesach Seder, it is dissolved in water and used to represent the tears of Israelite slaves.

Sour salt (citric acid) is a great favourite in the Ashkenazic kitchen and is used instead of lemon or vinegar to add a sour taste to dishes such as borscht.

Honey has been much loved by Jews since the biblical description of Israel as a land flowing with milk and honey. It is used to represent the sweetness of the year to come at Rosh Hashanah and is also used in baking – most famously in lekach, the honey cake eaten to celebrate a child's first day at school.

Rose water and orange flower water are fragrant essences used in sweet and savoury dishes. They are added to the syrups poured over sweet pastries, and to savoury tagines and couscous dishes.

Halek, also known as dibis, is a thick date syrup used to flavour sweet and savoury foods. It is readily available in jars, but you can easily make your own. Reconstitute dried dates in water, then boil in a little water until soft. Purée in a food processor, then strain into a clean pan and cook over a medium heat until thickened.

NOODLES, PANCAKES, DUMPLINGS AND SAVOURY PASTRIES

NOODLES

These were once the pride of the Ashkenazi kitchen and housewives were judged on their skills as home-makers (*balaboostas*) by how thin and delicate they could make their noodles. Noodles were cut into a variety of shapes, such as little squares (plaetschen) and small butterflies (varnishkes). Noodles were served in soup, tossed with sour cream or cheese, or layered with other ingredients such as fruit or cheeses and baked into delicious puddings known as kugels. Noodle dough could also be rolled thin and filled to make dumplings, such as the meat-filled kreplach; potato-, kasha- or cabbage-filled pierogi, or cheese- or fruit-filled varenikes.

Noodles were probably introduced to German Ashkenazic kitchens during the 14th century, via the Italian Jews. This was long before they reached the non-Jewish German kitchen during the 16th century. Pasta came to Poland at the same time, possibly through Central Asia, and the Yiddish word for noodles (lokshen) comes from the Polish word "lokszyn". The sauces of the Polish Yiddish kitchen also showed a Central Asian slant. They were based on yogurt, sour cream and fresh cheeses

Left: Kreplach are meat-filled pasta dumplings that are often enjoyed in chicken soup.

rather than the rich tomato sauces of Italian extraction. Sephardic cooking showed a stronger Italian or Spanish influence as evidenced in kelsonnes, dumplings filled with cheese and eaten at the festival of Shavuot, and calzonicchi, which are filled with spinach and enjoyed for Purim.

Making Noodle Dough

Egg noodles are still made at home for special occasions. This is easy to do with a pasta-rolling machine, but they can also be rolled by hand on a well-floured surface with a large rolling pin.

1 Sift 225g/8oz/2 cups plain (all-purpose) flour and 2.5ml/½ tsp salt into a bowl, making a well in the centre.

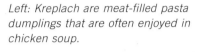

2 Pour 2 lightly beaten eggs into the flour and mix with a fork, gradually incorporating the eggs into the flour. Continue to stir, using a wooden spoon, until well combined. Alternatively, place all the ingredients in a food processor fitted with the metal blade and mix to form a dough. If the dough is sticky, add a little more flour.

3 Tip the dough on to a floured board and knead until smooth and elastic. Place the dough in a plastic bag, seal and leave for at least 30 minutes.

Right: (clockwise from top) Lokshen, farfel, varnishkes and plaetschen are just a few of the classic noodles from the Ashkenazic kitchen.

4 If using a pasta-rolling machine, roll out walnut-size balls of the dough, then, one at a time, feed the dough into the largest opening of the rollers. Fold the flattened dough and repeat, reducing the roller opening until the dough is the desired thickness.

5 If rolling by hand, divide the dough into three equal pieces, then roll out each piece on a floured surface, until it is extremely thin.

Making Noodle Shapes

Lightly sprinkle the sheets of freshly rolled noodle dough with flour, then cut into the desired shape. To cook, drop the pasta into a large pan of boiling salted water and cook for 2–4 minutes.

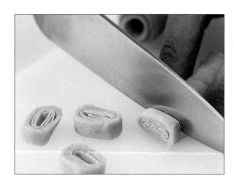

To make lokshen (flat noodles), roll a sheet of noodle dough into a tight scroll. Using a heavy sharp knife cut the scroll of dough crossways into narrow or wide strips, as desired. Unroll the strips, boil and serve with sauce, in soup or baked with other ingredients in a kugel.

To make plaetschen (little squares), cut a sheet of noodle dough into 1cm/½in squares. Boil and serve in soup.

To make varnishkes (butterflies), cut a sheet of noodle dough into 2.5cm/1in squares. Pinch each square in the centre to form a bow tie or butterfly. Boil and serve in soup or with kasha.

To make farfel (pellets), grate kneaded, unrolled noodle dough through the large holes of a grater to form pellets. Boil and add to soups.

Making Mandlen

These crisp soup garnishes are made from noodle dough. They take their name from the Yiddish word for almond, a reference to their shape and colour.

1 Preheat the oven to 190°C/375°F/ Gas 5. Beat 1 egg with 15ml/1 tbsp vegetable oil. Add 2.5ml/½ tsp salt, then mix in about 115g/4oz/1 cup plain (all-purpose) flour until the dough holds together. Knead for 10 minutes. Cover and leave for 20 minutes.

2 Divide the dough into two to four pieces and form each into a rope, about 1cm/½in wide. Cut each one into 1cm/ ½in pieces and place on an oiled baking sheet. Bake for 35–40 minutes. Alternatively, deep-fry, until just golden.

PANCAKES

Since biblical times pancakes have been popular. In times of plenty, they were made from the finest ingredients and fried in lots of oil. When times were hard, they were made from whatever wild greens and grains could be found and fried in a drop or two of fat.

Pancakes are usually either very thin and filled or thick and crispy. Crêpe-like blintzes are filled with cheese, meat, fruit or vegetables and are often folded into parcels and fried until crisp. Thick, hearty latkes are best known as a treat eaten at Chanukkah, consisting of grated potatoes formed into cakes and fried until golden brown. They can also be enjoyed at any time of year and can be made from spinach, grated apples or a mixture of cottage cheese, matzo meal and eggs. Hearty grains such as kasha can also be used.

Chremslach are thick pancakes eaten at Pesach, made from egg, matzo meal and seasonings. They are good served with a generous spoonful of cooling sour cream or yogurt.

Ataif are Egyptian pancakes, raised with yeast, and served with a sweet syrup and dollops of rich clotted cream. Like other dairy-filled pancakes, they are enjoyed at Shavuot, the festival when dairy products are traditionally eaten in abundance.

Below: Melawah are pancake flat breads eaten by Yemenite Jews, often with chopped tomatoes and spicy zchug.

DUMPLINGS

Generations of Jewish cooks have delighted in dumplings, especially knaidlach made from matzo meal and egg. The word "knaidlach" comes from "knodel", the German for dumpling. Knaidlach are as much a part of Yiddish cooking as dumplings are of Eastern European peasant food. Because they were made with matzo, knaidlach were eaten for Shabbat and other festivals, especially Pesach, when bread is forbidden.

Different Jewish communities added their distinctive flavour to knaidlach: some added chopped herbs such as parsley or chives, or aromatics such as garlic or grated onions. Others stuffed them with a bit of meat, while the Viennese Jews added a pinch of dried ginger to the mixture. Knaidlach can be big balls or small two-bite wonders and can be tender and light or solid and heavy. Cold cooked knaidlach can be cut into bitesize pieces and browned with eggs and mushrooms.

Sephardic dumplings are made from noodles stuffed with meat, then floated in soup. Alternatively, they may be made from rice as is the case with the Middle Eastern kobeba, meat-filled dumplings much like kibbeh, using rice instead of bulgur wheat.

Below: Knaidlach are the Ashkenazic matzo balls that are traditionally served in chicken soup.

Above: Kibbeh are classic Sephardic dumplings made of pounded bulgur wheat and minced (ground) meat.

SAVOURY PASTRIES

These are popular with both Ashkenazic and Sephardic Jews. Whenever there was something special to celebrate, the women of the community would gather and spend days preparing pastries.

Ashkenazi Pastries

Classic Ashkenazic pastries include knishes (half-moon shaped turnovers), strudels (wafer-thin pastry rolled around fillings) and piroshkis (small pies). They may be filled with kasha, mashed potatoes and onions, minced (ground) meat, browned cabbage, chopped egg and sometimes smoked salmon. The dough can be shortcrust (unsweetened) pastry or puff pastry, but there are also yeast doughs and even doughs made from mashed potato. The pastries may then be baked or fried.

Sephardic Pastries

The Sephardim have a virtually endless number of pastries, with many different types of pastry and filling. They are made in an array of shapes, including cigars, half moons, triangles, rectangles, squares, circles and even cones and round balls, and may be baked or deep-fried in oil.

Borekas are eaten wherever Turkish, Greek and Balkan Jews have settled. These pastries are flaky on the outside, with tender layers within. Borekas can be tiny one-bite pastries or made as tapadas – big trays to cut into individual portions. They are usually filled with aubergine (eggplant) and tomatoes, cheese, spinach or meat.

Iraqi Jews traditionally fill their pastries with mashed chickpeas and chicken. Also from Iraq are sambusaks, crisp shortcrust pastries filled with egg and cheese or vegetables or meat. They are usually topped with sesame seeds or a blend of za'atar herbs containing thyme. Italian Jews fill their savoury burricche with a variety of mixtures, from tuna to liver, and even make sweet pastries with pumpkin and glacé (candied) fruit. Pumpkin pastries are a speciality of Bukharan Jews.

The Spanish and Portuguese Jews have empanadas, crisp little pastries filled with meats, fish or vegetables.

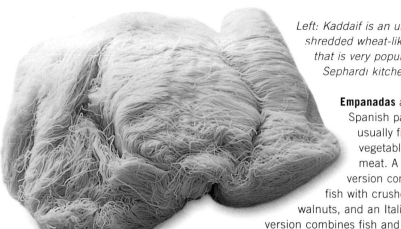

Left: Kaddaif is an unusual, shredded wheat-like pastry that is very popular in the Sephardi kitchen.

Bishak are Bukharan baked pastries made from pizza dough filled with sweet and peppery cooked pumpkin.

Brik are crisp, fried filo pastries, filled with tuna or meat, and a raw egg.

Borekas, sambusak, pasteles and buricche are crisp shortcrust pastries filled with cheese, aubergine (eggplant), and tomato or meat.

Boyos are little pies made from dough layered with mature (sharp) cheese, fried onions and vegetables.

Empanadas are crisp Spanish pastries, usually filled with vegetables and meat. A Turkish version combines fish with crushed walnuts, and an Italian version combines fish and anchovies with chopped parsley.

Filo pastry is a stretched, tissue-paper-thin pastry made from flour and water with a touch of oil for elasticity. It is brushed with oil or butter and rolled around a filling before being fried or baked. Filo pastry is bought ready-made as it requires great skill and years of practice to make it successfully.

Kaddaif is a shredded pastry that looks much like shredded wheat. It is also known as konafa. It is usually used for sweet pastries, which are stuffed with nuts, baked, then soaked in syrup. Like filo dough kaddaif is usually purchased ready-made, as preparing it requires great skill and dexterity.

Khatchapuri are yeast dough pastries filled with cheese from Georgia in Russia. Goat's cheese mixed with Gruyère is a very popular filling, sometimes with a little chopped coriander (cilantro).

Bulemas and rodanchas are made by rolling sheets of filo pastry around a filling, then coiling the rolls on a baking sheet. The dough is very delicate and needs to be handled with great care when being rolled around the filling.

Lamahjeen are small pizza-like pastries made with tomato, tamarind and meat; a speciality of the Jews of Aleppo.

A mina is a Sephardic pie made using soaked matzo as a kind of pastry. They are usually served for Pesach when bread and pastry are forbidden. Minas are often served in Mexico, where they are likened to tortillas.

Warka is similar to filo pastry. It is made by quickly tapping a ball of dough on to a hot surface, leaving behind a thin, wispy layer of tissue-thin pastry, which rapidly becomes crisp.

From the Deli Counter

Sweet noodle kugels may be sold cut into big squares and sold as dessert. Potato latkes can be bought all year round, but are particularly popular at Chanukkah. Blintzes are often sold in delis – hot, freshly cooked blintzes will often be on the menu for brunch, while take-away blintzes can be reheated at home.

Many delis sell hot or cold knishes or piroshkis, ready to eat on the spot or to take home for later, filled with anything from kasha to meat to spinach. Filo pastries can also be found – spinach and cheese is a particularly popular filling. Fresh filo pastry and kaddaif are also sold in delis, especially those with a Middle Eastern influence.

Right: Piroshkis and knishes from the Ashkenazic tradition are particular favourites on the deli counter.

BREADS

The world over, bread is very important to the Jews. A meal without bread is not a meal, according to the dictates of the Jewish religion. Without bread, there can be no Hamotzi (blessing over the bread that signals the start of a meal) and neither can there be the Birkat Hamazon (grace that usually concludes a meal). A meal without bread can only really be considered a snack.

ASHKENAZIC BREADS

In Jewish bakeries, it is usual for the breads to be pareve – made without butter or milk so that they can be eaten with either meat or dairy foods. There is challah, rye bread, pumpernickel, bagels, Kaiser rolls and onion rolls – the variety is astonishing and, if you happen to have wandered into an ethnic Jewish bakery, you may well encounter some wonderful regional specialities as well as the usual fare.

All ethnic groups have a wide variety of breads, both for everyday use and special occasions. When the Ukrainian Ashkenazim emigrated to America, they brought with them sourdough loaves of seeded rye, dark pumpernickel and onion-crusted rolls.

Right: Pumpernickel, from the Ashkenazic tradition, is dark and sour with a crisp crust.

Walking into one of their bakeries is a joy: the smells of baking – yeast, flour, a whiff of something sweet – mingling with the scent of the wood-burning stove.

Bagels are an Ashkenazic classic that travelled from the shtetlach and ghettos of Eastern Europe and are now enjoyed all over the world. They lend themselves to any number of different fillings and are satisfyingly chewy.

Bagels are usually made in bakeries that bake nothing else, because the procedure for making them is a special one. The dough rings are first briefly poached in huge vats of water before being glazed and baked. This technique creates the distinctive dense, chewy texture that has made bagels so popular. To walk past a bagel bakery without venturing in is just about impossible. The alluring smell inevitably entices you in, and you'll want to get yourself a nice hot bagel before setting off once more.

Above: Challah is the traditional bread of Shabbat and festivals and may be braided, round or shaped like a ladder, depending on the festival.

Sweet challah is the traditional Shabbat and festival bread of the Ashkenazic Jews. The dough is made with eggs and vegetable oil, which gives it a soft texture, similar to that of brioche, and is lightly sweetened with honey or sugar.

The loaves are usually braided, made with three, six or even twelve strands of dough. During Rosh Hashanah challah may be shaped into a round or crown, in honour of the Rosh Hashanah blessing: "The whole world will crown thee." On the eve of Yom Kippur, the challah is shaped like a ladder, raised arms or wings, representing prayers rising heavenwards.

Boulkas are small, individual challah rolls, shaped into rounds, braids or spirals and dusted with poppy seeds, that are frequently served at weddings.

SEPHARDIC BREADS

These vary greatly and are very different from the breads of the Ashkenazim. Some are risen; some are flat; some, such as melawah, are slightly puffed and fried to a crisp. One Sephardic bread most of us are familiar with is pitta, a flat bread favoured by Jews and Arabs alike, and by many other Middle Easterners as well. Iraqi pitta bread is a particularly large flat bread, which resembles an enormous, thick pancake.

Breads that are especially made for Shabbat include mouna, lahuhua and kubaneh. The latter is a coiled bread from Yemen, which is made from a rich yeast dough. It is prepared before Shabbat begins, then steamed in a very low oven overnight.

Israel produces a marvellous array of breads, from the simple everyday loaf, which is crusty on the outside and beautifully tender inside, to large flat breads, which are used for wrapping around vegetables or meat.

Left: Pitta bread came from the Middle East but is now enjoyed by Ashkenazim, Europeans and Americans alike.

MATZO

This is unleavened bread, made for Pesach, when leavened bread may not be eaten. The flat, brittle sheets are served at the table, and are also ground to make a meal that is transformed into cakes, biscuits and cookies. Matzo meal can be fine or coarse, while matzo farfel is lightly crushed matzo.

For Pesach, matzo is prepared under special guidelines and the packaging is always marked "Kosher for Pesach". Observant Jews often eat schmurah matzo as they are handmade to a very high specification.

Right: Jews eat unleavened matzos at Pesach but they are also enjoyed during the rest of the year.

From the Deli

Oy what sandwiches! A true Jewish deli sandwich is a thing of mammoth proportions. Piles of thinly sliced salami, billows of roasted turkey, peppery pastrami, corned or salt beef, bologna or steamed knockwurst are just some of the possible ingredients, and most likely there will be a combination of several of the above, at least 350g/12oz per sandwich, layered between thick slices of fresh, crusty, tender bread.

A sandwich from one of the legendary New York delis, such as the Carnegie or Second Avenue Deli, Katz's, the Stage Deli or Juniors will be far too thick for the average eater

to get his or her mouth around. It will be necessary to wrap up at least half for later – much, much later.

The Reuben, assumed by many to be a Jewish classic, is not actually kosher. Slices of seeded rye bread contain both corned beef and Swiss cheese – a forbidden combination.

Choosing the filling for your deli sandwich is taxing enough, but it can be even more difficult to decide precisely which bread to have. One thing everyone agrees on, however, is that a sandwich from the deli is never served on sliced white.

Left: A bagel spread generously with cream cheese and topped with wafer-thin slices of smoked salmon is the quintessential Jewish deli snack.

CAKES, PASTRIES AND SWEETMEATS

For Jews, whenever there is something to celebrate, be it a festival or a family occasion, cakes and other sweet treats are very much in evidence. Precisely what is on the table will largely depend on whether the hosts come from the Ashkenazic or Sephardic traditions, as these take very different approaches when it comes to baking.

During Pesach, the kosher kitchens of both Ashkenazim and Sephardim undergo a transformation. At this time, all food must be free of leaven, and eggs are used as the main raising agent instead. The result is a wealth of featherlight sponge cakes, often made with matzo meal and ground nuts.

THE ASHKENAZIC BAKERY

Visit an Eastern European bakery and you will find the shelves filled with a wide selection of delectable pastries, sweetmeats, crisp cookies, cakes and crunchy rolls. No one could possibly walk through without having a "little something". A cup of coffee is never just a cup of coffee: you must have a Danish – a pastry filled with jam and topped with icing – or a rugelach, or maybe a mohn cake or strudel, or perhaps an apfelkuchen. The choice and variety is seemingly endless.

Cakes of all kinds are baked in the Ashkenazic kitchen. Kuchen is closer to a sweet fruit bread than a cake. It is made from a moderately sweet dough, filled with fresh or dried fruit. Honey cake, also known as lekach, is

eaten for Rosh Hashanah and Shabbat, while almond cakes, plava and other leaven-free cakes are classic Pesach specialities. For Purim, the traditional treat is hamantashen, triangular cakes filled with seeds and fruit that resemble the three-cornered hat of Haman.

Cookies and sweet biscuits include croissant-shaped rugelach, almond mandelbrot and plain kichel. None of these are very sweet, and they make the perfect accompaniment to tea or coffee. Teiglach, from Lithuania, are rich with honey, so a little goes a very long way.

Candied citrus peel known as pomerantzen is a great favourite of all Jews, not just because it tastes so good, but because the peel that might otherwise have been discarded is transformed into an irresistible treat. Jews also love pastries, the most well known being strudel, which originated

Left: Pomerantzen (candied citrus peel) is a classic Ashkenazic sweetmeat.

Below: Sweet, fruit-filled strudel made with paper-thin pastry is one of the glories of the Eastern European Jews.

as a hefty pastry roll filled with vegetables or fruit. It was the Turks, invading Hungary in 1526, who introduced the thin multi-layered pastry that we now know as strudel dough.

Strudel is eaten for many festivals: with cabbage for Simchat Torah; with dried fruit for Tu b'Shevat; with crushed poppy-seed paste for Purim and with cheese for Shavuot. Fruit versions are filled with sliced apple, cherries or rhubarb, alone or with dried fruit.

Left: (left to right) Traditional Ashkenazic rugelach and mandelbrot cookies are delicious with a glass of hot tea.

Making Strudel Pastry

This is very like filo pastry, which can be bought ready-made and makes a good substitute for strudel pastry.

1 In a large bowl, beat 250g/9oz/ generous 1 cup butter with 30ml/2 tbsp sugar and 250ml/8fl oz/1 cup sour cream or softened vanilla ice cream. Add 2.5ml/½ tsp vanilla or almond extract and 1.5ml/¼ tsp salt, then stir in 500g/1¼lb/5 cups plain (all-purpose) flour. Mix to a soft dough.

2 Divide the dough into three pieces, wrap separately and chill overnight. (It may be frozen for up to 3 months.)

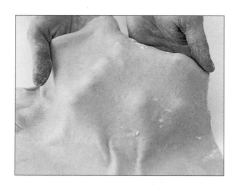

3 If necessary, thaw the dough. Place one piece on a floured board. Flatten it lightly, then, very gently, pull it out with your hands, pulling each side in turn until it is almost paper thin. It is now ready to fill and bake. (Take extra care if you have long fingernails.)

VARIATION

To make a non-dairy pastry, substitute 120ml/4fl oz/½ cup each of sweet wine and vegetable oil for the butter and sour cream or ice cream.

SEPHARDIC SWEET SPECIALITIES

These are Mediterranean in their origin. Every Sephardic community produces a wealth of moist, succulent almond and walnut cakes. Often a local dish was adapted for Jewish holidays – Greek Jews eat crisp, fried loukomades for Chanukkah, Israelis eat jam-filled sufganiot (doughnuts) and Tunisians enjoy syrup-soaked cakes for Purim.

During Pesach when leaven (and flour) may not be used, nuts are used to give body to desserts. Almond cakes and coconut macaroons are particularly popular, as is sesame seed halva.

Syrup-soaked filo pastries, such as nut-filled baklava, are popular among Sephardic Jews. Other pastries include kaddaif, a shredded pastry drenched in syrup, and felabis, deep-fried, pretzel-like pastries filled with syrup.

Making Simple Baklava

The secret to perfect baklava is to pour very cold syrup over a hot pastry, or very hot syrup over a cold pastry.

1 Preheat the oven to 200°C/400°F/ Gas 6. Layer six sheets of filo pastry in a shallow dish, brushing each layer with melted butter or oil.

2 Sprinkle chopped nuts on top of the pastry, to a depth of 1cm/½in. Sprinkle generously with sugar and cinnamon. Top with six more layers of buttered or oiled filo, then, using a sharp knife, cut the top layer of pastry into triangles.

3 Bake the baklava for 30 minutes until golden. Remove from the oven and pour over hattar, or a light syrup flavoured with orange flower water or rose water.

The Deli Cheesecake

This is one of the most popular desserts in the deli cabinet. It is often associated with Ashkenazim from Germany, who were famous for their fresh cheeses. It is eaten at Shavuot, reflecting the legend of the Jews who, on returning to camp after receiving the Torah, found that their milk had turned sour and had to sweeten it with honey.

Cheesecakes can be flavoured and topped with many ingredients from fruit to chocolate and it is not unusual to find delis offering upwards of 30 different types.

Below: Cheesecake is a deli classic, though purists argue that only a simple white cheesecake can be considered the real thing.

APPETIZERS

From chopped liver to herring to bean salads, Jewish appetizers are adored by
Jews and non-Jews alike. Festive meals from the weekly Shabbat to annual
holidays almost always include a selection of appetizers. In fact, what
often distinguishes an everyday meal from a celebration is the
serving of these delicacies. Both Ashkenazim and Sephardim
have a wealth of tasty morsels to sharpen the appetite
and enhance the sociability of the occasion.

CUCUMBER AND WALNUT YOGURT

WHEN MANY OF BULGARIA'S JEWS WENT TO ISRAEL, THEY TOOK WITH THEM THEIR PASSION AND SKILLS FOR EXCELLENT SALAD-STYLE YOGURTS, OF WHICH THIS IS ONE. IF POSSIBLE, ADD ANOTHER BULGARIAN FLOURISH BY USING ONE OF THEIR THICK SHEEP'S MILK YOGURTS.

SERVES SIX

INGREDIENTS

1 large cucumber
3–5 garlic cloves, finely chopped
250ml/8fl oz/1 cup sour cream or
   120ml/4fl oz/½ cup Greek
   (US strained plain) yogurt mixed
   with 120ml/4fl oz/½ cup double
   (heavy) cream
250ml/8fl oz/1 cup yogurt, preferably
   thick Greek or Bulgarian sheep's
   milk yogurt
2–3 large pinches of dried dill or
   30–45ml/2–3 tbsp chopped
   fresh dill
45–60ml/3–4 tbsp chopped walnuts
salt
sprig of dill, to garnish (optional)

1 Dice the cucumber finely and place in a large mixing bowl.

COOK'S TIP
If using very thick strained yogurt, you will be able to shape the mixture into balls and serve on a bed of salad leaves.

2 Add the garlic, sour cream or yogurt and cream, thick yogurt, dill and salt. Mix together, then cover and chill.

3 To serve, pile the mixture into a bowl and sprinkle with walnuts. Garnish with dill, if you like.

Energy 164Kcal/677kJ; Protein 4.7g; Carbohydrate 5.5g, of which sugars 5.4g; Fat 13.9g, of which saturates 5.8g; Cholesterol 26mg; Calcium 131mg; Fibre 0.5g; Sodium 53mg.

EGYPTIAN BROWN BEAN SALAD

RICH, ROBUST BROWN BEANS COULD BE CALLED THE EGYPTIAN NATIONAL DISH. THIS DISH IS ESPECIALLY DOTED ON BY EGYPTIAN JEWS BECAUSE IT CONTAINS NEITHER MEAT NOR DAIRY AND CAN BE EATEN AT ROOM TEMPERATURE FOR SHABBAT. ENJOY WITH A STACK OF SOFT, FRESH PITTA BREAD.

SERVES SIX

INGREDIENTS
  350g/12oz/1½ cups dried brown
    beans, or use canned
  3 thyme sprigs
  2 bay leaves
  1 onion, halved
  4 garlic cloves, crushed
  7.5ml/1½ tsp cumin seeds, crushed
  3 spring onions (scallions), finely
    chopped
  90ml/6 tbsp chopped fresh parsley
  20ml/4 tsp lemon juice
  90ml/6 tbsp olive oil
  3 hard-boiled eggs, shelled and
    roughly chopped
  1 pickled cucumber, roughly
    chopped, preferably Israeli or
    Middle Eastern
  salt and ground black pepper

1 Put the beans in a bowl with plenty of cold water and leave to soak overnight. Drain, transfer to a pan and cover with fresh water. Bring to the boil and boil rapidly for 10 minutes. Omit this step if using canned beans.

2 Reduce the heat and add the thyme, bay leaves and onion. Simmer very gently for about 1 hour (5–8 minutes if canned) until tender. Drain and discard the herbs and onion.

COOK'S TIP
The cooking time for dried beans can vary considerably. They may need only 45 minutes, or much longer, to become tender. For the busy cook, canned beans are of course more convenient.

3 Mix together the garlic, cumin, spring onions, parsley, lemon juice, oil and a little salt and pepper. Pour over the warm beans and toss the ingredients lightly together.

4 Serve immediately, garnished with chopped egg and pickled cucumber if you like.

Energy 301Kcal/1263kJ; Protein 16.6g; Carbohydrate 27.1g, of which sugars 2.5g; Fat 14.8g, of which saturates 2.5g; Cholesterol 95mg; Calcium 99mg; Fibre 10g; Sodium 50mg.

AVOCADO, ORANGE AND ALMOND SALAD

ISRAEL GROWS AVOCADOS AND ORANGES AND EXPORTS THEM ALL OVER THE WORLD. IMAGINE THE AMAZEMENT THE SETTLERS FROM EASTERN EUROPE MUST HAVE FELT AS THESE SUN-DRENCHED FRUIT GREW SO ABUNDANTLY FROM THEIR TREES AND GROVES! THIS IS A REFRESHING SALAD OF CONTRASTING TASTES AND TEXTURES, FULL OF FRESHNESS AND MEDITERRANEAN FLAVOUR.

SERVES FOUR

INGREDIENTS

   2 oranges
   2 well-flavoured tomatoes
   2 small avocados
   60ml/4 tbsp extra virgin olive oil
   30ml/2 tbsp lemon juice
   15ml/1 tbsp chopped fresh parsley
   1 small onion, sliced into rings
   salt and ground black pepper
   25g/1oz/¼ cup flaked (sliced)
     almonds and 10–12 black olives,
     to garnish

1 Plunge the tomatoes into boiling water for 30 seconds, then refresh in cold water. Peel away the skins, cut into quarters, remove the seeds and chop roughly.

2 Cut the avocados in half, remove the stones (pits) and carefully peel away the skin. Cut into chunks.

3 Mix together the olive oil, lemon juice and parsley. Season with salt and pepper. Toss the avocados and tomatoes in half of the dressing.

4 Peel the oranges and slice into thick rounds. Arrange the slices on a plate and sprinkle over the onion rings. Drizzle with the rest of the dressing. Spoon the avocados, tomatoes, almonds and olives on top.

Energy 240Kcal/993kJ; Protein 2.5g; Carbohydrate 10.9g, of which sugars 10.2g; Fat 20.9g, of which saturates 3.7g; Cholesterol 0mg; Calcium 63mg; Fibre 4g; Sodium 13mg.

GRILLED PEPPER SALAD

*ALSO KNOWN AS SALATA DE ARDEI, THIS IS THE ROMANIAN VERSION OF A DISH BELOVED IN
THE MEDITERRANEAN AND BALKANS. SERVE AS PART OF A MEZE (KNOWN AS VORSHPEIZ TO THE
ASHKENAZIM), ALONG WITH PICKLES, FETA CHEESE (FOR A DAIRY MEAL) AND SALAMI (FOR A MEAT
MEAL). THIS SALAD IS ALSO A TRADITIONAL ACCOMPANIMENT TO MINCED BEEF KEBABS.*

SERVES FOUR

INGREDIENTS
8 green and/or yellow, red or orange
(bell) peppers
3 garlic cloves, crushed
75ml/5 tbsp olive oil
60ml/4 tbsp wine vinegar
4 tomatoes, sliced
1 red onion, thinly sliced
salt and ground black pepper
2.5ml/$\frac{1}{2}$ tsp paprika
sprigs of fresh coriander (cilantro),
to garnish
black bread, to serve

1 Cut the peppers into quarters,
discarding the cores, seeds and tops.
Place under a preheated grill (broiler),
skin side up and cook until the skin
chars and blisters.

2 Place the grilled pepper quarters in a
plastic bag and seal tightly. Leave for
15 minutes.

3 Remove from the bag and scrape off
the skins using a sharp knife.

COOK'S TIP
Using a colourful range of peppers in the
dish will boost the presentation no end.
If different coloured bell peppers are not
available, substitute with long peppers.

4 Blend together the garlic, olive oil
and vinegar. Arrange the peppers,
tomatoes and onion on four serving
plates and pour over the garlic dressing.
Season, sprinkle with paprika, garnish
with sprigs of coriander and serve with
black bread.

Energy 242Kcal/1006kJ; Protein 3.9g; Carbohydrate 23.5g, of which sugars 22.3g; Fat 15.3g, of which saturates 2.4g; Cholesterol 0mg; Calcium 35mg; Fibre 6g; Sodium 22mg.

MUSHROOM CAVIAR WITH GARLIC-RUBBED RYE TOASTS

MIXTURES OF FINELY CHOPPED VEGETABLES ARE KNOWN AS IKRA, OR CAVIAR, AND ARE BELOVED DISHES IN THE ASHKENAZI KITCHEN. THEY RESEMBLE THE FAMOUS FISH ROE IN THEIR TEXTURE — HENCE THE NICKNAME — BUT ARE OF COURSE PERFECT VEGETARIAN TREATS.

SERVES FOUR

INGREDIENTS
  10–15g/¼–½oz dried porcini or
    other well-flavoured dried mushrooms
  120ml/4fl oz/½ cup water
  45ml/3 tbsp olive or vegetable oil
  450g/1lb mushrooms, roughly chopped
  5–10 shallots, chopped
  5 garlic cloves, 4 chopped and
    1 whole
  30ml/2 tbsp port
  juice of ¼ lemon, or to taste
  12–16 slices cocktail rye bread or
    2 ordinary slices, cut in halves,
    quarters or fingers
  salt
  2–3 spring onions (scallions), thinly
    shredded, and/or 15ml/1 tbsp
    chopped fresh parsley and
    1 roughly chopped hard-boiled egg,
    or sour cream, to garnish

1 Break up the dried mushrooms, put in a bowl and soak in the water for about 30 minutes.

2 Heat the oil in a pan, add the fresh mushrooms, shallots and chopped garlic and fry until browned. Season with salt. Add the soaked mushrooms and water and cook until all the liquid has evaporated. Add the port and lemon juice.

3 Continue cooking until the port and lemon juice have evaporated and the mixture is brown and dry.

4 Put the mixture in a food processor or blender and process briefly until a chunky paste is formed.

5 Toast the rye bread until golden on both sides, then rub with the whole garlic clove. Spoon the mushroom caviar into dishes and serve with the toast, or top each piece of garlic toast with the mushroom mixture and heat gently under the grill (broiler). Serve garnished with the spring onions, parsley, hard-boiled egg or sour cream.

COOK'S TIP
Depending on the size and strength of the shallots, you may wish to vary the quantity according to your own taste.

Energy 143Kcal/596kJ; Protein 3.7g; Carbohydrate 10.3g, of which sugars 3.7g; Fat 9.1g, of which saturates 1.1g; Cholesterol 0mg; Calcium 29mg; Fibre 2.4g; Sodium 80mg.

MUHAMMARA

MUHAMMARA IS A DISH OF THE SEPHARDIC TABLE, ESPECIALLY IN SYRIA AND TURKEY. A THICK,
SPICY, SWEET AND TANGY SALAD SPREAD, IT IS RICHLY RED IN COLOUR AND A DELICIOUS WAY
TO BEGIN ANY MEAL. ARMENIAN CHRISTIANS MAKE A SIMILAR MUHAMMARA, OCCASIONALLY
SPICING IT UP WITH A LITTLE CAYENNE PEPPER.

SERVES FOUR

INGREDIENTS

1½ slices Granary (whole-wheat)
  bread, day-old or toasted
3 red (bell) peppers, roasted, skinned
  and chopped
2 very mild chillies, roasted, skinned
  and chopped
115g/4oz/1 cup walnut pieces
3–4 garlic cloves, chopped
15–30ml/1–2 tbsp balsamic vinegar
  or pomegranate molasses
juice of ½ lemon
2.5–5ml/½–1 tsp ground cumin
2.5ml/½ tsp sugar, or to taste
105ml/7 tbsp extra virgin olive oil
salt

1 Break the Granary bread into small pieces and place in a food processor or blender with all the remaining ingredients except the extra virgin olive oil. Blend together until the ingredients are finely chopped.

2 With the motor running, slowly drizzle the extra virgin olive oil into the food processor or blender and process until the mixture forms a smooth paste. Tip the muhammara into a serving dish. Serve at room temperature.

Energy 425Kcal/1753kJ; Protein 6.1g; Carbohydrate 11.7g, of which sugars 7.8g; Fat 39.6g, of which saturates 4.5g; Cholesterol 0mg; Calcium 52mg; Fibre 3.1g; Sodium 48mg.

SUN-DRIED TOMATO <u>AND</u> PEPPER SALAD

THIS APPETIZER IS VERY MUCH A MODERN ISRAELI CREATION, BRIDGING TRADITIONAL MIDDLE EASTERN AND CONTEMPORARY EUROPEAN STYLES. IT IS DELICIOUS SERVED WITH SLICES OF VERY FRESH BREAD OR WEDGES OF FLAT BREAD.

SERVES FOUR TO SIX

INGREDIENTS

    10–15 sun-dried tomatoes
    60–75ml/4–5 tbsp olive oil
    3 yellow (bell) peppers, cut into
      bitesize pieces
    6 garlic cloves, chopped
    400g/14oz can chopped tomatoes
    5ml/1 tsp fresh thyme leaves, or
      more to taste
    large pinch of sugar
    15ml/1 tbsp balsamic vinegar
    2–3 capers, rinsed and drained
    15ml/1 tbsp chopped fresh parsley,
      or more to taste
    salt and ground black pepper
    fresh thyme, to garnish (optional)

1 Put the sun-dried tomatoes in a bowl and pour over boiling water to cover. Leave to stand for at least 30 minutes until plumped up and juicy, then drain and cut the tomatoes into halves or quarters.

2 Heat the olive oil in a pan, add the peppers and cook for 5–7 minutes until lightly browned but not too soft.

3 Add half the garlic, the tomatoes, thyme and sugar and cook over a high heat, stirring occasionally, until the mixture is reduced to a thick paste. Season with salt and pepper to taste. Stir in the sun-dried tomatoes, balsamic vinegar, capers and the remaining chopped garlic. Leave to cool to room temperature.

4 Serve the salad at room temperature, heaped into a serving bowl and sprinkled with chopped fresh parsley. Garnish with thyme, if you like.

Energy 121Kcal/499kJ; Protein 1.4g; Carbohydrate 7.3g, of which sugars 7g; Fat 9.7g, of which saturates 1.5g; Cholesterol 0mg; Calcium 17mg; Fibre 2.1g; Sodium 11mg.

LIBYAN SPICY PUMPKIN DIP

This spicy Sephardi dip from the Libyan-Jewish community in Israel is a beautiful orange colour. Many people love serving it for Sukkot and leftovers can be stored for at least a week in the refrigerator. Serve it with chunks of bread or raw vegetables to dip into it.

SERVES SIX TO EIGHT

INGREDIENTS

45–60ml/3–4 tbsp olive oil
1 onion, finely chopped
5–8 garlic cloves, roughly chopped
675g/1½lb pumpkin, peeled
  and diced
5–10ml/1–2 tsp ground cumin
5ml/1 tsp paprika
1.5–2.5ml/¼–½ tsp ground ginger
1.5–2.5ml/¼–½ tsp curry powder
75g/3oz canned chopped tomatoes or
  diced fresh tomatoes and 15–30ml/
  1–2 tbsp tomato purée (paste)
½–1 red jalapeño or serrano chilli,
  chopped, or cayenne pepper,
  to taste
pinch of sugar, if necessary
juice of ½ lemon, or to taste
salt
30ml/2 tbsp chopped fresh coriander
  (cilantro) leaves, to garnish

1 Heat the oil in a frying pan, add the onion and half the garlic and fry until softened. Add the pumpkin, then cover and cook for about 10 minutes, or until half-tender.

2 Add the spices to the pan and cook for 1–2 minutes. Stir in the tomatoes, chilli, sugar and salt and cook over a medium-high heat until the liquid has evaporated.

3 When the pumpkin is tender, mash to a coarse purée. Add the remaining garlic and taste for seasoning, then stir in the lemon juice to taste. Serve at room temperature, sprinkled with the chopped fresh coriander.

VARIATION
Use butternut squash, or any other winter squash, in place of the pumpkin.

Energy 54Kcal/224kJ; Protein 0.9g; Carbohydrate 2.9g, of which sugars 2.3g; Fat 4.4g, of which saturates 0.7g; Cholesterol 0mg; Calcium 37mg; Fibre 1.3g; Sodium 3mg.

BRIK À L'OEUF

THESE TRADITIONALLY NORTH AFRICAN PASTRIES ARE SOLD IN THE MARKETPLACES OF ISRAEL. MEN BALANCING FULL TRAYS OF BRIKS NEGOTIATE THE CROWDS IN A BID TO SELL THEIR CRISPY PASTRIES BEFORE THE MARKET CLOSES FOR THE LONG AFTERNOON SIESTA. TRADITIONALLY, BRIKS ARE MADE WITH A THIN PASTRY CALLED WARKA BUT FILO PASTRY IS MUCH EASIER.

2 Preheat the oven to 200°C/400°F/ Gas 6. Heat the oil in a pan until it browns a cube of bread in 30 seconds.

3 Working quickly, break an egg into a small bowl or cup, then carefully tip it into the corner of the pastry sheet with the onion. Quickly fold over the pastry to form a triangle and enclose the egg completely.

4 Carefully slide the parcel into the oil and fry until golden brown. (The egg inside should be lightly cooked and still soft.)

MAKES FOUR

INGREDIENTS
1 onion, finely chopped
30–45ml/2–3 tbsp chopped
  fresh parsley or coriander
  (cilantro), or a mixture
  of both
a pinch of chopped fresh
  chilli (optional)
4 filo pastry sheets
90–115g/3½–4oz can tuna,
  well drained
vegetable oil, for deep-frying
4 eggs
hot sauce, such as zchug, harissa
  or Tabasco, to serve

1 In a bowl, combine the onion, herbs and chilli, if using. Lay a sheet of pastry on some baking parchment. Put one quarter of the onion mixture at one corner, then add one quarter of the tuna.

VARIATION
Add a dab of mashed potato and a little grated cheese to the filling before rolling up and frying.

5 Remove the brik from the pan with a slotted spoon, drain on kitchen paper, then transfer to a baking sheet. Make three more pastries in the same way.

6 Bake the pastries for 5 minutes, or until crisp and golden brown. Do not overcook as the egg yolk must be served runny. Serve immediately, accompanied by hot sauce for dipping or drizzling over.

Energy 267Kcal/1111kJ; Protein 14.1g; Carbohydrate 11.2g, of which sugars 1.3g; Fat 18.9g, of which saturates 3.2g; Cholesterol 202mg; Calcium 75mg; Fibre 1.2g; Sodium 140mg.

REBECCHINE DE JERUSALEMME

THESE STUFFED POLENTA FRITTERS COME FROM THE JEWISH COMMUNITY OF ITALY. POLENTA, COOKED TO A THICK CONSISTENCY AND POURED OUT TO COOL INTO A FIRM BREAD-LIKE MIXTURE, IS THE "BREAD" OF THESE TINY FRIED SANDWICHES. ANCHOVIES ARE THE TRADITIONAL FILLING BUT HERE A LITTLE TOMATO, ROSEMARY AND CHEESE HAVE BEEN USED. PORCINI MUSHROOMS ALSO MAKE A GOOD FILLING.

SERVES SIX

INGREDIENTS
  250g/9oz/1½ cups polenta
  30–45ml/2–3 tbsp tomato
    purée (paste)
  30–45ml/2–3 tbsp diced ripe fresh or
    canned chopped tomatoes
  30ml/2 tbsp chopped fresh rosemary
  30–45ml/2–3 tbsp freshly grated
    Parmesan or Pecorino cheese
  130g/4½oz mozzarella, Gorgonzola
    or fontina cheese, finely chopped
  half vegetable and half olive oil,
    for frying
  1–2 eggs, lightly beaten
  plain (all-purpose) flour, for dusting
  salt
  diced red (bell) pepper, shredded
    lettuce and rosemary sprigs, to garnish

1 In a large pan, combine the polenta with 250ml/8fl oz/1 cup cold water and stir. Add 750ml/1¼ pints/3 cups boiling water and cook, stirring constantly, for about 30 minutes until the mixture is very thick and no longer grainy. If the mixture is thick but still not cooked through, stir in a little more boiling water and simmer until soft. Season.

2 Pour the mixture into an oiled baking tray, forming a layer about 1cm/½in thick. Lightly cover the polenta, then chill.

3 Using a 6–7.5cm/2½–3in plain pastry (cookie) cutter or the rim of a glass, cut the polenta into rounds.

4 In a small bowl, combine the tomato purée with the diced tomatoes.

5 Spread a little of the mixture on the soft, moist side of a polenta round, sprinkle with rosemary and a little of the grated and chopped cheeses, then top with another round of polenta, the moist soft side against the filling. Press the edges together to help seal the sandwiches. Fill the remaining polenta rounds in the same way.

VARIATION
If seeking a healthier alternative to this recipe, you can simply omit the frying. Instead, cut out rounds of cooked polenta, top with gorgonzola cheese and chopped sage, then grill (broil) until the cheese is melting – just divine.

6 Heat the oil in a wide, deep frying pan, to a depth of about 5cm/2in, until it is hot enough to brown a cube of bread in 30 seconds.

7 Dip a sandwich into the beaten egg, then coat in the flour. Gently lower it into the hot oil and fry for 4–5 minutes, turning once. Drain on kitchen paper. Cook the remaining polenta sandwiches in the same way. Serve warm, garnished with pepper, lettuce and rosemary.

COOK'S TIPS
• If the polenta is too thin the fritters will fall apart; if too thick they will be heavy.
• Do not use instant polenta as the sandwiches will fall apart on cooking.
• The fritters can be cooked ahead of time and reheated in the oven at 200°C/400°F/Gas 6 for 5–10 minutes.

Energy 333Kcal/1386kJ; Protein 11.4g; Carbohydrate 31.8g, of which sugars 1.3g; Fat 17.5g, of which saturates 5.3g; Cholesterol 49mg; Calcium 148mg; Fibre 1.2g; Sodium 171mg.

BISSARA DIP <u>WITH</u> ZAHTAR

BISSARA IS A BEAN DIP FLAVOURED WITH GARLIC, WHICH IS AS MUCH ENJOYED IN MOROCCO AS HUMMUS IS THROUGHOUT THE REST OF THE MIDDLE EAST. ZAHTAR REFERS BOTH TO WILD THYME AND TO A SPICE MIXTURE MADE UP OF WILD THYME, CUMIN, PAPRIKA, GROUND CORIANDER, SESAME SEEDS AND OFTEN SUMAC. IT IS DELICIOUS AND WORTH SEEKING OUT.

SERVES FOUR

INGREDIENTS

350g/12oz/1¾ cups dried broad
  (fava) beans, soaked overnight
4 garlic cloves
10ml/2 tsp cumin seeds
60–75ml/4–5 tbsp olive oil
salt
zahtar, paprika or dried thyme
  to garnish

COOK'S TIP
You may prefer to shell fresh broad (fava) beans for their flavour (as used in step 1). Fresh beans can even be bought ready-skinned.

1 Drain the beans, remove their wrinkly skins and place them in a large pan with the garlic and cumin seeds. Add enough water to cover the beans and bring to the boil. Boil for 10 minutes, then reduce the heat, cover the pan and simmer gently for about 1 hour, or until the beans are tender.

2 When cooked, drain the beans and, while they are still warm, pound or process them with the olive oil until the mixture forms a smooth dip. Season to taste with salt and serve warm or at room temperature, sprinkled with zahtar, paprika or thyme. Alternatively, simply drizzle with a little olive oil.

Energy 335Kcal/1413kJ; Protein 19.6g; Carbohydrate 39.2g, of which sugars 2.3g; Fat 12.2g, of which saturates 1.8g; Cholesterol 0mg; Calcium 88mg; Fibre 13.9g; Sodium 16mg.

FETA AND ROAST PEPPER DIP WITH CHILLIES

This meze, unknown in the rest of Greece, is from the beautiful city of Thessalonika, whose cuisine is greatly influenced by its Jewish heritage. If you stop for an ouzo in the area called Lathathika, which used to be part of the old market, you will inevitably be served a small plate of htipiti, as this dip is known.

SERVES FOUR

INGREDIENTS
1 yellow or green long or
  bell pepper
1 fresh green chilli
200g/7oz feta cheese, cubed
2 cloves garlic, chopped
60ml/4 tbsp extra virgin olive oil
juice of 1 lemon
45–60ml/3–4 tbsp yogurt
ground black pepper
a little finely chopped fresh flat leaf
  parsley, to garnish
slices of toast, to serve

1 Scorch the pepper and chillies by threading them on to metal skewers and turning them under the grill (broiler), until charred all over. Set aside until cool enough to handle.

2 When the pepper and chillies are cool enough to handle, peel off as much of their skins as possible. Slit them and discard the seeds and stem.

3 Slice and crumble the feta cheese into small pieces.

4 Put the pepper and chilli flesh into a food processor. Add the other ingredients except the parsley and blend, adding a little more yogurt if the consistency becomes too stiff. Spread on slices of toast, sprinkle a hint of parsley on top and serve immediately.

COOK'S TIP
Feta cheese is often soaked in brine when packaged. To reduce the salty taste, soak the whole cheese in cold water for up to 10 minutes.

Energy 244Kcal/1010kJ; Protein 8.8g; Carbohydrate 4.4g, of which sugars 4.3g; Fat 21.4g, of which saturates 8.5g; Cholesterol 35mg; Calcium 205mg; Fibre 0.7g; Sodium 731mg.

SHAKSHOUKA

SHAKSHOUKA MEANS ALL MIXED UP, AND IT IS A DIVINE MIXTURE OF RIPE FLAVOURFUL PEPPERS AND TOMATOES, USUALLY WITH EGGS EITHER SCRAMBLED OR POACHED IN THE MIXTURE. IT IS A BELOVED DISH OF ISRAELIS, ESPECIALLY OF NORTH AFRICAN HERITAGE. DISHES LIKE THIS ARE FOUND ALL OVER THE MEDITERRANEAN WITH REGIONAL VARIATIONS, SUCH AS FRENCH PIPÉRADE, GREEK STRAPATSATHA, OR TURKISH MEMENEN.

SERVES FOUR

INGREDIENTS
   90ml/6 tbsp extra virgin olive oil
   1 onion, finely chopped
   675g/1 ½lb sweet tomatoes,
    roughly chopped
   pinch of dried oregano or 5ml/1 tsp
    chopped fresh thyme
   2.5ml/½ tsp sugar
   6 eggs, lightly beaten
   salt and ground black pepper
   a handful of thyme leaves, to garnish
    (optional)

1 Heat the olive oil in a large frying pan and sauté the onion, stirring occasionally, until it appears glistening and translucent.

2 Stir in the tomatoes, herbs and sugar, with salt and pepper to taste. Cook over a low heat for about 15 minutes until most of the liquid has evaporated and the sauce is thick.

3 Add the beaten eggs to the pan and cook for 2–3 minutes, stirring continuously with a wooden spatula as when making scrambled eggs. The eggs should be just set, but not overcooked. Serve immediately, garnished with the thyme leaves.

Energy 307Kcal/1273kJ; Protein 11.2g; Carbohydrate 9.2g, of which sugars 8.8g; Fat 25.5g, of which saturates 4.9g; Cholesterol 285mg; Calcium 62mg; Fibre 2.6g; Sodium 123mg.

CRISP FRIED AUBERGINE

THE AUBERGINE IS NATIVE TO INDIA BUT WAS BROUGHT TO PERSIA IN THE 4TH CENTURY, AND THEN INTRODUCED BY THE ARABS TO SPAIN IN THE 13TH CENTURY. EVENTUALLY IT MADE ITS WAY TO SICILY, WHERE IT WAS EMBRACED BY THE JEWISH COMMUNITY LONG BEFORE MANY CHRISTIANS WERE TEMPTED TO EAT IT. AUBERGINE IS AN IMPORTANT VEGETABLE IN THE SEPHARDIC KITCHEN, AS IT CAN ACT AS AN ALTERNATIVE TO MEAT. THIS DISH IS FROM THE BENE ISRAEL, AN INDIAN-JEWISH COMMUNITY THAT DATES FROM THE YEAR 175BCE.

SERVES FOUR

INGREDIENTS
50g/2oz/½ cup gram flour
15ml/1tbsp semolina or ground rice
2.5ml/½ tsp onion seeds
5ml/1 tsp cumin seeds
2.5ml/½ tsp fennel seeds or aniseeds
2.5–5ml/½–1 tsp hot chilli powder
2.5ml/½ tsp salt, or to taste
1 large aubergine (eggplant)
vegetable oil, for deep-frying

1 Sift the gram flour into a large mixing bowl and add all of the remaining ingredients except the aubergine and the vegetable oil.

2 Halve the aubergine lengthways and cut each half into slices of around 5mm/¼in thickness. Rinse them and shake off the excess water, but do not pat dry.

COOK'S TIPS
• Choose a plump aubergine (eggplant) with an unblemished, glossy skin.
• There is no need to soak the aubergine in salted water after slicing, as today's aubergines generally have less bitterness in the skin than they used to.
• Avoid overcrowding the pan as this will lower the oil temperature, resulting in a soggy texture.

3 With some of the water still clinging to the slices, add them to the spiced gram flour mixture. Toss them around until they are evenly coated with the flour. Use a spoon if necessary to ensure that all the flour is incorporated.

4 Heat the oil in a deep-fat fryer or other suitable pan over a medium-high heat. If you have a thermometer, check that the oil has reached 190°C/375°F. Alternatively, drop a small piece of day-old bread into the oil. If it floats immediately, then the oil has reached the right temperature. Place the sliced aubergine in the fryer, in a single layer.

5 Fry until the aubergines are crisp and well browned. Remove, lightly shake off excess oil, and drain on kitchen paper. Serve with a chutney.

Energy 165Kcal/689kJ; Protein 2.3g; Carbohydrate 14g, of which sugars 1.3g; Fat 11.5g, of which saturates 1.4g; Cholesterol 0mg; Calcium 9mg; Fibre 1.6g; Sodium 3mg.

FATTOUSH

ISRAEL SHARES A PASSION FOR THIS SALAD OF CRISP VEGETABLES AND TOASTED PITTA WITH ITS NEIGHBOUR IN THE NORTH, LEBANON. IT IS EXQUISITELY REFRESHING ON A HOT SUMMER'S DAY AND A GREAT WAY TO USE UP PITTA THAT HAS LOST SOME OF ITS FRESHNESS.

SERVES FOUR

INGREDIENTS

1 yellow or red (bell) pepper
1 large cucumber
4–5 tomatoes
1 bunch spring onions (scallions)
30ml/2 tbsp finely chopped
  fresh parsley
45–60ml/3–4 tbsp finely chopped
  fresh mint
45–60ml/3–4 tbsp finely chopped
  fresh coriander (cilantro)
2 garlic cloves, crushed
75ml/5 tbsp olive oil
juice of 2 lemons
5ml/1 tsp sumac (optional)
salt and ground black pepper
4 pitta breads

1 Slice the pepper, discarding the seeds and core, then slice or chop the flesh. Leaving the skin on the cucumber, roughly chop it. Dice the tomatoes. Place them in a large salad bowl.

2 Slice the spring onions. Add to the cucumber, tomatoes and pepper with the parsley, mint and coriander.

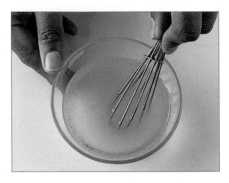

3 To make the dressing, mix the garlic with the olive oil and lemon juice. Whisk well, then season to taste.

4 Pour the dressing over the salad and toss lightly to mix. Sprinkle with sumac, if using. Serve with toasted pitta breads.

VARIATION
Toast the pitta breads in a toaster or under a hot grill (broiler) until crisp. Break them up and sprinkle them throughout the salad.

COOK'S TIP
Sumac is a tangy and tart berry which is dried and crushed and used as a spice throughout the Middle East. Popular in Iran sprinkled over rice, it is also found a great deal in Turkish, Lebanese and Israeli cuisine, favoured as a seasoning for salads thanks to its bright red colour.

Energy 177Kcal/732kJ; Protein 2.8g; Carbohydrate 8.7g, of which sugars 8.4g; Fat 14.8g, of which saturates 2.2g; Cholesterol 0mg; Calcium 80mg; Fibre 3.8g; Sodium 24mg.

COURGETTE AND FETA FRITTERS

THESE DELICIOUS FRITTERS ARE SIMILAR TO THE TURKISH MUNKVEN AND MAY HAVE COME TO GREECE VIA JEWISH MIGRANTS FROM TURKEY OR THE BALKANS. THEY ARE BEST SERVED PLAIN, WITH A SQUIRT OF LEMON, OR WITH A THICK YOGURT DIP ON THE SIDE.

SERVES SIX AS A SNACK

INGREDIENTS
500g/1¼lb courgettes (zucchini)
120ml/4fl oz/½ cup extra virgin
 olive oil
1 large onion, finely chopped
2 spring onions (scallions), green and
 white parts finely chopped
1 garlic clove, crushed
3 medium slices of country bread,
 sourdough or French/Italian bread
2 eggs, lightly beaten
200g/7oz feta cheese, crumbled
50g/2oz/½ cup freshly grated
 Greek Graviera
45–60ml/3–4 tbsp finely chopped
 fresh dill or 5ml/1 tsp dried oregano
50g/2oz/½ cup plain (all-purpose) flour
salt and ground black pepper
6 lemon wedges, to serve

1 Bring a pan of lightly salted water to the boil. Slice the courgettes into 4cm/1½in lengths and drop them into the boiling water. Cover and cook for about 10 minutes, or until very soft. Drain in a colander and let them cool completely.

2 Heat 45ml/3 tbsp of the olive oil in a frying pan, add the onion and spring onions and sauté until translucent. Add the garlic, then as soon as it becomes aromatic take the pan off the heat.

3 Squeeze the courgettes with your hands, to extract as much water as possible, then place them in a large bowl. Add the fried onion and garlic mixture and mix well.

4 Toast the bread, cut off and discard the crusts, then break up the toast and crumb it in a food processor. Add the crumbs to the courgette mixture, with the eggs, feta, grated Graviera.

5 Stir in the dill or oregano and add salt and pepper to taste. Mix well, using your hands to squeeze the mixture and make sure that all the ingredients are combined evenly. If the courgette mixture seems too wet, add a little flour.

COOK'S TIP
If you can't get hold of Graviera, Italian Pecorino is a good substitute.

6 Take about a heaped tablespoon of the courgette mixture, roll it into a ball and press it lightly to make the typical fritter shape. Make more fritters in the same way.

7 Coat the fritters lightly in the flour and dust off any excess. Heat the remaining olive oil in a large non-stick frying pan and fry the fritters, in batches if necessary, until they are crisp and brown, turning them over once or twice during cooking. Drain the fritters on a double layer of kitchen paper and serve on a warmed platter, with the lemon wedges.

Energy 340Kcal/1412kJ; Protein 12.8g; Carbohydrate 20g, of which sugars 4.1g; Fat 23.7g, of which saturates 8.3g; Cholesterol 32mg; Calcium 290mg; Fibre 2.1g; Sodium 677mg.

ROASTED BEETROOT WITH GARLIC SAUCE

BEETROOT IS SO OFTEN EATEN THROUGHOUT THE WORLD'S JEWISH COMMUNITIES, FROM EASTERN EUROPE TO EASTERN INDIA, THAT IT IS OFTEN DESCRIBED AS A "JEWISH VEGETABLE". BEETROOT IS ADORED IN GREECE, TOO, AND IT IS CLASSICALLY SERVED WITH THIS FRAGRANT GARLIC SAUCE, SKORTHALIA. OF COURSE, SOME JEWISH COMMUNITIES IN EASTERN EUROPE LIKED GARLIC SO MUCH THAT IT WAS THE GARLIC THAT COULD HAVE BEEN CALLED THE "JEWISH VEGETABLE".

SERVES FOUR

INGREDIENTS

   675g/1½lb medium or small beetroot
     (beets)
   75–90ml/5–6 tbsp extra virgin
     olive oil
   salt
For the garlic sauce
   4 medium slices of bread, crusts
     removed, soaked in water for
     10 minutes
   2–3 garlic cloves, chopped
   15ml/1 tbsp white wine vinegar
   60ml/4 tbsp extra virgin olive oil

1 Preheat the oven to 180°C/350°F/ Gas 4. Rinse the beetroot under running water to remove any grit. Be careful not to pierce the skin or the colour will run.

2 Line a roasting pan with a large sheet of foil and place the beetroot on top. Drizzle a little of the olive oil over them, sprinkle lightly with salt and fold over both edges of the foil to enclose the beetroot completely. Bake for about 1½ hours until perfectly soft.

COOK'S TIP
In Greece, the beetroot in this dish is often boiled rather than roasted, but opting for the latter method does bring out a more concentrated sweetness in the vegetables.

3 While the beetroot are cooking, make the garlic sauce. Squeeze most of the water out of the bread, but leave it quite moist. Place it in a blender or food processor. Add the garlic and vinegar, with salt to taste, and blend until smooth.

4 While the blender or processor is running, drizzle in the olive oil through the lid or feeder tube. The sauce should be runny. Spoon it into a bowl and set it aside.

5 Remove the beetroot from the foil package. When they are cool enough to handle, peel them. Slice them in thin round slices and arrange on a flat platter. Drizzle the remaining oil all over. Either spread a thin layer of garlic sauce on top, or hand it around separately. Serve with fresh bread to mop up the sauce, if you like.

Energy 372Kcal/1547kJ; Protein 5.1g; Carbohydrate 26.1g, of which sugars 12.5g; Fat 28.2g, of which saturates 3.9g; Cholesterol 0mg; Calcium 64mg; Fibre 3.6g; Sodium 252mg.

AUBERGINE CAVIAR <u>FROM</u> BESSARABIA

THIS TRADITIONAL DISH IS PART OF THE JEWISH CUISINE THROUGHOUT EASTERN EUROPE. SOME VERSIONS ARE MADE ONLY OF GARLIC, OTHERS ONLY OF ONION, STILL OTHERS INCLUDE GREEN PEPPERS WITH THE ONIONS, BOTH VEGETABLES ROASTED ALONG WITH THE AUBERGINE.

SERVES FOUR

INGREDIENTS

3 large aubergines (eggplants), total
  weight about 900g/2lb
1–2 onions, chopped
2 garlic cloves, crushed
juice of ½ lemon, or a little more
90–105ml/6–7 tbsp extra virgin
  olive oil or vegetable oil
salt and ground black pepper
4 tomatoes, diced
finely chopped fresh flat leaf parsley,
  to garnish
chicory (Belgian endive) and black
  and green olives, to serve

COOK'S TIP

If you have the means, do as the Greeks do when preparing this dish and cook the aubergines over charcoal. This traditional method will give the fruits a wonderful smoky flavour. Good-quality lumpwood charcoal can be used, but natural aromatics can also be added to the coals, such as hickory or oak, if you want to alter the flavour subtly.

1 Prick the aubergines and cook them on a barbecue over a low to medium heat for at least 1 hour, turning occasionally, until they are soft. If you are cooking the aubergines in a domestic oven, prick them and lay them directly on the shelves. Roast at 180°C/350°F/Gas 4 for 1 hour, or until soft. Turn them over twice.

2 When the aubergines are cool enough to handle, cut them in half. Spoon the flesh into a food processor and add the onion, garlic and lemon juice. Season and process until smooth.

3 With the motor running, drizzle in the olive oil through the feeder tube, until the mixture forms a smooth paste. Taste the mixture and adjust the seasoning, then spoon the mixture into a bowl and stir in the diced tomato. Cover and chill lightly. Garnish with parsley and serve with chicory leaves and bowls of olives.

Energy 200Kcal/829kJ; Protein 2.6g; Carbohydrate 8.9g, of which sugars 7.3g; Fat 17.5g, of which saturates 2.6g; Cholesterol 0mg; Calcium 35mg; Fibre 5.2g; Sodium 6mg.

SPINACH EMPANADILLAS

LITTLE PIES ARE PART OF THE MOORISH TRADITION IN SPAIN AND OF THE PEACEFUL INTERCHANGE OF FLAVOURS BETWEEN CHRISTIANS, JEWS AND MUSLIMS. THE SWEETNESS OF RAISINS WITH THE CRUNCH OF NUTS AND LEAFY FRESHNESS OF SPINACH IS A CLASSIC CULINARY SOUVENIR THROUGHOUT THE REGION.

MAKES TWENTY

INGREDIENTS
  25g/1oz/¼ cup raisins
  25ml/1½ tbsp olive oil
  450g/1lb fresh spinach
    leaves, washed, drained
    and chopped
  6 canned anchovies, drained
    and chopped
  2 garlic cloves, finely chopped
  25g/1oz/¼ cup pine nuts,
    roughly chopped
  1 egg, beaten
  350g/12oz puff pastry
  salt and ground black pepper

1 To make the filling, soak the raisins in a little warm water for 10 minutes. Drain well, then chop roughly.

2 Heat the olive oil in a large pan, add the spinach, stir, then cover and cook over a low heat until the spinach starts to wilt. Remove the lid, turn up the heat and cook until any liquid has evaporated.

3 Add the chopped anchovies, garlic and seasoning to the spinach and cook, stirring, for about 1 minute.

4 Remove the pan from the heat, then stir in the soaked raisins and pine nuts, and set aside to cool.

5 Meanwhile, preheat the oven to 180°C/350°F/Gas 4. Roll out the pastry on a lightly floured surface to a 3mm/⅛in thickness.

6 Using a 7.5cm/3in pastry (cookie) cutter, cut the pastry into 20 rounds, Place about 10ml/2 tsp of filling in the middle of each round, then brush the edges with a little water.

7 Fold the pastry in half and press the edges together with the back of a fork.

8 Brush the pies with egg and place, slightly apart, on a lightly greased baking sheet and bake for about 15 minutes, until puffed up and golden brown.

9 Transfer the pies to a wire rack to cool. They are best served while still slightly warm, but not hot.

VARIATIONS
• A Jewish speciality from Turkey is cooked pumpkin mixed with feta cheese.
• A Salonika Sephardic speciality is a filling of roasted aubergine (eggplant) mixed with feta, shredded Gruyère and beaten egg.
• A Moroccan favourite, filled with a canned tuna and vegetable stuffing, is a popular hot snack.

Energy 93Kcal/389kJ; Protein 2.4g; Carbohydrate 7.8g, of which sugars 1.5g; Fat 6.2g, of which saturates 0.3g; Cholesterol 10mg; Calcium 53mg; Fibre 0.5g; Sodium 125mg.

ROASTED RED PEPPERS WITH FETA

ROASTED RED PEPPERS, PARTICULARLY THE LONG, SLIM, HORN-SHAPED TYPE, WITH SWEET, THICK FLESH, ARE EATEN THROUGHOUT THE MIDDLE EAST AND MEDITERRANEAN REGIONS. THIS TUNISIAN JEWISH DISH IS DELICIOUS: SWEET, PUNGENT, TANGY AND SAVOURY.

SERVES FOUR

INGREDIENTS
    4 fleshy, red (bell) peppers
    200g/7oz feta cheese, crumbled
    30–45ml/2–3 tbsp olive oil
    30ml/2 tbsp capers
    peel of 1 preserved lemon, cut into
      small pieces
    salt

VARIATION
To add a dash more colour to the dish, substitute two of the red (bell) peppers for green ones.

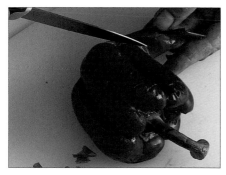

1 Preheat the grill (broiler) on the hottest setting. Roast the red peppers under the grill, turning frequently, until they soften and their skins begin to blacken. (Alternatively, spear the peppers on skewers and turn them over a gas flame, or roast them in a very hot oven or over a barbecue.) Place the peppers in a plastic bag, seal and leave them to stand for 15 minutes.

2 Peel, removing the stalks and seeds, then slice the flesh and arrange on a plate. Add the crumbled feta and pour over the olive oil. Sprinkle the capers and preserved lemon over the top and season with a little salt, if required (this depends on whether the feta is salty or not). Serve with chunks of fresh bread to mop up the delicious, oil-rich juices.

Energy 255Kcal/1058kJ; Protein 9.6g; Carbohydrate 12g, of which sugars 11.4g; Fat 19.1g, of which saturates 8.2g; Cholesterol 35mg; Calcium 194mg; Fibre 2.8g; Sodium 727mg.

SWEET AND SOUR ONIONS

THIS DISH, WHICH REFLECTS THE SWEET-SOUR FLAVOURS SO BELOVED BY THE ARABS, PROBABLY ORIGINATED IN SICILY. WHEN SICILY FELL UNDER SPANISH RULE, THE JEWISH COMMUNITY WAS FORCED TO FLEE AND CARRIED VERSIONS OF THIS DISH TO THE REST OF ITALY, TURKEY, GREECE AND FRANCE.

SERVES SIX

INGREDIENTS
    450g/1lb baby (pearl) onions, peeled
    50ml/2fl oz/¼ cup wine vinegar
    45ml/3 tbsp olive oil
    40g/1½oz/3 tbsp caster (superfine)
      sugar
    45ml/3 tbsp tomato purée (paste)
    a pinch each of cinnamon and
      allspice
    1 bay leaf
    2 parsley sprigs
    65g/2½oz/½ cup raisins
    salt and ground black pepper

1 Put all the ingredients in a pan with 300ml/½ pint/1¼ cups water. Bring to the boil and simmer gently, uncovered, for 45 minutes, or until the onions are tender and most of the liquid has evaporated.

2 Remove the bay leaf and parsley, check the seasoning and transfer to a serving dish. Leave to cool a little and serve at room temperature.

Energy 138Kcal/578kJ; Protein 1.5g; Carbohydrate 21.5g, of which sugars 19.7g; Fat 5.7g, of which saturates 0.8g; Cholesterol 0mg; Calcium 30mg; Fibre 1.5g; Sodium 27mg.

ROASTED PLUM TOMATOES WITH GARLIC

THIS IS CLASSIC MEDITERRANEAN FARE THAT CAN BE ENJOYED WITH EITHER A DAIRY OR A MEAT MEAL. IT MAKES A LOVELY ANTIPASTO OR MEZE, OR A SIDE DISH OR SALAD. FOR A PASTA SAUCE, SIMPLY PURÉE THE TOMATOES — YOU CAN USE YOUR HANDS TO SQUEEZE ALL THE JUICES OUT.

SERVES FOUR

INGREDIENTS

   60ml/4 tbsp extra virgin olive oil,
     plus extra for greasing
   12 plum tomatoes
   12 garlic cloves
   3 bay leaves
   salt and a pinch of sugar
   45ml/3 tbsp fresh oregano leaves,
     to garnish

COOK'S TIPS
• Use ripe plum tomatoes for this recipe as they keep their shape and do not fall apart when roasted at such a high temperature. Leave the stalks on, if possible.
• To give the tomatoes a bit of extra zing, add a couple of dashes of hot pepper sauce or a sprinkling of curry powder to the olive oil.

1 Preheat the oven to 230°C/450°F/ Gas 8. Select an ovenproof dish that will hold all the tomatoes snugly in a single layer. Grease it lightly with olive oil.

2 Cut the plum tomatoes in half lengthways. Place them in the dish, cut sides uppermost, and push the whole, unpeeled garlic cloves between them.

3 Drizzle the tomatoes with the oil, add the bay leaves and sprinkle with salt and sugar over the top. Roast for about 45 minutes until the tomatoes have softened and are sizzling in the dish. They should be charred around the edges. Season with oregano and serve warm, or leave to cool and enjoy at room temperature.

Energy 158Kcal/660kJ; Protein 3.1g; Carbohydrate 10.3g, of which sugars 8.4g; Fat 12g, of which saturates 1.9g; Cholesterol 0mg; Calcium 43mg; Fibre 3.6g; Sodium 27mg.

MARMOUNA

THIS DELICIOUS COLD MEDITERRANEAN DISH OF TUNISIAN-JEWISH HERITAGE IS A VARIATION ON SIMILAR LONG-SIMMERED MEDITERRANEAN DISHES EATEN THROUGHOUT THE REGION. AUBERGINE, INDISPENSABLE TO RATATOUILLE, IS NOT USUALLY INCLUDED IN MARMOUNA, BUT MAKES A NICE CHUNKY ADDITION.

SERVES SIX

INGREDIENTS
  900g/2lb ripe, well-flavoured
    tomatoes
  120ml/4fl oz/½ cup olive oil
  2 onions, thinly sliced
  2 red (bell) peppers, seeded and cut
    into chunks
  1 yellow or orange (bell) pepper,
    seeded and cut into chunks
  1 large aubergine (eggplant), cut
    into chunks
  2 courgettes (zucchini), cut into
    thick slices
  7 garlic cloves, coarsely chopped
  pinch of sugar, to taste
  15ml/1 tbsp chopped young thyme
  30ml/2 tbsp capers, drained of brine
  salt and ground black pepper
  15ml/1 tbsp chopped parsley

1 Plunge the tomatoes into boiling water for 30 seconds, then refresh in cold water. Peel away the skins and chop roughly.

2 Heat a little of the oil in a large, heavy pan and fry the onions for 5 minutes. Add the peppers and fry for a further 2 minutes. Add the aubergines and more oil and fry gently for 5 minutes or until lightly browned.

3 Add the remaining oil and courgettes and fry for 3 minutes. Remove from the pan and set aside.

4 Add the garlic and tomatoes to the pan with the sugar, thyme and a little salt and pepper. Cook gently until the tomatoes have softened and are turning pulpy, about 15 minutes.

5 Return all the vegetables to the pan and cook gently, stirring frequently, for 20–25 minutes, until fairly pulpy but retaining a little texture. Season with more salt and pepper to taste, stir in the capers and parsley, and serve.

COOK'S TIP
If the tomatoes lack flavour, add 30–45ml/2–3 tbsp tomato purée (paste) to the mixture along with the tomatoes.

Energy 197Kcal/816kJ; Protein 3.4g; Carbohydrate 14g, of which sugars 12.9g; Fat 14.5g, of which saturates 2.2g; Cholesterol 0mg; Calcium 40mg; Fibre 4.4g; Sodium 19mg.

FRIED PEPPERS WITH CHEESE

This traditional Bulgarian dish varies slightly from place to place in the Balkan area. Feta cheese makes a wonderful filling for this meze dish — if you can, use an Israeli-style feta, as these tend to be creamier than the Greek variety.

SERVES TWO TO FOUR

INGREDIENTS
4 bell peppers (red, yellow
  or green)
50g/2oz/½ cup plain (all-purpose)
  flour, seasoned
1 egg, beaten
olive oil, for shallow frying
cucumber and tomato salad,
  to serve
For the filling
  1 egg, beaten
  90g/3½oz/scant ½ cup feta cheese,
    finely crumbled
  30ml/2 tbsp chopped fresh parsley

1 Slit open the peppers lengthways, scoop out the seeds and remove the cores, but leave the peppers in one piece.

2 Carefully open out the peppers and place under a preheated grill (broiler), skin side up. Cook until the skin is charred and blackened. Place the peppers on a plate, cover with clear film (plastic wrap) and leave for 10 minutes.

3 Using a sharp knife, carefully peel away the skin from the peppers, taking care not to damage the flesh.

VARIATIONS
• A little chopped fresh chilli may be added to the cheese filling.
• Use long peppers for this recipe if you prefer. These are increasingly available.

4 In a bowl mix together all the filling ingredients until well combined. Divide evenly among the four peppers.

5 Reshape the peppers to look whole. Dip them into the seasoned flour, then the egg then the flour again.

6 Fry the peppers gently in a little olive oil for 6–8 minutes, turning once, or until golden brown and the filling is set. Lift the peppers out of the pan with a slotted spoon. Drain on kitchen paper before serving with a cucumber and tomato salad.

Energy 301Kcal/1253kJ; Protein 10g; Carbohydrate 23.1g, of which sugars 12.9g; Fat 19.4g, of which saturates 5.7g; Cholesterol 111mg; Calcium 144mg; Fibre 4g; Sodium 370mg.

LITTLE FINGER BISCUITS

THESE SAVOURY POLISH TREATS, PALUSZKI, ARE DELICIOUS SERVED WARM OR COLD WITH SOUP OR DIPS, AND ALSO MAKE AN EXCELLENT SNACK ON THEIR OWN.

MAKES THIRTY

INGREDIENTS
115g/4oz/8 tbsp butter, softened
115g/4oz/1⅓ cups mashed potato
150g/5oz/1¼ cups plain (all-
    purpose) flour, plus extra
    for dusting
2.5ml/½ tsp salt
1 egg, beaten
30ml/2 tbsp caraway seeds

VARIATIONS
• Though butter gives a lovely rich flavour, a little like shortbread, vegetable or olive oil may be used for a pareve food, or if serving with a meat meal.
• If you prefer not to use caraway seeds, other delicious toppings such as cracked wheat, poppy seeds or sesame seeds may be used.

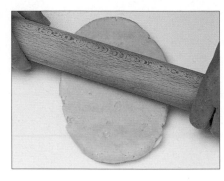

1 Preheat the oven to 220°C/425°F/Gas 7. Put the butter and mashed potato in a large bowl. Sift the flour and salt into the bowl, then mix to a soft dough.

2 Knead the dough on a lightly floured surface for a few seconds, or until smooth. Wrap in clear film (plastic wrap) and chill for 30 minutes.

3 Roll out the potato dough on a lightly floured surface until 8mm/⅓in thick. Brush with beaten egg, then cut into strips 2 x 7.5cm/¾ x 3in. Transfer to an oiled baking sheet and sprinkle with caraway seeds.

4 Bake for 12 minutes, or until lightly browned. Leave to cool on a wire rack. Store in an airtight container.

Energy 51Kcal/212kJ; Protein 0.8g; Carbohydrate 4.6g, of which sugars 0.1g; Fat 3.4g, of which saturates 2.1g; Cholesterol 15mg; Calcium 9mg; Fibre 0.2g; Sodium 26mg.

CHEESE SCROLLS

THESE DELICIOUS BULGARIAN CHEESE SAVOURIES ARE ONE OF THE MANY SEPHARDIC PASTRIES FOUND IN ISRAEL. THEY MAKE A TERRIFIC ACCOMPANIMENT TO A GLASS OF WINE OR TEA.

MAKES FOURTEEN TO SIXTEEN

INGREDIENTS
    450g/1lb/2 cups feta cheese, well
      drained and finely crumbled
    90ml/6 tbsp Greek (US strained
      plain) yogurt
    2 eggs, beaten
    14–16 sheets 40 x 30cm/16 x 12in
      ready-made filo pastry, thawed
      if frozen
    225g/8oz/1 cup unsalted (sweet)
      butter, melted
    sea salt and chopped spring onions
      (scallions) to garnish

1 Preheat the oven to 200°C/400°F/ Gas 6. In a large bowl mix together the feta cheese, yogurt and eggs, beating well until the mixture is smooth.

2 Fit a piping (pastry) bag with a large 1cm/½in plain round nozzle and fill with half of the cheese mixture.

COOK'S TIP
If possible, replace the feta with bryndza – a locally produced Slovakian cheese made from ewe's milk. It is a subtly flavoured, crumbly and moist cheese that resembles feta in texture, but its flavour is not quite as salty. Many Eastern European countries produce similar cheeses, such as brinza in Romania and brynza in Hungary.

3 Lay out one sheet of pastry, fold into a 30 x 20cm/12 x 8in rectangle and brush with a little melted butter. Along one long edge pipe the cheese mixture 5mm/¼in away from the edge.

4 Roll up the pastry to form a sausage shape and tuck in each end, to prevent the filling escaping. Brush with more melted butter.

5 Form the "sausage" into an "S" shape. Repeat with the remaining ingredients, refilling the piping bag as necessary.

6 Arrange the scrolls on a buttered baking sheet and sprinkle with a little sea salt and chopped spring onion. Bake for 20 minutes, or until golden brown and crispy. Cool before serving.

Energy 212Kcal/878kJ; Protein 6.2g; Carbohydrate 5.5g, of which sugars 0.7g; Fat 18.6g, of which saturates 11.7g; Cholesterol 73mg; Calcium 125mg; Fibre 0.2g; Sodium 503mg.

MEDITERRANEAN CHARRED ARTICHOKES
<u>WITH</u> LEMON AND ROASTED GARLIC DIP

ROASTING OR BARBECUING ARTICHOKES OVER AN OPEN FIRE IN SPRING AND SUMMER CONJURES UP IMAGES OF THE ANCIENT HEBREWS, AS THIS IS A DISH THAT EVOLVED FROM THAT TIME AND PLACE. THESE DAYS VARIATIONS OF THE DISH ARE FOUND IN SPAIN AND SICILY.

SERVES TWO TO FOUR

INGREDIENTS
  15ml/1 tbsp lemon juice or white
    wine vinegar
  2 globe artichokes, young and tender
  45ml/3 tbsp olive oil
  sea salt
  sprigs of fresh flat leaf parsley,
    to garnish
For the lemon oil dip
  12 garlic cloves, unpeeled
  1 lemon
  45ml/3 tbsp extra virgin olive oil

COOK'S TIP
If you do manage to get young, tender artichokes, they are delicious roasted over a barbecue.

1 Preheat the oven to 200°C/400°F/ Gas 6. Stir the lemon juice or vinegar into a bowl of cold water.

2 Cut each artichoke lengthways into wedges. Pull the hairy choke out from the centre of each wedge and drop the wedges into the acidulated water.

3 Drain the artichokes and place in a roasting pan with the garlic cloves. Toss in the oil. Sprinkle with salt and roast for 40 minutes, stirring once or twice, until the artichokes are tender.

4 Meanwhile, make the dip. Pare away two strips of rind from the lemon and scrape away any pith. Place the rind in a pan with water to cover. Simmer for 5 minutes, then drain, refresh in cold water and chop roughly.

5 Arrange the artichokes on a plate and set aside to cool for 5 minutes. Flatten the garlic cloves so that the flesh pops out of the skins. Transfer the garlic flesh to a bowl, mash to a purée then add the lemon rind. Squeeze the juice from the lemon, then, using a fork, whisk in the olive oil and lemon juice.

6 Serve the artichokes warm. Garnish them with parsley and accompany them with the lemon dip.

Energy 170Kcal/700kJ; Protein 1.7g; Carbohydrate 3.5g, of which sugars 0.7g; Fat 16.7g, of which saturates 2.4g; Cholesterol 0mg; Calcium 19mg; Fibre 1.2g; Sodium 23mg.

HALF-MOON CHEESE PIES <u>WITH</u> RAISINS <u>AND</u> PINE NUTS

THESE DELICIOUS SMALL PIES ARE FROM THE GREEK ISLAND OF CRETE. THE COMBINATION OF SALTY CHEESE, SWEET FRUIT AND RESINY PINE NUTS IS CLASSIC SEPHARDIC. THE PASTRIES ARE LIKELY TO HAVE BEEN BROUGHT TO CRETE BY SPANISH JEWS FROM SPAIN, SICILY OR TURKEY. THE CRETAN TOWN OF CHANIA HAD AN ANCIENT JEWISH NEIGHBOURHOOD UNTIL THE GERMAN OCCUPATION OF WORLD WAR II. SKALTSOUNAKIA CAN BE OFFERED WITH DRINKS OR PRESENTED AS PART OF A LARGE MEZE.

MAKES TWELVE TO FOURTEEN

INGREDIENTS
  1 large (US extra large) egg,
    plus 1 egg yolk for glazing
  150g/5oz feta cheese
  30ml/2 tbsp milk
  30ml/2 tbsp chopped fresh
    mint leaves
  15ml/1 tbsp raisins
  15ml/1 tbsp pine nuts, lightly
    toasted
  a little vegetable oil, for greasing
For the pastry
  225g/8oz/2 cups self-raising
    (self-rising) flour
  45ml/3 tbsp extra virgin olive oil
  15g/½oz/1 tbsp butter, melted
  90g/3½oz Greek (US strained
    plain) yogurt

1 To make the pastry, put the flour in a bowl and mix in the oil, butter and yogurt by hand. Cover and place in the refrigerator for 15 minutes.

2 Meanwhile, make the filling. Beat the egg lightly in a bowl. Crumble in the cheese, then mix in the milk, mint, raisins and pine nuts.

VARIATION
One of the many variations of this recipe has a filling of sautéed wild greens.

3 Preheat the oven to 190°C/375°F/ Gas 5. Cover half of the pastry, thinly roll out the remainder and cut out 7.5cm/3in rounds.

4 Place a heaped teaspoon of filling on each round and fold the pastry over to make a half-moon shape. Press the edges to seal, then place the pies on a greased baking sheet. Repeat with the remaining pastry. Brush the pies with egg yolk and bake for 20 minutes.

Energy 136Kcal/571kJ; Protein 4.4g; Carbohydrate 13.7g, of which sugars 1.5g; Fat 7.5g, of which saturates 2.9g; Cholesterol 26mg; Calcium 81mg; Fibre 0.7g; Sodium 174mg.

BESSARABIAN PANCAKES

THIS CHEESE AND SPINACH STUFFED PANCAKE IS FROM BESSARABIA, THE HISTORICAL NAME FOR MODERN MOLDOVA, IN ROMANIA. IT IS IDEAL FOR SHAVUOT, THE HOLIDAY OF DAIRY FEASTING.

SERVES FOUR TO SIX

INGREDIENTS
4 eggs, beaten
40g/1½oz/3 tbsp butter, melted
250ml/8fl oz/1 cup single
 (light) cream
250ml/8fl oz/1 cup soda water
175g/6oz/1½ cups plain (all-
 purpose) flour, sifted
pinch of salt
1 egg white, lightly beaten
oil, for frying
For the filling
350g/12oz/1½ cups feta
 cheese, crumbled
50g/2oz/⅔ cup Parmesan or other
 sharp, dry cheese, grated
2 spring onions (scallions), chopped
30ml/2 tbsp chopped fresh dill
40g/1½oz/3 tbsp butter
1 garlic clove, crushed
450g/1lb frozen spinach, thawed
shavings of Parmesan or other sharp,
 dry cheese, to garnish

1 Blend the eggs, butter, cream and water in a food processor or blender. With the motor running, spoon in the flour and salt through the feeder tube until the batter mixture is smooth and lump free. Leave to rest for 15 minutes, loosely covered with clear film (plastic wrap).

2 Lightly grease a 13–15cm/5–6in non-stick frying pan and place over a medium heat. When hot, pour in 45–60ml/3–4 tbsp of the batter, tilting the pan to spread the mixture thinly.

3 Cook for 1½–2 minutes or until the underside of the pancake is pale golden brown, then turn over and cook on the other side.

4 Repeat the process until you have used all the batter, stacking the pancakes on a warm plate as you go.

5 For the filling, mix together the crumbled feta and Parmesan cheese, butter and garlic clove until well combined. Thoroughly stir in the squeeze-dried spinach.

6 Place 30–45ml/2–3 tbsp of the filling mixture on to the centre of each pancake. Brush a little egg white around the outer edges of the pancakes and then fold them over. Press the edges down well to seal.

7 Fry the pancakes in a little oil on both sides, turning gently, until they are golden brown and the filling is hot. Serve immediately, garnished with the shavings of cheese.

Energy 584Kcal/2428kJ; Protein 23.6g; Carbohydrate 26g, of which sugars 3.7g; Fat 43.7g, of which saturates 23.5g; Cholesterol 227mg; Calcium 548mg; Fibre 2.8g; Sodium 1188mg.

TWISTED CHEESE PASTRIES

WRAP SAVOURY CHEESE UP IN DOUGH AND BAKE TILL FLAKY AND CRISP; DELICIOUS. THIS TYPICALLY EASTERN EUROPEAN DELICACY MAKES A DELICIOUS NIBBLE WITH A GLASS OF WINE.

MAKES ABOUT THIRTY

INGREDIENTS
    400g/14oz packet puff pastry
    1 large egg, beaten
    115–150g/4–5oz Liptauer cheese
    (see Cook's Tip), finely crumbled

COOK'S TIP
Hungarian Liptauer is a cheese spread made from a white sheep's milk cheese, liptó, spiced with paprika, salt and various other ingredients, such as onion, caraway seeds, mustard and capers. Liptauer has a heady, spicy flavour. If unavailable, use feta cheese or the Romanian brinza instead, mixed with a handful of herbs, some chopped onion and a sprinkling of paprika.

1 Preheat the oven to 200°C/400°F/ Gas 6. Roll out the puff pastry on a lightly floured surface to a 30cm/12in long oblong about 5mm/¼in thick. Cut the pastry in half crossways.

2 Glaze the pastry with the beaten egg, sprinkle over the Liptauer cheese and push it lightly into the pastry. Cut the pastry into 15 x 2.5cm/6 x 1in strips.

3 Twist the pastry strips to form long spiral shapes. Place on a non-stick baking sheet and bake for 10–15 minutes, or until golden brown. Cool on a wire rack.

Energy 62Kcal/258kJ; Protein 1.6g; Carbohydrate 5g, of which sugars 0.2g; Fat 4.2g, of which saturates 0.6g; Cholesterol 9mg; Calcium 23mg; Fibre 0g; Sodium 99mg.

MINI SAFFRON FISH CAKES <u>WITH</u> MINTY CUCUMBER SALAD

MINT-SCENTED CUCUMBER SALAD MAKES A SUPERBLY REFRESHING ACCOMPANIMENT FOR THESE SPICY FISH CAKES. THIS IS AN EXCELLENT DISH FOR SHABBAT LUNCH, AS IT MAY BE EATEN COLD. SERVED HOT, THE FISH CAKES ARE CRISP AND DELICIOUS AND TASTE OF THE MAGHREB.

SERVES FOUR

INGREDIENTS
  450g/1lb white fish fillets, such as
    sea bass, ling or haddock, skinned
    and cut into chunks
  10ml/2 tsp harissa
  rind of ½ preserved lemon,
    finely chopped
  small bunch fresh coriander
    (cilantro), finely chopped
  1 egg
  5ml/1 tsp honey
  pinch of saffron threads, soaked in
    5ml/1 tsp water
  salt and ground black pepper
  sunflower oil, for frying
  harissa or hot pepper sauce on the
    side (optional)
For the salad
  2 cucumbers, peeled and finely diced
  juice of ½ lemon
  1 garlic clove, chopped
  pinch of salt
  pinch of sugar
  handful of fresh mint, finely chopped

1 Make the salad in advance to allow time for chilling before serving. Combine the salad ingredients. Chill until ready to eat.

2 To make the fish cakes, put the fish in a food processor. Add the harissa, preserved lemon, coriander, egg, honey, saffron with its soaking water and seasoning, and blend until smooth.

3 Divide the mixture into 16 portions. Wet your hands under cold water to prevent the mixture from sticking to them, then roll each portion into a ball and flatten in the palm of your hand.

COOK'S TIP
If you are in a hurry and need to turn to store-cupboard (pantry) basics, canned tuna can be used instead of fresh fish.

4 Heat the oil in a large frying pan and fry the fish cakes in batches, until golden brown on each side. Drain the fish cakes on kitchen paper and keep hot until all the fish cakes are cooked. Serve immediately with the chilled cucumber salad.

Energy 228Kcal/951kJ; Protein 24.1g; Carbohydrate 3g, of which sugars 2.8g; Fat 13.4g, of which saturates 1.8g; Cholesterol 88mg; Calcium 82mg; Fibre 1.6g; Sodium 103mg

HERRING SALAD WITH BEETROOT AND SOUR CREAM

THIS SALAD, SERVED WITH BLACK PUMPERNICKEL BREAD OR RYE CRISPBREAD, IS A QUINTESSENTIAL SHABBAT DISH TO ENJOY AFTER MORNING SERVICES. HERRING IS A STRONG, PROVOCATIVE FLAVOUR, AND A VERY POPULAR ONE ON THE ASHKENAZIC TABLE.

SERVES EIGHT

INGREDIENTS

1 large tangy cooking apple
500g/1¼lb matjes herrings (schmaltz herrings), drained and cut into slices
2 small pickled cucumbers, diced
10ml/2 tsp caster (superfine) sugar, or to taste
10ml/2 tsp cider vinegar or white wine vinegar
300ml/½ pint/1¼ cups sour cream
2 cooked beetroot (beets), diced
lettuce, to serve
sprigs of fresh dill and chopped onion or onion rings, to garnish

1 Peel, core and dice the apple. Put in a bowl, add the herrings, cucumbers, sugar and cider or white wine vinegar and mix together. Add the sour cream and mix well to combine.

2 Add the beetroot to the herring mixture and chill in the refrigerator. Serve the salad on a bed of lettuce leaves, garnished with fresh dill and chopped onion or onion rings.

Energy 225Kcal/938kJ; Protein 12.1g; Carbohydrate 11.6g, of which sugars 11.4g; Fat 14.4g, of which saturates 4.7g; Cholesterol 49mg; Calcium 51mg; Fibre 0.5g; Sodium 554mg.

CHICKEN LIVER PÂTÉ <u>WITH</u> GARLIC

THE METHODS DEVELOPED BY THE JEWS OF ALSACE OF FATTENING GEESE AND DUCKS ARE SAID TO HAVE COME ORIGINALLY FROM ANCIENT EGYPT, VIA ANCIENT ROME, SPAIN, AND THE EXPULSION. THE ALSACIAN JEWS PURÉED THE LIVERS INTO A SAVOURY SPREAD, A FORERUNNER OF THE FRENCH PÂTÉS. TO COOK LIVERS IN A KOSHER WAY, WASH AND SPRINKLE WITH SALT BEFORE GRILLING (BROILING).

SERVES SIX TO EIGHT

INGREDIENTS

150–175g/4–6oz/½–¾ cup duck or
   goose fat
400g/14oz chicken livers, washed
45ml/3 tbsp port or cognac
1½ onions, chopped
3 large garlic cloves, finely chopped
5ml/1 tsp finely chopped fresh thyme
   or a pinch of dried thyme
pinch of ground allspice or cloves
salt and ground black pepper
3 or 4 bay leaves or fresh thyme
   sprigs, to garnish
toast and small pickled gherkins,
   to serve

1 Sprinkle the washed livers with salt. Lightly grill (broil), rinse and pat dry.

2 Melt 40g/1½oz/3 tbsp duck or goose fat in a frying pan and fry the grilled chicken livers for 4–5 minutes, or until browned. Stir frequently to ensure that the livers cook evenly. Do not overcook them or they will be tough.

3 Add 45ml/3 tbsp port or cognac and set it alight, then scrape the contents of the pan into a food processor or blender.

4 Melt 25g/1oz/2 tbsp duck or goose fat in the pan over a low heat and cook the onions for 5 minutes, or until soft. Add the garlic, thyme and allspice and cook for another 2–3 minutes. Add this mixture to the livers with the remaining duck or goose fat, then process until the texture is smooth.

5 Add about 7.5ml/1½ tsp each of salt and black pepper and more port or cognac to taste. Place 2 or 3 bay leaves in the bottom of a bowl. Scrape the pâté into the bowl. Top with another bay leaf, then with clear film (plastic wrap). Chill for at least 4 hours.

COOK'S TIP
This pâté is a delicious entrée to a meal with family or friends, and the flavour is even better the day after preparation. It is well worth preparing it in advance and chilling overnight if you can.

VARIATIONS
• Use duck livers instead of chicken and add 2.5ml/½ tsp grated orange rind.
• Use chopped fresh tarragon instead of the thyme.

Energy 229Kcal/945kJ; Protein 9.1g; Carbohydrate 2.2g, of which sugars 1.7g; Fat 19.8g, of which saturates 7.9g; Cholesterol 207mg; Calcium 9mg; Fibre 0.3g; Sodium 39mg.

CIRCASSIAN CHICKEN

THE DELICIOUS CREAMINESS OF THIS DISH COMES FROM PURÉED WALNUTS RATHER THAN DAIRY AND THEREFORE IT WAS A GREAT FAVOURITE OF THE JEWS OF TURKEY. AS IT IS EATEN COLD (AT ROOM TEMPERATURE), IT CAN BE MADE AHEAD, READY FOR SHABBAT LUNCH.

SERVES SIX

INGREDIENTS
1.6kg/3–3½lb chicken
2 onions, quartered
1 carrot, sliced
1 celery stick, trimmed and sliced
6 peppercorns
3 slices bread, crusts removed
2 garlic cloves, roughly chopped
400g/14oz/3½ cups chopped walnuts
15ml/1 tbsp walnut oil
salt and ground black pepper
chopped walnuts and paprika,
 to garnish

1 Place the chicken in a large pan, with the onions, carrot, celery and peppercorns. Add enough water to cover, and bring to the boil. Simmer for about 1 hour, uncovered, until the chicken is tender. Leave to cool in the stock. Drain the chicken, reserving the stock.

2 Tear up the bread and soak in 90ml/ 6 tbsp of the chicken stock. Transfer to a blender or food processor with the garlic and walnuts and add 250ml/8fl oz/ 1 cup of the remaining stock. Process until smooth, then transfer to a pan.

VARIATION
Try this Georgian variation (Satsivi). Add 2 chopped, sautéed onions to the sauce mixture before puréeing. Season with cinnamon, allspice, cloves and coriander, and sprinkle with paprika, cayenne pepper, plus a drizzle of pomegranate syrup.

3 Over a low heat, gradually add more chicken stock to the sauce, stirring continually, until it gradually thickens to pouring consistency.

4 Remove the pan from the heat and season the sauce with salt and pepper. Leave the sauce to cool. Skin and bone the cooked chicken, and cut it into bitesize chunks.

5 Place in a bowl and add a little of the sauce. Stir to coat the chicken, then arrange on a serving dish. Spoon the remaining sauce over the chicken, and drizzle with the walnut oil. Sprinkle with walnuts and paprika and serve.

VARIATION
This wonderfully thick sauce is equally delicious prepared for boiled vegetables such as potatoes and cauliflower.

Energy 639Kcal/2656kJ; Protein 40.9g; Carbohydrate 8.9g, of which sugars 2.1g; Fat 49.1g, of which saturates 4.3g; Cholesterol 88mg; Calcium 84mg; Fibre 2.5g; Sodium 150mg.

SAVOURY CIGARS

THROUGHOUT THE BALKANS, GREECE, TURKEY, THE MIDDLE EAST, NORTH AFRICA, ITALY AND SPAIN, SMALL SAVOURY PASTRIES HAVE BEEN A HALLMARK OF THE SEPHARDIC COMMUNITIES. EACH VILLAGE, TOWN AND CITY HAS ITS OWN VERSION. THESE PASTRIES ARE FILLED WITH MINCED LAMB OR BEEF, SPINACH OR CHEESE WITH HERBS AND ARE KNOWN AS BRIOUATS IN MOROCCO. EASY TO MAKE, THEY ARE ALWAYS SHAPED INTO CIGARS, THOUGH THE FILLINGS CAN BE VARIED TO SUIT INDIVIDUAL TASTES. THE FILLINGS CAN BE PREPARED AHEAD OF TIME, BUT THE PASTRY SHOULD ONLY BE UNWRAPPED WHEN YOU ARE READY TO MAKE THE PASTRIES, OTHERWISE IT WILL DRY OUT.

MAKES ABOUT THIRTY-TWO

INGREDIENTS
    8 sheets of warka or filo pastry
    sunflower oil, for deep-frying
For the feta cheese filling
    450g/1lb feta cheese
    4 eggs
    bunch of fresh coriander (cilantro),
      finely chopped
    bunch of flat leaf parsley,
      finely chopped
    bunch of mint, finely chopped
For the beef filling
    15–30ml/1–2 tbsp olive oil
    1 onion, finely chopped
    30ml/2 tbsp pine nuts
    5ml/1 tsp ras el hanout
    225g/8oz minced (ground) beef
    salt and ground black pepper
For the spinach filling
    50g/2oz/¼ cup butter
    1 onion, finely chopped
    275g/10oz fresh spinach, cooked,
      drained and chopped
    small bunch of fresh coriander
      (cilantro), finely chopped
    pinch of grated nutmeg
    salt and ground black pepper

1 First, choose one of the fillings for the cigars. To make the feta cheese filling, place the cheese in a bowl and mash with a fork, then beat in the eggs and chopped herbs.

2 To make the beef filling, heat the olive oil in a heavy frying pan. Add the onion and pine nuts and cook, stirring, until coloured. Stir in the ras el hanout, add the beef and cook for about 15 minutes, stirring, until browned. Season with salt and pepper, and leave to cool.

3 To make the spinach filling, melt the butter in a small heavy pan. Add the onion and cook over a low heat for 15 minutes until softened. Stir in the spinach and coriander. Season with nutmeg, salt and pepper, then cool.

4 Lay a sheet of warka or filo pastry on a work surface. Cut widthways into four strips.

5 Spoon a little filling mixture on the first strip, at the end nearest to you. Fold the corners of the pastry over the mixture to seal it, then roll up the pastry and filling, rolling in the direction away from you, until it forms a tight cigar.

6 As you reach the end of the strip, brush the edges with a little water and continue to roll up the cigar to seal in the filling. Repeat, placing the finished cigars under a damp cloth.

7 Heat the sunflower oil for deep-frying to 180°C/350°F, or until a cube of day-old bread browns in 30–45 seconds. Add the cigars to the oil in batches and fry over a medium heat until golden brown. Drain on kitchen paper and serve warm.

Feta filling: *Energy 169kcal/705kJ; Protein 10.4g; Carbohydrate 6.6g, of which sugars 0.9g; Fat 11.5g, of which saturates 6.8g; Cholesterol 108mg; Calcium 194mg; Fibre 0.5g; Sodium 678mg.*
Beef filling: *Energy 122kcal/508kJ; Protein 6.8g; Carbohydrate 6.6g, of which sugars 0.7g; Fat 7.8g, of which saturates 2.2g; Cholesterol 17mg; Calcium 25mg; Fibre 0.6g; Sodium 24mg.*
Spinach filling: *Energy 72kcal/299kJ; Protein 1.6g; Carbohydrate 6.8g, of which sugars 0.9g; Fat 4.4g, of which saturates 2.7g; Cholesterol 11mg; Calcium 60mg; Fibre 0.9g; Sodium 69mg.*

SHAMMI KEBABS

SHAMMI KEBABS ARE NOT, AS YOU MIGHT THINK FROM THE NAME, CHUNKS OF SKEWERED MEAT. RATHER, THEY ARE MADE OF SIMMERED LAMB, WHICH IS GROUND UP WITH SPICES AND MOULDED INTO PATTIES. ONCE COVERED IN GRAM FLOUR AND BEATEN EGG, THEY ARE THEN FRIED TO A CRISP. THE DISH IS PART OF THE INDIAN JEWISH CULINARY REPERTOIRE.

SERVES FIVE TO SIX

INGREDIENTS

2 onions, finely chopped
250g/9oz lean lamb, boned
  and cubed
50g/2oz chana dhal or yellow
  split peas
5ml/1 tsp cumin seeds
5ml/1 tsp garam masala
4–6 fresh green chillies
5cm/2in piece fresh root
  ginger, grated
175ml/6fl oz/¾ cup water
a few fresh coriander (cilantro)
  and mint leaves, chopped,
  plus extra coriander sprigs
  to garnish
juice of 1 lemon
15ml/1 tbsp gram flour
2 eggs, beaten
vegetable oil, for shallow-frying
salt

1 Put the first seven ingredients and the water into a large pan with salt, and bring to the boil. Simmer, covered, until the meat and dhal are cooked. Remove the lid and cook for a few more minutes to reduce the excess liquid. Set aside to cool.

VARIATION
Simmer 1 or 2 dried limes or lemons (often known as loomie) with the lamb. Remove before chopping the meat. If powdered loomie is available, use a few pinches to spice the meat mixture.

2 Mix the meat and dhal to a rough paste in a food processor or blender.

3 Put the paste into a large mixing bowl and add the chopped coriander and mint leaves, lemon juice and gram flour. Knead well with your hands.

4 Divide the mixture into 10–12 even-size portions and use your hands to roll each into a ball, then flatten slightly. Chill for 1 hour. Dip the kebabs in the beaten egg and shallow fry each side until golden brown. Pat dry on kitchen paper and serve hot.

Energy 207Kcal/861kJ; Protein 12.8g; Carbohydrate 7.7g, of which sugars 1g; Fat 14.1g, of which saturates 3.6g; Cholesterol 95mg; Calcium 40mg; Fibre 1.1g; Sodium 65mg.

STUFFED CABBAGE LEAVES

IN THE YEARS BEFORE THE POTATO WAS BROUGHT FROM THE NEW WORLD AND EMBRACED BY EASTERN EUROPEAN JEWS, CABBAGE WAS UBIQUITOUS IN THE FOODS OF THE JEWISH COMMUNITIES LIVING IN THOSE COLD NORTHERLY CLIMES. THIS IS A QUICK VERSION OF A SUMPTUOUS APPETIZER THAT IS PERFECT FOR ANY TIME OF YEAR, AND EASILY ADAPTED TO SUIT A VEGETARIAN DIET.

SERVES FOUR

INGREDIENTS
115g/4oz/generous ½ cup long
  grain rice
1–2 large green cabbages, total
  weight about 1.6–2kg/3½–4½lb
500g/1¼lb minced (ground) lamb,
  beef, or a mixture of lamb and beef
1 large onion, roughly grated
1 egg, lightly beaten
30ml/2 tbsp chopped fresh flat leaf
  parsley
45–60ml/3–4 tbsp chopped fresh dill
90ml/6 tbsp extra virgin olive oil
250ml/8fl oz beef stock
15ml/1 tbsp cornflour (cornstarch)
2 eggs
juice of 1½ lemons
salt and ground black pepper

2 Rinse the leaves and cabbage hearts in cold water, then drain them. Bring a large saucepan of water to the boil and blanch the leaves in batches for 1–2 minutes, until they become just pliable. Remove with a slotted spoon and place them in a colander. Put in the cabbage hearts and let them boil for slightly longer. Drain.

3 Prepare the stuffing by combining the minced meat, rice, onion, egg and fresh herbs in a bowl. Mix in half the olive oil and a generous amount of seasoning.

5 Carefully strip as many leaves as possible from the blanched cabbage heart and stuff them individually. Leave the inner heart intact, but open the leaves on the top, and put some stuffing in it, too.

6 Line a large heavy pan with the uncooked outer leaves. Layer the stuffed leaves in the pan, packing them tightly together. Season each layer as you go, then drizzle the remaining olive oil over the top.

7 Invert a small heatproof plate on top of the last layer of stuffed leaves. Pour in the stock and enough hot water to just cover the top layer. Cover and cook gently for about 50 minutes. As soon as the stuffed leaves are cooked, tilt the pan, holding the plate down firmly, and empty most of the liquid into a bowl. Let it cool slightly.

8 Mix the cornflour to a loose paste with a little water. Whisk the eggs in another bowl, then add the lemon juice and the cornflour mixture and whisk again. Continue to whisk, gradually adding tablespoons of the hot cooking liquid. As soon as the liquid has all been added, pour the sauce over the stuffed cabbage leaves and shake the pan gently to distribute it evenly. Return the pan to a very gentle heat and cook for 3 minutes to thicken the sauce, rotating the pan occasionally.

1 Soak the rice in cold water for 10 minutes, then drain, rinse it under cold water and drain again. Core the cabbages and strip off the outer leaves. Rinse these and set them aside. Peel off the inner leaves, cutting off more of the core as you proceed. When you reach the hard heart, stop peeling. Set the cabbage hearts aside.

VARIATION
For a pareve or dairy dish, you can substitute cooked brown or white rice for the meat.

4 Cut the larger leaves of the cabbage in half and trim any hard cores and veins. Place about 15ml/1 tbsp of the stuffing at one end of a leaf, fold the end of the leaf over so it looks like a short, fat cigar, then fold in the sides and roll up fairly tightly to make a neat package.

Energy 697Kcal/2902kJ; Protein 37.2g; Carbohydrate 51.5g, of which sugars 23.2g; Fat 38.4g, of which saturates 11.3g; Cholesterol 239mg; Calcium 270mg; Fibre 9.5g; Sodium 172mg.

SOUPS

Throughout Jewish history, soups have provided sustenance in times of scarcity and deprivation. Clear, golden chicken soup is perhaps the most famous, but warming, stew-like soups made of root vegetables, and light summer soups based on sorrel and beetroot are evocative of the shtetl life of the Ashkenazim. The spicy soups of the Yemenite Jews are reminiscent of the North African lands settled by the Sephardim.

FASOLADA

THIS ROBUST MEDITERRANEAN BEAN AND TOMATO SOUP IS A FAVOURITE THROUGHOUT THE JEWISH COMMUNITIES OF GREECE AND TURKEY, AS WELL AS THE NON-JEWISH COMMUNITIES. ENJOY WITH RUSTIC SOURDOUGH BREAD AND A PLATE OF OLIVES AND ONIONS.

SERVES FOUR

INGREDIENTS
275g/10oz/1½ cups dried cannellini
   beans, butter (lima) beans or Greek
   gigantes, soaked overnight in
   cold water
1 large onion, thinly sliced
1 celery stick, sliced
2–3 carrots, sliced in discs
400g/14oz can tomatoes
15ml/1 tbsp tomato purée (paste)
8 garlic cloves, half sliced,
   half chopped
150ml/¼ pint/⅔ cup extra virgin
   olive oil
5ml/1 tsp dried oregano
30ml/2 tbsp finely chopped fresh flat
   leaf parsley
salt and ground black pepper

1 Drain the beans, rinse them under cold water and drain them again. Tip them into a large pan, pour in enough water to cover and bring to the boil. Cook for about 3 minutes, then drain.

2 Return the beans to the pan, pour in fresh water to cover them by about 3cm/1¼in, then add the onion, celery and carrots.

VARIATION
Adding fairly thin vegetable stock instead of water will slightly enhance flavour and thicken texture.

3 Add the tomatoes and stir in the tomato purée, sliced garlic, olive oil and oregano. Season with a little pepper, but don't add salt at this stage, as it would toughen the skins of the beans.

4 Bring to the boil, lower the heat and cook for about 1 hour, until the beans are just tender. Season with salt, add the chopped garlic and the parsley, stir in the rest of the olive oil and serve.

Energy 455Kcal/1901kJ; Protein 16.8g; Carbohydrate 40g, of which sugars 10.3g; Fat 26.5g, of which saturates 3.9g; Cholesterol 0mg; Calcium 99mg; Fibre 13.4g; Sodium 46mg.

OLD COUNTRY MUSHROOM, BEAN AND BARLEY SOUP

THIS HEARTY ASHKENAZIC SOUP FROM EASTERN EUROPE IS PERFECT ON A FREEZING COLD DAY, OF WHICH THERE ARE MANY IN THE "OLD COUNTRY". SERVE IN WARMED BOWLS, WITH PLENTY OF RYE (PUMPERNICKEL) BREAD. THIS IS A PAREVE VERSION. FOR A MEAT VERSION, USE MEAT STOCK INSTEAD OF VEGETABLE AND ADD CHUNKS OF LONG-SIMMERED BEEF TO THE SOUP.

SERVES SIX TO EIGHT

INGREDIENTS

- 30–45ml/2–3 tbsp small haricot (navy) beans, soaked overnight
- 45–60ml/3–4 tbsp green split peas
- 45–60ml/3–4 tbsp yellow split peas
- 90–105ml/6–7 tbsp pearl barley
- 1 onion, chopped
- 2 carrots, sliced
- 3 celery sticks, diced or sliced
- ½ baking potato, peeled and cut into chunks
- 10g/¼oz or 45ml/3 tbsp mixed flavourful dried mushrooms
- 5 garlic cloves, sliced
- 2 litres/3½ pints/8 cups water
- 2 vegetable stock (bouillon) cubes
- salt and ground black pepper
- 30–45ml/2–3 tbsp chopped fresh parsley, to garnish

1 Put the beans, green and yellow split peas, pearl barley, onion, carrots, celery, potato, mushrooms, garlic and water into a large pan.

2 Bring the mixture to the boil, then reduce the heat, cover and simmer gently for about 1½ hours, or until the beans are tender.

3 Crumble the stock cubes into the soup and taste for seasoning. Ladle into warmed bowls, garnish with parsley and serve with rye or pumpernickel bread.

COOK'S TIP

Do not add the stock cubes until the end of cooking, as the salt they contain will prevent the beans from becoming tender.

Energy 130Kcal/553kJ; Protein 6.7g; Carbohydrate 26.1g, of which sugars 2.2g; Fat 0.6g, of which saturates 0.1g; Cholesterol 0mg; Calcium 24mg; Fibre 1.8g; Sodium 20mg.

BORSCHT

BEETROOT IS THE MAIN INGREDIENT OF BORSCHT. ITS FLAVOUR AND COLOUR DOMINATE THIS WELL-KNOWN SOUP, A CLASSIC OF BOTH RUSSIA AND POLAND. A TRADITIONAL JEWISH ACCOMPANIMENT IS COLD BOILED POTATOES, WHICH ARE ADDED AT THE TABLE, AS DESIRED.

SERVES FOUR TO SIX

INGREDIENTS
900g/2lb uncooked beetroot, peeled
2 carrots, peeled
2 celery sticks
40g/1½oz/3 tbsp butter
2 onions, sliced
2 garlic cloves, crushed
4 tomatoes, peeled, seeded and chopped
1 bay leaf
1 large parsley sprig
2 cloves
4 whole peppercorns
1.2 litres/2 pints/5 cups vegetable stock
150ml/¼ pint/⅔ cup beetroot kvas (see Cook's Tip) or the liquid from pickled beetroot
vinegar and sugar to taste, for sweet–sour effect
salt and ground black pepper
sour cream, garnished with chopped fresh chives or sprigs of dill, to serve

1 Cut the beetroot, carrots and celery into fairly thick strips. Melt the butter in a large pan and cook the onions over a low heat for 5 minutes, stirring occasionally.

2 Add the beetroot, carrots and celery and cook for a further 5 minutes, stirring occasionally.

3 Add the garlic and chopped tomatoes to the pan and cook, stirring, for 2 more minutes.

4 Place the bay leaf, parsley, cloves and peppercorns in a piece of muslin (cheesecloth) and tie with string.

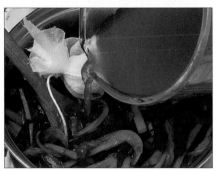

5 Add the muslin bag to the pan with the stock. Bring to the boil, reduce the heat, cover and simmer for 1¼ hours, or until the vegetables are very tender. Discard the bag. Stir in the beetroot kvas and season. Add sugar and vineger to taste. Bring to the boil. Ladle into bowls and serve with sour cream garnished with chives or dill.

COOK'S TIP
Beetroot kvas, fermented beetroot juice, adds an intense colour and a slight tartness. If unavailable, peel and grate 1 beetroot, add 150ml/¼ pint/⅔ cup stock and 10ml/2 tsp lemon juice. Bring to the boil, cover and leave for 30 minutes. Strain before using.

Energy 137Kcal/574kJ; Protein 3.7g; Carbohydrate 18.2g, of which sugars 16.3g; Fat 6g, of which saturates 3.6g; Cholesterol 14mg; Calcium 55mg; Fibre 4.6g; Sodium 157mg.

GRANDFATHER'S SOUP

A POTATO AND NOODLE COMBINATION IS IDEAL FARE IF YOU LIVE IN A COLD CLIMATE. THIS SOUP DERIVES ITS NAME FROM THE FACT THAT IT IS EASILY DIGESTED AND THEREFORE THOUGHT TO BE SUITABLE FOR THE ELDERLY.

SERVES FOUR

INGREDIENTS
  1 large onion, finely sliced
  25g/1oz/2 tbsp butter
  350g/12oz potatoes, peeled
    and diced
  900ml/1½ pints/3¾ cups
    vegetable stock
  1 bay leaf
  salt and ground black pepper
For the drop noodles
  75g/3oz/⅔ cup self-raising
    (self-rising) flour
  pinch of salt
  15g/½oz/1 tbsp butter
  15ml/1 tbsp chopped fresh
    parsley, plus a little extra
    to garnish
  1 egg, beaten
  chunks of bread, to serve

1 In a wide, heavy pan, cook the onion in the butter gently for 10 minutes, or until it begins to brown.

2 Add the diced potatoes and cook for 2–3 minutes, then pour in the stock. Add the bay leaf, salt and pepper. Bring to the boil, then reduce the heat, cover and simmer for 10 minutes.

COOK'S TIP
Use old potatoes, of a floury texture, such as King Edwards or Maris Pipers.

3 Meanwhile, make the noodles. Sift the flour and salt into a bowl and rub in the butter. Stir in the parsley, then add the egg to the flour mixture and mix to a soft dough.

4 Drop half-teaspoonfuls of the dough into the simmering soup. Cover and simmer gently for a further 10 minutes. Ladle the soup into warmed soup bowls, sprinkle over a little parsley, and serve immediately with chunks of bread.

Energy 241Kcal/1010kJ; Protein 5.7g; Carbohydrate 33.6g, of which sugars 4.9g; Fat 10.3g, of which saturates 5.7g; Cholesterol 69mg; Calcium 63mg; Fibre 2.5g; Sodium 91mg.

SPICY PUMPKIN SOUP

PUMPKIN WAS A GREAT FAVOURITE OF THE JEWS OF ITALY LONG BEFORE THE REST OF THE COUNTRY BEGAN TO EAT IT INSTEAD OF FEEDING IT TO THEIR LIVESTOCK. AS A RESULT, THE ITALIAN JEWISH COMMUNITY CONTRIBUTED MUCH TO THE PUMPKIN RECIPES IN ITALIAN CUISINE. PUMPKIN RECIPES LIKE THIS NORTH AFRICAN-SCENTED SOUP ARE VERY POPULAR WITH SEPHARDIC JEWS.

SERVES FOUR

INGREDIENTS
   900g/2lb pumpkin, peeled and
   seeds removed
   30ml/2 tbsp olive oil
   2 leeks, trimmed and sliced
   1 garlic clove, crushed
   5ml/1 tsp ground ginger
   5ml/1 tsp ground cumin
   900ml/1½ pints/3¾ cups
   vegetable stock
   salt and ground black pepper
   coriander (cilantro) leaves, to garnish
   60ml/4 tbsp natural (plain) yogurt,
   to serve

1 Cut the pumpkin into chunks. Heat the oil in a large pan and add the leeks and garlic. Cook gently until softened.

2 Add the ginger and cumin and cook, stirring, for a further minute. Add the pumpkin and the chicken stock and season with salt and pepper. Bring to the boil and simmer for 30 minutes, until the pumpkin is tender. Process the soup, in batches if necessary, in a blender or food processor.

3 Reheat the soup and serve in warmed individual bowls, with a swirl of yogurt on top and a garnish of coriander leaves.

VARIATION
For a pareve meal, omit the yogurt swirl.

Energy 98Kcal/409kJ; Protein 3g; Carbohydrate 7.5g, of which sugars 5.8g; Fat 6.4g, of which saturates 1.1g; Cholesterol 0mg; Calcium 86mg; Fibre 4.2g; Sodium 2mg.

AVGOLEMONO

EGG AND LEMON MIXED TOGETHER AND THEN COOLED TO MAKE A CREAMY SAUCE, HAS LONG BEEN A TRADITIONAL FAVOURITE OF JEWS THROUGHOUT THE MEDITERRANEAN. THIS IS A TRADITIONAL BREAK-THE-FAST DISH FOR YOM KIPPUR.

SERVES FOUR TO SIX

INGREDIENTS

1.75 litres/3 pints/7½ cups
  chicken stock
115g/4oz/½ cup orzo pasta
3 eggs
juice of 1 large lemon
salt and ground black pepper
lemon slices, to garnish

2 Beat the eggs until frothy, then add the lemon juice and a tablespoon of cold water. Slowly stir in a ladleful of the hot chicken stock, then add one or two more. Return this mixture to the pan, remove from the heat and stir well. Season with salt and pepper and serve immediately, garnished with lemon slices.

VARIATION
Make this dish with rice instead of orzo for a more classic – and heartier – soup.

1 Pour the stock into a large pan, and bring to boiling point. Add the pasta and cook for 5 minutes.

COOK'S TIP
Do not let the soup boil once the eggs have been added or it will curdle.

Energy 104Kcal/438kJ; Protein 5.5g; Carbohydrate 14.3g, of which sugars 0.7g; Fat 3.2g, of which saturates 0.8g; Cholesterol 95mg; Calcium 20mg; Fibre 0.6g; Sodium 117mg.

HUNGARIAN CHERRY SOUP

SOUPS MADE FROM SEASONAL FRUITS ARE A FAVOURITE CENTRAL EUROPEAN TREAT. CHERRY SOUP, ONE OF THE GLORIES OF THE HUNGARIAN TABLE, IS OFTEN SERVED IN ISRAEL AT THE START OF A DAIRY MEAL OR DURING THE FESTIVAL OF SHAVUOT WHEN DAIRY FOODS ARE TRADITIONALLY FEASTED UPON. IT IS DELICIOUS SERVED WITH AN EXTRA SPOONFUL OR TWO OF SOUR CREAM.

SERVES SIX

INGREDIENTS

   1kg/2¼lb fresh, frozen or canned
     sour cherries, such as Morello or
     Montmorency, pitted
   250ml/8fl oz/1 cup water
   175–250g/6–9oz/about 1 cup sugar,
     to taste
   1–2 cinnamon sticks, each about
     5cm/2in long
   750ml/1¼ pints/3 cups dry red wine
   5ml/1 tsp almond extract, or to taste
   250ml/8fl oz/1 cup single (light) cream
   250ml/8fl oz/1 cup sour cream or
     crème fraîche

VARIATION
When plums are in season, use them
instead of cherries.

1 Put the pitted cherries, water, sugar, cinnamon and wine in a large pan. Bring to the boil, reduce the heat and simmer for 20–30 minutes until the cherries are tender. Remove from the heat and add the almond extract.

2 In a bowl, stir a few tablespoons of single cream into the sour cream or crème fraîche to thin it down, then stir in the rest until the mixture is smooth. Stir the mixture into the cherry soup, then chill until ready to serve.

Energy 484Kcal/2037kJ; Protein 3.7g; Carbohydrate 64.1g, of which sugars 64.1g; Fat 16.3g, of which saturates 10.3g; Cholesterol 48mg; Calcium 125mg; Fibre 1g; Sodium 53mg.

Sweet <u>and</u> Sour Cabbage, Beetroot <u>and</u> Tomato Borscht

There are many variations of this classic Ashkenazic soup. This version is served hot and includes plentiful amounts of cabbage, tomatoes and potatoes. If you make the meat version, omit the sour cream and serve with unbuttered rye bread.

SERVES SIX

INGREDIENTS

1 onion, chopped
1 carrot, chopped
4–6 raw or vacuum-packed (cooked, not pickled) beetroot (beets),
  3–4 diced and 1–2 coarsely grated
400g/14oz can tomatoes
4–6 new potatoes, cut into bitesize pieces
1 small white cabbage, thinly sliced
1 litre/1¾ pints/4 cups vegetable stock
45ml/3 tbsp sugar
30–45ml/2–3 tbsp white wine, cider vinegar or sour salt (citric acid)
45ml/3 tbsp chopped fresh dill, plus extra to garnish
salt and ground black pepper
sour cream, to garnish
buttered rye bread, to serve

1 Put the onion, carrot, diced beetroot, tomatoes, potatoes, cabbage and stock in a large pan. Bring to the boil, reduce the heat and simmer for 30 minutes, or until the potatoes are tender.

VARIATION
To make meat borscht, place 1kg/2¼lb chopped beef in a large pan. Pour over water to cover and crumble in 1 beef stock (bouillon) cube. Bring to the boil, then reduce the heat and simmer until tender. Skim any fat from the surface, then add the vegetables and proceed as above. For kashrut, omit the sour cream and serve with unbuttered rye bread.

2 Add the grated beetroot, sugar, wine and vinegar or sour salt to the soup and cook for 10 minutes. Taste for a good sweet–sour balance and add more sugar and/or vinegar if necessary. Season.

3 Stir the chopped dill into the soup and ladle into warmed bowls immediately. If you like, garnish each bowl with a generous spoonful of sour cream and more dill. Serve with rye bread.

Energy 46Kcal/196kJ; Protein 1.6g; Carbohydrate 9.8g, of which sugars 6.4g; Fat 0.4g, of which saturates 0.1g; Cholesterol 0mg; Calcium 22mg; Fibre 1.9g; Sodium 29mg.

TOMATO SOUP WITH ISRAELI COUSCOUS

ISRAELI COUSCOUS IS A TOASTED, ROUND PASTA, MUCH LARGER THAN REGULAR COUSCOUS, WHICH IS DELICIOUS IN SAVOURY, ZESTY SOUPS SUCH AS THIS ONE. IT WORKS REALLY WELL IN SPICY FISH SOUPS SERVED WITH A WEDGE OF LEMON. IF YOU LIKE YOUR SOUP TO HAVE A STRONG GARLIC FLAVOUR, ADD AN EXTRA CLOVE OF CHOPPED GARLIC JUST BEFORE SERVING.

SERVES FOUR TO SIX

INGREDIENTS

  30ml/2 tbsp olive oil
  1 onion, chopped
  1–2 carrots, diced
  400g/14oz can chopped tomatoes
  6 garlic cloves, roughly chopped
  1.5 litres/2½ pints/6¼ cups
    vegetable or chicken stock
  200–250g/7–9oz/1–1½ cups
    Israeli couscous
  2–3 mint sprigs, chopped, or several
    pinches of dried mint
  1.5ml/¼ tsp ground cumin
  ¼ bunch fresh coriander (cilantro),
    or about 5 sprigs, chopped
  cayenne pepper, to taste
  salt and ground black pepper

1 Heat the oil in a large pan, add the onion and carrots and cook gently for about 10 minutes until softened. Add the tomatoes, half the garlic, the stock, couscous, mint, ground cumin and coriander, with the cayenne pepper, salt and pepper to taste.

2 Bring the soup to the boil, add the remaining chopped garlic, then reduce the heat slightly and simmer gently for 7–10 minutes, stirring occasionally, or until the couscous is just tender. Serve piping hot, ladled into individual serving bowls.

Energy 138Kcal/575kJ; Protein 2.8g; Carbohydrate 23.1g, of which sugars 5.3g; Fat 4.3g, of which saturates 0.6g; Cholesterol 0mg; Calcium 24mg; Fibre 1.6g; Sodium 13mg.

LUBIYA

This Sephardic Israeli soup of black-eyed beans and turmeric-tinted tomato broth is flavoured with tangy lemon and speckled with chopped fresh coriander. It is ideal for serving at parties — simply multiply the quantities as required. In Egypt, black-eyed bean soup was served at Rosh Hashanah as a symbol of fertility for the New Year.

SERVES FOUR

INGREDIENTS

175g/6oz/1 cup black-eyed
   beans (peas)
15ml/1 tbsp olive oil
2 onions, chopped
4 garlic cloves, chopped
1 medium-hot or 2–3 mild fresh
   chillies, chopped
5ml/1 tsp ground cumin
5ml/1 tsp ground turmeric
250g/9oz fresh or canned
   tomatoes, diced
600ml/1 pint/2½ cups chicken,
   beef or vegetable stock
25g/1oz fresh coriander (cilantro)
   leaves, roughly chopped
juice of ½ lemon
pitta bread, to serve

1 Put the beans in a pan, cover with cold water, bring to the boil, then cook for 5 minutes. Remove from the heat, cover and leave to stand for 2 hours. Drain the beans, return to the pan, cover with fresh cold water, then simmer for 35–40 minutes, or until the beans are tender. Drain and set aside.

2 Heat the oil in a pan, add the onions, garlic and chilli and cook for 5 minutes, or until the onion is soft. Stir in the cumin, turmeric, tomatoes, stock, half the coriander and the beans and simmer for 20–30 minutes. Stir in the lemon juice and remaining coriander and serve immediately with pitta bread.

Energy 172Kcal/727kJ; Protein 10.9g; Carbohydrate 25.4g, of which sugars 6g; Fat 3.7g, of which saturates 0.6g; Cholesterol 0mg; Calcium 73mg; Fibre 8.5g; Sodium 17mg.

A POTAGE OF LENTILS

THIS SOUP IS SOMETIMES KNOWN AS ESAU'S SOUP FOR THE ROLE IT PLAYED IN THAT BIBLICAL STORY.
RED LENTILS AND VEGETABLES ARE COOKED AND PURÉED, THEN SHARPENED WITH LOTS OF LEMON
JUICE. LENTILS MAY BE SERVED AS PART OF A MEAL FOR SHABBAT.

SERVES FOUR

INGREDIENTS

  45ml/3 tbsp olive oil
  1 onion, chopped
  2 celery sticks, chopped
  1–2 carrots, sliced
  8 garlic cloves, chopped
  1 potato, peeled and diced
  250g/9oz/generous 1 cup red lentils
  1 litre/1¾ pints/4 cups
    vegetable stock
  2 bay leaves
  1–2 lemons, halved
  2.5ml/½ tsp ground cumin, or
    to taste
  cayenne pepper or Tabasco sauce,
    to taste
  salt and ground black pepper
  lemon slices and chopped fresh
    flat leaf parsley or coriander
    (cilantro) leaves, to serve

1 Heat the oil in a large pan. Add the onion and cook for about 5 minutes, or until softened. Stir in the celery, carrots, half the garlic and all the potato. Cook for a few minutes until beginning to soften.

2 Add the lentils and stock to the pan and bring to the boil. Reduce the heat, cover and simmer for about 30 minutes, until the potato and lentils are tender.

3 Add the bay leaves, remaining garlic and half the lemons to the pan and cook the soup for a further 10 minutes. Remove the bay leaves. Squeeze the juice from the remaining lemons, then stir into the soup, to taste.

4 Pour the soup into a food processor or blender and process until smooth. (You may need to do this in batches.) Tip the soup back into the pan, stir in the cumin, cayenne pepper or Tabasco sauce, and season with salt and pepper.

5 Ladle the soup into bowls and top each portion with lemon slices and a sprinkling of parsley or coriander.

VARIATIONS
• On a hot day, serve this soup cold, with even more lemon juice.
• Add 25g/8oz chopped spinach leaves during the last 10 minutes of cooking for a traditional Egyptian lentil and spinach soup.

Energy 327Kcal/1379kJ; Protein 16.4g; Carbohydrate 47.4g, of which sugars 4.5g; Fat 9.3g, of which saturates 1.4g; Cholesterol 0mg; Calcium 51mg; Fibre 4.3g; Sodium 39mg.

RUSSIAN <u>AND</u> ROOT VEGETABLE SOUP <u>WITH</u> DILL

THIS IS A TYPICAL RUSSIAN SOUP, TRADITIONALLY PREPARED WHEN THE FIRST VEGETABLES OF SPRINGTIME APPEAR. EARTHY ROOT VEGETABLES, COOKED WITH FRESH SPINACH LEAVES, ARE ENLIVENED WITH A TART, FRESH TOPPING OF DILL AND LEMON. THE FRESH DILL REALLY INVIGORATES THE SOUP, SO DON'T EVEN CONSIDER DOING WITHOUT.

SERVES FOUR TO SIX

INGREDIENTS

1 small turnip, cut into chunks
2 carrots, sliced or diced
1 small parsnip, cut into large dice
1 potato, peeled and diced
1 onion, chopped or cut into chunks
1 garlic clove, finely chopped
¼ celeriac bulb, diced
1 litre/1¾ pints/4 cups vegetable or
  chicken stock
200g/7oz spinach, washed and
  roughly chopped
1 small bunch fresh dill, chopped
salt and ground black pepper
For the garnish
2 hard-boiled eggs, sliced
1 lemon, cut into slices
30ml/2 tbsp fresh parsley and dill

1 Put the turnip, carrots, parsnip, potato, onion, garlic, celeriac and stock into a large pan. Bring to the boil, then simmer for 25–30 minutes, or until the vegetables are very tender.

COOK'S TIP
For the best results, use a really good quality vegetable stock.

2 Add the spinach to the pan and cook for a further 5 minutes, or until the spinach is tender but still green and leafy. Season with salt and pepper.

3 Stir the dill into the soup, then ladle into bowls and serve garnished with egg, wedges of lemon and a sprinkling of parsley and dill.

Energy 49Kcal/207kJ; Protein 2.1g; Carbohydrate 9.4g, of which sugars 5.1g; Fat 0.7g, of which saturates 0.1g; Cholesterol 0mg; Calcium 83mg; Fibre 2.8g; Sodium 58mg.

FRESH CABBAGE SHCHI

*CABBAGE AND PICKLES ARE THE TWO ESSENTIAL VEGETABLES OF THE RUSSIAN JEWS. HERE, KOSHER
PICKLE BRINE AND FRESH DILL ADD A SPARKY SAVOUR TO LIVEN UP THE TASTEBUDS.*

SERVES FOUR TO SIX

INGREDIENTS

1 small turnip
2 carrots
40g/1½oz/3 tbsp butter
1 large onion, sliced
2 celery sticks, sliced
1 white cabbage, about 675g/1½lb
1.2 litres/2 pints/5 cups vegetable
  stock
1 sharp eating apple, cored, peeled
  and chopped
2 bay leaves
15ml/1 tbsp chopped fresh dill
15–30ml/1–2 tbsp pickled cucumber
  juice (preferably dill or kosher dill)
  or lemon juice
salt and ground black pepper
fresh herbs, to garnish
sour cream and black bread,
  to serve

1 Cut the turnip and carrots into
matchstick strips. Melt the butter in a
large pan and fry the turnip, carrot,
onion and celery for 10 minutes.

VARIATION
For a meat soup, use beef stock in place
of vegetable stock, and omit the butter
and sour cream (use oil instead of
butter). Add one or two potatoes in place
of the apple.

2 Shred the cabbage and add it to the
pan with the stock, apple, bay leaves
and dill and bring to the boil. Cover and
simmer for 40 minutes or until the
vegetables are really tender.

3 Remove the bay leaves, then stir in
the pickled cucumber juice or lemon
juice and season with plenty of salt and
pepper. Serve hot, garnished with fresh
herbs and accompanied by sour cream
and black bread.

Energy 106Kcal/442kJ; Protein 2.4g; Carbohydrate 11.5g, of which sugars 10.5g; Fat 5.9g, of which saturates 3.5g; Cholesterol 14mg; Calcium 81mg; Fibre 3.9g; Sodium 62mg.

CAULIFLOWER SOUP

THIS PUREÉD SOUP HAS THE LUXURIOUSLY SMOOTH TEXTURE TYPICAL OF CZECH SOUPS AND THE BOUNCY, PLUMP DUMPLINGS SO BELOVED OF ALL CZECH PEOPLE.

SERVES SIX TO EIGHT

INGREDIENTS
  1 large cauliflower, cut into florets
  1.5 litres/2½ pints/6¼ cups
    vegetable stock
  40g/1½oz/3 tbsp butter
  40g/1½oz/⅓ cup plain flour
  generous pinch of nutmeg or mace
  2 egg yolks
  300ml/½ pint/1¼ cups
    whipping cream
  flat leaf parsley, to garnish
  crusty bread, to serve
For the dumplings
  75g/3oz/1½ cups white breadcrumbs
  10g/¼oz/½ tbsp butter, softened
  1 egg, beaten
  10ml/2 tsp chopped fresh flat
    leaf parsley
  a little milk, to bind
  salt and ground black pepper

1 Cook the cauliflower in the vegetable stock for 12 minutes or until just tender. Remove and reserve the cooking liquid and a few florets of the cauliflower.

2 Make a sauce by melting the butter in a small pan. Add the flour and cook for 1–2 minutes, before adding about 150ml/¼ pint/⅔ cup of the reserved cauliflower cooking liquid and stirring well. Remove from the heat.

3 Purée the cooked cauliflower in a food processor or blender until smooth. Beat the nutmeg or mace and egg yolks into the cauliflower, then add to the pan of sauce.

4 Add enough cauliflower liquid to make up to 1.2 litres/2 pints/5 cups. Reheat the soup.

5 Make up the dumplings by mixing all the ingredients together. Roll into balls.

6 Poach the dumplings gently in the soup for 3–5 minutes before adding the whipping cream. Garnish with the sprigs of parsley and reserved cauliflower.

Energy 293Kcal/1216kJ; Protein 6.9g; Carbohydrate 14.8g, of which sugars 3.5g; Fat 23.3g, of which saturates 13.5g; Cholesterol 127mg; Calcium 72mg; Fibre 1.9g; Sodium 138mg.

MIDDLE EASTERN YOGURT <u>AND</u> CUCUMBER SOUP

ON A HOT SULTRY DAY, THERE IS NOTHING AS REFRESHING AS A BOWL — OR GLASS — OF COOLING YOGURT AND CUCUMBER SOUP. BELOVED THROUGHOUT THE MIDDLE EAST, AND ALSO IN VARIOUS GUISES IN EASTERN EUROPE, THIS IS A LIGHT DAIRY MEAL. BULGARIAN JEWS HAD A HUGE IMPACT ON ISRAELI FOOD WITH THEIR DELICIOUS YOGURT DISHES. IF POMEGRANATES ARE IN SEASON, SPRINKLE A HANDFUL OF THE SEEDS OVER THE TOP OF EACH BOWLFUL.

SERVES FOUR

INGREDIENTS
  1 large cucumber, peeled
  500ml/1 pint/2 cups thick yogurt
  2 garlic cloves, crushed
  30ml/2 tbsp white wine vinegar
  15ml/1 tbsp chopped fresh mint
  salt and ground black pepper
  sprigs of mint, to garnish

VARIATION
Instead of cucumber, you can use 250g/8oz/1 bunch cooked, chopped, squeeze-dried, spinach.

1 Grate the cucumber coarsely. Place in a bowl with the yogurt, garlic, vinegar and mint. Stir well and season to taste. Chill for at least two hours.

2 Just before serving, stir the soup again. Pour into individual bowls, garnish with mint sprigs and serve with Middle Eastern style flat bread.

Energy 77Kcal/322kJ; Protein 6.9g; Carbohydrate 10.3g, of which sugars 10.1g; Fat 1.3g, of which saturates 0.6g; Cholesterol 2mg; Calcium 255mg; Fibre 0.3g; Sodium 106mg.

LENTIL SOUP <u>WITH</u> ORZO

LENTILS ARE A WINTER STAPLE IN GREECE AND VERY DELICIOUS THEY ARE TOO. THIS SOUP OF LENTILS AND TINY PASTA, SHARPENED BY A SHAKE OF VINEGAR, IS OF GREEK SEPHARDIC HERITAGE. THE SECRET OF GOOD LENTIL SOUP, AS WITH ALL THESE WINTER DISHES FROM GREECE, IS TO BE GENEROUS WITH THE OLIVE OIL.

SERVES FOUR

INGREDIENTS
275g/10oz/1¼ cups brown-green
  lentils, preferably the small variety
150ml/¼ pint/⅔ cup extra virgin
  olive oil
1 onion, thinly sliced
5 garlic cloves, sliced into
  thin batons
1 carrot, sliced into thin discs
400g/14oz can chopped tomatoes
15ml/1 tbsp tomato purée (paste)
2.5ml/½ tsp dried oregano
1 litre/1¾ pints/4 cups hot water
60g/2oz/½ cup tiny pasta, such
  as orzo
salt and ground black pepper
30ml/2 tbsp roughly chopped parsley
  leaves, to garnish
a few shakes of vinegar

1 Rinse the lentils, drain them and put them in a large pan with cold water to cover. Bring to the boil and boil for 3–4 minutes. Strain, discarding the liquid, and set the lentils aside.

2 Wipe the pan clean, heat the olive oil in it, then add the onion and sauté until translucent. Stir in the garlic, then, as soon as it becomes aromatic, return the lentils to the pan.

3 Add the carrot, tomatoes, tomato purée and oregano. Stir in the hot water and a little pepper to taste.

4 Bring to the boil, then lower the heat, cover the pan and cook gently for 20–30 minutes until the lentils feel soft but have not begun to disintegrate. Halfway through, add the tiny pasta.

5 Add salt, the chopped parsley and a few shakes of vinegar just before serving the soup.

Energy 601Kcal/2523kJ; Protein 21.9g; Carbohydrate 72.3g, of which sugars 8.2g; Fat 26.9g, of which saturates 3.9g; Cholesterol 0mg; Calcium 60mg; Fibre 6.1g; Sodium 40mg

SCHAV

This refreshingly sharp, chilled sorrel soup is a culinary souvenir of the Ashkenazim of Russia. The sorrel, also known as sour spinach or sour grass, gives it a wonderful pale green colour and tangy flavour and the addition of lemon juice gives it a tart edge.

SERVES FOUR TO SIX

INGREDIENTS
  500g/1¼lb sorrel leaves,
    stems removed
  1 medium–large onion, thinly sliced
  1.5 litres/2½ pints/6¼ cups
    vegetable stock
  15–30ml/1–2 tbsp sugar
  60ml/4 tbsp lemon juice
  2 eggs
  150ml/¼ pint/⅔ cup sour cream
  salt
  3–4 spring onions (scallions), thinly
    sliced, to serve

COOK'S TIP
Shred the sorrel across the grain. This will help to prevent it from becoming stringy when it is cooked.

1 Finely shred the sorrel, then put in a large pan with the onion and stock. Bring to the boil, then reduce the heat and simmer for 10–15 minutes.

2 Add the sugar and half the lemon juice to the pan, stir and simmer for a further 5–10 minutes.

3 In a bowl, beat the eggs and mix in the sour cream, then stir in about 250ml/ 8fl oz/1 cup of the hot soup. Add another 250ml/8fl oz/1 cup of soup, stirring to ensure a smooth texture.

4 Slowly pour the egg mixture into the hot soup, stirring constantly to prevent the eggs curdling and ensure a smooth texture. Cook for just a few moments over a low heat until the soup thickens slightly. Season with a little salt to taste and stir in the remaining lemon juice.

5 Leave the soup to cool, then chill for at least 2 hours. Taste again for seasoning (it may need more salt or lemon juice) and serve sprinkled with the spring onions.

Energy 116Kcal/479kJ; Protein 5.5g; Carbohydrate 6.9g, of which sugars 6.2g; Fat 7.6g, of which saturates 3.7g; Cholesterol 78mg; Calcium 182mg; Fibre 2.1g; Sodium 151mg.

MIXED MUSHROOM SOLYANKA

THIS MUSHROOM SOUP HAS STRONG OVERTONES OF PICKLE, TYPICAL OF RUSSIAN-JEWISH CUISINE. TO BALANCE THE SEASONING, ADD A LITTLE PICKLE BRINE TO TASTE INSTEAD OF SALT. OFFER BOILED POTATOES ON THE SIDE, TO CUT UP AND ADD AS DESIRED. THE TART FLAVOURS OF PICKLED CUCUMBER, CAPERS AND LEMON ADD EXTRA BITE TO THIS RICH SOUP.

SERVES FOUR

INGREDIENTS

2 onions, chopped
1.2 litres/2 pints/5 cups
  vegetable stock
450g/1lb/6 cups mixed
  mushrooms, sliced
15–25ml/1–1½ tbsp tomato
  purée (paste)
1 pickled cucumber, dill or kosher
  dill pickle, chopped
1 bay leaf
15ml/1 tbsp capers in brine, drained
pinch of salt
6 peppercorns, crushed
lemon rind curls, green olives, spring
  onions (scallions) and sprigs of flat
  leaf parsley, to garnish

1 Put the onions in a large pan with 50ml/2fl oz/¼ cup of the stock. Cook, stirring occasionally, until the liquid has evaporated.

2 Add the remaining vegetable stock with the sliced mushrooms, bring to the boil, cover and simmer gently for 30 minutes.

3 In a small bowl, blend the tomato purée with 30ml/2 tbsp of stock.

4 Add the tomato purée to the pan with the pickled cucumber, bay leaf, capers, salt and peppercorns. Cook gently for 10 more minutes.

5 Ladle the soup into warmed bowls and sprinkle lemon rind curls, a few olives, a sprinkling of sliced spring onions and a sprig of flat leaf parsley over each bowl before serving.

Energy 54Kcal/224kJ; Protein 3.4g; Carbohydrate 8.9g, of which sugars 6.4g; Fat 0.8g, of which saturates 0.1g; Cholesterol 0mg; Calcium 33mg; Fibre 2.8g; Sodium 18mg.

BOURRIDE OF RED MULLET AND FENNEL WITH BLACK OLIVES

THE LAND OF PROVENCE IN THE SOUTH OF FRANCE HAS LONG HAD A JEWISH TRADITION, ALTHOUGH MANY COMMUNITIES HAVE NOW DISAPPEARED. THIS IS A JEWISH VERSION OF THE FAMOUS FISH SOUPS OF THE REGION, WITH ALL THE SUN-DRENCHED FLAVOUR, BUT NO SHELLFISH. IF YOU PREFER, SERVE THE OLIVES ON THE SIDE, RATHER THAN IN THE BOWL.

SERVES FOUR

INGREDIENTS
  25ml/1½ tbsp olive oil
  1 onion, chopped
  3 garlic cloves, chopped
  2 fennel bulbs, halved, cored and
    thinly sliced
  4 tomatoes, chopped
  1 bay leaf
  1 sprig fresh thyme
  1.2 litres/2 pints/5 cups fish stock
  675g/1½lb red mullet or snapper
  8 slices baguette
  1 garlic clove
  30ml/2 tbsp tomato purée (paste)
  12 black olives, pitted
    and quartered
  salt and ground black pepper
  fresh fennel fronds, to garnish
For the aioli
  2 egg yolks
  1–2 garlic cloves, crushed
  10ml/2 tsp lemon juice
  300ml/½ pint/1¼ cups extra virgin
    olive oil

1 Scale and fillet the red mullet. Hold the fish vertically by the tail with one hand and use the other to push a knife forward with the blade nearly flat, slicing just underneath the scales, taking care not to rupture the skin. Place the scaled fish on a chopping board and fillet by cutting through the skin behind the head to the backbone, then flat against the backbone to the tail. Turn the fish over to repeat on the other side.

2 Heat the olive oil in a large, heavy pan. Add the chopped onion and garlic and cook for 5 minutes, until softened. Add the fennel and cook for a further 2–3 minutes. Stir in the tomatoes, bay leaf, thyme and fish stock. Bring the mixture to the boil, then reduce the heat and simmer for 30 minutes.

3 Meanwhile, make the aioli. Put the egg yolks, garlic and lemon juice in a bowl. Season and whisk well. Whisk in the oil, a little at a time. As the mixture begins to emulsify and thicken, increase the speed with which you add the oil, from a few drops at a time to a slow trickle. Transfer to a large bowl and set aside.

4 Cut each mullet fillet into two or three pieces, then add them to the soup and cook gently for 5 minutes. Use a slotted spoon to remove the mullet and set aside.

5 Strain the cooking liquid, pressing the vegetables to extract as much flavour as possible. Whisk about a ladleful of the soup into the aioli, then whisk in the remaining soup in one go.

6 Return the soup to a clean pan and cook very gently, whisking continuously, until the mixture is very slightly thickened. Add the mullet to the soup and set it aside.

7 Toast the baguette slices on both sides. Rub each slice with the clove of garlic and spread with tomato purée. Divide the olives between the toasted bread slices.

8 Very gently reheat the soup, but do not allow it to boil, then ladle it into bowls. Top each portion with two toasts and garnish with fennel.

Energy 492Kcal/2079kJ; Protein 41.2g; Carbohydrate 53.6g, of which sugars 10g; Fat 14.1g, of which saturates 1.2g; Cholesterol 0mg; Calcium 256mg; Fibre 6.1g; Sodium 965mg.

SMOKED SALMON AND DILL SOUP

DILL IS THE PERFECT PARTNER FOR THIS CREAMY SOUP OF BOTH SMOKED AND FRESH SALMON. IT IS A FAVOURITE OF THE JEWISH COMMUNITY OF ALASKA, WHO JOKINGLY REFER TO THEMSELVES AS "THE FROZEN CHOSEN". IF PREPARING WITH SCRAPS OF SMOKED CHICKEN OR TURKEY INSTEAD OF THE SALMON, SUBSTITUTE OIL FOR BUTTER, WATER FOR MILK AND CREAM, AND USE CHICKEN STOCK.

SERVES FOUR

INGREDIENTS

20g/¾oz/1½ tbsp butter
1 onion, finely chopped
25g/1oz/¼ cup plain
  (all-purpose) flour
1.75 litres/3 pints/7 cups fish stock
2 medium potatoes, cut in
  1cm/½in cubes
50–75g/2–3oz smoked salmon
  scraps, cut into small pieces
250g/½lb salmon fillet, skinned and
  cut into 2cm/¾in cubes
175ml/6fl oz/¾ cup milk
120ml/4fl oz/½ cup whipping cream
30ml/2 tbsp chopped fresh dill
salt and ground black pepper

1 Melt the butter in a large pan. Add the onion and cook for 6 minutes until softened.

2 Stir in the flour. Reduce the heat to low and cook for 3 minutes, stirring occasionally with a wooden spoon.

3 Add the fish stock and potatoes to the mixture in the pan. Season with a little salt and ground black pepper. Bring to the boil, then reduce the heat, cover and simmer gently for about 20 minutes or until the potatoes are tender when tested with a fork.

4 Add the smoked salmon scraps and the cubed salmon, then simmer gently for 3–5 minutes until it is just cooked.

5 Stir the milk, cream and chopped dill into the contents of the pan. Cook until just warmed through, stirring occasionally, but do not allow to boil. Adjust the seasoning to taste, then ladle into warmed soup bowls to serve.

Energy 373Kcal/1556kJ; Protein 18.8g; Carbohydrate 20.8g, of which sugars 5.9g; Fat 24.5g, of which saturates 12g; Cholesterol 79mg; Calcium 107mg; Fibre 1.4g; Sodium 234mg

FISH SOUP WITH DUMPLINGS

JEWS FROM THE EASTERN EUROPEAN COMMUNITIES SHARED THEIR LOVE OF DUMPLINGS WITH THEIR NON-JEWISH NEIGHBOURS, ESPECIALLY THOSE FROM WHAT IS NOW THE CZECH REPUBLIC. THIS DELICIOUS SOUP TAKES VERY LITTLE TIME TO PREPARE, SO IS IDEAL AS A QUICK SUPPER.

SERVES FOUR TO EIGHT

INGREDIENTS
675g/1½lb assorted fresh fish,
   skinned, boned and diced
15–30ml/1–2 tbsp vegetable oil
15ml/1 tbsp paprika, plus extra
   to garnish
1.5 litres/2½ pints/6¼ cups
   fish stock
3 firm tomatoes, peeled and chopped
4 waxy potatoes, peeled and grated
5–10ml/1–2 tsp chopped fresh
   marjoram, plus extra to garnish
For the dumplings
75g/3oz/½ cup semolina or flour
1 egg, beaten
45ml/3 tbsp water
generous pinch of salt
15ml/1 tbsp chopped fresh parsley

1 Fry the pieces of assorted fish in the vegetable oil for 1–2 minutes, taking care not to break them up.

2 Sprinkle in the paprika, pour in the fish stock or water, bring to the boil and simmer for 10 minutes.

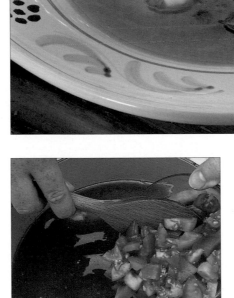

3 Stir the tomatoes, grated potato and marjoram into the pan. Cook for 10 minutes, stirring occasionally.

4 Meanwhile, make the dumplings. Mix all the ingredients together, then leave to stand, covered with clear film (plastic wrap), for 5–10 minutes.

5 Drop spoonfuls of the dumpling mixture into the soup and cook for 10 minutes. Serve hot, with a little marjoram and paprika.

COOK'S TIP
For the fish, use a variety of whatever kosher fresh fish is available. Good options include perch, cod, snapper or carp.

Energy 154Kcal/649kJ; Protein 18g; Carbohydrate 14.5g, of which sugars 1.8g; Fat 3g, of which saturates 0.5g; Cholesterol 63mg; Calcium 29mg; Fibre 1g; Sodium 67mg.

CHICKPEA SOUP WITH SPINACH

CHICKPEAS FORM PART OF THE STAPLE DIET IN THE BALKANS AND MEDITERRANEAN, USED EITHER WHOLE OR GROUND. THE FLAVOURS CAN BE VARIED ACCORDING TO WHICHEVER TASTE YOU PREFER — CUMIN IS PARTICULARLY DELICIOUS WITH CHICKPEAS.

SERVES FOUR TO SIX

INGREDIENTS

500g/1¼lb/3½ cups chickpeas,
   rinsed and drained
2 litres/3½ pints/8 cups
   vegetable stock
6 garlic cloves, sliced
3 large waxy potatoes, peeled and cut
   into bitesize chunks
50ml/2fl oz/¼ cup olive oil
225g/8oz spinach leaves, washed and
   drained well
salt and ground black pepper

VARIATION
For a meat meal, slice up smoked beef
or other kosher salami such as kosher
Polish sausage, and add to the soup
during the last 15–20 minutes.

1 Place the chickpeas in a bowl of cold water and leave overnight. The next day, drain them well and place in a large pan with the stock.

2 Bring to the boil, then reduce the heat and cook gently for about 55 minutes. Add the garlic, potatoes, olive oil and seasoning and cook for a further 20 minutes.

3 Five minutes before the end of cooking, add the spinach leaves. Serve in warmed soup bowls.

Energy 399Kcal/1681kJ; Protein 20.5g; Carbohydrate 58g, of which sugars 4g; Fat 10.9g, of which saturates 1.4g; Cholesterol 0mg; Calcium 203mg; Fibre 10.7g; Sodium 96mg.

CHICKEN SOUP WITH KNAIDLACH

ALL "BUBBAHS" (GRANDMOTHERS) TELL US THAT A BOWL OF JEWISH CHICKEN SOUP CAN HEAL THE SOUL. WHAT THEY HAVE ALSO TOLD US, AND MODERN DOCTORS ARE JUST NOW SCIENTIFICALLY PROVING, IS THAT CHICKEN SOUP ALSO HELPS TO CURE FLU AND THE COMMON COLD. THIS IS WHY THIS WARMING SOUP IS OFTEN KNOWN AS "JEWISH ANTIBIOTICS".

SERVES SIX TO EIGHT

INGREDIENTS

1–1.5kg/2¼–3¼lb chicken, cut
   into portions
2–3 onions
3–4 litres/5–7 pints/12–16 cups water
3–5 carrots, thickly sliced
3–5 celery sticks, thickly sliced
1 small parsnip, cut in half
30–45ml/2–3 tbsp roughly chopped
   fresh parsley
30–45ml/2–3 tbsp chopped
   fresh dill
1–2 pinches ground turmeric
2 chicken stock (bouillon) cubes
2 garlic cloves, finely chopped
   (optional)
salt and ground black pepper
For the knaidlach
175g/6oz/¾ cup medium matzo meal
2 eggs, lightly beaten
45ml/3 tbsp vegetable oil or rendered
   chicken fat
1 garlic clove, finely chopped (optional)
30ml/2 tbsp chopped fresh parsley,
   plus extra to garnish
½ onion, finely grated
1–2 pinches of chicken stock
   (bouillon) cube or powder (optional)
about 90ml/6 tbsp water
salt and ground black pepper

1 Put the chicken pieces in a very large pan. Keeping them whole, cut a large cross in the stem end of each onion and add to the pan with the water, carrots, celery, parsnip, parsley, half the fresh dill, the turmeric, and salt and black pepper.

2 Cover the pan and bring to the boil, then immediately lower the heat to a simmer. Skim and discard the scum that surfaces to the top. (Scum will continue to form but it is only the first scum that rises that will detract from the clarity and flavour of the soup.)

3 Add the crumbled stock cubes and simmer for 2–3 hours. When the soup is flavourful, skim off the fat. Alternatively, chill the soup and remove the layer of solid fat that forms.

4 To make the knaidlach, in a large bowl combine the matzo meal with the eggs, oil or fat, chopped garlic, if using, parsley, onion, salt and pepper. Add only a little chicken stock cube or powder, if using, as these are salty. Add the water and mix together until the mixture is of the consistency of a thick, soft paste.

5 Cover the matzo batter and chill for 30 minutes, during which time the mixture will become firm.

VARIATION
Instead of knaidlach, the soup can be served over rice, noodles or kreplach.

6 Bring a pan of water to the boil and have a bowl of water next to the stove. Dip a tablespoon into the water, then take a spoonful of the matzo batter. With wet hands, roll it into a ball, then slip it into the boiling water and reduce the heat so that the water simmers. Continue with the remaining matzo batter, working relatively quickly, then cover the pan and cook for 15–20 minutes.

7 Remove the knaidlach from the pan with a slotted spoon and transfer to a plate for about 20 minutes to firm up.

8 To serve, reheat the soup, adding the remaining dill and the garlic, if using. Put two or three knaidlach in each bowl, pour over the hot soup and garnish.

COOK'S TIP
To make lighter knaidlach, separate the eggs and add the yolks to the matzo mixture. Whisk the whites until stiff, then fold into the mixture.

Energy 266Kcal/1115kJ; Protein 25.7g; Carbohydrate 24g, of which sugars 6.6g; Fat 7.5g, of which saturates 1.2g; Cholesterol 109mg; Calcium 48mg; Fibre 2.7g; Sodium 86mg.

BULGARIAN SOUR LAMB SOUP

Sour soups, made tangy with vinegar, lemon, or pickle brine and thicker with beaten eggs, are traditional throughout Bulgaria and Romania. This recipe uses lamb, but it is just as delicious when prepared using poultry.

SERVES FOUR TO FIVE

INGREDIENTS
    30ml/2 tbsp vegetable oil
    450g/1lb lean lamb, trimmed
      and cubed
    1 onion, diced
    30ml/2 tbsp plain (all-purpose) flour
    15ml/1 tbsp paprika
    1 litre/1¾ pints/4 cups hot
      lamb stock
    3 parsley sprigs
    4 spring onions (scallions)
    30ml/2 tbsp chopped dill
    25g/1oz/scant ¼ cup long grain rice
    2 eggs, beaten
    30–45ml/2–3 tbsp or more vinegar or
      lemon juice
    salt and ground black pepper
    crusty bread, to serve
For the garnish
    30ml/2 tbsp olive oil
    5ml/1 tsp paprika
    a little parsley or lovage and dill

1 In a large pan, heat the oil and then brown the meat. Add the onion and cook until it has softened.

2 Sprinkle in the flour and paprika. Stir well, add the stock and cook for 10 minutes.

3 Tie the parsley, spring onions and dill together with string and add to the pan with the rice and a little salt and pepper. Bring to the boil, then simmer for 30–40 minutes, or until the lamb is tender.

COOK'S TIP
Reheat this soup very gently, as the eggs could become scrambled.

4 Remove the pan from the heat and add the beaten eggs, stirring continuously. Add the vinegar or lemon juice. Remove and discard the tied herbs and season to taste.

5 For the garnish, heat the oil and paprika together in a small pan. Ladle the soup into warmed serving bowls. Garnish with herbs and a little red paprika oil. Serve with thick wedges of crusty bread.

Energy 281Kcal/1173kJ; Protein 21.6g; Carbohydrate 11.3g, of which sugars 2g; Fat 16.9g, of which saturates 5.8g; Cholesterol 145mg; Calcium 39mg; Fibre 0.7g; Sodium 107mg.

BALKAN LAMB MEATBALL SOUP
WITH VEGETABLES

THIS HOMEY VEGETABLE SOUP WITH MEATBALLS IS OF EASTERN EUROPEAN HERITAGE. IT CAN BE STRETCHED TO FEED THE WHOLE FAMILY, AND YOUR NEIGHBOURS, TOO!

SERVES FOUR

INGREDIENTS
  1 litre/1¾ pints/4 cups lamb stock
  1 onion, finely chopped
  2 carrots, finely sliced
  ½ celeriac, finely diced
  75g/3oz/¾ cup frozen peas
  50g/2oz runner (green) beans, cut
    into 2.5cm/1in pieces
  3 tomatoes, seeded and chopped
  1 red (bell) pepper, seeded and
    finely diced
  1 potato, coarsely diced
  2 lemons, sliced
  salt and ground black pepper
  crusty bread, to serve
For the meatballs
  225g/8oz very lean minced
    (ground) lamb
  40g/1½oz/¼ cup short grain rice
  1 onion, chopped
  a pinch allspice
  a pinch cumin
  30ml/2 tbsp chopped fresh parsley
  plain (all-purpose) flour, for coating
  salt and ground black pepper

1 Put the stock, all of the vegetables, the slices of lemon and a little seasoning in a large pan. Bring to the boil, then reduce the heat and simmer for 15–20 minutes.

2 Meanwhile, for the meatballs, combine the minced meat, rice and parsley together in a bowl and season well.

3 Roll the mixture into small balls, roughly the size of walnuts, and toss them in the flour.

4 Drop the meatballs into the soup and simmer gently for 25–30 minutes, stirring occasionally, to prevent the meatballs from sticking. Adjust the seasoning to taste and serve the soup in warmed serving bowls, accompanied by crusty bread.

Energy 257Kcal/1076kJ; Protein 15.9g; Carbohydrate 30g, of which sugars 12.7g; Fat 8.7g, of which saturates 3.8g; Cholesterol 43mg; Calcium 77mg; Fibre 5.2g; Sodium 90mg.

FRAGRANT BEETROOT <u>AND</u> VEGETABLE SOUP
<u>WITH</u> SPICED LAMB KUBBEH

THIS INDIAN-JEWISH VERSION OF BORSCHT BEARS CULINARY HALLMARKS OF THE JEWISH BOGDODI COMMUNITY THAT ONCE FLOURISHED IN INDIA. YOU CAN ENJOY THE SOUP WITHOUT THE DUMPLINGS, AND ALSO THE DUMPLINGS WITHOUT THE SOUP; BOTH ARE DELICIOUS. TWO RECIPES IN ONE!

SERVES SIX TO EIGHT

INGREDIENTS

15ml/1 tbsp vegetable oil
½ onion, finely chopped
6 garlic cloves
1 carrot, diced
1 courgette (zucchini), diced
½ celery stick, diced (optional)
4–5 cardamom pods
2.5ml/½ tsp curry powder
4 vacuum-packed beetroot (beets),
  finely diced and juice reserved
1 litre/1¾ pints/4 cups
  vegetable stock
400g/14oz can chopped tomatoes
45–60ml/3–4 tbsp chopped fresh
  coriander (cilantro) leaves
2 bay leaves
15ml/1 tbsp sugar
salt and ground black pepper
15–30ml/1–2 tbsp white wine
  vinegar, to serve
For the kubbeh
2 large pinches of saffron threads
15ml/1 tbsp hot water
15ml/1 tbsp vegetable oil
1 large onion, chopped
250g/9oz lean minced (ground) lamb
5ml/1 tsp vinegar
½ bunch fresh mint, chopped
115g/4oz/1 cup plain (all-purpose) flour
2–3 pinches of salt
2.5–5ml/½–1 tsp ground turmeric
45–60ml/3–4 tbsp cold water
For the ginger and coriander paste
4 garlic cloves, chopped
15–25ml/1–1½ tbsp chopped
  fresh ginger
½–4 fresh mild chillies
½ large bunch fresh coriander
  (cilantro)
30ml/2 tbsp white wine vinegar
extra virgin olive oil

COOK'S TIP
Serve any leftover paste with meatballs, spread on sandwiches, or spooned over savoury dumplings such as kreplach.

1 To make the paste, put the garlic, ginger and chillies in a food processor and process. Add the coriander, vinegar, oil and salt and process to a purée. Set aside.

2 To make the kubbeh filling, place the saffron and hot water in a small bowl and leave to infuse (steep). Meanwhile, heat the oil in a pan and fry the onion until softened. Put the onion and saffron water in a food processor and blend. Add the lamb, season and blend. Add the vinegar and mint, then chill.

3 To make the kubbeh dough, put the flour, salt and turmeric in a food processor, then slowly add the water, processing until it forms a sticky dough. Knead on a floured surface for 5 minutes, wrap in a plastic bag and leave to stand for 30 minutes.

4 Divide the dough into 10–15 pieces. Roll each into a ball, then, using a pasta machine, roll into very thin rounds.

5 Lay the rounds on a well-floured surface. Place a spoonful of filling in the middle of each. Dampen the edges of the dough, then bring them together and seal. Set aside on a floured surface.

6 To make the soup, heat the oil in a pan, add the onion and fry for about 10 minutes, or until softened but not browned. Add half the garlic, the carrot, courgette, celery, if using, cardamom pods and curry powder, and cook for 2–3 minutes.

7 Add three of the diced beetroot, the stock, tomatoes, coriander, bay leaves and sugar to the pan. Bring to the boil, then reduce the heat and simmer for about 20 minutes.

8 Add the remaining beetroot, beetroot juice and garlic to the soup. Season with salt and pepper to taste and set aside until ready to serve.

9 To serve, reheat the soup and poach the dumplings in a large pan of salted boiling water for about 4 minutes. Using a slotted spoon, remove the dumplings from the water as they are cooked and place on a plate to keep warm.

10 Ladle the soup into bowls, adding a dash of vinegar to each bowl, then add two or three dumplings and a small spoonful of the ginger and coriander paste to each. Serve immediately.

Energy 54Kcal/226kJ; Protein 1.5g; Carbohydrate 5.7g, of which sugars 4.4g; Fat 3g, of which saturates 0.4g; Cholesterol 0mg; Calcium 34mg; Fibre 1.2g; Sodium 24mg.

HARIRA

Harira is a Moroccan meat and vegetable soup which is traditionally eaten during the month of Ramadan, when the Muslim population fasts between sunrise and sunset. Living together in the same communities, the Jews of Morocco also grew to love this hearty, herby-spicy lentil and lamb soup.

SERVES FOUR

INGREDIENTS
    450g/1lb well-flavoured tomatoes
    225g/8oz lamb, cut into pieces
    2.5ml/½ tsp ground turmeric
    2.5ml/½ tsp ground cinnamon
    30ml/2 tbsp vegetable oil
    60ml/4 tbsp chopped fresh coriander
      (cilantro)
    30ml/2 tbsp chopped fresh parsley
    1 onion, chopped
    50g/2oz/¼ cup split red lentils
    75g/3oz/½ cup dried chickpeas,
      soaked overnight in cold water
    600ml/1 pint/2½ cups water
    4 baby (pearl) onions or shallots
    25g/1oz/¼ cup fine noodles
    salt and ground black pepper
    fresh coriander (cilantro), lemon
      slices and ground cinnamon,
      to garnish

COOK'S TIPS
• The skins of the tomatoes can be left on, to save time.
• For maximum cinnamon flavour, grind a broken cinnamon stick in a spice grinder or a coffee grinder kept especially for the purpose.

1 Plunge the tomatoes into boiling water for 30 seconds, then refresh in cold water. Peel off the skins. Cut into quarters and remove the seeds. Chop the flesh roughly.

2 Put the pieces of lamb, ground turmeric, cinnamon, oil, fresh coriander, parsley and onion into a large pan, and cook over a medium heat, stirring, for 5 minutes.

3 Add the chopped tomatoes and continue to cook for 10 minutes, stirring the mixture frequently.

4 Rinse the lentils under running water and drain them well. Stir them into the contents of the pan, with the drained chickpeas and the measured water. Season with salt and pepper. Bring to the boil, lower the heat, cover, and simmer gently for 1½ hours.

5 Add the onions or shallots. Cook for 25 minutes. Add the noodles and cook for 5 minutes more. Spoon into bowls and garnish with the coriander, lemon slices and cinnamon.

Energy 303Kcal/1269kJ; Protein 20.1g; Carbohydrate 26.8g, of which sugars 5.7g; Fat 13.3g, of which saturates 6.4g; Cholesterol 56mg; Calcium 105mg; Fibre 5.2g; Sodium 118mg.

CHAMIM

THIS IS A MORE SOUPY VERSION OF A TRADITIONAL SEPHARDIC SHABBAT DISH. MEATS AND BEANS ARE BAKED IN A VERY LOW OVEN FOR SEVERAL HOURS. A PARCEL OF RICE IS OFTEN ADDED TO THE BROTH PART WAY THROUGH COOKING, TO PRODUCE A LIGHTLY PRESSED RICE WITH A SLIGHTLY CHEWY TEXTURE.

SERVES EIGHT

INGREDIENTS
250g/9oz/1 cup chickpeas,
    soaked overnight
45ml/3 tbsp olive oil
1 onion, chopped
10 garlic cloves, chopped
1 parsnip, sliced
3 carrots, sliced
5–10ml/1–2 tsp ground cumin
2.5ml/½ tsp ground turmeric
15ml/1 tbsp chopped fresh root ginger
2 litres/3½ pints/8 cups beef stock
1 potato, peeled and cut into chunks
½ marrow (large zucchini), sliced or
    cut into chunks
400g/14oz fresh or canned
    tomatoes, diced
45–60ml/3–4 tbsp brown or
    green lentils
2 bay leaves
250g/9oz salted meat such as
    salt beef (or double the quantity
    of lamb)
250g/9oz piece of lamb
½ large bunch fresh coriander
    (cilantro), chopped
200g/7oz/1 cup long grain rice
1 lemon, cut into wedges, and a
    spicy sauce such as zchug or fresh
    chillies, finely chopped, to serve

1 Preheat the oven to 120°C/250°F/ Gas ½. Drain the chickpeas.

2 Heat the oil in a large flameproof casserole, add the onion, garlic, parsnip, carrots, cumin, turmeric and ginger and cook for 2–3 minutes. Add the chickpeas, stock, potato, marrow, tomatoes, lentils, bay leaves, salted meat, lamb and coriander. Cover and cook in the oven for about 3 hours.

COOK'S TIP
Add 1–2 pinches of bicarbonate of soda (baking soda) to the soaking chickpeas to make them tender, but do not add too much as it can make them mushy.

3 Put the rice on a double thickness of muslin (cheesecloth) and tie together at the corners, allowing enough room for the rice to expand while it is cooking.

4 Two hours before the end of cooking, remove the casserole from the oven. Place the rice parcel in the casserole, anchoring the edge of the muslin parcel under the lid so that the parcel is held above the soup and allowed to steam. Return the casserole to the oven and continue cooking for a further 2 hours.

5 Carefully remove the lid and the rice. Skim any fat off the top of the soup and ladle the soup into bowls with a scoop of the rice and one or two pieces of meat. Serve with lemon wedges and a spoonful of hot sauce or chopped fresh chillies.

Energy 463Kcal/1941kJ; Protein 28.5g; Carbohydrate 60.5g, of which sugars 17g; Fat 12.7g, of which saturates 3.5g; Cholesterol 47mg; Calcium 130mg; Fibre 9.4g; Sodium 409mg.

DELI AND BRUNCH

New York deli culture, combined with the growing prosperity of American Jews who no longer needed to work on Sundays, gave way to the Sunday brunch. Each week, families throughout America buy bags of bagels from the bakery, schmears to spread on them and perhaps a few salads from the deli and gather together for brunch. Smoked salmon might be scrambled into eggs or piled on to bagels, matzos may be browned up with eggs into matzo brei, or smoked whitefish flaked into salad with mayonnaise and sour cream.

HUMMUS

ENJOYED THROUGHOUT THE MIDDLE EAST, HUMMUS IS A DELICIOUS PASTE OF CHICKPEAS AND RICH SESAME PURÉE, ENLIVENED WITH GARLIC AND SPIKED WITH TANGY LEMON. IT IS MOST FREQUENTLY SERVED WITH SOFT PITTA, NAAN, OR CRUSTY FRENCH BREAD.

SERVES FOUR TO SIX

INGREDIENTS

    400g/14oz can chickpeas, drained
    60ml/4 tbsp tahini
    2–3 garlic cloves, chopped
    juice of ½–1 lemon
    cayenne pepper
    small pinch to 1.5ml/¼ tsp ground
      cumin, or more to taste
    salt and ground black pepper

VARIATIONS

Throughout Israel you'll find many variations of this traditional hummus.
• Roasted red (bell) pepper hummus: purée one roasted, peeled, red pepper with the above recipe.
• Pine nut hummus: sprinkle pine nuts, paprika and olive oil over the top of the hummus.

1 Using a potato masher or food processor, coarsely mash the chickpeas. If you prefer a smoother purée, process them in a food processor or blender until smooth.

COOK'S TIP

Hummus also makes a delicious bed for shredded schwarna, dona kebab, roasted lamb or meatballs.

2 Mix the tahini into the chickpeas, then stir in the garlic, lemon juice, cayenne, cumin, and salt and pepper to taste. If needed, add a little water. Serve at room temperature.

Energy 138Kcal/577kJ; Protein 6.7g; Carbohydrate 10.9g, of which sugars 0.4g; Fat 7.8g, of which saturates 1g; Cholesterol 0mg; Calcium 97mg; Fibre 3.5g; Sodium 149mg.

MINT AND PARSLEY TAHINI SALAD

TAHINI IS A CREAMY SESAME SEED PASTE THAT FORMS THE BASIS FOR A WIDE VARIETY OF THE MEZE THAT START ISRAELI AND ARAB MEALS. TAHINI IS RICH, HEARTY AND EARTHY AND COMBINES WONDERFULLY WITH FRESH HERBS AND SUBTLE SPICES IN THIS SALAD TO MAKE A LIGHT AND REFRESHING DISH.

SERVES FOUR TO SIX

INGREDIENTS

115g/4oz/½ cup tahini
3 garlic cloves, chopped
½ bunch (about 20g/¾oz) fresh
  mint, chopped
½ bunch (about 20g/¾oz) fresh
  coriander (cilantro), chopped
½ bunch (about 20g/¾oz) fresh flat
  leaf parsley, chopped
juice of ½ lemon, or to taste
pinch of ground cumin
pinch of ground turmeric
pinch of ground cardamom seeds
cayenne pepper, to taste
salt
extra virgin olive oil, warmed pitta
  bread, olives and raw vegetables,
  to serve

1 Combine the tahini with the chopped garlic, fresh herbs and lemon juice in a bowl. Taste and add a little more lemon juice, if you like. Stir in a little water if the mixture seems too dense and thick. Alternatively, place the ingredients in a food processor. Process briefly, then stir in a little water if required.

2 Stir in the cumin, turmeric and cardamom to taste, then season with salt and cayenne pepper.

3 To serve, spoon into a shallow bowl or on to plates and drizzle with olive oil. Serve with warmed pitta bread, olives and raw vegetables.

Energy 122Kcal/505kJ; Protein 4.1g; Carbohydrate 0.9g, of which sugars 0.4g; Fat 11.4g, of which saturates 1.6g; Cholesterol 0mg; Calcium 151mg; Fibre 2.1g; Sodium 7mg.

SALAT HATZILIM

ALSO KNOWN AS BABA GHANOUSH, THIS CREAMY, SMOKY AUBERGINE DIP IS AT ITS BEST WHEN THE AUBERGINE IS VERY SMOKY AND THE MIXTURE IS SPARKY WITH GARLIC AND CUMIN. MAYONNAISE, INSTEAD OF TAHINI, IS A TRADITIONAL LEBANESE AND ISRAELI ADDITION TO MAKE THE SALAD CREAMY.

SERVES TWO TO FOUR

INGREDIENTS

   1 large or 2 medium
      aubergines (eggplants)
   2–4 garlic cloves, chopped, to taste
   30–45ml/2–3 tbsp mayonnaise
      or as needed
   juice of 1 lemon, or to taste
   1.5ml/¼ tsp ground cumin, or
      to taste
   salt
   extra virgin olive oil, for drizzling
   coriander (cilantro) leaves, hot
      pepper sauce and a few olives
      and/or pickled cucumbers and
      (bell) peppers, to garnish
   pitta bread or chunks of crusty
      French bread, to serve

1 Place the aubergine(s) directly over the flame of a gas stove or on the coals of a barbecue. Turn the aubergine(s) fairly frequently until they are deflated and the skin is evenly charred. Remove from the heat with a pair of tongs.

2 Put the aubergine(s) in a plastic bag or in a bowl and seal tightly. Leave to cool for 30–60 minutes.

3 Peel off the blackened skin from the aubergine(s), taking care not to remove much of the flesh, and reserve the juices. Chop the aubergine flesh, either by hand for a textured result or in a food processor for a smooth purée. Put the aubergine in a bowl and stir in the reserved juices.

4 Add the garlic and mayonnaise to the aubergine and stir until smooth and well combined.

5 Stir in the lemon juice, which will thicken the mixture. If the mixture becomes too thick, add a little more lemon juice, or olive oil if you like, to dilute. Season with cumin and salt to taste.

6 Spoon the mixture into a serving bowl. Drizzle with olive oil and garnish with fresh coriander leaves, hot pepper sauce, olives and/or pickled cucumbers and peppers. Serve at room temperature with pitta bread or chunks of crusty French bread.

VARIATION
Instead of mayonnaise use 90–150ml/ 6–10 tbsp tahini for a nuttier flavour.

Energy 91Kcal/375kJ; Protein 1g; Carbohydrate 2.2g, of which sugars 1.5g; Fat 8.8g, of which saturates 1.4g; Cholesterol 8mg; Calcium 8mg; Fibre 1.4g; Sodium 52mg

SMOKY AUBERGINE AND PEPPER SALAD

COOKING THE AUBERGINES WHOLE, OVER AN OPEN FLAME, GIVES THEM A DISTINCTIVE SMOKY FLAVOUR AND AROMA, AS WELL AS TENDER, CREAMY FLESH. THE SUBTLE FLAVOUR OF THE ROASTED AUBERGINE CONTRASTS WONDERFULLY WITH THE STRONG, SWEET FLAVOUR OF THE PEPPERS. THIS DISH IS A MIDDLE EASTERN TAKE ON MEDITERRANEAN ROASTED VEGETABLES. IT IS TYPICAL OF THE MODERN MEDITERRANEAN CUISINE FAVOURED IN ISRAEL TODAY.

SERVES FOUR TO SIX

INGREDIENTS

2 aubergines (eggplants)
2 red (bell) peppers
3–5 garlic cloves, chopped, or more
  to taste
2.5ml/½ tsp ground cumin
juice of ½–1 lemon, to taste
2.5ml/½ tsp sherry or wine vinegar
45–60ml/3–4 tbsp extra virgin
  olive oil
1–2 shakes of cayenne pepper,
  Tabasco or other hot pepper sauce
coarse sea salt
chopped fresh coriander (cilantro),
  to garnish
pitta bread wedges or thinly sliced
  French bread or ciabatta bread,
  sesame seed crackers and cucumber
  slices, to serve

1 Place the aubergines and peppers directly over a medium-low gas flame or on the coals of a barbecue. Turn the vegetables frequently until deflated and the skins are evenly charred.

2 Put the aubergines and peppers in a plastic bag or in a bowl and seal tightly. Leave to cool for 30–40 minutes.

3 Peel the vegetables, reserving the juices, and roughly chop the flesh. Put the flesh in a bowl and add the juices, garlic, cumin, lemon juice, vinegar, olive oil, hot pepper seasoning and salt. Mix well to combine. Turn the mixture into a serving bowl and garnish with coriander. Serve with bread, sesame seed crackers and cucumber slices.

Energy 74Kcal/308kJ; Protein 1g; Carbohydrate 4.7g, of which sugars 4.4g; Fat 5.9g, of which saturates 0.9g; Cholesterol 0mg; Calcium 9mg; Fibre 1.8g; Sodium 3mg.

TABBOULEH

THIS IS A WONDERFULLY REFRESHING, TANGY SALAD OF SOAKED BULGUR WHEAT AND MASSES OF FRESH MINT, PARSLEY AND SPRING ONIONS. LEMON MAKES IT TANGY, GOOD OLIVE OIL GIVES IT CHARACTER, AND THE FRESH VEGETABLES MAKE IT SO REFRESHING. YOU CAN ADD MORE HERBS, OR EVEN DOUBLE THE AMOUNT, FOR A GREENER, LIGHTER SALAD OR DO THE SAME WITH THE BULGAR WHEAT INSTEAD, FOR A HEARTIER DISH. TABBOULEH IS GREAT ALL SUMMER LONG, FOR A PICNIC OR SHABBAT LUNCH.

SERVES FOUR TO SIX

INGREDIENTS
250g/9oz/1½ cups bulgur wheat
1 large bunch spring onions
  (scallions), thinly sliced
1 cucumber, finely chopped or diced
3 tomatoes, chopped
1.5–2.5ml/¼–½ tsp ground cumin
1 large bunch fresh parsley, chopped
1 large bunch fresh mint, chopped
juice of 2 lemons, or to taste
60ml/4 tbsp extra virgin olive oil
salt
olives, lemon wedges, tomato wedges,
  cucumber slices and mint sprigs,
  to garnish (optional)
cos or romaine lettuce and natural
  (plain) yogurt, to serve (optional)

1 Pick over the bulgur wheat to remove any dirt. Place it in a bowl, cover with cold water and leave to soak for about 30 minutes. Tip the bulgur wheat into a sieve (strainer) and drain well, shaking to remove any excess water, then return it to the bowl.

2 Add the spring onions to the bulgur wheat, then mix and squeeze together with your hands to combine.

3 Add the cucumber, tomatoes, cumin, parsley, mint, lemon juice, oil and salt to the bulgur wheat and toss to combine.

4 Heap the tabbouleh on to a bed of lettuce and garnish with olives, lemon wedges, tomato, cucumber and mint sprigs. Serve with a bowl of natural yogurt, if you like.

VARIATION
The French community uses couscous soaked in boiling water in place of the bulgur wheat, and sometimes chopped fresh coriander (cilantro) instead of parsley.

Energy 179Kcal/746kJ; Protein 3.6g; Carbohydrate 24.2g, of which sugars 2.7g; Fat 8.1g, of which saturates 1.1g; Cholesterol 0mg; Calcium 44mg; Fibre 1.4g; Sodium 10mg.

AUBERGINE AND PEPPER CAVIAR

THE GRILLED GREEN PEPPERS GIVE THIS A VERY ROMANIAN FLAVOUR. SERVE AS A MEZE WITH A DAIRY MEAL OR MEAT MEAL, OR AS PART OF A LIGHT LUNCH.

SERVES SIX TO EIGHT

INGREDIENTS

675g/1½lb aubergines (eggplants),
  halved lengthways
2 green (bell) peppers, seeded
  and quartered
45ml/3 tbsp olive oil
2 firm ripe tomatoes, halved, seeded
  and finely chopped
45ml/3 tbsp chopped fresh parsley
  or coriander (cilantro)
2 garlic cloves, crushed
30ml/2 tbsp red wine vinegar
lemon juice, to taste
salt and ground black pepper
sprigs of parsley or coriander,
  to garnish
dark rye bread and lemon wedges,
  to serve

1 Place the aubergines and peppers under a preheated grill (broiler), skin side up, and cook until the skin blisters and chars. Turn the vegetables over and cook for a further 3 minutes. Place in a plastic bag and leave for 10 minutes.

2 Peel away the blackened skin and purée the aubergine and pepper flesh in a food processor.

3 With the motor running, pour the olive oil in a continuous stream through the feeder tube.

4 Carefully remove the blade and stir in the chopped tomatoes, parsley or coriander, garlic, vinegar and lemon juice. Season to taste, garnish with fresh parsley or coriander and serve with dark rye bread and wedges of lemon.

Energy 71Kcal/294kJ; Protein 1.6g; Carbohydrate 5.6g, of which sugars 5.3g; Fat 4.8g, of which saturates 0.7g; Cholesterol 0mg; Calcium 29mg; Fibre 3g; Sodium 8mg.

NEW YORK EGG CREAM

NO EGGS, NO CREAM, JUST THE BEST CHOCOLATE SODA YOU WILL EVER SIP. THIS LEGENDARY DRINK IS EVOCATIVE OF OLD NEW YORK, BUT YOU'LL FIND IT IN DINERS THROUGHOUT THE CITY TODAY. NO ONE KNOWS WHY IT IS CALLED EGG CREAM, BUT SOME SAY IT WAS A WITTY WAY OF DESCRIBING RICHNESS AT A TIME WHEN NO ONE COULD AFFORD TO PUT EXPENSIVE EGGS AND CREAM IN A DRINK.

SERVES ONE

INGREDIENTS
   45–60ml/3–4 tbsp good-quality
      chocolate syrup
   120ml/4fl oz/½ cup chilled milk
   175ml/6fl oz/¾ cup chilled
      carbonated water
   cocoa powder (unsweetened),
      to sprinkle

1 Pour the chocolate syrup into the bottom of a tall glass.

2 Pour the chilled milk on to the chocolate syrup. Pour the carbonated water into the glass, sip up any foam that rises to the top of the glass and continue to add the remaining water. Dust with cocoa powder and serve. Stir well before drinking.

COOK'S TIP
An authentic egg cream is made with an old-fashioned soda siphon (seltzer dispenser) that you press and shpritz.

VARIATION
Though chocolate is most popular, you'll find vanilla and strawberry egg creams, too.

Energy 302Kcal/1266kJ; Protein 6.9g; Carbohydrate 32.9g, of which sugars 32.5g; Fat 16.9g, of which saturates 5.8g; Cholesterol 8mg; Calcium 203mg; Fibre 0.4g; Sodium 74mg.

SWEET AND SOUR CUCUMBER WITH FRESH DILL

THIS IS HALF PICKLE, HALF SALAD — AND TOTALLY DELICIOUS. ENJOY AS AN APPETIZER BEFORE A ROASTED MEAT MAIN COURSE WITH THIN SLICES OF PUMPERNICKEL OR OTHER COARSE, DARK, FULL-FLAVOURED BREAD, OR AS A BAGEL BRUNCH.

SERVES FOUR

INGREDIENTS

1 large or 2 small cucumbers,
  thinly sliced
3 onions, thinly sliced
45ml/3 tbsp sugar
75–90ml/5–6 tbsp white wine vinegar
  or cider vinegar
30–45ml/2–3 tbsp water
30–45ml/2–3 tbsp chopped
  fresh dill
salt

COOK'S TIP
This salad can be kept in the refrigerator
for up to a week.

1 In a bowl, mix together the sliced cucumber and onion, season with salt and toss together until thoroughly combined. Leave to stand in a cool place for 5–10 minutes.

2 Add the sugar, white wine or cider vinegar, water and chopped dill to the cucumber mixture. Toss together until well combined, then chill for a few hours, or until ready to serve.

Energy 76Kcal/322kJ; Protein 1.3g; Carbohydrate 18.4g, of which sugars 16.7g; Fat 0.2g, of which saturates 0g; Cholesterol 0mg; Calcium 34mg; Fibre 1.4g; Sodium 5mg.

CHOPPED EGG AND ONIONS

THIS ASHKENAZIC DISH, ALTHOUGH THE ESSENCE OF MODERN WESTERN DELI FOOD, IS IN FACT ONE OF THE OLDEST DISHES IN JEWISH HISTORY. SOME SAY THAT IT GOES BACK TO ANCIENT EGYPTIAN TIMES. IT IS DELICIOUS PILED ON TO RYE BREAD OR ON TOP OF A TOASTED BAGEL.

SERVES FOUR TO SIX

INGREDIENTS
 8–10 eggs
 6–8 spring onions (scallions) and/or
  1 yellow or white onion, very finely
  chopped, plus extra to garnish
 60–90ml/4–6 tbsp mayonnaise or
  rendered chicken fat
 mild French wholegrain mustard, to
  taste (optional if using chicken fat)
 15ml/1 tbsp chopped fresh parsley
 salt and ground black pepper
 rye toasts or crackers, to serve

COOK'S TIP
The amount of rendered chicken fat or mayonnaise required will depend on how much onion you use in this dish.

1 Put the eggs in a large pan and cover with cold water. Bring the water to the boil and when it boils, reduce the heat and simmer over a low heat for 10 minutes.

2 Hold the eggs under cold running water, then remove the shells, dry the eggs and chop roughly.

3 Place the chopped eggs in a large bowl, add the onions, season generously with salt and pepper and mix well. Add enough mayonnaise or chicken fat to bind the mixture together. Stir in the mustard, if using, and the chopped parsley, or sprinkle the parsley on top to garnish. Chill before serving with rye toasts or crackers.

Energy 195Kcal/1002kJ; Protein 10.8g; Carbohydrate 0.5g, of which sugars 0.5g; Fat 16.9g, of which saturates 3.7g; Cholesterol 325mg; Calcium 57mg; Fibre 0.3g; Sodium 163mg.

ISRAELI WHITE CHEESE AND GREEN OLIVES

ISRAEL'S WONDERFUL CHEESES OF COW, SHEEP AND GOAT'S MILK ARE OFTEN ENJOYED AS PART OF AN ISRAELI BREAKFAST OR LIGHT SUPPER. THEY ARE USUALLY MIXED WITH SEASONINGS SUCH AS THIS ONE WITH PIQUANT GREEN OLIVES. SERVE WITH DRINKS AND LITTLE CRACKERS OR TOAST, OR AS A BRUNCH SPREAD, WITH CHUNKS OF BREAD OR BAGELS.

SERVES FOUR

INGREDIENTS
 175–200g/6–7oz soft white
  (farmer's) cheese
 65g/2½oz feta cheese, preferably
  sheep's milk, lightly crumbled
 20–30 pitted green olives, some
  chopped, the rest halved or quartered
 2–3 large pinches of fresh thyme,
  plus extra to garnish
 2–3 garlic cloves, finely
  chopped (optional)
 crackers, toast or bagels, to serve

VARIATION
Add 115g/4oz chopped smoked salmon and 2 thinly sliced spring onions (scallions) to the cheese mixture.

1 Place the soft cheese in a mixing bowl and stir with the back of a spoon until soft and smooth.

2 Add the crumbled feta cheese to the blended soft cheese and stir until thoroughly combined.

3 Add the olives, thyme and chopped garlic to the cheese mixture and mix well to combine.

4 Spoon the mixture into a bowl, sprinkle with thyme and serve with crackers, toast, chunks of bread or bagels.

Energy 242Kcal/1002kJ; Protein 13.8g; Carbohydrate 0.3g, of which sugars 0.3g; Fat 19.7g, of which saturates 12g; Cholesterol 54mg; Calcium 393mg; Fibre 0.6g; Sodium 972mg.

CRISP DELICATESSEN COLESLAW

THE KEY TO GOOD COLESLAW IS A ZESTY DRESSING AND AN INTERESTING SELECTION OF VEGETABLES.

SERVES SIX TO EIGHT

INGREDIENTS

1 large white or green cabbage, very
  thinly sliced
3–4 carrots, coarsely grated
½ red (bell) pepper, chopped
½ green (bell) pepper, chopped
1–2 celery sticks, finely chopped, or
  5–10ml/1–2 tsp celery seeds
1 onion, chopped
2–3 handfuls of raisins or sultanas
  (golden raisins)
45ml/3 tbsp white wine vinegar or
  cider vinegar
60–90ml/4–6 tbsp sugar, to taste
175–250ml/6–8fl oz/¾–1 cup
  mayonnaise, to bind
salt and ground black pepper

1 Put the cabbage, carrots, peppers, celery or celery seeds, onion, and raisins or sultanas in a salad bowl and mix to combine well. Add the vinegar, sugar, salt and ground black pepper and toss together. Leave to stand for about 1 hour.

2 Stir enough mayonnaise into the salad to lightly bind the ingredients together. Taste the salad for seasoning and sweet-and-sour flavour, adding more sugar, salt and pepper if needed. Chill. Drain off any excess liquid before serving.

Energy 215Kcal/891kJ; Protein 1.6g; Carbohydrate 15.1g, of which sugars 14.6g; Fat 16.8g, of which saturates 2.6g; Cholesterol 16mg; Calcium 46mg; Fibre 2.3g; Sodium 115mg.

POTATO SALAD ᵂᴵᵀᴴ EGG, MAYONNAISE ᴬᴺᴰ OLIVES

*A DELI WITHOUT POTATO SALAD IS UNTHINKABLE! BUT WHICH POTATO SALAD? THERE ARE SO MANY.
THIS VERSION INCLUDES A PIQUANT MUSTARD MAYONNAISE, CHOPPED EGGS AND GREEN OLIVES,
MAKING IT RICH, CREAMY AND ZESTY, AND KEEPING IT PAREVE.*

SERVES SIX TO EIGHT

INGREDIENTS

1kg/2¼lb waxy salad
  potatoes, scrubbed
1 red, brown or white onion,
  finely chopped
2–3 celery sticks, finely chopped
60–90ml/4–6 tbsp chopped
  fresh parsley
15–20 pimento-stuffed olives, halved
3 hard-boiled eggs, chopped
60ml/4 tbsp extra virgin olive oil
60ml/4 tbsp white wine vinegar
15–30ml/1–2 tbsp mild or
  wholegrain mustard
celery seeds, to taste (optional)
175–250ml/6–8fl oz/
  ¾–1 cup mayonnaise
salt and ground black pepper
paprika, to garnish

1 Cook the potatoes in a pan of salted boiling water until tender. Drain, return to the pan and leave for 2–3 minutes to cool and dry a little.

2 When the potatoes are cool enough to handle but still very warm, cut them into chunks or slices and place in a salad bowl.

3 Sprinkle the potatoes with salt and pepper, then add onion, celery, parsley, olives and the chopped eggs. In a jug (pitcher), combine the olive oil, vinegar mustard and celery seeds, if using, pour over the salad and toss to combine. Add enough mayonnaise to bind the salad together. Chill before serving, sprinkled with a little paprika.

Energy 331Kcal/1375kJ; Protein 5.1g; Carbohydrate 21.4g, of which sugars 2.6g; Fat 25.6g, of which saturates 4.2g; Cholesterol 88mg; Calcium 45mg; Fibre 2.1g; Sodium 358mg.

SCRAMBLED EGGS <u>WITH</u> SMOKED SALMON <u>AND</u> ONIONS

IT'S NOT SUNDAY MORNING WITHOUT SMOKED SALMON AND ONIONS, SCRAMBLED SOFTLY WITH EGGS, SERVED WITH FRESH BAGELS AND MUGS OF HOT COFFEE. AT LEAST, NOT IF YOU ARE FROM NEW YORK.

SERVES FOUR

INGREDIENTS
40g/1½oz/3 tbsp unsalted
  (sweet) butter
2 onions, chopped
150–200g/5–7oz smoked
  salmon trimmings
6–8 eggs, lightly beaten
ground black pepper
45ml/3 tbsp chopped fresh chives,
  plus whole chives, to garnish
bagels, to serve

VARIATIONS
Substitute 200–250g/7–9oz diced
kosher salami for the smoked salmon
and cook in oil or pareve margarine.

1 Heat half the unsalted butter in a frying pan, add the chopped onions and fry until softened and just beginning to brown. Add the smoked salmon trimmings to the onions and mix well to combine.

2 Pour the eggs into the pan and stir until soft curds form. Add the remaining butter and stir off the heat until creamy. Season with pepper. Spoon on to serving plates and garnish with chives. Serve with bagels.

Energy 288Kcal/1199kJ; Protein 22.5g; Carbohydrate 3g, of which sugars 2.2g; Fat 21.1g, of which saturates 8.6g; Cholesterol 415mg; Calcium 75mg; Fibre 0.5g; Sodium 907mg.

MATZO BREI

EVERY ASHKENAZIC FAMILY HAS ITS OWN VERSION OF THIS DISH OF SOAKED MATZOS, MIXED WITH EGG AND BROWNED IN A PAN. SOME ARE BIG, MOIST, SOFT PARCELS; SOME ARE SWEET, EATEN WITH JAM AND SOUR CREAM, AND SOME ARE SAVOURY. THIS VERSION IS CRISP, SALTY AND CAN BE BROKEN INTO PIECES AND SHARED AMONG FAMILY AND FRIENDS DURING A COMMUNAL MID-MORNING BRUNCH.

SERVES ONE

INGREDIENTS
    3 matzos, broken into bitesize pieces
    2 eggs, lightly beaten
    30–45ml/2–3 tbsp olive oil or
        25–40g/1–1½oz/2–3 tbsp butter
    salt
    sour cream and fresh dill,
        to serve (optional)

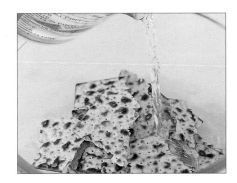

VARIATION
To make a sweet matzo brei pancake, soak the matzos in 250ml/8fl oz/1 cup milk for 5–10 minutes. Add the eggs, a large pinch of ground cinnamon, 15–30ml/ 1–2 tbsp sugar and 2.5ml/½ tsp vanilla extract. Fry the mixture in the oil or butter, turning once. Serve with jam or cinnamon, sugar and sour cream.

1 Put the matzos in a large bowl and pour over cold water to cover. Leave for 2–3 minutes, then drain. Add the eggs.

2 Heat the oil or butter in a frying pan, then add the matzo mixture. Lower the heat and cook for 2–3 minutes until the bottom is golden brown.

3 Break up the matzo brei into pieces, turn them over and brown their other side. Turn once or twice again until the pieces are crisp. (The more times you turn them, the smaller the pieces will become.) Sprinkle with a little salt and serve immediately, with sour cream and dill if you like.

Energy 554Kcal/2296kJ; Protein 15.2g; Carbohydrate 18.9g, of which sugars 0.6g; Fat 47.2g, of which saturates 7.8g; Cholesterol 381mg; Calcium 87mg; Fibre 0.8g; Sodium 258mg.

FALAFEL

THESE DEEP-FRIED CHICKPEA FRITTERS ARE EATEN THROUGHOUT THE MIDDLE EAST, AND ARE ISRAEL'S FAVOURITE STREET FOOD. THE SECRET TO GOOD FALAFEL IS USING WELL-SOAKED, BUT NOT COOKED, CHICKPEAS. DO NOT USE CANNED CHICKPEAS AS THE TEXTURE WILL BE MUSHY AND THE FALAFEL WILL FALL APART WHEN THEY ARE FRIED.

SERVES SIX

INGREDIENTS
  250g/9oz/generous 1⅓ cups
    dried chickpeas
  1 litre/1¾ pints/4 cups water
  45–60ml/3–4 tbsp bulgur wheat
  1 large or 2 small onions, finely chopped
  5 garlic cloves, crushed
  75ml/5 tbsp chopped fresh parsley
  75ml/5 tbsp chopped fresh coriander
    (cilantro) leaves
  45ml/3 tbsp ground cumin
  15ml/1 tbsp ground coriander
  5ml/1 tsp baking powder
  5m/1 tsp salt
  small pinch to 1.5ml/¼ tsp ground
    black pepper
  small pinch to 1.5ml/¼ tsp
    cayenne pepper
  5ml/1 tsp curry powder with a pinch
    of cardamom seeds added (optional)
  45–60ml/3–4 tbsp gram flour
  crumbled wholemeal (whole-wheat)
    bread or flour, if necessary
  vegetable oil, for deep-frying
  6 pitta breads, hummus, chopped
    vegetable salad relish, tahini,
    Tabasco or other hot pepper sauce,
    pickles, olives and salads, such as
    shredded cabbage, to serve

1 Place the chickpeas in a large bowl and pour over the water. Leave to soak for at least 4 hours, then drain and grind in a food processor.

2 Put the ground chickpeas in a bowl and stir in the bulgur wheat, onion, garlic, parsley, fresh coriander, ground cumin and coriander, baking powder, salt, black pepper and cayenne pepper, and curry powder, if using. Stir in 45ml/ 3 tbsp water and leave to stand for about 45 minutes.

3 Stir the gram flour into the falafel batter, adding a little water if it is too thick or a little crumbled wholemeal bread or flour if it is too thin.

4 Using a wet tablespoon and wet hands, shape heaped tablespoons of the falafel mixture into 12–18 balls.

5 Heat the oil for deep-frying in a pan until it is hot enough to brown a cube of bread in 30 seconds. Lower the heat.

6 Add the falafel to the hot oil in batches and cook for 3–4 minutes until golden brown. Remove the cooked falafel with a slotted spoon and drain on kitchen paper before adding more to the oil.

7 Serve the freshly cooked falafel tucked into warmed pitta bread with a spoonful of hummus, vegetable relish and a drizzle of tahini. Accompany with hot pepper sauce, pickles, olives and some salads.

COOK'S TIP
If you wish to prepare the falafel ahead of time, undercook them, then arrange them on a baking sheet and finish cooking them in the oven at 190°C/ 375°F/Gas 5 for about 10 minutes.

Energy 284Kcal/1190kJ; Protein 10.6g; Carbohydrate 31.6g, of which sugars 2.1g; Fat 13.7g, of which saturates 1.5g; Cholesterol 0mg; Calcium 115mg; Fibre 5.7g; Sodium 22mg.

KASHA AND MUSHROOM KNISHES

MADE IN TINY, ONE-BITE PASTRIES, KNISHES ARE DELICIOUS COCKTAIL OR APPETIZER FARE. WHEN MADE AS BIG, HANDFUL-SIZED PASTRIES, THEY ARE THE PERFECT ACCOMPANIMENT TO A LARGE BOWL OF BORSCHT. THEY CAN BE FILLED WITH DAIRY, MEAT OR PAREVE FILLINGS (ALTHOUGH WITH MEAT FILLINGS, OR FOR A MEAT MEAL, A DAIRY-FREE PASTRY SUCH AS PAREVE PUFF BRUSHED WITH OIL MUST BE USED). KNISHES ARE GREAT FOR BRUNCH, OR ALONGSIDE A BOWL OF SOUP ON A WINTER AFTERNOON.

MAKES ABOUT FIFTEEN

INGREDIENTS
40g/1½oz/3 tbsp butter (for a
    dairy meal), or vegetable oil
    (for a pareve filling)
2 onions, finely chopped
200g/7oz/scant 3 cups mushrooms,
    diced (optional)
200–250g/7–9oz/1–1¼ cups
    buckwheat, cooked
handful of mixed dried mushrooms,
    broken into small pieces
200ml/7fl oz/scant 1 cup hot stock,
    preferably mushroom
1 egg, lightly beaten
salt and ground black pepper
For the sour cream pastry
250g/9oz/2¼ cups plain
    (all-purpose) flour
5ml/1 tsp baking powder
2.5ml/½ tsp salt
2.5ml/½ tsp sugar
130g/4½oz/generous ½ cup plus
    15ml/1 tbsp unsalted (sweet)
    butter, cut into small pieces
75g/3oz sour cream or Greek
    (US strained plain) yogurt

1 To make the pastry, sift together the flour, baking powder, salt and sugar, then rub in the butter until the mixture resembles fine breadcrumbs. Add the sour cream or yogurt and mix together to form a dough. Add 5ml/1 tsp water if necessary. Wrap the dough in a plastic bag and chill for about 2 hours.

VARIATIONS
• To make chopped liver knishes, wash, salt and grill (broil) the livers before chopping them. Replace the sour cream pastry with 500g/1¼lb pareve puff or shortcrust pastry and fill with the liver.
• To make smoked salmon knishes, roll puff pastry into rounds about 4–5cm/1½–2in in diameter and fill with a little soft (cream) cheese, shreds of smoked salmon and fresh dill.

2 To make the filling, heat the butter, fat or oil in a pan, add the onions and fresh mushrooms, if using, and fry until soft and browned. Add the buckwheat and cook until slightly browned. Add the dried mushrooms and stock and cook over a medium-high heat until the liquid has been absorbed. Leave to cool, then stir in the egg and season well.

3 Preheat the oven to 200°C/400°F/Gas 6. Roll out the pastry on a lightly floured surface to about 3mm/⅛in thickness, then cut into rectangles (about 7.5 × 16cm/3 × 6¼in). Place 2–3 spoonfuls of the filling in the middle of each piece and brush the edges with water, fold up and pinch together to seal. Bake for 15 minutes.

Energy 210Kcal/876kJ; Protein 3.6g; Carbohydrate 22.7g, of which sugars 2.4g; Fat 12.3g, of which saturates 7.4g; Cholesterol 43mg; Calcium 44mg; Fibre 1.1g; Sodium 86mg.

YOGURT CHEESE IN OLIVE OIL

YOGURT CHEESE IS SIMPLY WELL-DRAINED YOGURT; SERVED WITH HERBS, OLIVE OIL AND ZAHTAR, THE WILD THYME HARVESTED FROM THE HILLS AND MOUNTAINS OF ISRAEL AND THE MIDDLE EAST. IT MAKES A TYPICAL ISRAELI BREAKFAST, ESPECIALLY IN THE COUNTRYSIDE SUCH AS THE GALILEE, AND IS OFTEN ACCDOMPANIED BY PITTA BREAD AND A LITTLE SLICED ONION.

SERVES ABOUT FOUR TO SIX

INGREDIENTS
1 litre/1¾ pints/4 cups Greek (US
    strained plain) sheep's yogurt
salt, to taste
about 300ml/½ pint/ 1¼ cups extra
    virgin olive oil
olives, to garnish
To serve
30ml/2 tbsp chopped fresh herbs,
    such as rosemary, thyme, oregano
    or coriander (cilantro)
several garlic cloves, chopped
zahtar, for sprinkling

VARIATION
Bottle the drained cheese with oil, dried chillies and your choice of fresh herbs to make a wonderful, unusual gourmet gift or an aromatic appetizer.

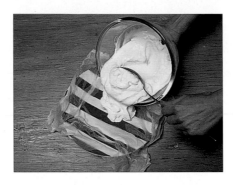 

1 Sterilize a 30cm/12in square of muslin (cheesecloth) by soaking it in boiling water. Drain and lay it over a large plate. Season the yogurt generously with salt and tip on to the centre of the muslin. Bring up the sides of the muslin and tie firmly with string.

2 Hang the bag on a kitchen cabinet handle or suitable position where it can be suspended over a bowl to catch the whey. Leave for 2–3 days until the yogurt stops dripping.

3 Sterilize two 450g/1lb glass preserving or jam jars by heating in the oven at 150°C/300°F/Gas 2 for 15 minutes.

4 Take teaspoonfuls of the cheese and roll into balls with your hands. Pack carefully into the glass jars.

5 Pour the oil over the cheese until completely covered. Store in the refrigerator for up to 2 weeks. To serve, spoon the cheese out of the jars with a little of the olive oil, garnish with olives and serve with the herbs, garlic and zahtar spread on slices of lightly toasted bread.

Energy 291Kcal/1202kJ; Protein 10.7g; Carbohydrate 3.3g, of which sugars 3.3g; Fat 28g, of which saturates 10.2g; Cholesterol 0mg; Calcium 250mg; Fibre 0g; Sodium 118mg.

EGGS WITH CAVIAR

STUFFED EGGS, THE YOLKS MOISTENED WITH MAYONNAISE AND A LITTLE ONION, MUSTARD AND PAPRIKA, IS A DELICIOUS DELI TREAT ON ITS OWN. TOPPED WITH CAVIAR, THOUGH, IT IS FIT FOR THE HAPPIEST OF OCCASIONS. THIS IS A DISH BELOVED OF ALL RUSSIANS, JEWS AND NON-JEWS ALIKE. A CAVIAR IS AS KOSHER AS THE FISH IT COMES FROM. THIS MEANS THAT SALMON, COD AND HERRING ROE ARE FINE, BUT STURGEON IS GENERALLY NOT EATEN. HOWEVER, SOME TURKISH JEWS DO CONSIDER STURGEON ACCEPTABLE BECAUSE IT HAS SCALES FOR THE FIRST FEW MONTHS OF ITS LIFE.

SERVES FOUR

INGREDIENTS
6 eggs, hard-boiled and halved, lengthways
4 spring onions (scallions), very finely sliced
30ml/2 tbsp mayonnaise
1.5ml/¼ tsp Dijon mustard
25g/1oz/2 tbsp caviar or black lumpfish roe
salt and ground black pepper
small sprigs of dill, to garnish
watercress or rocket (arugula), to serve

COOK'S TIP
There are many different kinds of caviar available to buy, and your choice can depend on how much colour you want to add to a meal or snack:
Beluga is the largest member of the sturgeon family and the eggs are a pearly-grey colour. Oscietra comes from a smaller sturgeon and the eggs have a golden tinge. Sevruga caviar is less expensive than other types, as it produces eggs at a much younger age. Lumpfish roe, not a true caviar, has black or orange eggs. Salmon roe, from the red salmon, has large, translucent pinky-orange eggs.

VARIATION
A new and interesting variation on the caviar theme is the version made from seaweed, which is – of course – 100% kosher. Availability in shops and delis is still limited, but this vegetarian caviar has found its way on to a number of restaurant menus and demand should increase in the coming years.

1 Remove the yolks from the halved eggs. Mash the yolks to a smooth paste in a bowl with the spring onions, mayonnaise and mustard. Mix well and season with salt and pepper.

2 Fill the egg whites with the yolk mixture and arrange them on a serving dish. Spoon a little caviar or roe on top of each before serving with watercress or rocket.

Energy 170Kcal/706kJ; Protein 10.4g; Carbohydrate 0.4g, of which sugars 0.4g; Fat 14.4g, of which saturates 3.3g; Cholesterol 309mg; Calcium 48mg; Fibre 0.2g; Sodium 272mg.

SMOKED SALMON PÂTÉ

SMOKED SALMON — LOX — AND CREAM CHEESE! IS THERE A MORE PERFECT COMBINATION? SMEAR IT ON A BAGEL, OR WHIP UP A CHIC LITTLE PÂTÉ SUCH AS THIS ONE. SALTED, BRINED AND SMOKED FISH WERE VERY POPULAR IN THE EASTERN EUROPEAN SHTETLACH, AS THEY KEPT THROUGH THE LONG, COLD WINTERS. CREAM CHEESE WAS A MUCH BELOVED DELICACY, SOLD FROM EARTHENWARE POTS.

SERVES FOUR

INGREDIENTS
  350g/12oz thinly sliced
    smoked salmon
  250g/8oz cream cheese
  1 shallot, chopped
  salt and ground black pepper
  few drops of lemon juice
  thin crisp toast, to serve

1 Line four small ramekins with clear film (plastic wrap). Line the dishes with 115g/4oz of the smoked salmon, cut into strips long enough to flop over the edges.

2 Put the remaining smoked salmon into a food processor and add the cream cheese. Process until smooth, then add the shallots, salt and ground black pepper. If the salmon is quite oily, it may also be necessary to add a few drops of lemon juice.

3 Pack the lined ramekins with the smoked salmon pâté. Fold over the loose strips of salmon to cover the pâté completely. Cover and chill for at least 30 minutes, then turn out of the moulds, lift off and discard the clear film, and serve with the Melba toast.

COOK'S TIP
Process the salmon in short bursts until it is just smooth. Don't over-process the pâté or it will thicken too much and the texture will be compromised.

VARIATIONS
• Try this with smoked trout, which has a lovely rosy colour and a more delicate flavour than smoked salmon.
• A little horseradish cream makes a good addition, but don't overdo it, or you won't be able to taste the smoked fish.
• Chopped chives, spring onion (scallions) or dill are all delicious added to the creamy filling.

Energy 401Kcal/1664kJ; Protein 24.3g; Carbohydrate 0.6g, of which sugars 0.4g; Fat 33.7g, of which saturates 19.3g; Cholesterol 90mg; Calcium 80mg; Fibre 0.1g; Sodium 1833mg.

HERRING SPREAD WITH HORSERADISH

VAST QUANTITIES OF HERRING ARE FISHED IN THE BALTIC SEA TO THE NORTH OF POLAND. THERE IS ONE THING YOU CAN BE SURE OF AT ANY EASTERN EUROPEAN OR RUSSIAN FEAST AND THAT IS THAT YOU'LL START WITH HERRING, HERRING, AND MORE HERRING. SERVE IT SPREAD ON THINLY SLICED RYE BREAD AS A SUNDAY BRUNCH.

SERVES FOUR

INGREDIENTS
    2 fresh herrings, filleted
    50g/2oz/4 tbsp butter, softened
    5ml/1 tsp creamed horseradish sauce
    freshly ground black pepper
To serve
    4 slices rye bread
    1 small onion, cut into rings
    1 red eating apple, cored and sliced
    15ml/1 tbsp lemon juice
    45ml/3 tbsp sour cream

COOK'S TIP
Ice-cold vodka makes another fantastic accompaniment – and is the perfect start to a lazy brunch!

1 Chop the herrings into pieces and put in a food processor with the butter, horseradish sauce and pepper. Process until smooth.

2 Spoon the pâté into a bowl. Cover with clear film and chill for 1 hour. Serve on rye bread, add onion rings and apple slices, tossed in lemon juice.

Energy 171Kcal/705kJ; Protein 7.2g; Carbohydrate 0.3g, of which sugars 0.2g; Fat 15.7g, of which saturates 7.9g; Cholesterol 47mg; Calcium 27mg; Fibre 0g; Sodium 133mg.

MARINATED HERRINGS

THIS IS A CLASSIC ASHKENAZIC DISH, SWEET-AND-SOUR AND LIGHTLY SPICED. IT IS DELICIOUS FOR SUNDAY BRUNCH AND IS ALWAYS WELCOME AT A SHABBAT MIDDAY KIDDUSH RECEPTION. IF THERE IS ANYTHING YOU CAN BE SURE OF AT AN ASHKENAZIC GATHERING, IT'S HERRING.

SERVES FOUR TO SIX

INGREDIENTS
2–3 herrings, filleted
1 onion, sliced
juice of 1 ½ lemons
30ml/2 tbsp white wine vinegar
25ml/1 ½ tbsp sugar
10–15 black peppercorns
10–15 allspice berries
1.5ml/¼ tsp mustard seeds
3 bay leaves, torn
salt

1 Soak the herrings in cold water for 5 minutes, then drain. Pour over water to cover and soak for 2–3 hours, then drain. Pour over water to cover and leave to soak overnight.

2 Hold the soaked herrings under cold running water and rinse very well, both inside and out.

3 Cut each fish into bitesize pieces, then place the pieces in a glass bowl or shallow dish.

4 Sprinkle the onion over the fish, then add the lemon juice, vinegar, sugar, peppercorns, allspice, mustard seeds, bay leaves and salt. Add enough water to just cover. Cover the bowl and chill for 2 days to allow the flavours to blend before serving.

Energy 115Kcal/481kJ; Protein 9g; Carbohydrate 5.2g, of which sugars 4.9g; Fat 6.6g, of which saturates 1.7g; Cholesterol 25mg; Calcium 35mg; Fibre 0.1g; Sodium 61mg.

WHITEFISH SALAD

SMOKED WHITEFISH IS ONE OF THE GLORIES OF THE DELI. IT'S DELICIOUS EATEN PLAIN, BUT WHEN MADE INTO A SALAD WITH MAYONNAISE AND SOUR CREAM, IT MAKES A WONDERFUL SUNDAY BRUNCH OR SHABBAT LUNCH. EAT IT WITH BAGELS, PUMPERNICKEL OR RYE BREAD AND CUCUMBER SALAD.

SERVES FOUR TO SIX

INGREDIENTS

1 smoked whitefish, skinned
  and boned
2 celery sticks, chopped
½ red, white or yellow onion
  or 3–5 spring onions
  (scallions), chopped
45ml/3 tbsp mayonnaise
45ml/3 tbsp sour cream or Greek
  (US strained plain) yogurt
juice of ½–1 lemon
1 round lettuce
ground black pepper
5–10ml/1–2 tsp chopped fresh
  parsley, to garnish

1 Break the smoked fish into bitesize pieces. In a bowl, combine the chopped celery, onion or spring onion, mayonnaise, and sour cream or yogurt, and add lemon juice to taste.

2 Fold the fish into the mixture and season with pepper. Arrange the lettuce leaves on serving plates, then spoon the whitefish salad on top. Serve chilled, sprinkled with parsley.

Energy 95Kcal/393kJ; Protein 5.8g; Carbohydrate 1.3g, of which sugars 1g; Fat 7.4g, of which saturates 1.8g; Cholesterol 24mg; Calcium 17mg; Fibre 0.3g; Sodium 61mg.

FISH DISHES

Fish is pareve and so may be eaten with either meat or dairy foods. This provides great variety and flexibility within the otherwise demanding laws of Kashrut. Having fish as a main course means that you can serve an elegant entertaining menu that has butter, cheeses and rich dairy desserts, without worrying about the lack of meat. Both Ashkenazim and Sephardim have many traditional fish dishes, from the fried fish of London's East End to whole fish baked with fragrant spices in Israel.

CLASSIC ASHKENAZIC GEFILTE FISH

GEFILTE MEANS STUFFED AND ORIGINALLY THIS MIXTURE OF CHOPPED FISH WAS STUFFED BACK INTO THE SKIN OF THE FISH BEFORE COOKING. OVER THE CENTURIES, IT HAS EVOLVED INTO THE CLASSIC BALLS OF CHOPPED FISH THAT ARE SERVED AT THE START OF MOST JEWISH FESTIVITIES. THE AMOUNT OF SUGAR AND PEPPER USED USUALLY REFLECTS THE REGION OF ORIGIN.

SERVES EIGHT

INGREDIENTS

1kg/2¼lb of 2–3 varieties of fish
   fillets, such as carp, whitefish,
   yellow pike, haddock and cod
2 eggs
120ml/4fl oz/½ cup cold water
30–45ml/2–3 tbsp medium
   matzo meal
15–45ml/1–3 tbsp sugar
fish stock, for simmering
2–3 onions
3 carrots
1–2 pinches of ground cinnamon
salt and ground black pepper
horseradish and beetroot (beets),
   to serve

1 Place the fish fillets on a plate, sprinkle with salt and chill for 1 hour, or until the flesh has firmed. Rinse the fish well, then put in a food processor or blender and process until minced (ground).

2 Put the fish into a bowl, add the eggs, mix, then gradually add the water. Stir in the matzo meal, then the sugar and seasoning. Beat until light and aerated; cover and chill for 1 hour.

3 Take 15–30ml/1–2 tbsp of the mixture and, with wet hands, roll into a ball. Continue with the remaining mixture.

4 Bring a large pan of fish stock to the boil, reduce to a simmer, then add the fishballs. Return to the boil, then simmer for about 1 hour. (Add more water during cooking, if necessary, to keep the balls covered with liquid.)

5 Add the onions, carrots, cinnamon and a little extra sugar, if you like, to the pan and simmer, uncovered, for 45–60 minutes. Add more water, if necessary, to keep the balls covered.

6 Leave the fish to cool slightly, then remove from the liquid. Serve warm or cold with horseradish and beetroot.

Energy 159kcal/667kJ; Protein 25.5g; Carbohydrate 8.7g, of which sugars 4.7g; Fat 2.6g, of which saturates 0.5g; Cholesterol 105mg; Calcium 37mg; Fibre 1.4g; Sodium 100mg.

BRITISH FRIED FISH PATTIES

THESE PATTIES OF CHOPPED, SEASONED FISH — THE FRIED VERSION OF GEFILTE FISH — ARE POPULAR WITH BRITISH JEWS. THEY WERE LIKELY TO HAVE BEEN MADE THIS WAY BY PORTUGUESE JEWS WHO CAME TO ENGLAND IN THE 16TH CENTURY.

MAKES TWELVE TO FOURTEEN

INGREDIENTS
  450g/1lb haddock fillet, skinned
  450g/1lb cod fillet, skinned
  2 eggs
  50–65g/2–2½oz matzo meal, plus
    extra for coating
  10ml/2 tsp salt
  5ml/1 tsp sugar
  15ml/1 tbsp vegetable oil
  15ml/1 tbsp chopped fresh parsley
  2 onions, chopped
  vegetable oil, for frying
  ground black pepper
  chrain or other spicy condiment,
    to serve

1 Mince (grind) or finely chop the fish in a food processor or by hand. Add the eggs, matzo meal, salt, sugar, oil, parsley, onions and a little pepper. Combine to form a batter.

2 The batter should be firm enough to shape into a soft patty. If it is too thin, add a little more matzo meal and if too thick, add 15–30ml/1–2 tbsp water. Cover and chill for at least 1 hour.

3 Form the mixture into round patties measuring about 6cm/2½in in diameter and 2cm/¾in thick.

4 Put some matzo meal on a plate and use to coat each patty. Place the coated patties on another plate.

5 Heat the oil in a pan until it is hot enough to brown a cube of bread in 30 seconds. Add the patties, and fry for 7–8 minutes, turning occasionally, until they are golden brown on both sides. Place on kitchen paper to drain. Serve hot or cold with one or more spicy condiments.

VARIATION

To make a Sephardi version, add a little chopped garlic to the fish mixture and fry the patties in olive oil.

Energy 123kcal/513kJ; Protein 13.4g; Carbohydrate 3.8g, of which sugars 0.9g; Fat 6.1g, of which saturates 0.8g; Cholesterol 54mg; Calcium 15mg; Fibre 0.2g; Sodium 332mg.

GINGER FISHBALLS IN TOMATO AND PRESERVED LEMON SAUCE

THESE SPICY BALLS OF FISH AND GINGER COOKED IN A SAUCE OF TOMATOES AND PRESERVED LEMON ARE A SPECIALITY OF THE JEWS OF MOROCCO. ENJOY THEM WITH RICE, COUSCOUS OR SOFT FLAT BREAD, TO SOAK UP THE DELICIOUS SAUCE.

SERVES SIX

INGREDIENTS
  65g/2½ oz bread (about 2 slices)
  1kg/2¼ lb minced (ground) fish such
    as cod, haddock or whiting
  2 onions, chopped
  8 garlic cloves, chopped
  2.5–5ml/½–1 tsp ground turmeric
  2.5ml/½ tsp ground ginger
  2.5ml/½ tsp ras al hanout or
    garam masala
  1 bunch fresh coriander (cilantro),
    chopped, plus extra to garnish
  1 egg
  cayenne pepper, to taste
  150ml/¼ pint/⅔ cup vegetable or
    olive oil or a combination of both
  4 ripe tomatoes, diced
  5ml/1 tsp paprika
  1 preserved lemon, rinsed and cut
    into small strips
  salt and ground black pepper
  ½ lemon, cut into wedges, to serve

1 Remove the crusts from the bread, put the bread in a bowl and pour over cold water. Leave to soak for about 10 minutes, then squeeze dry.

2 Add the fish to the bread with half the onions, half the garlic, half the turmeric, the ginger, half the ras al hanout or garam masala, half the coriander, the egg and cayenne pepper and seasoning. Mix together and chill while you make the sauce.

3 To make the sauce, heat the oil in a pan, add the remaining onion and garlic and fry for about 5 minutes, or until softened. Sprinkle in the remaining turmeric and ras al hanout or garam masala and warm through.

VARIATION
Use a fresh lemon, instead of the preserved lemon, if you prefer. Cut it into small dice and add with the tomatoes.

4 Add the diced tomatoes, paprika and half the remaining coriander to the pan and cook over a medium heat until the tomatoes have formed a sauce consistency. Stir in the strips of preserved lemon.

5 With wet hands, roll walnut-size lumps of the fish mixture into balls and flatten slightly. Place in the sauce. Cook gently, for 15–20 minutes, turning twice. Garnish with coriander and serve with lemon wedges for squeezing.

Energy 341kcal/1422kJ; Protein 33.4g; Carbohydrate 8.8g, of which sugars 4g; Fat 19.3g, of which saturates 2.5g; Cholesterol 108mg; Calcium 68mg; Fibre 1.8g; Sodium 169mg.

MOROCCAN GRILLED FISH BROCHETTES

SERVE THESE DELICIOUS KEBABS WITH POTATOES, AUBERGINE SLICES AND STRIPS OF RED PEPPER, WHICH CAN BE COOKED ON THE BARBECUE ALONGSIDE THE FISH BROCHETTES. THE SPICE AND HERB MARINADE IS CALLED CHERMOULA, AND IS A FAVOURITE OF MOROCCAN JEWS. THE JEWS OF FEZ ARE SAID TO MAKE A PARTICULARLY DELICIOUS CHERMOULA.

SERVES FOUR TO SIX

INGREDIENTS
5 garlic cloves, chopped
2.5ml/½ tsp paprika
2.5ml/½ tsp ground cumin
2.5–5ml/½–1 tsp salt
2–3 pinches of cayenne pepper
60ml/4 tbsp olive oil
30ml/2 tbsp lemon juice
30ml/2 tbsp chopped fresh coriander
  (cilantro) or parsley
675g/1½lb firm-fleshed white fish,
  such as haddock, halibut, sea bass,
  snapper or turbot, cut into
  2.5–5cm/1–2in cubes
3–4 green (bell) peppers, cut into
  2.5–5cm/1–2in pieces
2 lemon wedges, to serve

1 Put the garlic, paprika, cumin, salt, cayenne pepper, oil, lemon juice and coriander or parsley in a large bowl and mix together. Add the fish and toss to coat. Leave to marinate for at least 30 minutes, and preferably 2 hours, at room temperature, or chill overnight.

2 About 40 minutes before you are going to cook the brochettes, light the barbecue. The barbecue is ready when the coals have turned white and grey.

3 Meanwhile, thread the fish cubes and pepper pieces alternately on to wooden or metal skewers.

4 Grill the brochettes on the barbecue for 2–3 minutes on each side, or until the fish is tender and lightly browned. Serve with lemon wedges.

COOK'S TIP
If you are using wooden skewers for the brochettes, soak them in cold water for 30 minutes before using to prevent them from burning.

Energy 178kcal/743kJ; Protein 21.3g; Carbohydrate 45g, of which sugars 4.1g; Fat 8.4g, of which saturates 1.2g; Cholesterol 52mg; Calcium 17mg; Fibre 1.1g; Sodium 70mg.

MUSHROOM-STUFFED FRIED FISH FILLETS

MARINATED FISH ROLLED AROUND A MUSHROOM FILLING AND FINELY CRUMBED AND FRIED, THIS DISH BEARS THE HALLMARK OF THE RUSSIAN KITCHEN.

SERVES FOUR

INGREDIENTS

  8 sole, whiting or other white fish
    fillets, about 200g/7oz, skinned
  45ml/3 tbsp olive oil
  15ml/1 tbsp lemon juice
  25g/1oz/2 tbsp butter
  175g/6oz/2 cups button (white)
    mushrooms, very finely chopped
  4 anchovy fillets, finely chopped
  5ml/1 tsp chopped fresh thyme, plus
    extra to garnish
  2 eggs, beaten
  115g/4oz/2 cups white breadcrumbs
  oil, for deep frying
  salt and ground black pepper
  grilled (broiled) chicory (Belgian
    endive), to serve

1 Lay the fish fillets in a single layer in a glass dish. Mix together the oil and lemon juice and sprinkle over. Cover with clear film (plastic wrap) and marinate in the refrigerator for 1 hour.

2 Melt the butter in a pan and gently fry the mushrooms for 5 minutes, until tender and all the juices have evaporated. Stir in the chopped anchovies, thyme, salt and pepper.

3 Divide the mixture equally and spread evenly over the fish. Roll up and secure with cocktail sticks (toothpicks).

COOK'S TIP
To skin the fillets, slice the flesh away from the skin using a sharp knife. Keep the knife parallel to the fish and the skin taut.

4 Dip each fish roll in beaten egg, then in breadcrumbs to coat. Repeat this process. Heat the oil to 180°C/350°F/Gas 4.

5 Deep fry in 2 batches for 4–5 minutes, or until well browned and cooked through. Drain on kitchen paper. Remove the cocktail sticks and sprinkle with thyme. Serve with grilled chicory.

Energy 410kcal/1760kJ; Protein 17.2g; Carbohydrate 22.5g, of which sugars 0.9g; Fat 28.6g, of which saturates 6.6g; Cholesterol 133mg; Calcium 69mg; Fibre 1.1g; Sodium 442mg.

CARP WITH GREEN HORSERADISH SAUCE

THIS ASHKENAZIC DISH IS FROM ALSACE, FRANCE, WHERE FRESHWATER FISH, SUCH AS CARP,
ARE FAVOURED IN LOCAL CUISINE. SHARP HORSERADISH IS A TRADITIONAL PAIRING.

SERVES FOUR

INGREDIENTS
   675g/1½lb carp, skinned and filleted
   45ml/3 tbsp plain (all-purpose) flour
   1 egg, beaten
   115g/4oz/2 cups fresh white
     breadcrumbs
   sunflower oil, for frying
   salt and ground black pepper
   lemon wedges, to serve
For the sauce
   15g/½oz fresh horseradish,
     finely grated
   pinch of salt
   150ml/¼ pint/⅔ cup double
     (heavy) cream
   1 bunch watercress, trimmed and
     finely chopped
   30ml/2 tbsp chopped fresh chives
   2 eggs, hard-boiled and finely
     chopped (optional)

1 Cut the fish into thin strips, about 6cm/2½in long by 1cm/½in thick. Season the flour with salt and pepper. Dip the strips of fish in the flour, then in the beaten egg and finally coat in the breadcrumbs.

2 Heat 1cm/½in of oil in a frying pan. Fry the fish in batches for 3–4 minutes, until golden brown. Drain on kitchen paper and keep warm until all the strips are cooked.

3 For the sauce, put the horseradish, salt, cream and watercress in a small pan. Bring to the boil and simmer for 2 minutes. Stir in the chives and eggs, if using. Serve the sauce with the fish.

Energy 618kcal/2576kJ; Protein 36.2g; Carbohydrate 27.2g, of which sugars 1.9g; Fat 41.3g, of which saturates 15.8g; Cholesterol 212mg; Calcium 193mg; Fibre 1.4g; Sodium 354mg.

WHITEBAIT ESCABECHE

THE JEWISH COMMUNITY IN PERU DATES BACK TO THE TIME FOLLOWING THE SPANISH INQUISITION. MANY CAME TO PERU FROM RUSSIA IN THE 1920S, TO ALL PARTS OF SOUTH AMERICA TO FLEE THE NAZIS OR TO RELOCATE AFTER THE HOLOCAUST. PERU HAS A CONSTELLATION OF ESCABECHES AND CEVICHES. THIS ONE IS PARTICULARLY JEWISH AS NO SHELLFISH ARE INVOLVED.

3 Fry the fish in small batches, until golden brown, then put in a shallow serving dish and set aside.

4 In a separate pan, heat 30ml/2 tbsp of oil. Add the onions, cumin seeds, carrots, chillies and garlic and fry for 5 minutes, until the onions are softened. Add the vinegar, oregano and coriander, stir well and cook for 1–2 minutes.

5 Pour the onion mixture over the fried fish and leave to cool. Serve the fish at room temperature, garnished with slices of corn on the cob, black olives and coriander leaves.

COOK'S TIP
When selecting whitebait or any other smelt, make sure the fish are very tiny as they are eaten whole.

VARIATION
If you prefer, use chunks of any firm white fish such as cod or halibut instead of tiny whole fish.

SERVES FOUR

INGREDIENTS
800g/1¾lb whitebait
juice of 2 lemons
5ml/1 tsp salt
plain (all-purpose) flour, for dusting
vegetable oil, for frying
2 onions, chopped or thinly sliced
2.5–5ml/½–1 tsp cumin seeds
2 carrots, thinly sliced
2 jalapeño chillies, chopped
8 garlic cloves, roughly chopped
120ml/4fl oz/½ cup white wine or
   cider vinegar
2–3 large pinches of dried oregano
15–30ml/1–2 tbsp chopped fresh
   coriander (cilantro) leaves
slices of corn on the cob, black olives
   and coriander, to garnish

1 Put the fish in a bowl, add the lemon juice and salt and leave to marinate for 30–60 minutes. Remove the fish from the bowl and dust with flour.

2 Heat the oil in a deep frying pan until hot enough to turn a cube of bread golden brown in 30 seconds.

Energy 1087kcal/4504kJ; Protein 40.3g; Carbohydrate 18.5g, of which sugars 5.9g; Fat 95.3g, of which saturates 8.9g; Cholesterol 0mg; Calcium 1743mg; Fibre 2.3g; Sodium 471mg.

FILO-WRAPPED FISH

THIS DELICIOUS DISH COMES FROM JERUSALEM, WHERE WHOLE FISH ARE WRAPPED IN FILO PASTRY AND SERVED WITH A ZESTY TOMATO SAUCE. HOWEVER, IT IS MORE CONTEMPORARY TO PREPARE THIS DISH USING FRESH FILLETED FISH OR FISH STEAKS.

SERVES THREE TO FOUR

INGREDIENTS

    450g/1lb salmon or cod steaks
      or fillets
    1 lemon
    30ml/2 tbsp olive oil, plus extra
      for brushing
    1 onion, chopped
    2 celery sticks, chopped
    1 green (bell) pepper, diced
    5 garlic cloves, chopped
    400g/14oz fresh or canned
      tomatoes, chopped
    120ml/4fl oz/½ cup passata
      (bottled strained tomatoes)
    30ml/2 tbsp chopped fresh flat
      leaf parsley
    2–3 pinches of ground allspice or
      ground cloves
    cayenne pepper, to taste
    pinch of sugar
    about 130g/4½oz filo pastry
      (6–8 large sheets)
    salt and ground black pepper

1 Sprinkle the salmon or cod steaks or fillets with salt and black pepper and a squeeze of lemon juice. Set aside while you prepare the sauce.

2 Heat the olive oil in a pan, add the chopped onion, celery and pepper and fry for about 5 minutes, until the vegetables are softened. Add the garlic and cook for a further 1 minute, then add the tomatoes and passata and cook until the tomatoes are of a sauce consistency.

3 Stir the parsley into the sauce, then season with allspice or cloves, cayenne pepper, sugar and salt and pepper.

4 Preheat the oven to 200°C/400°F/ Gas 6. Take a sheet of filo pastry, brush with a little olive oil and cover with a second sheet. Place a piece of fish on top of the pastry, towards the bottom edge, then top with 1–2 spoonfuls of the sauce, spreading it evenly.

5 Roll the fish in the pastry, taking care to enclose the filling completely. Arrange on a baking sheet and repeat with the remaining fish and pastry. You should have about half the sauce remaining, to serve with the fish.

6 Bake for 10–15 minutes, or until golden. Meanwhile, reheat the remaining sauce if necessary. Serve immediately with the remaining sauce.

Energy 266kcal/1122kJ; Protein 24.6g; Carbohydrate 27.6g, of which sugars 8g; Fat 7.2g, of which saturates 1.1g; Cholesterol 52mg; Calcium 69mg; Fibre 3g; Sodium 158mg.

PIKE <u>AND</u> RUSSIAN SALMON MOUSSE

A LIGHT-TEXTURED LOAF OF PIKE MOUSSE LAYERED WITH POACHED SALMON, THIS DISH IS AN UNUSUAL TREAT FROM THE TRADITIONAL ASHKENAZIC REPERTOIRE.

<u>SERVES EIGHT</u>

INGREDIENTS
225g/8oz salmon fillets, skinned
600ml/1 pint/2½ cups fish stock
finely grated rind and juice of
  ½ lemon
900g/2lb pike fillets, skinned
4 egg whites
475ml/16fl oz/2 cups double
  (heavy) cream
30ml/2 tbsp chopped fresh dill
salt and ground black pepper
red salmon caviar and dill sprigs,
  to garnish

1 Preheat the oven to 180°C/350°F/
Gas 4. Line a 900g/2lb loaf tin (pan)
with greaseproof paper and oil.

2 Cut the salmon into 5cm/2in strips.
Place the stock and lemon juice in a
pan and bring to the boil, then turn off
the heat. Add the salmon strips, cover
and leave the mixture to bubble gently
for 2 minutes. Remove the salmon
with a slotted spoon.

3 Cut the pike into cubes and process
in a food processor or blender until
smooth. Lightly whisk the egg whites
with a fork. With the motor running,
slowly pour in the egg whites, then the
cream. Finally, add the lemon rind, dill
and seasoning.

4 Arrange the poached salmon strips
on top, then carefully spoon in the
remaining pike mixture.

5 Cover the loaf tin with foil and put in
a roasting pan. Add enough boiling
water to come halfway up the sides of
the loaf tin. Bake for 45–50 minutes, or
until firm.

6 Leave on a wire rack to cool, then
chill for at least 3 hours. Turn out on to
a serving plate and remove the lining
paper. Serve the mousse cut into
slices and garnished with red salmon
caviar and a sprig of dill.

Energy 477kcal/1977kJ; Protein 27.8g; Carbohydrate 1g, of which sugars 1g; Fat 40.3g, of which saturates 21.4g; Cholesterol 171mg; Calcium 89mg; Fibre 0g; Sodium 105mg.

SALMON KULEBYAKA

THIS LUXURIOUS COMBINATION OF SALMON, RICE AND PUFF PASTRY IS ONE OF RUSSIA'S MOST FAMOUS DISHES. ALTHOUGH THIS IS A SIMPLIFIED VERSION, IT IS STILL PERFECT FOR THE FESTIVE TABLE.

SERVES FOUR

INGREDIENTS

   50g/2oz/4 tbsp butter
   1 small onion, finely chopped
   175g/6oz/1 cup cooked long
     grain rice
   15ml/1 tbsp chopped fresh dill
   15ml/1 tbsp lemon juice
   450g/1lb thawed puff pastry
   450g/1lb salmon fillet, skinned
   3 eggs, hard-boiled and
     left to cool
   beaten egg, for sealing and glazing
   salt and ground black pepper
   watercress or rocket (arugula),
     to garnish

1 Preheat the oven to 200°C/400°F/Gas 6. Melt the butter in a pan, add the finely chopped onion and cook gently for 10 minutes, or until soft.

2 Stir in the cooked rice, dill, lemon juice, salt and pepper.

3 Roll out the puff pastry on a lightly floured surface to a 30cm/12in square. Spoon the rice mixture over half the pastry, leaving a 1cm/½in border around the edges.

4 Cut the salmon into 5cm/2in pieces and arrange on top of the bed of rice so that the pieces lie flat. Chop up the hard-boiled egg into little pieces and place in a small bowl.

5 Sprinkle the chopped eggs over the top of the salmon, using a fork, and press flat.

6 Brush the pastry edges with egg, fold it over the filling to make a rectangle and press the edges together firmly to seal.

7 Carefully lift the pastry on to a lightly oiled baking sheet. Glaze with beaten egg, then pierce the pastry a few times with a skewer to make holes for the steam to escape.

8 Bake on the middle shelf of the oven for 40 minutes, covering with foil after 30 minutes. Leave to cool on the baking sheet, before cutting into slices. Garnish with watercress or rocket.

Energy 933kcal/3888kJ; Protein 37.3g; Carbohydrate 77.8g, of which sugars 2.4g; Fat 54.6g, of which saturates 9.8g; Cholesterol 226mg; Calcium 125mg; Fibre 0.2g; Sodium 528mg.

FISH BAKED <u>IN A</u> DOUGH JACKET

WRAP A WHOLE FISH UP IN BREAD DOUGH THEN BAKE UNTIL THE DOUGH BECOMES A CRISP CASE AND THE FISH A FLAVOURFUL, TENDER FILLING. SERVE WITH A ZCHUG OR HOISIN SAUCE.

SERVES FOUR TO SIX

INGREDIENTS
 about 1kg/2¼lb whole fish, such as
  grey mullet, red snapper or
  pompano, skinned and cleaned
 flaked sea salt
 sprigs of fennel, to garnish
 lemon wedges and courgette
  (zucchini) and dill salad, to serve
For the dough
 225g/8oz/2 cups strong white bread
  flour, sifted
 1.5ml/¼ tsp salt
 7g/¼oz sachet easy-blend (rapid-rise)
  dried yeast
 1 egg, beaten
 100–120ml/3½–4fl oz/⅓–½ cup
  milk and warm water combined

1 Preheat the oven to 180°C/350°F/ Gas 4. Pat the fish dry with kitchen paper and sprinkle inside and out with salt. Cover and chill the fish until the dough is ready for use.

2 Put the flour and salt into a large mixing bowl and stir in the yeast evenly. Make a well in the centre. Whisk together the egg, milk and water, then pour half into the centre of the flour. Knead to make a soft dough.

3 Knead the dough until smooth on a very lightly floured surface. Divide the dough roughly in half, making one portion slightly larger than the other.

4 Carefully roll out the smaller piece of dough on a lightly floured surface to the shape of your fish, allowing a 5cm/2in border. Lay the dough on a large greased shallow baking sheet. Place the fish on top.

5 Roll out the remaining piece of dough until large enough to cover the fish, again allowing for a 5cm/2in border. Brush the edges of the pastry with water and seal well. Make criss-cross patterns across the top, using a sharp knife. Leave to rise for 30 minutes.

6 Glaze the dough with the remaining egg mixture. Make a small hole in the top of the pastry to allow steam to escape. Bake the fish for 25–30 minutes or until golden brown and well risen. Garnish with sprigs of fennel and serve with wedges of lemon and a salad of finely sliced courgette (zucchinis), tossed in melted butter and sprinkled with dill seeds.

Energy 235kcal/955kJ; Protein 20.6g; Carbohydrate 29.1g, of which sugars 0.6g; Fat 4.9g, of which saturates 0.3g; Cholesterol 32mg; Calcium 117mg; Fibre 1.2g; Sodium 194mg.

FISH KEBABS

These Balkan kebabs may be made from any firm-fleshed fish. While Turkish Jews consider swordfish kosher, other groups do not. Halibut, salmon or cod are good choices.

SERVES FOUR

INGREDIENTS
    900g/2lb fish, chunks
    5ml/1 tsp paprika, plus extra
      to garnish
    pinch of turmeric
    60ml/4 tbsp lemon juice
    45ml/3 tbsp olive oil
    6 fresh bay leaves
    4 small tomatoes
    2 green (bell) peppers, seeded and
      cut into 5cm/2in pieces
    2 onions, cut into 4 wedges each
    salt and ground white pepper
    extra bay leaves, to garnish
    lettuce leaves, sour cream, cucumber
      salad and lime or lemon wedges,
      to serve
For the sauce
    120ml/4fl oz/½ cup virgin olive oil
    juice of 1 lemon
    60ml/4 tbsp finely chopped
      fresh parsley
    salt and ground black pepper

1 Cut the fish into 5cm/2in cubes and place in a shallow dish.

2 Mix together the paprika, turmeric, lemon juice, olive oil and seasoning and pour over the fish. Crush 2 bay leaves over the fish. Leave, covered, in the refrigerator for at least 2 hours.

3 Carefully turn the fish cubes in the marinade once or twice.

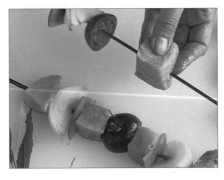

4 Thread the fish and vegetables on 4 large skewers; finish with a bay leaf.

5 Cook under a preheated grill (broiler) or over the hot coals of a barbecue, basting with any remaining marinade mixture from time to time. Turn the fish once during cooking.

6 Meanwhile, for the sauce, in a bowl whisk the oil, lemon juice, parsley and seasoning together until emulsified (thickened) and pour into a jug (pitcher). Arrange the kebabs on lettuce leaves, garnish with extra bay leaves and serve with the parsley and oil sauce, sour cream sprinkled with paprika, a cucumber salad and lime or lemon wedges.

COOK'S TIP
To help prevent the onion from falling apart during the cooking, keep the root end intact when preparing the onion. The root will hold the pieces together.

Energy 475kcal/1975kJ; Protein 42.9g; Carbohydrate 7.7g, of which sugars 6.7g; Fat 30.4g, of which saturates 4.4g; Cholesterol 104mg; Calcium 67mg; Fibre 2.5g; Sodium 147mg.

Spiced Sardines with Grapefruit and Fennel Salad

Sardines spiced with cumin and coriander are popular in the coastal regions of Morocco, both in restaurants and as street food. This grapefruit and fennel salad makes a juicy and refreshing counterpoint. It is thought that the Jews brought the love of fennel to Italy from the areas around the Mediterranean. Until recent times, Jews were the only Italians who ate the sweet, fragrant bulb.

SERVES FOUR TO SIX

INGREDIENTS

   12 fresh sardines, cleaned
   1 onion, grated
   60–90ml/4–6 tbsp olive oil
   5ml/1 tsp ground cinnamon
   10ml/2 tsp cumin seeds, roasted
     and ground
   10ml/2 tsp coriander seeds, roasted
     and ground
   5ml/1 tsp paprika
   5ml/1 tsp ground black pepper
   small bunch of fresh coriander
     (cilantro), chopped
   coarse salt
   2 lemons, cut into wedges, to serve
For the salad
   2 ruby grapefruits
   5ml/1 tsp sea salt
   1 fennel bulb
   2–3 spring onions (scallions),
     finely sliced
   2.5ml/½ tsp ground roasted cumin
   30–45ml/2–3 tbsp olive oil
   handful of black olives

1 Rinse the sardines and pat them dry on kitchen paper, then rub inside and out with a little coarse salt.

2 In a bowl, mix the grated onion with the olive oil, cinnamon, ground roasted cumin and coriander, paprika and black pepper. Make several slashes into the flesh of the sardines and smear the onion and spice mixture all over the fish, inside and out and into the gashes. Leave the sardines to stand for about 1 hour to allow the flavours of the spices to penetrate the flesh.

3 Meanwhile, prepare the salad. Peel the grapefruits with a knife, removing all the pith and peel in neat strips down the outside of the fruit. Cut between the membranes to remove the segments of fruit intact. Cut each grapefruit segment in half, place in a bowl and sprinkle with salt.

4 Trim the fennel, cut it in half lengthways and slice finely. Add the fennel to the grapefruit with the spring onions, cumin and olive oil. Toss lightly, then garnish with the olives.

5 Preheat the grill (broiler) or barbecue. Cook the sardines for 3–4 minutes on each side, basting with any leftover marinade. Sprinkle with fresh coriander and serve immediately, with lemon wedges for squeezing over and the refreshing grapefruit and fennel salad.

Energy 258kcal/1066kJ; Protein 11.7g; Carbohydrate 5.7g, of which sugars 5.4g; Fat 21g, of which saturates 3.6g; Cholesterol 0mg; Calcium 103mg; Fibre 2.7g; Sodium 441mg.

ROASTED FISH ON A BED OF LEMONS AND TOMATOES WITH TAHINI SAUCE

KNOWN AS MASGOUF, A WHOLE ROASTED FISH SITTING ON A BED OF LEMON AND TOMATO IS A FAVOURITE OF THE JEWS OF IRAQI HERITAGE. TAHINI SAUCE SERVED ALONGSIDE IS AN ISRAELI-MIDDLE EASTERN TWIST.

SERVES FOUR

INGREDIENTS
  1 whole fish, about 1.1kg/2½lb,
    scaled and cleaned
  10ml/2 tsp coriander seeds
  10ml/2 tsp ground cumin
  4 garlic cloves, sliced
  10ml/2 tsp harissa sauce
  90ml/6 tbsp olive oil
  6 plum tomatoes, sliced
  1 mild onion, sliced
  3 preserved lemons or 1 fresh lemon
  plenty of fresh herbs, such as bay
    leaves, thyme and rosemary
  salt and ground black pepper
For the sauce
  75ml/3fl oz/⅓ cup light tahini
  juice of 1 lemon
  1 garlic clove, crushed
  45ml/3 tbsp finely chopped fresh
    parsley or coriander (cilantro)
  extra herbs, to garnish

1 Preheat the oven to 200°C/400°F/
Gas 6. Grease the base and sides of
a large shallow ovenproof dish or
roasting pan.

2 Slash the fish diagonally on both
sides with a sharp knife. Finely crush
the coriander seeds, cumin and garlic
with a mortar and pestle. Mix with the
harissa sauce and about 60ml/4 tbsp of
the olive oil.

3 Spread a little of the harissa,
coriander, cumin and garlic paste inside
the cavity of the fish. Spread the
remainder over each side of the fish
and set aside.

4 Place the tomatoes, onion and
preserved or fresh lemon into the dish.
(Thinly slice the lemon if using fresh.)
Sprinkle with the remaining oil and
season with salt and pepper. Lay the
fish on top and tuck plenty of herbs
around it.

5 Bake, uncovered, for about
25 minutes, or until the fish has turned
opaque – test by piercing the thickest
part with a knife.

6 Meanwhile, make the sauce. Mix the
tahini, lemon juice, garlic and parsley or
coriander in a small bowl, then beat in
120ml/4fl oz/½ cup cold water. Season
to taste. Serve in a separate dish.

COOK'S TIP
The best fish to use in this recipe are
sea bass, hake, bream or snapper. If
you are having difficulty finding a
suitably large fish to dress, try a smaller
whole fish such as red mullet or snapper.
In an emergency, you can even use cod
or haddock steaks. Remember to reduce
the cooking time slightly as necessary
for smaller fry.

Energy 449kcal/1870kJ; Protein 31.3g; Carbohydrate 5.5g, of which sugars 5.1g; Fat 33.9g, of which saturates 4.1g; Cholesterol 0mg; Calcium 262mg; Fibre 3.5g; Sodium 157mg.

MIXED FISH GOULASH

The Jews of Hungary brought a taste for paprika, pepper and goulash to the lands they emigrated to. This is a really rich and satisying winter fish dish.

SERVES SIX

INGREDIENTS
2kg/4½lb mixed fish
4 large onions, sliced
4 garlic cloves, crushed
½ small celeriac, diced
handful of parsley stalks,
  finely chopped
30–45ml/2–3 tbsp paprika
500ml/18fl oz/2¼ cups dry
  white wine
500ml/18fl oz/2¼ cups
  fish stock
1 green (bell) pepper, seeded
  and sliced
60ml/4 tbsp tomato purée (paste)
salt
pinch of cayenne pepper
pinch of marjoram
90ml/6 tbsp sour cream, to serve

1 Skin and fillet the fish and cut the flesh into chunks. Put all the fish heads, skin and bones into a large pan, together with the onions, garlic, celeriac, parsley stalks, paprika and salt. Add the wine and stock and cover with water. Bring to the boil. Reduce the heat and simmer for 1¼–1½ hours. Strain the stock.

2 Place the fish and green pepper in a large frying pan and pour over the stock. Blend the tomato purée with a little stock and pour it into the pan.

3 Heat gently but do not stir, or the fish will break up. Cook for just 10–12 minutes but do not boil. Season with salt, cayenne pepper and marjoram to taste. Ladle into warmed deep plates or bowls and top with a generous spoonful of sour cream.

Energy 420kcal/1761kJ; Protein 64.1g; Carbohydrate 15.2g, of which sugars 12g; Fat 5.8g, of which saturates 2.2g; Cholesterol 162mg; Calcium 104mg; Fibre 3g; Sodium 259mg.

CRISP-CRUMBED FISH SAUSAGES

A favourite Hungarian dish, these fish sausages have been enjoyed by Jews and non-Jews alike since the 17th century for their satisfying, crunchy coating.

SERVES THREE TO FOUR

INGREDIENTS
    375g/13oz fish fillets, such as perch,
      pike, carp or cod, skinned
    1 white bread roll
    75ml/5 tbsp water
    25ml/1½ tbsp chopped fresh flat
      leaf parsley
    2 eggs, well beaten
    50g/2oz/½ cup plain
      (all-purpose) flour
    50g/2oz/1 cup fine fresh
      white breadcrumbs
    oil, for shallow frying
    salt and ground black pepper
    deep fried sprigs of parsley and
      lemon wedges, sprinkled with
      paprika, to serve

COOK'S TIP
For dairy meals, you may soak the
bread in milk.

1 Mince (grind) or process the fish
coarsely in a food processor or blender.
Soak the roll in the milk for about
10 minutes, then squeeze it out. Mix
the fish and bread together before
adding the chopped parsley, one of
the eggs and seasoning.

2 Using your fingers, shape the mixture
into 10cm/4in long sausages, about
2.5cm/1in thick.

3 Carefully roll the fish "sausages" into
the flour, then in the remaining egg and
then lastly in the breadcrumbs.

4 Heat the oil in a pan then slowly
cook the "sausages" until golden brown
all over. Drain well on crumpled kitchen
paper. Garnish with deep-fried parsley
sprigs and lemon wedges sprinkled
with paprika.

Energy 314kcal/1313kJ; Protein 23.5g; Carbohydrate 22.7g, of which sugars 0.7g; Fat 15g, of which saturates 2.5g; Cholesterol 138mg; Calcium 64mg; Fibre 0.8g; Sodium 222mg.

MARINATED FISH WITH ALLSPICE AND CAPERS

AN ASHKENAZIC DISH WITH POSSIBLE SEPHARDIC ROOTS. ENJOY THIS PICKLED, COOKED FISH WITH A GLASS OF COOL BEER, PUMPERNICKEL BREAD AND PICKLES.

SERVES SIX TO EIGHT

INGREDIENTS
    1.75kg/4lb tuna, carp or pike steaks
    75g/3oz/6 tbsp extra virgin olive oil
    50ml/2fl oz/¼ cup dry sherry
    salt and ground black pepper
For the marinade
    400ml/14fl oz/1⅔ cups water
    150ml/¼ pint/⅔ cup wine vinegar
    150ml/¼ pint/⅔ cup good fish stock
    1 onion, thinly sliced
    6 white peppercorns
    2.5ml/½ tsp allspice
    2 cloves
    1 bay leaf
    25ml/1½ tbsp capers, drained
      and chopped
    2 dill pickles, diced
    120ml/4fl oz/½ cup olive oil
    salad, dill pickles and bread,
      to serve

1 Preheat the oven to 180°C/350°F/ Gas 4. Put the fish steaks into an ovenproof dish and brush with the butter. Sprinkle over the sherry. Season well and bake for 20–25 minutes, or until just tender. Leave to cool.

COOK'S TIP
Use plump fillets of fish if tuna steaks are not available.

2 Meanwhile, boil the water, vinegar, fish stock, onion, spices and bay leaf together in a pan for 20 minutes. Leave to cool before adding the capers, dill pickle and olive oil.

3 Once the fish steaks have cooled, pour over the marinade.

4 Cover the dish with clear film (plastic wrap) and leave the fish to marinate for 24 hours in the refrigerator, basting occasionally. Serve with a green salad, dill pickles and slices of pumpernickel or rye bread.

Energy 342kcal/1436kJ; Protein 51.9g; Carbohydrate 0.1g, of which sugars 0.1g; Fat 14.2g, of which saturates 3.2g; Cholesterol 61mg; Calcium 36mg; Fibre 0g; Sodium 104mg.

HERBY SALMON PARCELS

WRAPPING THE FISH WITH LIME, TOMATO AND BASIL INTO AN ENVELOPE OF PAPER WHICH IS SEALED AND ROASTED, IS A DELICIOUS WAY TO PREPARE SALMON. THE AROMATIC MOISTURE OF THE CITRUS AND TOMATOES CREATES A PERFUMED STEAM TO COOK THE FISH IN. OPEN THE PARCEL AND WHOOSH! THE MOST FRAGRANT STEAM ESCAPES, LEAVING A SUCCULENT, PERFECTLY COOKED FISH.

SERVES FOUR

INGREDIENTS
  1 lime
  50g/2oz/¼ cup butter, softened
  30ml/2 tbsp finely chopped
    fresh basil
  4 plum tomatoes, sliced
  2 garlic cloves, sliced
  4 salmon fillets, each about
    200g/7oz
  15ml/1 tbsp olive oil

1 Grate the rind from the lime and put it in a small bowl. Cut the lime into eight slices and set aside. Add the butter and basil to the lime rind and mix well. Roll the mixture into a cylinder shape, wrap in greaseproof (waxed) paper or baking parchment and chill.

2 Preheat the oven to 190°C/375°F/ Gas 5. Cut out sheets of greaseproof paper or baking parchment, each large enough to enclose a salmon fillet easily.

4 Place the salmon fillets on the tomatoes. Cut the flavoured butter into pieces and place on each piece of salmon. Top with the reserved lime slices and drizzle with the olive oil.

5 Fold the paper or parchment around the topped salmon to make neat parcels. Place on a baking sheet and bake for 20 minutes or until the fish is cooked through. Serve immediately.

3 Arrange one sliced tomato on each piece of paper or parchment. Sprinkle each with one-quarter of the garlic and season with plenty of salt and pepper.

COOK'S TIP
The flavour of the tomatoes is central to the success of this dish. If you can obtain home-grown Italian plum tomatoes, such as San Marzano, so much the better. Alternatively, plump for sweet and juicy cherry tomatoes.

Energy 495Kcal/2057kJ; Protein 41.2g; Carbohydrate 3.2g, of which sugars 3.2g; Fat 35.3g, of which saturates 10.8g; Cholesterol 127mg; Calcium 51mg; Fibre 1g; Sodium 175mg.

BAKED SALT COD <u>WITH</u> POTATOES, TOMATOES <u>AND</u> BASIL

SALTED AND PRESERVED FISH HAVE LONG BEEN A FAVOURITE FOOD OF ASHKENAZIM DURING THE LONG WINTER, FAR FROM THE SHORES OF THE SEA. YOU MUST CHOOSE A PLUMP, THICK PIECE OF SALT COD, AND SOAK IT OVERNIGHT. YOU'LL BE REWARDED WITH A HEARTY, FIRM, FLAVOURFUL FISH, HERE COOKED BALKAN STYLE WITH POTATOES, TOMATOES AND AROMATICS. SERVED WITH PLENTY OF THICKLY SLICED FRESH BREAD, THIS DISH MAKES A MAIN COURSE FOR FOUR OR A DINNER PARTY FIRST COURSE FOR SIX. IT CAN ALSO BE SERVED COLD, AS PART OF THE MEZES, ANTIPASTO, OR VORSHPEIZ.

SERVES FOUR

INGREDIENTS
675g/1½lb salt cod
800g/1¾lb potatoes, peeled and cut into small wedges
1 large onion, finely chopped
5 garlic cloves, chopped
leaves from 1 fresh rosemary sprig, chopped
30ml/2 tbsp chopped fresh flat leaf parsley
120ml/4fl oz/½ cup extra virgin olive oil
400g/14oz can chopped tomatoes
15ml/1 tbsp tomato purée (paste)
300ml/½ pint/1¼ cups hot water or fish stock
5ml/1 tsp dried oregano
12 black olives
ground black pepper

COOK'S TIP
Salt cod can often be bought from Italian and Spanish groceries, as well as from Greek food stores. It is often sold in small squares, ready for soaking and draining. If you buy it in the piece, cut it into 7cm/2¾in squares after soaking.

1 Try to get a plump piece of good-quality salt cod. Soak the cod in cold water overnight, changing the water as often as possible in the course of the evening and during the following day – a minimum of five changes is desirable. The cod does not have to be skinned for this dish, but you should remove any obvious fins or bones from the fish after soaking.

2 Preheat the oven to 180°C/350°F/ Gas 4. Mix the potatoes, onion, garlic, rosemary and parsley in a large roasting pan. Grind in plenty of pepper. Add the olive oil and toss the mixture until it is well coated.

3 Drain the cod and cut it into serving pieces. Arrange the pieces of cod between the coated vegetables and spread the tomatoes over the surface. Stir the tomato purée into the hot water or stock until dissolved, then pour the mixture over the contents of the tin. Sprinkle the oregano on top. Bake for 1 hour, basting the fish and potatoes occasionally with the pan juices.

4 Remove the roasting pan from the oven, sprinkle the olives on top, then cook it for 30 minutes more, adding a little more hot water if the mixture seems to be drying out. Garnish with fresh herbs. Serve hot or cold.

Energy 404kcal/1698kJ; Protein 40.1g; Carbohydrate 26.7g, of which sugars 6.1g; Fat 16g, of which saturates 2.5g; Cholesterol 66mg; Calcium 62mg; Fibre 3g; Sodium 667mg.

COD IN MUSTARD BEURRE BLANC

THIS IS A LIGHT, MODERN EUROPEAN FISH DISH WITH STRONG OVERTONES OF GERMAN-JEWISH
CUISINE. ENJOY WITH BOILED POTATOES AND CARROTS.

SERVES FOUR

INGREDIENTS

900g/2lb cod fillets
1 lemon
1 small onion, sliced
15g/½oz/¼ cup chopped fresh flat
  leaf parsley, whole stalks reserved
6 allspice berries
6 whole black peppercorns
1 clove
1 bay leaf
1.2 litres/2 pints/5 cups water
30ml/2 tbsp wholegrain mustard
75g/3oz/6 tbsp butter
salt and ground black pepper
bay leaves, to garnish
boiled potatoes and carrots, to serve

1 Place the fish on a plate. Pare two thin strips of rind from the lemon, then squeeze the lemon for its juice. Sprinkle the juice over the fish.

2 Put the lemon rind in a large frying pan with the onion, the stalks from the parsley, the allspice, peppercorns, clove and bay leaf.

3 Pour in the water. Slowly bring to the boil, cover and simmer for 20 minutes. Add the fish, cover and cook very gently for 10 minutes.

4 Ladle 250ml/8fl oz/1 cup of the cooking liquid into a pan and simmer until reduced by half. Add the mustard and stir to combine with the hot liquid.

5 Whisk the butter, a little at a time, into the reduced stock. Taste and season with salt and pepper, if needed.

6 Remove the fish from the stock and place on warmed serving dishes. Pour over a little sauce and serve the rest separately in a jug (pitcher). Garnish with chopped parsley and bay leaves and serve with a dish of boiled potatoes and carrots.

COOK'S TIP
When using the peel or rind of any fruit in cooking, choose an unwaxed or organic fruit, or – if unable to find – scrub waxed fruit thoroughly before use.

Energy 337kcal/1404kJ; Protein 42.2g; Carbohydrate 1.7g, of which sugars 1.3g; Fat 17.8g, of which saturates 10g; Cholesterol 143mg; Calcium 44mg; Fibre 0.8g; Sodium 372mg.

BAKED COD <u>WITH</u> HORSERADISH SAUCE

THIS UKRAINIAN FISH DISH HAS TRAVELLED TO ISRAEL, TO THE AMERICAN JEWISH COMMUNITY AND WHEREVER ELSE UKRAINIAN JEWS HAVE EMIGRATED TO. BAKING FISH IN A SAUCE KEEPS IT MOIST. SERVE THE CREAMY PINK HORSERADISH SAUCE ON THE SIDE, AS A CONDIMENT.

SERVES FOUR

INGREDIENTS

   4 thick cod fillets or steaks
   15ml/1 tbsp lemon juice
   25g/1oz/2 tbsp butter
   25g/1oz/¼ cup plain (all-purpose)
     flour, sifted
   150ml/¼ pint/⅔ cup milk
   150ml/¼ pint/⅔ cup fish stock
   salt and ground black pepper
   parsley sprigs, to garnish
   potato wedges and chopped spring
     onions (scallions), fried, to serve
For the horseradish sauce
   30ml/2 tbsp tomato purée (paste)
   30ml/2 tbsp grated fresh horseradish
   250ml/8fl oz/1 cup sour cream

1 Preheat the oven to 180°C/350°F/ Gas 4. Place the fish in a buttered ovenproof dish in a single layer. Sprinkle with lemon juice.

2 Melt the butter in a small heavy pan. Stir in the flour and cook for 3–4 minutes until lightly golden. Stir to stop the flour sticking to the pan. Remove from the heat.

3 Gradually whisk the milk, and then the stock, into the flour mixture. Season with salt and pepper. Bring to the boil, stirring, and simmer for 3 minutes, still stirring.

4 Pour the sauce over the fish and bake for 20–25 minutes, depending on the thickness. Check by inserting a skewer into the thickest part: the flesh should be opaque.

5 For the horseradish sauce, blend the tomato purée and horseradish with the sour cream in a small pan. Slowly bring to the boil, stirring, and then simmer for 1 minute.

6 Pour the horseradish sauce into a serving bowl and serve alongside the fish. Serve the fish hot. Garnish with the parsley sprigs and serve with the potato wedges and fried chopped spring onions.

Energy 380kcal/1584kJ; Protein 40.7g; Carbohydrate 10.2g, of which sugars 5.4g; Fat 19.7g, of which saturates 11.7g; Cholesterol 145mg; Calcium 137mg; Fibre 0.5g; Sodium 222mg.

FISH BABKA

A LIGHT, SOUFFLÉ-LIKE DISH OF CHOPPED FISH, DELICATELY SEASONED WITH SAUTÉED ONION AND NUTMEG, THIS IS A TYPICALLY EASTERN EUROPEAN, ELEGANT BUT HOMEY WAY TO SERVE FISH.

SERVES FOUR

INGREDIENTS

   350g/12oz white fish fillets, skinned
      and cut into 2.5cm/1in cubes
   50g/2oz white bread, cut into
      1cm/½in cubes
   250ml/8fl oz/1 cup milk
   25g/1oz/2 tbsp butter
   1 small onion, finely chopped
   3 eggs, separated
   1.5ml/¼ tsp grated nutmeg
   salt and ground black pepper
   30ml/2 tbsp chopped fresh dill
   sliced courgettes (zucchini) and
      carrots, to serve

1 Preheat the oven to 180°C/350°F/ Gas 4 and grease a 1.5 litre/2½ pint/ 6¼ cup ovenproof dish with a little butter.

2 Place the fish cubes in a bowl. Add the bread, then sprinkle over the milk and leave to soak while you cook the chopped onion.

3 Melt the butter in a small pan and fry the onion for 10 minutes, until soft. Cool for a few minutes.

4 Add the onions to the fish and bread with the egg yolks, nutmeg, dill, salt and pepper. Mix well.

5 Whisk the egg whites in a large bowl until stiff, then gently fold into the fish.

6 Spoon the mixture into the dish. Cover with buttered foil and bake for 45 minutes, or until set.

7 Allow to stand for 5 minutes, then spoon out. Alternatively, loosen with a knife, turn out, remove the paper and cut into wedges. Garnish with dill and serve with courgettes and carrots.

Energy 224kcal/937kJ; Protein 23.3g; Carbohydrate 9.2g, of which sugars 3g; Fat 10.8g, of which saturates 4.9g; Cholesterol 198mg; Calcium 93mg; Fibre 0.4g; Sodium 225mg.

FISH STEAKS BAKED <u>WITH</u> ONIONS, TOMATOES <u>AND</u> WINE

A ZESTY ONION AND TOMATO SAUCE SPOONED OVER FISH STEAKS THEN LEFT TO BAKE RESULTS IN A MOIST, FLAVOURFUL, EASILY PREPARED FISH COURSE. CHOOSE A FIRM, WHITE FISH SUCH AS COD, GREY MULLET, RED SNAPPER OR POMPANO FOR THIS DISH.

<u>SERVES FOUR</u>

INGREDIENTS

 45ml/3 tbsp olive oil
 4 onions, finely chopped
 5ml/1 tsp sea salt
 45ml/3 tbsp water
 3 garlic cloves, crushed
 1 bay leaf
 6 allspice berries
 2.5ml/½ tsp paprika
 4 plum tomatoes, seeded and diced
 120ml/4fl oz/½ cup dry white wine,
 plus 45ml/3 tbsp
 4 skinless fish steaks, about 175g/
 6oz each
 lemon juice, for sprinkling
 8 lemon slices
 salt and ground black pepper
 15ml/1 tbsp chopped fresh parsley,
 to garnish
 crusty bread, to serve

1 Put the oil, onion, sea salt and water in a heavy pan. Stir well and cook gently, covered, over a very low heat for 45 minutes but do not allow the onion to brown. Preheat the oven to 180°C/350°F/Gas 4.

COOK'S TIP
For extra flavour and to firm the fish up, marinate the fish in the salt, pepper and lemon juice for 1–2 hours in a covered, non-metallic bowl before cooking.

2 Stir in the garlic and cook for 1 minute before adding the bay leaf, allspice, paprika, tomatoes, the 120ml/4fl oz/½ cup wine and seasoning. Cook for 10–15 minutes, stirring occasionally to prevent sticking. Remove and discard the allspice and bay leaf.

3 Spoon a layer of the onion mixture into the base of a shallow ovenproof dish and top with the fish steaks. Sprinkle with a little lemon juice and seasoning.

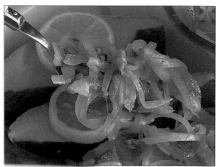

4 Sprinkle over the remaining white wine and place two lemon slices overlapping on top of each fish steak. Spoon the remaining onion sauce over the fish.

5 Bake the casserole in the oven for 15–20 minutes, or until the sauce thickens and the fish flakes easily. Garnish with a sprinkling of parsley and serve with crusty bread.

Energy 254kcal/1062kJ; Protein 33.5g; Carbohydrate 8.3g, of which sugars 6.5g; Fat 9.9g, of which saturates 1.4g; Cholesterol 81mg; Calcium 40mg; Fibre 1.8g; Sodium 114mg.

POACHED CARP <u>WITH</u> CARAWAY SEEDS

FROM ALSACE THROUGH THE BALKANS AND EASTERN EUROPE, JEWS HELPED TO SPREAD THE PRESENCE OF CARP. IMPORTED FROM CHINA IN THE 15TH CENTURY, THE FISH WAS BRED BY JEWS. CARP IS A FAVOURITE FRESHWATER FISH IN THE BALKANS AS IN CENTRAL EUROPE, FOR IT IS PLENTIFUL AND EASY TO COOK. OIL-RICH, IT DWELLS IN LAKES AND RIVERS AND IS GENERALLY SOLD ALIVE IN THE LOCAL MARKETS. THIS RECIPE USES FILLETS, AND IF VISITING A FISHMONGER ASK FOR FILLETED CARP WEIGHING 1.5–1.75KG/3–4LB. LARGER FISH TEND TO BE COARSE.

SERVES FOUR

INGREDIENTS
  4 carp fillets, about 175–200g/
    6–7oz each
  15ml/1 tbsp caraway seeds,
    roughly crushed
  40g/1½oz/3 tbsp butter
  30ml/2 tbsp chopped fresh chives
  1 onion, finely sliced
  juice of 1 lemon
  175ml/6fl oz/¾ cup dry white wine
  salt and ground black pepper
  fresh dill and mint, to garnish
  soft polenta and green beans,
    to serve

1 Wipe the fish fillets and pat dry with kitchen paper. Season well and press the roughly crushed caraway seeds into the flesh.

2 Heat half the butter in a large frying pan and stir in half the fresh chives, the onion, lemon juice and dry white wine. Bring to the boil, reduce the heat and gently simmer for 10–12 minutes.

3 Add the fish and poach gently for about 10 minutes. Carefully remove the fillets with a slotted spoon and keep them warm on a serving plate.

4 Continue cooking the stock to reduce it a little, then whisk in the remaining butter. Adjust the seasoning. Pour the sauce over the fish and top with the remaining chives. Garnish with the herbs and serve with soft polenta and green beans.

COOK'S TIP
The caraway seeds give the dish a very distinctive flavour, so be as liberal as you like with them.

Energy 333kcal/1391kJ; Protein 35.3g; Carbohydrate 1.5g, of which sugars 1.2g; Fat 17.7g, of which saturates 7g; Cholesterol 155mg; Calcium 104mg; Fibre 0.2g; Sodium 149mg.

FISH STEW WITH HERBY MASH

THIS STEW OF ANY FIRM FISH, IN A BROTH TINTED WITH TOMATOES AND TANGY WITH VINEGAR, IS
DELICIOUS SERVED WITH CREAMY, HERB-FLECKED MASHED POTATOES. USE SEA BREAM, TURBOT, TUNA
OR ANY FIRM FISH WITH FEW BONES. SERVE HOT OR COLD.

SERVES FOUR

INGREDIENTS
    45ml/3 tbsp olive oil
    1 onion, finely chopped
    2 garlic cloves, crushed
    30ml/2 tbsp tomato purée (paste)
    3 plum tomatoes, seeded
      and chopped
    15ml/1 tbsp vinegar
    1 bay leaf
    15ml/1 tbsp chopped fresh flat
      leaf parsley
    600ml/1 pint/2½ cups good
      fish stock
    675–900g/1½–2lb mixed fish fillets,
      cut into 10cm/4in cubes
    675g/1½lb old potatoes, peeled and
      cut into chunks
    60ml/4 tbsp sour cream
    small bunch chopped chives
    30–45ml/2–3 tbsp butter
    salt and ground black pepper
    chopped fresh flat leaf parsley, bay
      leaves and grated lemon rind,
      to garnish

1 Heat the olive oil in a large pan, and cook the onion and garlic for 2–3 minutes or until just soft. Add the tomato purée, tomatoes, vinegar, bay leaf and parsley. Stir well before pouring in the fish stock. Bring to the boil.

2 Add the pieces of fish to the pan. Bring to the boil again, then reduce the heat and cook for approximately 30 minutes, stirring occasionally.

3 Meanwhile, place the potatoes in a large pan of lightly salted water. Bring to the boil and cook for at least 20 minutes. Drain well.

4 Return the cooked potatoes to the pan, and add the sour cream and butter, and a little pepper. Mash well with a fork.

5 Season the fish to taste. Serve with mashed potato on individual plates or in bowls. Garnish with the parsley and bay leaves and sprinkle grated lemon rind over the mash.

COOK'S TIP
It's both quick and simple to make your own fish stock. Simply place all the bones, trimmings, head and any leftover fish pieces in a large pan; add 1–2 carrots, 1 onion, sprigs of fennel or dill, a few peppercorns and a dash of dry white wine. Cover with cold water, bring to the boil then simmer for 20 minutes. Strain through a fine sieve (strainer).

Energy 466kcal/1949kJ; Protein 35.3g; Carbohydrate 32.4g, of which sugars 7.1g; Fat 22.5g, of which saturates 9.3g; Cholesterol 111mg; Calcium 53mg; Fibre 2.9g; Sodium 219mg.

OREGANO-BAKED TUNA ᵂᴵᵀᴴ TOMATOES ᴬᴺᴰ GOLDEN-BROWN POTATOES

THIS IS A TYPICALLY GREEK, TURKISH OR SEPHARDIC WAY OF PREPARING TUNA. THE SAUCE IS ZESTY, AND PERMEATES THE HEARTY FISH. IN THE MEDITERRANEAN, SEPTEMBER IS OFTEN THE MONTH WHEN FISHERMEN LAND THEIR BIGGEST CATCHES OF TUNA, AND IT IS ALSO THE TIME WHEN THE LOCAL WOMEN ARE HARD AT WORK PREPARING THIS DISH. ON ALONNISOS, ONE OF THE GREEK SPORADES ISLANDS IN THE AEGEAN SEA, IT IS TRADITIONAL TO COOK THE DISH IN THE OVENS OF THE LOCAL BAKER, AFTER THE FINAL BREAD OF THE MORNING HAS BEEN BAKED. BY LUNCHTIME, THE AROMAS OF GARLIC AND OREGANO SIMPLY INTOXICATE ANYONE WHO WANDERS PAST.

SERVES FOUR

INGREDIENTS
  105ml/7 tbsp extra virgin
    olive oil
  juice of 1 large lemon
  3 garlic cloves, crushed
  4 medium-thick tuna steaks,
    total weight about 800g/1¾lb
  45ml/3 tbsp chopped fresh flat
    leaf parsley
  15ml/1 tbsp fresh oregano or
    5ml/1 tsp dried
  500g/1¼lb potatoes, peeled
    and cut into small cubes
  450g/1lb ripe tomatoes, peeled
    and chopped
  150ml/¼ pint/⅔ cup hot water
  salt and ground black pepper

COOK'S TIPS
• When buying tuna steaks, avoid those with heavy discolorations around the bone, or which are dull-looking and brownish all over. The flesh should be either pale beige-pink or deep red in colour, depending on the type bought, and firm and compact to touch.
• The best oregano hails from the Mediterranean, where it is gathered in huge bunches and hung in a shady place, for about a week, to dry. The aroma intensifies after the herb is dried, at which point the tops and leaves are crumbled and stored in glass jars for the dark winter months.

1 Whisk the olive oil with the lemon juice and garlic, and place in a shallow dish that will hold all the tuna steaks in a single layer. Stir in salt and pepper, then add the tuna steaks.

2 Sprinkle over the herbs and turn the steaks to coat them in the marinade. Leave to marinate for 1–2 hours. Lift the steaks out and lay them in a roasting pan.

3 Preheat the oven to 180°C/350°F/ Gas 4. Drop the cubes of potato into the marinating dish and turn them to coat in the olive oil mixture. Arrange them around the tuna steaks, drizzle over any remaining marinade and sprinkle the chopped tomatoes on top.

4 Pour the hot water into the roasting pan. Bake the tuna for 40 minutes, turning it over halfway through and stirring the potatoes.

5 Transfer the tuna to a heated platter and cover it with foil to keep it warm. Increase the oven temperature to 200°C/400°F/Gas 6. Add a little more hot water to the roasting pan if needed and cook the potatoes for about 15 minutes more to brown them and make them really crisp. Serve the tuna and potato mixture with an imaginative green salad.

Energy 553kcal/2318kJ; Protein 50.4g; Carbohydrate 23.7g, of which sugars 5.2g; Fat 29.2g, of which saturates 5.4g; Cholesterol 56mg; Calcium 55mg; Fibre 2.6g; Sodium 119mg.

TONNO CON PISELLI

This Jewish Italian dish of fresh tuna and peas, awash with rich tomato sauce, is delicious. When peas are not in season, chickpeas are traditionally used instead.

2 Sprinkle the tuna steaks on each side with salt and pepper. Add to the pan and cook for 2–3 minutes on each side until lightly browned. Transfer the tuna steaks to a shallow baking dish, in a single layer.

3 Add the canned tomatoes along with their juice and the wine or fish stock to the onions and cook over a medium heat for 5–10 minutes, stirring, until the flavours blend together and the mixture thickens slightly.

4 Stir the tomato purée, sugar, if needed, and salt and pepper into the tomato sauce, then add the fresh or frozen peas. Pour the mixture over the fish steaks and bake, uncovered, for about 10 minutes, or until tender.

SERVES FOUR

INGREDIENTS
- 60ml/4 tbsp olive oil
- 1 onion, chopped
- 4–5 garlic cloves, chopped
- 45ml/3 tbsp chopped fresh flat leaf parsley
- 1–2 pinches fennel seeds
- 350g/12oz tuna steaks
- 400g/14oz can chopped tomatoes
- 120ml/4fl oz/½ cup dry white wine or fish stock
- 30–45ml/2–3 tbsp tomato purée (paste)
- pinch of sugar, if needed
- 350g/12oz/3 cups fresh shelled or frozen peas
- salt and ground black pepper

1 Preheat the oven to 190°C/375°F/ Gas 5. Heat the olive oil in a large frying pan, then add the chopped onion, garlic, flat leaf parsley and fennel seeds, and fry over a low heat for about 5 minutes, or until the onion is softened but not browned.

VARIATIONS
This recipe works well with other fish. Use tuna fillets in place of steaks or try different fish steaks, such as salmon.

Energy 339kcal/1411kJ; Protein 28.1g; Carbohydrate 15.4g, of which sugars 7.2g; Fat 16.7g, of which saturates 3g; Cholesterol 25mg; Calcium 49mg; Fibre 5.5g; Sodium 71mg.

YEMENI POACHED FISH IN SPICY TOMATO HERB SAUCE

THE YEMENI SPICING OF THIS TRADITIONAL JEWISH DISH IS REFRESHING IN THE SULTRY HEAT OF THE MIDDLE EAST AND IS VERY POPULAR WITH ISRAELIS. SERVE THIS DISH WITH FLAT BREADS SUCH AS PITTA OR MATZOS, OR PLAIN RICE, WITH A HOT CHILLI SAUCE ALONGSIDE.

SERVES EIGHT

INGREDIENTS

300ml/½ pint/1¼ cups passata
   (bottled strained tomatoes)
150ml/¼ pint/⅔ cup fish stock
1 large onion, chopped
60ml/4 tbsp chopped fresh coriander
   (cilantro) leaves
60ml/4 tbsp chopped fresh parsley
5–8 garlic cloves, crushed
chopped fresh chilli or chilli paste,
   to taste
large pinch of ground ginger
large pinch of curry powder
1.5ml/¼ tsp ground cumin
1.5ml/¼ tsp ground turmeric
seeds from 2–3 cardamom pods
juice of 2 lemons, plus extra
   if needed
30ml/2 tbsp vegetable or olive oil
1.5kg/3¼lb mixed white fish fillets
salt and ground black pepper

1 Put the passata, stock, onion, herbs, garlic, chilli, ginger, curry powder, cumin, turmeric, cardamom, lemon juice and oil in a pan and bring to the boil.

VARIATIONS
• This dish is just as good using only one type of fish, such as cod or flounder.
• Instead of poaching the fish, wrap each piece in puff pastry and bake at 190°C/375°F/Gas 5 for 20 minutes, then serve with the tomato sauce.

2 Remove the pan from the heat and add the fish fillets to the hot sauce. Return to the heat and allow the sauce to boil briefly again. Reduce the heat and simmer very gently for about 5 minutes, or until the fish is tender. (Test the fish with a fork. If the flesh flakes easily, then it is cooked.)

3 Taste the sauce and adjust the seasoning, adding more lemon juice if necessary. Serve hot or warm.

Energy 191kcal/803kJ; Protein 35.1g; Carbohydrate 3.3g, of which sugars 2,7g; Fat 4.2g, of which saturates 0.5g; Cholesterol 86mg; Calcium 39mg; Fibre 0.9g; Sodium 202mg.

BRAISED TENCH AND VEGETABLES

TENCH IS A HARDY, FAT-BODIED FRESHWATER FISH, AND IS OFTEN TO BE FOUND ON THE MENU IN THE LAND-LOCKED COUNTRIES OF EASTERN EUROPE.

SERVES FOUR

INGREDIENTS
    900g/2lb tench, filleted and skinned
    15ml/1 tbsp lemon juice
    75g/3oz/6 tbsp butter
    1 onion, halved and cut into wedges
    1 celery stick, sliced
    1 carrot, halved lengthways
      and sliced
    115g/4oz/1½ cups small button
      (white) mushrooms, halved
    50ml/2fl oz/¼ cup vegetable stock
    salt and ground black pepper

VARIATION
Use small carp in this recipe, if you like. It tends to be a little sweeter in flavour than tench, and it also benefits from braising.

1 Cut the fish fillets into strips about 2.5cm/1in wide. Sprinkle them with the lemon juice and a little salt and pepper and set aside.

2 Melt the butter in a large flameproof casserole and cook the onion wedges for 5 minutes.

3 Add the celery, carrot and mushrooms and cook for a further 2–3 minutes, stirring to coat in the butter.

4 Pour the stock into the pan. Place the fish on top of the vegetables in a single layer. Cover the casserole with a lid and cook over a very low heat for 25–30 minutes, until the fish and vegetables are tender.

Energy 416kcal/1735kJ; Protein 40.6g; Carbohydrate 4.8g, of which sugars 3.7g; Fat 26.3g, of which saturates 11.9g; Cholesterol 191mg; Calcium 128mg; Fibre 1.4g; Sodium 222mg.

PLAICE WITH AN EGG AND BUTTER SAUCE

A SAUCE OF CHOPPED HARD-BOILED EGG WITH MELTED BUTTER IS KNOWN AS SAUCE POLONAISE, THOUGH THIS EASTERN EUROPEAN DISH IS NOT POLISH AT ALL. IT RAMBLES ACROSS THE BOUNDARIES OF EASTERN EUROPEAN COUNTRIES AND IS DELICIOUS WHEREVER IT IS EATEN.

SERVES FOUR

INGREDIENTS

4 plaice fillets, about 225g/8oz each
75g/3oz/6 tbsp butter
2 eggs, hard-boiled and
  finely chopped
30ml/2 tbsp chopped fresh dill
15ml/1 tbsp lemon juice
salt and ground black pepper
lemon slices, to garnish
boiled baby carrots, to serve

1 Put the fish, skin side down, on a sheet of greased foil on a grill (broiler) rack. Melt the butter in a small pan and brush a little over the fish. Season with salt and pepper.

2 Grill (broil) the fish under a moderate heat for 8–10 minutes, or until just cooked. Transfer to a warmed plate.

3 Add the eggs, dill and lemon juice to the melted butter in the pan. Heat gently for 1 minute. Pour over the fish just before serving. Garnish with lemon slices and serve with boiled baby carrots.

Energy 354kcal/1483kJ; Protein 40.8g; Carbohydrate 0.1g, of which sugars 0.1g; Fat 21.3g, of which saturates 11g; Cholesterol 230mg; Calcium 119mg; Fibre 0g; Sodium 419mg.

BLUE TROUT

*THE BLUE SHEEN OF BLAUE FORELLE IS A GERMAN SPECIALITY AND IS EASILY ACHIEVED BY FIRST
SCALDING THE FISH AND THEN FANNING TO COOL IT. COOKING THE FISH WITH SPICED VINEGAR
GIVES IT A TANGINESS WHICH IS PERFECTLY BALANCED BY A LITTLE MELTED BUTTER, PUNGENT
HORSERADISH, AND FRESH FRENCH BEANS.*

SERVES FOUR

INGREDIENTS

4 trout, about 175g/6oz each
5ml/1 tsp salt
600ml/1 pint/2½ cups white
  wine vinegar
1 onion, sliced
2 bay leaves
6 whole black peppercorns
bay leaves and lemon slices,
  to garnish
115g/4oz/½ cup melted butter,
  creamed horseradish sauce
  and French (green) beans,
  to serve

COOK'S TIP
The method of cooling the fish favoured
by German cooks was to leave the pan
in the draught of an open window,
enabling them to prepare other
ingredients in the meantime.

1 Preheat the oven to 180°C/350°F/
Gas 4. Rub both sides of the trout with
salt and place in a non-aluminium
roasting pan or fish kettle.

2 Bring the vinegar to the boil in a pan
and slowly pour over the trout so that it
is completely covered. Fan the fish as
it cools. This should take no more than
5 minutes.

3 Bring the vinegar back to the boil,
then add the sliced onion, bay leaves
and peppercorns.

4 Cover the pan with foil and cook in
the oven for 30 minutes, or until the
fish is cooked. Transfer the fish to
warmed serving dishes, garnish with
bay leaves and lemon slices and serve
with melted butter, creamed horseradish
sauce and French beans.

Energy 375kcal/1558kJ; Protein 27.5g; Carbohydrate 1.4g, of which sugars 1g; Fat 28.9g, of which saturates 16.2g; Cholesterol 173mg; Calcium 51mg; Fibre 0.2g; Sodium 768mg.

BAKED SALMON

ANY FISH, FRESHWATER OR SALT WATER, CAN BE PREPARED IN THIS SIMPLE WAY: BAKED IN ITS OWN JUICES, WITH BUTTER, LEMON AND CARAWAY SEEDS.

SERVES SIX

INGREDIENTS
  1.75kg/4lb whole salmon
  115g/4oz/½ cup butter, melted
  2.5–5ml/½–1 tsp caraway seeds
  45ml/3 tbsp lemon juice
  salt and ground black pepper
  sprigs of flat leaf parsley and lemon
    wedges, to garnish

1 Using a sharp knife, cut the fish in half lengthways.

2 Preheat the oven to 180°C/350°F/ Gas 4. Place the two halves of salmon, skin side down, in a lightly greased roasting pan and brush with the melted butter. Season, sprinkle over the caraway seeds and then brush with the lemon juice.

3 Bake the salmon in the oven, loosely covered with foil, for 25 minutes or until the flesh flakes easily.

4 Transfer the fish to a serving plate. Garnish with flat leaf parsley and lemon wedges. Serve hot or cold with a simple vegetable accompaniment of crisp green beans or boiled potatoes.

COOK'S TIP
Take care when cutting the fish. Dip your fingers into a little salt to help you to grip the fish without slipping.

Energy 656kcal/2730kJ; Protein 57.9g; Carbohydrate 0.1g, of which sugars 0.1g; Fat 47g, of which saturates 16.1g; Cholesterol 184mg; Calcium 65mg; Fibre 0g; Sodium 245mg.

BAKED SALMON <u>WITH</u> WATERCRESS SAUCE

WHOLE BAKED SALMON IS A CLASSIC DISH SERVED AT ANY SIMCHA BUFFET, BE IT BAR AND BAT MITZVAH FEASTS, WEDDING PARTIES OR ANY FESTIVAL CELEBRATION. BAKING THE SALMON IN FOIL PRODUCES A FLESH RATHER LIKE THAT OF A POACHED FISH BUT WITH THE EASE OF BAKING. THE SAUCE IS GREEN FLECKED, TANGY AND HOLLANDAISE-LIKE, YET EASY TO WHIP UP.

SERVES SIX TO EIGHT

INGREDIENTS

2–3kg/4½–6¾lb salmon,
  cleaned with head and tail
  left on
3–5 spring onions (scallions),
  thinly sliced
1 lemon, thinly sliced
1 cucumber, thinly sliced
fresh dill sprigs, to garnish
lemon wedges, to serve
For the watercress sauce
3 garlic cloves, chopped
200g/7oz watercress leaves,
  finely chopped
40g/1½oz fresh tarragon,
  finely chopped
300g/11oz mayonnaise
15–30ml/1–2 tbsp freshly squeezed
  lemon juice
200g/7oz/scant 1 cup unsalted
  (sweet) butter
salt and ground black pepper

1 Preheat the oven to 180°C/350°F/ Gas 4. Rinse the salmon and lay it on a large piece of foil. Stuff the fish with the sliced spring onions and layer the lemon slices inside and around the fish, then sprinkle with plenty of salt and ground black pepper.

2 Loosely fold the foil around the fish and fold the edges over to seal. Bake for about 1 hour.

3 Remove the fish from the oven and leave to stand, still wrapped in the foil, for about 15 minutes, then unwrap the parcel and leave the fish to cool.

4 When the fish is cool, carefully lift it on to a large plate, still covered with lemon slices. Cover the fish tightly with clear film (plastic wrap) and chill for several hours.

5 Before serving, discard the lemon slices around the fish. Using a blunt knife to lift up the edge of the skin, carefully peel the skin away from the flesh, avoiding tearing the flesh, and pull out any fins at the same time.

6 Arrange the cucumber slices in overlapping rows along the length of the fish, to resemble large fish scales.

COOK'S TIP
Do not prepare the sauce more than a few hours ahead of serving as the watercress will discolour the sauce.

7 To make the sauce, put the garlic, watercress, tarragon, mayonnaise and lemon juice in a food processor or blender or a bowl, and process or mix to combine.

8 Melt the butter, then add to the watercress mixture, a little at a time, processing or stirring, until the butter has been incorporated and the sauce is thick and smooth. Cover and chill before serving. Serve the fish, garnished with dill, with the sauce and lemon wedges.

VARIATION
Instead of cooking a whole fish, prepare 6–8 salmon steaks. Place each fish steak on an individual square of foil, then top with a slice of onion and a slice of lemon and season generously with salt and ground black pepper. Loosely wrap the foil up around the fish, fold the edges to seal and place the parcels on a baking sheet. Bake as above for 10–15 minutes, or until the flesh is opaque. Serve cold with watercress sauce, garnished with slices of cucumber.

Energy 843kcal/3490kJ; Protein 45.1g; Carbohydrate 2g, of which sugars 1.8g; Fat 72.6g, of which saturates 21.9g; Cholesterol 189mg; Calcium 114mg; Fibre 1.1g; Sodium 455mg.

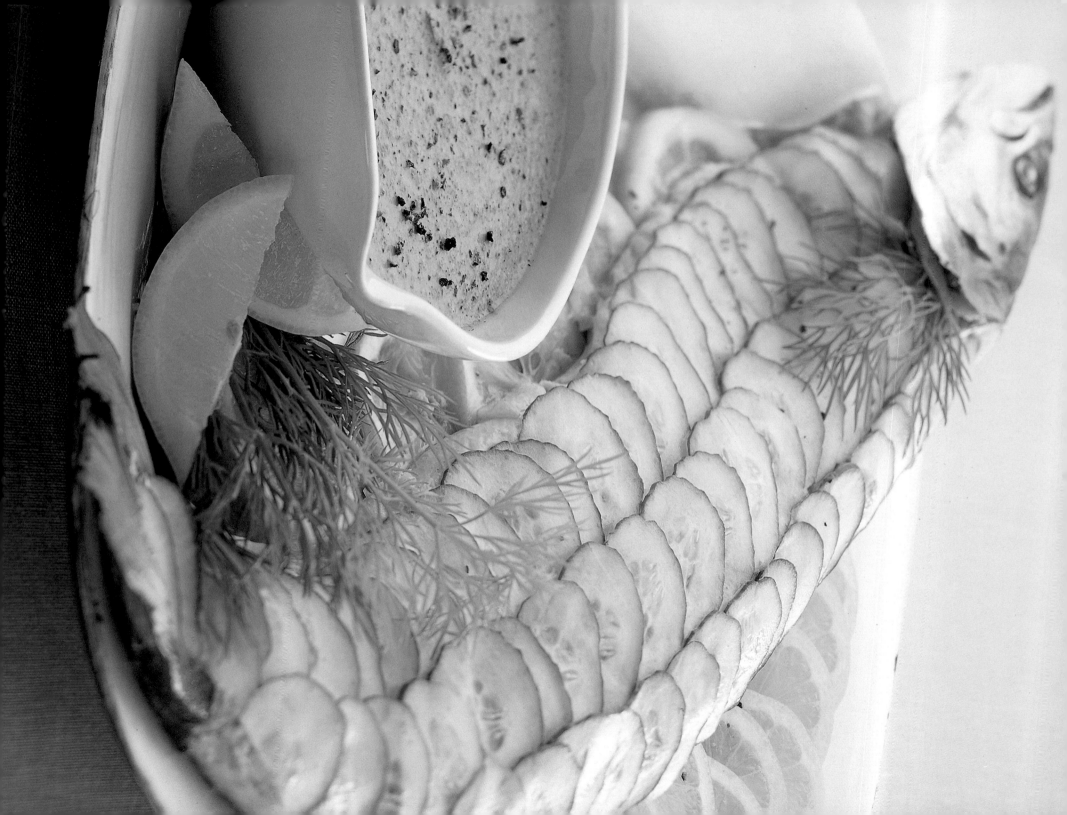

SINIYA

The name of this classic Israeli dish simply means fish and tahini sauce. In this lush and beautiful version, the fish is first wrapped in vine leaves, then spread with tahini and baked. A final sprinkling of pomegranate seeds adds a fresh, invigorating flavour.

SERVES FOUR

INGREDIENTS

   4 small fish, such as trout, sea
     bream, red mullet or snapper, each
     weighing about 300g/11oz, cleaned
   at least 5 garlic cloves, chopped
   juice of 2 lemons
   75ml/5 tbsp olive oil
   about 20 brined vine leaves
   tahini thinned with water and lemon
     juice, for drizzling
   1–2 pomegranates
   fresh mint and coriander (cilantro)
     sprigs, to garnish

VARIATION

Instead of whole fish, use fish fillets or steaks such as fresh tuna. Make a bed of vine leaves and top with the fish and marinade. Bake for 5–10 minutes until the fish is half cooked, then top with the tahini as above and grill (broil) until golden brown and lightly crusted on top.

1 Preheat the oven to 180°C/350°F/ Gas 4. Put the fish in a shallow, ovenproof dish, large enough to fit all the fish without touching each other. In a bowl, combine the garlic, lemon juice and oil; spoon over the fish. Turn the fish to coat.

2 Rinse the vine leaves well under cold water, then wrap the fish in the leaves. Arrange the fish in the same dish and spoon any marinade in the dish over the top of each. Bake for 30 minutes.

3 Drizzle the tahini over the top of each wrapped fish, making a ribbon so that the tops and tails of the fish and some of the vine leaf wrapping still show. Return to the oven and bake for a further 5–10 minutes until the top is golden and slightly crusted.

4 Meanwhile, cut the pomegranates in half and scoop out the seeds. Sprinkle the seeds over the fish, garnish with mint and coriander and serve.

Energy 301kcal/1254kJ; Protein 28.9g; Carbohydrate 1.5g, of which sugars 1.5g; Fat 20.1g, of which saturates 2g; Cholesterol 0mg; Calcium 109mg; Fibre 0.3g; Sodium 150mg.

DAG <u>HA</u> SFARIM

A WHOLE FISH, COOKED IN SPICES, IS A DISH FOR FESTIVALS AND CELEBRATIONS. SERVING A FISH WHOLE IS ESPECIALLY POPULAR AT ROSH HASHANAH, THROUGHOUT THE SEPHARDIC COMMUNITIES. THE WHOLENESS SYMBOLIZES THE FULL YEAR TO COME AND THE HEAD SYMBOLIZES THE WISDOM THAT WE ASK TO BE ENDOWED WITH IN THE MONTHS THAT FOLLOW.

SERVES SIX TO EIGHT

INGREDIENTS

1–1.5kg/2¼–3¼lb fish, such as red
    mullet or snapper, cleaned, with
    head and tail left on (optional)
2.5ml/½ tsp salt
juice of 2 lemons
45–60ml/3–4 tbsp extra virgin
    olive oil
2 onions, sliced
5 garlic cloves, chopped
1 green (bell) pepper, seeded
    and chopped
1–2 fresh green chillies, seeded
    and finely chopped
2.5ml/½ tsp ground turmeric
2.5ml/½ tsp curry powder
2.5 ml/½ tsp ground cumin
120ml/4fl oz/½ cup passata
    (bottled strained tomatoes)
5–6 fresh or canned tomatoes, chopped
45–60ml/3–4 tbsp chopped
    fresh coriander (cilantro) leaves
    and/or parsley
65g/2½oz pine nuts, toasted
parsley, to garnish

1 Prick the fish all over with a fork and rub with the salt. Put the fish in a roasting pan or dish and pour over the lemon juice. Leave to stand for 2 hours.

VARIATION
The spicy tomato sauce is very good served with fish patties. Omit step 1 and simply warm fried patties through in the spicy sauce.

2 Preheat the oven to 180°C/350°F/ Gas 4. Heat the oil in a pan, add the onions and half the garlic and fry for about 5 minutes, or until softened.

3 Add the pepper, chillies, turmeric, curry powder and cumin to the pan and cook gently for 2–3 minutes. Stir in the passata, tomatoes and herbs. ·

4 Sprinkle half of the pine nuts over the base of an ovenproof dish, top with half of the sauce, then add the fish and its marinade. Sprinkle the remaining garlic over the fish, then add the remaining sauce and the remaining pine nuts. Cover tightly with a lid or foil and bake for 30 minutes, or until the fish is tender. Garnish with parsley.

Energy 195kcal/815kJ; Protein 14.3g; Carbohydrate 6.7g, of which sugars 5.8g; Fat 12.6g, of which saturates 1g; Cholesterol 0mg; Calcium 62mg; Fibre 1.6g; Sodium 104mg.

BAKED HUNGARIAN PIKE <u>WITH</u> WILD MUSHROOMS

PIKE IS A LARGE FAMILY OF FRESHWATER FISH THAT RUN THROUGH THE RIVERS OF EUROPE. ITS FRESH FLAVOUR AND FIRM TEXTURE WHEN BAKED ARE PERFECTLY COMPLEMENTED BY CREAMY PAPRIKA SAUCE WITH WILD MUSHROOMS AND PEPPERS.

SERVES FOUR TO SIX

INGREDIENTS
    about 1.5kg/3lb whole pike, perch or
      any kosher firm-fleshed white fish
    115g/4oz/½ cup butter
    115g/4oz/½ cup finely sliced onion
    225g/8oz/3 cups wild mushrooms,
      roughly sliced
    15ml/1 tbsp paprika
    25ml/1½ tbsp flour
    250ml/8fl oz/1 cup sour cream
    15ml/1 tbsp finely chopped
      green (bell) pepper
    salt and ground black pepper

1 Clean, skin and fillet the fish and put the bones and skin in a large pan. Cover with cold water and bring to the boil. Reduce the heat, season and simmer for 30 minutes.

2 Preheat the oven to 190°C/375°F/ Gas 5. Butter a roasting pan, add the fillets and lightly season.

3 Melt the remaining butter in a pan and add the onion. Cook gently for 3–4 minutes, before adding the mushrooms. Cook for a further 2–3 minutes then sprinkle in the paprika.

COOK'S TIP
Serve with tiny pasta, or little dumplings such as spaetzel.

4 Strain the fish stock, ladle out 250ml/8fl oz/1 cup and pour into the onion and mushrooms.

5 Blend the flour with the sour cream, stir into the pan, then pour over the fish. Bake for 30 minutes or until just tender. Sprinkle the green pepper over the top of the onion and mushroom mixture just before serving.

Energy 385kcal/1598kJ; Protein 23g; Carbohydrate 6.6g, of which sugars 2.9g; Fat 29.8g, of which saturates 16.3g; Cholesterol 144mg; Calcium 110mg; Fibre 0.8g; Sodium 186mg.

CZECH CARP IN SPICY-SWEET SAUCE

IN THE "OLD COUNTRY", CARP IS GENERALLY SOLD ALIVE, OFTEN KEPT IN FRESH CLEAN WATER IN THE BATH UNTIL REQUIRED. EASTERN EUROPEAN JEWS BROUGHT THIS TRADITION TO NEW YORK, WHERE THE BATH TUB TRADITION ENDURED, TO THE BEMUSEMENT OF NEIGHBOURS AND LANDLORDS!

SERVES FOUR

INGREDIENTS

50g/2oz/4 tbsp butter
1 onion, sliced
2 carrots, diced
2 small parsnips, diced
¼ small celeriac, diced
juice of 1 lemon
50ml/2fl oz/¼ cup red wine vinegar
175ml/6fl oz/¾ cup dark ale
8 whole black peppercorns
2.5ml/½ tsp allspice
1 bay leaf
5ml/1 tsp chopped fresh thyme
2cm/¾in piece of root ginger, peeled and grated
1 strip of lemon peel
3 slices of dark pumpernickel bread, processed into crumbs
30ml/2 tbsp flour
15ml/1 tbsp sugar
40g/1½oz/⅓ cup raisins
6 ready-to-eat prunes
30ml/2 tbsp hazelnuts and almonds, roughly chopped
4 thick carp or sea bream steaks
salt and ground black pepper
chopped fresh chives, to garnish
dumplings and fresh bread, to serve

1 Melt half of the butter in a flame-proof casserole. Add the onion and cook for 2–3 minutes, then stir in the carrots, parsnips and celeriac. Cook for a further 5 minutes before adding the lemon juice, red wine vinegar and dark ale. Pour in just enough water to cover.

2 Place the peppercorns, allspice, bay leaf, thyme, ginger, lemon peel and a little seasoning, in a bowl. Stir in the breadcrumbs, mix well and add to the vegetables. Simmer for 15 minutes.

3 Meanwhile, melt the remaining butter in a small pan and sprinkle in the flour. Cook gently for 1–2 minutes before adding the sugar. Cook for a further 2–3 minutes or until the sugar begins to caramelize.

4 Gradually ladle all of the stock from the casserole into the flour mixture. Stir well, then pour this back into the vegetable mixture. Add the raisins, prunes, nuts and seasoning.

5 Place the fish steaks on top of the vegetables and cook for 12–15 minutes. To serve, arrange the fish on dishes, strain the vegetables, nuts and fruit and place them around the fish. Reduce the sauce by boiling quickly. Garnish with chopped chives and serve with dumplings and fresh bread.

Energy 504kcal/2115kJ; Protein 32.3g; Carbohydrate 41.6g, of which sugars 19.4g; Fat 22.5g, of which saturates 8.3g; Cholesterol 127mg; Calcium 171mg; Fibre 3.9g; Sodium 323mg.

CARP <u>WITH</u> WALNUT STUFFING

THIS JUDAEO-SPANISH WALNUT-STUFFED FISH IS A FAVOURITE IN THE BALKANS. THE FLAMBOYANT STUFFING AND DECORATIVE COAT MAKES IT A CENTRAL FEATURE OF FESTIVE GATHERINGS.

SERVES TEN

INGREDIENTS
    about 1.5kg/3lb whole carp, scaled,
      cleaned and roe reserved
    coarse sea salt
    2 tomatoes, sliced
    250ml/8fl oz/1 cup tomato juice
    salt and ground black pepper
    walnuts and fennel sprigs, to garnish
For the stuffing
    175ml/6fl oz/¾ cup walnut oil
    675g/1½lb onions, finely sliced
    5ml/1 tsp paprika
    pinch of cinnamon
    175g/6oz/1½ cups walnuts, chopped
    15ml/1 tbsp chopped fresh parsley
    10ml/2 tsp fresh lemon juice

1 Sprinkle the inside of the fish with a little sea salt. Remove any membrane or skin from the roe and roughly chop.

2 In a frying pan, heat the oil then cook the onions, paprika and cinnamon together until soft.

3 Add the roe and walnuts to the frying pan and cook, stirring all the time, for 5–6 minutes. Leave to cool before stirring in the parsley and lemon juice. Season to taste. Preheat the oven to 180°C/350°F/Gas 4.

4 Fill the cavity of the fish with half of the filling and secure with cocktail sticks (toothpicks). Spoon the remaining stuffing into the base of an ovenproof dish and then place the fish on top.

5 Arrange the sliced tomatoes over the top of the fish and spoon over the tomato juice. Bake in the oven for 30–45 minutes, or until the fish is browned and flakes easily.

6 Carefully transfer to a serving plate. Discard the cocktail sticks before serving the fish sprinkled with extra walnut pieces and sprigs of fennel.

Energy 344kcal/1425kJ; Protein 16.9g; Carbohydrate 7.3g, of which sugars 5.6g; Fat 27.7g, of which saturates 2.8g; Cholesterol 50mg; Calcium 73mg; Fibre 1.9g; Sodium 95mg.

STUFFED RED SNAPPER

SNAPPER, FILLED WITH A FETA, PICKLE AND HERB-INFUSED FISH MOUSSE AND ROASTED, MAKES A WONDERFUL MAIN COURSE FOR A DAIRY MEAL.

SERVES FOUR

INGREDIENTS

4 small red snapper, about 450g/1lb
  each, filleted and heads and
  fins removed
juice of 1 lemon
350g/12oz fish fillets, such as carp,
  pike or sole, skinned
1 egg white
2.5ml/½ tsp chopped fresh tarragon
1 dill pickle, sliced
40g/1½oz/¾ cup fresh breadcrumbs
40g/1½oz/¼ cup feta cheese or
  brinza, roughly crumbled
salt and ground white pepper
25g/1oz/2 tbsp butter, melted
sprigs of tarragon or sweet cicely plus
  pansies or other edible flowers,
  to garnish
lemon wedges, to serve

1 Preheat the oven to 180°C/350°F/ Gas 4. Wipe out the snapper and pat dry, removing any membrane with a little salt. Liberally rub the lemon juice inside the fish.

2 Put the fish fillets in a food processor with the egg white, tarragon, dill pickle, breadcrumbs and cheese. Season with a little ground white pepper.

3 Process the ingredients until they form a smooth paste, of suitable thickness for a stuffing.

4 Using a spoon, fill the fish with the fish fillet mixture and lay them in an ovenproof dish.

COOK'S TIP
The wooden satay sticks are left in place when the fish is served. They make a striking decoration and prevent the stuffing spilling out.

5 Secure the fish with wooden satay sticks and bake for 40–50 minutes. Spoon over the melted butter halfway through cooking.

6 Transfer the fish carefully to a serving plate. Serve with lemon wedges and garnish with fresh sprigs of tarragon or sweet cicely and edible flowers, if using.

Energy 500kcal/2108kJ; Protein 82g; Carbohydrate 8g, of which sugars 0.5g; Fat 16g, of which saturates 6.2g; Cholesterol 176mg; Calcium 194mg; Fibre 0.2g; Sodium 621mg.

GRILLED FISH IN VINE LEAVES WITH GREEN ZCHUG

ALMOST ANY KIND OF FIRM, WHITE FISH WILL DO FOR THESE KEBABS. THE FISH IS FIRST MARINATED IN A SPICY MIXTURE, THEN WRAPPED IN VINE LEAVES TO SEAL IN THE FLAVOURS. THE VINE-LEAF PARCEL BECOMES CRISP WHEN COOKED TO CONTRAST WITH ITS SUCCULENT, AROMATIC CONTENTS. THE GREEN, FRAGRANT, HOT-SPICED ZCHUG IS DELICIOUS ALONGSIDE.

SERVES FOUR

INGREDIENTS
  small bunch of fresh coriander
    (cilantro), finely chopped
  2–3 garlic cloves, chopped
  5–10ml/1–2 tsp ground cumin
  60ml/4 tbsp olive oil
  juice of 1 lemon
  salt
  about 30 preserved vine leaves
  4–5 large white fish fillets, skinned,
    such as haddock, ling or monkfish
For the green zchug
  6 cloves garlic, finely chopped
  1 fresh red chilli, finely chopped
  1 fresh green chilli, finely chopped
  1 small bunch coriander (cilantro)
    leaves, finely chopped
  1 small bunch mint, finely chopped
  10ml/2 tsp cumin
  2.5ml/½ tsp turmeric
  seeds of 3–5 cardamom pods
  2.5ml/½ tsp dried ginger
  juice of ½ lemon or lime
  salt to taste
  pinch of sugar
  30ml/2 tbsp olive oil

1 Combine the coriander, garlic, cumin, olive oil, lemon and salt. Set aside.

2 Rinse the vine leaves in a bowl, then soak them in cold water. Remove any bones from the fish and cut each fillet into about eight bitesize pieces. Coat the pieces of fish in the coriander-garlic mixture, cover and chill for 1 hour.

COOK'S TIP
Green zchug is a variation on the famous Israeli sauce, brought to that country by its Yemeni immigrants.

3 Meanwhile, prepare the green zchug. Combine the ingredients in a bowl and set aside.

4 Drain the vine leaves and pat dry on kitchen paper. Lay a vine leaf flat on the work surface and place a piece of marinated fish in the centre. Fold the edges of the leaf over the fish, then wrap up the fish and leaf into a small parcel. Repeat with the remaining pieces of fish and vine leaves.

COOK'S TIP
If using authentic wooden skewers, be sure to soak them in cold water first. Keeping them moist will prevent them from catching fire under a grill (broiler) or on a barbecue.

5 Thread the parcels on to wooden kebab skewers that have been soaked in water, and brush with leftover marinade.

6 Heat the grill (broiler) on the hottest setting and cook the kebabs for 2–3 minutes on each side. Serve immediately, with the sweet and sour zchug sauce for dipping.

Energy 354kcal/1477kJ; Protein 46.3g; Carbohydrate 0.7, of which sugars 0g; Fat 18.3g, of which saturates 2.6g; Cholesterol 115mg; Calcium 51mg; Fibre 0.1g; Sodium 152mg.

CARIBBEAN FISH STEAKS

THE JEWISH COMMUNITIES OF THE CARIBBEAN ISLANDS DATE BACK TO THE ARRIVAL OF SPANISH AND PORTUGUESE FAMILIES FLEEING THE SPANISH INQUISITION. THIS DISH, FULL OF CARIBBEAN FLAVOURS, CAN BE MADE WITH ANY KOSHER FISH — HERE IT IS COD.

SERVES FOUR

INGREDIENTS
45ml/3 tbsp sunflower oil
6 shallots
1 garlic clove
1 fresh green chilli, seeded and finely chopped
400g/14oz can chopped tomatoes
2 bay leaves
1.5ml/¼ tsp cayenne pepper
5ml/1 tsp ground allspice
juice of 2 limes
4 cod steaks
5ml/1 tsp muscovado (molasses) sugar
10ml/2 tsp angostura bitters
salt

1 Slowly heat the oil in a frying pan. Finely chop the shallots and add them to the frying pan. Cook for 5 minutes until soft. Crush a peeled garlic clove into the frying pan and add the chilli. Cook for a further 2 minutes, then stir in the tomatoes, bay leaves, cayenne pepper, allspice and lime juice, with a little salt to taste.

2 Cook gently for 15 minutes, then add the cod steaks and baste with the tomato sauce. Cover and cook for 10 minutes. Transfer the steaks to a warmed dish and keep hot while you prepare the sauce. Stir the sugar and angostura bitters into the sauce, simmer for 2 minutes, then pour over the fish.

Energy 266kcal/1114kJ; Protein 37.7g; Carbohydrate 6.5g, of which sugars 5.8g; Fat 10g, of which saturates 1.3g; Cholesterol 92mg; Calcium 33mg; Fibre 1.4g; Sodium 130mg.

RED MULLET WITH CHERMOULA AND PRESERVED LEMONS

CHERMOULA IS A CHUNKY, PASTE-LIKE MIXTURE OF CORIANDER, CHILLIES, SPICES AND CITRUS WHICH IS OFTEN SERVED WITH FISH. MOROCCO'S JEWISH COMMUNITIES WERE FAMOUS FOR THEIR CHERMOULAS. IT MAY BE USED AS A MARINADE, SPREAD, DIPPING SAUCE OR CONDIMENT AND IS AS DELICIOUS WITH VEGETABLES, EGGS, MEAT, SOUPS AND GRAINS AS IT IS WITH FISH.

SERVES FOUR

INGREDIENTS
- 30–45ml/2–3 tbsp olive oil, plus extra for brushing
- 1 onion, chopped
- 1 carrot, chopped
- ½ preserved lemon, finely chopped
- 4 plum tomatoes, peeled and chopped
- 600ml/1 pint/2½ cups fish stock or water
- 3–4 new potatoes, peeled and cubed
- 4 small red mullet or snapper, gutted and filleted
- handful of black olives, pitted and halved
- small bunch of fresh coriander (cilantro), chopped
- small bunch of mint, chopped
- salt and ground black pepper

For the chermoula
- small bunch of fresh coriander, (cilantro) finely chopped
- 2–3 garlic cloves, chopped
- 5–10ml/1–2 tsp ground cumin
- pinch of saffron threads
- 60ml/4 tbsp olive oil
- juice of 1 lemon
- 1 hot red chilli, seeded and chopped
- 5ml/1 tsp salt

COOK'S TIP
These mullet are delicious served as a main course, accompanied by spiced couscous and a delicious herb-filled salad. Alternatively, they may be eaten as an appetizer, perhaps with an extra helping of black olives.

1 To make the chermoula, pound the ingredients in a mortar with a pestle, or process them together in a food processor, then set aside.

2 Heat the olive oil in a pan. Add the onion and stir fry quickly, then add the carrot and cook until browned.

3 Stir in half the preserved lemon, along with 30ml/2 tbsp of the chermoula, the tomatoes and the stock or water. Bring to the boil, then reduce the heat, cover and simmer for about 30 minutes. Add the potatoes and simmer for a further 10 minutes, until they are tender.

4 Preheat the grill (broiler) on the hottest setting and brush a baking sheet or grill pan with oil. Brush the fish fillets with olive oil and a little of the chermoula. Season with salt and pepper, then place the fillets, skin side up, on the sheet or pan and cook under the grill for 5–6 minutes.

5 Meanwhile, stir the olives, the remaining chermoula and preserved lemon into the sauce and check the seasoning. Serve the fish fillets in wide bowls, spoon the sauce over and sprinkle liberally with chopped coriander and mint.

Energy 392kcal/1635kJ; Protein 22g; Carbohydrate 18.2g, of which sugars 6.6g; Fat 26.3g, of which saturates 3.3g; Cholesterol 0mg; Calcium 129mg; Fibre 3.6g; Sodium 549mg.

MEXICAN-STYLE SALT COD

THE SPANISH INQUISITION CAME ABOUT AROUND THE SAME TIME AS THE DISCOVERY OF THE NEW WORLD. JEWS, BOTH SECRET JEWS (MARRANOS) AND NEW CHRISTIANS WHO HAD CONVERTED FROM JUDAISM, WERE OFTEN LUCKY ENOUGH TO JOIN THE SPANISH SETTLERS. THEY TOOK WITH THEM A TASTE FOR SALT COD. THIS DISH IS A MEXICAN RENDITION AND INCLUDES PICKLED CHILLIES.

SERVES SIX

INGREDIENTS

450g/1lb dried salt cod
105ml/7 tbsp extra virgin olive oil
1 onion, halved and thinly sliced
4 garlic cloves, crushed
2 x 400g/14oz can chopped tomatoes
450g/½lb fresh tomatoes, chopped
pinch each of cumin, cinnamon
  and cloves
pinch of sugar
75g/3oz/¾ cup flaked (sliced) almonds
75g/3oz/½ cup pickled chilli slices
115g/4oz/1 cup green olives stuffed
  with pimiento
small bunch of fresh parsley,
  finely chopped
2–3 sprigs fresh coriander (cilantro)
salt and ground black pepper
fresh flat leaf parsley, to garnish
crusty bread, to serve

1 Put the cod in a large bowl and pour over enough cold water to cover. Soak for 24 hours, changing the water at least 5 times during this period.

2 Drain the cod and remove the skin. Shred the flesh finely using two forks, and put it into a bowl. Set it aside.

COOK'S TIP
Salt cod is available in specialist fishmongers, Spanish delicatessens and West Indian stores.

3 Heat half the oil in a large frying pan. Add the onion slices and fry over a medium heat, stirring often with a wooden spoon, until the onion has softened and is translucent. Do not let the onion slices burn.

4 Remove the onion from the pan and set aside. Make sure you transfer the oil with the onion as it is an important flavouring in this dish and must not be discarded.

5 Add the remaining olive oil to the frying pan. When it is hot but not smoking, add the crushed garlic and fry gently for 2 minutes, stirring constantly with the wooden spoon.

6 Add the tomatoes and their juice to the pan and stir to mix. Sprinkle with cumin, cinnamon, cloves and a pinch of sugar. Cook over a medium–high heat for about 20 minutes, stirring occasionally with the wooden spoon, until the mixture has reduced and thickened. Towards the end of the cooking time, stir the sauce more frequently to make sure it does not stick to the base of the pan as the liquid evaporates from it.

7 Meanwhile, spread out the flaked almonds in a single layer in a large heavy frying pan. Toast them over a medium heat for a few minutes, shaking the pan lightly throughout the process so that they turn golden brown all over. Do not let them burn.

8 Add the chilli slices and stuffed olives to the toasted almonds.

9 Stir in the shredded fish, mixing it in thoroughly, and cook for 20 minutes more, stirring occasionally, until the mixture is almost dry.

10 Season to taste, add the parsley and coriander, and cook for a further 2–3 minutes. Garnish with parsley leaves and serve in warmed bowls, with crusty bread.

Energy 342kcal/1425kJ; Protein 28.3g; Carbohydrate 5.8g, of which sugars 5.4g; Fat 23g, of which saturates 3g; Cholesterol 44mg; Calcium 69mg; Fibre 3g; Sodium 742mg.

COD PLAKI

THIS IS A CLASSIC DISH OF THE JEWS OF GREECE, WHICH — VARYING THE HERBS — IS EATEN IN ITALY, TURKEY AND OTHER PARTS OF THE MEDITERRANEAN. IT IS DELICIOUS EATEN HOT OR AT COOL ROOM TEMPERATURE AND MAKES A NICE SHABBAT LUNCH.

SERVES SIX

INGREDIENTS
300ml/½ pint/1¼ cups olive oil
2 onions, thinly sliced
3 large well-flavoured tomatoes,
  roughly chopped
5 garlic cloves, thinly sliced
5ml/1 tsp sugar
5ml/1 tsp chopped fresh dill
5ml/1 tsp chopped fresh mint
5ml/1 tsp chopped fresh
  celery leaves
15ml/1 tbsp chopped fresh parsley
6 cod steaks
juice of 1 lemon
salt and ground black pepper
extra dill, mint or parsley, to garnish

1 Heat the oil in a large heavy frying pan or flameproof dish. Add the onions and cook until pale golden. Add the tomatoes, garlic, sugar, dill, mint, celery leaves and parsley with 300ml/½ pint/1¼ cups water. Season with salt and pepper, then simmer, uncovered, for 25 minutes, until the liquid has reduced by one third.

2 Add the fish steaks and cook gently for 10–12 minutes, until the fish is just cooked. Remove from the heat and add the lemon juice. Cover and leave to stand for about 20 minutes before serving. Lift the cod out, arrange in a dish and spoon the sauce over. Garnish with herbs and serve warm or cold.

Energy 492kcal/2041kJ; Protein 37.7g; Carbohydrate 6.7g, of which sugars 5.6g; Fat 35g, of which saturates 5g; Cholesterol 92mg; Calcium 36mg; Fibre 1.4g; Sodium 128mg.

MACKEREL IN WHITE WINE SAUCE

A homely Eastern European dish of tomato and wine-baked fish. Once the sauce is ready, the mackerel is cooked quickly in batches, so you can prepare the first part of the dish ahead of time, if you like. It makes an excellent supper to share with family or friends on a cold evening.

SERVES FOUR

INGREDIENTS

    4 mackerel, filleted, with tails on
    50ml/2fl oz/¼ cup olive oil
    2 onions, finely sliced
    5 garlic cloves, finely chopped
    400g/14oz can plum tomatoes
    250ml/8fl oz/1 cup dry white wine
    salt and ground black pepper
    lemon slices, and parsley, to garnish
    crusty rye bread, to serve

1 Preheat the oven to 200°C/400°F/ Gas 6. Pat the fish fillets dry with kitchen paper.

2 In a flameproof casserole, cook the onions for 3–4 minutes. Stir in the garlic, followed by the tomatoes and seasoning. Cook for 20 minutes.

3 Carefully add two of the mackerel fillets, skin side up. Cook for 5 minutes on one side then remove and keep warm while you cook the remaining two mackerel. Using a slotted spoon, carefully transfer the four fillets to individual ovenproof dishes, cooked side up. Fold each fish loosely in half and pour in the tomato sauce, dividing it among the dishes.

4 Pour in the wine and cover each dish with foil. Cook in the oven for a further 25 minutes. Serve garnished with slices of lemon, sprigs of parsley and a little chopped parsley, accompanied by crusty rye bread.

Energy 504kcal/2096kJ; Protein 39.2g; Carbohydrate 4.7g, of which sugars 4.3g; Fat 32.1g, of which saturates 6.7g; Cholesterol 106mg; Calcium 39mg; Fibre 1.2g; Sodium 128mg.

MEDITERRANEAN COLD FISH <u>WITH</u> TOMATOES

FROM TURKEY AND GREECE TO NORTH AFRICA AND ISRAEL, FISH IS OFTEN COOKED WITH TOMATOES THEN COOLED AND EATEN AT COOL ROOM TEMPERATURE. THIS MAKES A TERRIFIC SHABBAT LUNCH.

SERVES FOUR

INGREDIENTS

- 60ml/4 tbsp extra virgin olive oil, or sunflower oil
- 900g/2lb red mullet or snapper
- 2 onions, sliced
- 1 green (bell) pepper, seeded and sliced
- 1 red (bell) pepper, seeded and sliced
- 3 garlic cloves, crushed
- 15ml/1 tbsp tomato purée (paste)
- 60ml/4 tbsp fish stock or water
- 5–6 tomatoes, peeled and sliced
- 400g/14oz can tomatoes
- 30ml/2 tbsp chopped fresh parsley
- 30ml/2 tbsp lemon juice
- 5ml/1 tsp paprika
- 15–20 green and black olives
- salt and ground black pepper
- bread and salad, to serve

VARIATION

One large fish looks spectacular, but it is tricky both to cook and serve. If you prefer, buy 4 smaller fish or fish steaks and cook for a shorter time, until just tender. The flesh should flake when tested with the tip of a knife.

1 Heat half the oil in a large roasting pan and fry the fish on both sides until golden brown. Remove from the pan, cover and keep warm.

COOK'S TIP

The delicate flesh of red mullet is highly perishable, so it is important to buy fish that is absolutely fresh and cook it as soon as possible after purchase. Ask the fishmonger to scale and clean it for you.

2 Heat the remaining oil in the pan and fry the onions for 2–3 minutes. Add the peppers and cook for 3–4 minutes, stirring occasionally, then add the garlic and stir-fry for 1 minute more.

3 Mix the tomato purée with the fish stock or water and stir into the pan with the fresh and canned tomatoes, parsley, lemon juice, paprika and seasoning. Simmer for 15 minutes.

4 Return the fish to the roasting pan and cover with the sauce. Cook for 10 minutes, then add the olives and cook for a further 5 minutes or until the fish is just cooked through.

5 Transfer the fish to a serving dish and pour the sauce over the top. Allow to cool, then cover and chill until completely cold. Serve cold, with chunks of bread and a mixed salad.

Energy 440kcal/1843kJ; Protein 45g; Carbohydrate 13.5g, of which sugars 12.9g; Fat 23.3g, of which saturates 2.3g; Cholesterol 0mg; Calcium 190mg; Fibre 4.5g; Sodium 798mg.

MARINATED FRIED FISH

INFUSED WITH SPICES AND FRIED WHOLE TO A CRISP OUTSIDE WITH A SUCCULENT INTERIOR, THIS FISH IS AN INDIAN JEWISH FAVOURITE. SERVE WITH TURMERIC-ROASTED POTATO CHUNKS.

SERVES FOUR TO SIX

INGREDIENTS
1 small onion, coarsely chopped
4 garlic cloves, crushed
5cm/2in piece fresh root
  ginger, chopped
5ml/1 tsp ground turmeric
10ml/2 tsp chilli powder
4 red mullet or snapper
vegetable oil, for shallow frying
5ml/1 tsp cumin seeds
3 fresh green chillies, finely sliced
salt
lemon or lime wedges, to serve

VARIATION
The fish may be roasted instead of fried. Drizzle with oil, then roast at 200–220°C/400–425°F/Gas 6–7 for 20–25 minutes.

1 In a food processor, grind the first five ingredients with salt to a smooth paste. Make several slashes on both sides of the fish and rub them with the paste. Leave to rest for 1 hour. Excess fluid will be released as the salt dissolves, so lightly pat the fish dry with kitchen paper without removing the coating of paste.

2 Heat the oil and fry the cumin seeds and sliced chillies for 1 minute. Add the fish. Cook in batches if necessary, and fry on one side. It is important not to overcrowd the pan. When the first side is sealed, turn them over very gently to ensure that they do not break. Fry until golden brown on both sides, drain and serve hot, with lemon or lime wedges.

Energy 150kcal/623kJ; Protein 13.1g; Carbohydrate 1.6g, of which sugars 1.3g; Fat 10.2g, of which saturates 0.9g; Cholesterol 0mg; Calcium 52mg; Fibre 0.3g; Sodium 68mg.

POULTRY DISHES

Many Jewish families in the shtetlach kept a few chickens, as these could be reared on a small amount of grain. When the birds reached the right plumpness — which, with luck, coincided with a family simcha or a festival — they were ritually slaughtered and examined for kashrut. Today, poultry is still beloved of Jews everywhere, and it is not difficult to see why, as it can be prepared and cooked in so many different ways. Whether a Friday night roast chicken, a Rosh Hashanah goose redolent of apples and honey, an Ethiopian stew of chicken and chillies or an Indian dish of curry and herbs, it would be hard to find a Jewish cook who did not make use of these meats. And when Ashkenazim arrived in what would one day be the state of Israel, and missed their delicate wiener schnitzel from the Old Country, what did they make? Schnitzel from turkey meat, arguably Israel's national dish.

ISRAELI BARBECUED CHICKEN

NEXT TO A SHABBAT ROAST CHICKEN, BARBECUED CHICKEN IS A FAVOURITE ISRAELI WAY WITH THIS TASTY BIRD. THE CINNAMON AND CUMIN TELL OF ITS EGYPTIAN HERITAGE.

SERVES FOUR

INGREDIENTS

  5 garlic cloves, chopped
  30ml/2 tbsp ground cumin
  7.5ml/1½ tsp ground cinnamon
  5ml/1 tsp paprika
  juice of 1 lemon
  30ml/2 tbsp olive oil
  1.3kg/3lb chicken, cut into
   8 portions
  salt and ground black pepper
  fresh coriander (cilantro) leaves,
   to garnish
  warmed pitta bread, salad and
   lemon wedges, to serve

VARIATION
For a Yemenite flavour, use 7.5ml/
1½ tsp turmeric and a pinch of ground
cardamom in place of the cinnamon.

1 In a bowl, combine the garlic, cumin, cinnamon, paprika, lemon juice, oil, salt and pepper. Add the chicken and turn to coat thoroughly. Leave to marinate for at least 1 hour or cover and place in the refrigerator overnight.

2 Light the barbecue and cook over hot coals for about 40 minutes.

3 Arrange the dark meat on the grill (broiler) and cook for 10 minutes, turning once.

4 Place the remaining chicken on the grill and cook for 7–10 minutes, turning occasionally, until golden brown and the juices run clear when pricked with a skewer. Serve immediately, with pitta breads, lemon wedges and salad.

Energy 516kcal/2140kJ; Protein 39.8g; Carbohydrate 1.2g, of which sugars 0.9g; Fat 39g, of which saturates 10.5g; Cholesterol 208mg; Calcium 20mg; Fibre 0.2g; Sodium 163mg.

CHICKEN, SPLIT PEA AND AUBERGINE KORESH

THIS IS A LIGHT CALIFORNIAN CHICKEN VERSION OF THE PERSIAN LAMB KORESH, A THICK, SAUCY STEW. IT IS A MAINSTAY OF THE HUGE PERSIAN-JEWISH COMMUNITY IN LOS ANGELES.

SERVES FOUR TO SIX

INGREDIENTS
50g/2oz/¼ cup green split peas
45–60ml/3–4 tbsp olive oil
1 large or 2 small onions,
  finely chopped
500g/1¼lb boneless
  chicken thighs
500ml/17fl oz/2¼ cups
  chicken stock
5ml/1 tsp ground turmeric
2.5ml/½ tsp ground cinnamon
1.5ml/¼ tsp grated nutmeg
2 aubergines (eggplants), diced
8–10 ripe tomatoes, diced
2 garlic cloves, crushed
30ml/2 tbsp dried mint
salt and ground black pepper
fresh mint, to garnish
rice, to serve

1 Put the split peas in a bowl, pour over cold water to cover, then leave to soak for about 4 hours. Drain well.

2 Heat a little of the oil in a pan, add two-thirds of the onions and cook for about 5 minutes. Add the chicken and cook until golden brown on all sides.

3 Add the soaked split peas to the chicken mixture, then the stock, turmeric, cinnamon and nutmeg. Cook over a medium-low heat for about 40 minutes, until the split peas are tender.

VARIATION
To make a traditional lamb koresh, use 675g/1½lb lamb stew chunks in place of the chicken. Add to the onions, pour over water to cover and cook for 1½ hours until tender, then proceed as above.

4 Heat the remaining oil in a pan, add the aubergines and remaining onions and cook until lightly browned. Add the tomatoes, garlic and mint. Season.

5 Just before serving, stir the aubergine mixture into the chicken and split pea stew. Garnish with fresh mint leaves and serve with rice.

Energy 278kcal/1166kJ; Protein 25.6g; Carbohydrate 14.1g, of which sugars 8.9g; Fat 13.6g, of which saturates 3g; Cholesterol 108mg; Calcium 47mg; Fibre 4.3g; Sodium 51mg.

CHICKEN TAGINE <u>WITH</u> GREEN OLIVES <u>AND</u> PRESERVED LEMONS

THIS MAY BE MOROCCO'S MOST FAMOUS DISH — IT'S CERTAINLY DELICIOUS, AND VERY POPULAR WITH MOROCCAN JEWS ALL OVER THE WORLD. IF YOU ARE UNABLE TO FIND PRESERVED LEMONS, CUT SEVERAL LEMONS INTO QUARTERS OR WEDGES AND BAKE THEM ALONG WITH THE CHICKEN. SIMILARLY, IF YOU CANNOT FIND CRACKED GREEN OLIVES, USE PIMIENTO-STUFFED ONES.

SERVES FOUR

INGREDIENTS
  1.3kg/3lb chicken
  3 garlic cloves, crushed
  small bunch of fresh coriander
    (cilantro), finely chopped
  juice of ½ lemon
  5ml/1 tsp coarse salt
  45–60ml/3–4 tbsp olive oil
  1 large onion, grated
  pinch of saffron threads
  5ml/1 tsp ground ginger
  5ml/1 tsp ground black pepper
  1 cinnamon stick
  175g/6oz/1½ cups cracked
    green olives
  2 preserved lemons,
    cut into strips

1 Rub the garlic, coriander, lemon juice and salt into the body cavity of the chicken.

2 Mix the olive oil with the grated onion, ginger and pepper, add a pinch of saffron and rub this over the chicken. Cover and stand in a deep dish for 30 minutes.

3 Transfer the chicken to a tagine or large, heavy flameproof casserole and pour the marinating juices over. Pour in enough water to come halfway up the chicken, add the cinnamon stick and bring the water to the boil. Reduce the heat, cover with a lid and simmer for about 1 hour, turning the chicken occasionally.

4 Preheat the oven to 150°C/300°F/ Gas 2. Using two slotted spoons, carefully lift the chicken out of the tagine or casserole and set aside on a plate, covered with foil. Turn up the heat and boil the cooking liquid for 5 minutes to reduce it.

5 Replace the chicken in the liquid and baste it thoroughly. Add the olives and preserved lemon and place the tagine or casserole in the oven for about 15 minutes. Serve the chicken immediately with your chosen accompaniments.

COOK'S TIP
This dish makes an interesting alternative to the traditional roast chicken served on Friday night.

Energy 585kcal/2422kJ; Protein 40.4g; Carbohydrate 0.4g, of which sugars 0.3g; Fat 46.7g, of which saturates 11.7g; Cholesterol 208mg; Calcium 68mg; Fibre 1.9g; Sodium 1151mg.

ROAST LEMON CHICKEN WITH POTATOES

CHICKEN, ROASTED WITH LEMONS AND POTATOES, ALL CRISP AND SUCCULENT IN ITS TANGY JUICES, IS A TRADITIONAL FRIDAY NIGHT DINNER FOR GREEK JEWS.

SERVES FOUR

INGREDIENTS

1 organic or free-range chicken,
  about 1.6kg/3½lb
5 garlic cloves, peeled but
  left whole
15ml/1 tbsp chopped fresh thyme or
  oregano, or 5ml/1 tsp dried,
  plus 2–3 fresh sprigs of thyme
  or oregano
800g/1¾lb potatoes
juice of 1 lemon
60ml/4 tbsp extra virgin olive oil
300ml/½ pint/1¼ cups
  chicken stock
salt and ground black pepper

1 Preheat the oven to 200°C/400°F/ Gas 6. Place the chicken, breast side down, in a large roasting pan, then tuck the garlic cloves and the thyme or oregano sprigs inside the bird.

2 Peel the potatoes and quarter them lengthways. Arrange them around the chicken.

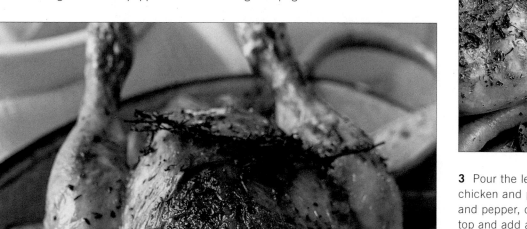

3 Pour the lemon juice over the chicken and potatoes. Season with salt and pepper, drizzle the olive oil over the top and add about three-quarters of the chopped fresh or dried thyme or oregano. Pour the chicken stock into the roasting pan.

4 Roast the chicken and potatoes for 30 minutes, then remove the roasting pan from the oven and carefully turn the chicken over. Season the bird with a little more salt and pepper, sprinkle over the remaining fresh or dried herbs, and add more hot water, if needed. Reduce the oven temperature to 190°C/375°F/ Gas 5.

5 Return the chicken and potatoes to the oven and roast them for another hour, or slightly longer, by which time both the chicken and the potatoes will be a golden colour. Serve with a crisp leafy salad.

Energy 643kcal/2678kJ; Protein 33.9g; Carbohydrate 32.2g, of which sugars 2.6g; Fat 42.8g, of which saturates 10.1g; Cholesterol 160mg; Calcium 25mg; Fibre 2g; Sodium 147mg.

SEPHARDIC SPICED CHICKEN RICE WITH LEMON AND MINT RELISH

INSPIRED BY A TRADITIONAL ISRAELI DISH, THIS SPICED CHICKEN AND CARROT RICE, SERVED WITH A LIVELY MINT RELISH, IS LIGHT AND VIVACIOUS.

SERVES FOUR

INGREDIENTS
  250g/9oz chicken, diced
  3 garlic cloves, chopped
  5ml/1 tsp ground turmeric
  30–45ml/2–3 tbsp olive oil
  2 small-medium carrots, diced
    or chopped
  seeds from 6–8 cardamom pods
  500g/1¼lb/2½ cups long grain rice
  250g/9oz tomatoes, chopped
  750ml/1¼ pints/3 cups
    chicken stock
For the lemon and mint relish
  3 tomatoes, diced
  1 bunch or large handful of fresh
    mint, chopped
  5–8 spring onions (scallions),
    thinly sliced
  juice of 2 lemons
  salt

1 To make the relish, put all the ingredients in a bowl and mix together. Chill until ready to serve.

2 Mix the diced chicken with half the garlic and the turmeric. Heat a little of the oil in a pan, add the chicken and fry briefly until the chicken has changed colour and is almost cooked. Remove from the pan and set aside.

3 Add the carrots to the pan with the remaining oil, then stir in the remaining garlic, cardamom and rice. Cook for 1–2 minutes.

4 Add the tomatoes and chicken stock to the pan and bring to the boil. Cover and simmer for about 10 minutes, until the rice is tender. A few minutes before the rice is cooked, fork in the chicken. Serve with the relish.

VARIATIONS
• Use the same quantity of pumpkin or butternut squash in place of the carrots.
• To make a vegetarian version, omit the chicken and add a 400g/14oz can of drained chickpeas to the rice just before the end of cooking.
• Dark chicken meat, such as thighs, is good in this recipe and less expensive than breast meat.

Energy 633kcal/2648kJ; Protein 26.1g; Carbohydrate 107.7g, of which sugars 7.7g; Fat 10.3g, of which saturates 1.6g; Cholesterol 44mg; Calcium 76mg; Fibre 3.1g; Sodium 64mg.

PETTI DI POLLO ALL'EBRAICA

THIS FRESH-TASTING DISH ORIGINATED AMONG THE ITALIAN-JEWISH COMMUNITY. FENNEL IS A TRADITIONAL JEWISH VEGETABLE AND THICKENING THE CHICKEN WITH EGG YOLKS CONTRIBUTES A CREAMINESS TO THE SAUCE, WHILE STILL ADHERING TO THE LAWS OF KASHRUT.

SERVES FOUR

INGREDIENTS
    4 skinless, chicken breast fillets
    plain (all-purpose) flour, for dusting
    30–45ml/2–3 tbsp olive oil
    1–2 onions, chopped
    ¼ fennel bulb, chopped (optional)
    15ml/1 tbsp chopped fresh parsley,
      plus extra to garnish
    7.5ml/1½ tsp fennel seeds
    75ml/5 tbsp dry Marsala
    120ml/4fl oz/½ cup chicken stock
    300g/11oz/2¼ cups petits pois
      (baby peas)
    juice of 1½ lemons
    2 egg yolks
    salt and ground black pepper

1 Season the chicken with salt and pepper, then dust generously with flour. Shake off the excess flour; set aside.

2 Heat 15ml/1 tbsp oil in a pan, add the onions, fennel, if using, parsley and fennel seeds. Cook for 5 minutes.

3 Add the remaining oil and the chicken to the pan and cook for 2–3 minutes on each side, until lightly browned. Remove the chicken and onion mixture from the pan and set aside.

4 Deglaze the pan by pouring in the Marsala and cooking over a high heat until reduced to about 30ml/2 tbsp, then pour in the stock. Add the peas.

5 Return the chicken and onion mixture to the pan. Cook over a very low heat while you prepare the egg mixture.

6 In a bowl, beat the lemon juice and egg yolks together, then slowly add about 120ml/4fl oz/½ cup of the hot liquid from the chicken and peas, stirring well to combine.

7 Return the mixture to the pan and cook over a low heat, stirring, until the mixture thickens slightly. (Do not allow the mixture to boil or the eggs will curdle and spoil the sauce.) Serve the chicken immediately, sprinkled with a little extra chopped fresh parsley.

VARIATION
Instead of peas, use young asparagus, thinly sliced artichokes, baby leeks or a combination of spring vegetables.

Energy 375kcal/1567kJ; Protein 43.4g; Carbohydrate 14.9g, of which sugars 7g; Fat 13.9g, of which saturates 2.7g; Cholesterol 206mg; Calcium 51mg; Fibre 4.5g; Sodium 99mg.

DORO WAT

ETHIOPIAN JEWS HAVE ADDED A LOT TO ISRAELI CULTURE. DORO WAT IS THEIR TRADITIONAL SHABBAT EVENING STEW. MADE FROM CHICKEN AND SPICES, WITH AN EGG SIMMERED IN THE SAUCE FOR EACH DINER, IT IS TRADITIONALLY SERVED WITH INJERA, A FLAT, PANCAKE-LIKE BREAD. SOFT PITTA BREAD OR RICE ARE GOOD ALTERNATIVES.

SERVES FOUR

INGREDIENTS
  90ml/6 tbsp vegetable oil
  6–8 onions, chopped
  6 garlic cloves, chopped
  10ml/2 tsp chopped fresh root ginger
  250ml/8fl oz/1 cup water or
    chicken stock
  250ml/8fl oz/1 cup passata (bottled
    strained tomatoes) or 400g/14oz
    can chopped tomatoes
  1.3kg/3lb chicken, cut into
    8–12 portions
  seeds from 5–8 cardamom pods
  2.5ml/½ tsp ground turmeric
  large pinch of ground cinnamon
  large pinch of ground cloves
  large pinch of grated nutmeg
  cayenne pepper, hot paprika or
    berbere, to taste
  4 hard-boiled eggs
  salt and ground black pepper
  fresh coriander (cilantro) and
    onion rings, to garnish
  injera, pitta bread or rice, to serve

3 Add the chicken and spices to the pan and turn the chicken in the sauce. Reduce the heat, then cover and simmer, stirring occasionally, for about 1 hour, or until the chicken is tender. Add a little more liquid if the mixture seems too thick.

4 Remove the shells from the eggs and then prick the eggs once or twice with a fork. Add the eggs to the sauce and heat gently until the eggs are warmed through. Garnish with coriander and onion rings and serve with injera, pitta bread or rice.

1 Heat the oil in a pan, add the onions and cook for 10 minutes until softened but not browned. Add the garlic and ginger and cook for 1–2 minutes.

2 Add the water or chicken stock and the passata or chopped tomatoes to the pan. Bring to the boil and cook, stirring continuously, for about 10 minutes, or until the liquid has reduced and the mixture has thickened. Season.

Energy 764kcal/3169kJ; Protein 48.8g; Carbohydrate 17.7g, of which sugars 13.1g; Fat 55.9g, of which saturates 13.2g; Cholesterol 398mg; Calcium 101mg; Fibre 3.2g; Sodium 382mg.

MILD GREEN CALCUTTA CURRY OF CHICKEN AND VEGETABLES

THIS CURRY HAS A RICH SAUCE THAT IS SWEETENED WITH DRIED AND FRESH FRUIT AND MADE FRAGRANT WITH HERBS. THE ADDITION OF COCONUT MILK MAKES A CREAMY SAUCE WITHOUT ADDING DAIRY, SO IT'S PERFECT FOR THE KOSHER KITCHEN.

SERVES FOUR

INGREDIENTS
    4 garlic cloves, chopped
    15ml/1 tbsp chopped fresh
      root ginger
    2–3 chillies, chopped
    ½ bunch fresh coriander (cilantro)
      leaves, roughly chopped
    1 onion, chopped
    juice of 1 lemon
    pinch of cayenne pepper
    2.5ml/½ tsp curry powder
    2.5ml/½ tsp ground cumin
    2–3 pinches ground cloves
    large pinch of ground coriander
    3 chicken breast fillets or
      thighs, skinned and cut into
      bitesize pieces
    30ml/2 tbsp vegetable oil
    2 cinnamon sticks
    250ml/8fl oz/1 cup chicken stock
    250ml/8fl oz/1 cup coconut milk
    15–30ml/1–2 tbsp sugar
    1–2 bananas
    ¼ pineapple, peeled and chopped
    handful of sultanas (golden raisins)
    handful of raisins or currants
    2–3 sprigs fresh mint, thinly sliced
    juice of ¼–½ lemon
    salt

1 Purée the garlic, ginger, chillies, fresh coriander, onion, lemon juice, cayenne pepper, curry powder, cumin, cloves, ground coriander and salt in a food processor or blender.

2 Toss together the chicken pieces with 15–30ml/1–2 tbsp of the spice mixture and set aside.

3 Heat the oil in a wok or frying pan, then add the remaining spice mixture and cook over a medium heat, stirring, for 10 minutes, or until the paste is lightly browned.

4 Stir the cinnamon sticks, stock, coconut milk and sugar into the pan, bring to the boil, then reduce the heat and simmer for 10 minutes.

5 Stir the chicken into the sauce and cook for 2 minutes, or until the chicken becomes opaque.

6 Meanwhile, thickly slice the bananas. Stir all the fruit into the curry and cook for 1–2 minutes. Stir in the mint and lemon juice. Check the seasoning and add more salt, spicing and lemon juice if necessary. Serve immediately.

Energy 383kcal/1622kJ; Protein 29.5g; Carbohydrate 52.8g, of which sugars 51.5g; Fat 7.5g, of which saturates 1.2g; Cholesterol 79mg; Calcium 92mg; Fibre 2.6g; Sodium 150mg.

CHICKEN BITKI

CHICKEN PATTIES, OR BITKI, ARE A FAVOURITE ASHKENAZIC DISH OF POLAND, RUSSIA AND EASTERN EUROPE. WHIPPED EGG WHITES ADDED TO THE CHICKEN MIXTURE LIGHTEN THE TEXTURE.

MAKES TWELVE

INGREDIENTS

60ml/4 tbsp vegetable oil
115g/4oz flat mushrooms,
  finely chopped
50g/2oz/1 cup fresh white
  breadcrumbs
350g/12oz skinless chicken breast
  fillets, thighs or guinea fowl,
  minced (ground) or finely chopped
2 eggs, separated
1.5ml/¼ tsp grated nutmeg
30ml/2 tbsp plain (all-purpose) flour
salt and ground black pepper
green salad and grated pickled
  beetroot (beets), to serve

1 Heat 15ml/1 tbsp of the oil in a pan and fry the mushrooms for 5 minutes until soft and all the juices have evaporated. Allow to cool.

2 Mix the crumbs, chicken, egg yolks, nutmeg, salt and pepper and flat mushrooms well.

3 Whisk the egg whites until stiff. Stir half into the chicken mixture, then fold in the remainder.

VARIATION

This is good served cold for lunch with a Russian salad and red cabbage coleslaw, plus a touch of horseradish.

4 Shape the mixture into 12 even meatballs, about 7.5cm/3in long and 2.5cm/1in wide. Roll in the flour to coat.

5 Heat the remaining oil in a frying pan and fry the bitki for 10 minutes, turning until evenly golden brown and cooked through. Serve hot with a green salad and pickled beetroot.

Energy 112kcal/470kJ; Protein 10.5g; Carbohydrate 5.6g, of which sugars 0.3g; Fat 5.5g, of which saturates 0.9g; Cholesterol 52mg; Calcium 21mg; Fibre 1.2g; Sodium 66mg.

CHICKEN COCHIN

A SIMPLE, STRAIGHTFORWARD CURRY FROM THE JEWISH COMMUNITY OF COCHIN. YOU CAN ADD VEGETABLES, SUCH AS CHUNKS OF POTATOES, TO THIS DISH IF YOU LIKE.

SERVES FOUR

INGREDIENTS
  450g/1lb chicken breast fillets,
  skinned
  45ml/3 tbsp tomato purée (paste)
  large pinch ground fenugreek
  1.5ml/¼ tsp ground fennel seeds
  5ml/1 tsp grated fresh root ginger
  7.5ml/1½ tsp ground coriander
  5ml/1 tsp crushed garlic
  5ml/1 tsp chilli powder
  1.5ml/¼ tsp ground turmeric
  30ml/2 tbsp lemon juice
  5ml/1 tsp salt
  300ml/½ pint/1¼ cups water
  45ml/3 tbsp vegetable oil
  2 onions, diced
  2–4 curry leaves
  2 fresh green chillies, seeded
  and chopped
  15ml/1 tbsp chopped fresh coriander
  (cilantro), plus extra sprigs
  to garnish
naan bread, to serve

1 Cut the chicken breast fillets into cubes. Mix the tomato purée in a bowl with the fenugreek, fennel, ginger, ground coriander, garlic, chilli powder, turmeric, lemon juice, salt and water.

2 Heat the oil in a wok, karahi or large pan and fry the onions with the curry leaves until the onions are golden. Add the chicken and stir for 1 minute to seal.

COOK'S TIP
Take care not to use too much ground fenugreek, as it can be quite bitter.

3 Pour the tomato sauce and spice mixture into the pan. Stir for 2 minutes to ensure the ingredients are well mixed.

4 Lower the heat and cook for 8–10 minutes, then add the chillies and fresh coriander. Garnish and serve.

Energy 229kcal/959kJ; Protein 28.5g; Carbohydrate 7.5g, of which sugars 5.8g; Fat 9.7g, of which saturates 1.3g; Cholesterol 79mg; Calcium 29mg; Fibre 1.4g; Sodium 588mg.

ROASTED CHICKEN WITH GRAPES AND FRESH ROOT GINGER

A FRESH, VIBRANTLY FLAVOURED CHICKEN DISH, INSPIRED BY MOROCCAN FLAVOURS BUT ENHANCED WITH FRESH GINGER RATHER THAN THE MORE TRADITIONAL DRIED VARIETY.

SERVES FOUR

INGREDIENTS

1–1.6kg/2¼–3½lb chicken
115–130g/4–4½oz fresh root
  ginger, grated
6–8 garlic cloves, roughly chopped
juice of 1 lemon
about 30ml/2 tbsp olive oil
2–3 large pinches of ground cinnamon
500g/1¼lb seeded red and green grapes
500g/1¼lb seedless green grapes
5–7 shallots, chopped
about 250ml/8fl oz/1 cup chicken stock
250ml/8fl oz/1 cup orange juice
salt, ground black pepper to taste

1 Rub the chicken with half of the ginger, the garlic, half of the lemon juice, the olive oil, cinnamon, salt and lots of pepper. Leave to marinate.

2 Meanwhile, cut the red and green seeded grapes in half, scraping out the seeds, and combine with the whole green seedless grapes.

3 Preheat the oven to 180°C/350°F/ Gas 4. Heat a heavy frying pan or flameproof casserole until hot.

4 Remove the chicken from the marinade, add to the pan and cook until browned on all sides. (There should be enough oil on the chicken to brown it but, if not, add a little extra.)

5 Put some of the shallots into the chicken cavity with the garlic and ginger from the marinade and as many of the red and green grapes that will fit inside. Roast in the oven for 40–60 minutes, or until the chicken is tender.

VARIATIONS
• This dish is good made with duck in place of the chicken. Marinate and roast as above, adding 15–30ml/1–2 tbsp honey to the pan sauce as it cooks.
• Use chicken breast fillets, with the skin still attached, instead of a whole chicken. Pan-fry the chicken fillets, rather than roasting them.

6 Remove the chicken from the pan and keep warm. Pour off any oil from the pan, reserving any sediment in the base of the pan. Add the remaining shallots to the pan and cook for about 5 minutes until softened.

7 Add half the remaining red and green grapes, the remaining ginger, the stock, orange juice and any juices from the roast chicken and cook over a medium-high heat until the grapes have cooked down to a thick sauce. Season with salt and ground black pepper and the remaining lemon juice to taste.

8 Serve the chicken on a warmed serving dish, surrounded by the sauce and the reserved grapes.

COOK'S TIP
Seeded Italia or muscat grapes have a delicious, sweet fragrance and are perfect for this recipe.

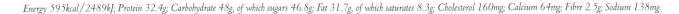

Energy 595kcal/2489kJ; Protein 32.4g; Carbohydrate 48g, of which sugars 46.8g; Fat 31.7g, of which saturates 8.3g; Cholesterol 160mg; Calcium 64mg; Fibre 2.5g; Sodium 138mg.

VARNA-STYLE CHICKEN

MUSHROOMS, THYME, TOMATOES AND SHERRY FLAVOUR THIS CHICKEN BRAISE FROM VARNA IN BULGARIA. SERVE WITH RICE, AND A CRISP SALAD AT THE SIDE.

SERVES EIGHT

INGREDIENTS

1.75kg/4lb chicken, cut into 8 pieces
2.5ml/½ tsp chopped fresh thyme
75ml/5 tbsp vegetable oil
5 garlic cloves, crushed
2 onions, finely chopped
salt and ground white pepper
basil and thyme leaves, to garnish
freshly cooked rice, to serve
For the sauce
  120ml/4fl oz/½ cup dry sherry
  45ml/3 tbsp tomato purée (paste)
  a few fresh basil leaves
  30ml/2 tbsp white wine vinegar
  generous pinch of granulated sugar
  5ml/1 tsp mild mustard, or more,
   to taste
  397g/14oz can chopped tomatoes
  225g/8oz/3 cups mushrooms, sliced

VARIATION
Replace the cultivated mushrooms with wild mushrooms, if you like.

1 Preheat the oven to 180°C/350°F/ Gas 4. Season the chicken with salt, pepper and thyme. In a large frying pan cook the chicken in the butter and oil, until golden brown. Remove from the frying pan, place in an ovenproof dish and keep hot.

2 Add the garlic and onion to the frying pan and cook for about 2–3 minutes, or until just soft.

3 For the sauce, mix together the sherry, tomato purée, salt and pepper, basil, vinegar and sugar. Add the mustard and tomatoes. Pour into the frying pan and bring to the boil.

4 Reduce the heat and add the mushrooms. Adjust the seasoning with more sugar or vinegar to taste.

5 Pour the tomato sauce over the chicken. Bake in the oven, covered, for 45–60 minutes, or until cooked thoroughly. Serve on a bed of rice, garnished with basil and thyme.

Energy 424kcal/1760kJ; Protein 28.5g; Carbohydrate 6.6g, of which sugars 5.4g; Fat 29.8g, of which saturates 7.4g; Cholesterol 140mg; Calcium 32mg; Fibre 1.7g; Sodium 132mg.

CHICKEN GHIVECI

BOTH ROMANIANS AND BULGARIANS MAKE GHIVECI, A DISH OF BRAISED CHICKEN WITH FRESH GARDEN VEGETABLES. IF GRAPES ARE IN SEASON, ADD A HANDFUL FOR A SWEET, JUICY ACCENT.

SERVES SIX

INGREDIENTS
60ml/4 tbsp vegetable oil or
   chicken fat
1 mild onion, thinly sliced
8 garlic cloves, sliced
2 red (bell) peppers, seeded
   and sliced
about 1.5kg/3½lb chicken
90ml/6 tbsp tomato purée (paste)
3 potatoes, diced
5ml/1 tsp chopped fresh rosemary
5ml/1 tsp chopped fresh marjoram
5ml/1 tsp chopped fresh thyme
3 carrots, cut into chunks
½ small celeriac, cut into chunks
120ml/4fl oz/½ cup dry white wine
2 courgettes (zucchini), sliced
salt, pinch of sugar and ground
   black pepper
chopped fresh rosemary and
   marjoram, to garnish
dark rye bread, to serve

COOK'S TIP
Chicken Ghiveci can be served with
polenta, as in Romania, or with rice,
as the Bulgarians are wont to do.

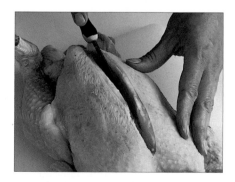

1 First, joint the chicken into 6 pieces by slicing through the middle, removing the wings and some of the breast meat, and finally the legs.

2 Heat the oil in a large flameproof casserole. Add the onion and garlic and cook for 1–2 minutes until soft and golden in colour.

3 Add the red peppers and stir fry for a further 3–4 minutes. Add the chicken joints to the casserole and brown gently on all sides for about 15 minutes.

4 Add the tomato purée, potatoes, herbs, carrots, celeriac and white wine, and season to taste with salt, a pinch of sugar and pepper. Cover and cook over a gentle heat for 40–50 minutes.

5 Add the courgette slices 5 minutes before the end of cooking. Adjust the seasoning to taste. Garnish with the herbs and serve with dark rye bread.

COOK'S TIP
Although fresh herbs contribute much to a recipe, if they are unavailable you can always replace them with 2.5ml/½ tsp dried herbs.

Energy 554kcal/2306kJ; Protein 34.9g; Carbohydrate 24.9g, of which sugars 12g; Fat 34.1g, of which saturates 8.6g; Cholesterol 160mg; Calcium 72mg; Fibre 4.4g; Sodium 207mg.

CHICKEN WITH LEMON AND GARLIC

POLLO CON LIMÓN MOST PROBABLY EVOLVED FROM THE SEPHARDIC CUISINE OF ANDALUCIA. THE SAUTÉED CHUNKS OF CHICKEN, WITH LOTS OF GARLIC AND LEMON, MAKE A SUPERB SUPPER OR, AT A SPECIAL OCCASION, SERVED AS PART OF A TERRIFIC MEZE.

SERVES TWO TO FOUR

INGREDIENTS

   2 skinless chicken breast fillets
   30ml/2 tbsp olive oil
   1 shallot, finely chopped
   6 garlic cloves, finely chopped
   5ml/1 tsp paprika
   juice of 1 lemon
   30ml/2 tbsp chopped fresh parsley
   salt and ground black pepper
   fresh flat leaf parsley, to garnish
   lemon wedges, to serve

VARIATION
You can use strips of turkey breast instead of the chicken breast. They need slightly longer cooking. The whites of spring onions (scallions) can replace the shallot and chopped green tops can replace the parsley.

1 Remove the little fillet from the back of each breast. If the breast still looks fatter than a finger, beat it with a rolling pin to make it thinner. Slice all the chicken meat into strips.

2 Heat the oil in a large frying pan. Stir-fry the chicken strips with the shallot, garlic and paprika over a high heat for about 3 minutes until cooked through.

3 Add the lemon juice and parsley and season with salt and pepper to taste. Serve hot with lemon wedges, garnished with flat leaf parsley.

Energy 164kcal/685kJ; Protein 24.4g; Carbohydrate 1.4g, of which sugars 1g; Fat 6.7g, of which saturates 1.1g; Cholesterol 70mg; Calcium 24mg; Fibre 0.6g; Sodium 63mg.

CRUMBED CHICKEN WITH GREEN MAYONNAISE

PECHUGAS DE POLLO REBOZADAS, SIMILAR TO SCHNITZEL, REFLECTS THE JEWISH INFLUENCE ON COOKING IN SOUTHERN SPAIN. LEMON WEDGES ARE A POPULAR ACCOMPANIMENT, AS IS THE TARTARE-STYLE CAPER MAYONNAISE SAUCE.

SERVES FOUR

INGREDIENTS

4 chicken breast fillets, each
  weighing about 200g/7oz
juice of 1 lemon
5ml/1 tsp paprika
plain (all-purpose) flour,
  for dusting
1–2 eggs
dried breadcrumbs, for coating
about 60ml/4 tbsp olive oil
salt and ground black pepper
lemon wedges (optional), to serve

For the mayonnaise

120ml/4fl oz/½ cup mayonnaise
30ml/2 tbsp pickled capers, drained
  and chopped
30ml/2 tbsp chopped fresh parsley
  or watercress

1 Start a couple of hours ahead, if you can. Skin the chicken fillets. Lay them upside down and, with a sharp knife, cut horizontally, almost through, from the rounded side. Open them up like a book. Press gently, to make a roundish shape, the size of a side plate. Sprinkle with lemon juice and paprika.

2 Set out three plates. Sprinkle flour over one, seasoning it well. Beat the egg with a little salt and pour into the second. Sprinkle the third with dried breadcrumbs. Dip the breasts first into the flour on both sides, then into the egg, then into the breadcrumbs. Chill the crumbed chicken, if you have time.

3 Put the mayonnaise ingredients in a bowl and mix well to combine.

4 Heat the oil in a heavy frying pan over a high heat. Fry the breast fillets, two at a time, turning after 3 minutes, until golden on both sides. Add more oil for the second batch if needed. Serve at once, with the mayonnaise and lemon wedges, if using.

Energy 584kcal/2437kJ; Protein 51.7g; Carbohydrate 10.5g, of which sugars 1g; Fat 37.6g, of which saturates 6g; Cholesterol 210mg; Calcium 56mg; Fibre 0.8g; Sodium 371mg.

BAKED CHICKEN WITH OKRA AND TOMATOES

LEGEND HAS IT THAT KING SOLOMON ORDERED 100 DISHES FOR A WELCOMING BANQUET FOR THE QUEEN OF SHEBA. THE CHEF COULD COME UP WITH ONLY 99 DISHES, SO WENT WALKING IN THE FIELDS, LOOKING FOR INSPIRATION. HE CAME UPON OKRA AND FOUND IT DELIGHTFUL SO MADE IT THE HUNDREDTH DISH, NAMING IT BEN-MAIYAH, OR "THE HUNDREDTH". OKRA — OR LADY'S FINGERS AS IT IS ALSO KNOWN — IS QUITE EXOTIC IN THE NORTH, BUT IN WARM LANDS THIS VEGETABLE IS A SUMMER STAPLE. IT IS COOKED ON ITS OWN, CAN BE COMBINED WITH LAMB OR BEEF, AND TASTES DELICIOUS IN THIS GREEK CHICKEN CASSEROLE.

SERVES FOUR

INGREDIENTS

1.6kg/3½lb organic or free-range
   roasting chicken
90ml/6 tbsp extra virgin olive oil
5ml/1 tsp dried oregano
400g/14oz can plum tomatoes,
   roughly chopped
3 garlic cloves, chopped
450ml/¾ pint/scant 2 cups hot water
600g/1lb 6oz okra
45ml/3 tbsp chopped fresh flat
   leaf parsley
salt and ground black pepper

COOK'S TIP

If you buy a larger chicken, or use large okra pods, you may need to increase the baking time. The chicken will be cooked when the joints move freely and the juices that flow when the thickest part of the thigh is pierced with a knife are no longer pink.

1 Preheat the oven to 200°C/400°F/ Gas 6. Place the chicken breast down in a large roasting pan. Drizzle half the olive oil over it and sprinkle over half the dried oregano. Add the tomatoes, garlic and 300ml/½ pint/1¼ cups of the hot water to the dish. Transfer to the oven and bake for 30 minutes.

2 Meanwhile, prepare the okra. Leave each okra pod whole and use a small sharp knife to peel the conical end. Be careful not to nick the pod and release the mucilaginous juices. You will soon get to grips with this task, but it is a good idea to get someone to help you. Rinse the okra thoroughly in cold water and then drain them well. Repeat until the water appears clear.

3 After 30 minutes, remove the pan from the oven and turn the chicken over. Add the okra, spreading it evenly around the bird. Drizzle the remaining oil over, then sprinkle with the rest of the oregano. Season and add the parsley and the remaining hot water. Turn the okra with a slotted spoon to coat it in the tomato sauce.

4 Reduce the oven temperature to 190°C/375°F/Gas 5 and bake the chicken for 1 hour more, or until it is fully cooked and the okra is tender. Take the dish out of the oven occasionally and baste both the chicken and the okra.

5 This dish is best served hot, but will happily wait for 30 minutes. It makes the perfect main course when accompanied by a salad and fresh bread.

Energy 567kcal/2350kJ; Protein 35.4g; Carbohydrate 7.6g, of which sugars 6.9g; Fat 44g, of which saturates 10.4g; Cholesterol 160mg; Calcium 260mg; Fibre 7g; Sodium 146mg.

CHARGRILLED CHICKEN <u>WITH</u> GARLIC <u>AND</u> PEPPERS

THOUGH THIS DISH HAS GREEK AND CALIFORNIAN AS WELL AS PROVENÇAL AND ITALIAN NOTES, IT IS FULL OF MEDITERRANEAN FLAVOURS. IT WOULD BE ESPECIALLY SUITED TO A BARBECUE, FOLLOWING A FIRST COURSE OF LITTLE SALADS SUCH AS HUMMUS, CHOPPED VEGETABLES AND OLIVES AND A BIG PILE OF FRESH PITTA BREAD.

SERVES FOUR TO SIX

INGREDIENTS
   1½ chickens, total weight about
      2.25kg/5lb, jointed, or
      12 chicken pieces
   2–3 red or green (bell) peppers,
      quartered, and seeded
   4–5 tomatoes, halved horizontally
   lemon wedges, to serve
For the marinade
   90ml/6 tbsp extra virgin olive oil
   juice of 1 large lemon
   5ml/1 tsp French mustard
   8 garlic cloves, crushed
   30–45ml/2–3 tbsp fresh rosemary,
      coarsely chopped
   salt and ground black pepper

1 If you are jointing the chicken yourself, divide the legs into two. Make a couple of slits in the deepest part of the flesh of each piece of chicken, using a small sharp knife. This will help the marinade to be absorbed more efficiently and let the chicken cook thoroughly.

3 Prepare the barbecue. When the coals are ready, lift the chicken pieces out of the marinade and place them on the grill. Add the pepper pieces and the tomatoes to the marinade and set it aside for 15 minutes. Cook the chicken pieces for 20–25 minutes. Watch them closely and move them away from the area where the heat is most fierce if they start to burn.

VARIATION
Instead of rosemary, use cumin and coriander leaves, and substitute harissa for mustard.

COOK'S TIP
You can, of course, cook these chicken pieces under the grill (broiler). Have the heat setting fairly high, but don't place the pieces of chicken too close. Allow about 15 minutes each side.

2 Beat together all the marinade ingredients in a large bowl. Add the chicken pieces and turn them over to coat them thoroughly in the marinade. Cover the bowl with clear film (plastic wrap) and place in the refrigerator for 4–8 hours, turning the chicken pieces over in the marinade a couple of times, if possible.

4 Turn the chicken pieces over and cook them for 20–25 minutes more. Meanwhile, thread the peppers on two long metal skewers. Add them to the barbecue grill, with the tomatoes, for the last 15 minutes of cooking. Remember to keep an eye on them and turn them over at least once. Serve with the lemon wedges.

Energy 497kcal/2060kJ; Protein 36.8g; Carbohydrate 6.3g, of which sugars 6.2g; Fat 36g, of which saturates 9.7g; Cholesterol 187mg; Calcium 25mg; Fibre 1.8g; Sodium 156mg.

MOROCCAN PIGEON PIE

B'Stillah, also known as La Pastilla, is a great dish of the Moroccan kitchen, a feast dish for special occasions. It is believed that Jews brought the dish to Morocco from Andalucia. Today it is also popular in Paris, as Moroccan Jews brought it with them from North Africa. It is especially appreciated at wedding feasts.

SERVES SIX

INGREDIENTS
  3 pigeons
  50g/2oz/4 tbsp olive oil, vegetable oil
    or pareve margarine
  1 onion, chopped
  1 cinnamon stick
  pinch of saffron threads
  2.5ml/½ tsp ground ginger
  30ml/2 tbsp chopped fresh
    coriander (cilantro)
  45ml/3 tbsp chopped fresh parsley
  pinch of ground turmeric and cloves
  1 litre/2 pints/4 cups chicken stock
    (cubed mixed with water is fine)
  15ml/1 tbsp caster (superfine) sugar
  2.5–5ml/½–1 tsp ground cinnamon
  115g/4oz/1 cup toasted almonds,
    finely chopped
  6 eggs, beaten
  salt and ground black pepper
  cinnamon and icing (confectioners')
    sugar, to garnish
For the pastry
  175g/6oz/¾ cup oil or
    pareve margarine
  16 sheets filo pastry
  1 egg yolk

1 Wash the pigeons and place in a pan with the oil, onion, cinnamon stick, saffron, ginger, coriander, parsley and turmeric. Season with salt and pepper. Add the stock and just enough water to cover and bring to the boil. Cover and simmer gently for about 1 hour, until the pigeon flesh is very tender.

COOK'S TIP
The traditional pastry used in this dish is warko, though filo is quicker and easier to work with.

2 Strain off the stock. Boil down until reduced by half. Reserve.

3 Skin and bone the pigeons and shred the flesh into bitesize pieces. Preheat the oven to 180°C/350°F/Gas 4. Mix together the sugar, cinnamon and almonds and set aside.

4 Measure 150ml/¼ pint/⅔ cup of the reserved stock into a small pan. Add the eggs and mix well. Stir over a low heat until creamy and very thick and almost set. Season with salt and pepper.

5 Brush a 30cm/12in diameter ovenproof dish with a little oil or pareve margarine and lay the first sheet of pastry in the dish. Brush this with a little more of the oil or fat, and continue with five more sheets of pastry. Top with the almond mixture, then half the egg mixture. Moisten with a little stock.

6 Layer four more sheets of filo pastry, brushing with a little oil or fat as before. Lay the pigeon meat on top, then add the remaining egg mixture and more stock. Cover with all the remaining pastry, brushing each sheet with the oil or fat, and tuck in any overlap.

7 Brush the pie with egg yolk and bake for 40 minutes. Raise the oven temperature to 200°C/400°F/Gas 6, and bake for 15 minutes more, until the pastry is crisp and golden. Garnish with a lattice design of cinnamon and icing sugar. Serve hot.

VARIATIONS
• For a Muslim version, use clarified butter instead of the pareve margarine and decorate more generously with icing sugar.
• Boneless and skinless chicken thighs may be used instead of pigeon.

Energy 628kcal/2607kJ; Protein 27.1g; Carbohydrate 15.1g, of which sugars 1.6g; Fat 51.7g, of which saturates 6.6g; Cholesterol 224mg; Calcium 113mg; Fibre 2.1g; Sodium 130mg.

ROAST GOOSE WITH APPLES

THE JEWS OF EASTERN EUROPE AND GERMANY ATE ROAST GOOSE WITH APPLES AS A CHANUKKAH TREAT, OFTEN SERVING IT SURROUNDED BY BRAISED RED CABBAGE.

SERVES SIX

INGREDIENTS
  115g/4oz/scant 1 cup raisins
  finely grated rind and juice of
    1 orange
  1 onion, finely chopped
  25g/1oz/2 tbsp vegetable oil
  75g/3oz/¾ cup hazelnuts, chopped
  175g/6oz/3 cups fresh white
    breadcrumbs
  15ml/1 tbsp clear honey
  15ml/1 tbsp chopped fresh marjoram
  30ml/2 tbsp chopped fresh parsley
  6 red eating apples
  15ml/1 tbsp lemon juice
  4.5–5kg/10–11lb oven-ready
    young goose
  salt and ground black pepper
  fresh herbs, to garnish
  orange wedges, red cabbage and
    French (green) beans, to serve

1 Preheat the oven to 220°C/425°F/Gas 7. Put the raisins in a bowl and pour over the orange juice. Gently cook the onion in the oil for 5 minutes.

2 Add the chopped nuts to the pan and cook for a further 4–5 minutes, or until beginning to brown.

3 Add the cooked onion and nuts to the raisins with 50g/2oz/1 cup of the breadcrumbs, the orange rind, honey, herbs and seasoning. Mix well.

4 Wash the apples and remove the cores to leave a 2cm/¾in hole. Using a sharp knife, make a shallow cut around the middle of each apple. Brush the cut and the cavity with the lemon juice to prevent it from browning.

5 Pack the centre of each apple with the nut and raisin stuffing.

6 Mix the remaining breadcrumbs into the stuffing and stuff the bird's tail end. Close with a small skewer.

7 Place the goose in a roasting pan, then prick the skin all over with a skewer. Roast for 30 minutes, then reduce the oven temperature to 180°C/350°F/Gas 4 and cook for a further 3 hours, pouring the excess fat out of the pan several times.

8 Arrange the apples around the goose and bake for 30–40 minutes, or until tender. Rest the goose in a warm place for 15 minutes, before carving. Garnish with fresh herbs, stuffed apples and orange wedges, with red cabbage and green beans.

COOK'S TIP
To test whether the goose is cooked, pierce the thigh with a thin skewer. The juice that runs out should be pale yellow. If it is tinged with pink, roast the goose for a further 10 minutes and test again.

Energy 822kcal/3437kJ; Protein 45.8g; Carbohydrate 45g, of which sugars 44.4g; Fat 15.1g, of which saturates 3g; Cholesterol 0mg; Calcium 87mg; Fibre 3.1g; Sodium 486mg.

DUCKLING TAPUZIM

*JEWS FROM CENTRAL EUROPE AND FRANCE HAVE TRADITIONALLY ENJOYED DUCK FOR THEIR
CELEBRATIONS, ESPECIALLY COOKED WITH SWEET FRUIT FOR ROSH HASHANAH. WHEN THESE JEWS
MADE THEIR WAY TO ISRAEL, THEY ADAPTED THE DUCK TO THE CITRUS AND ORCHARD FRUIT WHICH
GREW SO ABUNDANTLY. "TAPUZIM" MEANS ORANGE IN HEBREW. THIS CLASSIC DISH TASTES DELICIOUS,
AND IS VERY EASILY PREPARED.*

SERVES FOUR

INGREDIENTS
    1.75kg/4½lb duckling
    60ml/4 tbsp chopped fresh parsley
    1 lemon, quartered
    1 orange, cut into wedges
    3 carrots, sliced
    2 celery sticks, sliced
    1 onion, roughly chopped
    salt and ground black pepper
    apricots and sage flowers, to garnish
For the sauce
    425g/15oz can apricots in syrup
    50g/2oz/¼ cup granulated sugar
    10ml/2 tsp English mustard
    60ml/4 tbsp apricot jam
    15ml/1 tbsp lemon juice
    10ml/2 tsp freshly grated lemon rind
    100ml/4fl oz/½ cup fresh
      orange juice
    2.5ml/½ tsp ginger
    60–75ml/4–5 tbsp brandy

1 Preheat the oven to 220°C/425°F/
Gas 7. Clean the duck well and pat
dry with kitchen paper. Season the
skin liberally.

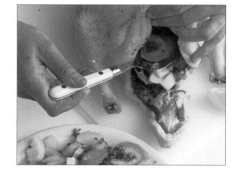

2 Mix together the chopped parsley,
lemon, carrots, celery sticks and onion
in a bowl, then carefully spoon this into
the cavity of the duck.

3 Cook the duck for 45 minutes on a
trivet set over a roasting pan. Baste the
duck occasionally with its juices.

4 Remove the duck from the oven and
prick the skin well. Return it to the
oven, reduce the temperature to 180°C/
350°F/Gas 4, and cook for a further
1–1½ hours or until the duck is golden
brown, tender and crispy.

5 Meanwhile, put the apricots and their
syrup, the sugar and mustard in a food
processor or blender. Add the jam
and process until smooth.

6 Pour the apricot mixture into a pan
and stir in the lemon juice and rind,
orange juice and spices. Bring to the
boil, add the brandy and cook for a
further 1–2 minutes. Remove from the
heat and adjust the seasoning.

7 Discard the fruit, vegetables and
herbs from inside the duck, pressing it
to extract their juices first. Arrange the
bird on a serving platter. Garnish with
fresh apricots and sage flowers. Serve
the sauce separately.

Energy 487kcal/2052kJ; Protein 45.8g; Carbohydrate 45g, of which sugars 44.4g; Fat 15.1g, of which saturates 3g; Cholesterol 248mg; Calcium 100mg; Fibre 2.6g; Sodium 287mg.

DUCK BREASTS WITH A WALNUT AND POMEGRANATE SAUCE

THIS IS A MODERN VERSION OF A TRADITIONAL DISH OF THE JEWS OF IRAQ AND IRAN. POMEGRANATES ARE CONSIDERED SPECIAL FRUIT, AS IT IS SAID THAT EACH ONE CONTAINS 613 SEEDS, THE SAME NUMBER AS THE NUMBER OF MITZVOT, OR COMMANDMENTS, WHICH JEWS ARE TAUGHT TO ADHERE TO. FOR THIS REASON, POMEGRANATES HOLD A SPECIAL PLACE ON MANY FAMILY TABLES.

SERVES FOUR

INGREDIENTS
60ml/4 tbsp olive oil
2 onions, very thinly sliced
2.5ml/½ tsp ground turmeric
400g/14oz/3½ cups walnuts,
  roughly chopped
1 litre/1¾ pints/4 cups duck or
  chicken stock
6 pomegranates
30ml/2 tbsp caster (superfine) sugar
60ml/4 tbsp lemon juice
4 duck breast fillets, about
  225g/8oz each
salt and ground black pepper

VARIATION
Preparing duck with pomegranates and walnuts dates back to the Jews of Iraq, Iran, and Syria. Traditionally, the dish comprised duck pieces simmered over a long period, with finely chopped walnuts and a thick, sweet and sour pomegranate syrup, as favoured by the Jews of these regions for centuries. Today, this traditional dish is only found in a handful of places, such as Los Angeles, or perhaps London, where there are large expatriot Iranian Jewish communities.

Our recipe is a contemporary, lighter version, in which the simmered duck pieces are replaced with lean, moist duck breasts, and the thick, treacle-like pomegranate molasses is replaced with the crisp juiciness of fresh, red, jewel-like pomegranate seeds.

COOK'S TIPS
• Choose pomegranates that are heavy with shiny, brightly coloured red skins. The juice stains, so take care when cutting them. Only the seeds are used in cooking, the pith is discarded.
• If using frozen duck, make sure that it is completely thawed before cooking.

1 Heat half the oil in a frying pan. Add the onions and turmeric, and cook gently until soft. Transfer to a pan, add the walnuts and stock, then season with salt and pepper. Stir, then bring to the boil and simmer the mixture, uncovered, for 20 minutes.

2 Cut the pomegranates in half and scoop out the seeds into a bowl. Reserve the seeds of one pomegranate and set aside. Transfer the remaining seeds to a blender or food processor and process to break them up. Strain to extract the juice, and stir in the sugar and lemon juice.

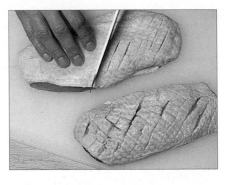

3 Score the skin of the duck breasts in a lattice fashion with a sharp knife. Heat the remaining oil in a frying pan or chargrill and place the duck breasts in it, skin side down.

4 Cook gently for 10 minutes, pouring off the fat from time to time if necessary, until the skin is dark golden and crisp. Turn them over and cook for a further 3–4 minutes. Transfer to a plate and leave to rest.

5 Deglaze the frying pan or chargrill with the pomegranate juice mixture, stirring with a wooden spoon, then add the walnut and stock mixture and simmer for 15 minutes until the sauce has thickened slightly. Serve the duck breasts sliced, drizzled with a little sauce and garnished with the reserved pomegranate seeds. Serve the remaining sauce separately.

Energy 1135kcal/4712kJ; Protein 59.9g; Carbohydrate 21.8g, of which sugars 19.9g; Fat 94.3g, of which saturates 10.1g; Cholesterol 248mg; Calcium 141mg; Fibre 5.4g; Sodium 258mg.

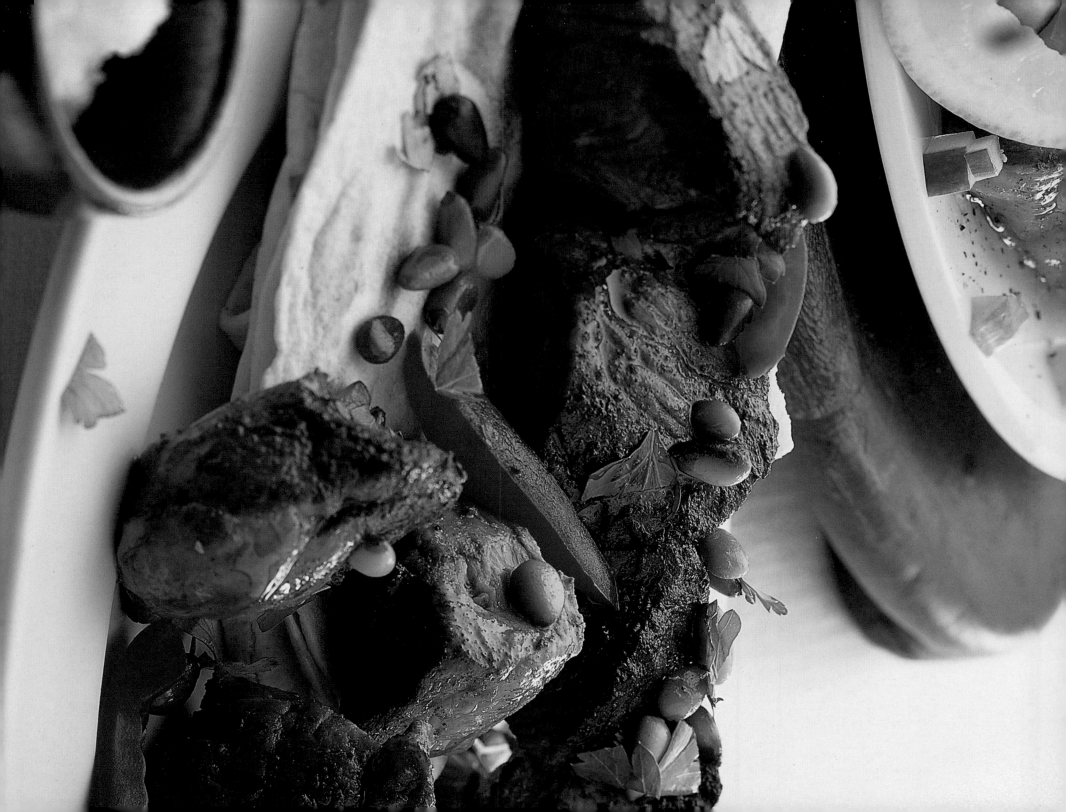

MEAT DISHES

The history of Jewish food shows a love and respect for meat and the Jewish kitchen holds it in very high esteem. A kosher butcher – or shochet – is required to be of the highest moral standing and of great learning, trained with exacting skills so that the animal does not suffer. Traditionally, in Eastern Europe, because meat was very expensive, many dishes bulked out the meat with other ingredients: meatballs are a great example. Dishes such as cholent, hamim, dafina, and all of the other long-braised dishes of beans, grains and meats were often served at special occasions such as Shabbat and festivals. They were warm and hearty and stretched a small amount of meat a long way.

JERUSALEM BARBECUED LAMB KEBABS

IN THE EARLY DAYS OF THE MODERN STATE OF ISRAEL, THE DAYS OF AUSTERITY, "LAMB" KEBABS WOULD HAVE BEEN MADE WITH TURKEY AND A LITTLE LAMB FAT, AND "VEAL" KEBABS WITH CHICKEN AND A SMALL AMOUNT OF VEAL. YOU MAY USE BEEF, CHICKEN, TURKEY OR VEAL IN PLACE OF THE LAMB IN THIS RECIPE IF YOU LIKE, BUT THE FRAGRANT SPICING IS DELICIOUS WITH LAMB.

SERVES FOUR TO SIX

INGREDIENTS
  800g/1¾lb tender lamb, cubed
  1.5ml/¼ tsp ground allspice
  1.5ml/¼ tsp ground cinnamon
  1.5ml/¼ tsp ground black pepper
  1.5ml/¼ tsp ground cardamom
  45–60ml/3–4 tbsp chopped
    fresh parsley
  2 onions, chopped
  5–8 garlic cloves, chopped
  juice of ½ lemon or 45ml/3 tbsp dry
    white wine
  45ml/3 tbsp extra virgin olive oil
  sumac, for sprinkling (optional)
  30ml/2 tbsp pine nuts
  salt
To serve
  flat breads, such as pitta bread,
    tortillas or naan bread
  tahini
  crunchy vegetable salad

1 Put the lamb, allspice, cinnamon, black pepper, cardamom, half the parsley, half the onions, the garlic, lemon juice or wine and olive oil in a bowl and mix together. Season with salt. Set aside and leave to marinate.

2 Meanwhile, light the barbecue and leave for about 40 minutes. When the coals are white and grey, the barbecue is ready for cooking. If using wooden skewers, soak them in water for about 30 minutes to prevent them from burning.

3 Thread the cubes of meat on to wooden or metal skewers, then barbecue for 2–3 minutes on each side.

4 Transfer the kebabs to a serving dish and sprinkle with the reserved onions, parsley, sumac, if using, pine nuts and salt. Serve the kebabs with warmed flat breads to wrap the kebabs in, a bowl of tahini for drizzling over and a crisp vegetable salad.

COOK'S TIPS
• If sumac is available, its tangy flavour is fresh and invigorating, and its red colour is appealing.
• These kebabs can also be cooked under a hot grill (broiler).

Energy 349kcal/1452kJ; Protein 27.8g; Carbohydrate 5.7g, of which sugars 4.1g; Fat 24.1g, of which saturates 8g; Cholesterol 101mg; Calcium 41mg; Fibre 1.4g; Sodium 119mg.

KOFTA KEBABS

These patties of minced lamb, spiced with aromatic herbs and seasonings, are doted on by both Jewish and non-Jewish communities from the Middle East right through to the Indian subcontinent. Serve a chopped vegetable salad on the side, or tender flatbread to wrap it up in, with a hot sauce such as zchug.

SERVES FOUR

INGREDIENTS

450g/1lb minced (ground) lamb
1–2 large slices of French bread,
  very finely crumbled
½ bunch fresh coriander (cilantro),
  finely chopped
5 garlic cloves, chopped
1 onion, finely chopped
juice of ½ lemon
5ml/1 tsp ground cumin
5ml/1 tsp paprika
15ml/1 tbsp curry powder
pinch each of ground cardamom,
  turmeric and cinnamon
15ml/1 tbsp tomato purée (paste)
cayenne pepper or chopped fresh
  chillies (optional)
1 egg, beaten, if needed
salt and ground black pepper
flat bread and salads, to serve

1 Put the lamb, crumbled bread, coriander, garlic, onion, lemon juice, spices, tomato purée, cayenne pepper or chillies and seasoning in a large bowl. Mix well. If the mixture does not bind together, add the beaten egg and a little more bread.

2 With wet hands, shape the mixture into four large or eight small patties.

3 Heat a heavy non-stick frying pan, add the patties and cook, taking care that they do not fall apart, turning once or twice, until browned. Serve hot with flat bread and salads.

VARIATION
Mix a handful of raisins or sultanas (golden raisins) into the meat mixture before shaping it into patties.

Energy 280kcal/1173kJ; Protein 23.9g; Carbohydrate 12.1g, of which sugars 1.4g; Fat 15.5g, of which saturates 7.1g; Cholesterol 87mg; Calcium 70mg; Fibre 1.2g; Sodium 214mg.

GRILLED SKEWERED LAMB

THERE IS NOTHING TO MATCH THE SIMPLE, HERB- AND LEMON-SPLASHED SUCCULENCE OF SOUVLAKIA — GRILLED LAMB KEBABS. YOU WILL FIND THEM IN ISRAELI CAFÉS AS WELL AS IN GREECE AND THEY ARE UTTERLY DELICIOUS. SOUVLAKIA ARE AT THEIR BEST SERVED WITH CUCUMBERS, OLIVES AND A LARGE TOMATO SALAD, ALONG WITH SOFT PITTA BREAD.

SERVES FOUR

INGREDIENTS

   1 small shoulder of lamb, boned and
     cut into 4cm/1½in cubes
   2–3 onions, preferably red onions
   2 red or green (bell) peppers,
     quartered and seeded
   75ml/5 tbsp extra virgin
     olive oil
   juice of 1 lemon
   5 garlic cloves, crushed
   15ml/1 tbsp dried oregano
   salt and ground black pepper

2 Put the oil, lemon juice, garlic and herbs in a large bowl. Season with salt and pepper and whisk well to combine.

4 Lift out the meat cubes, reserving the marinade, and thread them on long metal skewers, alternating each piece of meat with a piece of pepper and a piece of onion. Lay them across a grill (broiling) pan or baking tray and brush them with the reserved marinade.

1 Slice the onion into quarters and then separate each quarter into pieces composed of around two to three layers each. Slice each pepper quarter in half widthways.

COOK'S TIPS
• You can ask your butcher to trim the meat and cut it into cubes. A little fat will keep the souvlakia moist and succulent during cooking.
• If you are cooking the souvlakia on a barbecue you may need to cook them for longer, depending on the intensity of the heat.

3 Add the meat cubes, stirring to coat them in the mixture. Cover the bowl tightly and leave to marinate for 4–8 hours in the refrigerator, stirring several times.

VARIATION
If you prefer, you can use 4–5 best end neck (cross rib) fillets instead of shoulder of lamb.

5 Preheat a grill (broiler) until hot or prepare a barbecue. Cook the souvlakia under a medium to high heat or over the hot coals for 10 minutes, until they start to get scorched. If using the grill, do not place them too close to the heat source. Turn the skewers over, brush them again with the marinade or a little olive oil, and cook them for 10–15 minutes more. They should be served immediately.

Energy 358Kcal/1486kJ; Protein 21.4g; Carbohydrate 11.5g, of which sugars 9.6g; Fat 25.4g, of which saturates 7.3g; Cholesterol 76mg; Calcium 34mg; Fibre 2.5g; Sodium 92mg.

BAKED LAMB <u>WITH</u> TOMATOES, GARLIC <u>AND</u> PASTA

LAMB YIOUVETSI IS A VERY SPECIAL DISH IN GREECE AS IT MARKS THE END OF A LONG FASTING PERIOD. INDEED, THIS SUCCULENT, SLOW-BAKED STEW, ENRICHED WITH PASTA, MAKES WONDERFUL HEARTY FARE FOR ANY OCCASION. THE TURKISH JEWS HAVE THEIR OWN VERSION, IDENTICAL EXCEPT FOR THE OMISSION OF THE TRADITIONAL GRATED CHEESE TOPPING, FOR KASHRUT.

SERVES SIX

INGREDIENTS

1 shoulder of lamb, most of the fat
  removed, sliced into serving portions
600g/1lb 6oz ripe tomatoes, peeled
  and chopped, or 400g/14oz can
  chopped plum tomatoes
4–5 garlic cloves, chopped
75ml/5 tbsp extra virgin olive oil
5ml/1 tsp dried oregano
500ml/1 pint/2 cups beef stock
500ml/1 pint/2 cups hot water
400g/14oz/3½ cups orzo pasta, or
  spaghetti broken into short lengths
salt and ground black pepper

1 Preheat the oven to 190°C/375°F/ Gas 5. Rinse the meat to remove any obvious bone splinters and place it in a large roasting pan.

2 Add the fresh or canned tomatoes, with the garlic, olive oil and oregano. Season with salt and pepper and stir in the beef stock.

3 Place the lamb in the oven and bake for about 1 hour 10 minutes, basting and turning the pieces of meat over a couple of times.

4 Reduce the oven temperature to 180°C/350°F/Gas 4. Add the hot water to the roasting pan. Stir in the pasta and add more seasoning. Mix well.

5 Return the roasting pan to the oven and bake for 30–40 minutes more, stirring occasionally, until the meat is fully cooked and tender and the pasta feels soft.

COOK'S TIP
As yiouvetsi is quite a rich dish, serve with a salad to refresh the palate.

VARIATIONS
If possible, use ripe vine tomatoes, as it is their flavour that really makes the difference. The dish can also be made with young goat (kid) or beef.

Energy 447Kcal/1881kJ; Protein 21.8g; Carbohydrate 52.5g, of which sugars 5.3g; Fat 18.1g, of which saturates 5g; Cholesterol 51mg; Calcium 29mg; Fibre 2.9g; Sodium 68mg.

SPICY KEFTA IN TOMATO SAUCE WITH POACHED EGG

SPICY MEATBALLS ARE A GLORY OF THE MEDITERRANEAN KITCHEN AND THESE NORTH AFRICAN MEATBALLS, SIMMERED IN THE PAN WITH TOMATOES WITH EGGS POACHING IN THE RICH SAUCE, ARE UTTERLY DELICIOUS AND SATISFYING.

SERVES FOUR

INGREDIENTS

350g/12oz finely minced (ground)
  lamb or beef
1 onion, finely chopped
6 garlic cloves, coarsely chopped
50g/2oz fresh breadcrumbs
5 eggs
5ml/1 tsp ground cumin
5ml/1 tsp smoked or sweet
  paprika
1.5ml/¼ tsp cinnamon
large pinch ground ginger
5ml/1 tsp ras al hanout
1 bunch each flat leaf parsley
  and coriander (cilantro) leaves,
  finely chopped
30ml/2 tbsp olive oil
400g/14oz can chopped tomatoes
tiny pinch of sugar
salt and ground black pepper
crusty bread, to serve
extra coriander, to garnish

1 In a bowl, knead the minced lamb with the onion, half the garlic, breadcrumbs, 1 egg, half the cumin, half the paprika, ginger and half the cinnamon, half the ras al hanout, parsley and salt and pepper until well mixed. Lift the mixture in your hand and slap it down into the bowl several times. Take a small amount of mixture and shape it into a small ball about the size of a walnut. Repeat with the remaining mixture to make about 12 balls.

2 Heat the olive oil in a large heavy frying pan. Fry the meatballs until nicely browned, turning them occasionally so they cook evenly.

3 Stir in the remaining garlic, tomatoes, sugar, spices, ras el hanout and parsley and coriander. Bring to the boil, cook for a few minutes to reduce the liquid, and roll the balls in the sauce. Season.

4 Make room for the remaining four eggs in the pan and crack them into spaces between the meatballs. Cover the pan, reduce the heat and cook for about 3 minutes or until the eggs are just set.

5 Sprinkle with the extra coriander and serve in the pan, with chunks of bread to use as scoops.

COOK'S TIP
It is very authentic to serve this dish straight out of the pan. In North Africa and the Middle East it is known as "bus station kefta", and travellers waiting for connecting bus services often tuck into the meatballs to sustain themselves during a long journey. Alternatively, served in the comfort of the home, it would make a very good brunch.

Energy 330kcal/1381kJ; Protein 21.5g; Carbohydrate 16.7g, of which sugars 6.6g; Fat 20.4g, of which saturates 6.2g; Cholesterol 281mg; Calcium 97mg; Fibre 1.7g; Sodium 264mg.

LAMB GOULASH WITH TOMATOES AND PEPPERS

JEWS FROM HUNGARY HAVE THE REPUTATION OF BEING WONDERFUL COOKS, ABLE TO THROW TOGETHER SAVOURY, SPICY, PAPRIKA-GLOWING STEWS WITH ALL MANNER OF INGREDIENTS, INCLUDING BEEF, CHICKEN AND EVEN SMOKED SAUSAGES AND FRANKFURTERS. THIS DISH NO DOUBT STAYED A WHILE IN BULGARIA, FOR ITS MAIN INGREDIENT IS THE LAMB THAT BULGARIA IS SO FOND OF.

SERVES FOUR TO SIX

INGREDIENTS

30ml/2 tbsp vegetable oil
900g/2lb lean lamb, trimmed and cut
  into cubes
1 large onion, roughly chopped
5 garlic cloves, crushed
3 green (bell) peppers, seeded
  and diced
30ml/2 tbsp paprika
2 x 400g/14oz cans chopped
  plum tomatoes
15ml/1tbsp chopped fresh flat
  leaf parsley
5ml/1 tsp chopped fresh marjoram
30ml/2 tbsp plain (all-purpose) flour
60ml/4 tbsp cold water
salt and freshly ground black pepper
green salad, to serve

1 Heat up the oil in a frying pan. Fry the pieces of lamb for 5–8 minutes, or until browned on all sides. Season well.

2 Add the onion and garlic and cook for a further 2 minutes before adding the green peppers and paprika.

3 Pour in the tomatoes and enough water, if needed, to cover the meat in the pan. Stir in the herbs. Bring to the boil, turn down the heat, cover and simmer very gently for 1½ hours, or until the lamb is tender.

4 Blend the flour with the cold water and pour into the stew. Bring back to the boil then reduce the heat to a simmer and cook until the sauce has thickened. Adjust the seasoning and serve the lamb goulash with a crisp green salad.

Energy 396Kcal/1656kJ; Protein 32.6g; Carbohydrate 19.4g, of which sugars 13.8g; Fat 21.5g, of which saturates 8.5g; Cholesterol 114mg; Calcium 53mg; Fibre 4g; Sodium 147mg.

PASTRY-WRAPPED BALKAN LAMB

THIS LAMB ROAST, WRAPPED IN A BLANKET OF PASTRY AND BAKED WITH GARLIC UNTIL GOLDEN, IS A TREAT OF THE JEWISH COMMUNITY IN THE BALKANS.

SERVES SIX TO EIGHT

INGREDIENTS
1.5kg/3½lb shoulder roast of lamb, or if your butcher can kasher it, a leg of lamb, boned
40g/1½oz/3 tbsp olive oil
2.5ml/½ tsp each dried thyme, rosemary and oregano
8 garlic cloves, coarsely chopped
45ml/3 tbsp lemon juice
salt, for sprinkling
1 egg, beaten, for sealing and glazing
1 oregano or marjoram sprig, to garnish

For the pastry
450g/1lb/4 cups plain (all-purpose) flour, sifted
250g/9oz/generous 1 cup chilled vegetable shortening
150–250ml/¼–½ pint/⅔–1 cup iced water

1 Preheat the oven to 190°/375°F/Gas 5. To make the pastry, place the flour and vegetable shortening into a food processor or blender and process until the mixture resembles fine breadcrumbs. Add enough iced water to make a soft, but not sticky, dough. Knead gently and form into a ball. Wrap in clear film (plastic wrap) and refrigerate for 1–2 hours.

2 Meanwhile, put the lamb in a roasting pan, tie the joint with string and cut 20 small holes in the meat, with a sharp, narrow knife.

3 Mix together the olive oil, dried herbs, garlic and lemon juice and use to fill the small cuts in the lamb. Sprinkle the whole joint with salt and cook in a roasting pan for about 1 hour, then allow to cool. Remove the string.

COOK'S TIP
The meat juices from the lamb will make a wonderful gravy.

VARIATION
Use filo pastry instead of shortcrust.

4 Roll out the pastry on a lightly floured surface until large enough to wrap around the lamb in one piece. Seal the pastry edges with a little of the egg and place in a clean pan.

5 With any remaining scraps of pastry make leaves or other shapes to decorate the pastry. Brush with more of the egg. Return to the oven and bake for a further 30–45 minutes. Serve hot, in slices, garnished with a sprig of oregano or marjoram.

Energy 812Kcal/3380kJ; Protein 31.8g; Carbohydrate 44g, of which sugars 1.2g; Fat 57.7g, of which saturates 24.7g; Cholesterol 119mg; Calcium 89mg; Fibre 1.7g; Sodium 346mg.

LAMB <u>WITH</u> GLOBE ARTICHOKES

ITALIAN JEWS HAVE FAVOURED ARTICHOKES FOR MILLENNIA. THIS PROBABLY GOES BACK TO BIBLICAL TIMES IN THE LAND THAT IS NOW ISRAEL, WHERE THEY WERE GATHERED WILD. THE CLASSIC ROMAN DISH OF FRIED ARTICHOKES ALLA GIUDIA ACTUALLY CAME FROM THE OLD JEWS OF ROME AND CAN STILL BE ENJOYED AT ITS BEST IN THE RESTAURANTS OF THE GHETTO. THIS MAKES A LOVELY PESACH DISH.

SERVES SIX TO EIGHT

INGREDIENTS
  1 leg of lamb, about 2kg/4½lb
  1–2 garlic heads, divided into cloves,
    peeled and thinly sliced, leaving
    5–6 peeled but whole
  about 25g/1oz fresh rosemary,
    stalks removed
  500ml/17fl oz/2¼ cups dry
    red wine
  30–60ml/2–4 tbsp olive oil
  4 globe artichokes
  a little lemon juice
  5 shallots, chopped
  250ml/8fl oz/1 cup beef stock
  salt and ground black pepper
  crisp green salad, to serve (optional)

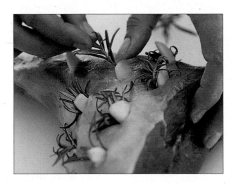

1 Using a sharp knife, make incisions all over the leg of lamb. Into each incision, put a sliver of garlic and as many rosemary leaves as you can stuff in. Season the lamb with salt and plenty of black pepper.

COOK'S TIPS
• Choose garlic heads that are plump and whose cloves are full and unshrivelled. Avoid any that are beginning to sprout.
• If you do not have access to a kosher leg of lamb with the sciatic nerve removed, use lamb riblets or shoulder of lamb. Vary cooking times accordingly.
• If you wish, you can marinate the lamb ahead of time. Cover and store the meat in the refrigerator for up to 1 day.

2 Put the lamb in a non-metallic dish and pour half the wine and all of the olive oil over the top. Set aside; leave to marinate until you are ready to roast the meat.

3 Preheat the oven to 230°C/450°F/ Gas 8. Put the meat and its juices in a roasting pan and surround with the remaining whole garlic cloves. Roast in the oven for 10–15 minutes, then reduce the temperature to 160°C/325°F/ Gas 3 and cook for a further 1 hour, or until the lamb is cooked to your liking. Test with a sharp knife.

4 Meanwhile, prepare the artichokes. Pull back their tough leaves and let them snap off. Trim the rough ends off the base. With a sharp knife, cut the artichokes into quarters and cut out the inside thistle heart. Immediately place the quarters into a bowl of water to which you have added the lemon juice. (The acidulated water will prevent the artichokes from discolouring.)

5 About 20 minutes before the lamb is cooked, drain the globe artichokes and place them around the meat.

6 When the lamb is cooked, transfer the meat and artichokes to a serving dish. Carefully pour the meat juices and roasted garlic into a pan.

7 Spoon off the fat from the pan juices and add the chopped shallots and the remaining red wine to the pan. Cook over a high heat until the liquid has reduced to a very small amount, then add the beef stock and cook, stirring constantly, until the pan juices are rich and flavourful.

8 To serve, coat the lamb and artichokes with the roasted garlic and red wine sauce and garnish with extra rosemary, if you wish. Serve immediately with green salad, if you like.

Energy 595Kcal/2487kJ; Protein 72.4g; Carbohydrate 2.2g, of which sugars 1.6g; Fat 28.3g, of which saturates 11.4g; Cholesterol 275mg; Calcium 53mg; Fibre 0.5g; Sodium 217mg.

LAMB TAGINE <u>WITH</u> HONEY <u>AND</u> PRUNES

THIS DISH IS EATEN BY MOROCCAN JEWS AT ROSH HASHANAH, WHEN SWEET FOODS ARE TRADITIONALLY SERVED IN ANTICIPATION OF A SWEET AND HARMONIOUS YEAR AHEAD. DRIED APRICOTS OR FIGS MAY BE ADDED TO THE BAKED LAMB STEW INSTEAD OF THE PRUNES.

SERVES SIX

INGREDIENTS

130g/4½ oz/generous ½ cup
  pitted prunes
350ml/12fl oz/1½ cups hot tea
1kg/2¼lb stewing or braising lamb such
  as shoulder, cut into chunky portions
1 onion, chopped
75–90ml/5–6 tbsp chopped
  fresh parsley
2.5ml/½ tsp ground ginger
2.5ml/½ tsp curry powder or
  ras al hanout
pinch of freshly grated nutmeg
10ml/2 tsp ground cinnamon
1.5ml/¼ tsp saffron threads
30ml/2 tbsp hot water
75–120ml/5–9 tbsp honey, to taste
250ml/8fl oz/1 cup beef or lamb stock
115g/4oz/1 cup blanched
  almonds, toasted
30ml/2 tbsp chopped fresh coriander
  (cilantro) leaves
3 hard-boiled eggs, cut into wedges
salt and ground black pepper

1 Preheat the oven to 180ºC/350ºF/ Gas 4. Put the prunes in a bowl, pour over the tea and cover. Leave to soak and plump up.

2 Meanwhile, put the lamb, chopped onion, parsley, ginger, curry powder or ras al hanout, nutmeg, cinnamon, salt and a large pinch of ground black pepper in a roasting pan. Cover and cook in the oven for about 2 hours, or until the meat is tender.

3 Drain the prunes; add their liquid to the lamb. Combine the saffron and hot water and add to the pan with the honey and stock. Bake, uncovered, for 30 minutes, turning the lamb occasionally.

4 Add the prunes to the pan and stir gently to mix. Serve sprinkled with the toasted almonds and chopped coriander, and topped with the wedges of hard-boiled egg.

Energy 523Kcal/2184kJ; Protein 40.6g; Carbohydrate 19g, of which sugars 18.3g; Fat 32.3g, of which saturates 10.3g; Cholesterol 222mg; Calcium 84mg; Fibre 2.8g; Sodium 185mg.

LAMB POT-ROASTED WITH TOMATO SAUCE, BEANS AND ONIONS

SLOW-BRAISED LAMB, PERFUMED WITH TOMATOES AND SIMMERED WITH GREEN BEANS (OR ANY VEGETABLE OF THE SEASON SUCH AS COURGETTE, SPINACH OR OKRA) IS A CLASSIC GREEK DISH MUCH APPRECIATED BY THE JEWS.

SERVES EIGHT

INGREDIENTS

1kg/2¼lb lamb on the bone
8 garlic cloves, chopped
2.5–5ml/½–1 tsp ground cumin
45ml/3 tbsp olive oil
juice of 1 lemon
2 onions, thinly sliced
about 500ml/17fl oz/2¼ cups
  lamb, beef or vegetable stock
75–90ml/5–6 tbsp tomato purée (paste)
1 cinnamon stick
2–3 large pinches of ground
  allspice or ground cloves
15–30ml/1–2 tbsp sugar
400g/14oz/scant 3 cups French or
  runner (green) beans
salt and ground black pepper
15–30ml/1–2 tbsp chopped
  fresh parsley, to garnish

1 Preheat the oven to 160°C/325°F/Gas 3. Coat the lamb with the garlic, cumin, olive oil, lemon juice, salt and pepper.

2 Heat a flameproof casserole. Sear the lamb on all sides. Add the onions and pour the stock over the meat to cover. Stir in the tomato purée, spices and sugar. Cover and cook in the oven for 2–3 hours.

3 Remove the casserole from the oven and pour the stock into a pan. Move the onions to the side of the dish and return to the oven, uncovered, for 20 minutes.

4 Meanwhile, add the beans to the hot stock and cook until the beans are tender and the sauce has thickened. Slice the meat and serve with the pan juices and beans. Garnish with parsley.

Energy 371Kcal/1544kJ; Protein 26.3g; Carbohydrate 7.9g, of which sugars 6.5g; Fat 26.4g, of which saturates 10.9g; Cholesterol 104mg; Calcium 40mg; Fibre 1.9g; Sodium 103mg.

SAFFRON LAMB PILAFF <u>WITH</u> PRUNES <u>AND</u> RAISINS

"PLOV" IS THE RUSSIAN AND UZBEKISTAN NAME FOR THIS RICE DISH WHICH IS POPULAR IN EASTERN EUROPE. IT IS ALSO KNOWN AS PILAU *IN TURKEY AND* PILAF *IN THE MIDDLE EAST.*

SERVES FOUR

INGREDIENTS

   50g/2oz/scant ½ cup raisins
   115g/4oz/½ cup pitted prunes
   15ml/1 tbsp lemon juice
   30ml/2 tbsp olive oil
   1 large onion, chopped
   450g/1lb lamb fillet, trimmed and
     cut into 1cm/½in cubes
   225g/8oz lean minced (ground) lamb
   2 garlic cloves, crushed
   600ml/1 pint/2½ cups lamb, beef or
     vegetable stock
   350g/12oz/scant 2 cups long
     grain rice
   large pinch of saffron threads
   salt and ground black pepper
   sprigs of flat leaf parsley, to garnish

1 Put the raisins and prunes in a small bowl and pour over enough water to cover. Add the lemon juice and leave to soak for at least 1 hour. Drain, then roughly chop the prunes.

2 Meanwhile, heat the olive oil in a large pan and cook the onion for 5 minutes. Add the lamb fillet, minced lamb and garlic. Fry for 5 minutes, stirring constantly until browned.

3 Pour in 150ml/¼ pint/⅔ cup of the stock. Bring to the boil, then lower the heat, cover and simmer for 1 hour, or until the lamb is tender.

4 Add the remaining stock and bring to the boil. Add the rice and saffron. Stir, then cover and simmer for 15 minutes, or until the rice is tender.

5 Stir in the raisins, chopped prunes, salt and pepper. Heat through for a few minutes, then turn on to a warmed serving dish and garnish with sprigs of flat leaf parsley.

Energy 777Kcal/3244kJ; Protein 40g; Carbohydrate 88.3g, of which sugars 18.5g; Fat 29.2g, of which saturates 11.5g; Cholesterol 128mg; Calcium 46mg; Fibre 1.9g; Sodium 118mg.

ROMANIAN KEBAB

MEAT, SKEWERED AND MARINATED, THEN COOKED OVER AN OPEN FIRE IS A ROMANIAN FAVOURITE SERVED WITH RICE OR POLENTA. IN TRUE ROMANIAN STYLE, THE MARINADE IS SO FULL OF GARLIC THAT ONE CAN BE SURE OF BEING QUITE SAFE FROM VAMPIRES!

SERVES SIX

INGREDIENTS
    675g/1½lb lean lamb, cut into
        4cm/1½in cubes
    12 shallots or button (pearl) onions
    2 green (bell) peppers, seeded and
        cut into 12 pieces
    12 small tomatoes
    12 small mushrooms
    sprigs of rosemary, to garnish
    lemon slices, freshly cooked rice and
        crusty bread, to serve
For the marinade
    juice of 1 lemon
    120ml/4fl oz/½ cup red wine
    1 onion, finely chopped
    8 garlic cloves, chopped
    60ml/4 tbsp olive oil
    2.5ml/½ tsp each dried sage
        and rosemary
    salt and ground black pepper

1 For the marinade, combine the lemon juice, red wine, onion, garlic, olive oil, herbs and seasoning in a bowl.

2 Stir the cubes of lamb into the marinade. Cover and refrigerate for up to 12 hours, stirring occasionally to re-coat the meat and thoroughly immerse it in the liquid.

3 Remove the lamb from the marinade and thread the pieces on to 6 skewers alternating with the onions, peppers, tomatoes and mushrooms.

4 Cook the kebabs over the hot coals of a barbecue or under a preheated grill (broiler) for 10–15 minutes, turning them once. Use the leftover marinade to brush over the kebabs during cooking to prevent the meat drying out.

5 Serve the kebabs on a bed of freshly cooked rice, sprinkled with fresh rosemary and accompanied by lemon slices and slices of crusty bread.

VARIATION
Sprinkle over 30ml/2 tbsp chopped fresh parsley and finely chopped onion, to garnish.

Energy 322Kcal/1340kJ; Protein 23.9g; Carbohydrate 7.6g, of which sugars 6.6g; Fat 20.5g, of which saturates 7g; Cholesterol 86mg; Calcium 28mg; Fibre 2.1g; Sodium 106mg.

AFGHAN LAMB PLOV

THE JEWISH COMMUNITY OF AFGHANISTAN WAS AN ANCIENT ONE, SPEAKING THE SAME TAJIKI LANGUAGE AS THE JEWS OF THE CITIES OF BUKHARA, TASHKENT AND SAMARKAND IN UZBEKISTAN. THIS DELICIOUS PLOV COMBINES STAPLES OF THESE REGIONS: RICE, LAMB, SPICES, NUTS AND FRUIT.

SERVES FOUR

INGREDIENTS

40g/1½oz/3 tbsp vegetable oil
1 large onion, finely chopped
450g/1lb lamb fillet, cut into
 small cubes
1 small carrot, diced
2.5ml/½ tsp ground cinnamon
30ml/2 tbsp tomato purée (paste)
45ml/3 tbsp chopped fresh parsley
115g/4oz/½ cup ready-to-eat dried
 apricots, halved
50g/2oz/¼ cup raisins
75g/3oz/¾ cup pistachio nuts
450g/1lb long grain rice, rinsed
salt and ground black pepper
flat leaf parsley, to garnish

1 Sauté the onion in the oil until soft and golden. Add the cubed lamb and carrots, and brown on all sides. Add the cinnamon and season with salt and pepper. Cover and cook gently for 10 minutes.

2 Add the tomato purée and enough water to cover the meat. Stir in the parsley, bring to the boil, cover and simmer very gently for 1½ hours, until the meat is tender. Chop the pistachio nuts.

3 Add enough water to the pan to make up to about 600ml/1 pint/2½ cups liquid. Add the apricots, raisins, pistachio nuts and rice, bring to the boil, cover tightly and simmer for about 20 minutes, until the rice is cooked. (You may need to add a little more water, if necessary.) Transfer to a warmed serving dish and garnish with parsley before serving.

VARIATION
Layer whole cloves of garlic with the rice and other ingredients. The garlic becomes soft as the rice cooks.

Energy 913Kcal/3814kJ; Protein 36.6g; Carbohydrate 119.4g, of which sugars 27.3g; Fat 32.3g, of which saturates 8.2g; Cholesterol 86mg; Calcium 105mg; Fibre 5.1g; Sodium 234mg.

LAMB <u>AND</u> COS LETTUCE CASSEROLE

*ONE OF THE CLASSIC GREEK DISHES, THIS IS FOUND THROUGHOUT THE COUNTRY, FROM THE IONIAN
TO THE AEGEAN SEA. THE EGG AND LEMON EMULSION USED TO THICKEN THE SAUCE, KNOWN AS
AVGOLEMONO, IS A BELOVED SEPHARDIC JEWISH TOUCH, ENJOYED IN TURKISH, GREEK AND ITALIAN
DISHES OF MEAT AND POULTRY WHEN DAIRY MIXTURES FOR CREAMINESS WOULD BE FORBIDDEN TO
COMBINE WITH THE MEAT. IT IS AN IDEAL CHOICE FOR SHABBAT EVENING, BECAUSE IT CAN BE
COOKED IN ADVANCE AND KEPT WARM UNTIL SERVING. MAKE SURE THAT THE FINAL DISH HAS QUITE A
LOT OF LIQUID, AS THIS WILL BE TRANSFORMED INTO THE DELICIOUS AVGOLEMONO SAUCE. SERVE IT
WITH PLENTY OF FRESH BREAD, TO ENJOY EVERY LAST DROP.*

SERVES FOUR TO SIX

INGREDIENTS
45ml/3 tbsp olive oil
1 onion, chopped
1kg/2¼lb leg of lamb, boned
  and kashered, sliced into
  4–6 medium steaks
2 cos or romaine lettuces,
  coarsely shredded
6 spring onions (scallions), sliced
60ml/4 tbsp roughly chopped fresh
  dill, plus extra to garnish (optional)
2 eggs
15ml/1 tbsp cornflour (cornstarch)
  mixed to a paste with 120ml/4fl oz/
  ½ cup water
juice of 1 lemon
salt

1 Heat the olive oil in a large, heavy pan. Add the chopped onion and sauté for 3–5 minutes, until it glistens and becomes translucent.

2 Increase the heat, then add the lamb steaks and cook, turning them over frequently, until all the moisture has been driven off, a process that will take about 15 minutes.

3 Add salt to taste and enough hot water to cover the meat. Cover the pan and simmer for about 1 hour, until the meat is only just tender.

4 Add the lettuces, spring onions and dill. If necessary, pour in a little more hot water so that all the vegetables are almost covered. Replace the lid on the pan and simmer for 15–20 minutes more. Remove from the heat and let the dish stand for 5 minutes while you prepare the ingredients for the sauce.

5 Beat the eggs lightly in a bowl, add the cornflour mixture and beat until smooth. Add the lemon juice and whisk briefly, then continue to whisk while gradually adding 75–90ml/5–6 tbsp of the hot liquid from the pan containing the lamb.

6 Pour the sauce over the meat. Do not stir; instead gently shake and rotate the pan until the sauce is incorporated with the remaining liquid. Return the pan to a gentle heat for 2–3 minutes, just long enough to warm the sauce through. Do not let it boil, or the sauce is likely to curdle. Serve on warmed plates and sprinkle over some extra chopped dill, if you like.

VARIATION
Substitute potato flour for the cornflour, if you plan to make this dish for Pesach.

Energy 437Kcal/1814kJ; Protein 35.2g; Carbohydrate 5g, of which sugars 2g; Fat 30.8g, of which saturates 12g; Cholesterol 188mg; Calcium 44mg; Fibre 0.9g; Sodium 130mg.

COCHIFRITO

The name of this sautéed lamb dish actually means "Fried Pork". The punishment for eating Jewish food in Spain during the dark days of the Inquisition was severe, so this dish was probably called pork as a protective act. Whatever the case, it is simple, savoury and delicious. Serve with roasted red peppers and a dish of simple rice.

SERVES FOUR

INGREDIENTS
  800g/1¾lb very well-trimmed, tender lamb, preferably shoulder, in cubes or strips
  30ml/2 tbsp olive oil, plus extra if necessary
  1 onion, chopped
  5 garlic cloves, finely chopped
  5ml/1 tsp paprika
  juice of 2 lemons
  15ml/1 tbsp finely chopped fresh parsley
  salt and ground black pepper

1 Season the lamb with salt and ground black pepper. Heat the 30ml/2 tbsp olive oil in a large frying pan or casserole over a high heat and add the meat in handfuls followed by the onion, pushing the meat around the pan to brown all over. Add more meat to the pan as each batch is sealed. Add the chopped garlic and a little more oil if necessary.

2 When the meat is golden and the onion soft, sprinkle with paprika and lemon juice. Cover and simmer for 15 minutes. Check the seasonings and add a sprinkling of parsley, then serve.

VARIATION
Non-Jews and non-Muslims may prefer to make this dish using pork in place of the lamb.

Energy 416Kcal/1732kJ; Protein 39.6g; Carbohydrate 1.4g, of which sugars 1g; Fat 28g, of which saturates 11.2g; Cholesterol 152mg; Calcium 35mg; Fibre 0.6g; Sodium 175mg.

RIÑONES ᴬᴸ JEREZ

KIDNEYS COOKED IN SHERRY ARE EXTREMELY POPULAR IN TAPAS BARS AND ALSO MAKE AN EXCELLENT FAMILY SUPPER. TRADITIONALLY, MEAT WAS NOT EATEN OFTEN IN JEWISH HOMES, BUT WHEN IT WAS, THE SEPHARDIM OFTEN CHOSE TO COOK OFFAL. THIS DISH COMES FROM ANDALUCIA IN SPAIN, A REGION BOASTING INFLUENCES FROM BOTH JEWISH AND MUSLIM CULTURES.

SERVES FOUR

INGREDIENTS

   12 plump lamb's kidneys, kashered
      for cooking
   60ml/4 tbsp olive oil
   1 large onion, chopped
   2 garlic cloves, finely chopped
   30ml/2 tbsp plain (all-purpose) flour
   150ml/¼ pint/⅔ cup fino sherry
   15ml/1 tbsp tomato purée (paste)
   30ml/2 tbsp chopped fresh parsley
   salt and ground black pepper
   new potatoes, boiled, to serve
      (optional)

1 Halve and skin the kidneys, then remove the cores. Trim if necessary. Heat half the oil in a large frying pan, add the onion and garlic and fry until softened. Remove to a plate.

2 Add the remaining oil to the pan and divide the kidneys into four batches. Put in one handful, and stir-fry over a high heat until sealed. Push them to the pan rim and stir-fry the next batch. They should be sealed, and not be allowed to give off juice. Remove to a plate and repeat until they are all cooked.

3 Return the onion mixture to the pan. Sprinkle with flour and cook, stirring gently. Add the sherry and stir until thickened. Add the tomato purée and parsley. Return the kidneys to the pan and heat through. Season well and serve hot with new potatoes, if using.

Energy 269Kcal/1120kJ; Protein 14.9g; Carbohydrate 13g, of which sugars 5.6g; Fat 13.3g, of which saturates 2.3g; Cholesterol 236mg; Calcium 54mg; Fibre 1.8g; Sodium 130mg.

LAMB CASSEROLE <u>WITH</u> GARLIC <u>AND</u> BROAD BEANS

THIS DELICATE SEPHARDIC STEW, FLAVOURED WITH SHERRY AND PLENTY OF GARLIC, IS PREPARED WITH SPRING'S FIRST BEANS. BECAUSE SEPHARDIM EAT BEANS DURING PESACH, UNLIKE ASHKENAZIM AND OTHER GROUPS, THIS DISH IS TRADITIONALLY SERVED FOR PESACH SEDAR.

SERVES SIX

INGREDIENTS
  45ml/3 tbsp olive oil
  1.5kg/3–3½lb fillet lamb, cut into
    5cm/2in cubes
  1 large onion, chopped
  6 large garlic cloves, unpeeled
  1 bay leaf
  5ml/1 tsp paprika
  120ml/4fl oz/½ cup dry white wine
  115g/4oz shelled fresh broad
    (fava) beans
  30ml/2 tbsp chopped fresh parsley
  salt and ground black pepper

3 Add the garlic cloves, bay leaf, paprika and wine. Season with salt and pepper. Bring to the boil, then cover and simmer very gently for 1½–2 hours, until the meat is tender.

4 Add the broad beans about 10 minutes before the end of the cooking time. Stir in the parsley just before serving.

1 Heat 30ml/2 tbsp of the oil in a large flameproof casserole. Add half the meat and brown well on all sides. Transfer to a plate. Brown the rest of the meat in the same way and remove from the casserole.

2 Heat the remaining oil in the pan, add the onion and cook for about 5 minutes until soft. Return the meat to the casserole.

COOK'S TIPS

• If fresh broad (fava) beans are not in season, you can substitute with dried or frozen beans.
• While beans are traditional Pesach fare for some Jewish communities, they are in fact forbidden to others.

Energy 541Kcal/2258kJ; Protein 50.8g; Carbohydrate 3.5g, of which sugars 1.2g; Fat 33.7g, of which saturates 13.8g; Cholesterol 190mg; Calcium 45mg; Fibre 1.6g; Sodium 221mg.

KOSHER CASSEROLE

CASSOULET IS A CLASSIC FRENCH DISH, USUALLY MADE TO INCLUDE MEATS AND SAUSAGES THAT ARE NOT KOSHER. IT IS BELIEVED, HOWEVER, THAT THE DISH ORIGINATED AS CHOLENT, A TRADITIONAL ASHKENAZIC SHABBAT DISH OF MEAT AND BEANS, WHICH WAS BROUGHT TO FRANCE BY THE JEWS FLEEING THE SPANISH INQUISITION.

SERVES SIX TO EIGHT

INGREDIENTS
675g/1½lb/3½ cups dried
   haricot (navy) beans
4 large duck breasts
900g/2lb stewing lamb
90ml/6 tbsp olive oil
2 onions, chopped
12 garlic cloves, crushed
2 bay leaves
1.5ml/¼ tsp ground cloves
60ml/4 tbsp tomato purée (paste)
8 spicy beef, duck or
   chicken sausages
4 tomatoes
75g/3oz/1½ cups stale breadcrumbs
half a bunch of parsley, chopped
salt and ground black pepper

1 Put the beans in a large bowl and cover with plenty of cold water. Leave to soak overnight.

2 Drain the beans thoroughly and put them in a large pan with fresh water to cover. Bring to the boil and boil rapidly for 10 minutes. Drain and set the beans aside.

5 Put the beans in a large, heavy pan with the onions, half the garlic, bay leaves, ground cloves and tomato purée. Stir in the browned lamb and just cover with water. Bring to the boil, then reduce the heat to the lowest setting and simmer, covered, for about 1½ hours until the beans are tender.

6 Preheat the oven to 180°C/350°F/ Gas 4. Heat 30ml/2 tbsp of the oil in a frying pan and fry the duck breasts and sausages until browned. Cut the sausages into smaller pieces.

7 Plunge the tomatoes into boiling water for 30 seconds. Peel and quarter.

8 Transfer the bean mixture to a large earthenware pot or ovenproof dish and stir in the fried sausages and duck breasts and chopped tomatoes with salt and pepper to taste.

9 Mix the breadcrumbs with the remaining oil, garlic and parsley. Sprinkle with an even layer of about half the breadcrumbs and bake in the oven for 45 minutes to 1 hour until the crust is golden. Using a spoon, cut the crust and turn it in. Sprinkle more crumb mix, return to the oven and bake for a further 15–20 minutes, then repeat. Sprinkle over the remaining crumbs and bake for a further 15 minutes.

3 Use a sharp knife to cut the duck breasts into chunks.

4 Heat 30ml/2 tbsp of the oil in a frying pan and fry the lamb in batches, until browned.

Energy 904Kcal/3784kJ; Protein 64g; Carbohydrate 59g, of which sugars 6.8g; Fat 48.3g, of which saturates 16g; Cholesterol 183mg; Calcium 242mg; Fibre 10.5g; Sodium 1404mg.

LIVER VARENYKY

ONE OF THE MANY UKRAINIAN SAVOURY DUMPLING RECIPES. ENJOY THIS DISH IN A BOWL ON ITS OWN, SPRINKLED WITH CHIVES, OR IN A BOWL OF CONSOMMÉ.

SERVES FOUR

INGREDIENTS
   200g/7oz/1¾ cups plain (all-
      purpose) flour
   1.5ml/¼ tsp salt
   2 eggs, beaten
   30ml/2 tbsp vegetable oil
   beaten egg, for sealing
For the filling
   15ml/1 tbsp sunflower oil
   ½ small onion, finely chopped
   225g/8oz chicken, calf's or lamb's
      liver, grilled (broiled) lightly first to
      make kosher, then roughly chopped
   30ml/2 tbsp chopped fresh chives,
      plus extra to garnish
   salt and ground black pepper

1 Sift the flour and salt into a bowl. Make a well in the centre. Add the eggs and vegetable oil and mix to a dough.

2 Knead the dough on a lightly floured surface for 2–3 minutes, until smooth. Wrap in clear film (plastic wrap) and leave to rest for 30 minutes.

3 For the filling, heat the oil in a pan and cook the onion for 5 minutes. Stir in the liver and cook for several minutes, until browned.

4 Put the liver mixture in a food processor or blender and process until it is finely chopped, but not smooth. Add the chopped chives and season with salt and pepper. Process for a few more seconds.

5 Roll out the dough on a lightly floured surface until 3mm/⅛in thick. Stamp out rounds of dough with a 5cm/2in cutter.

6 Spoon a teaspoonful of filling into the middle of each round. Brush the edges of the dough with beaten egg and fold in half to make half-moon shapes. Leave to dry on a floured dish towel for 30 minutes.

7 Bring a pan of salted water to the boil. Add the oil, then add the varenyky, in batches if necessary. Bring back to the boil and cook them at a gentle simmer for 10 minutes, until tender. Drain well and serve hot, garnished with chopped chives.

Energy 364Kcal/1529kJ; Protein 19.4g; Carbohydrate 40g, of which sugars 1.6g; Fat 15.2g, of which saturates 2.8g; Cholesterol 337mg; Calcium 92mg; Fibre 1.8g; Sodium 78mg.

MALSACHI LAMB

THIS IS A TYPICAL DISH OF THE BENE ISRAEL, A PEOPLE WHO HAVE LIVED ON THE WEST COAST OF INDIA SINCE THE 2ND CENTURY BCE AND WHO HAVE DEVELOPED A CUISINE THAT INCORPORATES THE FLAVOURS OF THE HINDUS AND CHRISTIANS WITH WHOM THEY LIVE. THE LAVISH USE OF BLACK PEPPER REFLECTS THE TIME BEFORE THE INTRODUCTION OF CHILLIES TO THE INDIAN SUBCONTINENT BECAME THE DOMINANT METHOD OF SPICING THERE.

SERVES FOUR

INGREDIENTS

1 large bunch fresh
  coriander (cilantro)
4 fresh green chillies, seeds and
  stems removed
8 garlic cloves, chopped
5cm/2in piece fresh root ginger,
  peeled and coarsely chopped
juice of 1 lime
8 cardamom pods
2.5ml/½ tsp cumin seeds
1 x 13cm/5in cinnamon stick, or
  5ml/1 tsp freshly ground cinnamon
6 cloves
15ml/1 tbsp coriander seeds
5ml/1 tsp turmeric
1.5ml/¼ tsp cayenne pepper
2.5–5ml/½–1 tsp ground
  black pepper
60–75ml/4–5 tbsp vegetable oil
1kg/2¼lb lamb shoulder, cut into
  bitesize chunks
4 large onions, chopped
4 ripe large tomatoes, diced
salt

1 In a blender or food processor, combine half the coriander with the chillies, garlic and ginger, and process with the lime juice until it forms a paste. Add a few spoonfuls of water if needed to make a smoother paste. Set aside.

2 In a small dry frying pan, over medium heat, lightly toast the cardamom, cumin, cinnamon, cloves and coriander, tossing them so that they do not burn, and removing them from the heat when they are fragrant, about 3 minutes. Leave to cool, then crush either in a coffee grinder reserved for spices or a mortar and pestle. Add the turmeric, cayenne and black pepper and set aside.

3 In a large shallow non-stick frying pan over medium-high heat, warm 15ml/1 tbsp of the oil. When hot, begin to brown the meat in batches very lightly, until lightly coloured. Continue to cook all the meat in this way.

4 To the same pan with the meaty flavours and juices from the frying, add the rest of the oil and the onions. Reduce the heat slightly and cook the onions, stirring, for about 10 minutes, until they are softened. Add the spice paste and cook, stirring, for a few minutes.

5 Add the tomatoes, cook for about 5 minutes until they soften, then add the reserved meat and its juices as well as the ground spice mixture, with salt to taste.

6 Cook over a low heat, gently, until the meat is very tender, about 1½ hours. The dish may be cooked in the oven at this point, making it particularly useful for Shabbat or Pesach Seder. Season to taste, adding more salt or ground black pepper as desired.

7 Serve the spicy lamb curry sprinkled with the reserved fresh coriander.

Energy 647Kcal/2698kJ; Protein 53.1g; Carbohydrate 20.5g, of which sugars 14.7g; Fat 39.9g, of which saturates 14.4g; Cholesterol 190mg; Calcium 104mg; Fibre 4.7g; Sodium 235mg.

WIENER SCHNITZEL

IN OLD VIENNA, VEAL WAS CUT THIN AND POUNDED THINNER, THEN FLOURED, EGGED AND CRUMBED, AND FLASH-FRIED INTO CRISP DISCS. WHEN GERMAN AND AUSTRIAN SURVIVORS OF THE HOLOCAUST REACHED ISRAEL THEY MADE THE SCHNITZEL WITH WHAT WAS AVAILABLE IN THE NEW LAND: TURKEY, CHICKEN AND EVEN AUBERGINE. THIS IS THE ORIGINAL VEAL.

SERVES FOUR

INGREDIENTS
    4 veal escalopes (US scallops),
        175g/6oz each
    75g/3oz/⅔ cup plain (all-purpose)
        flour, seasoned
    2 eggs, beaten
    115g/4oz/scant 2 cups dried
        breadcrumbs
    60ml/4 tbsp oil
    coarsely ground white pepper
    vegetable oil, for brushing
    chives and paprika, to garnish
    lemon wedges and tagliatelle, to serve

1 Place the veal escalopes in between 2 sheets of dampened plastic, clear film (plastic wrap) or greaseproof (waxed) paper and flatten with a meat mallet or rolling pin until half as large again. Press a little ground white pepper into both sides of the escalopes.

2 Tip the flour, eggs and breadcrumbs on to separate plates. Brush the meat with a little oil then dip into the flour. Shake off any extra flour. Then dip the escalopes into the egg and then finally the breadcrumbs. Leave, loosely covered, for 30 minutes.

3 Heat the oil in a large frying pan and gently fry the escalopes, one at a time, over a gentle to medium heat for 3–4 minutes on each side. Be aware that too much heat will cause the veal to toughen. Keep the escalopes warm while you cook the remainder.

4 Garnish with chives and a sprinkling of paprika. Serve with lemon wedges and tagliatelle, with a green salad or vegetable, if you like.

COOK'S TIP
To prevent the breadcrumb coating from cracking during cooking, use the back of a knife and lightly form a criss-cross pattern over the surface.

Energy 487kcal/2051kJ; Protein 48g; Carbohydrate 36.9g, of which sugars 1g; Fat 17.5g, of which saturates 3.2g; Cholesterol 186mg; Calcium 85mg; Fibre 1.2g; Sodium 357mg.

VITELLO <u>CON</u> PEPERONI

THIS TYPICALLY JEWISH-ITALIAN DISH IS OFTEN EATEN WHEN THE PEPPERS AND TOMATOES ARE STILL RIPE AND SWEET. SERVE WITH SOMETHING SUITABLY STARCHY, LIKE POLENTA.

SERVES FOUR TO SIX

INGREDIENTS

675g/1½lb veal, shoulder roast
  or breast
15ml/3 tsp olive oil
10–12 button (pearl) onions,
  whole, peeled
1 yellow (bell) pepper, seeded
  and sliced
1 orange or red (bell) pepper, seeded
  and sliced
5 tomatoes, peeled and quartered
4 garlic cloves, chopped
4 fresh basil sprigs
30ml/2 tbsp dry white wine
salt and black pepper

1 Cut the veal into cubes. Heat the oil in a frying pan and gently stir-fry the veal and onions until browned.

2 After a couple of minutes, add the peppers, tomatoes and garlic. Continue simmering for another 4–5 minutes.

3 Add half the basil leaves, roughly chopped (keep some for the garnish), the wine and seasoning. Cook, stirring frequently, over a low heat, for between 20 and 30 minutes, until the meat is tender.

4 Sprinkle with the remaining basil leaves and serve hot with rice, polenta or some warm crusty bread.

VARIATION
Chicken thighs may be used instead of veal, if you prefer.

Energy 168Kcal/705kJ; Protein 22.5g; Carbohydrate 7.7g, of which sugars 7.1g; Fat 5.1g, of which saturates 1.3g; Cholesterol 84mg; Calcium 23mg; Fibre 2g; Sodium 121mg.

YIDDISH HAIMESHEH HAMBURGERS

EVERY RUSSIAN AND EASTERN EUROPEAN HOUSEHOLD USED TO MAKE A VARIATION OF THIS DISH, WITH LAMB, BEEF AND SOMETIMES VEAL, AS HERE. THE KOSHER KITCHEN USES A GREAT DEAL OF GROUND MEAT AS IT TENDERIZES THE TOUGHER CUTS AND IS ALSO AN ECONOMICAL WAY TO STRETCH A SMALL AMOUNT OF MEAT INTO A MEAL.

SERVES FOUR

INGREDIENTS

   115g/4oz/2 cups fresh white
     breadcrumbs
   45ml/3 tbsp beef stock
   450g/1lb finely minced (ground) veal
   1 egg, beaten
   1 onion, finely chopped
   4 garlic cloves, chopped
   30ml/2 tbsp fresh tarragon
   30ml/2 tbsp plain (all-purpose) flour
   30ml/2 tbsp sunflower oil
   salt and ground black pepper
   pickled vegetables, such as
     cucumber, beetroot, turnips and
     peppers, and crispy fried onions,
     to serve

VARIATION
Instead of tarragon use 5ml/1 tsp dried thyme and a pinch of allspice.

1 Put the breadcrumbs in a bowl and spoon over the stock. Leave to soak for 10 minutes. Add the minced meat, egg, onion, garlic and tarragon, salt and pepper and mix all the ingredients together thoroughly.

2 Divide the mixture into 4 equal portions and shape into ovals, each about 10cm/4in long and 5cm/2in wide. Coat each with the flour.

3 Heat the oil in a frying pan and fry the burgers for about 8 minutes on each side so that they are hot right through. Serve with a tomato sauce, pickled vegetables and fried onions.

Energy 363Kcal/1524kJ; Protein 28.6g; Carbohydrate 29.3g, of which sugars 1.7g; Fat 15.4g, of which saturates 4.3g; Cholesterol 117mg; Calcium 69mg; Fibre 1.1g; Sodium 330mg.

VEAL WITH SAUERKRAUT

THIS TANGY SAUERKRAUT IS SIMMERED WITH VEAL AND ONIONS, TINTED WITH PAPRIKA AND SPICED WITH MUSTARD, REMINISCENT OF HUNGARIAN CUISINE. IT ALSO GETS A HIT OF HOT CHILLI!

SERVES FOUR

INGREDIENTS
    450g/1lb lean veal, diced
    1 onion, diced
    60ml/4 tbsp vegetable oil
    5ml/1 tsp paprika, or more as desired
    400g/14oz shredded sauerkraut,
      drained and well rinsed
    whole red chilli, chopped, or to taste
    1 bay leaf
    90ml/6 tbsp beef or chicken stock
    salt and ground black pepper
    coarse grain mustard, paprika and
      sage leaves, to garnish
    crusty bread, to serve

1 In a heavy frying pan, cook the veal in the oil until browned on all sides, then add the onions and continue to brown for 5 minutes or so.

2 Add the paprika and shredded sauerkraut. Stir well and transfer to a flameproof casserole.

3 Add the chilli and bay leaf to the casserole.

4 Add the stock to the casserole. Cover tightly and cook over a gentle heat for 1–1½ hours, stirring occasionally to prevent it sticking.

5 Season to taste before serving. Spoon on the mustard, sprinkle with paprika and garnish with sage leaves. Serve with crusty bread.

Energy 236Kcal/982kJ; Protein 25g; Carbohydrate 2.3g, of which sugars 2g; Fat 14.1g, of which saturates 2.3g; Cholesterol 95mg; Calcium 63mg; Fibre 2.4g; Sodium 714mg.

HOLISHKES

Stuffed cabbage — a quintessential Jewish dish — is enjoyed in a wide variety of guises among the Ashkenazim and some Sephardim. This main course version is sweet and sour, quite Russian, and served with a thick tomato sauce.

SERVES SIX TO EIGHT

INGREDIENTS

1kg/2¼lb lean minced (ground) beef
75g/3oz/scant ½ cup long grain rice
4 onions, 2 chopped and 2 sliced
5–8 garlic cloves, chopped
2 eggs
45ml/3 tbsp water
1 large head of white or green cabbage
2 × 400g/14oz cans chopped tomatoes
45ml/3 tbsp demerara (raw) sugar
pinch of citric acid
15–30ml/1–2 tbsp white wine
   vinegar, cider vinegar or lemon juice
pinch of ground cinnamon
salt and ground black pepper
lemon wedges, to serve

1 Put the beef, rice, 5ml/1 tsp salt, pepper, chopped onions and garlic in a bowl. Beat the eggs with the water, and combine with the meat mixture. Chill.

2 Cut the core from the cabbage in a cone shape and discard. Bring a very large pan of water to the boil, lower the cabbage into the water and blanch for 1–2 minutes, then remove from the pan. Peel one or two layers of leaves off the head, then re-submerge the cabbage. Repeat until all the leaves are removed.

3 Preheat the oven to 150°C/300°F/ Gas 2. Form the beef mixture into ovals, the size of small lemons, and wrap each in one or two cabbage leaves, folding and overlapping the leaves so that the mixture is completely enclosed.

4 Lay the cabbage rolls in the base of a large ovenproof dish, alternating with the sliced onions. Pour the tomatoes over and add the sugar, vinegar or lemon juice, salt, pepper and cinnamon. Cover and bake for 2 hours.

5 During cooking, remove the holishkes from the oven and baste them with the tomato juices two or three times.

6 After 2 hours, uncover the dish and cook for a further 30–60 minutes, or until the tomato sauce has thickened and is lightly browned on top. Serve hot with wedges of lemon.

COOK'S TIPS
• Any leaves that are too small to stuff, or that are left over when the stuffing has been used up, can be tucked into the side of the dish, alongside the stuffed cabbage rolls. Serve the cabbage leaves with the holishkes.
• Citric acid, also known as sour salt, indeed looks like salt. It is great for sweet and sour, because it doesn't fade unlike vinegar and lemon.

Energy 425Kcal/1773kJ; Protein 29.7g; Carbohydrate 27.5g, of which sugars 17.6g; Fat 22.3g, of which saturates 9.2g; Cholesterol 123mg; Calcium 86mg; Fibre 3.7g; Sodium 134mg.

HUNGARIAN CHOLENT

A CHOLENT IS A LONG-SIMMERED OR BAKED DISH OF BEANS, GRAINS, MEATS AND VEGETABLES, LEFT IN A WARM OVEN OVERNIGHT OR FOR THE AFTERNOON. IT IS EATEN IN ALL REGIONS OF EASTERN AND CENTRAL EUROPE WHEN THE FAMILY COMES HOME FROM SYNAGOGUE.

SERVES FOUR TO SIX

INGREDIENTS

250g/9oz/1⅓ cups white haricot (navy) or butter (lima) beans, soaked in water overnight
90ml/6 tbsp rendered chicken fat, goose fat, duck fat or olive oil
2 onions, chopped
14 garlic cloves, half chopped and half left whole
130g/4½oz pearl barley
25ml/1½ tbsp paprika
2–3 pinches of cayenne pepper
400g/14oz can chopped tomatoes
1 celery stick, chopped
3 carrots, sliced
1 small turnip, diced
2–3 baking potatoes, peeled and cut into large chunks and 1 potato, sliced (optional)
500g/1¼lb beef brisket, whole or cut into chunks
250g/9oz piece of smoked beef
250g/9oz stewing beef
4–6 eggs
1 litre/1¾ pints/4 cups water and 500ml/17fl oz/2¼ cups beef stock or 1.5 litres/2½ pints/6¼ cups water and 1–2 stock (bouillon) cubes
kishke or helzel (optional)
a handful of rice (optional)
salt and ground black pepper

1 Preheat the oven to 120°C/250°F/ Gas ½. Drain the beans. Heat the fat or oil in a flameproof casserole, add the onions and chopped garlic and cook for 5 minutes. Add the beans.

2 Add the whole garlic cloves, barley, paprika, cayenne pepper, tomatoes, celery, carrots, turnip, chopped potatoes, brisket, smoked beef, stewing beef, the eggs in their shells, water and stock or stock cubes to the casserole and season well. Cover and bake for 3 hours.

3 Place the kishke or helzel, if using, on top of the stew. Check if the cholent needs more water. (There should still be a little liquid on top.) Add a little water if necessary, or, if there is too much liquid, add the extra sliced potato or a handful of rice. Cover and bake for a further 1–2 hours. Season and serve hot, making sure each portion contains a whole egg.

VARIATION

To make a Russian cholent, add kasha to the stew. Lightly toast 130g/4½oz buckwheat in a heavy, dry frying pan, then add it to the cholent in place of the pearl barley.

Energy 674Kcal/2833kJ; Protein 46.4g; Carbohydrate 64.6g, of which sugars 10.5g; Fat 27.5g, of which saturates 6.4g; Cholesterol 258mg; Calcium 144mg; Fibre 7.9g; Sodium 190mg.

BRAISED MINCED BEEF PATTIES WITH ONIONS

THIS DISH IS BASED ON THE QUINTESSENTIAL RUSSIAN-JEWISH WAY OF COOKING BEEF. THE BASIC VERSION IS BRAISED, BEEF PATTIES STUDDED WITH GARLIC AND ONION, BUT MORE VEGETABLES SUCH AS GREEN BELL PEPPERS, MUSHROOMS AND BEANSPROUTS CAN BE ADDED TO THE PAN.

SERVES FOUR

INGREDIENTS

   500g/1¼lb lean minced
     (ground) beef
   4–6 garlic cloves, coarsely chopped
   4 onions, 1 finely chopped and
     3 sliced
   15–30ml/1–2 tbsp soy sauce
   15–30ml/1–2 tbsp vegetable oil
     (optional)
   2–3 green (bell) peppers, sliced
     lengthways into strips
   ground black pepper

COOK'S TIP
If the patties and onions become slightly dry during cooking, add a little water or beef stock.

1 Place the minced beef, garlic and chopped onion in a bowl and mix well. Season with soy sauce and pepper and form into four large or eight small patties.

2 Heat a non-stick pan, add a little oil, if you like, then add the patties and cook until browned. Splash over soy sauce.

3 Cover the patties with the sliced onions and peppers, add a little soy sauce, then cover the pan. Reduce the heat to very low; braise for 20–30 minutes.

4 When the onions are turning golden brown, remove the pan from the heat. Serve the patties piled with onions.

Energy 347Kcal/1442kJ; Protein 26.8g; Carbohydrate 13.8g, of which sugars 11.2g; Fat 20.8g, of which saturates 8.8g; Cholesterol 75mg; Calcium 44mg; Fibre 2.8g; Sodium 374mg.

SAUERBRATEN

*THE EASILY-PREPARED CLASSIC SWEET AND SOUR MARINADE GIVES THIS DISH OF POT-ROASTED BEEF —
WHICH ROUGHLY TRANSLATES AS "SOUR ROAST" — ITS NAME.*

SERVES SIX

INGREDIENTS
   1kg/2¼lb silverside (pot roast)
     of beef
   30ml/2 tbsp sunflower oil
   1 onion, sliced
   15ml/1 tbsp cornflour (cornstarch)
   50g/2oz/1 cup crushed ginger
     biscuits (cookies)
   flat leaf parsley, to garnish
   noodles, to serve
For the marinade
   2 onions, sliced
   1 carrot, sliced
   2 celery sticks, sliced
   600ml/1 pint/2½ cups water
   150ml/¼ pint/⅔ cup red vinegar
   1 bay leaf
   6 cloves
   6 whole black peppercorns
   15ml/1 tbsp soft dark brown sugar

VARIATION
Make meatballs of minced (ground) beef
with a little minced smoked beef.

1 To make the marinade, put the
onions, carrot and celery into a pan with
the water. Bring to the boil and simmer
for 5 minutes. Add the remaining
marinade ingredients and simmer for
a further 5 minutes. Cover and leave
to cool.

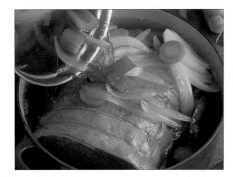

2 Put the joint in a casserole into
which it just fits. Pour over the
marinade, cover and leave to marinate
in the refrigerator for 3 days if possible,
turning the joint daily.

3 Remove the joint from the marinade
and dry thoroughly using kitchen paper.
Heat the oil in a large frying pan and
brown the beef over a high heat.
Remove the joint and set aside. Add
the sliced onion to the pan and fry for
5 minutes.

4 Strain the marinade, reserving the
liquid. Put the onion in a large
flameproof casserole or pan, then put
the beef on top. Pour over the marinade
liquid. Slowly bring to the boil, cover,
then simmer over a low heat for
1½ 2 hours, or until the beef is
very tender.

5 Remove the beef and keep warm.
Blend the cornflour in a cup with a little
cold water. Add to the cooking liquid
with the ginger biscuit crumbs and
bring to the boil, stirring. Thickly slice
the beef and serve on a bed of hot
noodles. Garnish with sprigs of fresh
flat leaf parsley and serve the gravy on
the side.

Energy 296Kcal/1244kJ; Protein 40.3g; Carbohydrate 7.4g, of which sugars 3.6g; Fat 11.9g, of which saturates 3.6g; Cholesterol 102mg; Calcium 23mg; Fibre 0.3g; Sodium 131mg.

SWEET AND SOUR TONGUE

TONGUE IS A FAVOURITE MEAT IN THE ASHKENAZIC KITCHEN, ALTHOUGH IN RECENT YEARS IT HAS RATHER GONE OUT OF FASHION. IT IS WONDERFUL SERVED HOT WITH A SWEET AND SOUR SAUCE AND LEFTOVERS ARE GOOD COLD, WITHOUT THE SAUCE, THINLY SLICED FOR SANDWICHES OR A SALAD.

SERVES ABOUT EIGHT

INGREDIENTS

1kg/2¼lb fresh tongue
2–3 onions, 1 sliced and
  1–2 chopped
3 bay leaves
½–1 stock (bouillon) cube or a small
  amount of stock powder
45ml/3 tbsp vegetable oil
60ml/4 tbsp potato flour
120ml/4fl oz/½ cup honey
150g/5oz/1 cup raisins
2.5ml/½ tsp salt
2.5ml/½ tsp ground ginger
1 lemon, sliced
fresh rosemary sprigs, to garnish

1 Put the tongue, sliced onion and bay leaves in a large pan. Pour over cold water to cover and add the stock cube or powder. Bring to the boil, reduce the heat, cover and simmer gently for 2–3 hours. Leave to cool.

2 In a small frying pan, heat the oil, add the chopped onion and cook for about 5 minutes, until softened.

3 Stir the potato flour into the onions and gradually add about 500ml/17fl oz/ 2¼ cups of the stock, stirring constantly to prevent lumps forming.

4 Stir the honey, raisins, salt and ginger into the sauce and continue to cook until it has thickened and is smooth. Add the lemon slices and set the sauce aside.

5 Slice the tongue thinly and serve generously coated with the sweet and sour sauce. Garnish with rosemary.

Energy 446Kcal/1864kJ; Protein 21g; Carbohydrate 30.6g, of which sugars 28.1g; Fat 27.6g, of which saturates 0.7g; Cholesterol 98mg; Calcium 34mg; Fibre 1.3g; Sodium 1528mg.

POT-ROASTED BRISKET

THIS BIG, POT-ROASTED MEAT DISH IS A FRIDAY NIGHT FAVOURITE. OCCASIONALLY, AS HERE, A HEAVY, SAUSAGE-SHAPED DUMPLING CALLED KISHKE IS ADDED TO THE POT AND COOKED WITH THE MEAT. POT-ROASTED BRISKET SHOULD COOK LONG AND SLOWLY AND BE MELTINGLY TENDER.

SERVES SIX TO EIGHT

INGREDIENTS
   5 onions, sliced widthways
   3 bay leaves
   1–1.6kg/2¼–3½lb beef brisket
   1 garlic head, broken into cloves
   4 carrots, thickly sliced
   5–10ml/1–2 tsp paprika
   about 500ml/17fl oz/2¼ cups
      beef stock
   3–4 baking potatoes, peeled
      and quartered
   salt and ground black pepper
For the kishke
   about 90cm/36in sausage casing
      (see Cook's Tip)
   250g/9oz/2¼ cups plain
      (all-purpose) flour
   120ml/4fl oz/½ cup semolina
      or couscous
   15–30ml/1–2 tbsp paprika
   1 carrot, grated and 2 carrots,
      diced (optional)
   250ml/8fl oz/1 cup rendered
      chicken fat
   30ml/2 tbsp crisp, fried onions
   ½ onion, grated and 3 onions,
      thinly sliced
   3 garlic cloves, chopped
   salt and ground black pepper

1 Preheat the oven to 180°C/350°F/ Gas 4. Put one-third of the onions and a bay leaf in an ovenproof dish, then top with the brisket. Sprinkle over the garlic, carrots and the remaining bay leaves, sprinkle with salt, pepper and paprika, then top with the remaining onions.

2 Pour in enough stock to fill the dish to about 5–7.5cm/2–3in and cover with foil. Cook in the oven for 2 hours.

3 Meanwhile, make the kishke. In a bowl, combine all the ingredients and stuff the mixture into the casing, leaving enough space for the mixture to expand. Tie into sausage-shaped lengths.

4 When the meat has cooked for about 2 hours, add the kishke and potatoes to the pan, re-cover and cook for a further 1 hour, or until the meat and potatoes are tender.

5 Remove the foil from the dish and increase the oven temperature to 190–200°C/375–400°F/Gas 5–6. Move the onions away from the top of the meat to the side of the dish and return to the oven for a further 30 minutes, or until the meat, onions and potatoes are beginning to brown and become crisp. Serve hot or cold.

COOK'S TIP
Traditionally, sausage casings are used for kishke but if unavailable, use cooking-strength clear film (plastic wrap) or a piece of muslin (cheesecloth).

Energy 727Kcal/3041kJ; Protein 33.8g; Carbohydrate 62.2g, of which sugars 10.1g; Fat 39.9g, of which saturates 15.9g; Cholesterol 97mg; Calcium 90mg; Fibre 4.7g; Sodium 105mg.

CALF'S LIVER WITH SLOW-COOKED ONIONS, MARSALA AND SAGE

THIS IS THE JEWISH VERSION OF THE FAMOUS VENETIAN DISH FEGATO ALLA VENEZIANA. THE JEWISH COMMUNITY IN VENICE IS ANCIENT. IT GREW SUBSTANTIALLY IN 1348 AS IT WAS A SAFE HAVEN FOR JEWS FROM NORTHERN EUROPE FLEEING PERSECUTION, AND AGAIN IN THE 1500s. SOON AFTER, THE JEWISH QUARTER, OR GHETTO, WAS ESTABLISHED.

SERVES FOUR

INGREDIENTS

  75ml/5 tbsp olive oil, plus extra for
    shallow-frying
  500g/1¼lb mild onions, thinly sliced
  small bunch of fresh sage leaves
  30ml/2 tbsp chopped fresh parsley,
    plus a little extra to garnish
  2.5ml/½ tsp caster (superfine) sugar
  15ml/1 tbsp balsamic vinegar
  30ml/2 tbsp plain (all-purpose) flour
  675g/1⅓lb calf's liver
  150ml/¼ pint/⅔ cup Marsala
  salt and ground black pepper

1 Heat half the oil in a large, wide, heavy pan and cook the onions, covered, over a very gentle heat for 30 minutes. Stir once or twice.

2 Chop 5 of the sage leaves and add them to the pan with the parsley, a pinch of salt, the sugar and balsamic vinegar. Cook, uncovered and stirring frequently, until very tender and golden. Taste for seasoning and add salt and pepper as necessary.

3 Heat a shallow layer of olive oil in a frying pan and fry the remaining sage leaves for 15–30 seconds, then drain them on kitchen paper.

4 Wash the liver, then sprinkle it with salt.

5 Under a grill (broiler) lightly brown the liver on both sides. Rinse, cool, and thinly slice.

6 Heat the oil in a frying pan over a high heat. Season the flour, then dip the liver in it and fry it quickly for about 2 minutes on each side until browned, but still pink in the middle. Use a slotted spoon to transfer the liver to warm plates and keep warm.

7 Immediately add the Marsala to the pan and let it bubble fiercely until reduced to a few tablespoons of sticky glaze. Distribute the onions over the liver and spoon over the Marsala juices. Sprinkle with the fried sage leaves and extra parsley and serve immediately.

VARIATIONS
• **Chicken liver and onion bruschetta**
Cook the onions as above, replacing the sage with 5ml/1 tsp chopped thyme. Fry 400g/14oz trimmed, kashered chicken livers in 45ml/3 tbsp oil until browned but still pink in the centre. Flame the chicken livers with 45ml/3 tbsp cognac, then mix with the cooked onions. Heap on to thick slices of toasted country bread rubbed with oil and garlic or on to slices of grilled (broiled) polenta. Serve sprinkled with chopped fresh parsley.
• In Tuscany, the mixture is puréed, seasoned with anchovy paste, then spread on crisp crostini (oil-browned thin toasts).

Energy 429Kcal/1788kJ; Protein 33.1g; Carbohydrate 20.2g, of which sugars 11.6g; Fat 19.8g, of which saturates 3.7g; Cholesterol 624mg; Calcium 54mg; Fibre 2g; Sodium 125mg.

SPICY MINCED BEEF KEBABS WITH HUMMUS

SPICY KEBABS ARE SERVED WITH HUMMUS THROUGHOUT THE MIDDLE EAST. THE EARTHY CHICKPEAS FORM THE BASIS OF THE ZESTY SAUCE. SPICE THE MEAT AS HOT AS YOU WISH, OR LEAVE IT MILD AND SERVE WITH A HOT SAUCE SUCH AS HARISSA OR ZCHUG. YOU WILL NEED METAL SKEWERS WITH WIDE BLADES FOR THESE KEBABS TO HOLD THE POUNDED MEAT IN PLACE SO THAT IT RESEMBLES A SHEATH ON A SWORD WHEN SERVING. THE WHOLE SHEATH CAN BE PUSHED OFF THE SKEWER.

SERVES SIX

INGREDIENTS
  500g/1¼lb finely minced
    (ground) beef
  1 onion, grated
  10ml/2 tsp ground cumin
  10ml/2 tsp ground coriander
  10ml/2 tsp paprika
  4ml/¾ tsp cayenne pepper
  5ml/1 tsp salt
  small bunch of flat leaf parsley,
    finely chopped
  small bunch of fresh coriander
    (cilantro), finely chopped
  salad and bread, to serve
For the hummus
  225g/8oz/1¼ cups dried chickpeas,
    soaked overnight, drained
    and cooked
  100ml/4fl oz/½ cup olive oil
  juice of 1 lemon
  2 garlic cloves, crushed
  5ml/1 tsp cumin seeds
  60ml/4 tbsp light tahini
  salt and ground black pepper

1 Mix the minced beef with the onion, cumin, ground coriander, paprika, cayenne, salt, parsley and chopped fresh coriander. Knead the mixture well, then pound it until smooth in a mortar with a pestle or in a food processor. Place in a dish, cover and leave to stand for 1 hour.

2 Meanwhile, make the hummus. In a food processor, process the chickpeas with half the olive oil, the lemon juice, garlic, cumin seeds and tahini. Season with salt and pepper and set aside.

3 Divide the meat mixture into six portions and mould each on to a metal skewer, so that the meat resembles a fat sausage. Heat the grill (broiler) on the hottest setting and cook the kebabs for 4–5 minutes on each side.

4 Pour a few tablespoons of the remaining olive oil over the hot hummus. Serve the kebabs with the hummus, salad and fresh bread.

Energy 490Kcal/2036kJ; Protein 26.6g; Carbohydrate 19.7g, of which sugars 1.7g; Fat 34.4g, of which saturates 8.7g; Cholesterol 50mg; Calcium 151mg; Fibre 5.3g; Sodium 86mg.

KOVBASA

SPICED SAUSAGES, FIRST POACHED, THEN SAUTÉED, ARE A FAVOURITE UKRAINIAN WAY WITH MINCED MEAT. THE RESULT IS RICH AND FLAVOURFUL.

SERVES SIX

INGREDIENTS

450g/1lb minced (ground) beef
450g/1lb minced veal
2 eggs, beaten
30ml/2 tbsp *peperivka* (see Cook's Tip) or pepper vodka
2.5ml/½ tsp ground allspice
1 onion, finely chopped
5ml/1 tsp salt
about 1.75 litres/3 pints/7½ cups chicken stock
fresh parsley, to garnish
mashed potato, to serve

VARIATIONS
• Use 900g/2lb minced beef instead of a combination of beef and veal.
• If you would prefer to serve the kovbasa with rice rather than mashed potatoes, use wild rice seasoned with chopped parsley as a fresh complement to the meaty richness of the kovbasa.

1 Combine the meat with the eggs, peperivka, allspice, onion and salt. Check the seasoning by frying a small piece of the mixture, then tasting it. Adjust if necessary.

COOK'S TIP
Spicing whisky with peppers to make peperivka is an old tradition in the Ukraine. Add 3 whole cayenne peppers, pricked all over with a fine skewer, to 150ml/¼ pint/⅔ cup whisky or bourbon and leave for at least 48 hours.

2 Form the meat mixture into sausages, about 15cm/6in long. Wrap in doubled, greased muslin (cheesecloth) and tie securely with string.

3 Bring a large pan of chicken stock to the boil, and allow to simmer gently for a couple of minutes.

4 Add the sausages and simmer gently, turning frequently, for 35–40 minutes, or until the juices run clear when the sausages are pierced with a fine skewer.

5 Leave the sausages in the stock for 20 minutes, then remove and leave to cool. Remove the muslin and sauté the sausages in oil to brown them. Garnish with parsley and serve with mashed potato or seasoned rice.

COOK'S TIP
These sausages can be made several days ahead and kept refrigerated.

Energy 305Kcal/1271kJ; Protein 32.2g; Carbohydrate 0.8g, of which sugars 0.6g; Fat 19.3g, of which saturates 7.9g; Cholesterol 155mg; Calcium 26mg; Fibre 0.1g; Sodium 146mg.

HUNGARIAN GOULASH

JEWS ARE SAID TO HAVE HELPED SPREAD NEW WORLD SPICES AND FOODS THROUGHOUT EUROPE, AS THE DISCOVERY OF THESE GOODS COINCIDED WITH THE EXPULSION FROM SPAIN, AND MANY JEWS TOOK THE NEW INGREDIENTS WITH THEM. HUNGARY CERTAINLY EMBRACED THE MILD DRIED PEPPER, PAPRIKA — ITS CUISINE HAS NOT BEEN THE SAME SINCE. GOULASH MIGHT BE DEFINED AS A STEW OR A SOUP, FULL OF MEAT AND RED WITH PAPRIKA. HERE IT IS ENRICHED WITH DUMPLINGS TO MAKE A CLASSIC OF HOT, FLAVOURSOME EASTERN EUROPEAN FOOD.

SERVES FOUR TO SIX

INGREDIENTS

  30ml/2 tbsp vegetable oil
  2 onions, chopped
  900g/2lb braising or stewing steak,
    trimmed and cubed
  1 garlic clove, crushed
  generous pinch of caraway seeds
  30ml/2 tbsp paprika
  1 firm ripe tomato, chopped
  2.4 litres/4 pints/10 cups beef stock
  2 green (bell) peppers, seeded
    and sliced
  450g/1lb potatoes, diced
  salt
For the dumplings
  2 eggs, beaten
  90ml/6 tbsp plain (all-purpose)
    flour, sifted

1 Heat the oil in a large, heavy pan. Add the onion and cook until soft.

2 Add the beef cubes to the pan and brown over a moderate heat for 10 minutes, stirring frequently to prevent the meat from sticking. Gradually add the garlic, caraway seeds and a light sprinkling of salt.

3 Remove the pan from the heat and stir in the paprika and tomato. Pour in the beef stock and cook, covered, over a gentle heat for 1–1½ hours, or until the meat is tender.

4 Add the peppers and potatoes to the pan and cook for a further 20–25 minutes, stirring occasionally.

5 Meanwhile, make the dumplings by mixing the beaten eggs together with the flour and a little salt. With lightly floured hands roll out the dumplings and drop them into the simmering stew for about 2–3 minutes, or until they rise to the surface of the stew. Adjust the seasoning and serve the goulash in warm dishes.

Energy 371Kcal/1562kJ; Protein 39.5g; Carbohydrate 29.2g, of which sugars 6.1g; Fat 11.5g, of which saturates 3.2g; Cholesterol 164mg; Calcium 52mg; Fibre 2.5g; Sodium 140mg.

BEEF CASSEROLE WITH BABY ONIONS AND RED WINE

THIS VERSION OF MOSHARI STIFATHO WITH TINY WHOLE ONIONS IS A SPECIALITY OF THE ISLAND OF CORFU AND WAS MUCH ENJOYED BY THE JEWS WHO ONCE LIVED THERE. THIS IS THE KIND OF EASY DISH THAT CAN BE LEFT SIMMERING IN THE OVEN FOR HOURS, SO IT IS PERFECT FOR THE SHABBAT EVENING MEAL. SERVE IT WITH RICE, PASTA, MASHED POTATOES OR OLIVE OIL-FRIED POTATOES.

SERVES FOUR

INGREDIENTS
  75ml/5 tbsp olive oil
  1kg/2¼lb good stewing or braising
    steak, cut into large cubes
  3 garlic cloves, chopped
  5ml/1 tsp ground cumin
  5cm/2in piece cinnamon stick
  175ml/6fl oz/¾ cup red wine
  30ml/2 tbsp red wine vinegar
  pinch of allspice
  2 bay leaves, crumbled
  30ml/2 tbsp tomato purée (paste)
    diluted in 1 litre/1¾ pints/4 cups
    hot water or stock
  675g/1½lb baby (pearl) onions,
    peeled and left whole
  15–30ml/1–2 tbsp demerara
    (raw) sugar
  salt and ground black pepper

1 Heat the olive oil in a large heavy pan and brown the meat cubes, in batches if necessary, until pale golden brown all over.

2 Stir in the garlic and cumin. Add the cinnamon stick and cook for a few seconds, then pour the wine and vinegar slowly over the mixture. Let the liquid bubble and evaporate for 3–4 minutes.

3 Add the rosemary and bay leaves, with the diluted tomato purée. Stir well, season with salt and pepper, then cover and simmer gently for about 1½ hours or until the meat is tender.

4 Dot the onions over the meat mixture and shake the pan to distribute them evenly. Sprinkle the demerara sugar over the onions, cover the pan and cook very gently for 30 minutes.

5 When the onions are soft but have not begun to disintegrate, add a little hot water if necessary. Do not stir once the onions have been added but gently shake the pan instead to coat them in the sauce. Remove the cinnamon stick and sprig of rosemary and serve.

COOK'S TIP
Stifatho can be cooked in the oven, if you prefer. Use a flameproof casserole. Having browned the meat and added the remaining ingredients, with the exception of the onions and sugar, transfer the covered casserole to an oven preheated to 160°C/325°F/Gas 3 and bake for about 2 hours, or until the meat is tender. Add the onions and sugar as above and return the casserole to the oven for 1 hour more.

Energy 590Kcal/2458kJ; Protein 57.6g; Carbohydrate 19.6g, of which sugars 14.6g; Fat 28.4g, of which saturates 8g; Cholesterol 158mg; Calcium 64mg; Fibre 2.9g; Sodium 187mg.

MEATBALLS WITH CUMIN AND CRACKED GREEN OLIVES

A DELICIOUS DISH THAT PROBABLY ORIGINATED WITH THE GREEKS WHO CAME FROM ASIA MINOR AFTER THE CATASTROPHIC WAR WITH TURKEY IN 1922. THE SPICING OF CUMIN REFLECTS THE SEPHARDIC JEWS WHO SETTLED IN THESSALONIKA, GREECE. THIS DISH IS IDEAL FOR ENTERTAINING AS IT CAN BE COOKED IN ADVANCE AND REHEATED AS NEEDED.

SERVES FOUR

INGREDIENTS
  2–3 medium slices of bread,
    crusts removed
  675g/1½lb minced (ground) lamb
    or beef
  2 garlic cloves, crushed
  15ml/1 tbsp ground cumin
  1 egg, lightly beaten
  25g/1oz/¼ cup plain
    (all-purpose) flour
  45ml/3 tbsp olive oil, for frying
  salt and ground black pepper
For the sauce
  45ml/3 tbsp extra virgin olive oil
  5ml/1 tsp cumin seeds
  400g/14oz can chopped tomatoes
  15ml/1 tbsp tomato purée (paste)
    diluted in 150ml/¼ pint/⅔ cup
    hot water
  2.5ml/½ tsp dried oregano
  12–16 green olives, preferably
    cracked ones, rinsed
    and drained

1 Soak the bread in water for 10 minutes, then drain, squeeze dry and place in a large bowl. Add the meat, garlic, cumin and egg. Season with salt and pepper, then mix either with a fork or your hands, until blended.

2 Take a small handful – the size of a large walnut – and roll it into a short, slim sausage. Set this aside. Continue until all the meat mixture has been used. Roll all the sausage-shaped meatballs lightly in flour, shaking each one to get rid of any excess.

3 Heat the oil in a large non-stick frying pan and fry the meatballs, in batches if necessary, until they are golden on all sides. Lift them out and place them in a bowl. Discard the oil remaining in the pan.

4 Make the sauce. Heat the olive oil in a large pan. Add the cumin seeds and swirl them around for a few seconds until they are aromatic. Add the tomatoes and stir with a wooden spoon for about 2 minutes to break them up. Pour in the diluted tomato purée and mix well.

VARIATION
The meatballs taste delicious when simmered in the cumin-flavoured tomato sauce, but their aroma is so seductive when they are first fried that you may not be able to wait that long. To eat them browned, without their sauce, serve with wedges of lemon instead.

5 Add the meatballs. Stir in the oregano and olives, with salt and pepper to taste. Spoon the sauce over the meatballs, then cover and cook gently for 30 minutes, shaking the pan occasionally to prevent them from sticking. Tip into a serving dish and serve immediately.

Energy 659Kcal/2739kJ; Protein 38.2g; Carbohydrate 18.1g, of which sugars 4.2g; Fat 48.7g, of which saturates 15g; Cholesterol 149mg; Calcium 76mg; Fibre 2.3g; Sodium 835mg.

STIR-FRIED BEEF WITH MANGETOUTS

The community of American Jews generally adore Chinese food: the crisp vegetables and light savoury sauces contrast with traditional, long-cooked Ashkenazic food. China has a history of Jewish culture, including the ancient community of Kaifung, the mid-20th century arrivals at Shanghai and Harbin and today's fledgling shul in Beijing.

SERVES FOUR

INGREDIENTS
   450g/1lb rump (round) steak
   45ml/3 tbsp soy sauce
   30ml/2 tbsp Chinese rice wine or
   dry sherry
   15ml/1 tbsp soft light brown sugar
   2.5ml/½ tsp cornflour (cornstarch)
   15ml/1 tbsp vegetable oil
   15ml/1 tbsp finely chopped fresh
   root ginger
   15ml/1 tbsp finely chopped garlic
   225g/8oz mangetouts (snow peas)

VARIATION
Broccoli, sugar snaps or Chinese leaves (Chinese cabbage) could be used in place of mangetouts.

1 Cut the steak into even-size, very thin strips.

2 Combine the soy sauce, rice wine or dry sherry, brown sugar and cornflour. Mix well and set aside.

3 Heat the oil in a preheated wok. Add the ginger and garlic and stir-fry for 30 seconds. Add the steak and stir-fry for 2 minutes, or until evenly browned.

4 Add the mangetouts and stir-fry for a further 3 minutes.

5 Stir the soy sauce mixture until smooth, then add to the wok. Bring to the boil, stirring constantly, lower the heat and simmer until the sauce is thick and smooth. Serve immediately.

Energy 188Kcal/790kJ; Protein 27.1g; Carbohydrate 3.3g, of which sugars 2.7g; Fat 7.5g, of which saturates 2.2g; Cholesterol 66mg; Calcium 31mg; Fibre 1.3g; Sodium 870mg.

BEEF WITH QUINCES

MEAT OR POULTRY COOKED WITH QUINCES IS ENJOYED BY MANY SEPHARDIC COMMUNITIES THROUGHOUT THE WORLD. THIS SWEET, SAVOURY AND AROMATIC DISH IS DELIGHTFUL TO ENJOY IN THE AUTUMN, WHEN QUINCES ARE IN SEASON.

SERVES FOUR

INGREDIENTS

   juice of ½ lemon
   2–3 large quinces, total weight about
     1kg/2¼lb
   75ml/5 tbsp extra virgin olive oil
   1kg/2¼lb good quality stewing beef
     steak, cut in large slices
   175ml/6fl oz/¾ cup white wine
   300ml/½ pint/1¼ cups hot water
   1 cinnamon stick
   45ml/3 tbsp demerara (raw) sugar
     mixed with 300ml/½ pint/1¼ cups
     hot water
   whole nutmeg
   salt

1 Have ready a bowl of water acidulated with the lemon juice. Using a sharp cook's knife, quarter each quince vertically. Core and peel the pieces and drop them into the acidulated water to prevent them from discolouring.

2 Heat the olive oil in a large heavy pan. When it is almost smoking, brown the meat on both sides, turning the pieces over once. As soon as all the meat has browned, lower the heat, pour the wine over and let it bubble and reduce slightly.

3 Pour the hot water into the pan and add the cinnamon stick. Cover the pan and cook over a gentle heat for about 1 hour or until the meat is tender. Add salt to taste.

4 Lift the quinces out of the acidulated water, and slice each piece vertically into 2–3 elongated pieces. Spread half the quince slices in a single layer in a large frying pan, pour half the sugared water over and cook them gently for 10 minutes, turning them over occasionally until all the liquid has been absorbed and they start to brown and caramelize.

5 Spread the caramelized quince slices over the meat in the pan and repeat the caramelizing process with the remaining quince slices. Having added them to the meat, finely grate about one-quarter of a whole nutmeg over the top. If necessary, add more hot water to cover the quince slices.

6 Cover the pan and cook for 30 minutes more until both the meat and the quince slices are meltingly soft and sweet. Do not stir the mixture after the quince has been added; instead, shake the pan from side to side occasionally so that the meat is prevented from sticking to the base. Serve hot.

COOK'S TIP
Quinces look a bit like elongated apples and can be as big as melons. The golden flesh surrounding the central core turns pink when cooked.

Energy 603Kcal/2529kJ; Protein 57.4g; Carbohydrate 36.9g, of which sugars 36.9g; Fat 22.7g, of which saturates 5.5g; Cholesterol 168mg; Calcium 49mg; Fibre 5.5g; Sodium 184mg.

BEEF AND AUBERGINE CASSEROLE

This colourful dish is eaten in many guises and with different spicing throughout the Mediterranean region. Sephardic Jews have a great affinity for the aubergine, and this dish of braised beef, scented with Greek spices and awash with tomatoes, makes the very best of this versatile vegetable.

SERVES FOUR

INGREDIENTS

about 120ml/4fl oz/½ cup extra
   virgin olive oil, or as needed
1kg/2¼lb good-quality stewing steak
   or feather steak, sliced in
  4 thick pieces
1 onion, chopped
2.5ml/½ tsp dried oregano
5 garlic cloves, chopped
175ml/6fl oz/¾ cup white wine
400g/14oz can chopped tomatoes
pinch of sugar
1 bay leaf
pinch of allspice
1.5ml/¼ tsp cinnamon
2–3 aubergines (eggplants), total
  weight about 675g/1½lb
45ml/3 tbsp finely chopped
  fresh parsley
salt and ground black pepper
toasted pitta bread or steamed rice,
  to serve

1 Heat a few tablespoons of olive oil in a large pan and brown the pieces of meat on both sides. As each piece browns, take it out and set it aside on a plate.

2 Add the chopped onion to the oil remaining in the pan and sauté until it turns translucent.

COOK'S TIP
Feather steak is a tender cut of beef from between the neck and rib, near the chuck. It is particularly good for braising. If you can't find it, stewing or braising steak makes a good substitute.

3 Add the oregano and the garlic, then, as soon as the garlic becomes aromatic, return the meat to the pan and pour the wine over, allowing it to bubble and evaporate over a few minutes. Add the tomatoes, sugar, bay leaf, cinnamon and allspice, with enough hot water to just cover the meat. Bring to the boil, lower the heat, cover and cook for about 1 hour or a little longer, until the meat is tender.

4 Meanwhile, trim the aubergines and slice them into 2cm/¾in thick rounds.

5 Heat a few tablespoons more olive oil and fry the aubergines briefly in batches over a high heat, turning them over as they become lightly browned. Repeat and cook in batches, adding more oil as needed. They do not have to cook thoroughly at this stage and should not be allowed to burn.

6 Lift the fried aubergines out of the pan and pat dry on a platter lined with kitchen paper. When all the aubergines have been fried, season them.

7 When the meat feels tender, season it, then add the aubergines and shake the pan to distribute them evenly. From this point, do not stir the mixture, as the aubergines will be quite fragile.

8 Add a little more hot water so that the aubergines are submerged in the sauce, cover the pan and simmer for 30 minutes more or until the meat is very tender and all the flavours have amalgamated.

9 Sprinkle the parsley over the top and simmer for a few more minutes before serving with toasted pitta bread or steamed rice.

COOK'S TIP
Instead of simmering on the stove, the meat can be baked, covered, at 170°C/325°F/Gas 3 for 1½ hours or until tender, then returned to the oven, once the aubergines have been added, for the remaining 30 minutes.

Energy 565Kcal/2364kJ; Protein 59.3g; Carbohydrate 8.6g, of which sugars 7.8g; Fat 29.9g, of which saturates 6.6g; Cholesterol 168mg; Calcium 67mg; Fibre 5.2g; Sodium 191mg.

VEGETARIAN DISHES

The Jewish table has a strong tradition of vegetarianism. When meat cannot be eaten, for example when kosher meat is unavailable or when there are no kosher pans to cook it in, vegetarian dishes are often chosen. The repertoire of Jewish vegetarian dishes is wide and varied, including dishes based on eggs, rice, beans, chickpeas, tahini and even tofu. Stuffed, rolled, stewed and fried, these dishes are perfect as light bites or zesty mains.

AUBERGINES <u>WITH</u> TOMATO TOPPING

GRIDDLED AUBERGINE, TOPPED WITH A RICH TOMATO AND ONION MIXTURE, IS EATEN IN VARIOUS GUISES THROUGHOUT THE BALKANS, MEDITERRANEAN AND MIDDLE EAST. THEY ARE OFTEN SERVED AS AN ACCOMPANIMENT TO A MEAT OR A DAIRY MEAL BUT ALSO MAKE A FABULOUS MAIN VEGETARIAN COURSE, PAIRED WITH A SIMPLE RICE DISH OR A COOLING SALAD WITH YOGURT.

SERVES FOUR

INGREDIENTS
3 medium aubergines (eggplants), total weight about 800g/1¾lb
150ml/¼ pint/⅔ cup olive oil
2 large onions, finely chopped
3 garlic cloves, finely chopped
900g/2lb fresh tomatoes, peeled if you like, and chopped (canned is fine)
2.5ml/½ tsp each dried oregano and thyme
2.5ml/½ tsp sugar, or to taste
45ml/3 tbsp chopped fresh parsley
15ml/1 tbsp tomato purée (paste) diluted in 150ml/¼ pint/⅔ cup hot water
salt and ground black pepper

2 Heat half the olive oil in a ridged griddle pan or large frying pan and shallow-fry the aubergines in batches, turning them over once, until light golden on both sides.

3 As each batch cooks, lift the slices out and pat them dry on kitchen paper, then arrange them side by side in a large roasting dish.

6 Preheat the oven to 190°C/375°F/ Gas 5. Stir the parsley into the sauce, then pile 15–30ml/1–2 tbsp of the mixture on each slice of aubergine.

7 Pour the diluted tomato purée into the dish, adding it to one corner, to avoid disturbing the aubergines. It will disperse through the dish while they are cooking. Bake the aubergines for 20–25 minutes, basting them once.

8 Remove the baked aubergines from the oven and either serve piping hot or set aside to cool a little until required.

COOK'S TIP
These savoury topped aubergines are just as delicious served as finger food at room temperature as when piping hot, so do not be afraid to put them to one side for a short period after cooking. This will give you valuable time to prepare any accompanying dishes.

1 Trim the aubergines, then slice them into rounds, about 1cm/½in thick.

COOK'S TIP
Be sure to heat the oil before adding the aubergine slices and do not be tempted to add more oil once the aubergines are cooking even if the amount in the pan seems a little sparse. They will absorb cold oil, resulting in a greasy dish.

4 Heat the rest of the oil in a heavy pan and sauté the onions until pale gold in colour.

5 Add the garlic and, when aromatic, add the tomatoes and a little water. Season, stir in the oregano, thyme and sugar, then cover and allow to simmer gently for 15 minutes, stirring the mixture occasionally.

Energy 332Kcal/1378kJ; Protein 4.8g; Carbohydrate 19.8g, of which sugars 17.1g; Fat 26.7g, of which saturates 4g; Cholesterol 0mg; Calcium 62mg; Fibre 7.8g; Sodium 36mg.

SEPHARDIC STUFFED ONIONS, POTATOES AND COURGETTES

STUFFED VEGETABLES ARE A HALLMARK OF THE SEPHARDIC KITCHEN — IT IS SAID THAT THE FILLING REPRESENTS ABUNDANCE. THE FLAVOURS AND AROMAS IN THIS STUFFING ORIGINATE FROM CARDAMOM AND ALLSPICE, TINTED WITH TOMATO. THESE ARE AS DELICIOUS SERVED COLD AS WARM.

SERVES FOUR

INGREDIENTS
    4 potatoes, peeled
    4 onions, skinned
    4 courgettes (zucchini),
      halved widthways
    2–4 garlic cloves, chopped
    45–60ml/3–4 tbsp olive oil
    45–60ml/3–4 tbsp tomato
      purée (paste)
    1.5ml/¼ tsp ras al hanout or
      curry powder
    large pinch of ground allspice
    seeds of 2–3 cardamom pods
    juice of ½ lemon
    30–45ml/2–3 tbsp chopped
      fresh parsley
    90–120ml/6–8 tbsp vegetable stock
    salt and ground black pepper
    salad, to serve (optional)

1 Bring a large pan of salted water to the boil. Starting with the potatoes, then the onions and finally the courgettes, add to the boiling water and cook until they become almost tender but not cooked through. Allow about 10 minutes for the potatoes, 8 minutes for the onions and 4–6 minutes for the courgettes. Remove the vegetables from the pan and leave to cool.

COOK'S TIP
Use a small melon baller or apple corer to hollow out the vegetables.

2 When the vegetables are cool enough to handle, hollow them out. Preheat the oven to 190°C/375°F/Gas 5.

3 Finely chop the cut-out vegetable flesh and put in a bowl. Add the garlic, half the olive oil, the tomato purée, ras al hanout or curry powder, allspice, cardamom seeds, lemon juice, parsley, salt and pepper and mix well together. Use the stuffing mixture to fill the hollowed vegetables.

4 Arrange the stuffed vegetables in a baking pan and drizzle with the stock and the remaining oil. Roast for 35–40 minutes, or until golden brown. Serve warm with a salad, if you like.

Energy 347Kcal/1452kJ; Protein 10.2g; Carbohydrate 56.7g, of which sugars 22.1g; Fat 10.3g, of which saturates 1.6g; Cholesterol 0mg; Calcium 135mg; Fibre 8.2g; Sodium 62mg.

CHEESE-STUFFED AUBERGINES
WITH TOMATO SAUCE

AT ONE TIME, JEWISH COMMUNITIES FLOURISHED ON CRETE AND RHODES. IT IS POSSIBLE THAT THIS ITALIAN-TINGED DAIRY DISH HAILED FROM ONE OF THOSE ISLANDS, WHERE THERE WERE STRONG HISTORICAL CONNECTIONS WITH VENETIAN AND IONIAN JEWS.

SERVES FOUR

INGREDIENTS
   2 aubergines (eggplants)
   olive oil, for shallow-frying
   450g/1lb soft white cheese, such as
      feta or pecorino, crumbled
   2–3 mint sprigs, to garnish
   salt and ground black pepper
For the tomato sauce
   15ml/1 tbsp olive oil
   6–8 garlic cloves, chopped
   400g/14oz can chopped tomatoes
   120ml/4fl oz/½ cup vegetable stock
   15ml/1 tbsp chopped fresh parsley
   large pinch of dried Greek
      oregano, crushed

1 Make the tomato sauce. Heat the oil in a small pan and fry the garlic for 1 minute or so or until softened. Add the tomatoes, vegetable stock and the parsley. Season well. Bring to the boil, then lower the heat and simmer for 10–12 minutes until slightly thickened, stirring constantly. Add a pinch of oregano, stir into the mixture, then remove the pan from the heat and set aside while you prepare the aubergines.

2 Preheat the oven to 190°C/375°F/ Gas 5. Slice the aubergines lengthways. Heat the oil in a large frying pan and fry the aubergine slices until they are golden brown on both sides. Drain on kitchen paper.

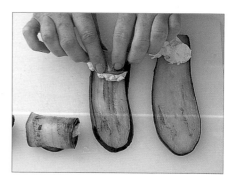

3 Place a generous spoonful of the cheese at one end of each aubergine slice and roll up. Arrange the rolls side by side in a shallow ovenproof dish. Pour the tomato sauce over the top and bake for 10–15 minutes until heated through. Garnish with the mint sprigs and serve.

VARIATION
Try this recipe with different varieties of soft cheese, such as ricotta, mozzarella or Gruyère.

Energy 421Kcal/1746kJ; Protein 19.7g; Carbohydrate 8.2g, of which sugars 7.9g; Fat 34.7g, of which saturates 17.2g; Cholesterol 79mg; Calcium 432mg; Fibre 4.1g; Sodium 1633mg.

CROATIAN COURGETTE RISOTTO

IT IS SAID THAT THE JEWS OF THE VENICE GHETTO PREPARED FAR MORE RISOTTO THAN DID THE REST OF THE NON-JEWISH VENETIAN POPULATION. VENETIAN JEWS MADE RISOTTO WITH EVERY VEGETABLE THE GARDEN AND MARKET OFFERED. PERHAPS THIS RISOTTO, FROM NEIGHBOURING CROATIA, IS AN INHERITANCE FROM THE JEWS OF VENICE.

SERVES FOUR

INGREDIENTS

1kg/2¼lb small or medium
   courgettes (zucchini)
60ml/4 tbsp olive oil
3 onions, finely chopped
5 garlic cloves, crushed
400g/14oz can chopped tomatoes
200g/7oz/1 cup risotto or short
   grain rice
600–750ml/1–1¼ pints/2½–3 cups
   vegetable stock
30ml/2 tbsp chopped fresh parsley
30ml/2 tbsp chopped fresh dill
pinch of cayenne pepper
salt and ground white pepper
sprigs of dill and olives, to garnish
thick natural (plain) yogurt, to serve

1 Preheat the oven to 190°C/375°F/ Gas 5. Trim the courgettes and slice into large chunks.

2 Heat half the olive oil in a large pan and gently fry the onions and garlic until just soft. Stir in the tomatoes and simmer for about 5–8 minutes before adding the courgettes and salt to taste.

3 Cook over a gentle to medium heat for 10–15 minutes, before stirring the rice into the pan.

4 Add the stock to the pan, cover and simmer for about 45 minutes or until the rice is tender. Stir the mixture occasionally to refresh the rice.

5 Remove from the heat and stir in pepper to taste, parsley, dill and cayenne pepper. Spoon into an ovenproof dish and bake for about 45 minutes.

6 Halfway through cooking, brush the remaining oil over the courgette mixture. Garnish with the dill and olives. Serve with the yogurt.

COOK'S TIP
Add extra liquid as necessary, during step 5, to prevent the mixture from sticking to the bottom of the pan.

Energy 199Kcal/826kJ; Protein 5.5g; Carbohydrate 29.8g, of which sugars 8g; Fat 6.5g, of which saturates 1g; Cholesterol 0mg; Calcium 66mg; Fibre 2.9g; Sodium 9mg.

STUFFED CELERIAC

CELERIAC IS THE ROOT OF THE CELERY PLANT, GROWN SPECIFICALLY TO DEVELOP THE ROOT RATHER THAN THE CRISP STALKS OR PUNGENT LEAVES. IN THIS DISH, LOVED BY TURKISH AND BALKAN JEWS, IT IS STUFFED WITH GARLIC AND PARSLEY AND COOKED WITH LOTS OF OLIVE OIL AND LEMON JUICE. ENJOY IT FOR A MAIN COURSE WITH RICE OR BREAD AND YOGURT, IF DESIRED.

SERVES FOUR

INGREDIENTS
    4 small celeriac, about 200–225g/
        7–8oz each
    juice of 2 lemons
    150ml/¼ pint/⅔ cup extra virgin
        olive oil
    lemon wedges and sprigs of flat leaf
        parsley, to garnish
For the stuffing
    6 garlic cloves, finely chopped
    2.5ml/½ tsp black peppercorns,
        finely crushed
    60–75ml/4–5 tbsp chopped
        fresh parsley
    salt

1 Peel the celeriac carefully with a sharp knife and quickly immerse them in a bowl of water and the lemon juice until ready to use. This will prevent them from browning.

COOK'S TIPS
• A knobbly root vegetable closely related to the more familiar swede, celeriac has a tangy flavour somewhere between aniseed, celery and parsley. It is one of the few root vegetables that should always be peeled before use. It can, however, be eaten raw in salads.
• It is necessary to add the lemon juice to acidulate the water, as this helps to prevent the peeled celeriac from discolouring and keeps it looking fresh.

2 Reserve the lemon water. Very carefully scoop out the flesh of each celeriac, leaving a shell about 2cm/¾in thick, in which to put the filling.

3 Working quickly, chop up the scooped out celeriac flesh and mix with the garlic and peppercorns. Add the parsley and season with salt.

4 Fill the shells with the stuffing and sit them in a large pan, making sure they remain upright throughout cooking. Pour in the olive oil and enough lemon water to come halfway up the celeriac.

5 Simmer very gently until the celeriac are tender and nearly all the cooking liquid has been absorbed. Serve the celeriac hot or cold with their juices, and garnish with lemon wedges and sprigs of parsley.

Energy 235Kcal/965kJ; Protein 0.8g; Carbohydrate 1.4g, of which sugars 0.6g; Fat 25.2g, of which saturates 3.6g; Cholesterol 0mg; Calcium 29mg; Fibre 1g; Sodium 32mg.

Split Pea or Lentil Fritters

These sumptuous fritters are likely cousins of ta'amia and falafel. Serve them with a wedge of lemon and a spoonful of hot, fragrant chutney.

SERVES FOUR TO SIX

INGREDIENTS

250g/9oz/generous 1 cup yellow split peas or red lentils, soaked overnight
3–5 garlic cloves, chopped
30ml/2 tbsp roughly chopped fresh root ginger
120ml/4fl oz/½ cup chopped fresh coriander (cilantro) leaves
2.5–5ml/½–1 tsp ground cumin
1.5–2.5ml/¼–½ tsp ground turmeric
large pinch of cayenne pepper or ½–1 fresh green chilli, chopped
120ml/4fl oz/½ cup gram flour
5ml/1 tsp baking powder
30ml/2 tbsp couscous
2 large or 3 small onions, chopped
vegetable oil, for frying
salt and ground black pepper
lemon wedges, to serve

1 Drain the split peas or lentils, reserving a little of the soaking water. Put the chopped garlic and ginger in a food processor or blender and process until finely minced (ground). Add the drained peas or lentils, 15–30ml/ 1–2 tbsp of the reserved soaking water and the chopped coriander, and process to form a purée.

2 Add the cumin, turmeric, cayenne or chilli, 2.5ml/½ tsp salt, 2.5ml/½ tsp pepper, the gram flour, baking powder and couscous to the mixture and combine. The mixture should form a thick batter. If it seems too thick, add a spoonful of soaking water and if it is too watery, add a little more flour or couscous. Mix in the onions.

3 Heat the oil in a wide, deep frying pan, to a depth of about 5cm/2in, until it is hot enough to brown a cube of bread in 30 seconds. Using two spoons, form the mixture into two bitesize balls and slip each gently into the hot oil. Cook until golden brown on the underside, then turn and cook the second side until golden brown.

4 Remove the fritters from the hot oil with a slotted spoon and drain well on kitchen paper. Transfer the fritters to a baking sheet and keep warm in the oven until all the mixture is cooked. Serve hot or at room temperature with lemon wedges.

Energy 360Kcal/1511kJ; Protein 14.1g; Carbohydrate 51.3g, of which sugars 8.3g; Fat 12.3g, of which saturates 1.4g; Cholesterol 0mg; Calcium 119mg; Fibre 5.3g; Sodium 26mg.

STUFFED VINE LEAVES

THE SPICING OF CUMIN, MINT, CINNAMON AND RAISINS IN THIS DISH IS DISTINCTLY SEPHARDIC. SERVE COLD WITH A YOGURT DIP FOR A LUSCIOUS MEZE OR BUFFET.

SERVES SIX TO EIGHT

INGREDIENTS
250g/9oz/1¼ cups brown rice
30–45ml/2–3 tbsp natural
 (plain) yogurt
3 garlic cloves, chopped
1 egg, lightly beaten
5–10ml/1–2 tsp ground cumin
2.5ml/½ tsp ground cinnamon
several handfuls of raisins
3–4 spring onions (scallions),
 thinly sliced
½ bunch fresh mint or 10ml/2 tsp
 dried mint, plus extra to garnish
about 25 preserved or fresh
 vine leaves
salt, if necessary
For steaming
8–10 unpeeled garlic cloves
juice of ½–1 lemon
90ml/6 tbsp olive oil
To serve
1 lemon, cut into wedges or half slices
15–25 Greek black olives
150ml/¼ pint/⅔ cup natural
 (plain) yogurt

1 Put the rice in a pan with 300ml/ ½ pint/1¼ cups water. Bring to the boil, reduce the heat, cover and simmer for 30 minutes, or until just tender. Drain well and leave to cool slightly.

2 Put the cooked rice in a bowl, add the yogurt, garlic, egg, ground cumin and cinnamon, raisins, spring onions and mint and mix together.

3 If you are using preserved vine leaves, rinse them well. If using fresh vine leaves, blanch in salted boiling water for 2–3 minutes, then rinse under cold water and drain.

VARIATION
For a twist to the classic stuffed vine leaf, other herbs such as dill or parsley can be used, and a handful of pine nuts can be added to the stuffing.

4 Lay the leaves on a board, shiny side down. Place 15–30ml/1–2 tbsp of the mixture near the stalk of each leaf. Fold each one up, starting at the bottom, then the sides, and finally rolling up towards the top to enclose the filling.

COOK'S TIP
Vine leaves are at their most tender when freshly picked in early summer, but if fresh leaves are not available, you can buy preserved ones in specialist grocers and some supermarkets.

5 Carefully layer the rolls in a steamer and stud with the whole garlic cloves. Fill the base of the steamer with water and drizzle the lemon juice and olive oil evenly over the rolls.

6 Cover the steamer tightly and cook over a medium-high heat for about 40 minutes. Add more water if necessary.

7 Remove the steamer from the heat and set aside to cool slightly. Arrange the vine leaves on a serving dish and serve hot or, alternatively, leave to cool further. Garnish and serve with lemon wedges or half slices, olives, and a bowl of yogurt, for dipping.

VARIATION
For a Syrian Jewish dish, make a filling of minced beef or lamb and omit the yogurt. Place the rolled vine leaves on a bed of cooked white beans mixed with tomatoes, onions and allspice. Steam.

Energy 220Kcal/924kJ; Protein 3.5g; Carbohydrate 31.1g, of which sugars 6g; Fat 9.9g, of which saturates 1.6g; Cholesterol 24mg; Calcium 27mg; Fibre 1.2g; Sodium 18mg.

RICE-STUFFED TOMATOES AND PEPPERS

CRUNCHY CHOPPED ALMONDS, TENDER RICE AND DICED VEGETABLES MAKE A SATISFYING VEGETARIAN FILLING FOR JUDAEO-SPANISH STUFFED VEGETABLE DISHES. THESE STUFFED PEPPERS ARE EQUALLY DELICIOUS EITHER SERVED WARM OR ALLOWED TO COOL TO ROOM TEMPERATURE.

3 Halve the peppers, leaving the cores intact. Scoop out the seeds. Brush the peppers with 15ml/1 tbsp of the oil.

4 Fry the onions and garlic in 30ml/ 2 tbsp oil. Stir in most of the almonds. Add the rice, tomato pulp, drained raisins, mint and 30ml/2 tbsp parsley. Season well, then spoon the mixture into the vegetable cases.

5 Bake uncovered for 20 minutes. Finely chop the remaining almonds and parsley in a food processor and sprinkle over the top. Drizzle with 15–30ml/ 1–2 tbsp olive oil. Return to the oven and bake for a further 20 minutes, or until turning golden. Serve, garnished with more parsley if you wish.

SERVES FOUR

INGREDIENTS
   2 large tomatoes
   1 green (bell) pepper
   1 yellow or orange (bell) pepper
   75ml/5 tbsp olive oil
   2 onions, finely chopped
   5 garlic cloves, finely chopped
   75g/3oz/¾ cup almonds, chopped
   175g/6oz/1½ cups cooked rice, or
      75g/3oz/scant ½ cup long grain
      rice, cooked and drained
   30ml/2 tbsp Malaga raisins or
      muscatels, soaked in hot water
   45ml/3 tbsp chopped fresh mint
   45ml/3 tbsp chopped fresh flat
      leaf parsley
   salt and ground black pepper

1 Preheat the oven to 190°C/375°F/ Gas 5. Cut the tomatoes in half and scoop out the pulp and seeds.

2 Put the tomato halves on kitchen paper with the cut sides down and leave to drain. Roughly chop the centres and seeds and place in a bowl.

VARIATION
Small aubergines (eggplants) or large courgettes (zucchini) are also good stuffed. Scoop out the centres, then oil the vegetable cases and bake for about 15 minutes. Chop the centres, fry to soften and add to the stuffing mixture, then fill and bake as for the peppers and tomatoes.

Energy 399Kcal/1657kJ; Protein 8.3g; Carbohydrate 36g, of which sugars 17.6g; Fat 25.1g, of which saturates 3g; Cholesterol 0mg; Calcium 105mg; Fibre 5.1g; Sodium 22mg.

STEWED AUBERGINE

THIS MOORISH DISH FROM ANDALUCIA, BERENJENA GUISADA, BEARS FLAVOURINGS CHARACTERISTIC OF BOTH ARAB AND JUDAEO-SPANISH TABLES. WHEN THE ARABS INTRODUCED THE AUBERGINE TO ANDALUCIA, IT WAS THE JEWS WHO WERE FIRST TO EMBRACE IT AND WHO SPREAD THEIR LOVE OF THE VEGETABLE THROUGHOUT THE REST OF EUROPE.

SERVES FOUR

INGREDIENTS

1 large aubergine (eggplant)
60–90ml/4–6 tbsp olive oil
2 shallots, thinly sliced
5 tomatoes, quartered
4–5 garlic cloves, thinly sliced
60ml/4 tbsp red wine, or juice of
  1 lemon
pinch of sugar, if needed
30ml/2 tbsp chopped fresh parsley,
  plus extra to garnish
30–45ml/2–3 tbsp virgin olive oil
salt and ground black pepper

1 Slice the aubergine into 1cm/½in rounds. Rinse well, then press between several layers of kitchen paper to remove any excess liquid.

2 Heat 30ml/2 tbsp of the oil in a large frying pan until smoking. Add one layer of aubergine slices and fry, turning once, until golden brown. Remove to a plate covered with kitchen paper. Heat more oil and fry the second batch in the same way.

3 Heat 15ml/1 tbsp of oil in a pan and cook the shallots for 5 minutes until golden. Cut the aubergine into strips. Add to the pan, with the tomatoes, garlic and wine or lemon juice. Cover and simmer for 30 minutes.

4 Stir in a pinch of sugar to taste, add the parsley, and check the seasoning. Sprinkle with a little more parsley and serve hot. Dribble a little virgin olive oil over the dish before it goes on the table.

Energy 148Kcal/614kJ; Protein 1.8g; Carbohydrate 6.8g, of which sugars 6.3g; Fat 11.7g, of which saturates 1.8g; Cholesterol 0mg; Calcium 26mg; Fibre 3.1g; Sodium 15mg.

THREE-VEGETABLE KUGEL

Shredded carrots and courgettes add colour and lightness to the traditional potato kugel. The lighter vegetable addition is a modern touch from places such as Israel, California and southern France. An excellent, traditional-style dish for Pesach.

SERVES FOUR

INGREDIENTS

2 courgettes (zucchini),
    coarsely grated
2 carrots, coarsely grated
2 potatoes, peeled and
    coarsely grated
1 onion, grated
3 eggs, lightly beaten
3 garlic cloves, chopped
pinch of sugar
15ml/1 tbsp finely chopped fresh
    parsley or basil
30–45ml/2–3 tbsp matzo meal
105ml/7 tbsp olive or vegetable oil
salt and ground black pepper

1 Preheat the oven to 180°C/350°F/ Gas 4. Put the courgettes, carrots, potatoes, onion, eggs, garlic, sugar, parsley or basil, salt and pepper in a bowl and combine. Add the matzo meal and mix together to form a thick batter.

2 Pour half the oil into an ovenproof dish, spoon in the vegetable mixture, then pour over the remaining oil. Bake for 40–60 minutes, or until the vegetables are tender and the top is golden brown. Serve hot.

Energy 358Kcal/1488kJ; Protein 9.2g; Carbohydrate 26.6g, of which sugars 5.7g; Fat 24.5g, of which saturates 4.2g; Cholesterol 143mg; Calcium 63mg; Fibre 2.9g; Sodium 71mg.

BROCCOLI AND CHEESE MINA

A MINA IS A SEPHARDIC-STYLE PIE, PREPARED FROM LAYERED MATZOS AND A SAVOURY SAUCE AND TOPPED WITH BEATEN EGG, WHICH HOLDS IT ALL TOGETHER AS IT BAKES. MINA CAN BE EITHER MEAT OR DAIRY. ENJOYED IN TURKEY AND MEXICO, IT COMBINES SPANISH AND JEWISH HERITAGE.

2 Wet four matzos and leave to soak for 2–3 minutes. Butter a baking sheet that is large enough to hold four matzo pieces in a single layer. If necessary, use two baking sheets.

3 Place the dampened matzos on the baking sheet, then top evenly with the broccoli, onion, Cheddar cheese, cottage cheese, Parmesan cheese, spring onions and dill.

SERVES FOUR

INGREDIENTS

1 large broccoli head
pinch of salt
pinch of sugar
8 matzo squares
50g/2oz/½ cup butter, plus extra
   for greasing
1 onion, chopped
250g/9oz/2¼ cups grated
   Cheddar cheese
250g/9oz/generous 1 cup
   cottage cheese
65g/2½oz/¾ cup freshly grated
   Parmesan cheese
2 spring onions (scallions), chopped
30–45ml/2–3 tbsp chopped fresh dill
4 eggs
30ml/2 tbsp water
8 garlic cloves, chopped

1 Preheat the oven to 190°C/375°F/ Gas 5. Remove the tough part of the stem from the broccoli, then cut the broccoli head into even-size florets. Cook the broccoli by either steaming above or boiling in water to which you have added a pinch of salt and sugar. Cook until bright green, then remove from the pan with a slotted spoon.

4 In a bowl, lightly beat together the eggs and water, then pour about half the egg over the cheese and broccoli mixture. Wet the remaining matzos and place on top of the broccoli. Pour the remaining beaten egg over the top, dot with half the butter and sprinkle half the chopped garlic over the top.

5 Bake for 20 minutes. Dot the remaining butter on top and sprinkle over the remaining chopped garlic. Return to the oven and bake for about 10 minutes more, or until the mina is golden brown and crisp on top. Serve hot or warm.

Energy 687Kcal/2852kJ; Protein 42.4g; Carbohydrate 23g, of which sugars 4.2g; Fat 45.6g, of which saturates 26.6g; Cholesterol 304mg; Calcium 816mg; Fibre 2.8g; Sodium 969mg.

BALKAN AUBERGINES <u>WITH</u> CHEESE

THIS WONDERFUL BULGARIAN—ISRAELI DISH OF LAYERED AUBERGINES IS CLOAKED IN A THICK CHEESE SAUCE THAT, WHEN COOKED, PRODUCES A WONDERFUL SOUFFLÉ-LIKE MIXTURE. IT IS DELICIOUS EATEN HOT BUT EVEN BETTER SERVED COLD, CUT INTO SQUARES. IT IS OFTEN EATEN FOR SHABBAT, OR MAY FEATURE AT A SUMMER PICNIC OR AFTERNOON GATHERING.

SERVES FOUR TO SIX

INGREDIENTS
   2 large aubergines (eggplants),
     cut into 5mm/¼in thick slices
   about 60ml/4 tbsp olive oil
   25g/1oz/2 tbsp butter
   30ml/2 tbsp plain (all-purpose) flour
   500ml/17fl oz/2¼ cups hot milk
   about ⅛ of a nutmeg, freshly grated
   cayenne pepper
   4 large (US extra large) eggs,
     lightly beaten
   400g/14oz/3½ cups grated cheese,
     such as Kashkaval, Gruyère, or a
     mixture of Parmesan and Cheddar
   salt and ground black pepper

1 Layer the aubergine slices in a bowl or colander, sprinkling each layer with salt, and leave to drain for at least 30 minutes. Rinse well, then pat dry with kitchen paper.

2 Heat the oil in a frying pan, then fry the aubergine slices until golden brown on both sides. Remove from the pan and set aside.

3 Melt the butter in a pan, then add the flour and cook for 1 minute, stirring. Remove from the heat and gradually stir in the hot milk. Return to the heat and slowly bring to the boil, stirring constantly, until the sauce thickens and becomes smooth. Season with nutmeg, cayenne pepper, salt and black pepper and leave to cool.

4 When the sauce is cool, beat in the eggs, then mix in the grated cheese, reserving a little to sprinkle on top of the dish. Preheat the oven to 180°C/350°F/Gas 4.

5 In an ovenproof dish, arrange a layer of the aubergine, then pour over some sauce. Repeat, ending with sauce. Sprinkle with the cheese. Bake for 35–40 minutes until golden and firm.

Energy 501Kcal/2084kJ; Protein 25.9g; Carbohydrate 10.9g, of which sugars 6.9g; Fat 38.4g, of which saturates 19.9g; Cholesterol 206mg; Calcium 650mg; Fibre 2.2g; Sodium 599mg.

MUSHROOM STROGANOFF

JEWS HAVE ADAPTED THE CREAMY RUSSIAN STROGANOFF TO THE MUSHROOM, IN KEEPING WITH THE RULES OF KASHRUT. SERVE WITH HEARTY BUCKWHEAT, NUTTY BROWN RICE, OR A WILD RICE MIX.

SERVES FOUR

INGREDIENTS

40–50g/1½–2oz/3–4 tbsp butter
500g/1¼lb button (white)
  mushrooms, quartered
250g/9oz assorted wild or interesting,
  unusual mushrooms, cut into
  bitesize pieces
6 garlic cloves, chopped
2 onions, chopped
30ml/2 tbsp plain (all-purpose) flour
120ml/4fl oz/½ cup dry white wine
250ml/8fl oz/1 cup vegetable stock
2.5ml/½ tsp dried basil
250g/9oz crème fraîche
large pinch of freshly grated nutmeg
juice of about ¼ lemon
salt and ground black pepper
chopped fresh parsley or chives,
  to garnish
buckwheat, brown rice or wild rice,
  to serve

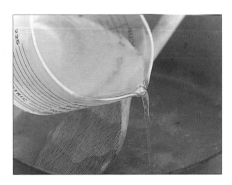

3 Remove the pan from the heat and gradually stir in the wine and half the stock. Return to the heat and slowly bring to the boil, stirring constantly, until the sauce thickens and becomes smooth. Gradually stir in the remaining stock and continue to cook until the sauce is thick.

4 Add the basil and mushrooms, including their juices, to the pan. Put the crème fraîche in a bowl and stir in a little sauce, then stir the mixture into the sauce. Season with nutmeg, lemon juice, salt and pepper. Serve hot, garnished with parsley or chives and accompanied by buckwheat or rice.

1 Melt a little of the butter in a pan and quickly fry the mushrooms, in batches, over a high heat, until brown. During cooking, sprinkle the mushrooms with a little of the garlic, reserving about half for use later. Transfer the mushrooms to a plate after cooking each batch.

2 Heat the remaining butter in the pan, add the chopped onions and fry for about 5 minutes until softened. Add the remaining garlic and cook for a further 1–2 minutes, then sprinkle over the flour and cook for 1 minute more, stirring continuously.

Energy 408Kcal/1685kJ; Protein 6.5g; Carbohydrate 14.3g, of which sugars 6.3g; Fat 34.4g, of which saturates 22.4g; Cholesterol 92mg; Calcium 81mg; Fibre 3.4g; Sodium 88mg.

TAGINE OF ARTICHOKE HEARTS, POTATOES, PEAS AND SAFFRON

IN THE BOOK OF GENESIS, 3:18, IT IS WRITTEN, "THORNS AND THISTLES SHALL THE EARTH BRING FORTH FOR YOU". RASHI, THE BIBLE AND TALMUD COMMENTATOR FROM MEDIEVAL TROYES, FRANCE, TELLS US THAT THIS REFERS TO THE WILD ARTICHOKES OF ANCIENT ISRAEL. THIS IS PERHAPS WHY JEWS THROUGHOUT EUROPE AND THE MIDDLE EAST ENJOYED ARTICHOKES BEFORE THE REST OF THEIR SURROUNDING COMMUNITIES. THIS IS TRULY A DISH OF THE MOROCCAN COUNTRYSIDE IN SPRING.

SERVES FOUR TO SIX

INGREDIENTS

6 fresh artichoke hearts
juice of 1 lemon
30–45ml/2–3 tbsp olive oil
1 onion, chopped
675g/1½lb new potatoes, peeled
   and quartered
small bunch of flat leaf
   parsley, chopped
small bunch of coriander
   (cilantro), chopped
small bunch of mint, chopped
pinch of saffron threads
5ml/1 tsp ground turmeric
about 350ml/12fl oz/1½ cups
   vegetable stock
finely chopped rind of
   ½ preserved lemon
250g/9oz/2¼ cups shelled or
   frozen peas
salt and ground black pepper
couscous or freshly baked bread,
   to serve

1 Prepare the artichokes by discarding the outer leaves, slicing lengthways and scooping out the hairy choke in the middle of the heart. Poach the hearts very gently in plenty of simmering water with half the lemon juice, for 10–15 minutes until tender. Drain and refresh with cold water, then drain again.

2 Heat the olive oil in a tagine or heavy pan. Add the chopped onion and cook over a low heat for about 15 minutes, or until softened but not browned.

VARIATIONS
• To save on preparation time, use frozen artichoke hearts instead of fresh.
• For a more Spanish or Italian flavour, omit the spices and preserved lemon, and use only parsley, no coriander.

COOK'S TIP
Once cut, the flesh of artichokes will blacken. To prevent this from happening, put the artichokes into acidulated water – you can use lemon juice or white wine vinegar as the acidic element.

3 Add the potatoes, most of the parsley, the coriander, mint, the remaining lemon juice, and the saffron and turmeric to the pan. Pour in the vegetable stock, bring to the boil, then reduce the heat. Cover the pan and cook for about 15 minutes, or until the potatoes are almost tender.

4 Stir the preserved lemon, artichoke hearts and peas into the stew and cook, uncovered, for a further 10 minutes. Season to taste, sprinkle with the remaining parsley, and serve with couscous or chunks of fresh bread.

Energy 162Kcal/678kJ; Protein 5.6g; Carbohydrate 25.5g, of which sugars 4.5g; Fat 4.9g, of which saturates 0.8g; Cholesterol 0mg; Calcium 59mg; Fibre 4.4g; Sodium 46mg.

GRILLED AUBERGINE IN HONEY AND SPICES

FIRE-GRILLED AUBERGINE, DRESSED WITH GARLIC, GINGER, CUMIN, HONEY AND LEMON GETS AN ADDITIONAL KICK FROM HARISSA, NORTH AFRICAN HOT PEPPER PASTE. LONG JAPANESE OR SMALL ROUND ITALIAN AUBERGINES ARE EXCELLENT VARIETIES TO CHOOSE FOR THIS DISH, AS ARE THE MORE USUAL LARGE, OBLONG AUBERGINES.

SERVES FOUR

INGREDIENTS
   2 aubergines (eggplants), peeled and
      thickly sliced
   olive oil, for frying
   5 garlic cloves, crushed
   5cm/2in piece of fresh root ginger,
      peeled and grated
   5ml/1 tsp ground cumin
   5ml/1 tsp harissa
   75ml/5 tbsp clear honey
   juice of 1 lemon
   salt
   fresh bread, to serve

VARIATION
If you prefer, substitute the aubergines in this recipe for 3 large courgettes (zucchini). Thickly slice the courgettes, and griddle in a little olive oil. Then cook with the garlic, honey and spices exactly as you would the aubergine slices.

COOK'S TIP
If you want to make a feature out of this sumptuous dish, serve it with other grilled (broiled) vegetables and fruit, such as (bell) peppers, chillies, tomatoes, oranges, pineapple and perhaps with mangoes.

1 Preheat the grill (broiler) or a ridged griddle pan. Dip each aubergine slice in olive oil and cook in a pan under the grill or in a griddle pan. Turn the slices so that they are lightly browned on both sides.

2 In a wide frying pan, fry the garlic in a little olive oil for a few seconds, then stir in the ginger, cumin, harissa, honey and lemon juice.

3 Add enough water to cover the base of the pan and to thin the mixture, then lay the aubergine slices in the pan. Cook the aubergines gently for about 10 minutes, or until they have absorbed all the sauce.

4 Add a little extra water, if necessary, season to taste with salt, and serve at room temperature, with chunks of fresh bread to mop up the juices.

Energy 151Kcal/631kJ; Protein 1.4g; Carbohydrate 17.6g, of which sugars 17.3g; Fat 8.9g, of which saturates 1.3g; Cholesterol 0mg; Calcium 16mg; Fibre 3g; Sodium 5mg.

THRACIAN TOMATO CASSEROLE

THIS TIAN, OR KUGEL, IS FROM THE REGION OF THRACE, WHICH BORDERS BULGARIA AND GREECE. IT IS A LAYERING OF THE FRESH TOMATOES OF LATE SUMMER, DRIZZLED WITH OLIVE OIL AND SPRINKLED WITH CRUMBS. THE CRUMBS HELP TO ABSORB THE SPICY JUICES OF THE TOMATOES AS THEY BAKE. AS DELICIOUS SERVED COLD AS IT IS HOT, IT IS A NICE DISH TO SERVE IN THE SUKKAH.

SERVES FOUR

INGREDIENTS

45ml/3 tbsp olive oil
45ml/3 tbsp chopped fresh flat
  leaf parsley
1kg/2¼lb firm ripe tomatoes
2.5–5ml/½–1 tsp caster
  (superfine) sugar
40g/1¼oz/scant 1 cup day-old
  breadcrumbs
5ml/1 tsp paprika
large pinch of chilli powder or
  cayenne pepper
salt
chopped parsley, to garnish
rye bread, to serve

1 Preheat the oven to 200°C/400°F/ Gas 6. Brush a large baking dish with 15ml/1 tbsp of the oil.

2 Sprinkle the chopped flat leaf parsley over the base of the dish. Cut the tomatoes into even slices, discarding the two end slices of each. Arrange the slices of tomato in the dish so that they overlap slightly. Sprinkle them with a little salt and the caster sugar and set aside while you prepare the topping.

VARIATION

For a tomato and courgette (zucchini) casserole, replace half the quantity of tomatoes with 450g/1lb courgettes. Slice the courgettes evenly and arrange alternate slices of courgette and tomato in the dish, overlapping the slices, for a colourful vegetable medley.

3 In a mixing bowl, stir together the breadcrumbs, the remaining oil, paprika and chilli powder or cayenne pepper, then sprinkle over the top of the tomatoes.

4 Bake in the oven for 40–50 minutes, covering with foil if the topping is getting too brown. Serve hot or cold, garnished with chopped parsley and accompanied by rye bread.

Energy 155Kcal/649kJ; Protein 3.1g; Carbohydrate 15.7g, of which sugars 8.2g; Fat 9.3g, of which saturates 1.4g; Cholesterol 0mg; Calcium 46mg; Fibre 3.1g; Sodium 101mg.

BALKAN SEPHARDIC VEGETABLE STEW

THIS BALKAN STEW LAYERS SUMMER VEGETABLES, SPLASHED WITH OLIVE OIL AND FLAVOURED WITH GARLIC, TO MAKE A HEARTY, VITAL VEGETARIAN CASSEROLE. ENJOY IT AS A MAIN COURSE, OR WITH EITHER A MEAT OR A DAIRY MEAL.

SERVES FOUR

INGREDIENTS
  1 aubergine (eggplant)
  4–5 garlic cloves, chopped
  115g/4oz/½ cup okra, halved lengthways
  225g/8oz/2 cups frozen peas
  225g/8oz/1½ cups French (green)
    beans, cut into 2.5cm/1in pieces
  4 courgettes (zucchini), cut into
    1cm/½in pieces
  2 onions, finely chopped
  450g/1lb old potatoes, diced into
    2.5cm/1in pieces
  1 red (bell) pepper, seeded and sliced
  397g/14oz can chopped tomatoes
  150ml/¼ pint/⅔ cup vegetable stock
  90ml/6 tbsp olive oil
  75ml/5 tbsp chopped fresh parsley
  5ml/1 tsp paprika
For the topping
  3 tomatoes, sliced
  1 courgette (zucchini), sliced

1 Preheat the oven to 190°C/375°F/ Gas 5. Dice the aubergine into 2.5cm/1in pieces. Sprinkle with chopped garlic as you add all the vegetables to a large casserole.

2 Stir in the canned tomatoes, stock, olive oil, parsley, paprika and salt to taste. Stir well.

3 Level the surface of the vegetables and arrange alternate slices of tomatoes and courgette attractively on top.

4 Put the lid on or cover the casserole tightly. Cook for 60–70 minutes. Serve either hot or cold with wedges of warm crusty bread.

Energy 422Kcal/1759kJ; Protein 14.4g; Carbohydrate 48.7g, of which sugars 23.5g; Fat 20.2g, of which saturates 3.3g; Cholesterol 0mg; Calcium 176mg; Fibre 13.9g; Sodium 40mg.

CAULIFLOWER IN COCONUT SAUCE

THERE ARE THREE COMMUNITIES OF JEWS IN INDIA. THE BENE ISRAEL OF MUMBAI ARE SAID TO HAVE SETTLED IN THIS PART OF INDIA AFTER THEIR SHIP WAS WRECKED AS THEY FLED THE CRUELTY OF ANTIOCHUS EPIPHANES OF JUDAEA. THE SECOND COMMUNITY IS THE COCHINESE, CONSISTING OF BOTH A "WHITE" AND "BLACK" COMMUNITY. THE THIRD COMPRISES THE BAGHDADI JEWS OF CALCUTTA. THEY WERE ALL SEPHARDIC, AND HAVE IN RECENT DECADES SCATTERED THROUGHOUT THE WORLD, DISAPPEARING FROM INDIA. THIS DISH IS FROM THE BENE ISRAEL OF BOMBAY.

SERVES FOUR TO SIX

INGREDIENTS
15ml/1 tbsp gram flour
120ml/4fl oz/½ cup water
5ml/1 tsp chilli powder
15ml/1 tbsp ground coriander
5ml/1 tsp ground cumin
5ml/1 tsp mustard powder
5ml/1 tsp ground turmeric
60ml/4 tbsp vegetable oil
6–8 curry leaves
5ml/1 tsp cumin seeds
1 cauliflower, broken into florets
175ml/6fl oz/¾ cup thick
  coconut milk
juice of 2 lemons
salt
lime slices, to garnish

1 Mix the gram flour with a little water to make a smooth paste. Add the chilli, coriander, cumin, mustard, turmeric and salt. Add the remaining water and mix to blend the ingredients.

2 Heat the oil in a wok, karahi or large pan, and fry the cumin seeds until they pop. Add the curry leaves and spice paste and simmer for about 5 minutes.

3 Add the cauliflower and coconut milk. Cook until the mixture bubbles gently, then reduce the heat, cover and simmer until the cauliflower is tender but crunchy in texture.

4 Turn down the heat, add the lemon juice and mix in thoroughly. Serve immediately while piping hot, and garnish with the lime slices.

Energy 374Kcal/1540kJ; Protein 3.5g; Carbohydrate 6.4g, of which sugars 2.2g; Fat 37.3g, of which saturates 26.3g; Cholesterol 0mg; Calcium 25mg; Fibre 1.7g; Sodium 8mg.

TOMATO AND SPINACH PLOV

THIS VEGETARIAN PLOV, OR UZBEK PILAFF, IS REDOLENT OF CUMIN AND CORIANDER, SPICES WHICH, ALONG WITH TURMERIC, ARE THE DISTINCTIVE FLAVOUR OF THE REGION. JEWS HAVE BEEN IN BUKHARA AND TASHKENT SINCE THE 16TH CENTURY. THEIR PRESENCE IN SAMARKAND DATES BACK EVEN EARLIER: RECORDS SUGGEST THEY FIRST ARRIVED IN THE YEAR 1170.

SERVES FOUR

INGREDIENTS
- 30ml/2 tbsp vegetable oil
- 15ml/1 tbsp ghee or unsalted (sweet) butter
- 1 onion, chopped
- 2 garlic cloves, crushed
- 3 tomatoes, peeled, seeded and chopped
- 225g/8oz/generous 1 cup basmati rice, soaked
- 5ml/1 tsp ground coriander
- 5ml/1 tsp ground cumin
- 2 carrots, coarsely grated
- 900ml/1½ pints/3¾ cups vegetable stock
- 275g/10oz young spinach leaves
- 50g/2oz/½ cup unsalted cashew nuts, toasted
- salt and ground black pepper
- naan bread, to serve

1 Heat the oil and ghee or butter in a wok, karahi or large pan, and fry the onion and garlic for 4–5 minutes until soft. Add the tomatoes and cook for 3–4 minutes, stirring, until thickened.

2 Drain the rice, add it to the pan and cook for a further 1–2 minutes, stirring, until the rice is coated.

COOK'S TIP
Leaving to rest for 6–8 minutes before serving makes the rice dry and fluffy.

3 Stir in the coriander and cumin, then add the carrots. Season with salt and pepper. Pour in the stock and stir well to mix.

COOK'S TIP
Ghee – a traditional Indian cooking fat – is clarified butter made from dairy milk. Vegetable ghee is also available and is lower in fat than its dairy equivalent.

4 Bring to the boil, then cover tightly and simmer over a very gentle heat for 10–15 minutes, until the rice is tender. Lay the spinach on the surface of the rice, cover again, and cook for a further 2–3 minutes, until the spinach has wilted. Fold the spinach into the rest of the rice and check the seasoning. Sprinkle with toasted cashews and serve with naan bread.

Energy 400Kcal/1664kJ; Protein 9.5g; Carbohydrate 53.9g, of which sugars 6.8g; Fat 16.1g, of which saturates 4g; Cholesterol 8mg; Calcium 148mg; Fibre 3.4g; Sodium 169mg.

SPAGHETTI WITH FRESH TOMATO SAUCE

DELICIOUS SIMPLICITY IS THE ORDER OF THE DAY IN THIS STRAIGHTFORWARD PASTA SAUCE OF SUMMER TOMATOES. BECAUSE OF ITS LACK OF MEAT, IT HAS LONG BEEN A FAVOURITE WITH ITALKIM. FOR A DAIRY MEAL ADD THE CHEESE; FOR A PAREVE MEAL, OMIT IT.

SERVES FOUR

INGREDIENTS
    675g/1½lb ripe Italian plum
        tomatoes or sweet cherry tomatoes
    60ml/4 tbsp olive oil
    1 onion, finely chopped
    3 garlic cloves, coarsely chopped
    350g/12oz dried spaghetti
    a small handful of fresh basil leaves
    salt and ground black pepper
    pinch of sugar
    coarsely shaved Parmesan cheese,
        to serve (optional)

1 With a sharp knife, cut a cross in the base end of each tomato. Plunge the tomatoes, a few at a time, into a bowl of boiling water. Leave for 30 seconds or so, then lift them out with a slotted spoon and drop them into a bowl of cold water. Drain well. The skin will have begun to peel back from the crosses. Remove it entirely.

2 Place the tomatoes on a chopping board and cut into quarters, then eighths, and then chop as finely as possible.

3 Heat the oil in a large pan, add the onion and garlic and cook over a low heat, stirring frequently, for about 5 minutes until softened and lightly coloured.

4 Add the tomatoes, season with salt and pepper to taste, add a pinch of sugar, and bring to a simmer, then turn the heat down to low and cover the pan with a lid. Cook, stirring occasionally, for 30–40 minutes until the mixture is thick.

VARIATION
Rigatoni or other pasta shapes may be used instead. Larger shapes may be made ahead and enjoyed cold, as a salad or Shabbat lunch.

5 Meanwhile, cook the pasta according to the instructions on the packet or until *al dente*. Shred the basil leaves finely and add to the sauce. Remove the pan from the heat so the herbs do not wilt.

6 Drain the spaghetti and tip into a bowl. Pour the sauce over and toss the mixture well. Serve immediately with shaved Parmesan, if using.

COOK'S TIPS
• The Italian plum tomatoes called San Marzano are the best variety to use. When fully ripe, they have thin skins that peel off easily.
• In Italy, cooks often make this sauce in bulk in the summer months and freeze it for later use. Let it cool, then freeze in usable quantities in rigid containers. Thaw before reheating.

Energy 155Kcal/642kJ; Protein 3.9g; Carbohydrate 8.2g, of which sugars 7.7g; Fat 12.1g, of which saturates 1.8g; Cholesterol 0mg; Calcium 39mg; Fibre 3.4g; Sodium 17mg.

CHICKPEA TAGINE

Sephardic Jews of the Middle East and North Africa love chickpeas. This dish probably has roots in Tunisia or Morocco, where Jewish communities once flourished but are now a mere shadow of their former selves. Serve with crusty bread or rice and cooling yogurt.

SERVES SIX TO EIGHT

INGREDIENTS
  150g/5oz/⅔ cup chickpeas, soaked
    overnight, or 2 x 400g/14oz cans
    chickpeas, drained
  45ml/3 tbsp olive oil
  1 large onion, thinly sliced
  5 garlic cloves, coarsely chopped
  1 yellow (bell) pepper, cut into
    thin strips
  5ml/1 tsp ground cumin
  2.5ml/½ tsp turmeric
  2.5ml/½ tsp paprika
  5 cardomom pods
  1.5ml/¼ tsp ground ginger
  2.5ml/½ tsp mild curry powder
  200g/7oz fresh tomatoes, peeled
    and puréed
  250ml/8fl oz/1 cup vegetable stock
  juice of 1 lemon
  salt and cayenne pepper, to taste
  30ml/2 tbsp chopped fresh
    coriander (cilantro)
  crusty bread and yoghurt, to serve

1 If using dried chickpeas, drain and cook in plenty of boiling water for 1–1½ hours until tender. Remove the skins by rubbing between the hands as shown.

2 Heat the oil in a large pan or flameproof casserole and lightly fry the onion, pepper and garlic until softened.

3 Sprinkle in the cumin, turmeric, paprika, cardomom pods, ginger and curry powder. Stir for a moment or two over the heat to warm the spices.

4 Stir in the tomatoes and then the stock. Cook for 20 minutes.

5 Add the chickpeas and simmer, uncovered, for 15 minutes more.

6 Add the lemon juice and stir into the chickpeas along with the coriander. Season the mixture with a pinch each of salt and cayenne pepper. Serve immediately with the bread and yogurt.

Energy 177Kcal/743kJ; Protein 8g; Carbohydrate 21.2g, of which sugars 4.6g; Fat 7.3g, of which saturates 0.9g; Cholesterol 0mg; Calcium 56mg; Fibre 5.2g; Sodium 224mg.

GRAINS, NOODLES, KUGELS AND PANCAKES

Noodles, once the glory of the Ashkenazi kitchen, were eaten in innumerable ways or filled to make dumplings. Kugels are the classic savoury pudding of noodles or vegetables, bound with egg and baked until firm and crispy, while pancakes — whether filled blintzes or crispy latkes — are definitively Jewish.

ITALIAN COLD PASTA

THIS IS A TRADITIONAL SHABBAT PASTA DISH KNOWN AS PASTA FREDDA TO THE ONCE LARGE AND VIBRANT TUSCAN JEWISH COMMUNITY. TODAY, AL DENTE NOODLES ARE DRESSED WITH GARLIC, PARSLEY AND OLIVE OIL AND EATEN COLD, AS SHABBAT IS THE DAY OF THE WEEK WHEN NO COOKING IS ALLOWED. SERVE AS A FIRST COURSE OR AS AN ACCOMPANIMENT TO A MEAT, FISH OR DAIRY MEAL.

SERVES FOUR

INGREDIENTS
  250g/9oz dried egg noodles
  30–60ml/2–4 tbsp extra virgin
    olive oil
  3 garlic cloves, finely chopped
  60–90ml/4–6 tbsp/¼–⅓ cup roughly
    chopped fresh parsley
  25–30 pitted green olives, sliced or
    roughly chopped
  salt

COOK'S TIP
Because this dish is so simple, always use the best quality ingredients.

1 Cook the noodles in salted boiling water as directed on the packet, or until just tender. Drain and rinse under cold running water.

2 Tip the pasta into a bowl, then add the olive oil, garlic, parsley and olives and toss together. Chill overnight before serving.

Energy 317Kcal/1333kJ; Protein 8.1g; Carbohydrate 45.1g, of which sugars 1.5g; Fat 12.8g, of which saturates 2.6g; Cholesterol 19mg; Calcium 52mg; Fibre 2.9g; Sodium 538mg.

KASHA VARNISHKES

THIS COMBINATION OF BUCKWHEAT GROATS, MUSHROOMS AND BOW-SHAPED PASTA IS A CLASSIC ASHKENAZIC DISH FROM POLAND, UKRAINE AND RUSSIA. IT MAY BE AN ACQUIRED TASTE, BUT FOR ANYONE WHO HAS GROWN UP EATING THIS, IT IS A TASTE OF HOME AND CHILDHOOD.

SERVES FOUR TO SIX

INGREDIENTS
  25g/1oz dried well-flavoured
    mushrooms, such as ceps
  500ml/17fl oz/2¼ cups boiling
    vegetable stock or water
  45ml/3 tbsp rendered chicken fat (for
    a meat meal), vegetable oil (for a
    pareve meal) or 40g/1½oz/3 tbsp
    butter (for a dairy meal)
  3–4 onions, thinly sliced
  250g/9oz mushrooms, sliced
  300g/11oz/1½ cups whole coarse,
    medium or fine buckwheat
  200g/7oz pasta bows
  salt and ground black pepper

1 Put the dried mushrooms in a bowl, pour over half the boiling stock or water and leave to stand for 20–30 minutes, until rehydrated. Remove the mushrooms from the liquid, then strain and reserve the liquid.

2 Heat the chicken fat, oil or butter in a frying pan, add the onions and fry for 5–10 minutes until softened and beginning to brown. Remove the onions to a plate, then add the sliced mushrooms to the pan and fry briefly. Add the soaked mushrooms and cook for 2–3 minutes. Return the onions to the pan and set aside.

VARIATION
To cook kasha without mushrooms, omit both kinds and simply add all of the boiling stock in step 4.

3 In a large, heavy frying pan, toast the buckwheat over a high heat for 2–3 minutes, stirring. Reduce the heat.

4 Stir the remaining boiling stock or water and the reserved mushroom soaking liquid into the buckwheat, cover the pan and cook for about 10 minutes until the buckwheat is just tender and the liquid has been absorbed.

5 Meanwhile, cook the pasta in a large pan of salted boiling water as directed on the packet, or until just tender, then drain.

6 When the kasha is cooked, toss in the onions and mushrooms, and the pasta. Season and serve hot.

Energy 377Kcal/1582kJ; Protein 10.3g; Carbohydrate 66.7g, of which sugars 5g; Fat 8.1g, of which saturates 3.6g; Cholesterol 14mg; Calcium 30mg; Fibre 3.5g; Sodium 46mg.

FARFEL

Farfel are little dumplings made of grated noodle dough. In Yiddish, farfallen means "fallen away", which describes the dough as it is grated. Farfel are eaten on Rosh Hashanah by Ashkenazim, while at Pesach they are made with matzo meal instead of flour. The many tiny dumplings represent fertility, while their round shape symbolizes a well-rounded year and the wholeness of life.

SERVES FOUR AS AN ACCOMPANIMENT

INGREDIENTS
225g/8oz/2 cups plain
  (all-purpose) flour
2 eggs
salt
chopped parsley, to garnish (optional)

COOK'S TIPS
• The dough can be made a day ahead and stored in the refrigerator.
• Farfel are delicious tossed with browned mushrooms or braised wild mushrooms.
• They can also be stuffed into the cavity of a small chicken or poussin and roasted.

1 Put the flour, eggs and a pinch of salt in a bowl and mix together. Gradually add 15–30ml/1–2 tbsp water until the dough holds together.

2 Continue mixing or kneading the dough, until it forms a smooth, non-sticky ball. Add a little more flour if needed. Place in a covered bowl and leave to rest for at least 30 minutes.

3 On a lightly floured surface, roll the dough into a thick rope using your hands. Leave at room temperature for at least 1 hour, and up to 2 hours, in order to let it dry out a little.

4 Cut the dough into chunks, then grate into barley-sized pieces, using the largest holes of a grater. Lightly toss the dumplings in flour and spread on a baking sheet or greaseproof (waxed) paper to dry.

5 To cook the dumplings, bring a pan of salted water to the boil, tip in the dumplings and boil for about 6 minutes, until just tender. Drain well and serve hot, in a bowl of chicken soup or as an accompaniment to a main dish. Garnish with parsley, if you like.

Energy 229Kcal/969kJ; Protein 8.4g; Carbohydrate 43.7g, of which sugars 0.9g; Fat 3.5g, of which saturates 0.9g; Cholesterol 95mg; Calcium 93mg; Fibre 1.8g; Sodium 37mg.

PIEROGI

These Polish "ravioli" are filled with spiced mashed potato and served with fried onions, melted butter or sour cream. Pierogi may be filled with cheese, sauerkraut, mushrooms, or any variety of fillings satisfying enough to ward off the coldest winter.

4 Place 15–30ml/1–2 tbsp of the potato filling in the centre of each square of dough or wrapper, then top with another sheet. Press the edges together and pinch with your fingers or use a fork to seal well. Set aside to allow the edges to dry out and seal firmly.

5 Bring a large pan of salted water to the boil, then lower the heat to a simmer. Carefully slip the dumplings into the water, keeping it simmering gently, and cook for about 2 minutes if using wonton wrappers and slightly longer for noodle dough until tender. (Do not overcrowd the pan.)

6 Using a slotted spoon, remove the dumplings from the water and drain. Serve the dumplings on plates or in bowls. Drizzle with butter and sour cream and garnish with chopped parsley.

VARIATIONS
• Add a sprinkling of chopped spring onions (scallions) to the topping.
• Top with slow-browned onions.

SERVES FOUR TO SIX

INGREDIENTS
675g/1½lb baking potatoes, peeled and cut into chunks
50–75g/2–3oz/4–5 tbsp unsalted (sweet) butter, plus extra melted butter to serve
3 onions, finely chopped
2 eggs, lightly beaten
1 quantity kreplach noodle dough or 250g/9oz packet wonton wrappers
salt and ground black pepper
chopped parsley, to garnish
sour cream, to serve

1 Cook the potatoes in a large pan of salted boiling water until tender. Drain well. Meanwhile, melt the butter in a frying pan, add the onions and fry over a medium heat for about 10 minutes, or until browned.

2 Mash the potatoes, then stir in the fried onions and leave to cool. When cool, add the eggs and mix together. Season generously.

3 If using noodle dough, roll out and cut into 7.5cm/3in squares. Brush the edges of the dough or wonton wrappers with a little water.

Energy 364Kcal/1532kJ; Protein 10.3g; Carbohydrate 55.9g, of which sugars 7.9g; Fat 12.7g, of which saturates 5.9g; Cholesterol 94mg; Calcium 55mg; Fibre 3.7g; Sodium 164mg.

KREPLACH

The three points of these stuffed pasta dumplings symbolize the three Patriarchs: Abraham, Isaac and Jacob. In Western Europe they were originally only filled with meat and eaten in soup, while in Slavic lands they were filled with cheese and eaten as a separate course as early as the 12th century. It was later, after a great meat shortage in Western and Central Europe, that fruit-filled kreplach, known as varenikes, became popular.

SERVES FOUR

INGREDIENTS
    225g/8oz/2 cups plain
        (all-purpose) flour
    2 eggs
    rendered chicken fat or vegetable
        oil (optional)
    salt
    whole and chopped fresh chives,
        to garnish
For the meat filling
    90–120ml/6–8 tbsp rendered chicken
        fat or vegetable oil
    1 large or 2 small onions, chopped
    400g/14oz leftover, pot-roasted meat
    2–3 garlic cloves, chopped
    salt and ground black pepper

1 To make the meat filling, fry the onions in the chicken fat or oil for 5–10 minutes. Mince (grind) or finely chop the meat. Add to the onion with the garlic, salt and pepper and stir.

2 Put the flour, eggs and a pinch of salt in a bowl and combine. Gradually add 15–30ml/1–2 tbsp water until the dough holds together. Continue mixing until the dough forms a non-sticky ball. Add more flour if needed. Place in a covered bowl and leave for 30 minutes.

3 Break off walnut-size pieces of dough and, on a lightly floured surface, roll out as thinly as possible. Cut the dough into squares measuring about 7.5cm/3in.

4 Working one at a time, dampen the edges of each square, then place a spoonful of filling in the centre (do not overfill). Fold the edges of the dough to form a triangular shape and press the edges together to seal.

5 Toss the dumplings in a little flour, then pile on to a non-stick baking sheet. Leave to stand for about 30 minutes.

6 Cook the dumplings in a pan of salted boiling water for about 5 minutes until just tender, then drain. If you like, heat a little chicken fat or oil in a pan and fry the dumplings until just turning brown. Serve, garnished with chives.

VARIATIONS
Kreplach are eaten at festive meals. The filling varies according to the holiday. For high days and holy days, meat-filled kreplach are served in chicken soup; for Purim they are filled with dried fruit and for Shavuot they are filled with cheese.

Energy 666kcal/2788kJ; Protein 41.4g; Carbohydrate 51.6g, of which sugars 6.5g; Fat 34.2g, of which saturates 8.5g; Cholesterol 186mg; Calcium 125mg; Fibre 3.2g; Sodium 91mg.

NOODLE KUGEL FLAVOURED WITH APPLE AND CINNAMON

BLISSFULLY BUTTERY, THIS NOODLE AND APPLE KUGEL IS FRAGRANT WITH CINNAMON AND ENRICHED WITH COTTAGE CHEESE. IT WAS ALLEGEDLY BROUGHT TO NORTH AMERICA FROM RUSSIA BY A JEWISH MIGRANT FLEEING THE TROUBLES IN SEARCH OF A BETTER LIFE, AND SIMPLY OOZES OLD COUNTRY CHARM. USE FLAT EGG NOODLES THAT ARE AT LEAST 1CM/½IN WIDE.

SERVES FOUR TO SIX

INGREDIENTS

- 350–500g/12oz–1¼lb egg noodles
- 130g/4½oz/generous ½ cup plus 15ml/1 tbsp unsalted (sweet) butter
- 2 well-flavoured cooking apples
- 250g/9oz/generous 1 cup cottage cheese
- 3–4 eggs, lightly beaten
- 10ml/2 tsp ground cinnamon
- 250g/9oz/1¼ cups sugar
- 2–3 handfuls raisins
- 2.5ml/½ tsp bicarbonate of soda (baking soda)
- salt

1 Preheat the oven to 180°C/350°C/ Gas 4. Set a pan of salted water over the stove and bring to the boil. Drop the clusters of noodles into the boiling water one by one, and cook according to the directions on the packet, or until they are tender. Drain thoroughly.

VARIATION

This kugel is just as delicious when cooked with pears as the principal fruit, and in fact this variation marks a strong tradition among Jewish communities in the Netherlands, where the pear is much loved as a fruit. Simply use two large, firm pears in place of the cooking apples and prepare the recipe in the same way. The flavour of the baked pears combines very well with the cinnamon.

2 In another pan, melt the butter over a low heat then toss in with the warm noodles. Coarsely grate the unpeeled cooking apples and mix in with the buttery noodle mixture. Stir in the cottage cheese and beaten eggs, then add the cinnamon, sugar, raisins, bicarbonate of soda and a tiny pinch of salt to season.

3 Tip the noodle mixture into a deep rectangular ovenproof dish, measuring about 38 × 20cm/15 × 8in and bake for 1–1¼ hours, until browned and crisp. Serve immediately.

COOK'S TIP

This kugel is also delicious served cold. Serve leftovers the next day, as a snack.

Energy 686kcal/2889kJ; Protein 16.2g; Carbohydrate 100.6g, of which sugars 59.9g; Fat 27.1g, of which saturates 14.4g; Cholesterol 165mg; Calcium 118mg; Fibre 2.4g; Sodium 409mg.

KUGEL YERUSHALAYIM

This traditional kugel, both sweet and peppery at the same time, is said to have been brought to the religious quarter of Mea Shearim in the 18th century by the Gaon of Vilna and his followers. The name means Jerusalem kugel and it is equally good cut into squares and served cold for breakfast or supper as it is for a festive or Shabbat dinner.

SERVES FOUR

INGREDIENTS

   200g/7oz very thin noodles, such as
      spaghellini or fine egg noodles
   60ml/4 tbsp olive oil
   130g/4$\frac{1}{2}$oz/$\frac{2}{3}$ cup sugar or
      demerara (raw) sugar
   2 eggs, lightly beaten
   5ml/1 tsp ground black pepper
   2.5–5ml/$\frac{1}{2}$–1 tsp ground cinnamon
   1–2 handfuls raisins
   salt

1 Preheat the oven to 180°C/350°F/ Gas 4. Cook the pasta in salted boiling water according to the directions on the packet, or until just tender, then drain.

VARIATION
Add about 250g/9oz grated pumpkin to the noodles when adding to the caramel.

2 Put the oil and half the sugar in a large, heavy pan and cook over a medium heat, stirring with a wooden spoon, until the oil and sugar combine and the mixture turns light brown.

3 Remove the pan from the heat (the mixture will continue to cook and turn brown), pour over the pasta and mix well to combine.

4 Add the remaining sugar, the eggs, pepper, ground cinnamon, raisins and 2–3 pinches of salt to the pasta and mix well.

5 Turn the mixture into an ovenproof dish, 33 × 25cm/13 × 10in and spread into an even layer. Bake for about 1 hour, or until set and the top is lightly browned. Serve hot or warm.

Energy 527Kcal/2224kJ; Protein 9.9g; Carbohydrate 87.1g, of which sugars 52.2g; Fat 18g, of which saturates 3.5g; Cholesterol 110mg; Calcium 57mg; Fibre 2g; Sodium 142mg.

POTATO KUGEL

A "PUDDING" OF SHREDDED POTATO AND EGG IS A TRADITIONAL ASHKENAZIC ACCOMPANIMENT TO FESTIVE MEALS. HERE IT IS PREPARED PAREVE, THAT IS, WITH OIL. FOR A MEAT MEAL YOU COULD USE DUCK OR GOOSE FAT, FOR A DAIRY MEAL USE BUTTER.

2 Place the grated potatoes in a large bowl and add the beaten eggs, matzo meal, salt and ground black pepper. Mix together until well combined. Stir in the grated onions, then add 90ml/ 6 tbsp of the vegetable oil.

3 Pour the remaining 30ml/2 tbsp vegetable oil into a baking tin (pan) that is large enough to spread the potato mixture out to a thickness of no more than 4–5cm/1½–2in. Heat the tin (pan) in the oven for about 5 minutes until the oil is very hot.

4 Carefully remove the baking tin (pan) from the oven. Spoon the potato mixture into the tin (pan), letting the hot oil bubble up around the sides and on to the top a little. (The sizzling oil helps to crisp the kugel as it cooks.)

5 Bake the kugel for 45–60 minutes, or until tender and golden brown and crisp on top. Serve immediately, cut into wedges.

SERVES SIX TO EIGHT

INGREDIENTS
2kg/4½lb potatoes
2 eggs, lightly beaten
120–180ml/8–12 tbsp medium matzo meal
10ml/2 tsp salt
3–4 onions, grated
120ml/4fl oz/½ cup vegetable oil
ground black pepper

1 Preheat the oven to 200°C/400°F/ Gas 6. Peel the potatoes and grate finely.

COOK'S TIPS
• Don't be tempted to grate the onions with a food processor, as the mechanical action of the blade creates a bitter flavour by breaking down the cells of the onions.
• For a dairy meal, this kugel can be made with any flavourful cheese such as Cheddar. Add about 350g/12oz/3 cups grated cheese to the grated potato and toss together, then continue as above.

Energy 361Kcal/1516kJ; Protein 8g; Carbohydrate 56.2g, of which sugars 6.8g; Fat 12.8g, of which saturates 1.8g; Cholesterol 48mg; Calcium 38mg; Fibre 3.7g; Sodium 538mg.

MATZO AND ONION KUGEL

LIGHTLY TOASTED, BROKEN-UP MATZOS LAYERED WITH SAVOURY SAUTÉED ONIONS MAKE A SUMPTUOUS KUGEL WHICH, AS A LEAVEN-FREE DISH, IS A PERFECT ACCOMPANIMENT TO SERVE DURING PESACH.

2 Heat the oil or fat in a frying pan, add the chopped onions and fry for 10 minutes, or until softened and browned. Season with salt and pepper.

3 Put the toasted matzos, onions and stock in an ovenproof dish and mix together, then add the eggs and stir well. Season with salt and pepper.

4 Bake the kugel for 25–30 minutes until tender and the top is golden brown. Serve immediately.

SERVES SIX TO EIGHT

INGREDIENTS
  500g/1¼lb matzos
  60ml/4 tbsp vegetable oil or rendered
   chicken fat
  3–4 onions, chopped
  500ml/17fl oz/2¼ cups hot chicken
   or mushroom stock
  3 eggs, lightly beaten
  salt and ground black pepper

1 Preheat the oven to 200°C/400°F/ Gas 6. Break the matzos into bitesize pieces and arrange on a baking sheet in a single layer. Bake for 5–10 minutes, turning frequently, until lightly toasted.

COOK'S TIP
This kugel is particularly good served alongside slowly roasted lamb.

VARIATIONS
• To make a matzo and mushroom kugel, add 250g/8oz thinly sliced, browned mushrooms to the onions, along with a handful of flavoursome dried mushrooms such as porcini or Polish field mushrooms, then continue as above.
• Instead of baking the kugel mixture, use it as a stuffing for a roast chicken or turkey. This is another great addition to a traditional Pesach meal.

Energy 375kcal/1574kJ; Protein 9.9g; Carbohydrate 52.3g, of which sugars 4.9g; Fat 15.5g, of which saturates 1.2g; Cholesterol 71mg; Calcium 101mg; Fibre 2.8g; Sodium 322mg.

MATZO MEAL AND COTTAGE CHEESE LATKES

CHEESE LATKES WERE PROBABLY ONCE THE FAVOURITE ASHKENAZIC DELICACY, POSSIBLY BECAUSE FLOUR, BUCKWHEAT AND MATZO MEAL LATKES WERE MORE COMMON. THE COTTAGE CHEESE GIVES A TANGY, SLIGHTLY GOOEY CONSISTENCY TO THE PANCAKE.

MAKES ABOUT TWENTY

INGREDIENTS
275g/10oz/1¼ cups
   cottage cheese
3 eggs, separated
5ml/1 tsp salt
250g/9oz/2¼ cups matzo meal
1 onion, coarsely grated, or
   3–5 spring onions (scallions),
   thinly sliced
2.5ml/½ tsp sugar
30–45ml/2–3 tbsp natural (plain)
   yogurt or water
vegetable oil, for shallow-frying
ground black pepper

1 In a bowl, mash the cottage cheese. Mix in the egg yolks, half the salt, the matzo meal, onion, spring onion, sugar, yogurt or water, and pepper.

2 Whisk the egg whites with the remaining salt until stiff. Fold one-third of the whisked egg whites into the batter, then fold in the remaining egg whites.

3 Heat the oil in a heavy frying pan to a depth of about 1cm/½in, until a cube of bread added to the pan turns brown immediately. Drop tablespoonfuls of the batter into the pan; fry over a medium-high heat until the undersides are golden brown. Turn carefully and fry the second side.

4 When cooked, remove the latkes from the pan with a slotted spoon and drain on kitchen paper. Serve immediately or place on a baking sheet and keep warm in the oven.

VARIATIONS
To make sweet latkes, omit the onion and add 15–30ml/1–2 tbsp sugar, chopped nuts and some ground cinnamon. Serve topped with a spoonful of jam or honey.

Energy 97kcal/405kJ; Protein 4.1g; Carbohydrate 10.3g, of which sugars 1g; Fat 4.6g, of which saturates 0.8g; Cholesterol 31mg; Calcium 40mg; Fibre 0.4g; Sodium 210mg.

MAMALIGA BAKED WITH TOMATO SAUCE

THIS DISH OF POLENTA OR CORNMEAL IS A STAPLE FOOD IN ITALY AND ROMANIA. LAYERED WITH HERBED TOMATO SAUCE AND CHEESE, IT IS EASY TO PUT TOGETHER AND DELICIOUS TO EAT.

SERVES FOUR

INGREDIENTS
 5ml/1 tsp salt
 250g/9oz/1½ cups quick-cook
  polenta
 30ml/2 tbsp extra virgin
  olive oil
 1 large onion, finely chopped
 5 garlic cloves, crushed
 2 x 400g/14oz cans chopped
  tomatoes, or 450g/1lb
  fresh tomatoes
 15ml/1 tbsp tomato purée (paste), or
  30ml/2 tbsp if using fresh tomatoes
 pinch of granulated sugar
 15ml/1 tbsp chopped fresh rosemary
 salt and ground black pepper
 75g/3oz Gruyère or other mild
  cheese, grated
 75g/3oz Parmesan or Pecorino
  cheese

1 Preheat the oven to 200°C/400°F/ Gas 6. Line a 28 x 18cm/11 x 7in baking tin (pan) with clear film (plastic wrap). Boil 1 litre/1¾ pints/4 cups water with the salt.

2 Pour in the polenta in a steady stream and cook, stirring continuously, for 5 minutes. Pour into the prepared tin and smooth the surface. Leave to cool.

3 Heat the oil in a pan and cook the onion and garlic until soft. Add the tomatoes, purée, sugar and rosemary. Season. Simmer for 20 minutes until the liquid has reduced a little.

4 Cut the polenta into 5cm/2in squares. Layer the polenta and tomato sauce in an ovenproof dish. Sprinkle with the cheeses and bake for 25 minutes, until golden. Serve immediately.

Energy 492kcal/2052kJ; Protein 20g; Carbohydrate 55.8g, of which sugars 8.4g; Fat 20.3g, of which saturates 8.8g; Cholesterol 37mg; Calcium 394mg; Fibre 3.6g; Sodium 861mg.

SPICY CHICKPEA AND AUBERGINE STEW

AUBERGINES WERE BROUGHT TO SPAIN AND ITALY BY THE ARABS. WHEN THE JEWS FLED THESE LANDS, THEY TOOK WITH THEM TO THE BALKAN LANDS TO THE NORTH THE LOVE OF THIS VERSATILE VEGETABLE. THIS DISTINCTLY MIDDLE EASTERN DISH OF AUBERGINES AND CHICKPEAS IN A SPICY TOMATO SAUCE IS A FAVOURITE OF MUSLIMS, CHRISTIANS AND JEWS.

SERVES FOUR

INGREDIENTS

3 large aubergines (eggplants), cubed
200g/7oz/1 cup chickpeas,
  soaked overnight
60ml/4 tbsp olive oil
3 garlic cloves, chopped
2 large onions, chopped
2.5ml/½ tsp ground cumin
2.5ml/½ tsp ground cinnamon
2.5ml/½ tsp ground coriander
3 x 400g/14oz cans chopped
  tomatoes
salt and ground black pepper
cooked rice, to serve
For the garnish
30ml/2 tbsp olive oil
1 onion, sliced
1 garlic clove, sliced
sprigs of coriander (cilantro)

1 Place the aubergines in a colander and sprinkle them with salt. Sit the colander in a bowl and leave for 30 minutes, to allow the bitter juices to escape. Rinse with cold water and dry on kitchen paper.

2 Drain the chickpeas and put in a pan with enough water to cover. Bring to the boil and simmer for 30 minutes, or until tender. Drain.

3 Heat the oil in a large pan. Add the garlic and onion and cook gently, until soft. Add the spices and cook, stirring, for a few seconds.

4 Add the aubergine and stir to coat with the spices and onion. Cook for 5 minutes. Add the tomatoes and gradually stir in the chickpeas. Season the mixture with salt and pepper. Cover and simmer for around 20 minutes.

5 To make the garnish, heat the oil in a frying pan and, when very hot, add the sliced onion and garlic. Fry until golden and crisp. Serve the stew with rice, topped with the onion and garlic and garnished with coriander.

Energy 360kcal/1512kJ; Protein 15g; Carbohydrate 43.3g, of which sugars 17.8g; Fat 15.4g, of which saturates 2.3g; Cholesterol 0mg; Calcium 135mg; Fibre 12.4g; Sodium 52mg.

COUSCOUS WITH DRIED FRUIT AND NUTS

To North African Jews, couscous is the definitive food. It is eaten for Shabbat, with soups, with barbecued food and with the spicy stews known as tagines. Enriched with dried fruit and nuts, it's a special dish served for celebrations such as Rosh Hashanah – the sweetness of the fruit represents a sweet new year.

SERVES SIX

INGREDIENTS

   500g/1¼lb medium couscous
   600ml/1 pint/2½ cups warm water
   5ml/1 tsp salt
   pinch of saffron threads
   15ml/1 tbsp sunflower oil
   75ml/5 tbsp olive oil
   a little butter, if for a dairy meal
   115g/4oz/½ cup ready-to-eat dried
     apricots, cut into slices
   75g/3oz/½ cup dried dates, chopped
   75g/3oz/generous ½ cup
     seedless raisins
   115g/4oz/1 cup blanched almonds,
     cut into slivers, plus a handful
     reserved whole for sprinkling
   75g/3oz/¾ cup pistachio nuts
   10ml/2 tsp ground cinnamon
   45ml/3 tbsp sugar

1 Preheat the oven to 180°C/350°F/ Gas 4. Place the weighed amounts of dried fruits and nuts into separate bowls, so they can be easily added during cooking. Set aside.

2 Mix the water, salt and saffron and pour it over the couscous, stirring to combine. Leave to stand for 10 minutes, or until the grains are plump and tender. Add the sunflower oil and, using your fingers, rub it through the grains so that they are thoroughly coated with the fat.

3 In a heavy pan, heat the olive oil and butter, if using, and stir in the apricots, dates, raisins, most of the almonds (reserving some for the garnish) and pistachio nuts. Cook until the raisins plump up.

4 Tip the nuts and fruit into the couscous and toss together. Put the mixture into an ovenproof dish and cover with foil. Place in the oven and heat through for about 20 minutes.

5 Toast the reserved whole almonds over a low heat until they begin to turn yellowish gold in colour. Pile the hot couscous in a mound on a large serving dish and sprinkle with the cinnamon and sugar. For a more decorative effect, place the cinnamon in stripes down the mound. Sprinkle the toasted almonds over the top and serve hot.

VARIATION
Reduce the amounts of dried fruits and nuts used in the recipe by around half. Add the following to the couscous, to taste: a large pinch of cumin followed by a smaller pinch of turmeric, ground coriander, ground ginger and cloves. Make a quick harissa sauce of 250ml/1 cup vegetable stock plus 1 tbsp each of hot chilli paste, lemon juice, cumin, chopped fresh coriander (cilantro) and olive oil. This accompaniment goes wonderfully with meatballs.

COOK'S TIP
By omitting the butter from the recipe and replacing it with a few shakes of rose water, you will be able to use this couscous mixture as a stuffing for roast chicken. Rub the outside of the chicken with a mixture of olive oil, garlic, cinnamon and salt and pepper before stuffing and roasting.

Energy 576Kcal/2403kJ; Protein 12.5g; Carbohydrate 73g, of which sugars 29.4g; Fat 27.8g, of which saturates 3.1g; Cholesterol 0mg; Calcium 102mg; Fibre 4.2g; Sodium 74mg.

POTATO LATKES

POTATO LATKES — FRIED CAKES OF GRATED RAW POTATO AND EGG — ARE AS MUCH A PART OF THE ASHKENAZIC CHANUKKAH AS ARE THE CANDLES. EATING FOODS FRIED IN OIL IS THE TRADITION FOR CHANUKKAH — THE OIL A COMMEMORATION OF THE OIL THAT BURNED FOR EIGHT DAYS IN THE REDEDICATED TEMPLE AT JERUSALEM. SERVE THE LATKES WITH APPLE SAUCE AND SOUR CREAM OR YOGURT FOR A DAIRY MEAL, OR SIMPLY WITH APPLE SAUCE FOR A MEAT MEAL.

SERVES ABOUT FOUR

INGREDIENTS

3 large baking potatoes, total weight
  about 675g/1½lb, peeled
2 onions, grated
60ml/4 tbsp matzo meal, or 30ml/
  2 tbsp matzo meal and 30ml/2 tbsp
  plain (all-purpose) flour
5ml/1 tsp baking powder
2 eggs, lightly beaten
2.5ml/½ tsp sugar
5ml/1 tsp salt
1.5ml/¼ tsp ground black pepper
vegetable oil, for shallow-frying
sour cream or natural (plain) yogurt,
  to serve (optional)
For the cranberry apple sauce
5 green cooking apples or a
  combination of cooking and
  eating apples
1 cinnamon stick
¼ lemon
about 90g/3½oz/½ cup sugar
225g/8oz/2 cups cranberries

1 To make the cranberry apple sauce, peel, core and roughly chop the apples and place them in a heavy pan with the cinnamon stick. Pare the rind from the lemon, then squeeze the lemon juice over the apples and add the lemon rind to the pan. Add the sugar, cover and cook over a low to medium heat for 15–20 minutes, until they are just tender but have not disintegrated. Stir occasionally so that the apples do not burn.

2 Add the cranberries to the pan, cover again and cook for 5–8 minutes more, or until the berries pop and are just cooked. Taste for sweetness and leave to cool.

3 To make the latkes, coarsely or finely (or a combination of both) grate the potatoes. Put in a sieve (strainer) and press out as much of their starchy liquid as possible with your hands.

4 Transfer the grated potato to a bowl, add the onion, matzo meal or matzo meal and flour, the baking powder, eggs, sugar, salt and pepper, and mix together until well combined.

5 Heat the oil in a heavy frying pan to a depth of about 1cm/½in, until a small piece of the potato mixture sizzles when added to the pan. Drop spoonfuls of the batter (depending on the size you want the latkes) into the pan. Fry over a medium heat for 3–4 minutes, until the undersides are brown and crisp. Turn and fry the second side.

6 When cooked, remove the latkes from the pan with a slotted spoon and drain on kitchen paper. Serve at once or keep warm on a baking sheet in the oven for up to 20 minutes. Serve with sour cream or yogurt, if you like, and the cranberry apple sauce.

Energy 489Kcal/2057kJ; Protein 9.4g; Carbohydrate 83.2g, of which sugars 44.4g; Fat 15.2g, of which saturates 2.2g; Cholesterol 95mg; Calcium 73mg; Fibre 5.9g; Sodium 61mg.

BLINTZES

THE ASHKENAZIC SPECIALITY OF BLINTZES ARE THIN, CRÊPE-LIKE PANCAKES, COOKED ON ONE SIDE, STUFFED, THEN ROLLED TO ENCLOSE THE FILLING AND PAN-FRIED UNTIL CRISP AND BROWN. BLINTZ BATTER IS USUALLY MADE WITH WATER SO YOU CAN FILL THEM WITH MEAT OR, IF THEY ARE FILLED WITH FRUIT, THEY CAN ACCOMPANY A MEAT MEAL. THIS VERSION IS DAIRY HOWEVER, FILLED WITH A LUSCIOUSLY SWEET, LEMONY COTTAGE CHEESE AND FRUIT FILLING.

4 Heat a pancake pan, add a slick of oil, then ladle a little batter into the pan, swirling it to form a thin pancake.

5 When the batter has set and the edges of the pancake begin to lift, gently loosen the edges and flip the pancake on to a plate. Continue with the remaining batter to make about 8–12 pancakes, stacking the pancakes as you cook them (they won't stick).

SERVES FOUR

INGREDIENTS
  4 eggs
  350ml/12fl oz/1½ cups water
  pinch of salt
  45ml/3 tbsp vegetable oil,
    plus extra, for frying
  350g/12oz/3 cups plain
    (all-purpose) flour
For the filling
  500g/1¼lb/2¼ cups cottage cheese
  1 egg, lightly beaten
  grated rind of ½–1 lemon
  15–30ml/1–2 tbsp sugar
  15–30ml/1–2 tbsp sour cream
  30–45ml/2–3 tbsp sultanas
    (golden raisins) (optional)

1 To make the filling, put the cottage cheese in a sieve (strainer) and leave for about 20 minutes to drain.

2 Put the cheese in a bowl and mash lightly with a fork. Add the beaten egg, lemon rind, sugar, sour cream and sultanas to the cheese and mix together.

3 To make the blintzes, whisk the eggs in a bowl, then add the water, salt and oil. Whisk in the flour and continue beating to form a smooth batter.

VARIATION
To make Lithuanian blintzes, omit the sugar and season with plenty of salt and ground black pepper.

6 Place 15–30ml/1–2 tbsp of the filling on the cooked side of a pancake and spread it out, leaving a border at the top and bottom. Fold in the top and bottom over the filling, then fold over one side and roll the pancake up carefully to enclose the filling completely.

7 To finish the blintzes, heat the pan, add a little oil, then place the pancakes in the pan and fry until the undersides are golden brown. Turn the blintzes over and fry the second side. Serve hot.

Energy 613Kcal/2578kJ; Protein 31.9g; Carbohydrate 75.9g, of which sugars 9.3g; Fat 21.9g, of which saturates 6.4g; Cholesterol 260mg; Calcium 322mg; Fibre 2.7g; Sodium 467mg.

LEEK, SPINACH AND COURGETTE KUGEL

FRESH DILL, SPRING ONIONS AND GARLIC GIVE THEIR FLAVOURS TO THE GREENS OF LEEKS, SPINACH AND COURGETTES IN THIS CRISP SEPHARDIC KUGEL. BOTH PERSIAN AND TURKISH JEWS FAVOUR LEEKS AT PESACH, PROBABLY BECAUSE THE YOUNG, TENDER LEEKS ARE FRESH IN THE GARDEN.

SERVES SIX TO EIGHT

INGREDIENTS
    90ml/6 tbsp olive oil
    2 large leeks, thinly sliced
    500g/1¼lb spinach, washed
    1 courgette (zucchini),
      coarsely grated
    1 baking potato
    3 garlic cloves, chopped
    3 spring onions (scallions), chopped
      or thinly sliced
    1–2 pinches of ground turmeric
    about 45ml/3 tbsp medium
      matzo meal
    15–30ml/1–2 tbsp chopped fresh
      dill, plus extra to garnish
    3 eggs, lightly beaten
    salt and ground black pepper
    lemon wedges, to serve

1 Preheat the oven to 200°C/400°F/ Gas 6. Heat half the oil in a pan, add the leeks and fry until just tender. Remove from the heat.

2 Cook the spinach in only the water that clings to it after washing until just tender. Drain and, when cool enough to handle, roughly chop. Add the spinach and courgette to the leeks, and stir to combine.

3 Peel and coarsely grate the potato, then squeeze in your hands to remove its excess starch and liquid. Add to the leeks with the garlic, spring onions, turmeric and plenty of salt and ground black pepper.

4 Add enough matzo meal to the vegetable mixture to form a thick dough consistency. Stir the dill into the eggs, then add to the vegetable mixture.

5 Pour the remaining oil into a baking pan and heat in the oven for about 5 minutes. When the oil is hot, spoon the vegetable mixture evenly into the pan, letting the hot oil bubble up around the sides and on to the top.

6 Bake the kugel for about 15 minutes, then reduce the oven temperature to 180°C/350°F/Gas 4 and bake for a further 15–20 minutes, until the kugel is firm to the touch and the top is golden brown and puffy. Sprinkle with chopped dill to garnish and serve hot or warm with the lemon wedges for squeezing over.

Energy 172Kcal/714kJ; Protein 6.4g; Carbohydrate 11.2g, of which sugars 2.9g; Fat 11.5g, of which saturates 1.9g; Cholesterol 71mg; Calcium 138mg; Fibre 3.1g; Sodium 118mg.

MEGADARRA

RICE MIXED WITH LENTILS AND SPICED WITH CUMIN AND CINNAMON IS A CLASSIC MEAL FOR BOTH JEWS AND ARABS, ENJOYED FROM EGYPT AND LIBYA TO GALILEE AND GREECE. IT IS OFTEN EATEN AS A DAIRY MEAL WITH A BOWL OF VEGETABLES, ANOTHER OF COOLING YOGURT, AND A PLATE OF CRISP SALAD.

2 Heat half the oil in a pan, add the chopped onion and fry for 5 minutes, or until golden brown. Stir in half the cumin and half the cinnamon.

3 Add the fried onion to the pan of lentils with the cardamom pods, rice and stock. Mix well, then bring to the boil. Reduce the heat, cover and simmer until the rice is tender and all the liquid has been absorbed. If the mixture appears a little too dry, add some extra water or stock. Season with salt and pepper to taste.

4 Meanwhile, heat the remaining oil in a pan, add the sliced onions and fry for about 10 minutes, until dark brown, caramelized and crisp. Sprinkle in the remaining cumin and cinnamon just before the end of cooking.

SERVES SIX TO EIGHT

INGREDIENTS
  400g/14oz/1¾ cups large brown or
    green lentils
  45ml/3 tbsp olive oil
  3–4 onions, 1 chopped and
    2–3 thinly sliced
  5ml/1 tsp ground cumin
  2.5ml/½ tsp ground cinnamon
  3–5 cardamom pods
  300g/11oz/1½ cups long grain
    rice, rinsed
  about 250ml/8fl oz/1 cup
    vegetable stock
  salt and ground black pepper
  natural (plain) yogurt, to serve

1 Put the lentils in a pan with enough water to cover generously. Bring to the boil, then simmer for about 30 minutes, or until tender. Skim off any scum that forms on top.

5 To serve, pile the rice and lentil mixture on to a serving dish, then top with the browned, caramelized onions. Serve immediately, with a cooling dish of natural yogurt.

Energy 353kcal/1486kJ; Protein 15.4g; Carbohydrate 63g, of which sugars 4.7g; Fat 5.1g, of which saturates 0.7g; Cholesterol 0mg; Calcium 48mg; Fibre 3.3g; Sodium 20mg.

USZKA

USZKA, MEANING "LITTLE EARS" IN POLISH, ARE PLUMP MUSHROOM DUMPLINGS. FOR A MEAT MEAL, ENJOY THEM IN CLEAR SOUPS, CHICKEN OR BEEF CONSOMMÉ. FOR A DAIRY MEAL, SERVE THEM WITH A LITTLE MELTED BUTTER AND CHOPPED FRESH HERBS.

MAKES TWENTY

INGREDIENTS
    75g/3oz/⅔ cup plain
      (all-purpose) flour
    pinch of salt
    30ml/2 tbsp chopped fresh parsley
    1 egg yolk
    40ml/2½ tbsp cold water
    fresh parsley, to garnish
    clear soup or melted herb butter,
      to serve
For the filling
    25g/1oz/2 tbsp butter or oil
    ½ small onion, very finely chopped
    50g/2oz/1 cup mushrooms,
      finely chopped
    1 egg white
    15ml/1 tbsp dried white
      breadcrumbs
    salt and ground black pepper

1 Sift the flour and salt into a bowl. Add the chopped parsley, egg yolk and water and mix to a dough. Lightly knead the dough on a floured surface until smooth.

2 To make the filling, melt the butter or oil in a pan. Add the onion and mushrooms and fry over a low heat for 10 minutes, or until the onion is very soft. Leave to cool.

3 Lightly whisk the egg white in a clean bowl with a fork. Add 15ml/1 tbsp of the egg white to the mushrooms, together with the dried breadcrumbs, salt and pepper. Mix together well.

4 Roll out the dough very thinly on a floured surface. Cut into 5cm/2in squares using a sharp knife or a pastry wheel, then lightly brush with the remaining egg white.

5 Spoon 2.5ml/½ tsp of mushroom mixture on to each square. Fold the dough in half to make a triangle, then pinch the outer edges together to seal them.

6 Bring a pan of boiling salted water to a brisk boil. Gently drop in the dumplings a few at a time and simmer for 5 minutes. Drain and add to a clear soup or toss in melted herb butter and serve.

Energy 29Kcal/123kJ; Protein 0.8g; Carbohydrate 3.6g, of which sugars 0.1g; Fat 1.4g, of which saturates 0.7g; Cholesterol 13mg; Calcium 11mg; Fibre 0.2g; Sodium 18mg.

DRACHENA

THIS RUSSIAN, VEGETABLE-RICH CROSS BETWEEN AN OMELETTE AND A PANCAKE MAY ALSO BE MADE SWEET, WITH SUGAR, FRUIT, HONEY OR JAM.

SERVES TWO TO THREE

INGREDIENTS

15ml/1 tbsp olive oil
1 bunch spring onions (scallions), sliced
1 garlic clove, crushed
4 tomatoes, peeled, seeded and chopped
45ml/3 tbsp wholemeal (whole-wheat) rye flour
60ml/4 tbsp milk
150ml/¼ pint/⅔ cup sour cream
4 eggs, beaten
30ml/2 tbsp chopped fresh parsley
25g/1oz/2 tbsp butter, melted
green salad, to serve

1 Preheat the oven to 180°C/350°F/ Gas 4. Heat the oil in a frying pan and gently cook the spring onions for 3 minutes. Add the garlic and cook for 1 more minute, or until the spring onions are soft.

2 Sprinkle the spring onions and garlic into the base of a lightly greased shallow 20cm/8in ovenproof dish followed by the tomatoes.

COOK'S TIP
To test whether the drachena is cooked, push a sharp knife into the very middle of the dish. If liquid seeps out, continue to cook for another 5–10 minutes.

3 Mix the flour to a smooth paste in a bowl with the milk. Gradually add the sour cream, then mix with the eggs. Stir in the parsley and melted butter. Season with salt and pepper.

4 Pour the egg mixture over the vegetables. Bake in the oven for 40–45 minutes.

5 Run a knife around the edge of the dish to loosen, then cut into wedges and serve immediately with a fresh green salad.

Energy 384Kcal/1598kJ; Protein 13.4g; Carbohydrate 19.4g, of which sugars 7.9g; Fat 28.9g, of which saturates 13.5g; Cholesterol 302mg; Calcium 155mg; Fibre 2.4g; Sodium 187mg.

BRAISED BARLEY AND VEGETABLES

BARLEY IS ONE OF THE OLDEST OF CULTIVATED CEREALS. IT IS A NUTTY, EARTHY GRAIN, DELICIOUS IN SOUPS AND STUFFINGS, OR WITH VEGETABLES, AS IN THIS CASSEROLE.

SERVES FOUR

INGREDIENTS
225g/8oz/1 cup pearl or pot barley
30ml/2 tbsp sunflower oil
1 large onion, chopped
2 celery sticks, sliced
2 carrots, halved lengthways
  and sliced
225g/8oz swede (rutabaga) or turnip,
  cut into 2cm/¾in cubes
225g/8oz potatoes, cut into 2cm/
  ¾in cubes
475ml/16fl oz/2 cups vegetable stock
salt and ground black pepper
celery leaves, to garnish

1 Put the barley in a measuring jug (cup) and add water to reach the 600ml/1 pint/2½ cup mark. Leave to soak in a cool place for at least 4 hours or, preferably, overnight.

2 Heat the oil in a large pan and fry the onion for 5 minutes. Add the sliced celery and carrots and cook for 3–4 minutes, or until the onion is starting to brown.

VARIATION
If you prefer a slightly nuttier texture, replace the barley in this recipe with 225g/8oz/1 cup buckwheat. Simply add the buckwheat after step 2, dry frying with the onion, celery and carrots for a couple of minutes. Double the quantity of vegetable stock added in step 3, and reduce the overall simmering time in step 4 by approximately one third.

3 Add the barley and its soaking liquid to the pan, stirring to combine. Then add the swede or turnip, potato and vegetable stock to the barley. Season with salt and pepper. Bring the mixture to the boil, then reduce the heat and cover the pan.

4 Simmer for 40 minutes, or until most of the stock has been absorbed and the barley is tender. Stir occasionally towards the end of cooking to prevent the barley from sticking to the base of the pan. Serve, garnished with celery leaves.

Energy 333Kcal/1407kJ; Protein 6.6g; Carbohydrate 65g, of which sugars 8.3g; Fat 7g, of which saturates 0.8g; Cholesterol 0mg; Calcium 69mg; Fibre 3.1g; Sodium 33mg.

PENNE <u>WITH</u> ARTICHOKES <u>AND</u> FENNEL

IN ROMAN COOKING, ARTICHOKES WERE ORIGINALLY A JEWISH FOOD. IT IS SAID THAT THE BITTERNESS OF ARTICHOKES PARTNERS THE HISTORICAL BITTERNESS OF JEWISH LIFE, BUT PERHAPS THE JEWS SIMPLY DISCOVERED THE POTENTIAL OF THESE EDIBLE THISTLES FIRST, GATHERING THEM WHERE THEY GREW WILD. THIS DELICIOUS PASTA DISH CAN BE MADE WITH FLAT PASTA, SUCH AS PAPPARDELLE, OR WITH BUTTERFLY-SHAPED FARFALLE. FOR MEAT MEALS, OMIT THE CHEESE.

SERVES SIX

INGREDIENTS
    juice of ½ lemon
    2 globe artichokes
    30ml/2 tbsp olive oil
    1 small fennel bulb, thinly sliced, or
     a pinch of fennel seed (optional)
    1 onion, finely chopped
    4 garlic cloves, finely chopped
    1 handful fresh flat leaf parsley or
     sweet basil, coarsely chopped
    150ml/¼ pint/⅔ cup dry white wine
    400g/14oz can chopped
     plum tomatoes
    350g/12oz dried penne
    10ml/2 tsp capers (pickled),
     drained and chopped
    salt and ground black pepper
    freshly grated Parmesan cheese,
     to serve

1 Fill a large mixing bowl with cold water and add the juice of half a lemon. To prepare the artichokes, cut or break off the artichoke stalks, peel and add to the lemon water, then pull off and discard the outer leaves until only the pale, firm inner leaves at the base of the chokes remain.

2 Slice off the tops of these inner leaves and discard. Cut the base in half lengthways, then prise the hairs out of the centre with the tip of the knife and discard. Cut the artichokes lengthways into 5mm/¼in slices, adding them immediately to the stems in the bowl of acidulated water to prevent them from discolouring.

3 Bring a large pan of salted water to the boil. Drain the artichokes and add them immediately to the water. Boil for 3–5 minutes, then drain and set aside.

4 Heat the oil in a large pan and add the fennel, onion, garlic and parsley. Cook over a low to medium heat, stirring frequently, for 10 minutes, or until the fennel has softened and is lightly coloured.

5 Add the wine, with salt and pepper to taste. Bring to the boil, and cook until the liquid has nearly evaporated. Add the tomatoes, reduce the heat, and simmer for 10–15 minutes.

6 Stir in the artichokes, replace the lid and simmer for 10 minutes more. Meanwhile, add the pasta to a large pan of lightly salted boiling water and cook according to the instructions on the packet.

7 Drain the pasta, reserving a little of the cooking water. Add the capers to the sauce, stir well, then taste for seasoning.

8 Tip the pasta into a warmed, large serving bowl, pour the sauce over and toss thoroughly to mix, adding a few spoonfuls of the reserved cooking water to bring it all together. Serve immediately, sprinkled with the Parmesan, with an extra serving of cheese on the side.

Energy 271Kcal/1146kJ; Protein 8.2g; Carbohydrate 47.1g, of which sugars 5.5g; Fat 5.1g, of which saturates 0.7g; Cholesterol 0mg; Calcium 49mg; Fibre 3.7g; Sodium 24mg.

CUBAN-STYLE RICE

THE JEWISH COMMUNITY OF CUBA DATES TO THE SPANISH–AMERICAN WAR OF 1898. OVER THE YEARS, THE CONGREGATION FLOURISHED, ABSORBING FIRST SEPHARDIC JEWS, THEN PEOPLE FLEEING THE HOLOCAUST. WHEN CASTRO CAME TO POWER, ABOUT 10,000 OF CUBA'S 12,000 JEWS FLED — MOST TO MIAMI. GARLIC RICE, SERVED WITH EGGS AND FRIED BANANAS OR PLANTAINS, IS A SIMPLE, TYPICAL DISH. SIMMERED BLACK BEANS ARE DELICIOUS SERVED ALONGSIDE.

SERVES FOUR

INGREDIENTS

   3 garlic cloves
   120ml/4fl oz/½ cup olive oil
   300g/11oz/1½ cups long grain rice
   15g/½oz/1 tbsp butter
   4 small or 2 large bananas
   4 large (US extra large) eggs
   salt and paprika
For the tomato sauce
   30ml/2 tbsp olive oil
   1 onion, chopped
   2 garlic cloves, finely chopped
   800g/1lb 12oz canned tomatoes
   4 thyme or oregano sprigs
   ground black pepper

1 Make the tomato sauce. Heat the oil in a pan, add the onion and garlic and fry gently, stirring, until soft. Stir in the tomatoes and thyme or oregano sprigs and simmer gently for 5 minutes. Add seasoning to taste. Remove the herb sprigs and keep the sauce warm.

2 Put 850ml/1 pint 8fl oz/3½ cups water in a pan with two of the garlic cloves and 15ml/1 tbsp oil. Bring to the boil, add the rice and cook for 18 minutes until it is done, and the liquid has been absorbed.

3 Heat a pan with 30ml/2 tbsp oil and gently fry one chopped garlic clove. Tip in the rice, stir, season well, then turn off the heat and cover the pan.

4 Heat the butter in a frying pan with 15ml/1 tbsp oil. When the fat begins to sizzle, halve each banana lengthways and fry briefly on both sides. Remove from the pan with a slotted spoon, set aside on a dish and cover with foil to keep them warm.

5 Add 60ml/4 tbsp oil to a non-stick pan and fry the eggs over a medium-high heat, so that the edges turn golden and curl inwards. Season with salt and paprika. Serve the rice surrounded by tomato sauce and garnished with the bananas and fried eggs.

Energy 723Kcal/3011kJ; Protein 14.5g; Carbohydrate 87.6g, of which sugars 25.4g; Fat 35.4g, of which saturates 7.4g; Cholesterol 198mg; Calcium 67mg; Fibre 3.2g; Sodium 112mg.

MARCOUDE DES LEGUMES

A MARCOUDE IS A NORTH AFRICAN SEPHARDIC DISH, SOMEWHERE BETWEEN AN OMELETTE AND A POTATO CAKE. THIS DELIGHTFULLY SIMPLE, LIGHTLY SPICED VEGETABLE RECIPE IS ALSO VERY POPULAR WITH JEWISH COMMUNITIES IN SOUTH-EASTERN EUROPE, THE GULF AND INDIA, AND VARIATIONS EXIST USING CHICKPEAS, SPINACH OR EVEN SAUTÉED PEPPERS AND TOMATOES.

SERVES TWO

INGREDIENTS
  30ml/2 tbsp vegetable oil
  1 onion, finely chopped
  2.5ml/½ tsp ground cumin
  2.5ml/½ tsp turmeric
  1 garlic clove, crushed
  1 or 2 fresh green chillies,
    finely chopped
  a few coriander (cilantro) sprigs,
    chopped, plus extra, to garnish
  1 firm tomato, chopped
  1 small potato, cubed and boiled
  25g/1oz/¼ cup cooked peas
  25g/1oz/¼ cup cooked corn, or
    canned corn, drained
  2 eggs, beaten
  25g/1oz/¼ cup grated cheese
  salt and ground black pepper
  green salad, to serve

1 Heat the vegetable oil in a wok or large pan, and fry the next ten ingredients until they are well blended but the potato and tomato are still firm. Season to taste with salt and ground black pepper.

VARIATION
You can use any vegetable with the potatoes. Try adding thickly sliced button (white) mushrooms in step 1.

2 Increase the heat and pour in the beaten eggs. Reduce the heat, cover and cook until the bottom layer is brown. Turn the omelette over and sprinkle with the grated cheese. Place under a hot grill (broiler) and cook until the egg sets and the cheese has melted.

3 Garnish the omelette with sprigs of coriander and serve with salad for a light lunch. Or, if you prefer, serve it as a Parsee-style breakfast.

VARIATION
If you prefer, replace the cooked corn with natural corn (white or yellow maize), which is not so sweet. In some countries, chickpeas are used in place of the corn, which gives the omelette a slightly nuttier taste and texture. If using fresh chickpeas, be sure to soak them beforehand.

Energy 102Kcal/422kJ; Protein 4.1g; Carbohydrate 5.6g, of which sugars 1.8g; Fat 7.1g, of which saturates 1.9g; Cholesterol 67mg; Calcium 46mg; Fibre 0.7g; Sodium 68mg.

CRISP-CRUMBED POTATO CAKES

POTATOES WERE INTRODUCED TO POLAND DURING THE REIGN OF JAN SOBIESKI, IN THE 17TH CENTURY. IT IS UNLIKELY THAT A SINGLE DAY HAS GONE BY SINCE IN WHICH POLISH JEWS HAVE NOT EATEN POTATOES. IN FACT, A YIDDISH FOLK SONG FROM EASTERN EUROPE HAS THE CHORUS "MONDAY POTATO, TUESDAY POTATO, WEDNESDAY, THURSDAY AND FRIDAY POTATO. SHABBAT, FOR A CHANGE, A LITTLE MORE POTATO ... POTATO, POTATO, POTATO..."

SERVES FOUR

INGREDIENTS

    450g/1lb potatoes, peeled and cut
      into large chunks
    25g/1oz/2 tbsp butter
    1 small onion, chopped
    45ml/3 tbsp sour cream
    2 egg yolks
    25g/1oz/¼ cup plain
      (all-purpose) flour
    1 egg, beaten
    25g/1oz/½ cup fresh white breadcrumbs

1 Cook the potatoes in a pan of boiling salted water for 20 minutes, or until tender. Drain well and mash. Allow to cool for a few minutes. Meanwhile, melt the butter in a small pan and fry the onion for 10 minutes, until soft.

2 Stir the butter and onion into the mashed potato and then mix in the sour cream and egg yolks. Preheat the oven to 180°C/350°F/Gas 4.

3 Sift the flour over the potato mixture, then mix it in well. Season with plenty of salt and pepper. Shape into rounds, then flatten slightly to make about 16 "doughnuts" 6cm/2½in across.

4 Place on a lightly oiled baking sheet and brush with beaten egg. Sprinkle the tops with breadcrumbs. Bake for 30 minutes, or until browned.

Energy 267Kcal/1116kJ; Protein 7.8g; Carbohydrate 29.5g, of which sugars 3g; Fat 13.9g, of which saturates 6.5g; Cholesterol 236mg; Calcium 66mg; Fibre 1.7g; Sodium 128mg.

PAMPUSHKI

JUST THE SOUND OF THE WORD "PAMPUSHKI" BRINGS A SMILE TO THE FACE OF THOSE LUCKY ENOUGH TO HAVE TASTED THEM IN THEIR CHILDHOOD. WHEN THESE CRUNCHY RUSSIAN POTATO DUMPLINGS ARE SPLIT OPEN, A TASTY CHEESE AND CHIVE FILLING IS REVEALED.

SERVES FOUR

INGREDIENTS
    675g/1½lb potatoes, peeled
    225g/8oz/2⅔ cups cooked
      mashed potato
    2.5ml/½ tsp salt
    75g/3oz/scant ½ cup curd
      (farmer's) cheese
    30ml/2 tbsp chopped fresh chives
    ground black pepper
    oil, for deep-frying

COOK'S TIP
Pampushki are traditionally cooked in stock or water. If you prefer to poach them, add 15ml/1 tbsp plain (all-purpose) flour and 1 beaten egg to the mixture and poach for 20 minutes.

1 Coarsely grate the raw potatoes and squeeze out as much water as possible. Put them in a bowl with the mashed potato, salt and black pepper. Mix together. In another bowl, mix the curd cheese and chives together.

2 Using a spoon and your fingers, scoop up a portion of the potato mixture, slightly smaller than an egg, and then flatten to a circle.

3 Put 5ml/1 tsp of the cheese filling into the middle, then fold over the edges and pinch to seal. Repeat with remaining potato and cheese mixtures, to make about 12 dumplings.

4 Heat the oil to 170°C/340°F. Deep-fry the dumplings for 10 minutes, or until deep brown and crisp. Drain on kitchen paper and serve hot.

Energy 202Kcal/852kJ; Protein 6.7g; Carbohydrate 36.6g, of which sugars 3.4g; Fat 4.4g, of which saturates 2.7g; Cholesterol 11mg; Calcium 39mg; Fibre 2.3g; Sodium 125mg.

SALADS

The Ashkenazic lands, which shivered in the cold for so much of the
year, did not give rise to a wealth of fresh salads. However, once
Ashkenazim migrated to lands where fresh vegetables were
plentiful, salads became an intrinsic part of every meal, even
if it was only a plate of raw spring onions, a few green
peppers or a cucumber cut into chunks. The Sephardic kitchen,
on the other hand, has a long tradition of a variety
of savoury vegetable salads, often cooked with
fragrant spices and golden, tasty olive oil.

ARTICHOKES <u>WITH</u> GARLIC, LEMON <u>AND</u> OLIVE OIL

ARTICHOKE DISHES IN ITALY, SUCH AS THIS ONE FROM TUSCANY, CAN BE TRACED BACK TO JEWISH CULINARY TRADITION. JEWS HAVE BEEN ENJOYING ARTICHOKES SINCE THE EARLIEST DAYS, AS THEY GREW WILD IN THE GALILEE. HERE THEIR FLAVOUR IS ENHANCED WITH GARLIC AND LEMON.

SERVES FOUR

INGREDIENTS
    4 globe artichokes
    juice of 1–2 lemons, plus extra to
      acidulate water
    60ml/4 tbsp olive oil
    1 onion, chopped
    5–8 garlic cloves, roughly chopped
      or thinly sliced
    30ml/2 tbsp chopped fresh parsley
    120ml/4fl oz/½ cup dry white wine
    120ml/4fl oz/½ cup vegetable
      stock or water
    salt and ground black pepper

COOK'S TIP
Placing trimmed artichokes in a bowl of acidulated water prevents them discolouring.

1 Prepare the artichokes. Pull back and snap off the tough leaves. Peel the tender part of the stems and cut into bitesize pieces, then put in a bowl of acidulated water. Cut the artichokes into quarters and remove the hairs inside. Add the hearts to the bowl.

2 Heat the oil in a pan, add the onion and garlic and fry for 5 minutes until softened. Stir in the parsley and cook for a few seconds. Add the wine, stock and drained artichokes. Season with half the lemon juice, salt and pepper.

3 Bring the mixture to the boil, then lower the heat, cover and simmer for 10–15 minutes until the artichokes are tender. Transfer the artichokes to a serving dish using a slotted spoon.

4 Bring the cooking liquid to the boil and boil until reduced to about half its volume. Pour the mixture over the artichokes and drizzle over the remaining lemon juice. Taste for seasoning and cool before serving.

Energy 129Kcal/534kJ; Protein 0.6g; Carbohydrate 2.1g, of which sugars 1.7g; Fat 11.2g, of which saturates 1.6g; Cholesterol 0mg; Calcium 37mg; Fibre 1g; Sodium 47mg.

BEETROOT <u>WITH</u> FRESH MINT

BEETROOT FIGURES PROMINENTLY IN JEWISH COOKING IN COMMUNITIES THROUGHOUT THE WORLD, BOTH ASHKENAZIC AND SEPHARDIC. THIS DISH IS PERFECT AS PART OF A SALAD SELECTION — PARTICULARLY IF THERE ARE CRACKERS AND GOAT'S CHEESE ON THE SIDE.

SERVES FOUR

INGREDIENTS

   4–6 cooked beetroot (beets)
   5–10ml/1–2 tsp sugar
   15–30ml/1–2 tbsp balsamic vinegar
   juice of ½ lemon
   30ml/2 tbsp extra virgin olive oil
   1 bunch fresh mint, leaves stripped
    and thinly sliced
   salt

VARIATIONS
• To make Tunisian beetroot, add harissa to taste and substitute fresh coriander (cilantro) for the mint.
• To make Ashkenazic beetroot, add a chopped onion and some dill.

1 Slice the beetroot or cut into even-size dice with a sharp knife. Put the beetroot in a bowl. Add the sugar, balsamic vinegar, lemon juice, olive oil and a pinch of salt and toss together to combine.

2 Add half the thinly sliced fresh mint to the salad and toss lightly until well combined. Place the salad in the refrigerator and chill for about 1 hour. Serve garnished with the remaining thinly sliced mint leaves.

Energy 122Kcal/511kJ; Protein 1.2g; Carbohydrate 17.8g, of which sugars 17.5g; Fat 5.6g, of which saturates 0.8g; Cholesterol 0mg; Calcium 21mg; Fibre 1g; Sodium 56mg.

UKRAINIAN CUCUMBER SALAD

SALTING THE CUCUMBER WITH THE ONIONS DRAWS OUT SOME OF THE MOISTURE, MAKES THE CUCUMBERS AND ONIONS SILKIER AND HELPS TO COMBINE THE FLAVOURS. SERVE AS PART OF A DAIRY LUNCH OR SELECTION OF SALADS, WITH HERRING, CHOPPED EGG AND ONION, AND BOILED POTATOES.

SERVES SIX TO EIGHT

INGREDIENTS
2 cucumbers, decorated with a
cannelle knife (zester) and
thinly sliced
5–10ml/1–2 tsp salt
1 onion, thickly sliced
45ml/3 tbsp chopped fresh dill
15ml/1 tbsp white wine vinegar
150ml/¼ pint/⅔ cup sour cream
ground black pepper
1 dill sprig, to garnish

VARIATION
You can use crème fraîche or natural (plain) yogurt instead of the sour cream if you prefer a less rich version of this dish.

1 Rinse the cucumber slices under cold running water, drain and place in a bowl.

2 Add the sliced onion to the bowl with the salt and chopped dill, and combine all ingredients well.

3 In another bowl, stir the vinegar into the sour cream and season the mixture with pepper.

4 Pour the sour cream over the cucumber and chill for 1 hour before turning into a serving dish. Garnish with a sprig of dill and serve.

Energy 45Kcal/185kJ; Protein 0.9g; Carbohydrate 1.9g, of which sugars 1.7g; Fat 3.8g, of which saturates 2.4g; Cholesterol 11mg; Calcium 26mg; Fibre 0.3g; Sodium 255mg.

BEETROOT AND POTATO SALAD

EASTERN EUROPEAN DISHES ABOUND WITH BEETROOT, POTATO AND DILL PICKLE. IN THIS RECIPE, ALL THE INGREDIENTS ARE COMBINED IN A QUINTESSENTIAL ASHKENAZIC WINTER SALAD. ENJOY FOR A SHABBAT LUNCH, PREFERABLY WITH SMOKED FISH.

SERVES FOUR

INGREDIENTS
    2 fresh beetroots (beets)
    1 or 2 medium-size potatoes,
      peeled
    ¼ onion, finely chopped
    red wine vinegar, to taste
    salt, to taste
    2.5ml/½ tsp sugar, or to taste
    2.5–5ml/½–1 tsp wholegrain
      mustard, or to taste
    1 medium dill pickle, diced
    15ml/1 tbsp chopped fresh mint
    30–45ml/2–3 tbsp sour cream to
      serve, if you like

COOK'S TIP
To save yourself time and energy, buy
ready cooked and peeled beetroot. They
are available in most supermarkets.

1 Boil the beetroot in a large pan, in
plenty of water, for 40 minutes or until
tender. Remove with a slotted spoon
and set aside to cool for a few minutes.

2 Meanwhile, boil the potatoes in a
separate pan for 20 minutes, until
just tender.

3 When the beetroot have cooled, rinse
and pull the skins off, chop into rough
pieces and place in a bowl. Drain the
potatoes, dice, and add to the bowl with
the onion. Add a shake of vinegar, salt
and sugar to taste, the wholegrain
mustard and pickle. Stir to combine.
Chill until ready to serve, then sprinkle
with the fresh dill.

Energy 59Kcal/248kJ; Protein 1.6g; Carbohydrate 10g, of which sugars 3.9g; Fat 1.7g, of which saturates 1g; Cholesterol 5mg; Calcium 21mg; Fibre 1.1g; Sodium 35mg.

SALAD <u>WITH</u> WATERMELON <u>AND</u> FETA CHEESE

THE COMBINATION OF SWEET AND JUICY WATERMELON WITH SALTY FETA CHEESE IS AN ISRAELI ORIGINAL, INSPIRED BY THE TURKISH AND RUSSIAN TRADITION OF EATING WATERMELON WITH SALTY WHITE CHEESE IN THE HOT SUMMER MONTHS. THE SPICES, SEEDS AND SALAD LEAVES PROVIDE A MODERN TWIST AND AN EXCITING VARIETY OF TASTE AND TEXTURE.

SERVES FOUR

INGREDIENTS
　　30–45ml/2–3 tbsp extra virgin
　　　olive oil
　　juice of ½ lemon
　　5ml/1 tsp vinegar of choice,
　　　or to taste
　　sprinkling of chopped fresh thyme
　　pinch of ground cumin
　　4 large slices of watermelon, chilled
　　1 frisée lettuce, core removed
　　130g/4½oz feta cheese,
　　　preferably sheep's milk feta,
　　　cut into bitesize pieces
　　handful of lightly toasted
　　　pumpkin seeds
　　handful of sunflower seeds
　　10–15 black olives

1 Pour the extra virgin olive oil, lemon juice and vinegar into a bowl or jug (pitcher). Add the chopped fresh thyme and ground cumin, and whisk all the ingredients together until they are well combined. Cover and set aside while you prepare the salad.

2 Cut the rind off the watermelon and remove as many seeds as possible. Cut the flesh into triangular shaped chunks.

3 Put the lettuce leaves in a bowl, pour over the dressing and toss together. Arrange the leaves on a serving dish or individual plates and add the watermelon, feta cheese, pumpkin and sunflower seeds and black olives. Serve the salad immediately.

COOK'S TIP
The best choice of olives for this recipe are plump black Mediterranean olives such as kalamata, other shiny, brined varieties or dry-cured black olives such as the Italian ones.

Energy 249Kcal/1035kJ; Protein 7.3g; Carbohydrate 13.2g, of which sugars 12.5g; Fat 18.9g, of which saturates 6.3g; Cholesterol 23mg; Calcium 161mg; Fibre 1.4g; Sodium 755mg.

GALILEE SALAD OF WILD GREENS, RAW VEGETABLES AND OLIVES

WILD GREENS WERE ONCE GATHERED IN THE GALILEE BY NECESSITY DURING TIMES OF AUSTERITY, YET THEY HAVE NOT ALWAYS PROVED TOO POPULAR IN THE MODERN AGE! NOW THEY HAVE COME INTO FASHION AND ARE CONSIDERED VERY CHIC, AS WELL AS DELICIOUS AND HEALTHY. SERVE THIS SALAD WITH TANGY YOGURT CHEESE.

SERVES FOUR

INGREDIENTS

1 large bunch wild rocket (arugula), about 115g/4oz
1 packet mixed salad leaves or wild salad greens
1/4 white cabbage, thinly sliced
1 cucumber, sliced
1 small red onion, chopped
2–3 garlic cloves, chopped
3–5 tomatoes, cut into wedges
1 green (bell) pepper, seeded and sliced
2–3 mint sprigs, sliced or torn
15–30ml/1–2 tbsp chopped fresh parsley and/or tarragon or dill
pinch of dried oregano or thyme
45ml/3 tbsp extra virgin olive oil
juice of 1/2 lemon
15ml/1 tbsp red wine vinegar
15–20 black olives
salt and ground black pepper

1 In a large salad bowl, put the rocket, mixed salad leaves, white cabbage, cucumber, onion and garlic. Toss gently with your fingers to combine the leaves and vegetables.

COOK'S TIP
Try to find mixed salad leaves that include varieties such as lamb's lettuce, purslane and mizuna.

2 Arrange the tomatoes, pepper, mint, fresh and dried herbs, salt and pepper on top of the greens and vegetables. Drizzle over the oil, lemon juice and vinegar, stud with the olives and serve.

VARIATION
Instead of serving with yogurt cheese, mash a little feta into natural (plain) yogurt and serve this instead.

Energy 126Kcal/523kJ; Protein 3.4g; Carbohydrate 11g, of which sugars 10.4g; Fat 7.9g, of which saturates 1.2g; Cholesterol 0mg; Calcium 108mg; Fibre 4.3g; Sodium 338mg.

ISRAELI CHOPPED VEGETABLE SALAD

ONE THING YOU CAN COUNT ON IN ISRAEL FOR BREAKFAST, LUNCH OR DINNER, IS A SALAD OF FINELY CHOPPED VEGETABLES. YOU CAN VARY THE HERBS, ADD A PINCH OF SPICE SUCH AS SUMAC OR CUMIN, AND OMIT THE CHILLI. LEMON OR LIME JUICE CAN BE ADDED INSTEAD OF VINEGAR, AND A HANDFUL OF OLIVES ALWAYS MAKES A GREAT ADDITION.

SERVES FOUR TO SIX

INGREDIENTS

1 each red, green and yellow (bell)
  pepper, seeded
1 carrot
1 cucumber
6 tomatoes
3 garlic cloves, finely chopped
3 spring onions (scallions),
  thinly sliced
30ml/2 tbsp chopped fresh coriander
  (cilantro) leaves
30ml/2 tbsp each chopped fresh dill,
  parsley and mint leaves
½–1 hot fresh chilli,
  chopped (optional)
45–60ml/3–4 tbsp extra virgin
  olive oil
juice of 1–1½ lemons
salt and ground black pepper

1 Using a sharp knife, finely dice the red, green and yellow peppers, carrot, cucumber and tomatoes and place them in a large mixing bowl.

2 Add the garlic, spring onions, coriander, dill, parsley, mint and chilli, if using, to the chopped vegetables and toss together to combine.

3 Pour the olive oil and lemon juice over the vegetables, season with salt and pepper to taste and toss together. Chill before serving.

COOK'S TIP
This classic chopped salad is the most commonly eaten dish of the land. It is particularly refreshing eaten for breakfast.

Energy 122Kcal/507kJ; Protein 2.1g; Carbohydrate 10.7g, of which sugars 10.4g; Fat 8.1g, of which saturates 1.3g; Cholesterol 0mg; Calcium 24mg; Fibre 3.1g; Sodium 16mg.

MOROCCAN VEGETABLE SALAD

ISRAELI JEWS OF MOROCCAN DESCENT ARE PARTICULARLY GOOD AT COMBINING THE DISTINCTIVE FLAVOURS OF THEIR LANDS WITH THE SALADS SO BELOVED IN ISRAEL.

SERVES FOUR

INGREDIENTS

 1 large cucumber, thinly sliced
 2 cold, boiled potatoes, sliced
 1 each red, yellow and green (bell)
   pepper, seeded and thinly sliced
 300g/11oz/2²⁄₃ cups pitted olives
 ½–1 hot fresh chilli, chopped or
   2–3 shakes of cayenne pepper
 3–5 garlic cloves, chopped
 3 spring onions (scallions), sliced
   or 1 red onion, finely chopped
 60–90ml/4–6 tbsp extra virgin olive oil
 15–30ml/1–2 tbsp white wine vinegar
 juice of ½ lemon, or to taste
 15–30ml/1–2 tbsp chopped fresh
   mint leaves
 15–30ml/1–2 tbsp chopped fresh
   coriander (cilantro) leaves
 salt (optional)

1 Arrange the cucumber, potato and pepper slices and the pitted olives on a serving plate or in a dish.

2 Sprinkle the chopped fresh chilli or cayenne pepper over the salad and season with salt, if you like. (Olives tend to be very salty so you may wish not to add any extra salt.)

3 Sprinkle the garlic, onions, olive oil, vinegar and lemon juice over the salad. Chill before serving, sprinkled with the chopped mint leaves and coriander leaves.

VARIATION
Serve the salad garnished with sliced or diced cooked beetroot (beet).

Energy 304Kcal/1257kJ; Protein 2.9g; Carbohydrate 17.1g, of which sugars 5.5g; Fat 25.2g, of which saturates 3.8g; Cholesterol 0mg; Calcium 66mg; Fibre 4.2g; Sodium 1700mg.

TURNIP SALAD IN SOUR CREAM

THIS ASHKENAZIC SOUR CREAM-DRESSED SALAD WAS ONCE EATEN BY ALL OF EASTERN EUROPE'S JEWS.
SOMETIMES IT WAS MADE WITH LARGE BLACK RADISHES INSTEAD OF TURNIPS.

SERVES FOUR

INGREDIENTS

2–4 young, tender turnips, peeled
¼–½ onion, finely chopped
2–3 drops white wine vinegar,
   or to taste
60–90ml/4–6 tbsp sour cream
salt and ground black pepper
chopped fresh parsley or paprika,
   to garnish

VARIATION
Crème fraîche can be used instead of the sour cream, if you like.

1 Thinly slice or coarsely grate the turnips. Alternatively, thinly slice half the turnips and grate the remaining half. Put in a bowl.

2 Add the onion, vinegar, salt and pepper, toss together then stir in the sour cream. Serve chilled, garnished with a sprinkling of parsley or paprika.

Energy 48Kcal/198kJ; Protein 1.1g; Carbohydrate 4.1g, of which sugars 3.7g; Fat 3.2g, of which saturates 1.9g; Cholesterol 9mg; Calcium 42mg; Fibre 1.4g; Sodium 14mg.

CURRIED RED CABBAGE SLAW

CABBAGE HAS LONG BEEN A FAVOURITE VEGETABLE AMONG JEWS AND, AT ONE TIME BEFORE POTATOES WERE INTRODUCED TO EUROPE, WAS ALMOST THE ONLY VEGETABLE OF THE ASHKENAZIM. SPICY SLAWS WITH LIGHT, TANGY DRESSINGS ARE FAVOURED THROUGHOUT ISRAEL. MIDDLE EASTERN, YEMENITE AND INDIAN JEWISH COMMUNITIES OFTEN CHOOSE TO SPICE VEGETABLE SALADS USING CURRY POWDER.

SERVES FOUR TO SIX

INGREDIENTS

½ red cabbage, thinly sliced
1 red (bell) pepper, chopped
  or very thinly sliced
½ red onion, chopped
60ml/4 tbsp red, white wine
  vinegar or cider vinegar
60ml/4 tbsp sugar, or to taste
60ml/2fl oz/¼ cup Greek
  (US strained plain) yogurt or
  natural (plain) yogurt
120ml/4fl oz/½ cup mayonnaise,
  preferably home-made
1.5ml/¼ tsp curry powder
2–3 handfuls of raisins
salt and ground black pepper

1 Put the cabbage, peppers and red onion in a bowl and toss to combine. In a small pan, heat the vinegar and sugar until the sugar has dissolved, then pour over the vegetables. Leave to cool slightly.

2 Combine the yogurt and mayonnaise, then stir into the cabbage mixture. Season to taste with curry powder, salt and ground black pepper, then mix in the raisins.

3 Chill the salad for at least 2 hours before serving. Just before serving, drain off any excess liquid and briefly stir the slaw again.

VARIATIONS
• To make a pareve slaw, suitable for serving with a meat meal, omit the yogurt and mayonnaise and add a little more vinegar.
• If you prefer, ready-made low-fat mayonnaise can be used.

Energy 268Kcal/1117kJ; Protein 2.8g; Carbohydrate 27.1g, of which sugars 26.6g; Fat 17.4g, of which saturates 3.4g; Cholesterol 15mg; Calcium 66mg; Fibre 1.6g; Sodium 119mg.

MOROCCAN CARROT SALAD

THE PRINCIPAL INGREDIENT OF A MOROCCAN CARROT SALAD CAN BE EITHER RAW OR COOKED, GRATED, SLICED OR CHOPPED. THIS VERSION FLAVOURS FINELY-SLICED COOKED CARROTS WITH A CUMIN AND CORIANDER VINAIGRETTE, AND WOULD BE SERVED BY BOTH Sephardim AND Ashkenazim.

SERVES FOUR TO SIX

INGREDIENTS

  3–4 carrots, thinly sliced
  pinch of sugar
  3–4 garlic cloves, chopped
  1.5ml/¼ tsp ground cumin,
    or to taste
  juice of ½ lemon
  30–45ml/2–3 tbsp extra virgin
    olive oil
  15–30ml/1–2 tbsp red wine vinegar
    or fruit vinegar, such as raspberry
  30ml/2 tbsp chopped fresh coriander
    (cilantro) leaves or a mixture of
    coriander and parsley
  salt and ground black pepper

1 Cook the carrots by either steaming or boiling in lightly salted water until they are just tender but not soft. Drain, leave for a few moments to dry, then put in a bowl.

2 Add the sugar, garlic, cumin, lemon juice, olive oil and vinegar to the carrots and toss together. Add the herbs and season. Serve immediately or chill before serving.

Energy 69Kcal/283kJ; Protein 0.5g; Carbohydrate 4.1g, of which sugars 3.8g; Fat 5.7g, of which saturates 0.8g; Cholesterol 0mg; Calcium 23mg; Fibre 1.5g; Sodium 14mg.

TUNISIAN POTATO AND OLIVE SALAD

CREAMY-FLESHED POTATOES, ENLIVENED WITH CUMIN AND CORIANDER THEN DRESSED IN OLIVE OIL AND VINEGAR, MAKE AN UNBEATABLE POTATO SALAD. TUNISIAN JEWS OFTEN SERVE SPICY, STRONG, VERY APPEALING FLAVOURS SUCH AS THIS.

SERVES FOUR

INGREDIENTS

   8 large new potatoes
   large pinch of salt
   large pinch of sugar
   3 garlic cloves, chopped
   15ml/1 tbsp vinegar of your choice,
     such as a fruit variety
   large pinch of ground cumin or whole
     cumin seeds
   pinch of cayenne pepper or hot
     paprika, to taste
   30–45ml/2–3 tbsp extra virgin
     olive oil
   30–45ml/2–3 tbsp chopped fresh
     coriander (cilantro) leaves
   10–15 dry-fleshed black
     Mediterranean olives

1 Chop the new potatoes into chunks. Put them in a pan, pour in water to cover and add the salt and sugar. Bring to the boil, then reduce the heat and boil gently for about 10 minutes, or until the potatoes are just tender. Drain well and leave in a colander to cool.

2 When cool enough to handle, slice the potatoes and put in a bowl.

3 Sprinkle the garlic, vinegar, cumin and cayenne or paprika over the salad. Drizzle with olive oil and sprinkle over coriander and olives. Chill before serving.

Energy 375Kcal/1581kJ; Protein 7.1g; Carbohydrate 64.5g, of which sugars 5.3g; Fat 11.6g, of which saturates 1.9g; Cholesterol 0mg; Calcium 43mg; Fibre 4.7g; Sodium 467mg.

ENSALADILLA

Known as Russian salad elsewhere, this "salad of little things" became extremely popular during the Spanish Civil War in the 1930s, when ingredients were scarce and it was easier to make a salad of whatever vegetables you had to hand, or could purchase cheaply. A favourite salad, this dish is welcome on any buffet table.

SERVES FOUR

INGREDIENTS

  8 new potatoes, scrubbed
    and quartered
  1 large carrot, diced
  115g/4oz French (green) beans,
    cut into 2cm/¾in lengths
  75g/3oz/¾ cup peas
  ½ Spanish (Bermuda) onion, chopped
  4 cornichons or small
    gherkins, sliced
  1 small red (bell) pepper, seeded
    and diced
  50g/2oz/½ cup pitted black olives
  15ml/1 tbsp drained pickled capers
  15ml/1 tbsp freshly squeezed
    lemon juice
  30ml/2 tbsp chopped fresh fennel
    or parsley, to garnish
  salt and ground black pepper
For the aioli
  2 garlic cloves, finely chopped
  2.5ml/½ tsp salt
  150ml/¼ pint/⅔ cup mayonnaise

1 Make the aioli. Crush the garlic with the salt in a mortar and whisk or stir into the mayonnaise.

2 Cook the potatoes and diced carrot in a pan of boiling lightly salted water for 5–8 minutes until almost tender.

3 Add the beans and peas to the pan and cook for 2 minutes, or until all the vegetables are tender. Drain well.

4 Tip the vegetables into a large bowl. Add the onion, cornichons or gherkins, red pepper, olives and capers. Stir in the aioli and season to taste with pepper and lemon juice.

5 Toss the vegetables and aioli together until well combined, check the seasoning and chill for about an hour. Serve the salad garnished with the sprigs of fresh fennel or parsley.

VARIATIONS
• This salad is delicious using any combination of chopped, cooked vegetables. Use the freshest available and adjust the cooking time accordingly.
• You may vary the quantity of garlic in the aioli according to taste.
• The addition of a little lime juice gives the aioli an extra citrus tang. Add with the mayonnaise.

Energy 461Kcal/1916kJ; Protein 6.5g; Carbohydrate 41.4g, of which sugars 9.1g; Fat 31g, of which saturates 4.9g; Cholesterol 28mg; Calcium 49mg; Fibre 5.2g; Sodium 479mg.

BALKAN BEANS <u>WITH</u> GREEN PEPPERS <u>IN</u> SPICY DRESSING

THIS DISH OF TENDER BEANS DRESSED WITH SWEET PEPPERS, HOT CHILLI AND LEMONY VINAIGRETTE IS A CULMINATION OF THE INFLUENCES BROUGHT TO ISRAEL BY JEWS OF TURKEY, BULGARIA AND GREECE. THIS SALAD IS BEST PREPARED AHEAD OF TIME AND ENJOYED AS PART OF THE SHABBAT FESTIVE MEAL, OR AS A FEATURE OF A WARM-WEATHER AL FRESCO FEAST.

SERVES FOUR

INGREDIENTS

750g/1²⁄₃lb tomatoes, diced
1 onion, finely chopped
½–1 mild fresh chilli, finely chopped
1 green (bell) pepper, seeded and chopped
pinch of sugar
4 garlic cloves, chopped
400g/14oz can butter (lima) beans, drained
45–60ml/3–4 tbsp olive oil
grated rind and juice of 1 lemon
15ml/1 tbsp cider vinegar or wine vinegar
salt and ground black pepper
chopped fresh parsley, to garnish

1 Put the tomatoes, onion, chilli, green pepper, sugar, garlic, butter beans, salt and plenty of ground black pepper in a large bowl and toss together until well combined.

2 Add the olive oil, grated lemon rind, lemon juice and vinegar to the salad and toss lightly to combine. Chill before serving, garnished with chopped parsley.

Energy 200Kcal/841kJ; Protein 7.8g; Carbohydrate 22.4g, of which sugars 10g; Fat 9.5g, of which saturates 1.5g; Cholesterol 0mg; Calcium 35mg; Fibre 7.3g; Sodium 438mg.

HALLOUMI AND GRAPE SALAD

IN CYPRUS, FIRM, SALTY HALLOUMI CHEESE IS OFTEN SERVED FRIED FOR BREAKFAST OR SUPPER. IT IS ALSO DELICIOUS WITH SWEET, JUICY FRUIT SUCH AS WATERMELON OR, AS HERE, WITH GRAPES. THIS UPDATED ISRAELI VERSION IS FABULOUS ON A SUMMER'S DAY.

SERVES FOUR

INGREDIENTS
For the dressing
  60ml/4 tbsp olive oil
  15ml/1 tbsp lemon juice
  2.5ml/½ tsp caster
   (superfine) sugar
  salt and ground black pepper
  15ml/1 tbsp chopped fresh thyme
   or dill
For the salad
  150g/5oz mixed green salad leaves
  75g/3oz seedless green grapes
  75g/3oz seedless black grapes
  250g/9oz halloumi cheese
  45ml/3 tbsp olive oil
  fresh young thyme leaves or dill,
   to garnish

1 To make the dressing, combine the olive oil, lemon juice and sugar in a bowl and beat together with a whisk. Season. Stir in the thyme or dill and set aside.

2 Toss together the salad leaves and the green and black grapes, then transfer to a large serving plate.

3 Thinly slice the cheese. Heat the oil in a large frying pan. Add the cheese and fry briefly until turning golden on the underside. Turn the cheese and cook the other side.

4 Arrange the cheese over the salad. Pour over the dressing and garnish with thyme or dill.

Energy 362Kcal/1497kJ; Protein 12.1g; Carbohydrate 6.4g, of which sugars 6.4g; Fat 32.2g, of which saturates 11.4g; Cholesterol 36mg; Calcium 242mg; Fibre 0.6g; Sodium 249mg.

MEDITERRANEAN POTATO <u>AND</u> FETA SALAD

LESS A POTATO SALAD THAN AN INSPIRED MEDLEY OF FLAVOURS AND TEXTURES. THE TENDER NEW POTATOES MUST SHARE THE LIMELIGHT WITH SALTY FETA, FRESH HERBS, TANGY OLIVES AND CAPERS, IN A DRESSING ENRICHED WITH YOGURT AND FLAVOURED WITH ANCHOVIES.

SERVES FOUR

INGREDIENTS
    500g/1¼lb small new potatoes
    5 spring onions (scallions), green and
      white parts, finely chopped
    15ml/1 tbsp pickled capers, rinsed
    8–10 black olives
    115g/4oz feta cheese, cut into
      small cubes
    45ml/3 tbsp finely chopped fresh
      flat leaf parsley
    30ml/2 tbsp finely chopped
      fresh mint
    salt and ground black pepper
For the vinaigrette
    90–120ml/6–8 tbsp extra virgin
      olive oil
    juice of 1 lemon, or to taste
    2 salted or preserved anchovies,
      rinsed and finely chopped
    45ml/3 tbsp Greek (strained
      plain) yogurt
    45ml/3 tbsp finely chopped fresh dill
    5ml/1 tsp French mustard

1 Bring a pan of lightly salted water to the boil and cook the potatoes in their skins for 25–30 minutes, until they are tender. Drain them thoroughly and set aside to cool a little while you prepare the vinaigrette.

2 Place the oil in a bowl with the lemon juice and anchovies. Whisk thoroughly until the dressing emulsifies and thickens. Whisk in the yogurt, dill and mustard, with salt and pepper to taste.

3 When the potatoes are cool enough to handle, peel them and place in a large bowl. If they are very small, keep them whole; otherwise cut them into large cubes.

4 Add the spring onions, capers, olives, feta and fresh herbs to the potatoes and toss gently to mix.

5 Dress the salad in the vinaigrette while the potatoes are still warm, tossing lightly to combine. Serve on its own, or as a light second course.

COOK'S TIP
The salad tastes even better if it has had time to sit for an hour or so at room temperature before being served. This will allow the flavours of the vinaigrette to seep into the potatoes and cheese. Similarly, any leftover salad will be delicious the next day. Remove from the refrigerator about an hour before it is due to be served, drain off any juices that have accumulated overnight and refresh the salad with a few drops of fresh lemon juice and a drizzle of olive oil to wake up the flavours again.

Energy 343Kcal/1425kJ; Protein 8.4g; Carbohydrate 21.4g, of which sugars 2.9g; Fat 25.5g, of which saturates 7.3g; Cholesterol 21mg; Calcium 165mg; Fibre 2.3g; Sodium 780mg.

BULGARIAN CUCUMBER AND TOMATO SALAD

RICH, THICK YOGURT GIVES BODY TO THE DRESSING FOR THIS REFRESHING VEGETABLE SALAD.
THIS IS A FAVOURITE IN ISRAEL.

SERVES FOUR

INGREDIENTS
    450g/1lb firm ripe tomatoes
    ½ cucumber
    1 onion
    ½ green (bell) pepper, diced
    2–3 garlic cloves, chopped
    salt, to taste
    ½ small hot chilli, seeded
        and chopped
    2.5cm/1in lengths of chives,
        to garnish
    crusty bread, to serve
For the dressing
    60ml/4 tbsp olive or vegetable oil
    90ml/6 tbsp Greek (US strained
        plain) yogurt
    30ml/2 tbsp chopped fresh parsley
        or chives
    5ml/1 tsp vinegar
    salt and ground black pepper

1 Skin the tomatoes by first cutting a cross in the base of each tomato. Place in a bowl and cover with boiling water for 1–2 minutes, or until the skin starts to split, then drain and plunge into cold water and peel thoroughly. Cut the tomatoes into quarters, seed and chop.

2 Chop the cucumber and onion into pieces the same size as the tomatoes, add the pepper, garlic and salt and put them all in a bowl.

3 Mix all the dressing ingredients together and season to taste. Pour over the salad and toss all the ingredients together. Sprinkle over black pepper, the chopped chilli and chives to garnish and serve with crusty bread.

COOK'S TIP
To add mild spice to the dressing, stir in half the chopped chilli with the dressing ingredients, then toss with the salad as normal. Use the rest as garnish.

Energy 146Kcal/605kJ; Protein 2.5g; Carbohydrate 8.3g, of which sugars 7.8g; Fat 11.7g, of which saturates 1.5g; Cholesterol 0mg; Calcium 60mg; Fibre 1.9g; Sodium 31mg.

TOMATO SALAD WITH BLACK OLIVES AND SARDINES

TANGY, SUMMER-FRESH TOMATO SALAD IS DELICIOUS WITH THE PUNGENT, SAVOURY TASTE OF SATISFYING SARDINES AND BLACK OLIVES.

SERVES SIX

INGREDIENTS
8 large firm ripe tomatoes
1 large red onion
60ml/4 tbsp wine vinegar
90ml/6 tbsp extra virgin olive oil
18–24 small sardines, cooked
75g/3oz/¾ cup black oil-covered or
 other Mediterranean olives,
 drained well
salt and ground black pepper
45ml/3 tbsp chopped fresh parsley,
 to garnish

1 Cut the tomatoes into 5mm/¼in slices. Slice the red onion thinly and separate into rings.

2 Arrange the tomatoes on a serving plate, overlapping the slices, then top with the red onion.

3 Whisk together the wine vinegar, olive oil and seasoning and spoon over the tomatoes.

4 Top with the sardines and black olives and sprinkle the chopped parsley over the sardines before serving.

VARIATION
If you like, replace the sardines with 6 shelled and halved hard-boiled eggs.

Energy 248Kcal/1032kJ; Protein 14.9g; Carbohydrate 4.9g, of which sugars 4.7g; Fat 18.9g, of which saturates 3.7g; Cholesterol 0mg; Calcium 76mg; Fibre 1.8g; Sodium 374mg.

FENNEL, ORANGE <u>AND</u> ROCKET SALAD

ALTHOUGH ORIGINALLY FROM CORFU, THIS LIGHT AND REFRESHING SALAD IS A FAVOURITE OF ITALIAN JEWS. ORANGE BLENDS PERFECTLY WITH THE DELICATE FLAVOUR OF FENNEL AND THE PEPPERY ROCKET.

SERVES FOUR

INGREDIENTS

   2 oranges, such as Jaffa, Shamouti or
     blood oranges
   1 fennel bulb
   115g/4oz rocket (arugula) leaves
   50g/2oz/⅓ cup black olives
For the dressing
   30ml/2 tbsp extra virgin olive oil
   15ml/1 tbsp balsamic vinegar
   1 small garlic clove, crushed
   salt and ground black pepper

1 With a vegetable peeler, cut strips of rind from the oranges, leaving the pith behind, and cut into thin strips. Cook in boiling water for a few minutes. Drain and set aside. Peel the oranges, removing all the white pith. Slice them into thin rounds and discard any seeds.

2 Trim the fennel bulb, then cut in half lengthways and slice across the bulb as thinly as possible, preferably in a food processor fitted with a slicing disc or using a mandolin.

3 Combine the slices of orange and fennel in a serving bowl and toss with the rocket leaves.

4 To make the dressing, mix together the oil, vinegar, garlic and seasoning. Pour over the salad, toss together well and leave to stand for a few minutes. Sprinkle with the black olives and strips of orange. Serve.

VARIATION
Substitute mineolas for the oranges.

Energy 123Kcal/511kJ; Protein 2.1g; Carbohydrate 6.7g, of which sugars 6.6g; Fat 10g, of which saturates 1.4g; Cholesterol 0mg; Calcium 98mg; Fibre 3.2g; Sodium 330mg.

AUBERGINE, LEMON AND CAPER SALAD

LEMON SUBTLY UNDERSCORES THE FLAVOUR OF MELTINGLY SOFT AUBERGINE IN THIS CLASSIC SICILIAN DISH. IT IS DELICIOUS SERVED AS AN ACCOMPANIMENT TO A PLATTER OF COLD MEATS, WITH PASTA OR SIMPLY ON ITS OWN WITH SOME GOOD CRUSTY BREAD.

SERVES FOUR

INGREDIENTS
  1 large aubergine (eggplant),
    weighing about 675g/1½lb
  60ml/4 tbsp olive oil
  grated rind and juice of 1 lemon
  30ml/2 tbsp pickled capers, rinsed
  12 pitted green olives
  30ml/2 tbsp chopped fresh flat
    leaf parsley
  salt and ground black pepper

COOK'S TIP
This salad will taste even better when it is prepared the day before it is to be served. It will keep well, covered in the refrigerator, for up to 4 days. Return to room temperature before serving.

1 Cut the aubergine into 2.5cm/1in cubes. Heat the olive oil in a large, heavy frying pan. Add the aubergine cubes and cook over a medium heat for about 10 minutes, tossing frequently, until golden and softened. You may need to do this in two batches. Remove with a slotted spoon, drain on kitchen paper and sprinkle with a little salt.

2 Place the aubergine cubes in a large serving bowl, toss with the lemon rind and juice, capers, olives and chopped parsley and season well with salt and pepper. Serve at room temperature.

VARIATION
Add toasted pine nuts and shavings of Parmesan cheese for extra bulk.

Energy 137Kcal/567kJ; Protein 1.6g; Carbohydrate 3.7g, of which sugars 3.4g; Fat 13.1g, of which saturates 2g; Cholesterol 0mg; Calcium 25mg; Fibre 3.7g; Sodium 285mg.

BEETROOT SALAD <u>WITH</u> ORANGES

THE COMBINATION OF SWEET BEETROOT, ZESTY ORANGE AND WARM CINNAMON IS REFRESHINGLY UNUSUAL, BUT WORKS PERFECTLY. IT IS A COLOURFUL AND INVIGORATING WAY TO BEGIN A COUSCOUS FEAST OR A HOLIDAY CELEBRATION.

SERVES FOUR TO SIX

INGREDIENTS

675g/1½lb beetroot (beets), steamed
  or boiled, then peeled
1 orange, peeled and sliced
30ml/2 tbsp orange flower water
15ml/1 tbsp sugar
5ml/1 tsp ground cinnamon
salt and ground black pepper

COOK'S TIP
This salad can be made with shop-bought, vacuum-packed cooked beetroot if you are short of time.

1 Quarter the cooked beetroot, then slice the quarters. Arrange the beetroot on a plate with the orange slices or toss them together in a bowl.

2 Gently heat the orange flower water with the sugar, stir in the cinnamon and season to taste. Pour the sweet mixture over the beetroot and orange salad and chill for at least 1 hour before serving.

COOK'S TIP
To cook raw beetroot always leave the skin on and trim off only the tops of the leaf stalks. Cook in boiling water or steam over rapidly boiling water for 1–2 hours, depending on size. Small beetroot are tender in about 1 hour, medium roots take 1–1½ hours, and larger roots can take up to 2 hours.

Energy 58Kcal/247kJ; Protein 2.2g; Carbohydrate 12.9g, of which sugars 12.2g; Fat 0.1g, of which saturates 0g; Cholesterol 0mg; Calcium 33mg; Fibre 2.5g; Sodium 75mg.

CABBAGE SALAD WITH LEMON VINAIGRETTE AND BLACK OLIVES

THIS CRISP, REFRESHING SALAD IS ENJOYED THROUGHOUT THE MIDDLE EAST. THIS PARTICULAR VERSION IS FAVOURED BY THE JEWS OF KURDISTAN.

SERVES FOUR

INGREDIENTS
 1 white cabbage
 12 black olives
For the vinaigrette
 75–90ml/5–6 tbsp extra virgin
  olive oil
 30ml/2 tbsp lemon juice
 1 garlic clove, crushed
 30ml/2 tbsp finely chopped fresh flat
  leaf parsley
 salt

1 Cut the cabbage in quarters, discard the outer leaves and trim off any thick, hard stems as well as the hard base.

VARIATION
Use half red cabbage and half white cabbage. The olives may be omitted.

2 Lay each quarter on its side and cut into long, very thin slices until you reach the central core, which should be discarded. Place the shredded cabbage in a bowl and stir in the black olives.

COOK'S TIP
The key to a perfect cabbage salad is to shred the cabbage as finely as possible.

3 Make the vinaigrette by whisking the olive oil, lemon juice, garlic, parsley and salt together in a bowl until all the ingredients are thoroughly combined. Pour the dressing over the salad, and toss the cabbage and olives together until they are evenly coated in the vinaigrette. Serve at room temperature as a refreshing side to a main meal.

Energy 160Kcal/658kJ; Protein 1.1g; Carbohydrate 3.1g, of which sugars 3.1g; Fat 15.9g, of which saturates 2.3g; Cholesterol 0mg; Calcium 42mg; Fibre 1.9g; Sodium 426mg.

SIDE DISHES

Jews throughout the world ate the vegetables that grew around them. The vegetables
of the Old Country were often simple: cabbage, beetroot and onion. In the
spring, however, the new young vegetables would be cooked and served with
sour cream and fresh herbs. Leafy greens such as spinach, chard and leeks
were put into pancakes, and whatever vegetables were available would
often be shredded and baked into a kugel. The Sephardic kitchen, on the
other hand, was abundant with a lavish array of vegetables: okra,
aubergine, courgettes, pumpkin, artichokes, peppers and tomatoes,
as well as fragrant olive oil.

SUMMER SQUASH AND BABY NEW POTATOES IN WARM DILL SOUR CREAM

IN ASHKENAZIC EASTERN EUROPE, BABY NEW POTATOES AND SQUASH WERE DRESSED IN RICH BUTTER AND SOUR CREAM, WITH MASSES OF FRAGRANT DILL.

SERVES FOUR

INGREDIENTS

400g/14oz mixed squash, such as yellow and green courgettes (zucchini), and green patty pans
400g/14oz tiny, baby new potatoes
pinch of sugar
40–75g/1½–3oz/3–5 tbsp butter
2 bunches spring onions (scallions), thinly sliced
1 large bunch fresh dill, finely chopped
300ml/½ pint/1¼ cups sour cream or Greek (US strained plain) yogurt
salt and ground black pepper

COOK'S TIP
Choose small specimens of squash with bright skins that are free of blemishes and bruises.

1 Cut the squash into pieces about the same size as the potatoes. Put the potatoes in a pan and add water to cover, with the sugar and salt. Bring to the boil, then simmer for about 10 minutes, until almost tender. Add the squash and continue to cook until the vegetables are just tender, then drain.

2 Melt the butter in a large pan; fry the spring onions until just wilted, then gently stir in the dill and vegetables.

3 Remove the pan from the heat and stir in the sour cream or yogurt. Return to the heat and heat gently until warm. Season with salt and pepper and serve.

Energy 317Kcal/1317kJ; Protein 5.8g; Carbohydrate 21g, of which sugars 6.1g; Fat 23.9g, of which saturates 14.8g; Cholesterol 66mg; Calcium 105mg; Fibre 2g; Sodium 104mg.

BAKED WINTER SQUASH IN TOMATO SAUCE

THIS DISH IS VENETIAN-JEWISH IN ORIGIN, FOR VENICE'S JEWISH COMMUNITY HAS CONTRIBUTED AN ENDURING APPRECIATION OF PUMPKIN IN ITALIAN CUISINE.

SERVES FOUR TO SIX

INGREDIENTS

   45–75ml/3–5 tbsp olive oil
   1kg/2½lb pumpkin or orange winter
     squash, peeled and sliced
   1 onion, chopped
   3–5 garlic cloves, chopped
   2 × 400g/14oz cans chopped tomatoes
   pinch of sugar
   2–3 sprigs of fresh rosemary, stems
     removed and leaves chopped
   salt and ground black pepper

VARIATION
Acorn, butternut or Hubbard squash can all be used in this recipe.

1 Preheat the oven to 160°C/325°F/ Gas 3. Heat 45ml/3 tbsp of the oil in a pan and fry the pumpkin slices in batches until golden brown, removing them from the pan as they are cooked.

2 In the same pan, add the onion, with more oil if necessary, and fry for about 5 minutes until softened.

3 Add the garlic to the pan and cook for 1 minute, then add the tomatoes and sugar and cook over a medium-high heat until the mixture is of a sauce consistency. Stir in the rosemary and season with salt and pepper to taste.

4 Layer the pumpkin slices and tomato sauce in an ovenproof dish, ending with some sauce. Bake for 35 minutes, or until the top is lightly glazed and beginning to brown, and the pumpkin is tender. Serve immediately.

Energy 97Kcal/407kJ; Protein 2.2g; Carbohydrate 8.6g, of which sugars 7.5g; Fat 6.3g, of which saturates 1.1g; Cholesterol 0mg; Calcium 60mg; Fibre 3.1g; Sodium 12mg.

CAULIFLOWER WITH GARLIC CRUMBS

SUCH IS THE SIMPLICITY OF THIS ASHKENAZIC SPECIALITY, IT CAN BE SERVED WITH JUST ABOUT ANY MAIN COURSE DISH. OMIT THE PARMESAN CHEESE FOR A PAREVE DISH.

2 Heat 60–75ml/4–5 tbsp of the olive or vegetable oil in a pan, add the breadcrumbs and cook over a medium heat, tossing and turning, until browned and crisp. Add the garlic, turn once or twice, then remove from the pan and set aside.

3 Heat the remaining oil in the pan, then add the cauliflower, mashing and breaking it up a little as it lightly browns in the oil. (Do not overcook but just cook lightly in the oil.)

4 Add the garlic breadcrumbs and cumin to the pan and cook, stirring, sprinkling with a little Parmesan every so often as you do, until well combined and some of the cauliflower is still holding its shape. Season with salt and pepper and serve hot or warm.

SERVES FOUR TO SIX

INGREDIENTS
  1 large cauliflower, cut into
    bitesize florets
  pinch of sugar
  90–120ml/6–8 tbsp olive or
    vegetable oil
  130g/4½oz/2¼ cups dry white or
    wholemeal (whole-wheat)
    breadcrumbs
  3–5 garlic cloves, thinly sliced
    or chopped
  5ml/1 tsp cumin seeds
  60–90ml/4–6 tbsp freshly grated
    Parmesan cheese
  salt and ground black pepper

1 Bring a pan of water to the boil and add the pinch of sugar, and one of salt. Drop in the cauliflower florets and steam until just tender. Drain and leave to cool.

COOK'S TIPS
• Serve, as they do in Italy, with cooked pasta such as spaghetti or rigatoni.

Energy 244Kcal/1016kJ; Protein 8.9g; Carbohydrate 18.8g, of which sugars 2.2g; Fat 15.3g, of which saturates 3.8g; Cholesterol 10mg; Calcium 162mg; Fibre 1.7g; Sodium 280mg.

DEEP-FRIED ARTICHOKES

CARCIOFI ALLA GIUDIA IS AN ANCIENT DISH NAMED AFTER THE ROMAN GHETTO, GIUDIA, AND A GREAT SPECIALITY OF THE JEWS OF ROME. THE ARTICHOKES ARE PRESSED TO OPEN THEM, THEN PLUNGED INTO HOT OIL WHERE THEIR LEAVES BROWN AND TWIST INTO CRISPY FLOWERS.

SERVES FOUR

INGREDIENTS

2–3 lemons, halved
4–8 small globe artichokes
olive or vegetable oil, for deep-frying
salt

1 Fill a large bowl with cold water and stir in the juice of one or two of the lemons. Trim and discard the stems of the artichokes, then trim off their tough end and remove all the tough outer leaves until you reach the pale pointed centre.

2 Carefully open the leaves of one of the artichokes by pressing it against the table or poking them open. Trim the tops if they are sharp. (Take care not to knock off the remaining leaves.)

3 If there is any hairiness inside the artichoke, remove it with a melon baller or small pointed spoon. Put the artichoke in the acidulated water and prepare the remaining artichokes in the same way.

4 Put the artichokes in a large pan and pour over water to cover. Bring to the boil and cook over a medium-high heat for 15 minutes, or until the artichokes are partly cooked. If the artichokes are small, cook them for only 10 minutes.

5 Remove the artichokes from the pan, place upside down on a baking sheet and leave to cool. When they are cool enough to handle, press them open gently but firmly, being careful not to break them apart.

6 Fill a wok or pan with oil to a depth of 5–7.5cm/2–3in and heat until hot.

7 Add one or two artichokes to the oil, with the leaves uppermost, and press down with a slotted spoon to open up the leaves, being careful not to splash the hot oil. Fry for 5–8 minutes, turning, until golden and crisp. Remove from the pan, and drain on kitchen paper. Serve immediately or place on a baking sheet and keep warm in the oven.

Energy 132Kcal/546kJ; Protein 0.6g; Carbohydrate 1.1g, of which sugars 1.1g; Fat 14g, of which saturates 1.6g; Cholesterol 0mg; Calcium 51mg; Fibre 1.4g; Sodium 75mg.

ARTICHOKES WITH NEW POTATOES

THIS IS SUCH A SPRING-LIKE DISH, POPULAR AMONG THE JEWS WHO COME FROM GREECE, TURKEY AND OTHER AREAS OF THE BALKANS. IT IS JUST AS DELICIOUS AT COOL ROOM TEMPERATURE AS IT IS WARM, SO IT'S PERFECT TO MAKE A DAY AHEAD!

SERVES FOUR

INGREDIENTS

   4 globe artichokes
   juice of 1½ lemons
   150ml/¼ pint/⅔ cup extra virgin
     olive oil
   1 large onion, thinly sliced
   3 carrots, sliced into long batons
   300ml/½ pint/1¼ cups hot water
   400g/14oz small new potatoes,
     scrubbed or peeled
   4–5 spring onions (scallions),
     chopped
   60–75ml/4–5 tbsp chopped
     fresh dill
   salt and ground black pepper

COOK'S TIP

Although easy to neglect, it is important to soak the artichoke hearts as instructed after preparing them for cooking. The acidulated water will preserve firmness, flavour and colour while the other ingredients are being sautéed.

1 Prepare the artichokes by discarding the outer leaves and stalk, slicing in half lengthways and scooping out the hairy part at the centre. Drop the hearts into a bowl of water acidulated with about one-third of the lemon juice.

2 Heat the olive oil in a wide, heavy pan and sauté the onion slices gently until they become translucent. Add the carrot batons and sauté them for about 3 minutes. Add the remaining lemon juice and the hot water and bring to the boil.

3 Drain the artichokes and add them to the pan with the potatoes, spring onions and seasoning. The vegetables should be almost covered with the sauce, so add a little more hot water if needed. Cover and cook gently for 40–45 minutes. Sprinkle the dill over the top and cook for 2–3 minutes more.

VARIATION

For a slightly different flavour, add some chopped garlic to the pan when frying the onions during step 2, and omit the dill entirely.

Energy 342Kcal/1420kJ; Protein 3.2g; Carbohydrate 26.1g, of which sugars 9.8g; Fat 25.7g, of which saturates 3.8g; Cholesterol 0mg; Calcium 60mg; Fibre 4g; Sodium 60mg.

BRAISED ARTICHOKES <u>WITH</u> FRESH PEAS

THE COMBINATION OF FRESH PEAS WITH ARTICHOKES MAKES ANOTHER LIGHT, SPRINGTIME ARTICHOKE DISH BELOVED OF JEWS AND NON-JEWS ALIKE THROUGHOUT GREECE.

SERVES FOUR

INGREDIENTS
4 globe artichokes
juice of 1½ lemons
150ml/¼ pint/⅔ cup extra virgin
   olive oil
1 onion, thinly sliced
4–5 spring onions (scallions),
   roughly chopped
2 carrots, sliced in rounds
1.2kg/2½lb fresh peas in pods,
   shelled (this will give you about
   500–675g/1¼–1½lb peas)
450ml/¾ pint/scant 2 cups hot water
60ml/4 tbsp finely chopped fresh dill
salt and ground black pepper

1 First, prepare the artichokes as instructed opposite, by discarding the outer leaves and stalk, slicing in half lengthways and scooping out the heart. Drop the chokes into a bowl of water acidulated with about one-third of the lemon juice.

2 Heat the olive oil in a wide, shallow pan and add the onion and spring onions, and then a minute later, add the carrots. Sauté the mixture, stirring constantly, for a few seconds, then add the peas and stir for 1–2 minutes to coat them in the oil.

3 Pour in the remaining lemon juice. Let it bubble and evaporate for a few seconds, then add the hot water and bring to the boil. Drain the artichokes and add them to the pan, with salt and pepper to taste. Cover and cook gently for 40–45 minutes, stirring occasionally. Add the dill and cook for 5 minutes more, or until the vegetables are beautifully tender. Serve hot or at room temperature.

Energy 355Kcal/1465kJ; Protein 9.4g; Carbohydrate 19.7g, of which sugars 7.9g; Fat 27.1g, of which saturates 4g; Cholesterol 0mg; Calcium 63mg; Fibre 7.8g; Sodium 44mg.

WILTED SPINACH AND DILL PILAFF

FRESH, SPRINGTIME SPINACH AND FRAGRANT, HERBY DILL MAKE THIS A REFRESHINGLY LIGHT PILAFF.
ENJOY WITH EITHER A MEAT OR DAIRY MEAL, WITH EXTRA LEMON WEDGES IF IT'S A MEAT MEAL, OR
WITH A BOWL OF THICK, STRAINED YOGURT FOR A DAIRY MEAL.

SERVES FOUR TO SIX

INGREDIENTS
  675g/1½lb fresh spinach, trimmed of
    any hard stalks
  105ml/7 tbsp extra virgin olive oil
  1 large onion, chopped
  juice of ½ lemon
  150ml/¼ pint/⅔ cup water
  115g/4oz/generous ½ cup long
    grain rice
  45ml/3 tbsp chopped fresh dill, plus
    extra sprigs to garnish
  salt and ground black pepper

1 Thoroughly wash the spinach in
several changes of cold water until
clean, then drain it in a colander. Shake
off the excess water and shred the
spinach coarsely.

2 Heat the olive oil in a large pan and
sauté the onion until it is translucent.
Add the spinach and stir for a few
minutes to coat it with the oil.

COOK'S TIP
It is important that you use the
measured quantity of water for cooking
the rice if the dish is to be successful.

3 As soon as the spinach looks wilted,
add the lemon juice and the measured
water and bring to the boil. Add the rice
and dill, saving a few sprigs for the
garnish, then cover and cook gently for
about 10 minutes or until the rice is
cooked to your taste. If it looks too dry,
add a little hot water.

4 Spoon into a serving dish and
sprinkle the little sprigs of dill over the
top. Serve hot or at room temperature.

VARIATION
This dish can be made using several
varieties of spinach or with other
seasonal vegetables such as spring
greens, green or, for a colourful
alternative, ruby chard.

Energy 224Kcal/928kJ; Protein 5g; Carbohydrate 19.7g, of which sugars 3.6g; Fat 13.9g, of which saturates 2g; Cholesterol 0mg; Calcium 203mg; Fibre 2.8g; Sodium 159mg.

YEMENITE SPICY CABBAGE <u>WITH</u> TOMATOES, TURMERIC <u>AND</u> PEPPERS

THIS DISH OF HUMBLE CABBAGE IS PERFUMED WITH AN ARRAY OF AROMATIC SPICES AND THEN BRAISED. THE LEAVES BECOME SILKY AND THE SPICES BECOME MORE COMPLEX IN THEIR BALANCE. THE DISH IS DELICIOUS EATEN EITHER WARM OR COOL.

SERVES FOUR TO SIX

INGREDIENTS

1 green or white cabbage,
 thinly sliced
30–60ml/2–4 tbsp olive oil
2 onions, chopped
5–8 garlic cloves, chopped
½ green (bell) pepper, chopped
2.5ml/½ tsp curry powder
2.5ml/½ tsp ground cumin
2.5ml/½ tsp ground turmeric,
 or more to taste
seeds from 3–5 cardamom pods
1 mild fresh chilli, chopped, or
 2–3 pinches dried chilli flakes
400g/14oz can tomatoes
pinch of sugar
juice of ½–1 lemon
45–60ml/3–4 tbsp chopped fresh
 coriander (cilantro) leaves

1 Cook the cabbage in a pan of boiling water for 5–8 minutes, or until tender. Drain well and set aside.

2 Meanwhile, heat the oil in a pan, add the onions and fry until softened, then add half the garlic and the green pepper and cook for 3–4 minutes, or until the pepper softens but the garlic does not turn brown.

VARIATION
Pan-fry meatballs until browned all over, then add them to the cabbage with the tomatoes and cook as above.

3 Sprinkle all the spices into the pan, stir and cook for 1–2 minutes to bring out their flavour. Add the reserved cabbage, the tomatoes and sugar, cover the pan and cook over a low heat for 15–30 minutes, or until the sauce is thick and flavoursome. If necessary, remove the lid and cook off any excess liquid.

4 Add the lemon juice and remaining garlic to the cabbage and cook for about 10 minutes. Stir in the chopped coriander and serve immediately. Alternatively, leave the cabbage to cool slightly before serving the dish warm, or allow to cool completely then chill and serve as a cold salad.

Energy 81Kcal/338kJ; Protein 1.9g; Carbohydrate 9.6g, of which sugars 8.3g; Fat 4.1g, of which saturates 0.6g; Cholesterol 0mg; Calcium 43mg; Fibre 2.7g; Sodium 12mg.

STUFFED BANANAS

STUFFED VEGETABLES ARE A SPECIALITY OF THE SEPHARDIC KITCHEN, FROM THE MEDITERRANEAN EASTWARDS AND EVEN WEST INTO THE NEW WORLD OF LATIN AMERICA. THIS DISH, FROM THE BENE ISRAEL OF INDIA, CAN BE ENJOYED FOR ROSH HASHANAH.

SERVES FOUR

INGREDIENTS

4 green bananas or plantains
30ml/2 tbsp ground coriander
15ml/1 tbsp ground cumin
5ml/1 tsp chilli powder
2.5ml/½ tsp salt
1.5ml/¼ tsp ground turmeric
5ml/1 tsp granulated sugar
15ml/1 tbsp gram flour
45ml/3 tbsp chopped fresh coriander
  (cilantro), plus extra sprigs
  to garnish
90ml/6 tbsp vegetable oil
1.5ml/¼ tsp cumin seeds
1.5ml/¼ tsp black mustard seeds

1 Trim the bananas or plantains and cut each crossways into three equal pieces, leaving the skin on. Make a lengthways slit along each piece of banana, without cutting all the way through the flesh.

2 On a plate, mix together the ground coriander, cumin, chilli powder, salt, turmeric, sugar, gram flour, chopped fresh coriander and 15ml/1 tbsp of the oil. Use your fingers to combine well.

3 Carefully stuff each piece of banana with the spice mixture, taking care not to break the bananas in half.

4 Heat the remaining oil in a wok or large pan, and fry the cumin and mustard seeds for 2 minutes or until they begin to splutter. Add the bananas and toss gently in the oil. Cover and simmer over a low heat for 15 minutes, stirring from time to time, until the bananas are soft but not mushy.

5 Garnish with the fresh coriander sprigs, and serve with warm chapatis, if you like.

COOK'S TIP
Baby courgettes (zucchini) make a delicious alternative to bananas.

Energy 256Kcal/1067kJ; Protein 1.6g; Carbohydrate 26.1g, of which sugars 21g; Fat 16.8g, of which saturates 2g; Cholesterol 0mg; Calcium 11mg; Fibre 1.2g; Sodium 1mg.

SPICED BROAD BEANS AND CARROTS

A SELECTION OF SPICY VEGETABLES FORM A TYPICAL, REFRESHING START OR SIDE DISH FOR MANY MIDDLE EASTERN MEALS. ALTHOUGH CALLED SALADS, THEY ARE OFTEN SIMPLY COOKED VEGETABLES, SPLASHED WITH A SPRIGHTLY SAUCE AND EATEN WARM OR COOL. BROAD BEANS ARE ESPECIALLY ASSOCIATED WITH SEPHARDIM BECAUSE IT IS SAID THAT THESE TENDER YOUNG BEANS ARE WHAT THE HEBREWS ATE IN THEIR EGYPTIAN BONDAGE, AND CARROTS ARE A GREAT FAVOURITE OF EASTERN JEWS. THESE SALADS ARE DELICIOUS SERVED WITH THICK YOGURT FOR A DAIRY MEAL, FLAVOURED WITH A LITTLE GARLIC, CHOPPED FRESH DILL AND SALT.

SERVES FOUR

INGREDIENTS
For the broad bean salad
  2kg/4½lb broad (fava) beans in
    the pod
  60–75ml/4–5 tbsp olive oil
  juice of ½ lemon
  2 garlic cloves, chopped
  5ml/1 tsp ground cumin
  10ml/2 tsp paprika
  small bunch of fresh coriander
    (cilantro), finely chopped
  1 preserved lemon, chopped
  handful of black olives, to garnish
  salt and ground black pepper
For the carrot salad
  450g/1lb carrots, cut into batons
  30–45ml/2–3 tbsp olive oil
  juice of 1 lemon
  2–3 garlic cloves, crushed
  10ml/2 tsp sugar
  5–10ml/1–2 tsp cumin seeds, roasted
  5ml/1 tsp ground cinnamon
  5ml/1 tsp paprika
  small bunch of fresh coriander
    (cilantro), finely chopped
  small bunch of mint, finely chopped
  salt and ground black pepper

1 First, pod the beans. Boil them for about 2 minutes, then drain and refresh under cold water. Slip off the thick outer skin to reveal the bright green flesh.

2 Put the beans in a heavy pan and add the olive oil, lemon juice, garlic, cumin and paprika. Cook the beans gently over a low heat for about 10 minutes, then season to taste with salt and pepper and leave to cool in the pan.

3 Tip the beans into a serving bowl, scraping all the juices from the pan. Toss in the fresh coriander and preserved lemon and garnish with the black olives.

4 To make the carrot salad, steam the carrots over boiling water for about 15 minutes, or until tender. While they are still warm, toss the carrots in a serving bowl with the olive oil, lemon juice, garlic and sugar. Season to taste, then add the cumin seeds, cinnamon and paprika. Finally, toss in the fresh coriander and mint, and serve warm or at room temperature.

COOK'S TIP
Stir the cumin seeds in a heavy pan over a low heat until they change colour slightly and emit a warm, nutty aroma.

Energy 344Kcal/1437kJ; Protein 15.9g; Carbohydrate 31.2g, of which sugars 11.1g; Fat 18.1g, of which saturates 2.7g; Cholesterol 0mg; Calcium 158mg; Fibre 15.5g; Sodium 47mg.

CHEESE DUMPLINGS

HOW MANY KINDS OF DUMPLINGS ARE THERE IN EASTERN EUROPE? THESE ARE ENRICHED WITH TANGY WHITE CHEESE AND HAIL FROM UKRAINE. SERVE AS A SIDE DISH TO A DAIRY SUPPER, PERHAPS ALONGSIDE A BIG VEGETABLE CASSEROLE.

SERVES FOUR

INGREDIENTS
   115g/4oz/1 cup self-raising
      (self-rising) flour
   25g/1oz/2 tbsp butter
   25g/1oz/⅓ cup crumbled feta,
      dry brinza (sheep's milk cheese),
      or a mixture of Caerphilly
      and Parmesan
   30ml/2 tbsp chopped
      fresh herbs
   60ml/4 tbsp cold water
   salt and ground black pepper
   parsley sprigs, to garnish
For the topping
   40g/1½oz/3 tbsp butter
   50g/2oz/1 cup slightly dry
      white breadcrumbs

1 Sift the flour into a bowl. Rub in the butter until the mixture resembles fine breadcrumbs.

2 Stir the cheese and herbs into the mixture. Season with salt and pepper. Add the cold water and mix to a firm dough. Rinse your hands to prevent the mixture sticking to them, then shape the dough into 12 balls.

3 Bring a pan of salted water to the boil. Add the dumplings, cover and gently simmer for 20 minutes, until light and fluffy. Remove with a slotted spoon.

4 For the topping, melt the butter in a frying pan. Add the breadcrumbs and cook for 2–3 minutes, until the crumbs are golden and crisp. Sprinkle over the dumplings and garnish with the parsley.

Energy 276Kcal/1155kJ; Protein 5.1g; Carbohydrate 31.6g, of which sugars 0.9g; Fat 15.2g, of which saturates 9.4g; Cholesterol 39mg; Calcium 142mg; Fibre 1.2g; Sodium 387mg.

LECSÓ

THIS IS A THICK, FLAVOURFUL MIXTURE OF LONG-SIMMERED PEPPERS AND TOMATOES. A FAVOURITE DISH OF HUNGARY, IT MAY BE EATEN ON ITS OWN OR ADDED TO ALMOST ANYTHING ELSE: CHICKEN, STEWS, EGGS, OR SIMPLY PREPARED AS A SALAD.

SERVES SIX TO EIGHT

INGREDIENTS
5 green (bell) peppers
30ml/2 tbsp vegetable oil
1 onion, sliced
8 garlic cloves, sliced
450g/1lb plum tomatoes, peeled and chopped
15ml/1 tbsp paprika
sugar and salt, to taste
crusty bread, to serve

1 Wipe the green peppers, remove the cores and seeds and slice the flesh into strips.

2 Heat the oil gently in a large pan, then add the onion and cook over a low heat for 5 minutes until just softened and pale gold in colour.

3 Add the garlic and fry quickly with the onion, then add the strips of pepper and cook gently for 10 minutes, stirring regularly, until the peppers have lost some of their firmness.

4 Add the chopped tomatoes and paprika to the pan and season to taste with a little sugar and salt.

5 Simmer the vegetables over a low heat for 20–25 minutes, until some of the liquid has reduced and they are plump and tender. Serve immediately, accompanied by wedges of thick, crusty bread to mop up the juices.

VARIATIONS
• Add some lightly scrambled eggs to the cooked vegetables immediately before serving.
• For a dash of colour, prepare the dish with red and yellow (bell) peppers in addition to, or instead, of the green.

Energy 80Kcal/333kJ; Protein 1.9g; Carbohydrate 11.1g, of which sugars 9.9g; Fat 3.4g, of which saturates 0.5g; Cholesterol 0mg; Calcium 21mg; Fibre 2.7g; Sodium 10mg.

TZIMMES

Hearty vegetables braised with dried fruit, and sometimes with orchard fruit such as apple or pear too, is a traditional Ashkenazic dish. Some versions contain meat and can be served as a main dish rather than as an accompaniment. The Yiddish expression gantze tzimmes, meaning a "big deal", is inspired by this dish, because it is full of rich, sweet and spicy flavours.

SERVES SIX

INGREDIENTS
  250g/9oz carrots, peeled and sliced
  1 sweet potato, peeled and cut
    into chunks
  1 potato, peeled and cut into chunks
  pinch of sugar
  25g/1oz/2 tbsp butter or 30ml/2 tbsp
    vegetable oil
  1 onion, chopped
  10 pitted prunes, halved
    or quartered
  30–45ml/2–3 tbsp currants
  5 dried apricots, roughly chopped, or
    30ml/2 tbsp sultanas (golden raisins)
  30ml/2 tbsp honey
  5–10ml/1–2 tsp chopped fresh
    root ginger
  1 cinnamon stick or 2–3 shakes of
    ground cinnamon
  juice of ½ lemon
  salt

1 Preheat the oven to 160°C/325°F/Gas 3. Put the carrots, sweet potato and potato into a pan of sugared and salted boiling water and cook until they are almost tender. Drain, reserving the cooking liquid, and set aside.

VARIATION
To make a meat tzimmes, braise about 500g/1¼lb beef, cut into chunks, for 1–1½ hours until tender. In step 2 use oil rather than butter and add the meat to the pan with the vegetables.

2 Heat the butter or oil in a flameproof casserole, add the onion and fry until softened. Add the cooked vegetables and enough of the cooking liquid to cover the vegetables completely, then add the remaining ingredients.

3 Cover the casserole with a lid and cook in the oven for about 40 minutes. Towards the end of cooking time, check the amount of liquid in the casserole. If there is too much liquid, remove the lid for the last 10–15 minutes.

Energy 143Kcal/601kJ; Protein 1.9g; Carbohydrate 26.8g, of which sugars 15.9g; Fat 3.9g, of which saturates 2.3g; Cholesterol 9mg; Calcium 36mg; Fibre 2.9g; Sodium 55mg.

SEPHARDIC STEWED OKRA <u>WITH</u> TOMATOES <u>AND</u> ONIONS

THE SPICY, FRAGRANT FLAVOURS OF YEMEN, IRAQ AND INDIA ARE ALL DELICIOUS WITH TOMATO-SIMMERED OKRA. THIS DISH IS GOOD EATEN WARM OR COOL.

SERVES FOUR TO SIX

INGREDIENTS

90–120ml/6–8 tbsp olive oil
2 onions, thinly sliced
5–8 garlic cloves, roughly chopped
90ml/6 tbsp chopped fresh coriander
  (cilantro) leaves
800g/1¾lb okra
1kg/2¼lb fresh tomatoes, diced or
  400g/14oz can tomatoes plus 30–60ml/
  2–4 tbsp tomato purée (paste)
1.5–2.5ml/¼–½ tsp ground cumin
pinch of ground cinnamon
pinch of ground cloves
5ml/1 tsp sugar, or to taste
cayenne pepper
salt and ground black pepper
1 lemon, to serve

3 Add the tomatoes, cumin, cinnamon and cloves to the pan, then season to taste with the sugar, cayenne pepper, salt and pepper, and cook until the liquid boils. Reduce the heat to low, then simmer for 20–30 minutes until the okra is tender, stirring occasionally.

4 Taste for spicing and seasoning, and adjust if necessary, then stir in the remaining olive oil and coriander. If serving hot or warm, squeeze in the lemon juice and add to the okra or, if serving cold, cut the lemon into wedges and serve with the okra.

1 Heat about half the oil in a pan. Add the onions, garlic and half the coriander and fry for about 10 minutes until the onions are softened and turning brown.

2 Add the okra to the onions and stir-fry for 2–3 minutes.

COOK'S TIP
Trimming the okra and leaving them whole means that they will be succulent and not slimy.

VARIATION
For an Indian-inspired flavour, fry 7.5ml/1½ tsp curry powder, 5ml/1 tsp ground turmeric and 2.5ml/½ tsp ground ginger with the onion and garlic.

Energy 195Kcal/810kJ; Protein 6g; Carbohydrate 14.8g, of which sugars 12.6g; Fat 12.9g, of which saturates 2.1g; Cholesterol 0mg; Calcium 243mg; Fibre 7.9g; Sodium 49mg.

HATZILIM PILPEL

IN HEBREW, THE WORD HATZILIM MEANS "AUBERGINE" AND PILPEL MEANS "SPICY AND PEPPERY".
THIS TELLS YOU EVERYTHING YOU NEED TO KNOW ABOUT THIS DISH. EAT IT ON ITS OWN OR SERVE
IT ALONGSIDE A ROASTED CHICKEN OR FISH, OR WITH BEEF OR LAMB KEBABS.

SERVES FOUR TO SIX

INGREDIENTS

about 60ml/4 tbsp olive oil
1 large aubergine (eggplant) cut
  into bitesize chunks
2 onions, thinly sliced
3–5 garlic cloves, chopped
1–2 green (bell) peppers, thinly
  sliced or chopped
1–2 fresh hot chillies, chopped
4 fresh or canned tomatoes, diced
30–45ml/2–3 tbsp tomato purée
  (paste), if using fresh tomatoes
5ml/1 tsp ground turmeric
pinch of curry powder or
  ras al hanout
cayenne pepper, to taste
400g/14oz can chickpeas, drained
  and rinsed
juice of ½–1 lemon
30–45ml/2–3 tbsp chopped fresh
  coriander (cilantro) leaves
salt

2 Heat the remaining oil in the pan, add the onions, garlic, peppers and chillies and fry until softened. Add the diced tomatoes, tomato purée, if using, spices and salt, and cook, stirring, until the mixture is of a sauce consistency. Add a little water if necessary.

3 Add the chickpeas to the sauce and cook for about 5 minutes, then add the aubergine, stir to mix and cook for 5–10 minutes until the flavours are well combined. Add lemon juice to taste, then add the coriander leaves. Chill before serving.

1 Heat half the oil in a frying pan, add the aubergine chunks and fry until brown, adding more oil if necessary. When cooked, transfer the aubergine to a sieve (strainer), standing over a bowl, and leave to drain.

VARIATION

To make a Middle Eastern-style ratatouille, cut 2 courgettes (zucchini) and one red (bell) pepper into chunks. Add to the pan with the onions and garlic and continue as before.

Energy 220Kcal/922kJ; Protein 8g; Carbohydrate 25.5g, of which sugars 13.1g; Fat 10.3g, of which saturates 1.5g; Cholesterol 0mg; Calcium 68mg; Fibre 7.8g; Sodium 172mg.

LEEK FRITTERS

THESE CRISPY FRIED MORSELS FEATURE PROMINENTLY IN THE SEPHARDIC KITCHEN. ACCORDING TO ACCOUNTS OF THE FLEEING HEBREW SLAVES, LEEKS AND GARLIC WERE MISSING FROM THEIR DIET AND LIFE WITHOUT THEM WAS HARDLY WORTH LIVING.

SERVES FOUR

INGREDIENTS

4 large leeks, total weight about
   1kg/2¼lb, thickly sliced
120–175ml/4–6fl oz/½–¾ cup
   coarse matzo meal
2 eggs, lightly beaten
large pinch of dried thyme
   or basil
freshly grated nutmeg
olive or vegetable oil, for
   shallow-frying
salt and ground black pepper
lemon wedges, to serve

1 Cook the leeks in salted boiling water for 5 minutes, or until just tender and bright green. Drain and leave to cool.

2 Chop the leeks roughly. Put in a bowl and combine with the matzo meal, eggs, herbs, nutmeg and seasoning.

3 Heat 5mm/¼in oil in a frying pan. Using two tablespoons, carefully spoon the leek mixture into the hot oil. Cook over a medium-high heat until golden brown on the underside, then turn and cook the second side. Drain on kitchen paper. Cook the rest of the mixture, adding oil if needed. Serve with lemon wedges and salt.

VARIATION

To make spinach or chard fritters, replace the leeks with 400–500g/ 14oz–1¼lb fresh spinach or chard leaves and 1 finely chopped onion. Cook the spinach or chard leaves, in only the water that clings to their leaves after washing, until wilted. Leave to cool, reserving the cooking liquid. Roughly chop the greens and continue as in the recipe above, adding enough of the cooking liquid to make a thick batter.

Energy 326Kcal/1356kJ; Protein 10g; Carbohydrate 29.2g, of which sugars 5.5g; Fat 18.8g, of which saturates 2.6g; Cholesterol 95mg; Calcium 75mg; Fibre 6.2g; Sodium 40mg.

BULGARIAN BRAISED CABBAGE WITH TOMATOES

CABBAGE, CABBAGE AND MORE CABBAGE WAS THE MAINSTAY OF THE ASHKENAZIC KITCHEN. TOMATOES FEATURE HEAVILY IN THE BALKAN DIET, AND THIS DISH IS AT HOME IN ROMANIA AND BULGARIA.

SERVES FOUR

INGREDIENTS
  1 green or white cabbage, about
    675g/1½lb
  15ml/1 tbsp light olive oil
  30ml/2 tbsp water
  45–60ml/3–4 tbsp vegetable stock
  4 firm, ripe tomatoes, peeled
    and chopped
  3–5 garlic cloves, chopped
  5ml/1 tsp paprika
  large pinch of chilli
  salt
  15ml/1 tbsp chopped fresh parsley or
    fennel, to garnish (optional)
For the topping
  3 firm ripe tomatoes, thinly sliced
  15ml/1 tbsp olive oil
  salt and ground black pepper

1 Preheat the oven to 180°C/350°F/ Gas 4. Finely shred the leaves and the core of the cabbage. Heat the oil in a frying pan with the water and add the cabbage. Cook over a very low heat, to allow the cabbage to sweat, for 5–10 minutes with the lid on. Stir occasionally.

2 Add the stock and stir in the tomatoes. Cook for a further 10 minutes. Season with the garlic, paprika and chilli as well as a little salt.

3 Tip the cabbage mixture into the base of an ovenproof dish. Level the surface of the cabbage and arrange the sliced tomatoes on top. Season and brush with the oil to prevent them drying out. Cook for 30–40 minutes, or until the tomatoes are just starting to brown. Serve hot, garnished with a little parsley or fennel sprinkled over the top, if you like.

COOK'S TIPS
• To vary the taste, add seeded, diced red or green (bell) peppers to the cabbage with the tomatoes.
• If you have a shallow flameproof casserole, you could cook the cabbage in it on the stove and then simply transfer it to the oven for baking.

Energy 123Kcal/513kJ; Protein 3.5g; Carbohydrate 13.5g, of which sugars 13.3g; Fat 6.3g, of which saturates 1g; Cholesterol 0mg; Calcium 94mg; Fibre 5.2g; Sodium 27mg.

COURGETTES <u>A LA</u> NIÇOISE

PURÉED, COOKED COURGETTES, PERFUMED WITH GARLIC AND BASIL THEN BAKED UNDER A BLANKET OF CRUMBS, IS A DISH FROM NICE, FRANCE, WHICH IS ENJOYED BY JEWS AND NON-JEWS ALIKE.

SERVES FOUR TO SIX

INGREDIENTS

6 courgettes (zucchini), about
200g/7oz each
65g/2½oz/5 tbsp olive oil
1 onion, finely chopped
3–4 garlic cloves, crushed
60ml/4 tbsp day-old breadcrumbs
salt
olives, lemon slices and sprig of fresh
parsley, to garnish

1 Trim the courgettes and cut into 1cm/½in slices. Add to a pan of boiling water and cook for 5–8 minutes, or until just tender. Drain very well.

2 Using a potato masher, mash the courgettes or blend in a food processor or blender until smooth.

VARIATION
Replace the courgettes with two large marrows (large zucchini) that have been peeled, seeded and diced.

3 Heat half the olive oil in a frying pan and cook the onion until soft, then stir in the garlic and the puréed courgettes. Cook without browning for a further 2–3 minutes, before spooning into a warm ovenproof serving dish.

4 Dot the courgette with the remaining olive oil and sprinkle over the breadcrumbs. Cook under a preheated grill (broiler) until golden brown. Garnish with olives, lemon slices and a sprig of parsley just before serving.

Energy 157Kcal/653kJ; Protein 4.9g; Carbohydrate 12.1g, of which sugars 4.2g; Fat 10.2g, of which saturates 1.5g; Cholesterol 0mg; Calcium 66mg; Fibre 2.2g; Sodium 78mg.

BAKED PEPPERS <u>AND</u> TOMATOES

A CLASSIC MEDITERRANEAN DISH, PAN-ROASTED PEPPERS ARE ENJOYED IN ISRAEL AND THROUGHOUT THE REGION. FOR A DAIRY MEAL, EAT ALONGSIDE A FRESH, TANGY GOAT'S CHEESE.

SERVES EIGHT

INGREDIENTS

2 red (bell) peppers
2 yellow (bell) peppers
1 red onion, sliced
4 garlic cloves, sliced
6 plum tomatoes, quartered
50g/2oz/½ cup oil-cured or other Mediterranean black olives
5ml/1 tsp soft light brown sugar
45ml/3 tbsp balsamic vinegar
3–4 fresh rosemary sprigs
30ml/2 tbsp olive oil
salt and ground black pepper
crusty bread, to serve

1 Slice the red and yellow peppers in half, remove the cores and seeds, then cut each half into about four individual strips.

2 Preheat the oven to 200°C/400°F/ Gas 6. Place the peppers, onion, garlic, tomatoes and olives in a large roasting pan. Sprinkle over the sugar, then pour over the balsamic vinegar. Season well, cover with foil and bake for 45 minutes.

3 Remove the foil from the pan and stir the vegetable and olive mixture well. Add the rosemary sprigs.

4 Drizzle over the olive oil. Return the pan to the oven for a further 30 minutes until the vegetables are tender and full of flavour. Serve hot, with warm bread for mopping up the juices.

Energy 78Kcal/324kJ; Protein 1.6g; Carbohydrate 9.2g, of which sugars 8.8g; Fat 4g, of which saturates 0.7g; Cholesterol 0mg; Calcium 19mg; Fibre 2.5g; Sodium 152mg.

SPICED TURNIPS WITH SPINACH AND TOMATOES

A LUSTY MIDDLE EASTERN VEGETABLE STEW, DELICIOUS IN THE SUMMER WHEN THE TURNIPS ARE GETTING FAIRLY LARGE AND THE TOMATOES RIPE AND FULL OF FLAVOUR. SUCH STEWS ARE A FAVOURITE OF SEPHARDIM, ESPECIALLY BAGHDADI JEWS. ENJOY WITH RICE OR A STACK OF WARM PITTA BREAD.

SERVES SIX

INGREDIENTS
  450g/1lb plum tomatoes
  2 onions
  60ml/4 tbsp olive oil
  450g/1lb turnips, peeled
  5ml/1 tsp paprika
  1.5ml/¼ tsp turmeric
  1.5ml/¼ tsp cumin
  seeds of 2 cardamom pods
  2.5ml/½ tsp sugar
  60ml/4 tbsp chopped fresh
    coriander (cilantro)
  450g/1lb fresh young spinach
  salt and ground black pepper

VARIATION
Use celery hearts, fennel or even canned artichoke hearts instead of baby turnips.

1 Cut a small cross in the bottom of the tomatoes, plunge them into boiling water for 30 seconds, then refresh in cold water. Drain, peel away the tomato skins and chop the flesh roughly.

2 Slice the onions. Heat the olive oil in a large frying pan or sauté pan and gently fry the onion slices for about 5 minutes until golden. Ensure that they do not blacken.

3 Add the baby turnips, tomatoes, paprika, turmeric, cumin and cardamom seeds to the pan with 60ml/4 tbsp water and cook until the tomatoes are pulpy. Cover the pan with a lid and continue cooking for a few minutes more until the baby turnips have softened.

4 Stir in the sugar and coriander, then add the spinach and a little salt and ground black pepper. Cook the mixture for a further 2–3 minutes until the spinach has wilted. The side dish is delicious served either warm or cold.

Energy 61Kcal/256kJ; Protein 3.7g; Carbohydrate 9.7g, of which sugars 8.7g; Fat 1.1g, of which saturates 0.2g; Cholesterol 0mg; Calcium 177mg; Fibre 4.6g; Sodium 124mg.

POTATOES <u>AND</u> ONIONS

TWO SIMPLE INGREDIENTS ARE PREPARED SEPARATELY AND THEN TOSSED TOGETHER TO CREATE THE PERFECT COMBINATION. THESE POTATOES GO VERY WELL WITH A SIMPLE MEAT DISH, SUCH AS STEAK OR ROAST CHICKEN. ALTERNATIVELY, SERVE THEM WITH A BOWL OF GREEN BEANS TOSSED IN BUTTER.

SERVES SIX

INGREDIENTS

900g/2lb floury potatoes
olive oil or vegetable oil, for
   shallow-frying
45ml/3 tbsp olive oil
2 medium onions, sliced
   into rings
sea salt
15ml/1 tbsp chopped fresh parsley
   and 2 cloves chopped garlic,
   to garnish

1 Scrub the potatoes clean and cook in a large pan with plenty of boiling water for 10 minutes.

2 Drain the potatoes through a colander and leave to cool slightly. When the potatoes are cool enough to handle, peel and finely slice them.

3 Heat the olive oil or vegetable oil and shallow-fry the potatoes in two batches for about 10 minutes until crisp, turning occasionally.

4 Meanwhile, heat the olive oil in a frying pan and fry the onions for 10 minutes until golden. Drain on kitchen paper.

5 Remove the potatoes with a slotted spoon and drain on kitchen paper. Toss with sea salt and carefully mix with the onions. Sprinkle with the parsley and garlic.

VARIATION
If serving with a dairy meal, the onions can be cooked in butter instead of oil.

COOK'S TIP
Make sure you use floury, rather than waxy, potatoes for this recipe.

Energy 189Kcal/793kJ; Protein 3.2g; Carbohydrate 28.1g, of which sugars 4.8g; Fat 7.9g, of which saturates 1.2g; Cholesterol 0mg; Calcium 22mg; Fibre 2.2g; Sodium 18mg.

BOMBAY POTATOES

THE BENE ISRAEL ENJOY SIMILAR SPICED POTATOES TO THOSE OF THEIR NON-JEWISH NEIGHBOURS. USING OIL INSTEAD OF BUTTER MEANS THE DISH MAY BE EATEN WITH MEAT MEALS.

SERVES FOUR TO SIX

INGREDIENTS
450g/1lb new or small salad potatoes
5ml/1 tsp turmeric
60ml/4 tbsp vegetable oil
2 dried red chillies
6–8 curry leaves
2 onions, finely chopped
2 fresh green chillies,
  finely chopped
50g/2oz coriander (cilantro) leaves,
  coarsely chopped
1.5ml/¼ tsp asafoetida
2.5ml/½ tsp each cumin, mustard,
  onion, fennel and nigella seeds
about 1.5ml/¼ tsp lemon juice
salt
fresh fried curry leaves,
  to garnish

COOK'S TIP
You can omit the lemon juice at the end of the recipe if you prefer.

1 Chop the potatoes into small chunks and cook in boiling, lightly salted water with 2.5ml/½ tsp of the turmeric until tender. Drain, then coarsely mash. Set aside.

2 Heat the oil in a large heavy pan and fry the red chillies and curry leaves until the chillies are nearly burnt. Add the onions, green chillies, coriander, remaining turmeric, asafoetida and spice seeds and cook until the onions are tender.

3 Fold in the potatoes and add a few drops of water. Cook on a low heat for about 10 minutes, mixing well to ensure the even distribution of the spices. Remove the dried chillies and curry leaves. Reserve the leaves for the garnish.

4 Remove the pan from the heat and squeeze a little lemon juice over the top of the potato mixture. Garnish with the fresh fried curry leaves and serve piping hot.

Energy 143Kcal/595kJ; Protein 2.1g; Carbohydrate 17.4g, of which sugars 4.7g; Fat 7.7g, of which saturates 0.9g; Cholesterol 0mg; Calcium 21mg; Fibre 1.7g; Sodium 10mg.

POTATOES IN YOGURT SAUCE

THE POTATO WAS FIRST INTRODUCED TO INDIA BY DUTCH TRADERS AND WAS WHOLEHEARTEDLY EMBRACED BY THAT SPICY CUISINE. THIS IS A TYPICAL BENE ISRAEL DISH. THE BENE ISRAEL OF WESTERN AND NORTHERN INDIA ENJOYED THE FOODS AND FLAVOURS OF THEIR MUSLIM AND HINDU NEIGHBOURS AND ADDED THEIR OWN TOUCHES. THEIR FOOD IS LESS CHILLI-HOT THAN THAT OF THE COCHINESE JEWS OR BAGHDADI JEWS OF CALCUTTA.

SERVES FOUR

INGREDIENTS
  12 new potatoes, halved
  300ml/½ pint/1¼ cups natural
    (plain) yogurt, whisked
  200ml/7fl oz/1 cup water
  1.5ml/¼ tsp ground turmeric
  5ml/1 tsp chilli powder
  5ml/1 tsp ground coriander
  2.5ml/½ tsp ground cumin
  5ml/1 tsp salt
  15ml/1 tbsp gram flour mixed with
    60ml/4 tbsp water
  30ml/2 tbsp vegetable oil
  5ml/1 tsp cumin seeds
  15ml/1 tbsp chopped fresh coriander
    (cilantro), plus extra sprigs to
    garnish (optional)
  2 fresh green chillies, sliced

1 Boil the halved new potatoes with their skins on in a large pan of salted water, until they are just tender. Drain the potatoes and set aside.

2 Mix together the natural yogurt, water, turmeric, chilli powder, ground coriander, ground cumin, salt and gram flour mixture in a bowl. Set the mixture aside.

3 Heat the vegetable oil in a wok, karahi or large pan, and add the cumin seeds. Fry gently until they begin to splutter.

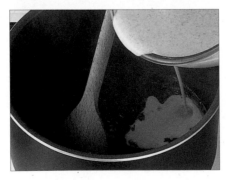

4 Reduce the heat, stir in the yogurt mixture and cook for about 3 minutes, stirring constantly.

COOK'S TIP
Do not allow the yogurt mixture to boil or it will curdle.

5 Add the chopped fresh coriander, green chillies and cooked potatoes. Blend everything together and cook for a further 5–7 minutes, stirring the mixture occasionally.

6 Transfer to a warmed serving dish and garnish with the coriander sprigs, if you like. This dish goes very well with hot chapatis.

Energy 161Kcal/677kJ; Protein 5.9g; Carbohydrate 24.7g, of which sugars 7g; Fat 5.1g, of which saturates 1g; Cholesterol 1mg; Calcium 154mg; Fibre 1.1g; Sodium 73mg.

CAULIFLOWER WITH TOMATOES AND CUMIN

CAULIFLOWER IS A POPULAR VEGETABLE IN THE SEPHARDIC KITCHEN. THIS HAS YEMENITE FLAVOURS, AND IS AS DELICIOUS AT ROOM TEMPERATURE AS IT IS WARM, MAKING IT PERFECT FOR SHABBAT OR OTHER HOLIDAYS WHEN COOKING IS FORBIDDEN. AS IT IS PAREVE, YOU CAN ENJOY IT WITH EITHER A MEAT OR A DAIRY MEAL.

SERVES FOUR

INGREDIENTS
  4 tomatoes
  30ml/2 tbsp olive oil
  1 onion, chopped
  4 garlic cloves, crushed
  1 small cauliflower, broken into florets
  5ml/1 tsp cumin seeds
  a good pinch each of ground ginger
    and turmeric
  15–30ml/1–2 tbsp lemon juice
  30ml/2 tbsp chopped fresh
    coriander (cilantro) (optional)
  salt and ground black pepper or
    red cayenne pepper

1 Cut a small cross in the bottom of the tomatoes, plunge them into boiling water for 30 seconds, then refresh in cold water. Peel, cut into quarters and remove the seeds.

2 Heat the oil in a flameproof casserole, add the onion and garlic and stir-fry for 2–3 minutes, or until the onion is softened. Add the cauliflower and stir-fry for a further 2–3 minutes, or until the cauliflower is flecked with brown. Add the cumin seeds, ginger and turmeric, fry briskly for 1 minute, and then add the tomatoes, 175ml/6fl oz/ ¾ cup water and some salt and pepper.

3 Bring to the boil and then reduce the heat, cover with a plate or with foil and simmer for 6–7 minutes, or until the cauliflower is just tender.

4 Stir in a little lemon juice to sharpen the flavour, taste and adjust the seasoning if necessary. Sprinkle over the chopped coriander, if using, and serve immediately.

Energy 119Kcal/493kJ; Protein 4.9g; Carbohydrate 10.1g, of which sugars 8.4g; Fat 6.8g, of which saturates 1.1g; Cholesterol 0mg; Calcium 41mg; Fibre 3.5g; Sodium 20mg.

BREADS AND BAKES

At the Jewish table, a meal begins with a blessing over the bread. Bread is one of the most basic foods in the Jewish diet. The variety is staggering, from sweet and tender challah eaten on Shabbat, to hefty sourdough ryes of the Ukraine, flat breads of the Middle East and crisp unleavened matzos that Jews all over the world eat ritually for Pesach. This section also includes a variety of sweet and spicy bakes, many based on Ashkenazic treats from the Old Country.

CHALLAH

SWEET, SHINY CHALLAH IS THE TRADITIONAL BRAIDED ASHKENAZIC BREAD SERVED AT CELEBRATIONS. EACH SHABBAT, IT IS CHALLAH THAT USHERS IN THE OBSERVANCES, ALONG WITH WINE AND CANDLES. AT ROSH HASHANAH, CANDIED FRUIT, RAISINS AND SULTANAS ARE KNEADED IN FOR A SWEET NEW YEAR.

MAKES TWO LOAVES

INGREDIENTS
  15ml/1 tbsp active dried yeast
  15ml/1 tbsp sugar
  250ml/8fl oz/1 cup lukewarm water
  500g/1¼lb/4½ cups strong white
    bread flour, plus extra if needed
  30ml/2 tbsp vegetable oil
  2 eggs, lightly beaten, plus 1 extra
    for glazing
  pinch of sugar
  salt
  poppy or sesame seeds,
    for sprinkling

1 In a mixer, food processor or large bowl, mix together the yeast, sugar and 120ml/4fl oz/½ cup water. Sprinkle the mixture with a little flour, cover and leave for about 10–12 minutes until bubbles appear on the surface.

2 Beat 5ml/1 tsp salt, the oil, remaining water and eggs into the mixture until well mixed, then add the flour, slowly at first until completely absorbed, then more quickly. Knead for 5–10 minutes until the mixture forms a dough that leaves the sides of the bowl. If the dough is still sticky, add a little more flour and knead again.

3 Place the dough in a lightly oiled bowl. Cover with a clean dish towel and leave in a warm place for 1½–2 hours, or until doubled in size.

4 Turn the dough on to a lightly floured surface and knead gently, then return to the bowl. Cover and place in the refrigerator overnight to rise.

5 Turn the dough on to a lightly floured surface, knock back (punch down) and knead until shiny and pliable. Divide the dough into two equal pieces, then divide each piece into three. Roll each into a long sausage shape.

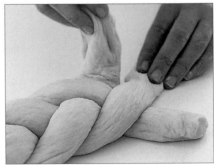

6 Pinch the ends of three pieces together, then braid into a loaf. Repeat with the remaining dough and place the loaves on a non-stick baking sheet. Cover with a dish towel and leave to rise for 1 hour, or until doubled in size.

7 Preheat the oven to 190°C/375°F/ Gas 5. In a bowl, combine the remaining egg, the sugar and salt, and brush over the loaves, then sprinkle with the poppy or sesame seeds. Bake for 40 minutes, or until well browned. Leave to cool on a wire rack.

VARIATION
Leftover challah makes excellent pain perdu (eggy bread or French toast). It can also be used to make divine bread and butter pudding.

Energy 1055Kcal/4464kJ; Protein 29.8g; Carbohydrate 202.1g, of which sugars 11.6g; Fat 19.8g, of which saturates 3.4g; Cholesterol 190mg; Calcium 383mg; Fibre 7.8g; Sodium 78mg.

MOUNA

THIS DELICATE, SWEET EGG BREAD OF THE ALGERIAN JEWISH COMMUNITY IS PERFECT FOR A SHABBAT BREAKFAST, OR TO BREAK THE FAST OF YOM KIPPUR.

MAKES TWO LOAVES

INGREDIENTS
  500g/1¼lb/4½ cups unbleached
    plain (all-purpose) flour
  130g/4½oz/scant ⅔ cup sugar
  7g packet easy-blend (rapid-rise)
    dried yeast
  45ml/3 tbsp lukewarm water
  105ml/7 tbsp lukewarm milk
  4 eggs
  130g/4½oz/generous ½ cup butter
  grated rind of 1 orange
  oil, for greasing
  90–120ml/6–8 tbsp jam
  15ml/1 tbsp cold water
  icing (confectioners') sugar,
    for dusting (optional)

1 Combine half the flour, half the sugar and the yeast in a large bowl. Stir the water and milk into the dry ingredients and mix until thoroughly combined. Cover and leave in a warm place for about 1 hour until doubled in size.

2 Whisk together half the remaining sugar and three of the eggs. Mix in the butter and orange rind. Gradually add the remaining flour and knead the mixture in the bowl until it is smooth.

3 Knead the yeast mixture into the egg mixture for about 10 minutes until it is smooth and elastic. Rinse your hands and rub a little oil over them, then shape the dough into a large ball. Place the dough in a bowl, cover and leave in a warm place for about 1 hour, or until roughly doubled in size.

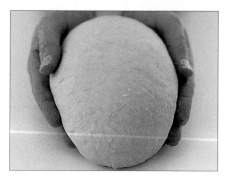

4 Turn the dough on to a lightly floured surface and knock back (punch down). Knead for 3–4 minutes, then divide the dough in half and shape each piece into a round loaf. Make a large indentation in each loaf and spoon in the jam. Close up and pinch the dough together.

VARIATION
Add 15–30ml/1–2 tbsp aniseed in place of the orange rind.

5 Lightly oil two baking sheets and then sprinkle with flour, or use non-stick baking sheets. Place the loaves on the prepared baking sheets and cut slits around the sides of the loaves, taking care not to let any jam leak out.

6 Cover the loaves with a clean dish towel and leave to rise for 45–60 minutes, or until doubled in size.

7 Preheat the oven to 190°C/375°F/ Gas 5. In a small bowl, beat the remaining egg with the cold water. Brush the glaze on to the loaves, then sprinkle over the remaining sugar. Bake the loaves for about 20 minutes, or until golden brown. Dust with icing sugar, if you like.

VARIATION
Instead of jam, add a handful of raisins and a pinch of saffron to the dough.

Energy 1881Kcal/7922kJ; Protein 38.8g; Carbohydrate 296.1g, of which sugars 105.6g; Fat 68.7g, of which saturates 38g; Cholesterol 522mg; Calcium 522mg; Fibre 7.8g; Sodium 581mg.

NEW YORK SEEDED CORN RYE SOURDOUGH

YOU DO NOT HAVE TO BE JEWISH TO LOVE THIS EASTERN EUROPEAN JEWISH BREAD. IT IS SURPRISINGLY EASY TO MAKE, ALTHOUGH YOU NEED TO PREPARE IT WELL IN ADVANCE, AS THE STARTER TAKES A FEW DAYS TO FERMENT. SADLY, THIS WONDERFUL BREAD IS BECOMING RARER IN NEW YORK.

MAKES TWO LOAVES

INGREDIENTS
  1.6kg/3½lb/14 cups unbleached
    strong white bread flour
  7g packet easy-blend (rapid-rise)
    dried yeast
  250ml/8fl oz/1 cup lukewarm water
  60ml/4 tbsp caraway or dill seeds
  15ml/1 tbsp salt
  cornmeal, for sprinkling
For the sourdough starter
  250g/9oz/2¼ cups unbleached strong
    white bread flour or a mixture of
    ¾ strong white bread flour and
    ¼ wholemeal (whole-wheat) flour
  7g easy-blend (rapid-rise) dried yeast
  250ml/8fl oz/1 cup lukewarm water
For the sponge
  200g/7oz/1¾ cups rye flour
  250ml/8fl oz/1 cup lukewarm water

1 To make the sourdough starter, put the flour into a large bowl and stir in the yeast. Make a central well, stir in the water and mix together. Cover tightly. Leave at room temperature for 2 days or in the refrigerator for 1 week.

2 To make the sponge, put the rye flour into a large bowl, mix in the sourdough starter and water. Cover tightly. Leave at room temperature for 8 hours or in the refrigerator for up to 2 days.

3 Put the flour into a large bowl and add the sponge mixture, yeast, water, caraway or dill seeds and salt and mix to form a soft, slightly sticky dough.

4 Turn the dough into a large, clean bowl, sprinkle the top with flour, cover with a clean dishtowel and leave to rise in a warm place for about 2 hours, or until doubled in size.

5 Turn the dough on to a lightly floured surface and knock back (punch down). Knead for 3–4 minutes until smooth and elastic. Divide the dough in half, then shape each piece into a round loaf.

6 Sprinkle two baking sheets with cornmeal. Place the loaves on the top and score each one with a sharp knife.

7 Cover each loaf loosely with a clean dish towel and leave in a warm place to rise for about 45 minutes, or until doubled in size.

8 Preheat the oven to 220°C/425°F/ Gas 7. Fill a roasting pan with boiling water and place in the bottom of the oven. Alternatively, if you have a tile or pizza stone place this in the oven – it will help to create a thick, crunchy crust. Bake the loaves for about 35 minutes until lightly browned and hollow-sounding when tapped on the bottom. Cool on a wire rack.

Energy 3496Kcal/14863kJ; Protein 96.4g; Carbohydrate 796.4g, of which sugars 15.4g; Fat 13.3g, of which saturates 2.1g; Cholesterol 0mg; Calcium 1436mg; Fibre 31.8g; Sodium

PUMPERNICKEL

Dark bread was the mainstay of most meals during the centuries of Jewish life in Poland, Russia and the Baltic states. It might be spread with butter, chicken fat or sour cream, or simply rubbed with onion or garlic. There are many theories as to the origins of the name. A popular notion is that Napoleon Bonaparte described it, rather dismissively, as "pain pour Nicol" – bread fit only for his horse, Nicol! This recipe, sweetened with cocoa, would surely sway even the fiercest critic.

MAKES TWO LOAVES

INGREDIENTS

65g/2½oz plain (semi-sweet) chocolate or cocoa powder (unsweetened)
7g packet easy-blend (rapid-rise) dried yeast
200g/7oz/1¾ cups rye flour
300–400g/11–14oz/2¾–3½ cups strong white bread flour
5ml/1 tsp salt
2.5ml/½ tsp sugar
15ml/1 tbsp instant coffee powder
15ml/1 tbsp caraway seeds (optional)
105ml/7 tbsp warm dark beer
15ml/1 tbsp vegetable oil
90ml/6 tbsp treacle (molasses)
cornmeal, for sprinkling

1 Place a bowl over a pan of water and heat the chocolate or cocoa with 50ml/2fl oz/¼ cup water. Stir to combine, then set aside.

2 Combine the yeast, flours, salt, sugar, coffee and caraway seeds, if using.

3 Make a well in the flour mixture, then pour in the chocolate or cocoa, 175ml/6fl oz/¾ cup water, the beer, oil and treacle. Mix well to form a dough.

4 Turn the dough out on to a lightly floured surface and knead for about 10 minutes, or until smooth.

5 Place the dough in a lightly oiled bowl and turn the dough to coat in oil. Cover with a dish towel and leave to rise for 1½ hours, or until doubled in size.

6 Oil a baking sheet and sprinkle with cornmeal. Turn the dough on to a lightly floured surface and knock back (punch down). Knead for 3–4 minutes, then divide the dough and shape into two round or oval loaves. Place the loaves on the baking sheet, cover with a clean dish towel and leave to rise in a warm place for 45 minutes, or until doubled in size.

7 Preheat the oven to 185°C/360°F/Gas 4½. Bake the loaves for about 40 minutes, or until they sound hollow when tapped on the base. Leave to cool on a wire rack.

COOK'S TIP

Time spent kneading the dough is well spent as it is important to continue until the dough is smooth.

Energy 1276Kcal/5400kJ; Protein 27.3g; Carbohydrate 246.4g, of which sugars 42.4g; Fat 24.3g, of which saturates 8.6g; Cholesterol 5mg; Calcium 395mg; Fibre 9.1g; Sodium 187mg.

KESRA

FLAT AROMATIC ROUNDS OF BREAD ARE EATEN THROUGHOUT THE MIDDLE EAST, BOTH TO SCOOP UP THE SOUPY STEWS, AS WELL AS FOR THEIR OWN GOODNESS. THIS IS A MOROCCAN VERSION.

MAKES TWO ROUND LOAVES

INGREDIENTS
    sunflower or vegetable oil
    75g/3oz/¾ cup cornmeal
    2.5ml/½ tsp dried active yeast
    scant 5ml/1 tsp sugar
    600ml/1 pint/2½ cups
      lukewarm water
    450g/1lb/4 cups unbleached strong
      white bread flour
    5ml/1 tsp salt
    30ml/2 tbsp melted butter
    sesame seeds, to sprinkle

1 Lightly oil two baking sheets and dust them with 15ml/1 tbsp of the cornmeal. In a small bowl, dissolve the yeast and sugar in about 50ml/2fl oz/¼ cup of the lukewarm water. Sift the flour, remaining cornmeal and salt into a bowl.

2 Make a well in the centre and pour in the yeast mixture and the melted butter. Gradually add the remaining water and mix the ingredients into a dough.

3 Knead the dough on a floured surface for about 10 minutes until smooth and elastic. Divide the dough in half and knead each piece into a ball.

4 Flatten and stretch the balls of dough into circles, about 20cm/8in in diameter. Place on the baking sheets and sprinkle with sesame seeds. Cover the loaves with damp cloths and leave in a warm place for about an hour, until doubled in size.

5 Preheat the oven to 220°C/425°F/ Gas 7. Pinch the tops of the loaves with your fingers or prick them with a fork.

VARIATIONS
• To make a satisfying breakfast bread, simply use half and half wholemeal (whole-wheat) and white flours and add a little honey to the dough with the lukewarm water.
• Add 15–30ml/1–2 tbsp anise or fennel seeds to the dough for a spicier bread.

6 Bake the loaves for about 15 minutes, then reduce the oven temperature to 180°C/350°F/Gas 4 and bake for a further 15 minutes, or until the loaves are crusty, golden and sound hollow when tapped underneath. Cool on a wire rack.

COOK'S TIPS
• Add a little more flour to the dough at the end of step 2 if it becomes too sticky.
• The dough can also be shaped into individual rolls before baking.

Energy 1017Kcal/4299kJ; Protein 24.8g; Carbohydrate 202.4g, of which sugars 3.5g; Fat 16.5g, of which saturates 8.3g; Cholesterol 32mg; Calcium 319mg; Fibre 7.8g; Sodium 1080mg

LAVASH

THIN AND CRISPY, THIS FLAT BREAD IS UNIVERSALLY EATEN THROUGHOUT THE MIDDLE EAST AND IS IDEAL FOR SERVING WITH SOUPS AND APPETIZERS.

MAKES TEN

INGREDIENTS
275g/10oz/2½ cups unbleached
   white bread flour
175g/6oz/1½ cups wholemeal
   (whole-wheat) flour
5ml/1 tsp salt
15g/½oz fresh yeast
250ml/8fl oz/1 cup lukewarm water
60ml/4 tbsp natural (plain) yogurt
   or milk

1 Sift the white and wholemeal flours and salt together into a large bowl and make a well in the centre. Mix the yeast with roughly half the lukewarm water until creamy, then stir in the remaining water.

2 Add the yeast mixture and yogurt or milk to the centre of the flour. Mix into a soft dough and turn out on to a lightly floured surface.

3 Knead for 8–10 minutes until smooth and elastic. Place in a lightly oiled bowl, cover with oiled clear film (plastic wrap) and leave to rise in a warm place for about an hour, or until doubled in size. Knock back (punch down) the dough, re-cover with a fresh sheet of oiled clear film and leave to rise for 30 minutes.

4 Turn the dough back out on to a lightly floured surface. Knock back (punch down) and gently divide into 10 equal pieces.

5 Shape the dough into balls, then flatten into discs with the palm of your hand. Cover and leave for 5 minutes. Meanwhile, preheat the oven to 230°C/450°F/Gas 8 and place three or four baking sheets in the oven to warm.

6 Roll the dough as thinly as possible, then lift it over the backs of your hands and gently stretch and turn it. If necessary, let the dough rest after rolling for a few minutes as this may help to avoid tearing.

7 As soon as the lavash are ready, place four of them on to the baking sheet and bake for 6–8 minutes, or until they start to brown. Stack the remaining uncooked lavash, layered with clear film or baking parchment, and cover to keep moist. Transfer to a wire rack to cool while you cook the remaining lavash.

COOK'S TIP
Pile the lavash on a plate in the centre of the table so that guests can break off pieces as desired.

Energy 151kcal/644kJ; Protein 5.1g; Carbohydrate 33g, of which sugars 1.2g; Fat 0.8g, of which saturates 0.1g; Cholesterol 0mg; Calcium 57mg; Fibre 2.4g; Sodium 203mg.

BAGELS

THESE RING-SHAPED ROLLS ARE A GASTRONOMICAL GIFT TO THE WORLD FROM THE EASTERN EUROPEAN JEWISH COMMUNITY OF LONG AGO. THE DOUGH IS FIRST BOILED TO GIVE IT A CHEWY TEXTURE AND THEN BAKED. FRESH BAGELS ARE EATEN WARM, SPREAD WITH BUTTER, CREAM CHEESE OR A MIXTURE OF CREAM CHEESE AND VEGETABLES OR ONIONS. WHEN A DAY OR SO OLD, THEY MUST BE TOASTED.

MAKES TEN TO TWELVE

INGREDIENTS
 7g packet easy-blend (rapid-rise)
  dried yeast
 25ml/1½ tbsp salt
 500g/1¼lb/4½ cups strong
  white bread flour
 250ml/8fl oz/1 cup lukewarm
  water
 oil, for greasing
 30ml/2 tbsp sugar
 cornmeal, for sprinkling
 1 egg yolk

1 In a bowl, combine the yeast, salt and flour. Pour the lukewarm water into a separate large bowl.

2 Gradually add half the flour to the lukewarm water, beating until it forms a smooth, soft batter.

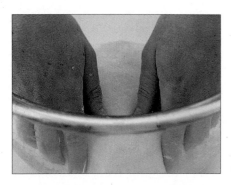

3 Knead the remaining flour into the batter until the mixture forms a fairly firm, smooth dough.

4 On a lightly floured surface, knead the dough by hand for 10–20 minutes or, if using a bread machine, 5–8 minutes, until shiny and smooth. If the dough is sticky, add a little more flour. (The dough should be much firmer than ordinary bread dough.)

5 Lightly oil a bowl. Place the dough in it and turn to coat it completely in oil. Cover with a clean dish towel and leave in a warm place for about 40 minutes, or until doubled in size.

6 Turn the dough on to a lightly floured surface and knock back (punch down). Knead for 3–4 minutes, or until smooth and elastic.

7 Divide the dough into 10–12 balls. Poke your thumb through each one then, working with your fingers, open the hole to form a bagel measuring 6–7.5cm/2½–3in in diameter. Place on a floured board and leave to rise for 20 minutes, or until doubled in size.

8 Preheat the oven to 200°C/400°F/ Gas 6. Bring 3–4 litres/5–7 pints/ 2½–3½ quarts water to the boil in a large pan and add the sugar. Lower the heat to a gentle boil. Lightly oil a baking sheet and sprinkle with cornmeal. Beat the egg yolk with 15ml/1 tbsp water.

9 Add the bagels one at a time to the boiling water, until you have a single layer of bagels, and cook for 8 minutes, turning occasionally so that they cook evenly. Remove from the pan with a slotted spoon, drain and place on the prepared baking sheet.

10 Brush each bagel with the egg mixture. Bake for 25–30 minutes until well browned. Cool on a wire rack.

VARIATIONS
Add dried onions, garlic granules or poppy seeds to the bagel dough or top the bagels with poppy seeds, sesame seeds, caraway seeds, dried onion or garlic granules before baking.

Energy 157Kcal/667kJ; Protein 4.2g; Carbohydrate 35g, of which sugars 3.2g; Fat 1g, of which saturates 0.2g; Cholesterol 17mg; Calcium 62mg; Fibre 1.3g; Sodium 821mg.

ONION ROLLS

THESE SWEET-SMELLING, TENDER ROLLS ARE RICH WITH ONIONS, AND MANY JEWS WILL REMEMBER THEM FROM CHILDHOOD, THOUGH PERHAPS WITH VARIATIONS ON THE TOPPINGS. THEY WERE MADE BY ROBUST WOMEN WHO WERE ALWAYS SMILING AND COVERED IN FLOUR. NOTHING TASTED SO GOOD!

MAKES TWELVE TO FOURTEEN

INGREDIENTS
15ml/1 tbsp dried active yeast
15ml/1 tbsp sugar
250ml/8fl oz/1 cup lukewarm
   water
30ml/2 tbsp vegetable oil
2 eggs, lightly beaten
500g/1¼lb/4½ cups strong
   white bread flour
3–4 onions, very, very
   finely chopped
60ml/4 tbsp poppy seeds
salt

1 In a mixer fitted with a dough hook, a food processor fitted with a dough blade, or a large bowl, mix together the yeast, sugar and water. Sprinkle the mixture with a little flour, cover and leave for 10–12 minutes until bubbles appear on the surface.

2 Beat 5ml/1 tsp salt, the oil and one of the eggs into the mixture until well mixed, then gradually add the flour and knead for 5–10 minutes until the dough leaves the sides of the bowl. If the dough is still slightly sticky, add a little more flour.

3 Lightly oil a bowl. Place the dough in it and turn. Cover with a dish towel. Leave to rise in a warm place for about 1½ hours, or until doubled in size.

4 Turn the dough on to a lightly floured surface, knock back (punch down) and knead the dough for 3–4 minutes, then knead half the onions into the dough. Form the dough into egg-size balls, then press each ball into a round 1cm/½in thick. Place on a baking sheet.

5 Lightly beat the remaining egg with 30ml/2 tbsp water and a pinch of salt. Press an indentation on top of each round of dough and brush with the egg mixture. Sprinkle the remaining onions and the poppy seeds on to the rolls and leave to rise in a warm place, uncovered, for around 45 minutes, or until doubled in size.

6 Preheat the oven to 190°C/375°F/ Gas 5. Bake the rolls for 20 minutes, or until pale golden brown. Serve hot from the oven or leave to cool.

Energy 161Kcal/681kJ; Protein 4.6g; Carbohydrate 31.1g, of which sugars 3.3g; Fat 2.9g, of which saturates 0.5g; Cholesterol 27mg; Calcium 62mg; Fibre 1.5g; Sodium 12mg.

PITTA BREAD

THROUGHOUT THE MEDITERRANEAN, FLATBREADS KNOWN AS PITTA ARE THE BREAD PAR EXCELLENCE. THERE ARE VERY FLAT ONES, PITTAS WITH POCKETS, AND THICK, CUSHIONY PITTAS. THE BEST PITTA BREAD IS ALWAYS SOFT, TENDER AND MOIST.

5 Heat a large, heavy frying pan over a medium-high heat. When smoking hot, gently lay one piece of flattened dough in the pan and cook for 15–20 seconds. Carefully turn it over and cook the second side for about 1 minute.

6 When large bubbles start to form on the bread, turn it over again. It should puff up. Using a clean dish towel, gently press on the bread where the bubbles have formed. Cook for a total of 3 minutes, then remove the pitta from the pan. Repeat with the remaining dough until all the pittas have been cooked.

7 Wrap the pitta breads in a clean dish towel, stacking them as each one is cooked. Serve the pittas hot while they are soft and moist.

MAKES TWELVE

INGREDIENTS
    500g/1¼lb/4½ cups strong white
      bread flour, or half white and
      half wholemeal (whole-wheat)
    7g packet easy-blend (rapid-rise)
      dried yeast
    15ml/1 tbsp salt
    15ml/1 tbsp olive oil
    250ml/8fl oz/1 cup water

1 Combine the flour, yeast and salt. In a large bowl, mix together the oil and water, then stir in half of the flour mixture, stirring in the same direction, until the dough is stiff. Knead in the remaining flour mixture.

2 Place the dough in a clean bowl, cover with a clean dish towel and leave in a warm place for at least 30 minutes and up to 2 hours.

3 Knead the dough for 10 minutes, or until smooth. Lightly oil the bowl, place the dough in it, cover again and leave to rise in a warm place for about 1 hour, or until doubled in size.

4 Divide the dough into 12 equal-size pieces. With lightly floured hands, flatten each piece, then roll out into a round measuring about 20cm/8in and about 5mm–1cm/¼–½in thick. Keep the rolled breads covered with a clean dish towel while you make the remaining pittas.

VARIATION
To cook the breads in the oven, preheat the oven to 220°C/425°F/Gas 7. Fill an unglazed or partially glazed dish with hot water and place in the bottom of the oven. Alternatively, arrange a handful of unglazed tiles in the bottom of the oven. Use either a non-stick baking sheet or a lightly oiled ordinary baking sheet and heat in the oven for a few minutes. Place two or three pieces of flattened dough on to the hot baking sheet and place in the hottest part of the oven. Bake for 2–3 minutes. They should puff up. Repeat with the remaining dough until all the pittas have been cooked.

Energy 150Kcal/638kJ; Protein 3.9g; Carbohydrate 32.4g, of which sugars 0.6g; Fat 1.5g, of which saturates 0.2g; Cholesterol 0mg; Calcium 58mg; Fibre 1.3g; Sodium 165mg.

SOUR RYE BREAD

MAKING YOUR OWN STARTER IS WHAT GIVES THIS BREAD ITS DISTINCTIVE FLAVOUR. EACH TIME YOU MAKE BREAD, SET ASIDE A LITTLE OF THE DOUGH TO ACT AS STARTER FOR YOUR NEXT BATCH. THIS WAY THE BREAD GETS INCREASINGLY SOUR EACH TIME.

MAKES TWO LOAVES

INGREDIENTS
   450g/1lb/4 cups rye flour, plus extra
      for dusting (optional)
   450g/1lb/4 cups strong white
      bread flour
   15ml/1 tbsp salt
   7g/¼oz packet easy-blend (rapid-rise)
      dried yeast
   25g/1oz/2 tbsp butter, softened
   600ml/1 pint/2½ cups warm water
   15ml/1 tbsp caraway seeds or
      buckwheat, for sprinkling (optional)
For the sourdough starter
   60ml/4 tbsp rye flour
   45ml/3 tbsp warm milk

1 For the starter, mix the rye flour and milk together in a small bowl. Cover with clear film (plastic wrap) and leave in a warm place for 1–2 days, or until it smells pleasantly sour.

2 To make the loaves, sift together the flour and salt into a large bowl. Next stir in the yeast. Make a well in the centre and add the butter, water and sourdough starter already prepared. Mix well until you have a soft dough.

COOK'S TIP
Sour rye bread keeps fresh for up to a week. This recipe can also be made without yeast, but it will be much denser.

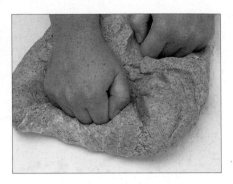

3 Turn out the dough on to a lightly floured surface and knead for 10 minutes, until smooth and elastic. Put in a clean bowl, cover with clear film and leave in a warm place to rise for 1 hour, or until doubled in size.

4 Knead for 1 minute, then divide the dough in half. Shape each piece into a round 15cm/6in across. Transfer to 2 greased baking sheets. Cover with oiled clear film and leave to rise for 30 minutes.

5 Preheat the oven to 200°C/400°F/ Gas 6. Brush the loaves with water, then sprinkle with caraway seeds or buckwheat, or dust with rye flour.

6 Bake for 35–40 minutes, or until the loaves are browned and sound hollow when tapped on the bottom. Cool on a wire rack.

VARIATION
If preferred, top the loaves with sesame or poppy seeds before baking.

Energy 1715Kcal/7278kJ; Protein 45.3g; Carbohydrate 368.3g, of which sugars 8.2g; Fat 16.8g, of which saturates 7.7g; Cholesterol 28mg; Calcium 691mg; Fibre 14.7g; Sodium 100mg.

YEMENITE SPONGE FLAT BREADS

KNOWN AS LAHUAH, THESE PANCAKE-LIKE BREADS ARE MADE FROM A BATTER. BUBBLY AND SOFT, THEY ARE SIMILAR TO A THIN CRUMPET AND ARE DELICIOUS DIPPED INTO THE ISRAELI HOT SAUCE ZCHUG.

SERVES FOUR

INGREDIENTS
  15ml/1 tbsp dried active yeast
  15ml/1 tbsp sugar
  500ml/17fl oz/2¼ cups
    lukewarm water
  350g/12oz/3 cups plain
    (all-purpose) flour
  5ml/1 tsp salt
  50g/2oz/¼ cup butter, melted, or
    60ml/4 tbsp vegetable oil

COOK'S TIP
Use two or three frying pans at the same time so that the flat breads are ready together and can be eaten piping hot.

1 In a bowl, dissolve the dried yeast and a pinch of the sugar in about 75ml/2½fl oz/⅓ cup of the water. Leave in a warm place for about 10 minutes, or until frothy.

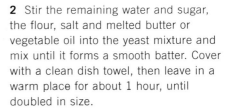

2 Stir the remaining water and sugar, the flour, salt and melted butter or vegetable oil into the yeast mixture and mix until it forms a smooth batter. Cover with a clean dish towel, then leave in a warm place for about 1 hour, until doubled in size.

3 Stir the thick, frothy batter and, if it seems too thick to ladle out, add a little extra water. Cover and leave in a warm place for about 1 hour.

4 Cook the flat breads in a non-stick frying pan. Ladle 45–60ml/3–4 tbsp of batter (or less for smaller breads) into the pan and cook over a low heat until the top is bubbling and the colour has changed. (Traditionally these breads are only cooked on one side but they can be turned over and the second side cooked for just a moment if you wish.)

5 Remove the cooked flat bread from the pan and keep warm in a clean dish towel. Repeat until you have used up all the remaining batter.

Energy 406Kcal/1714kJ; Protein 8.3g; Carbohydrate 72g, of which sugars 5.3g; Fat 11.4g, of which saturates 6.7g; Cholesterol 27mg; Calcium 127mg; Fibre 2.7g; Sodium 79mg.

HUNGARIAN SPLIT FARMHOUSE LOAF

TOPPED WITH FRAGRANT FENNEL SEEDS, THIS MOIST WHITE LOAF IS PARTICULARLY DELICIOUS WHEN IT IS SLATHERED WITH BUTTER AND JAM.

MAKES ONE LOAF

INGREDIENTS
   450g/1lb/4 cups unbleached white
      bread flour
   10ml/2 tsp salt
   2.5ml/½ tsp fennel seeds, crushed
   15ml/1 tbsp caster (superfine) sugar
   20g/¾oz fresh yeast
   275ml/9fl oz/1⅛ cups lukewarm
      water
   25g/1oz/2 tbsp butter, melted
For the topping
   1 egg white
   pinch of salt
   10ml/2 tsp fennel seeds,
      for sprinkling

1 Sift the white bread flour and salt together into a large bowl and stir in the crushed fennel seeds and caster sugar.

2 Cream the yeast with a little of the lukewarm water, then stir in the remaining water. Make a well at the centre of the flour and pour in the yeast, using your fingers to gradually combine with flour from the edge of the well until a batter forms. Leave in a warm place for 30 minutes, or until the sponge starts to bubble and rise.

3 Mix in the melted butter and any remaining flour so that a firm dough forms. Turn out on to a lightly floured surface and knead for 8–10 minutes until smooth and elastic. Place in a lightly oiled bowl, cover with lightly oiled clear film (plastic wrap) and leave to rise, in a warm place, for 45–60 minutes, or until doubled in bulk.

4 Turn out on to a lightly floured surface and knock back (punch down). Shape into an oval and place on a lightly oiled baking sheet. Cover with lightly oiled clear film and leave to rise, in a warm place, for 30–40 minutes, or until doubled in size.

5 Meanwhile, preheat the oven to 220°C/425°F/Gas 7. Mix the egg white and salt together, and brush this glaze over the loaf. Sprinkle with fennel seeds and then, using a sharp knife, slash along its length. Bake for 20 minutes, then reduce the oven temperature to 180°C/350°F/Gas 4 and bake for 10 minutes more, or until sounding hollow when tapped on the base. Transfer to a wire rack to cool.

Energy 1791Kcal/7591kJ; Protein 45.4g; Carbohydrate 365.5g, of which sugars 22.6g; Fat 26.4g, of which saturates 13.9g; Cholesterol 53mg; Calcium 644mg; Fibre 13.9g; Sodium 227mg.

RUSSIAN POTATO BREAD

THE RUSSIANS USE POTATOES FOR EVERYTHING — WHEN THEY'RE NOT EATING THEM, THEY'RE MAKING VODKA WITH THEM OR, AS IN THIS RECIPE, BAKING BREAD.

MAKES ONE LOAF

INGREDIENTS
  225g/8oz potatoes, peeled
    and diced
  7g packet easy-blend (rapid-rise)
    dried yeast
  350g/12oz/3 cups unbleached white
    bread flour
  115g/4oz/1 cup wholemeal
    (whole-wheat) bread flour,
    plus extra for sprinkling
  2.5ml/½ tsp caraway
    seeds, crushed
  10ml/2 tsp salt
  25g/1oz/2 tbsp butter

1 Lightly grease a baking sheet. Add the potatoes to a pan of boiling water and cook until tender. Drain and reserve 150ml/¼ pint/⅔ cup of the cooking water. Mash and press the potatoes through a sieve (strainer) and leave to cool.

2 Mix the yeast, bread flours, caraway seeds and salt together in a large bowl. Add the butter and rub in. Mix the reserved potato water and sieved potatoes together. Gradually work this mixture into the flour mixture to form a soft dough.

3 Turn out on to a lightly floured surface and knead for 8–10 minutes until smooth and elastic. Place in a lightly oiled bowl, cover with oiled clear film (plastic wrap) and leave in a warm place, for 1 hour, or until doubled in bulk.

4 Turn out on to a lightly floured surface, knock back (punch down) and knead gently. Shape into a plump oval loaf, about 18cm/7in long. Place on the prepared baking sheet and sprinkle the surface with a little wholemeal bread flour.

5 Cover the dough with lightly oiled clear film and leave to rise, in a warm place, for 30 minutes, or until doubled in size. Meanwhile, preheat the oven to 200°C/400°F/Gas 6.

6 Using a sharp knife, slash the top with 6–8 diagonal cuts to make a criss-cross effect. Bake for 30–35 minutes, or until golden and sounding hollow when tapped on the base. Transfer to a wire rack to cool.

VARIATION
Add dill seeds in place of the caraway seeds, and about 30ml/2 tbsp dried onions, or thinly-sliced spring onions (scallions). You can also experiment with different types of cheese.

Energy 1894Kcal/8026kJ; Protein 51.5g; Carbohydrate 381.8g, of which sugars 10.7g; Fat 28.3g, of which saturates 14.3g; Cholesterol 53mg; Calcium 553mg; Fibre 23.4g; Sodium 4120mg.

STOLLEN

THIS RICH, SWEET DESSERT BREAD WAS MADE DURING THE WINTERTIME FESTIVITIES IN GERMANY. JEWS ADOPTED IT FROM THEIR CHRISTIAN NEIGHBOURS.

SERVES TWELVE

INGREDIENTS
   375g/13oz/3 cups strong white
    bread flour
   pinch of salt
   50g/2oz/¼ cup caster
    (superfine) sugar
   10ml/2 tsp easy-blend (rapid-rise)
    dried yeast
   150ml/¼ pint/⅔ cup milk
   115g/4oz/½ cup butter
   1 egg, beaten
   175g/6oz/1 cup mixed dried fruit
   50g/2oz/¼ cup glacé (candied)
    cherries, quartered
   50g/2oz/½ cup blanched
    almonds, chopped
   finely grated rind of 1 lemon
   225g/8oz/1 cup marzipan
   icing (confectioners') sugar,
    for dredging

1 Sift the flour, salt and sugar. Stir in the yeast. Make a well in the centre. Over a low heat, gently melt the butter in the milk. Cool, then mix with the egg and pour into the centre of the sifted dry ingredients.

2 Turn out the dough on to a lightly floured surface and knead for 10 minutes, until smooth and elastic. Put in a clean bowl, cover with clear film (plastic wrap) and leave in a warm place to rise for about 1 hour, or until doubled in size.

3 On a lightly floured surface, knead in the dried fruit, cherries, almonds and lemon rind so that they are evenly dispersed through the dough.

4 Roll out the dough to a rectangle, about 25 x 20cm/10 x 8in in size. Roll the marzipan into a sausage shape, slightly shorter in length than the dough.

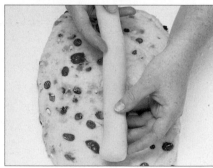

5 Place the marzipan in the centre of the dough and fold both sides across to enclose it completely. Place the folded dough seam side down on a greased baking sheet. Cover and leave in a warm place to rise for about 40 minutes, until doubled in size. Preheat the oven to 190°C/375°F/Gas 5.

6 Bake for 30–35 minutes, or until golden and hollow sounding when tapped on the underside. Leave to cool on a wire rack. Dust with icing sugar.

Energy 266Kcal/1128kJ; Protein 6.1g; Carbohydrate 50.5g, of which sugars 26.6g; Fat 5.8g, of which saturates 0.7g; Cholesterol 17mg; Calcium 97mg; Fibre 2g; Sodium 25mg.

RUSTIC MOROCCAN SEED BREAD

RUSTIC BREAD, ENRICHED WITH CORNMEAL AND A TRILOGY OF SEEDS — SUNFLOWER, PUMPKIN AND SESAME — IS DELICIOUS SERVED WITH A SPICY, SAUCY TAGINE OF THE REGION.

MAKES ONE LOAF

INGREDIENTS

275g/10oz/2½ cups unbleached
  white bread flour
50g/2oz/½ cup cornmeal
5ml/1 tsp salt
20g/¾oz fresh yeast
120ml/4fl oz/½ cup lukewarm water
120ml/4fl oz/½ cup lukewarm milk
15ml/1 tbsp pumpkin seeds
15ml/1 tbsp sesame seeds
30ml/2 tbsp sunflower seeds

1 Grease a baking sheet. Sift the flour, cornmeal and salt into a large bowl.

2 Cream the yeast with a little of the water in a jug (pitcher). Stir in the remainder of the water and the milk. Pour into the centre of the flour and mix to a fairly soft dough.

3 Turn out the dough on to a lightly floured surface and knead for about 5 minutes until smooth and elastic.

4 Place in a lightly oiled bowl, cover with lightly oiled clear film (plastic wrap) and leave in a warm place, for about 1 hour, or until doubled in bulk.

VARIATIONS
Incorporate all the seeds in the dough in step 5 and leave the top of the loaf plain. Alternatively, use sesame seeds instead of sunflower seeds for the topping and either incorporate the sunflower seeds in the loaf or leave them out.

5 Turn out the dough on to a lightly floured surface and knock back (punch down). Gently knead the pumpkin and sesame seeds into the dough. Shape into a round ball and flatten slightly.

6 Place on the prepared baking sheet, cover with lightly oiled clear film or slide into a large, lightly oiled plastic bag and leave to rise, in a warm place, for 45 minutes, or until doubled in bulk.

7 Meanwhile, preheat the oven to 200°C/400°F/Gas 6. Brush the top of the loaf with water and sprinkle evenly with the sunflower seeds. Bake the loaf for 30–35 minutes, or until it is golden and sounds hollow when tapped on the base. Transfer the loaf to a wire rack to cool.

Energy 1391Kcal/5869kJ; Protein 38.7g; Carbohydrate 250.6g, of which sugars 4.3g; Fat 31.3g, of which saturates 4.3g; Cholesterol 0mg; Calcium 688mg; Fibre 13.2g; Sodium 17mg.

SOUFGANIYOT

At Chanukkah time, Jews eat foods cooked in oil: latkes for Ashkenazim, syrup-dipped flat fritters for Tunisians, loukomades for Greek Jews. Israeli Jews eat soufganiyot, wonderful jam-filled doughnuts.

MAKES TEN TO TWELVE

INGREDIENTS
    225g/8oz/2 cups strong white bread
      flour, warmed
    2.5ml/½ tsp salt
    7g packet easy-blend (rapid-rise)
      dried yeast
    1 egg, beaten
    60–90ml/4–6 tbsp milk
    15ml/1 tbsp granulated sugar
    about 60ml/4 tbsp cherry jam
    oil, for deep-frying
    50g/2oz/¼ cup caster
      (superfine) sugar
    2.5ml/½ tsp cinnamon

1 Sift the flour into a bowl with the salt. Stir in the yeast. Make a well and add the egg, milk and sugar.

2 Mix together well to form a soft dough, adding a little more milk if necessary to make a smooth, but not sticky, dough.

3 Beat well, cover with clear film (plastic wrap) and leave to rise in a warm place for 1–1½ hours, or until the dough has doubled in size.

COOK'S TIP
Make sure that the warm place in which you set the dough to rise is not hot enough to kill the yeast.

4 Knead the dough on a lightly floured surface and divide it into 10–12 pieces.

5 Shape each into a round and put 5ml/1tsp of jam in the centre.

6 Dampen the edges of the dough with water, then draw them up to form a ball, pressing firmly to ensure that the jam will not escape during cooking. Place on a greased baking sheet and leave to rise for 15 minutes.

7 Heat the oil in a large pan to 180°C/350°F, or until a 2.5cm/1in piece of bread turns golden in 60–70 seconds. Fry the doughnuts fairly gently for 5–10 minutes, until golden brown. Drain well on kitchen paper.

8 Mix the caster sugar and cinnamon together on a plate or in a plastic bag and use to coat the doughnuts liberally.

COOK'S TIP
These doughnuts should really be eaten on the day of preparation. Even if stored overnight in an airtight container they will have lost much of their moistness by the following day.

VARIATION
You can substitute the traditional cherry jam filling for a number of different-flavoured fruit jams, such as apricot, strawberry and raspberry.

Energy 190Kcal/796kJ; Protein 2.5g; Carbohydrate 23.9g, of which sugars 9.6g; Fat 10g, of which saturates 1.3g; Cholesterol 16mg; Calcium 38mg; Fibre 0.6g; Sodium 10mg.

LEPESHKI

THE SWEET SMELL OF VANILLA AND ALMOND ANNOUNCES THESE TASTY, CRISP COOKIES FROM RUSSIA.

MAKES TWENTY-FOUR

INGREDIENTS
  225g/8oz/2 cups self-raising
    (self-rising) flour
  pinch of salt
  90g/3½oz/½ cup caster
    (superfine) sugar
  1 egg, separated
  120ml/4fl oz/½ cup sour cream
  2.5ml/½ tsp each vanilla extract
    and almond extract
  15ml/1 tbsp milk
  50g/2oz/½ cup flaked
    (sliced) almonds

1 Preheat the oven to 200°C/400°F/ Gas 6. Sift the flour, salt and sugar into a mixing bowl and make a well in the centre.

2 Reserve 10ml/2 tsp of the egg white. Mix the remainder with the egg yolk, sour cream, vanilla and almond extract and milk. Add to the dry ingredients and mix to form a soft dough.

3 Roll out the dough on a lightly floured surface until it is about 8mm/ ⅓in thick, then stamp it out into rounds using a 7.5cm/3in cutter.

COOK'S TIP
These biscuits will store for up to a week but are best eaten fresh.

4 Transfer the circles to lightly oiled baking sheets. Brush with the reserved egg white and sprinkle with the flaked almonds.

5 Bake for 10 minutes, until light golden brown. Transfer to a wire rack and allow to cool.

Energy 73Kcal/308kJ; Protein 1.8g; Carbohydrate 11.6g, of which sugars 4.4g; Fat 2.5g, of which saturates 0.8g; Cholesterol 11mg; Calcium 27mg; Fibre 0.4g; Sodium 6mg.

POPPY SEED ROLL

THIS DELICIOUS ASHKENAZIC CAKE CONSISTS OF POPPY SEED AND DRIED FRUIT PASTE, WRAPPED IN A SWEET YEAST DOUGH. ENJOY WITH COFFEE, TEA, OR A GLASS OF SCHNAPPS.

SERVES TWELVE

INGREDIENTS
  450g/1lb/4 cups plain
    (all-purpose) flour
  pinch of salt
  30ml/2 tbsp caster
    (superfine) sugar
  10ml/2 tsp easy-blend (rapid-rise)
    dried yeast
  175ml/6fl oz/¾ cup milk
  finely grated rind of 1 lemon
  50g/2oz/4 tbsp butter
For the filling and glaze
  50g/2oz/4 tbsp butter
  115g/4oz/⅔ cup poppy seeds
  50ml/2fl oz/¼ cup set honey
  65g/2½oz/½ cup raisins
  65g/2½oz/scant ½ cup finely
    chopped candied orange peel
  50g/2oz/½ cup ground almonds
  1 egg yolk
  50g/2oz/¼ cup caster
    (superfine) sugar
  15ml/1 tbsp milk
  60ml/4 tbsp apricot jam
  15ml/1 tbsp lemon juice
  15ml/1 tbsp rum or brandy
  25g/1oz/¼ cup toasted
    flaked (sliced) almonds

1 Sift the flour, salt and sugar into a bowl. Stir in the easy-blend dried yeast. Make a well in the centre.

2 Heat the milk and lemon rind in a pan with the butter, until melted. Cool a little, then add to the dry ingredients and mix to a dough.

3 Knead the dough on a lightly floured surface for 10 minutes, until smooth and elastic. Put in a clean bowl, cover and leave in a warm place to rise for 45–50 minutes, or until doubled in size.

COOK'S TIP
The gritty texture of the poppy seeds used in this recipe helps to keep the cake moist, so use liberally.

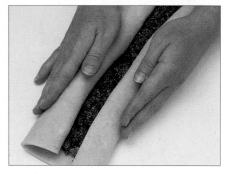

4 For the filling, melt the butter in a pan. Reserve 15ml/1 tbsp poppy seeds, then process the rest and add to the pan with the honey, raisins and peel. Cook gently for 5 minutes. Stir in the ground almonds and leave to cool.

5 Whisk the egg yolk and sugar together in a bowl until pale, then fold into the poppy seed mixture. Roll out the dough on a lightly floured surface into a rectangle 30 x 35cm/12 x 14in. Spread the filling to within 2.5cm/1in of the edges.

6 Roll both ends towards the centre. Cover with oiled clear film (plastic wrap) and leave to rise for 30 minutes. Preheat the oven to 190°C/375°F/Gas 5.

7 Brush with the milk, then sprinkle with the reserved poppy seeds. Bake for 30 minutes, until golden brown.

8 Heat the jam and lemon juice gently until bubbling. Strain, then stir in the rum or brandy. Brush over the roll while still warm and sprinkle the almonds on top.

Energy 362Kcal/1518kJ; Protein 7.6g; Carbohydrate 46.4g, of which sugars 17.6g; Fat 17.2g, of which saturates 5.8g; Cholesterol 36mg; Calcium 165mg; Fibre 2.7g; Sodium 82mg.

WALNUT AND RAISIN SQUARES

THE EASTERN EUROPEAN JEWISH KITCHEN WAS FULL OF FRAGRANT SWEET THINGS, SUCH AS THESE CZECH WALNUT SQUARES. THIS LIGHT AND DELICIOUS CZECH RECIPE IS GOOD WITH COFFEE IN THE MORNING OR CAN BE SERVED AS A DESSERT.

MAKES ABOUT TWENTY-FOUR

INGREDIENTS
225g/8oz/1 cup unsalted
  (sweet) butter
225g/8oz/generous 1 cup caster
  (superfine) sugar
3 egg yolks
175g/6oz/1½ cups plain
  (all-purpose) flour, sifted
4 eggs, beaten
175g/6oz/1½ cups ground walnuts
20g/¾oz/scant ⅓ cup day-old
  white breadcrumbs
cocoa powder (unsweetened),
  for sprinkling
For the topping
3 egg whites
150g/5oz/¾ cup caster
  (superfine) sugar
115g/4oz/1 cup ground walnuts
75g/3oz/½ cup raisins, chopped
25g/1oz/¼ cup cocoa powder, sifted

1 Preheat the oven to 150°C/300°F/
Gas 2. Grease and line a 28 x 18 x 4cm/
11 x 7 x 1½in Swiss roll tin (jelly roll pan).

2 Cream the butter and sugar together
until pale and fluffy, then beat in the
egg yolks.

3 Fold half the flour into the mixture,
then beat in the whole eggs before
stirring in the remaining flour and nuts.

4 Sprinkle the prepared Swiss roll tin
with the breadcrumbs before spooning
in the walnut mixture. Level the mixture
with a round-bladed knife. Bake for
30–35 minutes or until cooked and pale
golden brown.

5 Meanwhile, make the topping. Whisk
the egg whites in a grease-free bowl
until stiff. Slowly whisk in the sugar until
glossy, before folding in the walnuts,
raisins and cocoa powder.

6 Spread the topping mixture over the
cooked base and cook for a further
15 minutes. Leave to cool in the tin.
When cold, peel away the lining paper.
Cut into squares or fingers, and sprinkle
with cocoa powder.

COOK'S TIP
Do not be tempted to skip lining the
Swiss roll tin. It is an essential step if
the base is not to stick.

Energy 239Kcal/993kJ; Protein 3g; Carbohydrate 19.7g, of which sugars 18.9g; Fat 17g, of which saturates 5.9g; Cholesterol 46mg; Calcium 28mg; Fibre 0.6g; Sodium 85mg.

LEBKUCHEN

THIS IS A SPICY TREAT, SCENTED WITH CINNAMON, CLOVES, NUTMEG AND CARDAMOM AND TOPPED WITH A RUM-FLAVOURED ICING. IT MAKES ANY TEA-TIME A FESTIVAL, ESPECIALLY AT SUKKOT, BECAUSE OF THE FRUIT AND NUTS.

MAKES TWENTY

INGREDIENTS
115g/4oz/1 cup blanched almonds, finely chopped
50g/2oz/⅓ cup candied orange peel, finely chopped
finely grated rind of ½ lemon
3 cardamom pods
5ml/1 tsp cinnamon
1.5ml/¼ tsp nutmeg
1.5ml/¼ tsp ground cloves
2 eggs
115g/4oz/scant ¾ cup caster (superfine) sugar
150g/5oz/1¼ cups plain (all-purpose) flour
2.5ml/½ tsp baking powder
rice paper (optional)
For the icing
½ egg white
75g/3oz/¾ cup icing (confectioners') sugar, sifted
5ml/1 tsp white rum

1 Preheat the oven to 180°C/350°F/ Gas 4. Set aside some of the almonds for sprinkling and put the remainder in a bowl with the candied orange peel and lemon rind.

2 Remove the black seeds from the cardamom pods and crush using a mortar and pestle. Add to the bowl with the cinnamon, nutmeg and cloves and mix well.

3 Whisk the eggs and sugar in a mixing bowl until thick and foamy. Sift in the flour and baking powder and gently fold into the eggs before adding to the nut and spice mixture.

4 Spoon dessertspoons of the mixture on to sheets of rice paper, if using, or baking parchment placed on baking sheets, allowing room for the mixture to spread. Sprinkle over the reserved almonds.

5 Bake for 20 minutes, until golden. Allow to cool for a few minutes, then break off the surplus rice paper or remove the biscuits from the baking parchment and cool on a wire rack.

6 Put the egg white for the icing in a bowl and lightly whisk with a fork. Stir in a little of the icing sugar at a time, then add the rum. Drizzle over the lebkuchen and leave to set. Keep in an airtight container for 2 weeks before serving.

Energy 105Kcal/444kJ; Protein 2.4g; Carbohydrate 16.3g, of which sugars 11.7g; Fat 3.9g, of which saturates 0.4g; Cholesterol 19mg; Calcium 33mg; Fibre 0.7g; Sodium 16mg.

MAALI

MAMALIGA, OR CORNMEAL, IS ONE OF THE BASIC STAPLE INGREDIENTS OF THE BALKANS — IT EVEN FEATURES IN OLD YIDDISH FOLK SONGS ABOUT ROMANIA! CHEESE CAN BE ADDED TO THIS LIGHT GOLDEN BREAD TO GIVE IT A SAVOURY TASTE.

MAKES ONE LOAF OR NINE SMALL BUNS

INGREDIENTS
    75g/3oz/⅔ cup self-raising
      (self-rising) flour
    7.5ml/1½ tsp baking powder
    75g/3oz/¾ cup cornmeal
    2.5ml/½ tsp salt
    1 egg
    150ml/¼ pint/⅔ cup milk
    25g/1oz/¼ cup Cheddar cheese,
      finely grated (optional)

1 Preheat the oven to 200°C/400°F/ Gas 6. Place the self-raising flour, baking powder, cornmeal and salt into a large mixing bowl. Mix well, then make a well in the centre.

2 Add the egg, milk and Cheddar cheese, if using. Mix well with a wooden spoon.

COOK'S TIP
Cook this loaf immediately after making, otherwise the raising agent will be less effective and the loaf will not be so light.

3 Pour the mixture into a greased 15cm/6in round cake tin (pan) or a 9-hole bun tin.

4 Bake for 20–25 minutes or until well risen, golden and firm to the touch. Cool briefly on a wire rack. Serve warm in thick slices.

Energy 74Kcal/312kJ; Protein 2.8g; Carbohydrate 13.2g, of which sugars 0.9g; Fat 1.3g, of which saturates 0.4g; Cholesterol 22mg; Calcium 53mg; Fibre 0.4g; Sodium 45mg.

GEORGIAN KHATCHAPURI

THESE SAVOURY BUNS ARE SOLD FROM STREET STALLS AS WARM SNACKS. WHEN THE PASTRY BAKES, THE CHEESE FILLING MELTS. THEY ARE EXCELLENT SERVED WITH A PASTE OF FRESH HERBS, INCLUDING MINT, TARRAGON, DILL AND SPRING ONIONS.

3 Meanwhile, put the cheeses in a bowl and stir in the egg and softened butter for the filling. Season with plenty of salt and pepper.

4 Turn the dough out on to a lightly floured surface and knead for 2–3 minutes. Divide into four equal pieces and roll each out into a 20cm/8in circle.

MAKES FOUR BUNS

INGREDIENTS
   225g/8oz/2 cups unbleached white
     bread flour
   5ml/1 tsp salt
   15g/½oz fresh yeast
   150ml/¼ pint/⅔ cup lukewarm milk
   25g/1oz/2 tbsp butter, softened
For the filling
   225g/8oz/2 cups grated mature (sharp)
     Cheddar cheese
   225g/8oz Munster or Taleggio cheese,
     cut into small cubes
   1 egg, lightly beaten
   15ml/1 tbsp butter, softened
   salt and ground black pepper
For the glaze
   1 egg yolk
   15ml/1 tbsp water

VARIATIONS
• Use Red Leicester or Parmesan in place of the Cheddar.
• Make one large loaf instead of the buns. Bake for 50–55 minutes.

1 Lightly grease a Yorkshire pudding tin (muffin pan) with four 10cm/4in holes. Sift the flour and salt into a large bowl. Cream the yeast with the milk, add to the flour and mix to a dough. Knead in the butter, then knead on a lightly floured surface until smooth and elastic.

2 Place in a lightly oiled bowl, cover with lightly oiled clear film (plastic wrap) and leave to rise, in a warm place, for 1–1½ hours, or until doubled in size.

5 Place one dough circle in one hole of the Yorkshire pudding tin and fill with a quarter of the cheese filling. Gather the overhanging dough into the centre and twist to form a topknot. Repeat with the remaining dough and filling. Cover with lightly oiled clear film and leave to rise, in a warm place, for 20–30 minutes.

6 Meanwhile, preheat the oven to 180°C/350°F/Gas 4. Mix the egg yolk and water, and brush over the dough. Bake for 25–30 minutes, or until light golden. Cool for 2–3 minutes in the tin, then turn out on to a wire rack. Serve warm.

Energy 837Kcal/3491kJ; Protein 40.7g; Carbohydrate 45.7g, of which sugars 2.8g; Fat 53.2g, of which saturates 33.6g; Cholesterol 243mg; Calcium 1062mg; Fibre 1.8g; Sodium 1002mg.

PRETZELS

Pretzels or brezeln, as they are known in Germany, are said to be derived from the Latin bracellae or arms, referring to the crossed "arms" of dough inside the oval shape. The best pretzels are sold on the streets of New York, warm and chewy, covered with grains of salt and smeared with a golden stripe of mustard.

MAKES TWELVE

INGREDIENTS
For the yeast sponge
  7g/¼oz fresh yeast
  75ml/5 tbsp water
  15ml/1 tbsp unbleached plain
  (all-purpose) flour
For the dough
  7g/¼oz fresh yeast
  150ml/¼ pint/⅔ cup lukewarm water
  75ml/5 tbsp lukewarm milk
  400g/14oz/3½ cups unbleached
  white bread flour
  7.5ml/1½ tsp salt
  25g/1oz/2 tbsp butter, melted
For the topping
  1 egg yolk
  15ml/1 tbsp milk
  sea salt and caraway seeds
  for sprinkling
  mustard, to serve

1 Lightly flour a baking sheet. Also grease two baking sheets. Cream the yeast for the yeast sponge with the water, then mix in the flour, cover with clear film (plastic wrap) and leave to stand at room temperature for 2 hours.

2 Mix the yeast for the dough with the water until dissolved, then gradually stir in the milk.

3 Sift 350g/12oz/3 cups of the flour and the salt into a large bowl. Add the yeast sponge mixture and the butter; mix for 3–4 minutes. Turn out on to a lightly floured surface and knead in the remaining flour to make a medium firm dough. Place in a lightly oiled bowl, cover with lightly oiled clear film and leave to rise, in a warm place, for 30 minutes, or until almost doubled in bulk.

4 Turn out on to a lightly floured surface and knock back (punch down) the dough. Knead into a ball, return to the bowl, re-cover and leave to rise for at least 30 minutes.

5 Turn out the dough on to a lightly floured surface. Divide the dough into 12 equal pieces and form into balls. Take one ball of dough and cover the remainder with a dish towel. Roll into a thin stick 46cm/18in long and about 1cm/½in thick in the middle and thinner at the ends. Bend each end of the dough stick into a horseshoe. Cross over and place the ends on top of the thick part of the pretzel. Set aside and repeat this action with the remaining dough balls.

6 Place on the floured baking sheet to rest for 10 minutes. Meanwhile, preheat the oven to 190°C/375°F/Gas 5. Bring a large pan of water to the boil, then reduce to a simmer. Add the pretzels to the simmering water in batches, about 2–3 at a time and poach for about 1 minute. Drain the pretzels on a dish towel and place on the greased baking sheets, spaced well apart.

7 Mix the egg yolk and milk together and brush this glaze over the pretzels. Sprinkle with sea salt or caraway seeds and bake the pretzels for 25 minutes, or until they are deep golden. Transfer to a wire rack to cool. Serve piled high on a plate with a little pot of mild mustard, or mustard mayonnaise, as a dip.

Energy 142Kcal/601kJ; Protein 3.8g; Carbohydrate 27.2g, of which sugars 0.9g; Fat 2.8g, of which saturates 1.4g; Cholesterol 22mg; Calcium 60mg; Fibre 1.1g; Sodium 263mg.

CRISP SPICED BREADSTICKS

CRISP BREADSTICKS ARE EATEN THROUGHOUT THE MIDDLE EAST BY ALL RELIGIONS. THEY ARE MENTIONED IN BOTH THE TALMUD AND IN MEDIEVAL ARAB TEXTS. IT IS POSSIBLE THAT THE SEPHARDIC SPANISH JEWS HELPED TO SPREAD THEM THROUGHOUT EUROPE. THOUGH MORE TRADITIONALLY MADE IN BRACELET-LIKE CIRCLES, THEY LOOK FETCHING SERVED LIKE THIS, IN LONG CRISP FINGERS.

MAKES TWENTY

INGREDIENTS
  225g/8oz/2 cups unbleached white
    bread flour
  7.5ml/1½ tsp salt
  2.5ml/½ tsp ground cumin
  1.5ml/¼ tsp ground coriander
  15ml/3 tsp easy-blend (rapid-rise)
    dried yeast
  135ml/4½fl oz/scant ⅔ cup
    lukewarm water
  30ml/2 tbsp olive oil, plus extra
    for brushing
  poppy seeds or coarse sea salt,
    for coating

1 Combine the flour, salt, cumin, coriander and easy-blend dried yeast in a large bowl.

2 In a bowl, cream the yeast with the water and pour into the centre of the flour, gradually adding the olive oil to form a soft dough.

3 Turn out on to a lightly floured surface and knead until smooth and elastic. This should take around 10 minutes. Lightly oil two baking sheets.

4 Roll the dough into a rectangle about 15 x 20cm/6 x 8in. Brush with olive oil, cover with lightly oiled clear film (plastic wrap) and leave to rise, in a warm place until doubled in bulk.

5 Preheat the oven to 200°C/400°F/ Gas 6. Spread out the sesame seeds. Cut the dough into two 7.5 x 10cm/3 x 4in rectangles. Then cut each rectangle into ten 7.5/3in strips. Stretch each strip gently until it is about 30cm/12in in length.

6 Roll the breadsticks in poppy seeds or sea salt. Space well apart on the baking sheets. Brush lightly with olive oil, cover with clear film (plastic wrap) and leave in a warm place for 10–15 minutes. Bake for 15–20 minutes, or until golden, turning once. Transfer to a wire rack to cool.

Energy 42kcal/177kJ; Protein 1g; Carbohydrate 5.8g, of which sugars 0.1g; Fat 1.8g, of which saturates 0.3g; Cholesterol 0mg; Calcium 22mg; Fibre 0.4g; Sodium 92mg.

Desserts, Pastries Cakes and Sweetmeats

No Bar or Bat Mitzvah kiddush would be complete without a table of sweetmeats, whether the cookies of the Ashkenazim or the syrupy, exotic cakes of the Sephardim. Many cakes are made without flour, just with nut meal or matzo meal, and risen with beaten egg whites, to eat during the festival of Pesach.

TROPICAL-SCENTED RED AND ORANGE FRUIT SALAD

A FRAGRANT FRUIT SALAD, PREPARED WITH EXOTIC FRUITS, IS A WONDERFUL WAY TO END A FESTIVE MEAL. FRESH FRUIT IS HELD IN HIGH REGARD IN JEWISH CUISINE FOR ITS HEALTH-GIVING PROPERTIES.

SERVES FOUR TO SIX

INGREDIENTS
350–400g/12–14oz/3–3½ cups
  strawberries, hulled and halved
3 oranges, peeled and segmented
3 small blood oranges, peeled
  and segmented
1–2 passion fruit
120ml/4fl oz/½ cup dry white wine
sugar, to taste

VARIATION
Pear, kiwi fruit and banana also work
well, and blood oranges add colour.

1 Put the strawberries and oranges into a serving bowl. Halve the passion fruit and spoon the flesh into the bowl.

2 Pour the wine over the fruit and add sugar to taste. Toss gently and then chill until ready to serve.

Energy 80Kcal/339kJ; Protein 2.1g; Carbohydrate 15.3g, of which sugars 15.3g; Fat 0.2g, of which saturates 0g; Cholesterol 0mg; Calcium 74mg; Fibre 3.1g; Sodium 12mg.

ICED MELON SOUP WITH MELON AND MINT SORBET

THE HOT CLIMATE OF ISRAEL MAKES IT PERFECT FOR GROWING MELONS. THIS SOUP IS TYPICAL OF MODERN ISRAELI CUISINE. IT IS LIGHT AND FULL OF NATURAL, HOME-GROWN FLAVOURS.

SERVES SIX TO EIGHT

INGREDIENTS
  2.25kg/5–5¼lb very ripe melon
  45ml/3 tbsp orange juice or sweet
    white wine
  30ml/2 tbsp lemon juice
  mint leaves, to garnish
For the melon and mint sorbet
  25g/1oz/2 tbsp granulated sugar
  120ml/4fl oz/½ cup water
  2.25kg/5–5¼lb very ripe melon
  juice of 2 limes
  30ml/2 tbsp fresh mint leaves

1 Put the sugar and water in a pan and heat gently until the sugar dissolves. Bring to the boil and simmer for 4–5 minutes, then remove from the heat and leave to cool.

2 Halve the melon. Scrape out the seeds, then cut it into large wedges and scoop out the flesh. Weigh about 1.5kg/3–3½lb melon. Reserve the rest.

3 Process the melon in a food processor or blender with the cooled syrup and lime juice. Chop the mint leaves into small pieces and stir in.

4 Pour the mixture into an ice-cream maker. Churn, according to the manufacturer's instructions, or until the sorbet is smooth and firm. Alternatively, pour the mixture into a suitable container and freeze until icy around the edges. Transfer to a food processor or blender and process until smooth. Repeat the freezing and processing two or three times or until smooth and holding its shape, then freeze until firm.

5 To make the chilled melon soup, prepare the remaining melon as in step 2 and process it in a food processor or blender. Pour the purée into a bowl and stir in the orange juice and the lemon juice. Place the soup in a refrigerator and chill for 30–40 minutes.

6 Ladle the soup into bowls or tall glasses and add a large scoop of the sorbet to float at the surface of each one. Garnish with the mint leaves. Set the bowls or glasses on ice if possible and serve immediately.

COOK'S TIP
• Do not chill the soup in the refrigerator for longer than specified as its flavour will be dulled if it becomes too cold.
• You can use a combination of different melons for the soup, so long as they match the required total weight. Try Chanterais and Ogen or cantaloupe and Galia.

Energy 152Kcal/646kJ; Protein 3g; Carbohydrate 35.7g, of which sugars 35.5g; Fat 0.6g, of which saturates 0g; Cholesterol 0mg; Calcium 84mg; Fibre 2.3g; Sodium 176mg.

DRIED FRUIT COMPOTE

DRIED FRUIT, RICH WITH CONCENTRATED FLAVOUR, IS DELICIOUS AND REFRESHING WHEN STEEPED IN A COMPOTE. THIS IS ESPECIALLY WONDERFUL IN WINTER WHEN FRESH FRUIT IS SCARCE.

SERVES FOUR

INGREDIENTS
  225g/8oz/1⅓ cups mixed
    dried fruit
  75g/3oz/⅔ cup dried cherries
  75g/3oz/⅔ cup sultanas
    (golden raisins)
  10 dried prunes
  10 dried apricots
  hot, freshly brewed fragrant tea,
    such as Earl Grey or jasmine,
    to cover
  15–30ml/1–2 tbsp sugar
  ¼ lemon, sliced
  60ml/4 tbsp brandy

1 Put the dried fruits in a bowl and pour over the hot tea. Add sugar to taste and the lemon slices. Cover with a plate, set aside and leave to cool to room temperature.

2 When the fruits have cooled sufficiently, chill in the refrigerator for at least 2 hours and preferably overnight. Just before serving, pour in the brandy and stir well.

Energy 327Kcal/1390kJ; Protein 2.6g; Carbohydrate 74.6g, of which sugars 74.6g; Fat 0.4g, of which saturates 0g; Cholesterol 0mg; Calcium 77mg; Fibre 3g; Sodium 39mg.

POMERANTZEN

THIS CANDIED CITRUS PEEL IS A SPECIALITY OF JEWS WHOSE ORIGINS LIE IN GERMANY. IT IS EASY TO MAKE, AND APPEALS TO THE FRUGAL, AS THE PEEL WOULD USUALLY BE THROWN AWAY RATHER THAN BEING TRANSFORMED INTO SUCH A TREAT. POMERANTZEN ARE DELICIOUS CHOPPED UP AND ADDED TO CAKES AND BREADS, OR DIPPED INTO DARK CHOCOLATE.

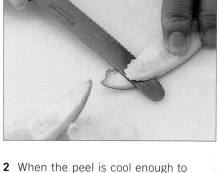

2 When the peel is cool enough to handle, gently scrape off as much of the white pith as possible. Cut the peel lengthways into narrow strips.

3 Put the sugar, water and golden syrup in a pan and bring to the boil. When clear, add the peel. Simmer for 1 hour until translucent, taking care that it does not burn.

SERVES FOUR TO SIX

INGREDIENTS
   3 grapefruit and 5–6 oranges or
    6–8 lemons, unwaxed
   300g/11oz/1¾ cups sugar
   300ml/½ pint/1¼ cups water
   30ml/2 tbsp golden (light corn) syrup
   caster (superfine) sugar (optional)

4 Stand a rack over a baking sheet. Remove the peel from the pan and arrange the slices on the rack. Leave to dry for 2–3 hours, then put in a plastic container or jar, cover and store in the refrigerator until required.

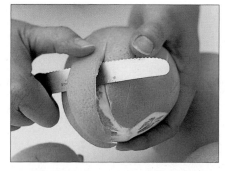

5 If serving as a sweetmeat, cover a large flat plate with caster (superfine) sugar and toss the drained peel slices in the sugar. Leave to dry for 1 hour. Sprinkle with sugar again and place in a covered container or jar. Store in a cool, dry place for up to 2 weeks or in the refrigerator for up to 2 months.

COOK'S TIP
If you find it too much trouble to remove the pith from the fruit, omit this step as once the pith has been simmered, its bitterness fades.

1 Score the fruit, to remove the peel neatly, then peel. Put the peel in a pan, fill with cold water and bring to the boil. Simmer for 20 minutes, then drain.

Energy 116Kcal/492kJ; Protein 0.2g; Carbohydrate 29.6g, of which sugars 29.6g; Fat 0.5g, of which saturates 0g; Cholesterol 0mg; Calcium 65mg; Fibre 2.4g; Sodium 140mg.

HAMANTASHEN

THESE TRIANGULAR-SHAPED TREATS ARE EATEN AT THE FESTIVAL OF PURIM, WHICH CELEBRATES THE STORY OF ESTHER, MORDECAI AND HAMAN. THEIR SHAPE REPRESENTS THE HAT OF HAMAN, WHOSE PLOT TO EXTERMINATE ALL THE JEWS OF PERSIA WAS FOILED. THESE ASHKENAZIC PASTRIES ORIGINATED IN THE 11TH CENTURY IN EASTERN FRANCE (THE HOME OF THE GREAT COMMENTATOR RASHI). THEY CAN BE MADE WITH A COOKIE DOUGH OR A YEAST DOUGH AND WITH VARIOUS SWEET FILLINGS, INCLUDING POPPY SEED, PRUNE, APRICOT, FIG OR ALMOND.

MAKES ABOUT TWENTY-FOUR

INGREDIENTS
  115g/4oz/½ cup unsalted (sweet)
    butter, at room temperature
  250g/9oz/1¼ cups sugar
  30ml/2 tbsp milk
  1 egg, beaten
  5ml/1 tsp vanilla extract or
    almond extract
  pinch of salt
  200–250g/7–9oz/1½–2¼ cups plain
    (all-purpose) flour
  icing (confectioners') sugar, for
    dusting (optional)
For the apricot filling
  250g/9oz/generous 1 cup dried
    apricots
  1 cinnamon stick
  45ml/3 tbsp sugar
For the poppy seed filling
  130g/4½oz/1 cup poppy seeds,
    coarsely ground
  120ml/4fl oz/½ cup milk
  75g/3oz/½ cup sultanas (golden
    raisins), roughly chopped
  45–60ml/3–4 tbsp sugar
  30ml/2 tbsp golden (light corn) syrup
  5–10ml/1–2 tsp grated lemon rind
  5ml/1 tsp vanilla extract
For the prune filling
  250g/9oz/generous 1 cup pitted
    ready-to-eat prunes
  hot, freshly brewed tea or water,
    to cover
  60ml/4 tbsp plum jam

1 In a large bowl, cream the butter and sugar until pale and fluffy.

2 In a separate bowl mix together the milk, egg, vanilla or almond extract and salt. Sift the flour into a third bowl.

3 Beat the creamed butter mixture with one-third of the flour, then gradually add the remaining flour, in three batches, alternating with the milk mixture. The dough should be the consistency of a loose shortbread dough. If it is too stiff, add a little extra milk. Cover and chill for at least 1 hour.

4 To make the apricot filling, put the dried apricots, cinnamon stick and sugar in a pan and add enough water to cover. Heat gently, then simmer for 15 minutes, or until the apricots are tender and most of the liquid has evaporated. Remove the cinnamon stick, then process the apricots in a food processor or blender with a little of the cooking liquid until they form a consistency like thick jam.

5 To make the poppy seed filling, put all the ingredients, except the vanilla extract, in a pan and simmer for 5–10 minutes or until the mixture has thickened and most of the milk has been absorbed. Stir in the vanilla extract.

6 To make the prune filling, put the prunes in a bowl and add enough hot tea or water to cover. Cover the bowl, then set aside for about 30 minutes, or until the prunes have absorbed the liquid. Drain, then process in a food processor or blender with the jam.

7 To make the hamantashen, preheat the oven to 180°C/350°F/Gas 4. On a lightly floured surface, roll out the dough to a thickness of about 3–5mm/ ⅛–¼in, then cut into rounds about 7.5cm/3in in diameter using a pastry (cookie) cutter.

8 Place 15–30ml/1–2 tbsp of filling in the centre of each round, then pinch the pastry together to form three corners, leaving a little of the filling showing in the middle of the pastry.

9 Place the pastries on a baking sheet and bake for about 15 minutes, or until pale golden. Serve warm or cold, dusted with icing sugar, if you like.

COOK'S TIPS
• Every Jewish family has its own favourite filling for this hefty little pastry-cake. Experiment until you find yours. The size of the hamantashen can also vary, from small and dainty to the size of a hand – it just depends on your traditions and preference.
• A chocolate cookie-style dough is easily prepared by replacing about 25g/1oz/ ¼ cup of the flour with the same amount of unsweetened cocoa powder. Add 50g/2oz/½ cup chocolate chips to the dough and mix in thoroughly. Apricot works well as a filling for this.

Energy 202Kcal/852kJ; Protein 3.1g; Carbohydrate 32.3g, of which sugars 25.9g; Fat 7.6g, of which saturates 3.1g; Cholesterol 19mg; Calcium 78mg; Fibre 2g; Sodium 44mg.

APRICOT AND ALMOND "FUDGE"

THIS IS A WONDERFUL EASTERN EUROPEAN SWEET TO MAKE IN THE WINTER WHEN FRESH FRUIT IS SCARCE. DRIED APRICOTS HAVE AN EVEN STRONGER, MORE "APRICOT" FLAVOUR THAN THE FRESH AND ARE DELICIOUS EATEN WITH ALMONDS.

SERVES SIX

INGREDIENTS

225g/8oz/1 cup ready-to-eat
 dried apricots, chopped
45ml/3 tbsp water
50g/2oz/¼ cup caster
 (superfine) sugar
50g/2oz/½ cup chopped almonds
50g/2oz/⅓ cup chopped candied
 orange peel
icing (confectioners') sugar,
 for dusting
whipped cream, to serve
ground cinnamon, to decorate

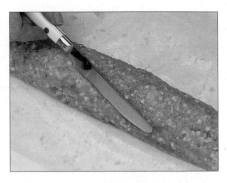

1 Put the apricots and water in a heavy pan. Cover and simmer, stirring, for about 20 minutes, until a thick paste has formed.

2 Stir in the caster sugar and simmer, stirring, for a further 10 minutes until quite dry. Remove from the heat and stir in the almonds and chopped orange peel. Allow to cool for around 10–15 minutes until the mixture is partially set. Scoop out with a wooden spoon and place on a piece of baking parchment, well dusted with icing sugar.

3 Using a knife, flatten and spread the mixture over the parchment, then push the edges inwards so that it forms a sausage of about 5cm/2in thickness.

4 Leave to dry in a cool place for at least 3 hours. Cut into slices and serve with whipped cream and sprinkled with a little cinnamon.

Energy 162Kcal/686kJ; Protein 3.3g; Carbohydrate 27.9g, of which sugars 27.7g; Fat 5g, of which saturates 0.4g; Cholesterol 0mg; Calcium 63mg; Fibre 3.4g; Sodium 30mg.

STEAMED BLACK BREAD SLICES TOPPED WITH CHERRY JAM

This sweet, spiced, steamed bread is traditionally eaten with a topping of sour cream and cherry jam. It is hearty winter fare, popular in many Eastern European countries.

MAKES TWO LOAVES

INGREDIENTS

50g/2oz/½ cup rye flour
40g/1½oz/⅓ cup plain
   (all-purpose) flour
4ml/¾ tsp baking powder
2.5ml/½ tsp salt
1.5ml/¼ tsp cinnamon
1.5ml/¼ tsp nutmeg
50g/2oz/⅓ cup fine semolina
125g/4oz/½ cup sugar
60ml/4 tbsp black treacle (molasses)
200ml/7fl oz/scant 1 cup
   cultured buttermilk
cherry jam, sour cream and a little
   ground allspice, to serve

1 Grease and line 2 x 400g/14oz fruit cans. Sift the flours, baking powder, salt and spices into a large bowl. Stir in the semolina and sugar.

2 Add the black treacle and buttermilk and mix thoroughly.

3 Divide the mixture equally between the two cans, then cover each with a double layer of greased, pleated foil. Secure the foil around the rim of each can with a rubber band.

COOK'S TIP
• If you cannot get hold of buttermilk, it is acceptable to use ordinary milk instead. Sour it before you use it with 5ml/1 tsp lemon juice.
• Check the water level occasionally when steaming the breads to make sure that the pan does not boil dry.

4 Place the cans on a trivet in a large pan and pour in enough hot water to come halfway up the sides. Cover tightly and steam for 2 hours.

5 Carefully remove the cans from the pan. Turn the bread out on to a wire rack and cool completely. Wrap in foil and use within one week.

6 When ready to eat, cut the bread into thick slices and spread with cherry jam. If you like, top with a spoonful of sour cream and a sprinkling of allspice.

Energy 578Kcal/2460kJ; Protein 10.2g; Carbohydrate 139.9g, of which sugars 90.1g; Fat 1.4g, of which saturates 0.3g; Cholesterol 4mg; Calcium 360mg; Fibre 4g; Sodium 105mg.

BOYER CREAM

THIS CREAMY MOUSSE IS FLUFFY AND LIGHT. SCENTED WITH ROSE WATER AND FLAVOURED WITH BERRIES, IT IS A SUMMER TREAT.

SERVES FOUR TO SIX

INGREDIENTS
225g/8oz/1 cup full-fat soft white
  (farmer's) cheese
75ml/5 tbsp sour cream
2 eggs, separated
50g/2oz/¼ cup vanilla sugar
115g/4oz/⅔ cup raspberries
115g/4oz/1 cup strawberries
icing (confectioners') sugar, sifted,
  to taste
15ml/1 tbsp rose water
halved strawberries, mint leaves and
  small pink roses, to decorate

VARIATION
Try using different fresh summer berries
and fruit to vary this recipe. Use
whatever is seasonally available.

COOK'S TIP
This cream dessert looks beautiful served
in dishes placed on saucers decorated
with halved strawberries and mint leaves.

1 Beat the cheese in a bowl with
the sour cream and egg yolks until the
cheese has thoroughly softened. Stir in
half of the sugar.

2 Whisk the egg whites in another
bowl until they are stiff, then whisk in
the remaining sugar. Fold the egg
whites into the cheese mixture and
set aside to chill while you prepare
the fruit sauce.

3 To make the sauce, purée the
raspberries and strawberries. Press
through a sieve (strainer) to remove
pips; add icing sugar, to taste.

4 Swirl 4–6 glass dishes with a little
rose water and divide three-quarters of
the sauce between the dishes. Top
with the cheese mixture. Add the
remaining sauce, swirling it into
the cheese.

Energy 258Kcal/1068kJ; Protein 4.1g; Carbohydrate 11.2g, of which sugars 11.2g; Fat 22.2g, of which saturates 13.2g; Cholesterol 107mg; Calcium 70mg; Fibre 0.7g; Sodium 143mg.

BULGARIAN RICE PUDDING

BALKAN RICE PUDDING IS A SUPERLATIVE TRADITIONAL DISH. THE CREAMY, SWEET RICE ACTS AS A BACKGROUND TO THE FANCIER FLAVOURS. THIS PUDDING, WITH ITS CINNAMON SCENT, PISTACHIOS AND ROSES IS A TYPICALLY IMAGINATIVE AND AROMATIC BULGARIAN OFFERING.

SERVES FOUR TO SIX

INGREDIENTS
    75g/3oz/scant ½ cup short grain
      or pudding rice
    45ml/3 tbsp granulated sugar
    900ml/1½ pints/3¾ cups full-
      cream (whole) milk
    25g/1oz/2 tbsp unsalted
      (sweet) butter
    1 cinnamon stick
    strip of lemon rind
    halved pistachios and rose petals,
      to decorate

COOK'S TIP
For an extra creamy rice pudding, fold in 150ml/¼ pint/⅔ cup lightly whipped double (heavy) cream, just before you are ready to serve.

1 Put the rice, sugar, milk, butter, cinnamon stick and lemon rind into a large double or heavy pan.

VARIATION
If you like, use thinly sliced blanched almonds instead of the pistachios. Toast lightly until golden in colour.

2 Cook over a very gentle heat, stirring occasionally, for about 1½ hours, or until thick and creamy. Remove and discard the cinnamon stick and lemon rind.

3 Spoon into serving dishes and sprinkle with halved pistachios and rose petals, to decorate.

Energy 205Kcal/852kJ; Protein 5.9g; Carbohydrate 24.6g, of which sugars 14.6g; Fat 9.3g, of which saturates 5.9g; Cholesterol 30mg; Calcium 184mg; Fibre 0g; Sodium 90mg.

BUTTERED CHALLAH PUDDING WITH PEARS, CHERRIES AND ALMONDS

BREAD AND BUTTER PUDDING, PREPARED WITH CHALLAH, IS DIVINE. THIS SWEET TWIST ON A CLASSIC JEWISH BREAD IS A GREAT REASON TO MAKE OR BUY AN EXTRA CHALLAH.

SERVES SIX TO EIGHT

INGREDIENTS

75–115g/3–4oz/6–8 tbsp butter or pareve margarine, softened, plus extra for greasing
900ml/2 pints/4 cups milk
4–5 eggs, lightly beaten
2.5ml/½ tsp vanilla extract
2.5ml/½ tsp almond extract
1.5ml/¼ tsp salt
500g/1¼lb leftover, slightly dry challah, thickly sliced and lightly toasted
130g/4½oz/1 cup dried cherries
3 firm, ripe pears
350g/12oz/2 cups demerara (raw) sugar
130g/4½oz/generous 1 cup flaked (sliced) almonds
cream, to serve (optional)

1 Preheat the oven to 190ºC/375ºF/ Gas 5. Butter a 25cm/10in square or oval baking dish. Mix together the milk, eggs, vanilla, almond extract and salt.

2 Spread the challah toast with butter, reserving 40g/1½oz/3 tbsp, then cut the challah into bitesize chunks.

VARIATION
To make an apple version, replace the almond extract with more vanilla extract and add 15ml/1 tbsp ground cinnamon to the milk. Use raisins instead of dried cherries, broken walnuts in place of the almonds, and apples instead of pears.

3 Add the buttered challah and dried cherries to the milk mixture and fold in gently so that all of the bread is coated with the liquid.

4 Core and dice the pears but do not peel. Layer the bread, sugar, almonds and pears in the dish, ending with a layer of sugar. Dot with butter. Bake for 40–50 minutes, or until caramelized. Serve with cream, if you like.

Energy 631Kcal/2660kJ; Protein 17.2g; Carbohydrate 95.8g, of which sugars 63.3g; Fat 22.7g, of which saturates 7.6g; Cholesterol 122mg; Calcium 221mg; Fibre 4.1g; Sodium 491mg.

COCONUT RICE PUDDINGS
WITH GRILLED ORANGES

RICE PUDDINGS ARE A REGULAR FEATURE OF JEWISH FESTIVITIES, OFTEN PREPARED WITH CARDAMOM-SCENTED RICE AND COCONUT MILK IN THE INDIAN STYLE. THE SEPHARDIM EAT RICE PUDDING DURING ROSH HASHANAH, THE BENE ISRAEL DURING PESACH AND PERSIAN JEWS DURING SHAVUOT.

SERVES FOUR

INGREDIENTS

  2 oranges, such as Valencia
  175g/6oz/scant 1 cup jasmine rice
  400ml/14fl oz/1⅔ cup coconut milk
  2.5ml/½ tsp grated nutmeg
  small pinch of salt
  60ml/4 tbsp golden caster (superfine)
    sugar, plus extra for sprinkling
  oil, for greasing
  orange peel twists, to decorate

1 Using a sharp knife, cut away the peel and pith from the oranges, then cut the flesh into rounds. Set aside.

2 Rinse and drain the rice. Place in a pan, cover with water, and bring to the boil. Cook for 5 minutes, until the grains are just beginning to soften. Place the rice in a muslin-lined (cheesecloth-lined) steamer, then make a few holes in the muslin to allow the steam to get through. Steam the rice for 15 minutes, or until tender.

3 Put the steamed rice in a heavy pan with the coconut milk, nutmeg, salt and sugar and cook over a low heat until the mixture begins to simmer. Simmer for about 5 minutes, or until the mixture is thick and creamy, stirring frequently to prevent the rice from sticking.

4 Spoon the rice mixture into four lightly oiled 175ml/6fl oz/¾ cup dariole moulds or ramekins and leave to cool.

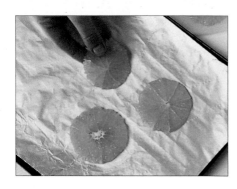

5 Preheat the grill (broiler) to high. Line a baking tray or the grill rack with foil and place the orange slices on top. Sprinkle the oranges with a little sugar, then grill (broil) for 6 minutes, or until lightly golden, turning the slices halfway through cooking.

6 When the rice mixture is completely cold, run a knife around the edge of the moulds or ramekins and turn out the rice. Decorate with orange peel twists and serve with the warm orange slices.

Energy 261Kcal/1103kJ; Protein 4.3g; Carbohydrate 60.8g, of which sugars 25.9g; Fat 0.6g, of which saturates 0.2g; Cholesterol 0mg; Calcium 75mg; Fibre 1.1g; Sodium 114mg.

CLASSIC AMERICAN CHEESECAKE

BAKED CHEESECAKE IS SYNONYMOUS WITH NEW YORK DELI CULTURE, AND THIS VERSION, WITH JUST A HINT OF VANILLA, IS THE REAL CLASSIC. IT IS PERFECT FOR A CELEBRATION BUFFET, FOR A FAMILY GATHERING, OR AS A TREAT FOR SUNDAY BRUNCH.

SERVES SIX TO EIGHT

INGREDIENTS
  130g/4½oz/generous ½ cup butter,
    melted, plus extra for greasing
  350g/12oz digestive biscuits
    (graham crackers), finely crushed
  350–400g/12–14oz/1¾–2 cups
    caster (superfine) sugar
  350g/12oz/1½ cups full-fat
    soft white (farmer's) cheese
  3 eggs, lightly beaten
  15ml/1 tbsp vanilla extract
  350g/12oz/1½ cups sour cream
  strawberries, blueberries, raspberries
    and icing (confectioners') sugar,
    to serve (optional)

1 Butter a deep 23cm/9in springform tin (pan). Put the biscuit crumbs and 60ml/4 tbsp of the sugar in a bowl and mix together, then add the melted butter and mix well. Press the mixture into the prepared tin to cover the base and sides. Chill for about 30 minutes.

2 Preheat the oven to 190ºC/375ºF/Gas 5. Using an electric mixer, food processor or wooden spoon, beat the cheese until soft. Beat in the eggs, then 250g/9oz/1½ cups of the sugar and 10ml/2 tsp of the vanilla extract.

3 Pour the mixture over the crumb base and bake for 45 minutes, or until a cocktail stick (toothpick), inserted in the centre, comes out clean. Leave to cool slightly for about 10 minutes. (Do not turn the oven off.)

4 Meanwhile, combine the sour cream and remaining sugar, to taste, and stir in the remaining vanilla extract. When the cheesecake has cooled, pour the topping over the base, spreading it out evenly. Return to the oven and bake for a further 5 minutes to glaze.

5 Leave the cheesecake to cool to room temperature, then chill. Serve with a few fresh strawberries, blueberries and raspberries, dusted with icing sugar, if you like.

VARIATIONS
• To make a strawberry cheesecake, in place of the sour cream, mix together 130g/4½oz/generous 1 cup fresh strawberries, sliced, with 30–45ml/2–3 tbsp melted redcurrant jelly. Spread the mixture over the top of the cheesecake and return to the oven until warmed through. Leave to cool, then chill before serving.
• For a lemon cheesecake, instead of the vanilla extract, flavour the cheesecake with the grated rind and juice of 1 lemon.

Energy 634Kcal/2628kJ; Protein 7.8g; Carbohydrate 31.8g, of which sugars 7.7g; Fat 53.8g, of which saturates 31.5g; Cholesterol 192mg; Calcium 137mg; Fibre 1g; Sodium 536mg.

CREAMY LEMON CHEESECAKE TOPPED WITH FRUIT KISEL

IF YOU LIKE YOUR CHEESECAKE WITH JUST THAT LITTLE BIT EXTRA, THIS IS THE RECIPE FOR YOU. THE CREAMY, LEMON-SCENTED FILLING IN A PASTRY CRUST IS PERFECTLY COMPLEMENTED BY KISEL — A SLIGHTLY TART FRUIT SAUCE TOPPING FROM RUSSIA.

SERVES EIGHT TO TEN

INGREDIENTS
   225g/8oz/2 cups plain
      (all-purpose) flour
   115g/4oz/½ cup butter
   15g/½ oz/1 tbsp caster
      (superfine) sugar
   finely grated rind of ½ lemon
   1 egg, beaten
   sprigs of mint, to decorate
For the filling
   675g/1½lb/3 cups quark (very
      low-fat soft cheese)
   4 eggs, separated
   150g/5oz/¾ cup caster sugar
   45ml/3 tbsp cornflour (cornstarch)
   150ml/¼ pint/⅔ cup sour cream
   finely grated rind and juice of
      ½ lemon
   5ml/1 tsp vanilla extract
For the kisel
   450g/1lb/4–4½ cups prepared red
      fruit, such as strawberries,
      raspberries, red currants, cherries
   50g/2oz/¼ cup caster sugar
   120ml/4fl oz/½ cup water
   15ml/1 tbsp arrowroot

1 Begin by making the pastry for the cheesecake. Sift the flour into a bowl. Rub in the butter until the mixture resembles fine breadcrumbs. Stir in the caster sugar and lemon rind, then add the beaten egg and mix to a dough. Wrap in clear film (plastic wrap) and chill for at least 15 minutes.

2 Roll out the pastry on a lightly floured surface and use to line the base and sides of a 25cm/10in springform cake tin (pan). Chill for 1 hour.

3 Put the quark for the filling in a fine sieve (strainer) set over a bowl and leave to drain for 1 hour.

4 Preheat the oven to 200°C/400°F/ Gas 6. Prick the chilled pastry case base with a fork, fill it with crumpled foil and bake for 5 minutes. Remove the foil and bake for a further 5 minutes. Remove the pastry case from the oven and reduce the oven temperature to 180°C/350°F/Gas 4.

5 Put the drained quark in a bowl with the egg yolks and caster sugar and mix together. Blend the cornflour in a cup with a little sour cream, then add to the bowl with the remaining sour cream, the lemon rind and juice, and the vanilla extract. Mix well.

6 Whisk the egg whites in a greaseproof bowl until stiff, then fold into the quark mixture, one-third at a time. Pour the filling into the pastry case and bake for 1–1¼ hours, until golden and firm. Turn off the oven and leave the door ajar. Let the cheesecake cool, then chill for 2 hours.

7 To make the kisel, put the prepared fruit, caster sugar and water into a pan and cook over a low heat until the sugar dissolves and the juices run. Remove the fruit with a slotted spoon and set aside.

8 Blend the arrowroot in a cup with a little cold water, stir into the fruit juices in the pan and bring to the boil, stirring all the time. Return the fruit to the pan and allow to cool, before serving it with the well-chilled cheesecake, decorated with sprigs of mint.

VARIATION
Use whichever red fruit is seasonally available for the kisel.

Energy 426Kcal/1783kJ; Protein 16.3g; Carbohydrate 48.2g, of which sugars 26.9g; Fat 21g, of which saturates 12.2g; Cholesterol 145mg; Calcium 159mg; Fibre 1.2g; Sodium 413mg.

RAISIN CHEESECAKE

RAISIN AND LEMON-SCENTED CHEESECAKE IN AN ALMOND CRUST IS A DELICIOUS SEASONAL TREAT, OFTEN SERVED IN CAFÉS DURING THE EASTERN EUROPEAN SPRING.

SERVES EIGHT

INGREDIENTS
   50g/2oz/4 tbsp butter
   115g/4oz/1 cup plain
     (all-purpose) flour
   15ml/1 tbsp caster (superfine) sugar
   25g/1oz/¼ cup almonds, very
     finely chopped
   30ml/2 tbsp cold water
   15ml/1 tbsp icing (confectioners')
     sugar, for dusting
For the filling
   115g/4oz/8 tbsp butter
   150g/5oz/¾ cup caster sugar
   5ml/1 tsp vanilla extract
   3 eggs, beaten
   25g/1oz/¼ cup plain flour, sifted
   400g/14oz/1¾ cups curd
     (farmer's) cheese
   grated rind and juice of 2 lemons
   65g/2½oz/½ cup raisins

4 For the filling, cream the butter, sugar and vanilla extract together. Beat in one egg, then stir in the flour. Whisk the cheese until soft in another bowl, then gradually mix in the remaining eggs. Blend this into the butter mixture. Stir in the lemon rind, juice and raisins.

5 Pour the filling over the pastry base. Bake in the oven for 1½ hours, until firm. Turn off the oven, leave the door ajar and allow to cool before removing. Dust with icing sugar.

1 Rub the butter into the flour until it resembles fine breadcrumbs. Stir in the sugar and almonds. Add the water and mix to a dough. Gently knead on a floured surface, wrap in clear film (plastic wrap) and chill for 30 minutes.

2 Preheat the oven to 200°C/400°F/ Gas 6. Roll out the pastry and use it to line the base and sides of a 20cm/8in tart tin (pan). Trim with a knife.

3 Prick with a fork, cover with oiled foil and bake for 6 minutes. Remove the foil and bake for 6 more minutes. Allow to cool and reduce the temperature to 150°C/300°F/Gas 2.

Energy 429Kcal/1794kJ; Protein 12.5g; Carbohydrate 42.9g, of which sugars 29.5g; Fat 25g, of which saturates 14.1g; Cholesterol 127mg; Calcium 119mg; Fibre 0.9g; Sodium 377mg.

CRÊPES AU FROMAGE

THE JEWS OF ALSACE WERE PROUD OF THE MANY DELICATE SWEETS IN THEIR REPERTOIRE. THIS ONE IS A SAVOURY-SWEET CLASSIC, AND A QUINTESSENTIAL FRENCH PASTRY.

MAKES SIX

INGREDIENTS
   115g/4oz/1 cup plain
    (all-purpose) flour
   pinch of salt
   pinch of grated nutmeg, plus extra
    for dusting
   1 egg, separated
   200ml/7fl oz/scant 1 cup milk
   30ml/2 tbsp sunflower oil
   25g/1oz/2 tbsp butter
   icing (confectioners') sugar, to dust
   lemon slices, to garnish
For the filling
   225g/8oz/1 cup curd
    (farmer's) cheese
   60ml/4 tbsp caster (superfine) sugar,
    to taste
   5ml/1 tsp vanilla extract
   50g/2oz/scant ½ cup sultanas
    (golden raisins)

1 Sift the flour, salt and nutmeg together in a large bowl. Make a well in the centre. Add the egg yolk and about half of the milk. Beat until smooth, then gradually beat in the remaining milk.

2 Whisk the egg white in a bowl until stiff. Fold into the batter.

3 Heat 5ml/1 tsp sunflower oil and a little of the butter in an 18cm/7in frying pan. Pour in enough of the batter to cover the base.

4 Cook for 2 minutes, until golden brown, then turn over and cook for a further 2 minutes.

5 Make five more pancakes in the same way, using more oil and butter as necessary. Stack up the pancakes and keep them warm.

6 To make the filling, put the curd cheese, sugar and vanilla extract in a bowl and beat together. Mix in the sultanas. Divide among the pancakes, fold them up and dust with grated nutmeg and icing sugar. Garnish with lemon slices.

Energy 269Kcal/1129kJ; Protein 9.9g; Carbohydrate 34g, of which sugars 19.4g; Fat 11.9g, of which saturates 5.2g; Cholesterol 52mg; Calcium 127mg; Fibre 0.8g; Sodium 218mg.

APPLE PANCAKES

CENTRAL EUROPEAN JEWS MADE PANCAKES FOR EVERY OCCASION. THESE ARE TENDER AND THIN AND FILLED WITH DELECTABLE CINNAMON-SCENTED SUGARED APPLES.

SERVES SIX

INGREDIENTS

115g/4oz/1 cup plain
  (all-purpose) flour
pinch of salt
2 eggs, beaten
175ml/6fl oz/¾ cup milk
120ml/4fl oz/½ cup water
25g/1oz/2 tbsp butter, melted
sunflower oil, for frying
cinnamon sugar or icing
  (confectioners') sugar and lemon
  wedges, to serve (optional)
For the filling
75g/3oz/6 tbsp butter
1.5kg/3lb eating apples, cored,
  peeled and sliced
50g/2oz/¼ cup caster
  (superfine)sugar
5ml/1 tsp cinnamon

1 Melt the butter for the filling in a heavy frying pan. When the foam subsides, add the apple slices. Sprinkle a mixture of the sugar and cinnamon over the apples. Cook, stirring occasionally, until the apples are soft and golden brown. Set aside.

VARIATION
Try using sliced pears instead of apples.

2 Sift the flour and salt into a mixing bowl and make a well in the middle. Add the eggs and gradually mix in the flour.

3 Slowly add the combined milk and the water, beating until smooth. Stir in the melted butter.

4 Heat 10ml/2 tsp oil in a crêpe or small frying pan. Pour in about 30ml/ 2 tbsp of the batter, tipping the pan to coat the base evenly.

5 Cook the pancake until the underside is golden brown, then turn over and cook the other side. Slide on to a warm plate, cover with foil and set the plate over a pan of simmering water to keep warm. Repeat with the remaining batter mixture, until it is all used up.

6 Divide the apple filling among the pancakes and roll them up. Sprinkle with cinnamon sugar or a dusting of icing sugar, if you like. Serve with lemon wedges to squeeze over.

Energy 348Kcal/1,464kJ; Protein 5.8g; Carbohydrate 47.3g, of which sugars 32.7g; Fat 16.6g, of which saturates 9.6g; Cholesterol 101mg; Calcium 89mg; Fibre 4.6g; Sodium 143mg.

SPICY APPLE CAKE

APFELKUCHEN IS A CAKE WHICH IS FAVOURED BY GERMAN AND EASTERN EUROPEAN JEWS. ENJOY IT FOR TEA, OR SERVE AT A HAPPY EVENT. HUNDREDS OF GERMAN CAKES AND DESSERTS INCLUDE THIS VERSATILE FRUIT. THIS MOIST AND SPICY APFELKUCHEN CAN BE FOUND ON THE MENU OF KONDITOREIEN, COFFEE AND TEA HOUSES, EVERYWHERE.

SERVES TWELVE

INGREDIENTS
  115g/4oz/1 cup plain
    (all-purpose) flour
  115g/4oz/1 cup wholemeal
    (whole-wheat) flour
  10ml/2 tsp baking powder
  5ml/1 tsp cinnamon
  2.5ml/½ tsp mixed (apple pie) spice
  225g/8oz cooking apple, cored,
    peeled and chopped
  75g/3oz/6 tbsp butter
  175g/6oz/generous ¾ cup soft light
    brown sugar
  finely grated rind of 1 small orange
  2 eggs, beaten
  30ml/2 tbsp milk
  whipped cream dusted with
    cinnamon, to serve
For the topping
  4 eating apples, cored and
    thinly sliced
  juice of ½ orange
  10ml/2 tsp caster (superfine) sugar
  45ml/3 tbsp apricot jam, warmed
    and strained

1 Preheat the oven to 180°C/350°F/ Gas 4. Grease and line a 23cm/9in round springform tin (pan).

3 Cream the butter, brown sugar and orange rind together until light and fluffy. Gradually beat in the eggs, then fold in the flour mixture, the chopped apple and the milk.

2 Sift the flours, baking powder and spices together in a bowl. Toss the chopped cooking apple in 30ml/2 tbsp of the flour mixture.

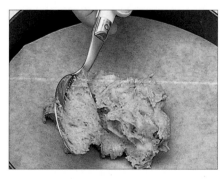

4 Spoon the mixture into the cake tin and level the surface.

5 For the topping, toss the apple slices in the orange juice and set them in overlapping circles on top of the cake mixture, pressing down lightly.

6 Sprinkle the caster sugar over the top and bake for 1–1¼ hours, or until well risen and firm. Cover with foil if the apples brown too much.

7 Cool in the tin for 10 minutes, then remove to a wire rack. Glaze the apples with the strained jam. Cut into wedges and serve with whipped cream, sprinkled with cinnamon.

Energy 205Kcal/865kJ; Protein 3.5g; Carbohydrate 35.5g, of which sugars 22.2g; Fat 6.5g, of which saturates 3.6g; Cholesterol 45mg; Calcium 36mg; Fibre 1.9g; Sodium 55mg.

DOBOS TORTA

THIS WELL-KNOWN HUNGARIAN CAKE WAS FIRST CREATED BY A CHEF CALLED JOZEP DOBOS IN THE LATE 1880S. JEWS AND NON-JEWS ALIKE HAVE DOTED ON IT EVER SINCE.

SERVES TEN TO TWELVE

INGREDIENTS
  6 eggs, separated
  150g/5oz/1¼ cups icing
    (confectioners') sugar, sifted
  5ml/1 tsp vanilla sugar
  130g/4½oz/generous 1 cup plain
    (all-purpose) flour, sifted
For the filling
  75g/3oz plain (semi sweet)
    chocolate, broken into pieces
  175g/6oz/¾ cup unsalted
    (sweet) butter
  130g/4½oz/generous 1 cup
    icing (confectioner's) sugar
  30ml/2 tbsp vanilla sugar
  1 egg
For the caramel topping
  150g/5oz/¾ cup sugar
  30–45ml/2–3 tbsp water
  10g/¼oz/½ tbsp butter, melted

1 Preheat the oven to 220°C/425°F/ Gas 7. Whisk the egg yolks and half the icing sugar together in a bowl until pale in colour, thick and creamy.

2 Whisk the egg whites in a grease-free bowl until stiff; whisk in half the remaining icing sugar until glossy, then fold in the vanilla sugar.

COOK'S TIP
Be careful when making and pouring the caramel topping, as it is very hot indeed.

3 Fold the egg whites into the egg yolk mixture, alternating carefully with spoonfuls of the flour.

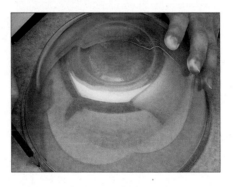

4 Line four baking sheets with baking parchment. Draw a 23cm/9in circle on each piece of paper. Lightly grease the paper and dust with flour.

5 Divide the mixture between the paper circles. Bake for 10 minutes, then leave to cool before stacking. Place a board over the top to weigh down the layers.

6 To make the filling, melt the chocolate in a small heatproof bowl set over a pan of gently simmering water. Stir until smooth.

7 Cream the butter and icing sugar together well in a bowl. Beat in the melted chocolate, vanilla sugar and egg.

8 Sandwich the four sponge circles together with the chocolate filling, then spread the remainder over the top and around the sides of the cake.

9 To make the caramel topping, put the sugar and water in a heavy pan and dissolve slowly over a very gentle heat. Add the butter.

10 When the sugar has dissolved, increase the heat and cook until the mixture turns golden brown. Quickly pour the caramel on to a greased baking sheet. Leave to set and shatter into shards when cold. Place the pieces of caramel on top of the cake, and cut it into slices to serve.

VARIATION
Try adding chopped nuts or candied peel to the chocolate filling.

Energy 368Kcal/1543kJ; Protein 5.3g; Carbohydrate 49.9g, of which sugars 41.6g; Fat 17.8g, of which saturates 10g; Cholesterol 144mg; Calcium 56mg; Fibre 0.5g; Sodium 137mg.

PALACSINKEN TORTE

IN HUNGARY, PANCAKES WERE ORIGINALLY VERY BASIC FOOD, MADE ONLY WITH FLOUR AND WATER AND THEN COOKED OVER AN OPEN FIRE. THEY COULD THEN BE ROLLED, FOLDED, WRAPPED OR STACKED WITH SAVOURY OR SWEET FILLINGS IN BETWEEN. THIS LAYERING OF SWEET ALMOND FILLING, TOPPED WITH SOUR CREAM AND BAKED UNTIL GOLDEN BROWN, IS ELEGANT AND DELICIOUS.

SERVES SIX

INGREDIENTS
  5 eggs, separated
  50g/2oz/¼ cup caster
    (superfine) sugar
  175ml/6fl oz//¾ cup milk
  50g/2oz/½ cup self-raising
    (self-rising) flour, sifted
  50g/2oz/4 tbsp unsalted
    (sweet) butter, melted
  175ml/6fl oz/¾ cup sour cream
  sifted icing (confectioners') sugar,
    for dredging
  lemon wedges, to serve
For the filling
  3 eggs, separated
  25g/1oz/¼ cup icing (confectioners')
    sugar, sifted
  grated rind of 1 lemon
  2.5ml/½ tsp vanilla sugar
  115g/4oz/1 cup ground almonds

1 Preheat the oven to 200°C/400°F/ Gas 6. Grease and line a deep 20–23cm/8–9in springform tin (pan). Whisk the egg yolks and caster sugar together in a bowl until thick and creamy, before whisking in the milk.

2 Whisk the egg whites in a grease-free bowl until stiff, then fold into the batter mixture, alternating with spoonfuls of the flour and half the melted butter. Continue to whisk until smooth.

3 Take a frying pan of similar size to the springform tin, and lightly grease with a little of the remaining melted butter. Tilt to cover the surface.

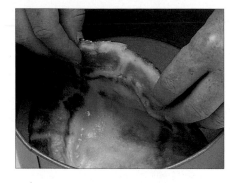

4 Tip one-quarter of the batter into the frying pan. Fry the thick pancake on each side until golden brown, then slide it into the prepared cake tin. Use the rest of the batter to make three more pancakes in the same way and set them aside while you make the filling.

5 For the filling, whisk the egg yolks in a bowl with the icing sugar until thick and creamy. Stir in the grated lemon rind and the vanilla sugar.

6 Whisk the egg whites in a separate bowl, then fold them into the egg yolk mixture, before adding the ground almonds. Mix together well.

7 Spread one-third of the mixture on top of the first pancake.

8 Repeat twice more with the second and third pancakes, then top with the final pancake.

9 Spread the sour cream over the top and bake for 20–25 minutes, or until the top is pale golden brown.

10 Leave in the tin for 10 minutes before removing the lining paper. Serve warm, cut into wedges, liberally dusted with icing sugar and accompanied by lemon wedges.

VARIATION
There are endless variations possible on pancake fillings. Try using pistachio nuts instead of the almonds in this recipe.

Energy 428Kcal/1783kJ; Protein 15.1g; Carbohydrate 23.4g, of which sugars 16.5g; Fat 31.4g, of which saturates 11.2g; Cholesterol 291mg; Calcium 166mg; Fibre 1.7g; Sodium 172mg.

CLASSIC STRUDEL

THIS CRISP PASTRY ROLL, FILLED WITH FRUIT AND JAM, IS A CLASSIC ASHKENAZIC PASTRY, WHICH HAS LONG BEEN A FAVOURITE IN BUDAPEST AND VIENNA. A SLICE OF STRUDEL SERVED WITH A GLASS OF LEMON TEA IS A PRETTY IRRESISTIBLE OFFER.

MAKES THREE

INGREDIENTS
  250g/9oz/generous 1 cup
    butter, softened
  250g/9oz/generous 1 cup sour cream
  30ml/2 tbsp sugar
  5ml/1 tsp vanilla extract
  large pinch of salt
  250g/9oz/2¼ cups plain
    (all-purpose) flour
  icing (confectioners') sugar, sifted,
    for dusting
For the filling
  2–3 cooking apples
  45–60ml/3–4 tbsp sultanas (golden
    raisins) or raisins
  45ml/3 tbsp light muscovado
    (brown) sugar
  115g/4oz/1 cup walnuts,
    roughly chopped
  5–10ml/1–2 tsp ground cinnamon
  60ml/4 tbsp apricot jam

1 To make the pastry, beat the butter until light and fluffy, then add the sour cream, sugar, vanilla extract and salt, and beat together.

2 Stir the flour into the mixture, then put in a plastic bag; chill overnight or longer.

COOK'S TIPS
• Pastry tends to dry out quickly, so always cover when not using.
• To follow a meat meal, substitute the butter and sour cream with 120ml/4fl oz/½ cup sweet white wine and 120ml/4fl oz/½ cup vegetable oil.

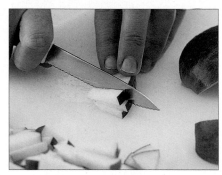

3 Preheat the oven to 180°C/350°F/Gas 4. To make the filling, core and finely chop the apples but do not peel. Put the apples in a bowl, add the sultanas or raisins, sugar, walnuts, cinnamon and apricot jam and mix together until well combined.

4 Divide the pastry into three equal pieces. Place one piece on a sheet of lightly floured greaseproof (waxed) paper and roll out to a rectangle measuring about 45 × 30cm/18 × 12in.

5 Spread one-third of the filling over the pastry, leaving a 1–2cm/½–¾in border. Roll up the pastry to enclose the filling and place, seam-side down, on a non-stick baking sheet. Repeat with the remaining pastry and filling. Bake the strudels for 25–30 minutes until golden brown all over.

6 Remove the strudels from the oven and leave for 5 minutes to become slightly firm, then cut into slices. Allow to cool, then dust with icing sugar.

Energy 1566Kcal/6519kJ; Protein 17.3g; Carbohydrate 129g, of which sugars 65.2g; Fat 112.6g, of which saturates 56.1g; Cholesterol 228mg; Calcium 274mg; Fibre 5.8g; Sodium 560mg.

RUGELACH

THESE CRISP, FLAKY COOKIES, ROLLED AROUND A SWEET FILLING, RESEMBLE SNAKES OR CROISSANTS. THEY ARE THOUGHT TO HAVE COME FROM POLAND WHERE THEY ARE A TRADITIONAL SWEET TREAT AT CHANUKKAH. THEY ARE VERY POPULAR IN THE UNITED STATES, ESPECIALLY MADE WITH CHOCOLATE CHIPS.

MAKES FORTY-EIGHT TO SIXTY

INGREDIENTS
- 115g/4oz/½ cup unsalted (sweet) butter
- 115g/4oz/½ cup full-fat soft white (farmer's) cheese
- 15ml/1 tbsp sugar
- 1 egg
- 2.5ml/½ tsp salt
- about 250g/9oz/2¼ cups plain (all-purpose) flour
- about 250g/9oz/generous 1 cup butter, melted
- 250g/9oz/scant 2 cups sultanas (golden raisins)
- 130g/4½oz/generous 1 cup chopped walnuts or walnut pieces
- about 225g/8oz/generous 1 cup caster (superfine) sugar
- 10–15ml/1–2 tsp ground cinnamon

1 To make the pastry, put the butter and cheese in a bowl and beat with an electric mixer until creamy. Beat in the sugar, egg and salt.

4 Preheat the oven to 180°C/350°F/ Gas 4. Divide the dough into six equal pieces. On a lightly floured surface, roll out each piece into a round about 3mm/½in thick, then brush with a little of the melted butter and sprinkle over the sultanas, chopped walnuts, a little sugar and the cinnamon.

COOK'S TIP
Always chill the dough sufficiently. It will be too soft if not allowed to cool to a low enough temperature.

5 Cut the rounds into eight to ten wedges and carefully roll the large side of each wedge towards the tip. (Some of the filling will fall out.) Arrange the rugelach on baking sheets, brush with a little butter and sprinkle with the sugar. Bake for 15–30 minutes until lightly browned. Leave to cool before serving.

VARIATION
Roll about 250g/8oz plain (semisweet) chocolate chips into the dough in place of the cinnamon, sugar and walnuts.

2 Fold the flour into the creamed mixture, a little at a time, until the dough can be worked with the hands. Continue adding the flour, kneading with the hands, until it is a consistency that can be rolled out. (Add only as much flour as needed.)

3 Shape the dough into a ball, then cover and chill for at least 2 hours or even overnight.

Energy 111Kcal/464kJ; Protein 1g; Carbohydrate 10.4g, of which sugars 7.2g; Fat 7.6g, of which saturates 3.9g; Cholesterol 18mg; Calcium 16mg; Fibre 0.3g; Sodium 45mg.

APPLE STRUDEL

This famous fruit-filled strudel is a classic Ashkenazic dish, and so rewarding when made at home rather than bought. Don't be put off if time is tight: just use ready-made pastry.

SERVES EIGHT TO TEN

INGREDIENTS

500g/1¼lb packet large sheets of
  filo pastry, thawed if frozen
115g/4oz/½ cup unsalted
  (sweet) butter, melted
icing (confectioners') sugar,
  for dredging
cream, to serve
For the filling
  1kg/2¼lb apples, cored, peeled
    and sliced
  115g/4oz/2 cups fresh breadcrumbs
  50g/2oz/4 tbsp unsalted (sweet)
    butter, melted
  150g/5oz/¾ cup sugar
  5ml/1 tsp cinnamon
  75g/3oz/generous ½ cup raisins
  finely grated rind of 1 lemon

1 Preheat the oven to 180°C/350°F/
Gas 4. For the filling, place the sliced
apples in a bowl. Stir in the
breadcrumbs, butter, sugar, cinnamon,
raisins and grated lemon rind.

2 Lay 1 or 2 sheets of pastry on a
floured surface and brush them with
melted butter. Place another 1 or 2
sheets on top, and continue until there
are 4–5 layers in all.

3 Put the apple on the pastry, with a
2.5cm/1in border all around.

4 Fold in the two shorter sides to
enclose the filling, then roll up like a
Swiss roll. Place the strudel on a lightly
buttered baking sheet.

5 Brush the pastry with the remaining
butter. Bake for 30–40 minutes or until
golden brown. Leave to cool before
dusting with icing sugar. Serve in thick
diagonal slices.

VARIATION
Add dried cherries or cranberries or any
other dried fruit in place of the raisins.

Energy 397Kcal/1676kJ; Protein 5.3g; Carbohydrate 66g, of which sugars 30.7g; Fat 14.4g, of which saturates 8.7g; Cholesterol 35mg; Calcium 82mg; Fibre 3.1g; Sodium 196mg.

LINZERTORTE

A classic, very tasty pastry which is filled with jam and baked. You can make these into little one-portion tartlets, if you prefer, rather than one big torte. This sweet recipe was named not, as is commonly thought, after the town of Linz, but after Linzer, chef to the Archduke Charles of Austria, victor over Napoleon at Aspern in 1809.

SERVES EIGHT TO TEN

INGREDIENTS
  200g/7oz/scant 1 cup butter
    or pareve margarine
  200g/7oz/1 cup caster
    (superfine) sugar
  3 eggs, beaten
  1 egg yolk
  2.5ml/½ tsp cinnamon
  grated rind of ½ lemon
  115g/4oz/2 cups fine sweet
    biscuit (cookie) crumbs
  150g/5oz/1¼ cups ground almonds
  225g/8oz/2 cups plain (all-purpose)
    flour, sifted
  225g/8oz/¾ cup raspberry jam
  1 egg yolk, for glazing
  icing (confectioners')
    sugar, to decorate

1 Cream the butter or margarine and sugar together in a mixing bowl until light and creamy. Add the eggs and egg yolk slowly, beating all the time, before adding the cinnamon and the lemon rind.

2 Stir the biscuit crumbs and ground almonds into the mixture. Mix well together before adding the sifted flour. Knead the pastry mixture lightly, then wrap it in clear film (plastic wrap) and allow it to chill for 30 minutes. During this time, preheat the oven to 190°C/375°F/Gas 5.

3 Roll out two-thirds of the pastry on a lightly floured surface and use to line a deep 25cm/10in loose-based flan tin (tart pan). Smooth down the surface.

4 Spread the raspberry jam evenly over the base of the pastry case. Roll out the remaining pastry into a long oblong. Cut this into strips and arrange in a lattice pattern over the jam.

5 Brush the pastry with the beaten egg yolk to glaze. Bake the flan for 35–50 minutes, or until golden brown. Leave to cool in the tin before turning out on to a wire rack. Serve warm or cold with custard and sift over a little icing sugar.

Energy 537Kcal/2247kJ; Protein 8.5g; Carbohydrate 63g, of which sugars 39.1g; Fat 29.7g, of which saturates 12.8g; Cholesterol 125mg; Calcium 106mg; Fibre 2.1g; Sodium 223mg.

BAKED PEACHES

THIS BULGARIAN RECIPE USES FRESH PEACHES WITH A HINT OF CLOVES TO GIVE AN AROMATIC, SPICY FLAVOUR. ENJOY IT WITH ICE CREAM AND FRESH BERRIES FOR A WONDERFUL SUMMERTIME DESSERT.

SERVES SIX

INGREDIENTS

40g/1½oz/3 tbsp unsalted
  (sweet) butter
6 firm ripe peaches, washed
12 whole cloves
90g/3½oz/½ cup vanilla sugar
45ml/3 tbsp brandy or dry white wine
  (optional)
pistachios, mint leaves and a little
  sifted icing (confectioners') sugar,
  to decorate
whipped cream or ice cream, to serve
fresh berries, to serve (optional)

COOK'S TIP
• The quality and ripeness of the peaches used will make a huge difference to the flavour of this dessert.
• You could add cinnamon to give the dish an extra spicy savour.

1 Preheat the oven to 180°C/350°F/ Gas 4. Spread half the butter around an ovenproof dish, making sure both the sides and base are well coated.

2 Halve the peaches and remove the stones (pits). Place the peaches skin side down in the dish. Push a whole clove into the centre of each peach half.

3 Sprinkle with the sugar and dot the remaining butter into each peach half. Drizzle over the brandy or wine, if using. Bake for 30 minutes, or until the peaches are tender.

4 Serve the peaches hot or cold, with freshly whipped cream, pistachio nuts and sprigs of mint, and sprinkled with a little icing sugar.

Energy 153Kcal/643kJ; Protein 1g; Carbohydrate 22.1g, of which sugars 22.1g; Fat 5.6g, of which saturates 3.5g; Cholesterol 14mg; Calcium 15mg; Fibre 1.3g; Sodium 42mg.

ALCOHOLIC FRUIT COMPOTE

ADDING A SHOT OF ALCOHOL — COGNAC, BRANDY, TEQUILA, CALVADOS; LIQUEURS SUCH AS FRAISES DE BOIS OR COINTREAU, OR EVEN A LITTLE FLAVOURFUL WINE — HELPS TO MAKE A SIMPLE BOWL OF FRUIT SALAD A DIGESTIBLE YET FESTIVE WAY TO END A CELEBRATORY MEAL.

SERVES SIX

INGREDIENTS
    350g/12oz/2 cups mixed dried fruits,
      such as apples, pears, prunes,
      peaches or apricots
    1 cinnamon stick
    300ml/½ pint/1¼ cups (hard) cider
      or water
    65g/2½oz/½ cup raisins
    30ml/2 tbsp clear honey
    juice of ½ lemon
    mint leaves, to decorate

1 Put the mixed dried fruit in a large pan with the cinnamon and cider or water. Heat gently until almost boiling, then cover the pan, lower the heat and cook gently for 12–15 minutes, to soften the fruit.

2 Remove the pan from the heat and stir in the raisins and honey. Cover the pan and leave to cool for a few minutes. Remove the cinnamon stick and then stir in the lemon juice.

3 Transfer the compote to a serving bowl, cover with clear film (plastic wrap) and keep refrigerated until needed. Allow the fruit compôte to come to room temperature before serving, decorated with a few mint leaves.

COOK'S TIP
This compote will keep in the refrigerator for up to a week and will even improve with age.

VARIATION
It is up to you what fruits and combinations you use in this dish, so you can really experiment creatively.

Energy 154Kcal/656kJ; Protein 2.6g; Carbohydrate 33.9g, of which sugars 33.9g; Fat 0.4g, of which saturates 0g; Cholesterol 0mg; Calcium 52mg; Fibre 3.9g; Sodium 19mg.

STEWED FRUIT

A DELICIOUS AND SIMPLE DESSERT THAT MAKES WONDERFUL USE OF A WINDFALL OF FRUIT WHETHER FROM YOUR GARDEN OR FROM THE MARKET. USE AN INTERESTING COMBINATION OF SWEET AND TART FLAVOURS TO MAKE THE MEDLEY EVEN TASTIER. SERVE CHILLED.

SERVES SIX

INGREDIENTS

115–175g/4–6oz/½–¾ cup sugar, depending on the tartness of the fruit
250ml/8fl oz/1 cup cold water
juice and strip of rind from ½ lemon
1 cinnamon stick, broken into two
900g/2lb prepared fruit, such as cored, peeled and sliced apples, pears, quince; stoned (pitted) plums, peaches, apricots; trimmed gooseberries; cranberries, blueberries, strawberries
30ml/2 tbsp arrowroot
caster (superfine) sugar and cream (optional), to serve

1 Put the sugar and water into a stainless steel pan and bring to the boil. Add the lemon juice and rind and the two pieces of cinnamon stick. Cook for 1 minute.

2 Add the prepared fruit to the pan and cook for 2–3 minutes only. Remove the fruit and cinnamon stick with a slotted spoon.

3 Blend the arrowroot with a little cold water, stir into the fruit juices and bring to the boil. Return the fruit to the pan and allow the fruit to cool before chilling. Discard the cinnamon stick if you wish.

4 Serve the fruit sprinkled with the caster sugar, and with whipped cream, if you like.

Energy 146Kcal/625kJ; Protein 0.6g; Carbohydrate 38.1g, of which sugars 33.4g; Fat 0.2g, of which saturates 0g; Cholesterol 0mg; Calcium 17mg; Fibre 2.4g; Sodium 4mg.

SWEET CHEESE DUMPLINGS

EASTERN EUROPEAN DESSERTS HAVE LONG FEATURED DUMPLINGS, DUMPLINGS AND MORE DUMPLINGS. SERVE THESE CHEESE-FILLED TREATS WITH SUGARED BERRIES OR COMPOTE.

SERVES FOUR TO SIX

INGREDIENTS

40g/1½oz/3 tbsp unsalted
  (sweet) butter
3 eggs, separated
450g/1lb/2 cups curd
  (farmer's) cheese
50g/2oz/⅓ cup semolina
15ml/1 tbsp double (heavy) cream
15–30ml/1–2 tbsp plain
  (all-purpose) flour
sifted icing (confectioners') sugar
  and sprigs of mint, to decorate

1 Cream the butter and beat in the egg yolks, one at a time. Stir in the curd cheese, semolina and cream. Mix well, cover and stand for 45 minutes.

2 Whisk the egg whites in a grease-free bowl until stiff, then carefully fold into the curd cheese mixture together with the flour.

3 Boil a very large pan of salted water. Scoop spoonfuls of mixture about the size of a plum and roll into ovals or balls with damp hands.

4 Drop the dumplings into the boiling water and simmer for about 6–7 minutes. Remove with a slotted spoon and drain well. Serve warm, dredged liberally with icing sugar and decorated with sprigs of mint.

Energy 236Kcal/980kJ; Protein 15.5g; Carbohydrate 11.1g, of which sugars 2.8g; Fat 15.8g, of which saturates 9g; Cholesterol 131mg; Calcium 109mg; Fibre 0.3g; Sodium 406mg.

CHEESE-FILLED JERUSALEM KODAFA DRENCHED <u>WITH</u> SYRUP

IN JERUSALEM, KODAFA IS A TRADITIONAL PALESTINIAN SWEET, ADORED BY BOTH ARAB AND JEW. YOU CAN SEE TRAYS BEING CARRIED THROUGH THE STREETS ON THE VENDORS' HEADS. A SWEET PASTRY, IT IS USUALLY MADE WITH KADAIF, A SHREDDED WHEAT-LIKE PASTRY THAT CAN BE BOUGHT READY MADE. THIS VERSION USES COUSCOUS, WHICH GIVES AN EQUALLY DELICIOUS RESULT.

SERVES SIX

INGREDIENTS

200–250g/7–9oz/1–1½ cups
  couscous
500ml/17fl oz/2¼ cups
  boiling water
130–200g/4½–7oz/½–scant 1 cup
  butter, cut into small pieces
1 egg, lightly beaten
pinch of salt
400g/14oz/1¾ cups ricotta cheese
175–200g/6–7oz cheese, such as
  mozzarella, Taleggio or Monterey
  Jack, grated or finely chopped
350ml/12fl oz/1½ cups
  clear honey
2–3 pinches saffron threads
  or ground cinnamon
120ml/4fl oz/½ cup water
5ml/1 tsp orange flower water or
  lemon juice
90ml/6 tbsp roughly chopped shelled
  pistachio nuts

3 Stir the butter into the couscous, then stir in the beaten egg and salt.

4 Preheat the oven to 200°C/400°F/ Gas 6. Spread half the couscous into a 25–30cm/10–12in round cake tin (pan).

5 In a bowl, combine the cheeses and 30ml/2 tbsp of the honey. Spread on top of the couscous, then top with the remaining couscous. Press down gently and bake for 10–15 minutes.

6 Meanwhile, put the remaining honey, the saffron threads or cinnamon, and the water in a pan. Bring to the boil, then boil for 5–7 minutes, or until the liquid forms a syrup. Remove from the heat and stir in the orange flower water or lemon juice.

7 When the kodafa is cooked, place under the grill (broiler) and cook until it is lightly browned on top and a golden crust is formed.

8 Sprinkle the pistachio nuts on top of the kodafa. Serve warm, cut into wedges, with the syrup.

VARIATIONS
• Other versions of this dish are made with biscuit (cookie) crumbs and broken pistachio nuts.
• If you like, warm the kodafa through in the microwave before serving with strong coffee or mint tea.

1 Put the couscous in a large bowl and pour over the boiling water. Stir together with a fork, then leave to soak for about 30 minutes until the water has been completely absorbed.

2 When the couscous is cool enough to handle, break up all the lumps with your fingers.

Energy 748Kcal/3119kJ; Protein 19.5g; Carbohydrate 65.1g, of which sugars 47.7g; Fat 46.6g, of which saturates 25.1g; Cholesterol 134mg; Calcium 250mg; Fibre 0.9g; Sodium 440mg.

POLISH HAZELNUT TORTE

Sweetened with honey and made from hazelnuts and crumbs, this Eastern European cake is delicious, and a perfect sweet treat for Rosh Hashanah. For Pesach, prepare this cake with matzo meal instead of breadcrumbs.

SERVES FOUR

INGREDIENTS
   15g/1/2oz/1 tbsp olive oil
   115g/4oz/2 cups slightly dry fine
      white breadcrumbs
   175g/6oz/³⁄₄ cup set strong flavoured
      honey, plus extra to serve
   50g/2oz/¹⁄₄ cup soft light
      brown sugar
   4 eggs, separated
   115g/4oz/1 cup hazelnuts, chopped
      and toasted, plus extra to decorate

1 Preheat the oven to 180°C/350°F/ Gas 4. Brush a 1.75 litre/3 pint/7½ cup fluted brioche tin (pan) with the olive oil. Sprinkle with 15g/½oz/¼ cup of the breadcrumbs.

2 Put the honey in a large bowl and set over a pan of barely simmering water. When the honey liquefies, add the sugar and egg yolks. Whisk until light and frothy. Remove from the heat.

3 Mix the remaining breadcrumbs with the hazelnuts and fold into the egg yolk and honey mixture. Whisk the egg whites in a separate bowl, until stiff, then gently fold into the other ingredients, half at a time.

4 Spoon the mixture into the tin. Bake for 40–45 minutes, until golden brown. Leave to cool in the tin for 5 minutes, then turn out on to a wire rack to cool. Sprinkle over nuts and drizzle with some extra melted honey to serve.

COOK'S TIP
The cake will rise during cooking and sink slightly as it cools – this is quite normal.

Energy 562Kcal/2361kJ; Protein 13.9g; Carbohydrate 70.5g, of which sugars 48.4g; Fat 27.1g, of which saturates 3.3g; Cholesterol 190mg; Calcium 115mg; Fibre 2.5g; Sodium 296mg.

PLUM STREUSEL SLICES

BUTTERY, NUTTY, CRUMBLY STREUSEL TOPPING WAS CARRIED FROM EASTERN EUROPE WITH THE WAVES OF EMIGRANTS AFTER WORLD WAR II. THIS DESSERT IS ESPECIALLY APPRECIATED AT ROSH HASHANAH, WHEN THE PLUMS USED ARE IN SEASON. APPLE STREUSEL IS EQUALLY DELICIOUS.

MAKES FOURTEEN

INGREDIENTS
    225g/8oz/1⅓ cups plums,
        stoned (pitted) and chopped
    15ml/1 tbsp lemon juice
    50g/2oz/¼ cup sugar
    115g/4oz/½ cup butter, softened
    50g/2oz/¼ cup caster
        (superfine) sugar
    1 egg yolk
    150g/5oz/1¼ cups plain
        (all-purpose) flour
For the topping
    150g/5oz/1¼ cups plain
        (all-purpose) flour
    2.5ml/½ tsp baking powder
    75g/3oz/6 tbsp butter, chilled
    50g/2oz/¼ cup soft light brown sugar
    50g/2oz/½ cup chopped hazelnuts

1 Preheat the oven to 180°C/350°F/ Gas 4. Grease and base-line a 20cm/8in square cake tin (pan). Put the plums and lemon juice in a pan and cook over a low heat for 5 minutes, until soft.

2 Add the sugar to the pan and cook gently until dissolved. Simmer for 3–4 minutes until very thick, stirring occasionally. Leave to cool.

3 Beat the butter and caster sugar together in a bowl until light and fluffy. Beat in the egg yolk, then mix in the flour to make a soft dough. Press the mixture into the base of the prepared cake tin. Bake for 15 minutes. Remove from the oven and spoon the cooked plums over the base.

4 Meanwhile, to make the topping, sift the flour and baking powder into a bowl. Rub in the butter until the mixture resembles breadcrumbs. Stir in the sugar and chopped nuts.

5 Sprinkle the topping mixture over the plums and press it down gently. Return the tin to the oven and bake for a further 30 minutes, or until the topping is lightly browned. Leave to cool for 15 minutes, then cut into slices. Remove from the tin when the streusel is completely cold.

COOK'S TIP
Fresh apricots are a delicious alternative to plums in this recipe.

Energy 236Kcal/985kJ; Protein 2.9g; Carbohydrate 25.8g, of which sugars 9.4g; Fat 14.1g, of which saturates 7.4g; Cholesterol 43mg; Calcium 45mg; Fibre 1.2g; Sodium 85mg.

BITTER CHOCOLATE MOUSSE

SABRA IS AN ISRAELI CHOCOLATE-ORANGE LIQUEUR. IF YOU DON'T HAVE IT, USE AN ORANGE LIQUEUR SUCH AS COINTREAU. WITH NO BUTTER OR CREAM, THIS IS A DELICIOUS AND STRONGLY CHOCOLATE DESSERT THAT MAY BE ENJOYED WITH EITHER MEAT OR DAIRY MEALS.

SERVES EIGHT

INGREDIENTS
  250g/10oz dark (bittersweet)
    chocolate, chopped
  30ml/2 tbsp sabra liqueur
  5 large (US extra large)
    eggs, separated
  45ml/3 tbsp caster (superfine) sugar

1 Place the chocolate and 60ml/4 tbsp water in a heavy pan. Melt over a low heat, stirring. Off the heat, whisk in the Sabra or orange liqueur. Beat the egg yolks until thick and creamy, then slowly beat into the melted chocolate until well blended.

2 In a clean, grease-free bowl, use an electric mixer to slowly whisk the egg whites until frothy. Increase the speed and continue until the egg whites form soft peaks. Gradually sprinkle the sugar over the egg white mixture and continue beating until the whites are stiff and glossy.

3 Using a rubber spatula or large metal spoon, stir a quarter of the egg whites into the chocolate mixture to lighten it, then gently fold in the remaining whites, cutting down to the bottom of the bowl, along the sides and up to the top in a semicircular motion until they are just combined. Don't worry about a few white streaks.

4 Gently spoon the mixture into eight individual dishes or a 2 litre/3½ pint/ 8 cup bowl. Chill for at least 2 hours until set before serving.

COOK'S TIPS
• Sabra is Hebrew for the prickly pear cactus fruit. Prickly on the outside, it is sweet within. The term also refers to native-born Israelis; tough on the outside, tender inside. And as a term for the native born, it is also the name of a popular Israeli dessert, which combines chocolate with the oranges that grow so beautifully in Israel.
• Be careful not to over-whisk the egg whites. The addition of 1.5ml/¼ tsp cream of tartar to the egg whites while they are being whisked will help them to stabilize and to hold their volume.

Energy 236Kcal/988kJ; Protein 5.5g; Carbohydrate 25.7g, of which sugars 25.4g; Fat 12.2g, of which saturates 6.2g; Cholesterol 121mg; Calcium 31mg; Fibre 0.8g; Sodium 46mg.

BAKED COFFEE CUSTARDS

SWEET, FRAGRANT CAFÉ AU LAIT, BAKED INTO A CUSTARD. EATEN COOL, IT MELTS HAPPILY IN THE MOUTH AND MAKES A LOVELY DESSERT FOR ANY FESTIVITY.

SERVES FOUR

INGREDIENTS
   35g/1½oz/8 tbsp finely ground
      strong coffee
   300ml/½ pint/1¼ cups milk
   150ml/¼ pint/⅔ cup single
      (light) cream
   2 eggs, beaten
   30ml/2 tbsp caster (superfine) sugar
   whipped cream and cocoa powder
      (unsweetened), to decorate

1 Preheat the oven to 190°C/375°F/ Gas 5. Put the ground coffee in a jug (pitcher). Heat the milk in a pan until it is nearly boiling. Pour over the coffee and leave to stand for 5 minutes.

2 Strain the coffee-flavoured milk back into the pan. Add the cream and heat again until nearly boiling.

3 Beat the eggs and sugar in a bowl. Pour the hot coffee-flavoured milk into the bowl, whisking all the time.

4 Strain the mixture into the rinsed jug then pour into four 150ml/¼ pint/⅔ cup ramekins. Cover each ramekin with a piece of foil.

COOK'S TIP
Make sure that the mixture does not boil once the cream has been added in step 2, or it will curdle.

5 Stand the ramekins in a roasting pan and pour in enough hot water to come halfway up the sides. Bake for 40 minutes, or until lightly set.

6 Remove the ramekins from the roasting pan and allow to cool. Chill for 2 hours. Decorate with a swirl of whipped cream and a sprinkle of cocoa powder, if you like, before serving.

Energy 173Kcal/725kJ; Protein 7g; Carbohydrate 12.2g, of which sugars 12.2g; Fat 11.2g, of which saturates 6.1g; Cholesterol 120mg; Calcium 142mg; Fibre 0g; Sodium 79mg.

LEKACH

THIS CAKE DATES BACK TO THE 12TH CENTURY, WHEN A SLICE WAS TAKEN TO JEWISH/HEBREW SCHOOL BY YOUNG BOYS ON THEIR FIRST DAY, WITH THE HOPE THAT THEIR LEARNING IN THE YEARS TO FOLLOW WOULD BE AS SWEET AS THIS MOIST CAKE.

SERVES ABOUT EIGHT

INGREDIENTS
175g/6oz/1½ cups plain
  (all-purpose) flour
75g/3oz/⅓ cup caster
  (superfine) sugar
2.5ml/½ tsp ground ginger
2.5–5ml/½–1 tsp ground cinnamon
5ml/1 tsp mixed (apple pie) spice
5ml/1 tsp bicarbonate of soda
  (baking soda)
225g/8oz/1 cup clear honey
60ml/4 tbsp vegetable or olive oil
grated rind of 1 orange
2 eggs
75ml/5 tbsp orange juice
10ml/2 tsp chopped fresh root
  ginger, or to taste

1 Preheat the oven to 180°C/350°F/ Gas 4. Line a rectangular baking tin (pan), measuring 25 × 20 × 5cm/ 10 × 8 × 2in, with baking parchment. In a large bowl, mix together the flour, sugar, ginger, cinnamon, mixed spice and bicarbonate of soda.

2 Make a well in the centre of the flour mixture and pour in the clear honey, vegetable or olive oil, orange rind and eggs. Using a wooden spoon or electric whisk, beat until smooth, then add the orange juice. Stir in the chopped ginger.

3 Pour the cake mixture into the prepared tin, then bake for about 50 minutes, or until firm to the touch.

4 Leave the cake to cool in the tin, then turn out and wrap tightly in foil. Store at room temperature for 2–3 days before serving to allow the flavours of the cake to mature.

COOK'S TIP
This honey cake keeps very well. It can be made in two loaf tins (pans), so that one cake can be eaten, while the other is wrapped in clear film (plastic wrap) and stored or frozen for a later date.

Energy 264Kcal/1115kJ; Protein 3.8g; Carbohydrate 49.1g, of which sugars 32.4g; Fat 7.2g, of which saturates 1.1g; Cholesterol 48mg; Calcium 45mg; Fibre 0.7g; Sodium 23mg.

PLUM AND ALMOND TART

THIS GERMAN JEWISH TART IS ENJOYED FOR ROSH HASHANAH, WHEN SWEET THINGS ARE EATEN FOR A SWEET NEW YEAR. IN SOUTHERN GERMANY THE PLUMS WERE RIPENING DURING THE TIME OF THE NEW YEAR CELEBRATIONS, AND SO THIS TART EVOLVED AS A SEASONAL TREAT.

SERVES SIX

INGREDIENTS
  175g/6oz/1½ cups plain
    (all-purpose) flour
  115g/4oz/8 tbsp butter, chilled
  60ml/4 tbsp sour cream
For the topping
  50g/2oz/4 tbsp butter, softened
  50g/2oz/¼ cup caster (superfine)
    sugar, plus 30ml/2 tbsp
    for sprinkling
  2 eggs, beaten
  115g/4oz/1 cup ground almonds
  about 6 plums, quartered and
    stoned (pitted)
  115g/4oz/scant ½ cup plum jam
  60ml/4 tbsp flaked (sliced) almonds

VARIATION
Make 4 individual tarts, like the one shown here. Thickly slice the plums instead of cutting them into quarters.

VARIATION
Apricots or greengages can be used instead of plums, if you like.

1 Sift the flour into a mixing bowl. Dice the butter and rub in until the mixture resembles fine breadcrumbs. Stir in the sour cream to make a soft dough. Wrap in clear film (plastic wrap) and chill for at least 30 minutes.

2 For the topping, cream the butter and sugar until light. Add the eggs, alternating with the ground almonds.

3 Preheat the oven to 220°C/425°F/ Gas 7. Roll out the pastry on a lightly floured surface to a 30cm/12in round, then transfer to a large baking sheet. Prick all over.

4 Spread the almond mixture over the pastry, leaving a border of about 4cm/1½in. Arrange the plums on top. Sprinkle with the 30ml/2 tbsp caster sugar. Turn in the border.

5 Bake the tart for 35–40 minutes, or until browned. Warm the plum jam in a small pan, press through a sieve (strainer) and brush over the tart to glaze. Sprinkle flaked almonds on top to decorate.

COOK'S TIP
Make sure the pastry is thoroughly chilled before using.

Energy 614Kcal/2562kJ; Protein 11.6g; Carbohydrate 49.7g, of which sugars 26.7g; Fat 42.5g, of which saturates 17g; Cholesterol 126mg; Calcium 142mg; Fibre 3.6g; Sodium 208mg.

BLACK FOREST CHERRY CAKE

ASHKENAZIC JEWS, ESPECIALLY FROM GERMANY, VIENNA, ALSACE AND HUNGARY, HAD A GREAT LOVE OF RICH, CREAMY CAKES. THIS LAYERING OF CHOCOLATE CAKE, CHERRY, KIRSCH, WHIPPED CREAM AND CHOCOLATE CURLS HAS NO RELIGIOUS SYMBOLISM. IT IS, HOWEVER, ONE OF THE MOST IRRESISTIBLE DELICACIES YOU COULD ASK FOR AND IS FIRMLY ENTRENCHED IN THE HIGH TEA CULTURE AS THE PERFECT ACCOMPANIMENT TO AN AFTERNOON CUP OF COFFEE.

SERVES TWELVE

INGREDIENTS
 200g/7oz plain (semisweet)
  chocolate, broken into squares
 115g/4oz/½ cup unsalted
  (sweet) butter
 3 eggs, separated
 115g/4oz/½ cup soft dark
  brown sugar
 45ml/3 tbsp Kirsch
 75g/3oz/⅔ cup self-raising
  (self-rising) flour, sifted
 50g/2oz/½ cup ground almonds
For the filling and topping
 130g/5oz plain
  (semi sweet) chocolate
 45ml/3 tbsp Kirsch
 425g/15oz can pitted black cherries,
  drained, with their juices reserved
 600ml/1 pint/2½ cups double
  (heavy) cream, lightly whipped
 12 fresh cherries with stalks

1 Preheat the oven to 180°C/350°F/ Gas 4. Grease and base-line a deep 20cm/8in round cake tin (pan) with greased baking parchment.

2 Melt the plain chocolate and butter in a heatproof bowl set over a pan of simmering water, stirring to mix. Remove from the heat and leave until barely warm.

3 Whisk the egg yolks and sugar in a bowl until very thick, then fold in the chocolate mixture and the Kirsch. Fold in the flour with the ground almonds. Whisk the egg whites in a grease-free bowl until stiff, then gently fold into the mixture.

4 Pour the mixture into the prepared cake tin and bake in the oven for 40 minutes, or until firm to the touch.

5 Allow the sponge to cool in the tin for 5 minutes, then turn out and cool on a wire rack. Use a long serrated knife to cut the cake horizontally into three even layers.

6 Meanwhile, make the chocolate curls. Melt the chocolate in a heatproof bowl set over a pan of simmering water, as before. Cool for around 5 minutes, then pour on to a board to set. Use a vegetable peeler to shave off thin curls.

7 Mix the Kirsch with 90ml/6tbsp of the reserved cherry juice. Place the bottom layer of sponge on a serving plate and sprinkle with 45ml/3 tbsp of the Kirsch syrup.

8 Spread one-third of the whipped cream over the sponge layer and sprinkle over half the cherries. Place the second layer of sponge on top and repeat with another third of the Kirsch syrup and cream and the remaining cherries. Place the final sponge layer on top and sprinkle the remaining Kirsch syrup over it.

9 Spread the remaining cream over the top of the cake. Sprinkle over the chocolate curls and top with the fresh cherries.

VARIATION
Try strawberries rather than cherries – both toppings are delicious.

Energy 604Kcal/2509kJ; Protein 5.5g; Carbohydrate 40g, of which sugars 34.9g; Fat 46.2g, of which saturates 26.9g; Cholesterol 138mg; Calcium 85mg; Fibre 1.4g; Sodium 115mg.

TORTE MIGDALOWY

AN EASTERN EUROPEAN TART, RICH WITH ALMONDS AND FLAVOURED WITH COFFEE ALMOND CREAM.
ENJOY IT AS A TREAT ON A FESTIVE AFTERNOON VISIT.

SERVES EIGHT TO TEN

INGREDIENTS
  75g/3oz/½ cup blanched almonds
  225g/8oz/1 cup butter, softened
  225g/8oz/generous 1 cup caster
    (superfine) sugar
  4 eggs, beaten
  150g/5oz/1¼ cups self-raising
    (self-rising) flour, sifted
For the icing
  175g/6oz/1 cup blanched almonds
  40g/1½oz/9 tbsp ground coffee
  75ml/5 tbsp near-boiling water
  150g/5oz/¾ cup caster
    (superfine) sugar
  90ml/6 tbsp water
  3 egg yolks
  225g/8oz/1 cup unsalted
    (sweet) butter

1 Preheat the oven to 190°C/375°F/
Gas 5. Lightly grease and base-line
3 x 18cm/7in round cake tins (pans)
with baking parchment.

2 Put the blanched almonds on a
baking sheet and roast in the oven for
7 minutes, or until golden brown.

3 Allow to cool, then transfer to a
processor or a blender and process
until fine.

4 Cream the butter and sugar together
in a bowl until pale and fluffy. Gradually
add the eggs, a little at a time, beating
well after each addition. Fold in the
ground roasted almonds and the flour.

5 Divide the cake mixture evenly
between the three prepared tins and
bake for 25–30 minutes, until well risen
and firm to the touch, swapping the
position of the top and bottom cakes
halfway through cooking. Turn out and
cool on a wire rack.

6 For the icing, put the blanched
almonds in a bowl and pour over
enough boiling water to cover. Leave
until cold, then drain the almonds and
cut each one lengthways into 4 or 5
slivers with a sharp knife. Roast on a
baking sheet for 6–8 minutes.

7 Put the ground coffee in a jug
(pitcher), spoon over the water and
leave to stand. Gently heat the sugar
and 90ml/6 tbsp water in a small heavy
pan until dissolved. Simmer for 3
minutes, until the temperature reaches
107°C/225°F on a sugar thermometer.

8 Put the egg yolks into a bowl and
pour over the syrup in a thin stream,
whisking all the time until very thick.
Cream the butter until soft, then
gradually beat the egg mixture into it.

9 Pour the coffee through a strainer
and beat it into the icing. Use about
two-thirds of the coffee cream to
sandwich the cakes together. Spread
the remainder over the top and press in
the almond slivers to create a tightly-
packed nut topping.

Energy 733Kcal/3050kJ; Protein 10.4g; Carbohydrate 52.5g, of which sugars 40.7g; Fat 55g, of which saturates 25.7g; Cholesterol 233mg; Calcium 159mg; Fibre 2.3g; Sodium 363mg.

WALNUT AND COFFEE SLICE

A BASE OF THIN FILO PASTRY IS TOPPED WITH A GROUND WALNUT MIXTURE AND COFFEE BUTTERCREAM. THIS IS QUINTESSENTIAL EASTERN EUROPEAN PATISSERIE.

SERVES EIGHT TO TWELVE

INGREDIENTS
   4 sheets of filo pastry
   50g/2oz/4 tbsp unsalted (sweet)
      butter, melted
   4 eggs, separated
   175g/6oz/scant 1 cup caster
      (superfine) sugar
   90g/3½oz/scant 1 cup walnuts,
      finely ground
   walnut pieces and sifted icing
      (confectioners') sugar, to decorate
For the topping
   200g/7oz/scant 1 cup unsalted
      butter, at room temperature
   1 egg yolk
   150g/5oz/¾ cup caster sugar
   45ml/3 tbsp cold strong coffee

1 Preheat the oven to 180°C/350°F/ Gas 4. Grease and line a deep 20cm/8in square cake tin (pan). Brush the sheets of filo pastry with the butter, fold them over and place them in the base of the prepared tin.

2 Whisk the egg yolks and sugar in a mixing bowl until thick and pale, and the whisk leaves a trail.

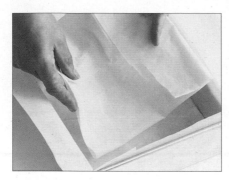

3 Whisk the egg whites until stiff. Fold in the ground nuts.

4 Fold the egg white into the egg yolk mixture. Spoon into the prepared tin. Bake for about 25–30 minutes, until firm. Allow to cool.

5 Meanwhile, for the topping, cream the ingredients well. Spread on the cake with a round-bladed knife. Sprinkle over the walnut pieces. Chill for at least 3–4 hours or overnight. Sprinkle with icing sugar and cut into fingers, triangles or squares.

VARIATION
Use pistachios in place of the walnuts if you prefer, grinding them in a food processor or blender.

Energy 357Kcal/1489kJ; Protein 4.1g; Carbohydrate 31.9g, of which sugars 28.7g; Fat 24.6g, of which saturates 11.9g; Cholesterol 125mg; Calcium 42mg; Fibre 0.4g; Sodium 153mg.

TORTE VARAZDIN

*THIS DARK CHOCOLATE CAKE FILLED WITH CHESTNUT CREAM AND ICED WITH CHOCOLATE GLAZE IS
AN EASTERN EUROPEAN TREAT FOR CHOCOLATE LOVERS*

SERVES EIGHT TO TWELVE

INGREDIENTS
   225g/8oz/1 cup butter, at
     room temperature
   225g/8oz/generous 1 cup caster
     (superfine) sugar
   200g/7oz plain (semisweet)
     chocolate, melted
   6 eggs, separated
   130g/4½oz/generous 1 cup plain
     (all-purpose) flour, sifted
   chocolate curls, to decorate
For the filling
   250ml/8fl oz/1 cup double (heavy)
     cream, lightly whipped
   450g/1lb/1¾ cups canned
     chestnut purée (paste)
   115g/4oz/generous ½ cup caster
     (superfine) sugar
For the topping
   150g/5oz/10 tbsp unsalted
     (sweet) butter
   150g/5oz/1¼ cups icing
     (confectioners') sugar, sifted
   115g/4oz plain (semisweet)
     chocolate, melted

1 Preheat the oven to 180°C/350°F/
Gas 4. Grease and line the base and
sides of a 20–23cm/8–9in round cake
tin (pan). Cream the butter and sugar
together in a bowl until pale and fluffy.
Stir in the melted chocolate and egg
yolks. Fold the flour carefully into the
chocolate mixture.

COOK'S TIP
Use good-quality chocolate with at least
70 per cent cocoa solids, if you can.

2 In a grease-free bowl, whisk the egg
whites until stiff. Add a spoonful of the
egg white to the chocolate mixture to
loosen it, then carefully fold in the
remainder. Spoon the cake mixture into
the prepared tin.

3 Bake the cake for 45–50 minutes, or
until firm to the touch and a skewer
inserted into the middle comes out
clean. Cool on a wire rack. When cold,
peel off the lining paper and slice the
cake in half horizontally.

4 Meanwhile, gently mix the filling
ingredients together in a bowl.
Sandwich the two cake halves together
firmly with the chestnut filling.

5 In a mixing bowl, cream together the
butter and sugar for the topping before
stirring in the melted chocolate. Using a
dampened knife, spread the chocolate
topping over the sides and top of the
cake. If possible, chill for 60 minutes
before serving, decorated with
chocolate curls.

Energy 731Kcal/3055kJ; Protein 3.8g; Carbohydrate 82g, of which sugars 62.4g; Fat 45.4g, of which saturates 27.9g; Cholesterol 97mg; Calcium 79mg; Fibre 2.5g; Sodium 202mg.

SUN-DRENCHED YOGURT AND LEMON CAKE

EASTERN EUROPE YOGURT COMBINES WONDERFULLY WITH A ZESTY ISRAELI-INSPIRED CITRUS TANG IN THIS MOIST, ROMANIAN-STYLE CAKE.

MAKES SIXTEEN

INGREDIENTS
  50g/2oz/4 tbsp butter, softened
  115g/4oz/generous ½ cup caster
    (superfine) sugar
  2 large eggs, separated
  115g/4oz/½ cup Greek (US strained
    plain) yogurt
  grated rind of 2 lemons
  juice of ½ lemon
  150g/5oz/1¼ cups self-raising
    (self-rising) flour
  2.5ml/½ tsp baking powder
  curls of lemon rind, to decorate
For the syrup
  juice of ½ lemon
  60ml/4 tbsp honey
  45ml/3 tbsp water
  1 small cinnamon stick

1 Preheat the oven to 190°C/375°F/ Gas 5. Grease and line a shallow 18cm/ 7in square cake tin (pan). Cream together the softened butter and sugar in a bowl until pale and fluffy.

2 Slowly add the egg yolks, yogurt and lemon rind and juice. Beat until smooth. In a separate, grease-free bowl, whisk the egg whites until they are just stiff.

3 Sift together the flour and baking powder. Fold into the yogurt mixture, then fold in the egg whites.

4 Spoon the mixture into the prepared cake tin. Bake for about 25 minutes, or until golden brown and firm to the touch. Turn out on to a plate and peel off the base paper.

5 Meanwhile, to make the syrup, put the lemon juice, honey, water and cinnamon stick together in a small pan. Stir until boiling then cook until the mixture is syrupy.

6 Remove the pan from the heat. Remove and discard the cinnamon stick. Spoon the warm syrup over the cake, then sprinkle with the lemon rind. Leave to cool completely before cutting into 16 pieces.

COOK'S TIP
Try a scented honey. The Romanian honey used in the local version has a natural perfume from the pollen of wild plants growing in the fruit orchards.

Energy 111Kcal/467kJ; Protein 2.1g; Carbohydrate 17.6g, of which sugars 10.7g; Fat 4.1g, of which saturates 2.2g; Cholesterol 30mg; Calcium 52mg; Fibre 0.3g; Sodium 67mg.

CITRUS RICOTTA SQUARES

TWO SPONGE LAYERS ARE FILLED WITH LEMON-SCENTED RICOTTA CHEESE IN THIS TASTY CAKE WHICH IS PERFECT FOR TEA-TIME ANYWHERE.

MAKES SIXTEEN

INGREDIENTS
    3 large eggs, separated
    175g/6oz/scant 1 cup caster
      (superfine) sugar
    45ml/3 tbsp hot water
    185g/6½oz/1⅔ cups plain
      (all-purpose) flour, sifted
    2.5ml/½ tsp baking powder
    icing (confectioners') sugar, sifted,
      for dredging
    long strands of lemon rind,
      to decorate
    fresh fruit, to serve
For the filling
    500g/1¼lb/2½ cups ricotta cheese
    100ml/3½fl oz/½ cup double
      (heavy) cream, lightly whipped
    25g/1oz/2 tbsp caster
      (superfine) sugar
    10ml/2 tsp lemon juice
    rind from 1 lemon

2 Fold the hot water into the egg yolks, together with the flour and baking powder. Lightly whisk the egg whites in a grease-free bowl and then fold these into the egg yolks.

3 Pour the sponge mixture into the prepared tin, tilting it to help ease the mixture into the corners. Bake for 15–20 minutes, or until golden brown and firm to the touch. Turn out and cool on a wire rack, then carefully slice in half horizontally.

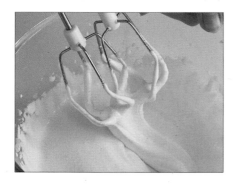

1 Preheat the oven to 190°C/375°F/ Gas 5. Grease a 30 x 20cm/12 x 8in Swiss roll tin (jelly roll pan). Whisk together the egg yolks and caster sugar in a large bowl until the mixture is pale and the whisk leaves a trail when lifted. (The mixture should triple in volume.)

COOK'S TIP
An ideal way of serving the citrus ricotta squares is with seasonal soft fruits such as blackberries, peaches or apricots which have been soaked in a little cherry brandy (maraska).

4 Make the filling by beating the ricotta cheese in a bowl and then stirring in the cream, caster sugar and lemon juice and lemon rind. Spread the filling on top of the base sponge then top with the remaining sponge half. Press down lightly on the top layer.

5 Chill the cake for 3–4 hours. Just before serving, dredge with a little icing sugar and decorate with the lemon rind. Cut into 16 squares and serve with fresh fruit.

Energy 146Kcal/611kJ; Protein 5.2g; Carbohydrate 11.7g, of which sugars 2.9g; Fat 9.1g, of which saturates 5.2g; Cholesterol 57mg; Calcium 25mg; Fibre 0.4g; Sodium 15mg.

TUSCAN LEMON SPONGE

THIS IS THE CLASSIC LEMON CAKE OF PESACH. IT MAY HAVE ORIGINATED IN THE LITTLE TUSCAN TOWN OF PITIGLIANO, WHOSE RICH JEWISH TRADITION DATES BACK TO THE 13TH CENTURY.

SERVES TEN TO TWELVE

INGREDIENTS

12 eggs, separated
300g/11oz/1½ cups caster
 (superfine) sugar
120ml/4fl oz/1 cup fresh lemon juice
grated rind of 2 lemons
50g/2oz/½ cup potato flour, sifted
90g/3½oz/¾ cup fine matzo meal
 or matzo meal flour, sifted
large pinch of salt
icing (confectioners') sugar,
 for dusting (optional)

1 Preheat the oven to 160°C/325°F/ Gas 3. Whisk the egg yolks until pale and frothy, then whisk in the sugar, lemon juice and lemon rind.

2 Fold the sifted flours into the egg mixture. In a clean bowl, whisk the egg whites with the salt until stiff, then fold into the egg yolk mixture. The consistency should be slightly thick and soufflé-like.

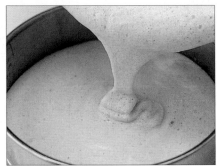

3 Pour the cake mixture into two deep, ungreased 25cm/10in cake tins (pans) and bake for about 1 hour, or until a cocktail stick (toothpick), inserted in the centre, comes out clean. Leave to cool in the tins.

4 When cold, turn out the cakes and invert on to a serving plate. Dust with a little icing sugar before serving, if you wish.

COOK'S TIPS
• If you don't have a cocktail stick (toothpick) to hand when testing to see if the cake is cooked, use a strand of raw dried spaghetti instead – it will work just as well.
• Serve this light and fluffy dessert with a refreshing fruit salad. Citrus fruits such as orange or grapefruit complement the lemon tang of the sponge very well.

Energy 169Kcal/716kJ; Protein 4.2g; Carbohydrate 33.1g, of which sugars 26.3g; Fat 3g, of which saturates 0.8g; Cholesterol 95mg; Calcium 29mg; Fibre 0.3g; Sodium 37mg.

PESACH ALMOND CAKES

ALMOND CAKE SUCH AS THIS PROBABLY HAS ITS ORIGINS IN THE JEWISH COMMUNITY OF VENICE. ITS POPULARITY WAS SPREAD BY CATHERINE DE MEDICI WHEN SHE BECAME QUEEN OF FRANCE IN 1547.

3 Put the oil, sugars, egg yolks, almond extract, vanilla extract, orange juice and half the brandy in a separate bowl. Stir, then add the almond mixture to form a thick batter. (You may find it is slightly lumpy.)

4 Whisk the egg whites until stiff. Fold one-third of the egg whites into the mixture to lighten it, then fold in the rest. Pour the mixture into the prepared tins and bake for 25–30 minutes.

5 Meanwhile, mix the remaining brandy with the icing sugar. If necessary, add a little water to make an icing with the consistency of single (light) cream. Remove the cake from the oven and prick the top all over with a skewer.

6 Pour the icing evenly over the top of the cake, then return the cake to the oven for a further 10 minutes, or until the top is crusty.

7 Leave the cake to cool in the tins, then serve cut into squares.

SERVES SIXTEEN

INGREDIENTS
  350g/12oz/3 cups ground almonds
  50g/2oz/½ cup matzo meal
  1.5ml/¼ tsp salt
  30ml/2 tbsp vegetable oil
  250g/9oz/1¼ cups sugar
  300g/11oz/1⅓ cups brown sugar
  3 eggs, separated
  7.5ml/1½ tsp almond extract
  5ml/1 tsp vanilla extract
  150ml/¼ pint/⅔ cup orange juice
  150ml/¼ pint/⅔ cup brandy
  200g/7oz/1¾ cups icing
    (confectioners') sugar
  90g/3½oz/scant 1 cup flaked
    (sliced) almonds

1 Preheat the oven to 180°C/350°F/Gas 4. Lightly grease two 30–38cm/12–15in square cake tins (pans).

2 Put the ground almonds, matzo meal and salt in a bowl and mix together.

Energy 415Kcal/1742kJ; Protein 7.6g; Carbohydrate 54g, of which sugars 51g; Fat 17.9g, of which saturates 1.7g; Cholesterol 36mg; Calcium 97mg; Fibre 2.1g; Sodium 21mg.

POLISH APPLE CAKE

THIS TRADITIONAL CAKE IS FIRM AND MOIST, WITH PIECES OF APPLE PEEKING THROUGH THE TOP. IT ORIGINATED IN POLAND AND HAS BEEN CARRIED TO THE FOUR CORNERS OF THE EARTH BY EMIGRANTS. IT IS POPULAR AMONG PERUVIAN JEWS AS PASTEL DE MANZANA.

2 Put the sliced apples in a bowl and mix with the cinnamon and 75ml/5 tbsp of the sugar.

3 In a separate bowl, beat together the eggs, remaining sugar, vegetable oil, orange juice and vanilla extract until well combined. Sift in the remaining flour and salt and stir into the mixture.

4 Pour two-thirds of the cake mixture into the prepared tin, top with one-third of the apples, then pour over the remaining cake mixture and top with the remaining apple. Bake for about 1 hour, or until golden brown.

5 Leave the cake to cool in the tin to allow the juices to soak in. Serve while still warm, cut into squares.

COOK'S TIP

This sturdy little cake is good to serve with tea on a Shabbat afternoon. Using orange juice instead of milk is typical of Jewish baking, as it allows the cake to be eaten with both meat and dairy meals.

SERVES SIX TO EIGHT

INGREDIENTS
  375g/13oz/3¼ cups self-raising
    (self-rising) flour
  3–4 large cooking apples, or
    a mixture of cooking and
    eating apples
  10ml/2 tsp ground cinnamon
  500g/1¼ lb/2½ cups caster
    (superfine) sugar
  4 eggs, lightly beaten
  250ml/8fl oz/1 cup vegetable oil
  120ml/4fl oz/½ cup
    orange juice
  10ml/2 tsp vanilla extract
  2.5ml/½ tsp salt

1 Preheat the oven to 180°C/350°F/ Gas 4. Grease a 30 × 38cm/12 × 15in square cake tin (pan) and dust with a little of the flour. Core and thinly slice the apples, but do not peel.

Energy 653Kcal/2751kJ; Protein 7.8g; Carbohydrate 105.4g, of which sugars 70.6g; Fat 25.2g, of which saturates 3.4g; Cholesterol 95mg; Calcium 215mg; Fibre 2.1g; Sodium 210mg.

RUSSIAN POPPY SEED CAKE

THIS PLAIN AND SIMPLE CAKE IS MADE FROM GROUND BLACK POPPY SEEDS WHICH GIVE IT A DISTINCTIVE TASTE THAT IS UTTERLY DELICIOUS. TRADITIONALLY CALLED MOHN TORTE OR KINDLI, IT IS THE STAPLE OF RUSSIAN BAKERIES, WHERE IT IS SERVED WITH GLASSES OF HOT TEA AND LEMON.

SERVES ABOUT EIGHT

INGREDIENTS

130g/4½oz/generous 1 cup
self-raising (self-rising) flour
5ml/1 tsp baking powder
2.5ml/½ tsp salt
2 eggs
225g/8oz/generous 1 cup caster
(superfine) sugar
5–10ml/1–2 tsp vanilla
extract
200g/7oz/scant 1½ cups poppy
seeds, ground
15ml/1 tbsp grated lemon rind
120ml/4fl oz/½ cup milk
130g/4½oz/generous ½ cup
unsalted (sweet) butter, melted
and cooled
30ml/2 tbsp vegetable oil
icing (confectioners') sugar, sifted,
for dusting

1 Preheat the oven to 180°C/350°F/
Gas 4. Grease a deep 23cm/9in
springform tin (pan). Sift together the
flour, baking powder and salt.

2 Using an electric whisk, beat
together the eggs, sugar and vanilla
extract for 4–5 minutes until pale and
fluffy. Stir in the poppy seeds and the
lemon rind.

VARIATION
To make a poppy seed tart, pour the cake
mixture into a par-cooked pastry case
(pie shell), then bake for 30 minutes, or
until the filling is firm and risen.

3 Gently fold the sifted ingredients
into the egg and poppy seed mixture,
working in three batches and alternating
with the milk, then fold in the melted
butter and vegetable oil.

4 Pour the mixture into the tin and
bake for 40 minutes, or until firm. Cool
in the tin for 15 minutes, then invert
the cake on to a wire rack. Serve cold,
dusted with icing sugar.

Energy 485Kcal/2023kJ; Protein 8.3g; Carbohydrate 42.7g, of which sugars 30.5g; Fat 32.4g, of which saturates 11.4g; Cholesterol 83mg; Calcium 267mg; Fibre 2.5g; Sodium 188mg.

M'HANNCHA

THIS CRISP-CRUSTED, PERFUMED, ALMOND-FILLED PASTRY IS A FAVOURITE OF SEPHARDIC JEWS FROM TUNISIA AND, ESPECIALLY, MOROCCO. ENJOY IT WITH A SMALL CUP OF MINT TEA.

SERVES EIGHT TO TEN

INGREDIENTS
  115g/4oz/1 cup blanched almonds
  300g/11oz/2¾ cups ground almonds
  50g/2oz/½ cup icing
    (confectioners') sugar
  115g/4oz/⅔ cup caster
    (superfine) sugar
  115g/4oz/½ cup butter, softened,
    plus 20g/¾oz for cooking nuts
  5–10ml/1–2 tsp ground cinnamon
  15ml/1 tbsp orange flower water
  3–4 sheets filo pastry
  1 egg yolk
For the topping
  icing (confectioners') sugar
  ground cinnamon

1 Fry the blanched almonds in a little butter until golden brown, then pound them using a pestle and mortar until they resemble coarse breadcrumbs.

VARIATION
Use pistachios instead of the blanched almonds and pound in the same way.

2 Place the nuts in a bowl and add the ground almonds, icing sugar, caster sugar, butter, cinnamon and orange flower water. Use your hands to form the mixture into a smooth paste. Cover and chill in the refrigerator for about 30 minutes.

3 Preheat the oven to 180°C/350°F/ Gas 4. Open out the sheets of filo pastry, keeping them in a pile so they do not dry out, and brush the top one with a little melted butter.

4 Take lumps of the almond paste and roll them into fingers. Place them end to end along the long edge of the top sheet of filo, then roll the filo up into a roll the thickness of your thumb, tucking in the ends to stop the filling oozing out. Repeat with the other sheets of filo, until all the filling is used up.

5 Grease a large round baking tin (pan) or the widest baking sheet you can find. Lift one of the filo rolls in both hands and gently push it together from both ends, like an accordion, to relax the pastry before coiling it in the centre of the tin or baking sheet. Do the same with the other rolls, placing them end to end to form a tight coil like a snake.

6 Mix the egg yolk with a little water and brush this over the pastry, then bake for 30–35 minutes, until crisp and lightly browned. Top the freshly cooked pastry with a liberal sprinkling of icing sugar, and add lines of cinnamon in the form of the spokes of a wheel. Serve at room temperature.

Energy 421Kcal/1750kJ; Protein 9.5g; Carbohydrate 22.5g, of which sugars 19.1g; Fat 33.2g, of which saturates 8g; Cholesterol 45mg; Calcium 117mg; Fibre 3.2g; Sodium 78mg.

TUNISIAN ALMOND CIGARS

A VARIATION ON M'HANNCHA, THESE PASTRIES ARE A GREAT FAVOURITE OF THE JEWS OF NORTH AFRICA, ESPECIALLY TUNISIA. SERVE THEM WITH A SMALL CUP OF FRAGRANT MINT TEA OR STRONG, DARK COFFEE.

MAKES EIGHT TO TWELVE

INGREDIENTS
250g/9oz almond paste, prepared according to the instructions opposite (reduce the amounts of all ingredients by about a third), or ready-made
1 egg, lightly beaten
15ml/1 tbsp rose water or orange flower water
5ml/1 tsp ground cinnamon
1.5ml/¼ tsp almond extract
8–12 sheets filo pastry
melted butter, for brushing
icing (confectioners') sugar and ground cinnamon, for dusting
mint tea or black coffee, to serve

1 Knead the almond paste until soft, then put in a bowl, and mix in the egg, flower water, cinnamon and almond extract. Chill for 1–2 hours.

2 Preheat the oven to 190°C/375°F/Gas 5. Lightly grease a baking sheet. Place a sheet of filo pastry on a piece of greaseproof (waxed) paper, keeping the remaining pastry covered with a damp cloth, and brush with the melted butter.

3 Shape 30–45ml/2–3 tbsp of the almond filling mixture into a cylinder and place at one end of the pastry. Fold the pastry over to enclose the ends of the filling, then roll it up to form a fat cigar shape. Place it on the baking sheet and make 7–11 more cigars in the same way.

4 Bake the pastries for about 15 minutes, or until golden. Leave to cool. Dust with sugar and cinnamon, and serve with tea or coffee.

VARIATION
Instead of dusting with sugar, drench the pastries in syrup. In a pan, dissolve 250g/9oz/1¼ cups sugar in 250ml/8fl oz/1 cup water and boil until thickened. Stir in a squeeze of lemon juice and a few drops of rose water and pour over the pastries. Allow the syrup to soak in before serving.

COOK'S TIP
If you lack the time and ingredients to prepare your own almond paste, you can of course use ready-made blocks, bought from a confectioner or supermarket. Choose a good quality brand.

Energy 109Kcal/458kJ; Protein 2.2g; Carbohydrate 18.9g, of which sugars 14.2g; Fat 3.2g, of which saturates 0.4g; Cholesterol 16mg; Calcium 25mg; Fibre 0.6g; Sodium 10mg.

BAKLAVA

THIS MIDDLE EASTERN PASTRY MADE OF CRISP FILO, FILLED WITH CRUSHED NUTS AND DRENCHED IN FRAGRANT SYRUP, IS FAMOUSLY DOTED ON IN GREECE AND TURKEY, AND IS AS MUCH A FAVOURITE OF THE SEPHARDIC JEWS AS IT IS OF ARAB COMMUNITIES.

MAKES TWENTY-FOUR PIECES

INGREDIENTS

175g/6oz/¾ cup butter, melted
400g/14oz packet filo pastry, thawed
  if frozen
30ml/2 tbsp lemon juice
60ml/4 tbsp clear thick honey
50g/2oz/¼ cup caster
  (superfine) sugar
finely grated rind of 1 lemon
10ml/2 tsp cinnamon
200g/7oz/1¾ cups blanched
  almonds, chopped
200g/7oz/1¾ cups walnuts, chopped
75g/3oz/¾ cup pistachios or
  hazelnuts, chopped
chopped pistachios, to decorate
For the syrup
350g/12oz/1¾ cups caster
  (superfine) sugar
115g/4oz/½ cup clear honey
600ml/1 pint/2½ cups water
2 strips of thinly pared lemon rind
5ml/1 tsp orange flower or rose water,
  or to taste

1 Preheat the oven to 160°C/325°F/ Gas 3. Brush the base of a shallow 30 x 20cm/12 x 8in loose-bottomed or Swiss roll tin (jelly roll pan) with a little of the melted butter.

2 Using the tin as a guide, cut the sheets of filo pastry with a sharp knife so that they fit the tin exactly.

3 Place one sheet of pastry in the base of the tin, brush with a little melted butter, then repeat until you have used half of the pastry sheets. Set the remaining pastry aside and cover with a clean dish towel.

4 To make the filling, place the lemon juice, honey and sugar in a pan and heat gently until dissolved. Stir in the lemon rind, cinnamon and chopped nuts. Mix thoroughly.

5 Spread half the filling over the pastry, cover with three layers of the filo pastry and butter then spread the remaining filling over the pastry.

COOK'S TIP
It is important to leave the baklava to soak in the syrup for long enough to thoroughly combine before serving. Allow plenty of time to do this. You would preferably make it the day before.

6 Finish by using up the remaining sheets of pastry and butter on top, and brush the top of the pastry liberally with butter.

7 Using a sharp knife, carefully mark the pastry into squares, almost cutting through the filling. Bake in the preheated oven for 1 hour, or until crisp and golden brown.

8 Meanwhile, make the syrup. Place the caster sugar, honey, water and lemon rind in a pan and stir over a low heat until the sugar and honey have dissolved. Bring to the boil, then boil for a further 10 minutes until the mixture has thickened slightly.

9 Take the syrup off the heat and leave to cool slightly. Remove the baklava from the oven. Remove and discard the lemon rind from the syrup and stir in the orange flower or rose water, then pour over the pastry. Leave to soak for 6 hours. Cut into squares and serve, decorated with chopped pistachios.

Energy 308Kcal/1289kJ; Protein 4.9g; Carbohydrate 33.2g, of which sugars 23.3g; Fat 18.2g, of which saturates 4.9g; Cholesterol 16mg; Calcium 59mg; Fibre 1.5g; Sodium 65mg.

KOURABIETHES

SUGAR-DUSTED SHORTBREADS ARE ADORED BY BOTH ASHKENAZIM AND SEPHARDIM ALIKE, FROM THE ROUND LITTLE MELT-IN-THE-MOUTH BALLS OF EASTERN EUROPE TO THESE GREEK STARS. THE STAR SHAPE MAKES THEM AN IDEAL BREAK-THE-FAST TREAT FOR YOM KIPPUR, WHEN YOU MUST COUNT THREE STARS IN THE SKY FOR THE DAY, AND THE FAST, TO BE OVER.

MAKES TWENTY TO TWENTY-TWO

INGREDIENTS
  225g/8oz/1 cup unsalted
    (sweet) butter
  150g/5oz/⅔ cup caster
    (superfine) sugar
  2 egg yolks
  5ml/1 tsp vanilla extract
  2.5ml/½ tsp bicarbonate of soda
    (baking soda)
  45ml/3 tbsp brandy
  500g/1¼lb/5 cups plain (all-purpose)
    flour, sifted with a pinch of salt
  150g/5oz/1¼ cups blanched
    almonds, toasted and coarsely
    chopped
  350g/12oz/3 cups icing
    (confectioners') sugar

1 Cream the butter and beat in the caster sugar gradually, until light and fluffy. Beat in the egg yolks one at a time, then the vanilla. Mix the bicarbonate of soda with the brandy and stir into the mixture. Add the flour sifted with salt and mix to a firm dough. Knead lightly, add the almonds and then knead again.

2 Preheat the oven to 180°C/350°F/ Gas 4. Cover half the dough with clear film (plastic wrap) and set aside.

VARIATION
Another variation on the nocturnal theme is to cut the pastry into half-moon shapes, which can be done very easily using a round object or pastry cutter. Or cut a combination of stars and moons.

3 Roll out the remaining dough until about 2.5cm/1in thick. Press out star shapes, using pastry cutters. Repeat with the remaining dough. Place on the baking sheets and bake for 20–25 minutes, or until pale golden. Do not let them brown.

4 Meanwhile, sift a quarter of the icing sugar on to a platter. As soon as the kourabiethes come out of the oven, dust them generously with icing sugar. Let them cool for a few minutes, then place them on the sugar-coated platter.

5 Sift the remaining icing sugar over them. The aim is to give them a generous coating, so they are almost pure white in colour.

Energy 305Kcal/1280kJ; Protein 4.5g; Carbohydrate 41.9g, of which sugars 24.4g; Fat 13.9g, of which saturates 6.1g; Cholesterol 73mg; Calcium 68mg; Fibre 1.2g; Sodium 67mg.

GUIRLACHE

VARIATIONS OF THIS NUT BRITTLE ARE EATEN IN BOTH ASHKENAZIC AND SEPHARDIC KITCHENS. YOU SEE THEM SOLD ON THE STREETS OF JERUSALEM, OR SERVED ON A HOLIDAY TABLE. THE ASHKENAZIC VERSIONS USE HONEY AND REMAIN CHEWY. THIS SPANISH VERSION SHOULD BE CRISP AND CRUNCHY. IT IS DELICIOUS WITH TEA OR COFFEE, OR COARSELY GROUND AND FOLDED INTO VANILLA ICE CREAM!

MAKES ABOUT TWENTY-FOUR PIECES

INGREDIENTS
115g/4oz/1 cup almonds, half
  blanched, half unblanched
115g/4oz/1 cup hazelnuts, half
  blanched, half unblanched
5ml/1 tsp almond oil or
  a flavourless oil
200g/7oz/1 cup granulated sugar
15ml/1 tbsp lemon juice

COOK'S TIP
Guirlache may be served as an after-dinner treat. It is very good when pulverized and used as a topping for mousses and whipped cream. It also makes wonderful ice cream.

1 Preheat the oven to 150°C/300°F/Gas 2. Sprinkle the nuts on a baking sheet and toast for about 30 minutes, shaking the sheet occasionally. The nuts should smell pleasant, have turned brown and be very dry.

2 Coarsely chop the toasted nuts or crush them roughly with a rolling pin. Cover another baking sheet with foil and grease it generously with the oil.

3 Put the sugar in a pile in a small pan and pour the lemon juice round it. Cook over a high heat, shaking the pan, until the sugar turns a coffee colour. (As it cooks, the pile of sugar will melt and collapse into caramel.)

4 Immediately tip in the nuts and stir once, then pour the mixture on to the foil and spread out into a thin, even layer. Leave the mixture to harden.

5 Once set, break up the caramel into pieces and store in an airtight tin.

VARIATION
Use 250g/8oz sesame seeds instead of the almonds and hazelnuts.

Energy 93Kcal/390kJ; Protein 1.7g; Carbohydrate 9.3g, of which sugars 9.1g; Fat 5.7g, of which saturates 0.4g; Cholesterol 0mg; Calcium 23mg; Fibre 0.7g; Sodium 1mg.

COCONUT MACAROONS

In America, coconut macaroons are synonymous with Pesach. Finely grated coconut gives these soft-centred cookies a rich creaminess. Although they are often purchased from confectioners in tins, these macaroons can be easily prepared at home and, when cooked, can be stored in an airtight container for up to one week.

MAKES SIXTEEN TO EIGHTEEN

INGREDIENTS
   50g/2oz/1 cup creamed coconut,
     chilled (or 60ml/4 tbsp/
     ¼ cup coconut cream)
   2 large (US extra large) egg whites
   90g/3½oz/½ cup caster
     (superfine) sugar
   75g/3oz/1 cup desiccated (dry
     unsweetened shredded) coconut

VARIATIONS
• Add 45ml/3 tbsp cocoa in step 2.
• Add some almond extract in step 2.
• Add about 120–175g/4–6oz small
plain (semi sweet) chocolate chips
in step 2.

1 Preheat the oven to 180°C/350°F/
Gas 4. Line a large baking sheet with
baking parchment. If using creamed
coconut, grate this finely.

2 Use an electric beater to whisk the
egg whites in a large bowl until stiff.
Whisk in the sugar, a little at a time, to
make a stiff and glossy meringue. Fold
in the grated creamed coconut (or
coconut cream), and desiccated
coconut, using a large metal spoon.

COOK'S TIP
Cooking these sweet treats on baking
parchment ensures that they can be
easily removed from the baking sheet.

3 Place dessertspoonfuls of the
mixture, spaced slightly apart, on the
baking sheet. Bake for 15–20 minutes,
until slightly risen and golden brown.
Leave to cool on the parchment, then
transfer to an airtight container.

Energy 65Kcal/270kJ; Protein 0.7g; Carbohydrate 5.7g, of which sugars 5.7g; Fat 4.5g, of which saturates 3.9g; Cholesterol 0mg; Calcium 4mg; Fibre 0.6g; Sodium 9mg.

RICH CHOCOLATE BROWNIES

*CAN YOU IMAGINE AN AMERICAN BAR MITZVAH SPREAD WITHOUT DELICIOUS CHOCOLATE BROWNIES?
THIS VERSION IS PACKED WITH CHOCOLATE. MANY OF THE MARRANO (SECRET) JEWS WERE IMPORT-
EXPORTERS OF CHOCOLATE FROM VENEZUELA AND HELPED TO SPREAD CHOCOLATE THROUGH EUROPE
VIA BAYONNE, BORDEAUX AND AMSTERDAM.*

MAKES SIXTEEN

INGREDIENTS
   300g/12oz plain (semisweet)
     chocolate chunks
   175g/6oz/¾ cup unsalted
     (sweet) butter
   75g/3oz/⅔ cup self-raising
     (self-rising) flour
   125g/4oz/½ cup sugar, or to taste
   3 large (US extra large) eggs, beaten
   a few drops of vanilla extract
   a tiny pinch of salt
   150g/6oz chocolate chips

1 Preheat the oven to 180°C/350°F/
Gas 4. Line the base and sides of a
20cm/8in square cake tin (pan) with
baking parchment.

2 Put the plain chocolate in a
heatproof bowl with the butter. Melt
over a pan of barely simmering water,
stirring frequently.

3 Stir the flour, sugar and eggs into the
melted chocolate until evenly combined,
then add the vanilla and salt.

4 Add the chocolate chips, then turn
the mixture into the prepared tin,
spreading it into the corners.

5 Bake the brownies for 30–35
minutes, until risen and just firm to the
touch. Leave to cool in the tin, then cut
the mixture into squares. Store the
brownies in an airtight container.

COOK'S TIP
If you can, use good-quality chocolate
with at least 70 per cent cocoa solids.
It will bring out the very best results
in this recipe.

Energy 285Kcal/1190kJ; Protein 3.1g; Carbohydrate 29.6g, of which sugars 25.9g; Fat 18g, of which saturates 10.7g; Cholesterol 61mg; Calcium 37mg; Fibre 0.9g; Sodium 98mg.

TISHPISHTI

TISHPISHTI IS A SEPHARDIC SPECIALITY, A NUT-RICH CAKE, DRENCHED IN SYRUP AND CUT INTO DIAMOND SHAPES OR SMALL WEDGES. IT IS TRADITIONALLY EATEN DURING PESACH BY THE JEWS OF TURKEY, GREECE AND SPAIN, THOUGH THE INGREDIENTS USED TEND TO VARY A LITTLE. THIS VERSION IS A SUPER-DELUXE ONE, PREPARED WITH WALNUTS, ALMONDS AND A HANDFUL OF PINE NUTS.

SERVES SIX TO EIGHT

INGREDIENTS
 500g/1¼lb/2½ cups caster
  (superfine) sugar
 1 litre/1¾ pints/4 cups cold water
 1 cinnamon stick
 15ml/1 tbsp rose water
 15ml/1 tbsp lemon juice
 5 eggs
 125g/4oz walnuts
 100g/4oz blanched almonds
 30ml/2 tbsp pine nuts
 5ml/1 tsp ground cinnamon

2 Grind the walnuts and almonds and mix with the eggs, remaining sugar and pine nuts.

1 Put two-thirds of the sugar in a heavy pan, pour in the water and add the cinnamon stick. Bring the mixture to the boil, stirring until the sugar dissolves, then boil without stirring for about 4 minutes to make a syrup. Set aside and when it is cool, add the rose water and lemon.

3 Scrape the mixture into a 30cm/ 12in round cake tin (pan), which is preferably non-stick. Bake at 350°C/180°F/Gas 4 for 1 hour.

4 Pour the cold syrup over the hot cake and sprinkle with cinnamon. Leave to cool and serve at room temperature.

COOK'S TIP
Whichever version of this cake you choose to prepare, as with all syrup-drenched desserts it will be much better if prepared a day before being eaten.

COOK'S TIP
The all-hazelnut version of this cake, kalbel louz, originated among Jews from Algeria, and the "louz" of the name actually means "hazelnuts".

VARIATIONS
Tishpishti exists in so many different forms, according to the culture that prepares it. Varying either the nutty or syrupy components will produce quite different results, so try experimenting with the following:
• Halvas: The Greek version is perhaps the most straightforward, as it omits the baking. To make the nutty mixture, use 350g/12oz/2 cups coarse semolina, 50g/2oz/½ cup blanched almonds and 30ml/2 tbsp pine nuts. Prepare the syrup as for step 1 of the recipe given opposite. Brown the semolina in a pan until light brown and almost smoking. Add the almonds and pine nuts and brown together over a low heat. Add the hot, sugary cinnamon syrup to the semolina mixture. It will hiss and spit at this point, so do stand well clear and use an oven glove. Return the pan, which now contains all the ingredients, to a gentle heat and stir until the syrup has been absorbed and the mixture is smooth. Scrape into a cake tin as for step 3, but do not bake – simply leave to cool. Dust with a sprinkle of ground cinnamon when cool enough to serve.
• Kalbel louz: Use only 100g/4oz hazelnuts and no other nuts. Instead, add 100g/4oz fine matzo meal to the ground hazelnuts in step 2 and then mix the nutty paste with the eggs and sugar, before following the directions for steps 3 and 4.
• Orange-almond tishpishti is just a slight variation on the tishpishti *recipe* given here. For step 1, omit the rosewater completely, and substitute half the cold water for 500ml/1 pint/2 cups fresh orange juice. Add the zest of 1 orange when bringing the liquid to the boil. For step 2, omit the walnuts, using 125g/4oz matzo meal in their place.

Energy 502Kcal/2108kJ; Protein 9.7g; Carbohydrate 66.8g, of which sugars 66.4g; Fat 23.7g, of which saturates 2.6g; Cholesterol 119mg; Calcium 96mg; Fibre 1.5g; Sodium 50mg.

MOIST AND ALMOND CAKE

*THIS MAY WELL BE THE FIRST TIME YOU HAVE GROUND AN ORANGE UP WHOLE, TO USE IN A CAKE.
THE KEY TO THIS RECIPE IS TO COOK THE ORANGE SLOWLY FIRST, SO THAT IT IS COMPLETELY TENDER
BEFORE IT IS BLENDED. DO NOT BE TEMPTED TO USE A MICROWAVE TO SPEED THINGS UP, AS IT WILL
IMPAIR THE FLAVOUR OF THIS SPECIAL CAKE.*

SERVES EIGHT

INGREDIENTS

   1 large Valencia or Navelina orange
   butter or oil, for greasing
   3 eggs
   225g/8oz/generous 1 cup caster
    (superfine) sugar
   5ml/1 tsp baking powder (omit
    for Pesach)
   225g/8oz/2 cups ground almonds
   25g/1oz/¼ cup plain (all-purpose)
    flour
   icing (confectioners') sugar,
    for dusting

1 Pierce the orange with a skewer. Put
it in a deep pan and pour over water to
cover it. Bring to the boil, then cover
and simmer for 1 hour until the skin is
soft. Drain, then cool.

2 Preheat the oven to 180°C/350°F/
Gas 4. Lightly grease a 20cm/8in round
cake tin (pan) and line it with baking
parchment. Cut the cooled orange in
half and discard all the pips (seeds).
Place the orange, peel, skin and all, in
a food processor or blender and
process until smooth and pulpy.

3 In a bowl, whisk the eggs and sugar
until thick. Fold in the baking powder,
almonds and flour. Fold in the
processed orange.

4 Pour into the prepared tin, level the
surface and bake for 1 hour, or until a
skewer inserted into the middle comes
out clean. Cool the cake in the tin for
10 minutes, then turn out on to a wire
rack, peel off the lining paper and cool
completely. Dust the top liberally with
icing sugar and serve.

COOK'S TIPS
• Serve with a compote of sliced oranges
dressed with sugar, orange flower water,
and a sprinkle of cinnamon.
• For Pesach, substitute fine matzo meal
for the plain (all-purpose) flour.

Energy 327Kcal/1369kJ; Protein 8.9g; Carbohydrate 35g, of which sugars 31.9g; Fat 17.8g, of which saturates 1.8g; Cholesterol 71mg; Calcium 105mg; Fibre 2.4g; Sodium 33mg.

LEMON AND LIME SYRUP CAKE

SIMPLE CAKES, DRENCHED IN CITRUS JUICE AND ZESTY WITH RIND, ARE PART OF A TRADITION OF SWEET TREATS CARRIED BY THE SPANISH JEWISH COMMUNITY, PROBABLY OF SEVILLE, TO NORTH AFRICA. LEMON, LIME AND ORANGE JUICE ARE ALL DELICIOUS. WHEN ISRAEL CAME INTO EXISTENCE AND BEGAN TO GROW ABUNDANT CITRUS FRUITS, CAKES LIKE THIS BECAME EXTREMELY POPULAR.

SERVES EIGHT

INGREDIENTS
225g/8oz/1 cup butter, softened, plus extra for greasing
225g/8oz/2 cups self-raising (self-rising) flour
5ml/1 tsp baking powder
225g/8oz/generous 1 cup caster (superfine) sugar
4 eggs, beaten
grated rind of 2 lemons
30ml/2 tbsp lemon juice
For the topping
finely pared rind of 1 lime
juice of 2 limes
150g/5oz/¾ cup caster (superfine) sugar

VARIATION
Use lemon rind and juice instead of lime for the topping if you like. You will need only one large lemon.

1 Preheat the oven to 160°C/325°F/ Gas 3. Grease and line a 20cm/8in round cake tin (pan). Sift the flour and baking powder into a bowl. Add the caster sugar, butter and eggs and beat until the mixture is smooth and creamy.

2 Beat in the lemon rind and juice. Spoon the mixture into the tin, smooth the surface and gently indent the top with the back of a spoon.

3 Bake for 1¼–1½ hours, or until the cake is golden on top and spongy when lightly pressed, and a skewer inserted in the centre comes out clean.

4 Meanwhile, mix the ingredients for the topping together. As soon as the cake is cooked, remove it from the oven and pour the topping evenly over the surface. Leave the cake to cool fully in the tin before removing and serving.

Energy 527Kcal/2209kJ; Protein 6.2g; Carbohydrate 71g, of which sugars 49.6g; Fat 26.3g, of which saturates 15.5g; Cholesterol 155mg; Calcium 84mg; Fibre 0.9g; Sodium 209mg.

PICKLES AND CONDIMENTS

Kosher dill pickles, resplendent with garlic and dill, are a deli treat taken to America from Eastern Europe. These are not the only one of their kind in the Jewish kitchen, however. There is a wide variety of pickles and condiments, from pink pickled turnips to the golden mixed vegetables of the Sephardic kitchen. Hot peppers, herbs and other aromatics make up a grand array of condiments too, from the green chutneys of Indian Jews to the spiced chilli sauces of Israel's Yemenite and North African Jews.

KOSHER DILL PICKLES

REDOLENT OF GARLIC AND SALT, DILL PICKLES CAN BE SUPPLE AND SUCCULENT OR CRISP AND CRUNCHY. THIS IS THE PICKLE OF NEW YORK CITY, JUST SALT BRINE, NO VINEGAR!

MAKES ABOUT FOUR JARS

INGREDIENTS
20 small, ridged or knobbly
  pickling cucumbers
2 litres/4 pints/2 quarts water
175g/6oz/generous ¾ cup kosher salt
  or coarse sea salt
15–20 garlic cloves, unpeeled
2 bunches fresh dill
15ml/1 tbsp dill seeds
30ml/2 tbsp mixed
  pickling spice
½ hot chilli, quartered

1 Scrub the cucumbers and rinse well in a bowl of cold water. Leave to dry.

2 Put the measured water and kosher or sea salt in a large pan and bring to the boil. Turn off the heat and leave to cool to room temperature.

3 Using the flat blade of a knife or a wooden mallet, lightly crush each garlic clove, breaking the papery skin.

4 Pack the cucumbers tightly into four 1.2 litre/2 pint wide-necked, sterilized jars, layering them with the garlic, fresh dill, dill seeds and mixed pickling spice. Add one piece of chilli to each jar. Pour over the cooled brine, making sure that the cucumbers are completely covered.

5 Cover the jars and leave to stand at room temperature for 4–7 days before serving. Store in a refrigerator.

COOK'S TIPS
• If you cannot find ridged or knobbly pickling cucumbers, use any kind of small cucumbers instead.
• If you have a dishwasher, prepare the jars by running them through on the highest heat setting.

Energy 50Kcal/200kJ; Protein 3.5g; Carbohydrate 7.5g, of which sugars 7g; Fat 0.5g, of which saturates 0g; Cholesterol 0mg; Calcium 93mg; Fibre 3g; Sodium 9840mg.

PRESERVED LEMONS

THESE ARE WIDELY USED IN MOROCCAN COOKING. THE INTERESTING THING ABOUT PRESERVED LEMONS IS THAT YOU ACTUALLY ONLY EAT THE PEEL. THIS CONTAINS THE ESSENTIAL FLAVOUR OF THE LEMON AND GETS SILKY AS IT PICKLES, WHILE ITS LEMON SCENT INTENSIFIES. TRADITIONALLY, WHOLE LEMONS ARE USED, BUT THIS RECIPE USES WEDGES WHICH ARE EASILY PACKED INTO JARS.

MAKES ABOUT TWO JARS

INGREDIENTS
  10 unwaxed lemons
  about 200ml/7fl oz/scant 1 cup fresh
    lemon juice or a combination
    of fresh and preserved
  boiling water
  sea salt

1 Wash the lemons well and cut each into six to eight wedges. Press a generous amount of salt into the cut surfaces, pushing it into every crevice.

2 Pack the salted lemon wedges into two 1.2 litre/2 pint sterilized jars. To each jar, add 30–45ml/2–3 tbsp salt and 90ml/6 tbsp lemon juice, then top up with boiling water, to cover the lemons. (If using larger jars, use more lemon juice and less boiling water.)

3 Cover the jars and leave to stand for 2–4 weeks before serving.

4 To serve, rinse the preserved lemons well to remove some of the salty flavour, then pull off the flesh and discard. Cut the lemon peel into strips or leave in chunks and use as desired.

COOK'S TIP
The salty, well-flavoured juice that is used to preserve the lemons can be added to salads or hot sauces, such as zchug, horef and harissa.

Energy 143Kcal/593kJ; Protein 7.5g; Carbohydrate 24g, of which sugars 24g; Fat 2.3g, of which saturates 0.8g; Cholesterol 0mg; Calcium 640mg; Fibre 0g; Sodium 7898mg.

TORSHI

This Middle Eastern speciality of pickled turnips is prepared by Jews and non-Jews of Persia, Israel and Arab lands. The turnips, rich red in their beetroot-spiked brine, not only look gorgeous in their jars but also make a delicious pickle to add to falafel or as part of an assortment of appetizers.

MAKES ABOUT FOUR JARS

INGREDIENTS

1kg/2¼lb young turnips
3–4 raw beetroot (beets)
about 45ml/3 tbsp kosher salt
  or coarse sea salt
about 1.5 litres/2½ pints/
  6¼ cups water
juice of 1 lemon

1 Wash the turnips and beetroot, but do not peel them, then cut into slices about 5mm/¼in thick. Put the salt and water into a bowl, stir and leave until the salt has completely dissolved.

2 Sprinkle the beetroot with lemon juice and place in the bases of four 1.2 litre/2 pint sterilized jars. Top with the slices of turnip, packing them in very tightly. Pour over the brine, making sure that the vegetables are covered.

3 Seal the jars and leave in a cool place for 7 days. Serve chilled.

COOK'S TIP
It is important to store the torshi for at least a week before serving as the pickles will be crisper in texture.

VARIATION
For a pink-jewelled effect, dice torshi and sprinkle them on a plate. So beautiful to look at, so pungent to eat!

Energy 85Kcal/361kJ; Protein 3.5g; Carbohydrate 17.5g, of which sugars 16.5g; Fat 0.8g, of which saturates 0g; Cholesterol 0mg; Calcium 136mg; Fibre 7.4g; Sodium 4508mg.

CHRAIN

THIS ASHKENAZIC HORSERADISH AND BEETROOT SAUCE IS OFTEN EATEN AT PESACH, FOR WHICH HORSERADISH IS ONE OF THE TRADITIONAL BITTER FLAVOURS. HOWEVER, IT IS A DELICIOUS ACCOMPANIMENT TO GEFILTE FISH, FRIED FISH PATTIES OR ROASTED MEAT AT ANY TIME OF THE YEAR, AND MANY PEOPLE WOULDN'T COUNTENANCE A DELI SANDWICH WITHOUT A FEW DABS ON THE SIDE.

SERVES ABOUT EIGHT

INGREDIENTS
  150g/5oz grated fresh horseradish
  2 cooked beetroot (beets), grated
  about 15ml/1 tbsp sugar
  15–30ml/1–2 tbsp red wine vinegar
  salt

1 Put the horseradish and beetroot in a bowl and mix together, then season with sugar, vinegar and salt to taste.

2 Spoon the sauce into a sterilized jar, packing it down firmly, and seal. Store in the refrigerator where it will keep for up to 2 weeks.

COOK'S TIPS
• Fresh horseradish is very potent so, when grating the fresh root, protect yourself well. Horseradish may also be purchased ready-grated.
• You can use either fresh cooked beetroot or beetroot pickled in vinegar for this recipe.

Energy 18Kcal/74kJ; Protein 0.5g; Carbohydrate 4g, of which sugars 3.9g; Fat 0.1g, of which saturates 0g; Cholesterol 0mg; Calcium 14mg; Fibre 0.7g; Sodium 17mg.

TURKISH GREEN OLIVE AND TOMATO RELISH

THIS RELISH OF GREEN OLIVES IN A SAUCE OF TOMATOES AND SWEET PEPPERS IS WONDERFUL. PUT IT ON THE TABLE ANY TIME, FOR MEZE, FOR LUNCH, FOR DINNER, OR FOR BREAKFAST, ISRAELI STYLE.

SERVES ABOUT TEN

INGREDIENTS
    45ml/3 tbsp extra virgin olive oil
    1 green (bell) pepper, chopped
      or sliced
    1 red (bell) pepper, chopped
      or sliced
    1 onion, chopped
    2–3 mild, large red and green
      chillies, thinly sliced
    1–2 hot, small chillies, chopped or
      thinly sliced (optional)
    5–7 garlic cloves, roughly chopped or
      thinly sliced
    5–7 tomatoes, quartered or diced
    5ml/1 tsp curry powder or hawaij
    1.5ml/¼ tsp ground cumin
    1.5ml/¼ tsp turmeric
    large pinch of ground ginger
    15ml/1 tbsp tomato purée (paste)
    juice of ¼ lemon, or to taste
    200g/7oz/1¾ cups pitted or
      pimiento-stuffed green olives

1 Heat the extra virgin olive oil in a pan, add the chopped or sliced peppers, the onion and chillies, and fry for 5–10 minutes, or until the vegetables have softened.

COOK'S TIP
This relish is extremely popular in Israel and is particularly good with chunks of tuna as a cooling lunch on a hot afternoon. It is also good with cold pasta or a diced potato salad.

2 Add the garlic and tomatoes to the pan and fry for a further 2–3 minutes, until the tomatoes have become the consistency of a sauce, then add the curry powder or hawaij, the cumin, turmeric, ginger and tomato purée, then remove from the heat.

3 Stir the lemon juice into the mixture, then add the olives. Leave to cool, then chill in the refrigerator, preferably overnight, before serving.

Energy 72Kcal/299kJ; Protein 1g; Carbohydrate 4.3g, of which sugars 4g; Fat 5.8g, of which saturates 0.9g; Cholesterol 0mg; Calcium 20mg; Fibre 1.7g; Sodium 456mg.

CHOPPED VEGETABLE SALAD RELISH

THIS RELISH IS A TYPICAL ISRAELI FUSION. IT COMBINES THE FRESHNESS AND CRUNCHINESS OF THE SALADS POPULAR IN ARAB COUNTRIES WITH THE CHOPPED VEGETABLES ADORED BY THE EASTERN EUROPEANS. IN THE SULTRY CLIMATE OF A MEDITERRANEAN SUMMER, FEW THINGS ARE AS REFRESHING.

SERVES ABOUT FOUR

INGREDIENTS
    2–3 ripe tomatoes, finely chopped
    ½ cucumber, finely chopped
    ½ green (bell) pepper,
      finely chopped
    1–2 garlic cloves, chopped
    2 spring onions (scallions), sliced
    30ml/2 tbsp finely chopped
      fresh mint, dill or coriander
      (cilantro) leaves
    30ml/2 tbsp finely chopped
      fresh parsley
    grated rind and juice of 1 lemon
    ⅛ red cabbage, chopped (optional)
    salt

1 Put the tomatoes, cucumber, pepper, garlic, spring onions, herbs and lemon rind and juice in a bowl. Mix together well, then chill in the refrigerator until ready to serve.

2 If using red cabbage, add to the relish just before serving, as its colour will run and spoil the fresh and vibrant colours of the other vegetables. Add a little salt to taste and stir to mix.

Energy 30Kcal/126kJ; Protein 1.2g; Carbohydrate 5.5g, of which sugars 5.4g; Fat 0.5g, of which saturates 0.1g; Cholesterol 0mg; Calcium 14mg; Fibre 1.6g; Sodium 10mg.

HOREF

THE WORD HOREF IS ROUGHLY TRANSLATED FROM HEBREW AS HOT PEPPER AND USUALLY REFERS TO A SPICY HOT CHILLI SAUCE. THIS ISRAELI RELISH SIMMERS SWEET AND HOT PEPPERS ALONG WITH TOMATOES AND MIDDLE EASTERN SPICES. IT IS GOOD WITH ROASTED OR BARBECUED MEATS, CHICKEN OR SCRAMBLED EGGS, OR SIMPLY SERVED TO DIP INTO WITH FRESH PITTA BREAD.

SERVES FOUR TO SIX

INGREDIENTS
45ml/3 tbsp olive oil
1 green (bell) pepper, chopped
   or sliced
2–3 mild, large chillies,
   thinly sliced
1–2 hot, small chillies, chopped
   or thinly sliced (optional)
5–7 garlic cloves, roughly chopped
   or thinly sliced
5–7 tomatoes, quartered or diced
5ml/1 tsp curry powder or hawaij
seeds from 3–5 cardamom pods
large pinch of ground ginger
15ml/1 tbsp tomato purée (paste)
juice of ¼ lemon
salt

1 Heat the olive oil in a large, heavy pan, add the chopped or sliced green pepper, large and small chillies and garlic. Fry over a medium heat, stirring, for about 10 minutes, or until the peppers are softened. (Be careful not to let the garlic brown.)

2 Add the tomatoes, curry powder or hawaij, cardamom seeds and ginger to the pan and cook until the tomatoes have softened to a sauce. Stir the tomato purée and lemon juice into the mixture, season with salt and leave to cool. Chill until ready to serve.

Energy 79Kcal/328kJ; Protein 1.3g; Carbohydrate 5.4g, of which sugars 5.3g; Fat 6g, of which saturates 0.9g; Cholesterol 0mg; Calcium 12mg; Fibre 1.5g; Sodium 17mg.

HARISSA

THIS RECIPE IS A QUICKLY PREPARED HOME-MADE VERSION OF HARISSA, THE NORTH AFRICAN CHILLI SAUCE THAT'S UBIQUITOUS WITH COUSCOUS, BRIKS, SANDWICHES, SOUPS AND ALMOST EVERYTHING.

SERVES FOUR TO SIX

INGREDIENTS
45ml/3 tbsp paprika
2.5–5ml/½–1 tsp cayenne pepper
1.5ml/¼ tsp ground cumin
250ml/8fl oz/1 cup water
juice of ¼–½ lemon
2–3 pinches of caraway
   seeds (optional)
salt
15ml/1 tbsp chopped coriander
   (cilantro) leaves, to serve

VARIATION
For a long-keeping harissa, soak about 3 dried red chillies, then process with a little water to make a purée. Continue as above, using only 5ml/1 tsp paprika.

1 Put the paprika, cayenne pepper, ground cumin, water or stock in a large, heavy pan and season with salt to taste.

2 Bring the spice mixture to the boil, then immediately remove the pan from the heat.

3 Stir the lemon juice and caraway seeds, if using, into the hot spice mixture and leave to cool.

4 Just before serving, pour the sauce into a serving dish and sprinkle with the chopped coriander leaves.

Energy 22Kcal/92kJ; Protein 1.1g; Carbohydrate 2.7g, of which sugars 0g; Fat 1g, of which saturates 0.2g; Cholesterol 0mg; Calcium 14mg; Fibre 0g; Sodium 3mg.

ZCHUG

This is the Yemenite chilli sauce that has become Israel's national condiment. It is hot with chillies, pungent with garlic and fragrant with exotic cardamom. Eat it with rice, couscous, soup or meat. Zchug may be red, green or, as here, somewhere in between.

MAKES ABOUT 475ML/16FL OZ/2 CUPS

INGREDIENTS
    5–8 garlic cloves, chopped
    2–3 medium-hot chillies, such
        as jalapeño
    5 fresh or canned tomatoes, diced
    1 small bunch coriander (cilantro),
        roughly chopped
    1 small bunch parsley, chopped
    30ml/2 tbsp extra virgin olive oil
    10ml/2 tsp ground cumin
    2.5ml/½ tsp turmeric
    2.5ml/½ tsp curry powder
    seeds from 3–5 cardamom pods
    juice of ½ lemon
    pinch of sugar, if necessary
    salt

1 Put all the ingredients except the sugar and salt in a food processor or blender. Process until well combined, then season with sugar and salt.

2 Pour the sauce into a serving bowl, cover and chill in the refrigerator until ready to serve.

VARIATIONS
• To make a spicy Yemenite dip, put 400g/14oz chopped fresh tomatoes, or a combination of chopped fresh and canned tomatoes in a bowl. Stir in 120ml/4fl oz/½ cup zchug, or to taste, and season with salt, if necessary. Spread the dip on to wedges of flat breads or serve in a bowl with strips of raw vegetables for dipping.

• To make hilbeh, a spicy tomato relish, soak 30ml/2 tbsp fenugreek seeds in cold water for at least 2 hours and preferably overnight. Drain, then grind the seeds in a spice grinder or pound them in a mortar with a pestle until they form a smooth paste. In a bowl, combine the paste with 15ml/1 tbsp zchug and 2 diced tomatoes. Season with salt and black pepper to taste.

Energy 326Kcal/1361kJ; Protein 7.1g; Carbohydrate 21.4g, of which sugars 17.5g; Fat 24.3g, of which saturates 3.7g; Cholesterol 0mg; Calcium 142mg; Fibre 8.6g; Sodium 63mg.

CORIANDER, COCONUT AND TAMARIND CHUTNEY

COOLING, FRAGRANT CHUTNEYS MADE OF FRESH CORIANDER AND MINT ARE AS POPULAR WITH NON-JEWS AS THEY ARE WITH JEWS OF INDIAN ORIGIN. THIS DELICIOUS BLEND OF CORIANDER, MINT AND COCONUT, SPICED WITH A HINT OF CHILLI AND SWEETENED WITH DATES, IS A CONDIMENT OF THE BENE ISRAEL TABLE. IT IS THE PERFECT ALTERNATIVE TO A YOGURT RAITA FOR A MEAT MEAL.

MAKES ABOUT 450G/1LB/2 CUPS

INGREDIENTS
30ml/2 tbsp tamarind paste
30ml/2 tbsp boiling water
1 large bunch fresh coriander
  (cilantro), roughly chopped
1 bunch fresh mint, roughly chopped
8–10 pitted dates, roughly chopped
75g/3oz dried coconut or
  50g/2oz creamed coconut,
  coarsely grated
2.5cm/1in piece fresh root
  ginger, chopped
3–5 garlic cloves, chopped
2–3 fresh chillies, chopped
juice of 2 limes or lemons
about 5ml/1 tsp sugar
salt
30–45ml/2–3 tbsp water for a meat
  meal, or natural (plain) yogurt for a
  dairy meal, to serve

3 Add the coconut, ginger, garlic and chillies to the chopped herbs and dates and stir in the tamarind. Season with citrus juice, sugar and salt. Spoon into sterilized jars, seal and chill.

4 To serve, thin the chutney with the water, if serving with a meat meal, or with yogurt for a dairy meal.

COOK'S TIPS
• This chutney can be stored in the refrigerator for up to 2 weeks.
• Serve with any vegetable dish or simple boiled rice. It is also good spooned over a spicy couscous salad.
• Make this chutney as mild or as fiery as you like by adjusting the amount of ginger, garlic and chillies.

1 Place the tamarind paste in a jug (pitcher) or bowl and pour over the boiling water. Stir thoroughly until the paste is completely dissolved and set aside.

2 Place the fresh coriander, mint and pitted dates in a food processor and process briefly until the ingredients appear finely chopped. Alternatively, chop finely by hand using a sharp knife. Place in a bowl.

Energy 536Kcal/2232kJ; Protein 10.1g; Carbohydrate 47g, of which sugars 39.4g; Fat 35.4g, of which saturates 29.8g; Cholesterol 0mg; Calcium 144mg; Fibre 6.5g; Sodium 39mg.

FRAGRANT PERSIAN HALEK

THIS HALEK EXUDES THE SWEET FLAVOURS OF ROSE WATER, DRIED FRUITS AND NUTS, WHICH MAKES IT SO POPULAR AMONG PERSIAN JEWS. HALEK IS AN EASTERN VERSION OF THE ASHKENAZIC CHAROSSET, WHICH IS EATEN AT PESACH SEDER.

SERVES ABOUT TEN

INGREDIENTS
60ml/4 tbsp blanched almonds
60ml/4 tbsp unsalted pistachio nuts
60ml/4 tbsp walnuts
15–30ml/1–2 tbsp skinned hazelnuts
30ml/2 tbsp unsalted shelled
  pumpkin seeds
90ml/6 tbsp raisins, chopped
90ml/6 tbsp pitted prunes, diced
90ml/6 tbsp dried apricots, diced
60ml/4 tbsp dried cherries
sugar or honey, to taste
juice of ½ lemon
30ml/2 tbsp rose water
seeds from 4–5 cardamon pods
pinch of ground cloves
pinch of grated nutmeg
1.5ml/¼ tsp ground cinnamon
fruit juice of choice, if necessary

1 Roughly chop the almonds, pistachio nuts, walnuts, hazelnuts and pumpkin seeds and put in a bowl.

2 Add the chopped raisins, prunes, apricots and cherries to the nuts and seeds and toss to combine. Stir in sugar or honey to taste and mix well until thoroughly combined.

3 Add the lemon juice, rose water, cardamom seeds, cloves, nutmeg and cinnamon to the fruit and nut mixture and mix until thoroughly combined.

4 If the halek is too thick, add a little fruit juice to thin the mixture. Pour into a serving bowl, cover and chill in the refrigerator until ready to serve.

Energy 207Kcal/863kJ; Protein 5.1g; Carbohydrate 14.9g, of which sugars 14.5g; Fat 14.6g, of which saturates 1.4g; Cholesterol 0mg; Calcium 66mg; Fibre 2.8g; Sodium 42mg.

ASHKENAZIC CHAROSSET

CHAROSSET IS A PASTE OF FRUIT THAT IS HELD TOGETHER WITH SWEET WINE. IT IS EATEN DURING THE PESACH RITUAL MEAL, OR SEDER. THIS RECIPE IS THE CLASSIC COMBINATION OF APPLE, WALNUT AND SWEET WINE THAT IS FAVOURED BY ASHKENAZI JEWS.

SERVES SIX TO EIGHT

INGREDIENTS
    3 apples
    75–115g/3–4oz/¾–1 cup
      walnut pieces
    7.5ml/1½ tsp ground cinnamon
    75–90ml/5–6 tbsp sweet Pesach
      red wine
    sugar or honey, to taste

COOK'S TIP
This will keep in the refrigerator for the duration of the Pesach festival. It can be eaten as a snack or as part of a meal. It is usually spread on matzos.

1 Quarter the apples and remove their cores but do not peel them. Grate them by hand or chop the fruit very finely using a sharp knife.

2 Put the apples and all the remaining ingredients in a bowl and mix together. Tip into a serving bowl, cover and chill in the refrigerator until ready to serve.

Energy 84Kcal/349kJ; Protein 1.5g; Carbohydrate 3.7g, of which sugars 3.6g; Fat 6.5g, of which saturates 0.5g; Cholesterol 0mg; Calcium 11mg; Fibre 0.9g; Sodium 2mg.

INSTANT SEPHARDIC PICKLE OF MIXED VEGETABLES

Fresh, crisp vegetables, brined and spiced, make this favourite Sephardic relish, or pickle. The turmeric gives it a golden hue, as well as warmth of flavour. It is delicious — some say irreplaceable — with falafel.

SERVES TWELVE

INGREDIENTS
½ cauliflower head, cut into florets
2 carrots, sliced
2 celery sticks, thinly sliced
¼–½ cabbage, thinly sliced
115g/4oz/1 cup runner (green)
  beans, cut into bitesize pieces
6 garlic cloves, sliced
1–4 fresh chillies, whole or sliced
30–45ml/2–3 tbsp sliced fresh
  root ginger
1 red (bell) pepper, sliced
2.5ml/½ tsp turmeric
105ml/7 tbsp white wine vinegar
15–30ml/1–2 tbsp sugar
60–90ml/4–6 tbsp olive oil
juice of 2 lemons
salt

1 Toss the cauliflower, carrots, celery, cabbage, beans, garlic, chillies and ginger, and season with salt. Leave to stand in a colander for 4 hours.

COOK'S TIP
This spicy pickle can be stored in the refrigerator for up to 2 weeks.

2 Transfer the salted vegetables to a bowl and add the turmeric, vinegar, sugar to taste, the oil and lemon juice. Toss to combine, then add enough water to balance the flavours.

3 Cover and chill for at least 1 hour, or until ready to serve.

Energy 78Kcal/321kJ; Protein 1.3g; Carbohydrate 5.2g, of which sugars 5g; Fat 5.8g, of which saturates 0.9g; Cholesterol 0mg; Calcium 23mg; Fibre 1.5g; Sodium 11mg.

TAHINI SAUCE

Made of ground sesame seeds and spiced with garlic and lemon juice, this is Israel's most famous sauce. Drizzle it on to hamburgers, koftas, falafel, a bowl of warm chickpeas, roasted peppers, boiled cauliflower — almost anything. It's also the quintessential dip, served with soft pitta bread.

SERVES FOUR TO SIX

INGREDIENTS
150–175g/5–6oz/²/₃–³/₄ cup tahini
3 garlic cloves, finely chopped
juice of 1 lemon
1.5ml/¼ tsp ground cumin
small pinch of ground coriander
small pinch of curry powder
50–120ml/2–4fl oz/¼–½ cup water
cayenne pepper
salt
For the garnish
15–30ml/1–2 tbsp extra virgin
  olive oil
chopped fresh coriander (cilantro)
  leaves or parsley
handful of olives and/or
  pickled vegetables
a few chillies or a hot
  pepper sauce

1 Put the tahini and garlic in a food processor or bowl and mix together well. Stir in the lemon juice, cumin, ground coriander and curry powder.

COOK'S TIP
Tahini sauce forms the basis of many of the salads and dips found in Israel and the Middle East.

2 Slowly add the water to the tahini, beating all the time. The mixture will thicken, then become thin. Season with cayenne pepper and salt.

3 To serve, spread the mixture on to a serving plate, individual plates or into a shallow bowl. Drizzle over the oil and sprinkle with the other garnishes.

Energy 175Kcal/725kJ; Protein 5.2g; Carbohydrate 1.2g, of which sugars 0.3g; Fat 16.7g, of which saturates 2.4g; Cholesterol 0mg; Calcium 184mg; Fibre 2.5g; Sodium 7mg.

Tapas of Almonds, Olives and Cheese

Meze, mazza, kemia, tapas...regardless of what you call them, these are delectable little nibbles to go with drinks, be it wine, schnapps or juice. They can be eaten before a meal, or simply offered to family and friends when they stop by to visit, especially during Shabbat in the Sephardic manner.

SERVES SIX TO EIGHT

INGREDIENTS

For the marinated olives
    2.5ml/½ tsp coriander seeds
    2.5ml/½ tsp fennel seeds
    2 garlic cloves, crushed
    10ml/2 tsp chopped fresh
        coriander (cilantro) leaves
    15–30ml/1–2 tbsp lemon juice
    30ml/2 tbsp olive oil
    115g/4oz/⅔ cup black olives
    115g/4oz/⅔ cup green olives
For the marinated cheese
    150g/5oz Boucheron or other
        firm goat's cheese
    90ml/6 tbsp olive oil
    15ml/1 tbsp white wine vinegar
    5ml/1 tsp black peppercorns
    1 garlic clove, sliced
    fresh thyme or tarragon sprigs
    fresh flat leaf parsley or tarragon
        sprigs, to garnish (optional)
For the salted almonds
    30ml/2 tbsp sea salt
    25g/1oz/2 tbsp butter
    60ml/4 tbsp olive oil
    200g/7oz/1¾ cups blanched
        almonds
    extra salt for sprinkling (optional)

1 To make the marinated olives, crush the coriander seeds in a mortar with a pestle. Work in the garlic, then add the coriander leaves, lemon juice and olive oil. Cover the olives with the marinade. Cover with clear film (plastic wrap) and chill for up to one week.

2 To make the marinated cheese, cut the cheese into bitesize pieces, removing any hard rind, and put in a small bowl. Combine the oil, vinegar, peppercorns, garlic, thyme or tarragon and pour over the cheese. Cover with clear film and chill for up to 3 days.

3 To make the salted almonds, combine the cayenne pepper and salt in a bowl. Melt the butter with the oil in a frying pan. Add the almonds and stir-fry them for 5 minutes, or until golden.

VARIATION
There is an infinite variety of tapas with which you can extend the basic idea of this recipe. It is an interesting exercise to provide half a dozen different types of olives and nuts, so that your guests can have a good tasting session. Toasted macadamia nuts are a good alternative to salted almonds. Some tapas dishes beautifully combine pine nuts and plump raisins with pulses such as chickpeas.

4 Tip the almonds into the salt mixture and toss until the almonds are coated. Leave to cool, then store in an airtight container for up to 1 week.

5 To serve, arrange the almonds, olives and cheese in three separate small, shallow dishes. Garnish the cheese with fresh herbs if you like and sprinkle the almonds with a little more salt, to taste. Provide cocktail sticks (toothpicks) for guests to pick up the cheese and olives with, and a little dish for the used sticks.

COOK'S TIPS
• Whole olives, sold with the stone (pit), invariably taste better than pitted ones. Don't serve them directly from the brine, but drain and rinse them, then pat dry with kitchen paper. Put the olives in a jar and pour over extra virgin olive oil to cover. Seal and store in the refrigerator for 1–2 months; the flavour of the olives will become enriched. Serve the olives as a tapas dish, or add to salads. When the olives have been eaten, the fruity oil can be used as a dressing for hot food, or made into flavoursome salad dressings.
• A number of exotic stuffed olives are exported from Spain and are widely available in most large supermarkets. Popular varieties include pimiento-stuffed olives, which have been in existence for more than half a century, olives stuffed with salted anchovies, and olives filled with roasted garlic.

Energy 432Kcal/1784kJ; Protein 10.3g; Carbohydrate 1.8g, of which sugars 1.1g; Fat 42.3g, of which saturates 9.7g; Cholesterol 25mg; Calcium 217mg; Fibre 2.7g; Sodium 805mg.

GLOSSARY OF TERMS AND FOODS

Adeni spice mixtures Adeni Jews have many different spice mixtures. The one for cooking is made of coriander, cumin, cardamom and pepper; the one for tea is made of cinnamon, cloves and cardamom; and the one for strong black coffee is made of ginger, cardamom, cloves and cinnamon.

Afikomen The piece of matzo, broken from the middle of the three matzos used at the Pesach Seder, that is wrapped and put aside to be searched for as part of the ceremony.

Ashkenazim Central and Eastern European Jews, including Yiddish-speaking Jews and their descendants.

Bagels Bread rolls with a hole in the middle, symbolizing the endless circle of life. They are boiled before being baked.

Baklava A crisp pastry of filo and nuts soaked in a honey syrup, which is often flavoured with rose or orange flower water or sweet spices.

Bar/Bat Mitzvah The coming of age ceremony for a boy (bar) or girl (bat) in which they assume the religious duties and responsibilities of an adult. A boy reaches this age at 13 years old, a girl at 12 years old.

Berbere The mixture of chillies and fragrant spices such as cardamom, black cardamom and ginger that forms the main flavouring of the Ethiopian cuisine. It is also the name of a certain type of chilli.

Besan *See* gram flour.

Betza/beitzah/baitzah Hebrew for egg. Betza are eaten by all Jewish communities and are considered pareve; they play an important role in the ritual plate for the Pesach Seder.

Betzel A Jewish North African cheese cracker, light and crisp, usually enjoyed for tea.

Bishak A Sephardic Bukharan pastry filled with pumpkin.

Blintz A thin pancake rolled around a savoury or sweet filling. They are often fried.

Borekas The flaky savoury pastries beloved by Turkish Jews. Borekas are usually half-moon shaped and have many different fillings. They may be made with filo dough, but a true boreka is made with a home-made dough.

Borscht Soup of Ashkenazic origin made from beetroot (beet) and sometimes other vegetables; it is eaten hot or cold.

Botarga Sephardic salted or smoked dried fish roe such as sea bass and grey mullet. It can be purchased or home-made; if purchased it should have certification to show that it is from a kosher fish.

Brik A deep-fried Moroccan-Tunisian pastry made from warka dough. Tuna and egg is a very popular filling.

Buricche Little Sephardic savoury pies of Italian/Turkish/Mediterranean origin. Fillings include chicken liver, tuna, pumpkin and chickpeas.

Challah The braided Ashkenazic Shabbat and holiday bread.

Chanukkah The festival of lights commemorating the Maccabean victory over the Seleucians in 165BCE (BC). Also known as Hanukkah.

Charosset/Charosses The paste of nuts, spices, wine and fruit eaten at Pesach to symbolize the mortar used by the Jews to build the pyramids. Also known as Harosset.

Chassidim A movement of very Observant Jews originating in Poland, the Ukraine and Galicia.

Chellou Persian rice, cooked with butter and allowed to form a crisp bottom crust. Vegetables, herbs, fruits and nuts may be added.

Chermoula A Moroccan spice and herb paste, often used with fish.

Chickpea flour *See* gram flour.

Cholent Ashkenazic, long-simmered stew of meat and beans. Adafina, dafina, hamim, cocido and skhena are Sephardic equivalents.

Chrain Horseradish and beetroot condiment of Ashkenazic origin.

Chremslach Ashkenazi matzo meal pancakes, often eaten at Pesach. They may be savoury or eaten with sweet spices.

Dafina A long-baked Shabbat stew, made of beef (often with a cow's foot), potato, beans and hard-boiled eggs. It is a speciality of Moroccan Jews.

Dairy Refers to a meal made with milk products.

Desayuno Sephardic Shabbat breakfast.

Einbren flour Flour browned with fat. Traditionally, it is used to thicken soup in the German Ashkenazic kitchen.

Eingemachts A sweet preserve made from beetroot (beets), radishes, carrots, cherries, lemons or walnuts, eaten with a spoon along with tea. It is favoured at Pesach.

Etrog Large yellow citron used to celebrate Sukkot.

Falafel Deep-fried chickpea or broad (fava) bean croquettes, adopted from the Arabs. They are eaten with salads, tucked into pitta bread.

Farfel Pellet-shaped dumplings made from grated noodle dough or crumbled matzo.

Fasolada/Fasolia White beans, often stewed with meats and vegetables, eaten as an appetizer, soup or stew, popular with the Jews of Greece and Turkey.

Fleyshig Yiddish for meat meals or products.

Forspeizen Yiddish for a tasty appetizer.

Gefilte fish Ashkenazic balls of minced (ground) fish, eaten cold, poached and jellied or fried. Gefilte means stuffed, and originally the fish was stuffed back into its skin.

Glatt A particularly stringent form of Kashrut, favoured by Chassidic Jews.

Gram flour Also known as chickpea flour and besan. It is made from ground chickpeas and is used in Indian pakoras, spicy pastries and falafel. It is also used in Mediterranean cooking: in Nice it is made into a pancake called socca and in Provence into cakes known as panisses.

Haimishe Yiddish for traditional home-made food.

Halek Date syrup, eaten for Pesach by the Jews of Iraq, India and Yemen, in addition to or in place of Charosset. In the Bible, "halek" is thought to refer to honey.

Halva A sweetmeat made from sesame paste and sugar or honey, and flavourings, then pressed into blocks and dried. Chocolate, pistachio nuts or almonds may also be added. Halva is popular with Jews from Middle Eastern and Balkan lands.

Hamantashen Triangular-shaped, Ashkenazic cookies with various fillings such as prunes, poppy seeds, apricots or nuts; eaten at Purim.

Hamim See Cholent.

Hanukkah See Chanukkah.

Harissa North African fiery paste of red chillies and spices, often served with mild foods such as couscous.

Harosset/Harosseth See Charosset/Charosses.

Havdalah The ceremony that marks the end of Shabbat and the start of the new week. Prayers are said over wine, special spices are smelled, and a braided candle is lit.

Hawaij A Yemeni spice mixture that includes cardamom, saffron and turmeric; used in most Yemenite cooking.

Helzel Yiddish for a stuffed chicken, turkey, goose or duck neck, filled with kishke stuffing and roasted so that the skin becomes crisp.

Hilbeh A pungent spice paste of soaked ground fenugreek seeds, often served with spicy zchug. Hilbeh is slighly bitter and has a unique aroma, almost like brown sugar. Yemenite in origin, it is eaten in Sephardic restaurants in Israel.

Holishkes Ashkenazic stuffed cabbage, often simmered or baked in a sweet-and-sour tomato sauce.

Horef Hebrew for hot pepper or spicy. Used in Israel to describe the spicy sauce or peppers eaten with falafel.

Huevos Haminados Sephardi long-cooked eggs; often placed in meat stews.

Injeera Ethiopian flat bread made from teff flour, a grain specific to Ethiopia. It is made from a fermented batter, which gives it a slightly sour flavour, formed into a huge pancake. It is used as a plate and pieces are used to pick up food.

Kaddaif Shredded dough used in Middle Eastern pastries to wrap around nuts, then baked and soaked in syrup.

Kaes The Yiddish word for cheese. Any dish that has kaes attached to its name has cheese as a component.

Kama A Moroccan spice mixture of pepper, turmeric, ginger, cumin and nutmeg, used for stews and soups.

Kapparot The symbolic ritual that takes place on the eve of Yom Kippur whereby a chicken is swung over the head and offered as ransom in atonement for a person's sins. Nowadays, a coin is often used instead of a chicken.

Karpas The parsley, lettuce or herbs placed on the Seder plate and dipped in salt water.

Kasha Toasted buckwheat.

Kashrut Jewish dietary laws dictating what may be eaten.

Katchapuri Flaky pastries filled with goat's cheese or feta cheese; brought to Israel from Georgian Russia.

Khoresht The sweet and sour Persian stew that is ladled over rice and features in the everyday diet of Persian Jews.

Kubbeh/Kibbeh Dumplings of Middle Eastern origin made from minced (ground) lamb and soaked bulgur wheat. Can be eaten raw, made into patties, or layered with vegetables and baked.

Kichelach Light, crisp, slightly sweet cookies of Lithuanian Ashkenazic origin. They are traditional in areas where there is a large Ashkenazic population, such as South Africa and the USA.

Kiddush Sanctifying blessing over the wine and challah.

Kindli Another name for Ashkenazic poppy-seed cake or mohn torte.

Kishke Stuffed intestine filled with matzo, chicken fat, onion and paprika. It is served roasted or poached.

Klops Meatloaf or meatballs of Ashkenazic German origin.

Knaidlach/Knaidl Matzo meal dumplings.

Knish Savoury pastry filled with meat, cheese, potato or kasha.

Kosher Term used to describe any food deemed fit to eat by the laws of Kashrut.

Kosher salt Large grains of salt for sprinkling on to meat, to drain out blood, as stipulated in the laws of Kashrut.

Kreplach Small meat-filled dumplings made of noodle dough, often served in chicken soup. At Shavuot they are filled with cheese and eaten with fruit and sour cream.

Krupnik Ashkenazic mushroom and barley soup. It is a traditional dish in Eastern Europe, particularly Poland, Lithuania and the Ukraine.

Kubaneh A Sephardi Shabbat breakfast dish cooked for a long time, often overnight.

Kubbeh Meat dumplings favoured by Iraqi Jews as well as those who emigrated to India and Israel. Kubbeh are eaten in soups and stews, and may also be steamed or fried.

Kuchen An Ashkenazic yeast raised cake that is slightly sweet and often stuffed with fruit. It is eaten with coffee or tea for morning or afternoon breaks, or as dessert for festivals or holiday meals.

Kugel Baked dish of noodles, vegetables, potatoes or bread; it may be sweet or savoury.

Lag b'Omer Holiday falling on the 33rd day of the counting of the Omer, the days between Pesach and Shavuot.

Lahuhua A Yemenite flat bread cooked in a frying pan. It has a crumpet-like texture and is eaten with soups and stews, often spread with zchug.

Latkes Fried potato pancakes eaten by Ashkenazic Jews at Chanukkah. Latkes can also be made with other vegetables or matzo meal.

Lekakh Traditional honey cake.

Lokshen Yiddish for noodles.

Lox Yiddish for smoked salmon.

Lubia Black-eyed beans (peas), popular in Sephardi cooking, especially in Israel where they are added to spicy soups and stews.

Lulav The palm branch carried and waved as part of the Sukkot observance.

Mamaliga A creamy porridge-like mixture of cornmeal, similar to polenta, eaten as the starchy staple by Romanians. It can be eaten hot or cold.

Mandelbrot Amond cookies resembling Italian biscotti. They are double-baked, giving a crisp, hard texture.

Mandlen The Yiddish word for almonds, which are favoured in Ashkenazic cooking (most famously in mandelbrot). Also the name of the crisp, baked or fried soup garnishes made from noodle dough.

Maror Bitter herbs eaten at Pesach.

Matjes herring *See* Salt herring.

Matzo/Matzah The unleavened, thin brittle bread ritually eaten during Pesach.

Matzo cake meal A fine flour made from crushed matzo, used to make cakes, cookies and other baked goods. Matzo cake meal may be used for Pesach, as long as it is labelled as matzo for Pesach.

Matzo meal A meal made from crushed matzo, used to coat fish and other foods for frying, bind together patties of meat, fish or vegetables and as the main ingredient for knaidlach. Matzo meal is available in medium or fine grade.

Megillah Scroll of the Book of Esther, read aloud at Purim as part of the observance.

Melawah Crisp North African pancakes made from pastry brushed with butter and rolled up thinly, similar to a Chinese spring roll pancake. When rolled out and baked, the layers puff up and become rich and flaky.

Menorah Also known as Chanukkia, the candelabra used at Chanukkah. It has spaces for eight candles, plus an extra in the middle, which is used for lighting the others.

Milshig Yiddish for milk or dairy, as opposed to meat.

Minhag Yiddish for different families' or communities' traditions and customs.

Mohn torte The Russian poppy-seed cake. Mohn means poppy seeds in Yiddish. *See* Kindli.

Mouna North African yeasted sweet tea bread, often stuffed with jam, served for Shabbat or a festival breakfast.

Muhammara A Middle Eastern paste of red (bell) pepper and bulgur wheat, particularly popular among Turks.

Nosh Yiddish, meaning to eat; can be a noun, meaning something to eat.

Oy Yiddish exclamation for any occasion: "Oy yoy yoy" and "oy vay s'mear" are variations.

Pareve Yiddish, describing the neutral foods that are neither dairy nor meat.

Pastrami A cured dried beef that is considered a speciality of the USA, though some say it was adapted from pastirma of Turkey, Romania and the Balkans. Traditional American pastrami is cured in salt, spices, pepper and garlic, then smoked and steamed.

Pesach/Passover The festival that celebrates the Israelites' exodus from Egypt.

Petcha Calf's foot jelly, once a very traditional Ashkenazic dish that is now less popular.

Pierogi Little pasta dumplings, of Polish origin, filled with fillings such as cabbage, mashed potatoes, onions, cheese and kasha and served with sour cream. The sweet, dessert version is varenikes.

Piroshki Ashkenazic savoury pastries of Russian origin made with a yeast dough and filled with cabbage, meat and hard-boiled egg, spinach and cheese, or kasha. They may be tiny, one-bite appetizers or large pastries, and either baked or fried.

Pitta bread Known as khubz in Arabic, pitta is a round flat bread that is cooked on a flat pan and puffs up as it cooks. The bread may be slashed open and its hollow inside filled like a sandwich. In addition to the pitta that we know in the West, there are many other pittas, for pitta simply means bread.

Plaetschen Ashkenazic term for little squares of pasta, which are eaten in soup.

Plava Very simple Ashkenazic sponge cake. It was once the favourite British Jewish cake and every bakery in London's East End had its own version.

Plotz Yiddish, meaning to faint, as in: "Oy, so delicious I could plotz!"

Pomerantzen Candied citrus peel, a classic sweet treat of the Ashkenazic Jews of Eastern Europe, especially Germany. Sometimes it may be dipped in chocolate.

Porge To ritually remove the blood and fat from meat.

Potato flour Used as a light and translucent thickening agent for sauces and cakes. It is popular during Pesach when grain flours are forbidden.

Preserved lemons A North African speciality, lemons are salted and layered in jars, which imparts a tangy flavour. They are often added to dishes such as tagines and salads.

Purim Festival celebrating the rescue of the Jewish people from Haman, as described in the Book of Esther.

Ras al hanout A Moroccan spice mixture that literally means head of the shop. Ras al hanout can contain myriad ingredients, and each spice shop guards its own secret recipe. For this reason, Kashrut is a consideration; many ras al hanout mixtures contain spices derived from insects or other ingredients that are not kosher. Check for a Kashrut certification insignia.

Rosh Hashanah The Jewish New Year, literally meaning head of the year.

Rugelach Crisp, Ashkenazic cinnamon-and-sugar layered biscuits (cookies).

Rye bread A typical bread from Eastern Europe, especially the Ukraine, where it is made with sourdough studded with caraway seeds. It is often baked on a cornmeal-coated baking sheet and is, therefore, sometimes known as corn rye.

Salt herring Herring preserved in wooden barrels in layers of salt. Ashkenazic salt herring need to be soaked in cold water before being eaten.

Sambousak Crisp half-moon pastries, of Sephardi Middle Eastern origin, often filled with cheese and hard-boiled egg, and coated in sesame seeds. They are popular in Israel and may be eaten hot or cold, dipped into zahtar.

Sauerkraut Fermented, pickled cabbage, made by salting shredded cabbage. It is a staple of the people of Eastern and parts of Western Europe.

Schav A refreshing, sour green soup made from sorrel and eaten cold. It is a traditional Ashkenazic soup and can be bought in bottles in American delis. It is sometimes referred to as green borscht.

Schmaltz Yiddish for fat, usually referring to rendered chicken fat.

Schmaltz herring *See* Salt herring.

Schnitzel Tender escalopes (scallops) of meat or poultry, coated in crumbs and fried. They originated in Vienna.

Seder The ceremonial dinner eaten on the eve of Pesach, commemorating the flight of the Jews from Egypt.

Sephardim Jews who settled in Iberia (Spain and Portugal), after the destruction of the Second Temple. This group, and their descendants, later spread to Greece, Turkey, the Middle East, England, the Netherlands and the Americas.

Shabbat The religious day of rest, which falls on a Saturday.

Shalach manot Food given at Purim. Shalach manot is often given to friends and family and people who are less well off.

Shalet Baked Ashkenazic dessert of apple and eggs, favoured by the Jews of Alsace. Other ingredients such as matzo, challah, dried fruit and spices may be added.

Shavuot Feast of the weeks, commemorating the revelation of the Ten Commandments.

Shochet The ritual butcher, licensed to slaughter and prepare meat according the laws of Kashrut.

Shtetl Yiddish for the Jewish villages of Eastern Europe.

Shulchan Arukh A code of Jewish law.

Simchat Torah The festival of the Torah, celebrated by parading the Torah through the synagogue.

Sour salt Citric acid, a souring agent used in Russia and in traditional Jewish cooking. It is available in crystals or grains.

Spaetzel Tiny dumplings made of noodle dough batter, dripped into boiling water. Also known as farfel.

Strudel Eastern European speciality of crisp, layered pastry filled with fruit, sprinkled with sugar and served as a mid-afternoon treat with tea. Strudel can be savoury, filled with vegetables, meat and sometimes fish.

Sufganiot Israeli jam-filled doughnuts, eaten to celebrate Chanukkah.

Sukkot The autumn harvest festival, the celebration of which includes eating meals in gaily decorated three-walled huts known as sukkah.

Sumac A sour-tasting, red spice made from ground berries of the sumac plant. Israelis, and some Sephardim, sprinkle the spice over salads, breads and rice.

Tahini/Tahina A Middle Eastern paste of toasted hulled sesame seeds, mixed with lemon juice, garlic and spices, and thinned with water. It is eaten as a sauce, dip, or used in dishes such as hummus.

Tapadas Big Sephardic pies of Turkish origin, filled with a similar filling to that of Borekas. They are served cut into individual-sized pieces.

Teiglach Ashkenazic cookies that have been cooked in honey. They are a Lithuanian speciality, popular in communities that celebrate their Lithuanian origins, such as South Africa. They are favoured at Rosh Hashanah when sweet foods are eaten in hope of a sweet new year.

Tisha b'Av A mourning and fast day in commemoration of the destruction of the First and Second Temples in Jerusalem. It is observed on the 9th of the month of Av.

Torah The scroll used in the synagogue, consisting of the first five books of the Bible, which include the Ten Commandments. The Torah was given to the Jews by God on Mount Sinai.

Torshi Pickled vegetables, eaten throughout the Middle East, especially Persia. All kinds of vegetables are made into torshi, particularly turnips, which are pickled in a tangy vinegar and salt brine, with the addition of beetroot (beets) to give the pale-coloured turnips a bright pink hue.

Treyf Meaning not kosher. Also known as tref and trefah.

Tu b'Shevat Festival known as the birthday of the trees.

Tzimmes A sweet dish of carrots, vegetables, dried fruit and sweetening agent such as honey or sugar. Spices, and sometimes meat, are added.

Varenikes Ashkenazic fruit-filled pasta dumplings. They may be filled with apricots, cherries or prunes.

Varnishkes Noodles shaped like bow ties or butterflies, often served with kasha.

Warka Very thin, transparent pastry from Morocco.

Wats/Wots Spicy Ethiopian stews, enjoyed by the Bene Israel (Ethiopian Jews). They are often eaten for Shabbat.

Yom Kippur The Day of Atonement, a solemn holy day upon which fasting is strictly observed.

Zahtar/Za'atar This is both the name of the wild thyme/hyssop that grows in the hillsides of Israel and the Middle East, and the name of the spice mixture made with it, which includes zahtar, ground cumin, toasted sesame seeds, coriander seeds and sometimes a little sumac and/or crushed toasted hazelnuts. Zahtar is eaten for breakfast, as a dip with fresh pitta bread, a drizzle of olive oil and fresh goat's cheese.

Zchug/Zhug/Zhoug This Yemenite seasoning paste is one of Israel's most popular spice mixtures. It may be red, based on chillies, garlic, spices, coriander (cilantro) and parsley, or it may be green, with more herbs and fewer or no tomatoes. Zchug is eaten as a dip with bread or as a relish or sauce.

Zeroa A lamb's bone, often a shank, roasted and placed on the ritual plate for Pesach. It represents the sacrificial lambs eaten on the eve of the flight of the Jews from Eygpt.

KOSHER FOODS: WEB LINKS AND BOOKS

WEBSITES
International
limmud.org (United Kingdom)
www.limmud.ca (Canada)
limmudny.org (New York, USA)
www.limmudoz.com.au (Australia)
Limmud is a festival of Jewish learning, periodically held at locations in the above. Includes a food fest.

www.israelim.com
Website of useful international links.

www.kosherdelight.com
Useful resource on Jewish foods and restaurants.

www.mavensearch.com
A comprehensive Web Directory on Jewish life.

yeahthatskosher.com
Kosher and Jewish travel guide US website.

Australia
www.jewishaustralia.com
Excellent resource on Jewish life and culture in Australia.

United Kingdom
Supermarkets in Jewish communities carry a large selection of kosher foods. Selfridges, in London's Oxford Street, has an excellent selection.

www.kosher.org.uk
A guide to suppliers of kosher foods and Judaica throughout the United Kingdom.

www.kosherpages.com
Excellent resource on where to buy Jewish foods in the United Kingdom.

United States
Many supermarkets in the United States, especially in areas with large Jewish communities, sell a varied selection of kosher foods and products.

www.empirekosher.com
Directory of outlets selling kosher foods, plus listings of restaurants and recipes – not limited to poultry!

www.aaronsgourmet.com
Outlet for kosher meats including glatt beef, buffalo, veal, poultry, fish and deli products.

www.thekoshercook.com
A North American outlet an extensive line of high-quality culinary products and utensils and general information on adhering to the Kashrut rules of hygiene in the kosher kitchen.

PUBLICATIONS

Avnon, Naf and Sella, Uri. *So Eat, My Darling; A Guide to the Yiddish Kitchen* (Massada Ltd, Israel, 1977)

Cohen, Elizabeth Wolf. *New Jewish Cooking* (Apple Publishing, London, 1997)

Ganor, Avi and Ron Maiberg. *Taste of Israel* (Galahad Books, New York, 1993)

Jackson, Judy. *Jewish: Traditional Recipes From a Rich Culinary Heritage* (Lorenz Books, London, 1998)

Leonard, Leah. *Jewish Cookery* (Crown Publishers, New York, 1949)

Lebewohl, Sharon and Bulkin, Rena. *The 2nd Ave Deli Cookbook* (Villard, New York, 1999)

Machlin, Edda Servi. *The Classic Cuisine of the Italian Jews* (Dodd Mead and Co, New York, 1982)

Marks, Copeland. *The Great Book of Couscous* (Donald I Fine Books, New York, 1994)

Marks, Copeland. *Sephardic Cooking* (Donald I Fine Books, New York, 1994)

Nathan, Joan. *The Jewish Holiday Kitchen* (Schocken Books, New York, 1988)

Roden, Claudia, *The Book of Jewish Food* (Viking Books, London, 1997)

Rose, Evelyn. *The Essential Jewish Festival Cookbook* (Robson Books, London, 2000)

Van Strajen, Michael. *The Healthy Jewish Cookbook Morocco* (Harper Trade, 1987)

Author's Acknowledgements
Thanks to Alan "Kishke" McLaughlan, Dr Leah Spieler and Rev Jon Harford, Gretchen Spieler, Paula Aspin and Chris, Jojo and India Aspin, Dr Esther Novak and John Chendo, Etty, Natalie and Bruce Blackman, Shirely at the Jewish Vegetarian Society, Paul Richardson, Nigel Patrick and Graham Ketteringham, Saara Rimm of Finn facts, Rabbi Brod Bloom, Graham and Janey Mills of Hedonica Marketing, Fran McCullough, Sotiris Kitrilakis, Rabbi Mona Alfi, the late Rabbi Jason Gaber, so sadly missed, UK Chief Rabbi Sir Jonathan Sachs, with whom I appeared on BBC "Jewish London" and have been a fan of ever since; Sandy Waks, Kamala Friedman, Amanda and Tim Hamilton Hemmeter, Gayle Merksamer, Antonietta Stefanic and her girls Charlotte and Caroline, Faye Levy, Joan Nathan, Lance Forman, whose family business, Forman's Smoked Fish, makes the best smoked salmon in the United Kingdom and beyond; Josephine Bacon, Susie Morgenstern and her sister Effie who took me to eat hummus in Jaffa; to my sister-in-law Ma-Tao, and her husband A J Morgan, my brother's brother; also my late brother Bryan Smith who preferred Chinese food to Jewish food, though he loved Kosher dill pickles.

Miriam Morgen and Michael Bauer of the *San Francisco Chronicle* for letting me write about so many delicious subjects; the wonderful Kim Severson of the *New York Times*, and *Saveur Magazine*, who sent me to Israel to write about falafel.

To my own Jewish family: parents Caroline and Izzy Smith (the famous baseball player, really!), aunt and uncle Sy and Estelle Opper, aunties Ella Smith and Sarah Rackusin who can rustle up latkes and cheesecake at the drop of a hat, and finally my editor on this project, Catherine Stuart, who was a great pleasure to work with.

INDEX